I0592398

Franz Delitzsch

Biblical commentary on the Book of Job

Vol. 2

Franz Delitzsch

Biblical commentary on the Book of Job
Vol. 2

ISBN/EAN: 9783337735968

Printed in Europe, USA, Canada, Australia, Japan

Cover: Foto ©ninafisch / pixelio.de

More available books at **www.hansebooks.com**

BIBLICAL COMMENTARY

ON

THE BOOK OF JOB.

BY

F. DÉLITZSCH, D.D.,

PROFESSOR OF THEOLOGY.

TRANSLATED FROM THE GERMAN

BY THE

REV. FRANCIS BOLTON, B.A.,

ELLAND.

VOL. II.

EDINBURGH:

T. AND T. CLARK, 38, GEORGE STREET.

LONDON: HAMILTON, ADAMS, & CO. DUBLIN: JOHN ROBERTSON & CO.

MDCCCLXVI.

TRANSLATOR'S PREFACE.

It is with no ordinary feeling of relief and satisfaction that I am at length able to send forth the second and concluding volume of this Commentary. And I am confident that the trifling delay in this year's issues of the Foreign Theological Library will be readily pardoned, when the tedious toil involved in carrying such a work through the press amidst the pressure of other duties is considered. No pains have been spared to render the work worthy its position; and the care bestowed upon the work by myself has been fully seconded by the attention of the printers.

The duties of translation have been carefully discharged, and it has been my aim to preserve the complexion of the original as far as possible, even sometimes at the expense of an easy flow of language. Conscious of imperfection in the working out of my design, I have nevertheless sought to put the reader in the position of a student of the original volume. The task which I imposed upon myself has not been confined to *mere* translation; but close attention has been given to the accurate reproduction of the critical portions, with the hope of contributing in some small degree to the diffusion of sound exegetical knowledge for the elucidation of one of the grandest and most practical books of the Old Testament Scriptures, and from a conviction of the need there is for the cultivation of the cognate Semitic languages. This latter branch of study is specially applicable and necessary in the interpretation of the book of Job, and the established scholarship of Dr Delitzsch eminently qualifies him for the effective execution of the work.

Further explanation need scarcely be added, except in reference to the retention of the word *Chokma*, and the character of the translation of the text. As to the former, I regret that I did not append a note to vol. i. p. 5, to the effect that the word *Chokma* (חָכְמָה, *Wisdom*) was reproduced because used technically by the author. I presumed that students of the volume would at once recognise the word ; but from the consideration that the Commentary may also be used, so far as the practical parts are concerned, even by readers unacquainted with Hebrew, this explanation has been deemed needful.

And it may further suffice, in connection with the second section of the Introduction, to define *Chokma* as the one word for the lofty spirit of wisdom which dwelt in the minds of the wise men of Israel in the Salomonic age,—a wisdom taught, inspired, by the Holy Spirit of God—the culmination of which is found in Solomon himself. In brief, the *Chokma* is the divine philosophy of the Jewish church.

With reference to the new rendering of the text: it aims at a literal and faithful reproduction of Dr Delitzsch's translation, as representing his " sense and appreciation of the original," and as the embodiment of the results of the critical notes. Therefore I have not felt at liberty to use that freedom of expression which I regard as most desirable in adapting the translation of the original text to the requirements of the general reader. This portion of my undertaking has not been free from difficulty; and occasionally an amount of stiffness has seemed unavoidable, owing to the different structure of the Hebrew and English languages, while, from the plastic nature of the German language, the author is enabled to mould his translation closely after the original text, and still render it elegant, and at times rhythmical.

A note on the transcription of Arabic words will be found at the end of the Appendix. The references have been verified, so far as the means of verification have been accessible; and I believe I may speak with confidence of those that I have not been able to verify, from the general accuracy I found in the others.

To clear up the misapprehension which has been manifested in many quarters, I would add that this Commentary forms a part of the *Biblical Commentary on the Old Testament* by Drs Keil and Delitzsch. But the name of the latter only is appended to these volumes, because Dr Delitzsch is the writer of this portion, just as Dr Keil only is the author of the *Commentary on the Pentateuch*, and all the other volumes that have appeared to this date.

I have still to acknowledge the kind promptitude with which my esteemed friend Dr Delitzsch has, in more than one instance, given me an explanation of a difficult point, and favoured me with an additional amendment of the original work during the progress of this translation through the press.

b

In the hope that the usefulness of Dr Delitzsch's valuable contribution to Biblical Exegesis may be extended beyond his original design, I commend it to all earnest students of the Holy Word, with the prayer that the blessing of the Spirit of Jehovah may rest upon the labours of *our* hands.

F. B.

ELLAND, *November* 2, 1866.

TABLE OF CONTENTS.

THE BOOK OF JOB.

SECOND PART.—THE ENTANGLEMENT.

CHAP. IV.-XXVI.

THE THIRD COURSE OF THE CONTROVERSY.— CHAP. XXII.-XXVI.

(CONTINUED.)

Job's First Answer.—Chaps. xxiii. xxiv.

Schema: 8. 8. 8. 8. | 8. 9. 9. 9. 5. 10. 9.

[Then began Job, and said :]

2 *Even to-day my complaint still biddeth defiance,*
   My hand lieth heavy upon my groaning.
3 *Oh that I knew where I might find Him,*
   That I might come even to His dwelling-place!
4 *I would lay the cause before Him,*
   And fill my mouth with arguments :
5 *I should like to know the words He would answer me,*
   And attend to what He would say to me.

SINCE מְרִי (for which the LXX. reads ἐκ τοῦ χειρός μου, מִידִי; Ew. מִידוֹ, from his hand) usually elsewhere signifies obstinacy, it appears that ver. 2a ought to be explained: My complaint is always accounted as rebellion (against God); but by this rendering ver. 2b requires some sort of expletive,

VOL. II.   A in order to furnish a connected thought: *although* the hand which is upon me stifles my groaning (Hirz.); or, according to another rendering of the עַל: *et pourtant mes gémissements n'égalent pas mes souffrances* (Renan, Schlottm.). These interpretations are objectionable on account of the artificial restoration of the connection between the two members of the verse, which they require; they lead one to expect וְיָדִי (as a circumstantial clause; LXX., *Cod. Vat. καὶ ἡ χείρ αὐτοῦ*). As the words stand, it is to be supposed that the definition of time, גַּם־הַיּוֹם (even to-day still, as Zech. ix. 12), belongs to both divisions of the verse. How, then, is מְרִי to be understood? If we compare ch. vii. 11, x. 1, where מַר, which is combined with שִׂיחַ, signifies *amarum = amaritudo*, it is natural to take מְרִי also in the signification *amaritudo, acerbitas* (Targ., Syr., Jer.); and this is also possible, since, as is evident from Ex. xxiii. 21, comp. Zech. xii. 10, the verbal forms מָרַר and מָרָה run into one another, as they are really cognates.[1] But it is more satisfactory, and more in accordance with the relation of the two divisions of the verse, if we keep to the usual signification of מְרִי; not, however, understanding it of ob-

---

[1] מָרַר and מָרָה both spring from the root מַר [*vid. supra*, i. p. 279, note], with the primary signification *stringere*, to beat, rub, draw tight. Hence مَرَّ, to touch lightly, smear upon (to go by, over, or through, to move by, etc.), but also *stringere palatum*, of an astringent taste, strong in taste, to be bitter, *opp.* حَلَّ, soft and mild in taste, to be sweet, as in another direction חָלָה, to be loose, weak, sick, both from the root حَلَّ in حَلَّ, *solvit, laxavit*. From the signification to be tight come *amarra*, to stretch tight, *istamarra*, to stretch one's self tight, to draw one's self out in this state of tension—of things in time, to continue unbroken; *mirreh*, string, cord; מָרָה, to make and hold one's self tight against any one, *i.e.* to be obstinate: originally of the body, as تَمَارَ, مَارَ, to strengthen themselves in the contest against one another; then of the mind, as تَمَارَى، مَارَى, to struggle against anything, both outwardly by contradiction and disputing, and inwardly by doubt and unbelief.—Fl.

stinacy, revolt, rebellion (viz. in the sense of the friends), but, like מֹרֶה, 2 Kings xiv. 26 (which describes the affliction as stiff-necked, obstinate), of stubbornness, defiance, continuance in opposition, and explain with Raschi: My complaint is still always defiance, *i.e.* still maintains itself in opposition, viz. against God, without yielding (Hahn, Olsh.: unsubmitting); or rather: against such exhortations to penitence as those which Eliphaz has just addressed to him. In reply to these, Job considers his complaint to be well justified even to-day, *i.e.* even now (for it is not, with Ewald, to be imagined that, in the mind of the poet, the controversy extends over several days,—an idea which would only be indicated by this one word).

In ver. 2*b* he continues the same thought under a different form of expression. My hand lies heavy on my groaning, *i.e.* I hold it immoveably fast (as Fleischer proposes to take the words); or better: I am driven to a continued utterance of it.[1] By this interpretation ידי retains its most natural meaning, *manus mea*, and the connection of the two members of the verse without any particle is best explained. On the other hand, all modern expositors, who do not, as Olsh., at once correct ידי into ידו, explain the suffix as objective: the hand, *i.e.* the destiny to which I have to submit, weighs upon my sighing, irresistibly forcing it out from me. Then ver. 2*b* is related to ver. 2*a* as a confirmation; and if, therefore, a particle is to be supplied, it is כִּי (Olsh.) and no other. Thus, even the Targ. renders it מְחָתִי, *plaga mea*. Job's affliction is frequently traced back to the hand of God, ch. xix. 21, comp. i. 11, ii. 5, xiii. 21; and on the suffix used objectively (pass.) we may compare ver. 14, חֻקִּי; ch. xx. 29, אִמְרוֹ; and

---

[1] The idea might also be: My hand presses my groaning back (because it would be of no use to me); but ver. 2*a* is against this, and the Arab. *kamada*, to restrain inward pain, anger, etc. by force (*e.g.* mât kemed, he died from suppressed rage or anxiety), has scarcely any etymological connection with כבד.

especially xxxiv. 6, חֵצִי. The interpretation : the hand upon
me is heavy above my sighing, *i.e.* heavier than it (Ramban,
Rosenm., Ges., Schlottm., Renan), also accords with the connection. עַל can indeed be used in this comparative meaning,
Ex. xvi. 5, Eccl. i. 16 ; but כבדה יד על is an established
phrase, and commonly used of the burden of the hand upon
any one, Ps. xxxii. 4 (comp. ch. xxxiii. 7, in the division
in which Elihu is introduced; and the connection with אֶל,
1 Sam. v. 6, and שָׂם, 1 Sam. v. 11); and this usage of the
language renders the comparative rendering very improbable.
But it is also improbable that "my hand" is = the hand [that
is] upon me, since it cannot be shown that יד was directly
used in the sense of *plaga;* even the Arabic, among the
many turns of meaning which it gives to يد, does not support
this, and least of all would an Arab conceive of يُدَّ passively,
plaga quam patior. Explain, therefore : his complaint now,
as before, offers resistance to the exhortation of the friends,
which is not able to lessen it, his (Job's) hand presses upon
his lamentation so that it is forced to break forth, but —
without its justification being recognised by men. This
thought urges him on to the wish that he might be able to
pour forth his complaint directly before God. מִי־יִתֵּן is at
one time followed by an accusative (ch. xiv. 4, xxix. 2, xxxi.
31, 35, to which belongs also the construction with the inf.,
ch. xi. 5), at another by the *fut.,* with or without *Waw* (as
here, ver. 3*b*, ch. vi. 8, xiii. 5, xiv. 13, xix. 23), and at
another by the *perf.,* with or without *Waw* (as here, ver. 3*a :*
utinam noverim, and Deut. v. 26). And יָדַעְתִּי is, as in ch.
xxxii. 22, joined with the *fut.:* *scirem* (*noverim*) *et invenirem*
instead of *possim invenire eum* (לִמְצָאוֹ), Ges. § 142, 3, *c.* If
he but knew [how] to reach Him (God), could attain to His
throne; תְּכוּנָה (everywhere from כּוּן, not from תָּכַן) signifies
the setting up, *i.e.* arrangement (Ezek. xliii. 11) or establish-
ment (Nah. ii. 10) of a dwelling, and the thing itself which is

set out and established, here of the place where God's throne is established. Having attained to this, he would lay his cause (*instruere causam*, as ch. xiii. 18, comp. xxxiii. 5) before Him, and fill his mouth with arguments to prove that he has right on his side (תּוֹכָחוֹת, as Ps. xxxviii. 15, of the grounds of defence, or proof that he is in the right and his opponent in the wrong). In ver. 5 we may translate: I would, or: I should like (to learn); in the Hebrew, as in *cognoscerem*, both are expressed; the substance of ver. 5*a* makes the optative rendering more natural. He would like to know the words with which He would meet him,[1] and would give heed to what He would say to him. But will He condescend? will He have anything to do with the matter?—

6 *Will He contend with me with great power?*
  No, indeed; He will only regard me!
7 *Then the upright would be disputing with Him,*
  And I should for ever escape my judge.
8 *Yet I go eastward, He is not there,*
  And westward, but I perceive Him not;
9 *Northwards where He worketh, but I behold Him*
  not;
  He turneth aside southwards, and I see Him not.

The question which Job, in ver. 6*a*, puts forth: will He contend with me in the greatness or fulness of His strength, *i.e.* (as ch. xxx. 18) with a calling forth of all His strength? he himself answers in ver. 6*b*, hoping that the contrary may be the case: no, indeed, He will not do that.[2] לֹא is here

---

[1] אֵדְעָה is generally accented with *Dechî*, מֵלִּים with *Munach*, according to which Dachselt interprets: *scirem, quæ eloquia responderet mihi Deus*, but this is incorrect. The old editions have correctly אֵדְעָה *Munach*, מֵלִּים *Munach* (taking the place of *Dechî*, because the *Athnach*-word which follows has not two syllables before the tone-syllable; *vid. Psalter*, ii. 104, § 4).

[2] With this interpretation, לֹא should certainly have *Rebia mugrasch*;

followed not by the 'ﬤ, which is otherwise customary after a
negation in the signification *imo*, but by the restrictive ex-
ceptive אַךְ, which never signifies *sed*, sometimes *verum tamen*
(Ps. xlix. 16; comp. *supra*, ch. xiii. 15, vol. i. p. 215), but
here, as frequently, *tantummodo*, and, according to the hyper-
baton which has been mentioned so often (vol. i. pp. 72, 238,
and also 215), is placed at the beginning of the sentence,
and belongs not to the member of the sentence immediately
following it, but to the whole sentence (as in Arabic also
the restrictive force of the اِنَّمَا never falls upon what immediately follows it): He will do nothing but regard me
(שִׂים, *scil.* לֵב, elsewhere with עַל of the object of regard or
reflection, ch. xxxiv. 23, xxxvii. 15, Judg. xix. 30, and without an ellipsis, ch. i. 8; also with אֶל, ch. ii. 3, or לְ, 1 Sam. ix.
20; here designedly with בְּ, which unites in itself the significations of the Arab. ب and ف, of seizing, and of plunging
into anything). Many expositors (Hirz., Ew., and others)
understand ver. 6*b* as expressing a wish: "Shall He contend
with me with overwhelming power? No, I do not desire that;
only that He may be a judge attentive to the cause, not a
ruler manifesting His almighty power." But ver. 6*a*, taken
thus, would be purely rhetorical, since this question (shall
He, etc.) certainly cannot be seriously propounded by Job;
accordingly, ver. 6*b* is not intended as expressing a wish, but
a hope. Job certainly wishes the same thing in ch. ix. 34,
xiii. 21; but in the course of the discussion he has gradually
acquired new confidence in God, which here once more
breaks through. He knows that God, if He could but be
found, would also condescend to hear his defence of himself,

its accentuation with *Mercha* proceeds from another interpretation, probably *non utique ponet in me* (*manum suam*), according to which the
Targ. translates. Others, following this accentuation, take לֹא in the
sense of לְהַ (*vid.* in Dachselt), or are at pains to obtain some other
meaning from it.

that He would allow him to speak, and not overwhelm him with His majesty.

Ver. 7. The question arises here, whether the שָׁם which follows is to be understood locally (נֻם) or temporally (נֻם); it is evident from ch. xxxv. 12, Ps. xiv. 5, lxvi. 6, Hos. ii. 17, Zeph. i. 14, that it may be used temporally; in many passages, e.g. Ps. xxxvi. 13, the two significations run into one another, so that they cannot be distinguished. We here decide in favour of the temporal signification, against Rosenm., Schlottm., and Hahn; for if שָׁם be understood locally, a "then" must be supplied, and it may therefore be concluded that this שָׁם is the expression for it. We assume at the same time that נוכח is correctly pointed as *part.* with *Kametz;* accordingly it is to be explained: then, if He would thus pay attention to me, an upright man would be contending with Him, *i.e.* then it would be satisfactorily proved that an upright man may contend with Him. In ver. 7b, פֵּלֵּט, like מִלֵּט, ch. xx. 20 (comp. פָּתַח, to have open, to stand open), is intensive of *Kal:* I should for ever escape my judge, *i.e.* come off most completely free from unmerited punishment. Thus it ought to be if God could be found, but He cannot be found. The הֵן, which according to the sense may be translated by "yet" (comp. ch. xxi. 16), introduces this antithetical relation: Yet I go towards the east (הֵן with *Mahpach,* קֶדֶם with *Munach*), and He is not there; and towards the west (אָחוֹר, comp. אחרנים, *occidentales,* ch. xviii. 20), and perceive Him not (expressed as in ch. ix. 11; בִּין לְ elsewhere: to attend to anything, ch. xiv. 21, Deut. xxxii. 29, Ps. lxxiii. 17; here, as there, to perceive anything, so that לֹו is equivalent to אֹתוֹ). In ver. 9 the left (שְׂמֹאול, Arab. *shemâl,* or even without the substantival termination, on which comp. *Jesurun,* pp. 222-227, *sham, shâm*) is undoubtedly an appellation of the north, and the right (יָמִין, Arab. *jemîn*) an appellation of the south; both words are locatives which outwardly are undefined. And if the usual signification of עשׂה and עטף are retained, it is to be explained thus: northwards or in the north, if He should be active—I behold not; if He veil himself southwards or in the south—I see not. This explanation is also satisfactory so far as ver. 9a is concerned, so·that it is unnecessary to understand בַּעֲשֹׂתוֹ other than in ch. xxviii. 26, and with Blumenfeld to translate according to the phrase עָשָׂה דַרְכּוֹ, Judg. xvii. 8 : if He makes His way northwards; or even with Umbr. to call in the assistance of the Arab. غشى (to cover), which neither here nor ch. ix. 9, xv. 27, is admissible, since even then שְׂמֹאול בעשׂתו cannot signify : if He hath concealed himself on the left hand (in the north). Ewald's combination of עשׂה with עטה, in the assumed signification "to incline to" of the latter, is to be passed over as useless. On the other hand, much can be said in favour of Ewald's trans- lation of ver. 9b : "if He turn to the right hand—I see Him not ;" for (1) the Arab. عطف, by virtue of the radical notion,[1] which is also traceable in the Heb. עטף, signifies both trans. and intrans. to turn up, bend aside ; (2) Saadia translates : "and if He turns southwards ('atafa 'gunûban);" (3) Schultens correctly observes : עטף significatione operiendi commodum non efficit sensum, nam quid mirum si quem occul- tantem se non conspiciamus. We therefore give the preference to this Arabic rendering of יעטף. If יעטף, in the sense of obvelat se, does not call to mind the חַדְרֵי תֵמָן, penetralia austri, ch. ix. 9 (comp. خدر, velamen, adytum), neither will בעשׂתו

---

[1] The verb عطف signifies trans. to turn, or lay, anything round, so that it is laid or drawn over something else and covers it ; hence عطاف, a garment that is cast round one, تعطّف with ب of a garment : to cast it or wrap it about one. Intrans. to turn aside, depart from, of deviating from a given direction, deflectere, declinare ; also, to turn in a totally opposite direction, to turn one's self round and to go back.—FL.

point to the north as the limit of the divine dominion. Such conceptions of the extreme north and south are nowhere found among the Arabs as among the Arian races (*vid.* Isa. xiv. 13);[1] and, moreover, the conception of the north as the abode of God cannot be shown to be biblical, either from ch. xxxvii. 22, Ezek. i. 4, or still less from Ps. xlviii. 3. With regard to the syntax, יַעְטֹף is a hypothetical *fut.*, as ch. xx. 24, xxii. 27 sq. The use of the *fut. apoc.* אָחַז, like אֵשׁ, ver. 11, without a voluntative or aoristic signification, is poetic. Towards all quarters of the heavens he turns, *i.e.* with his eyes and the longing of his whole nature, if he may by any means find God. But He evades him, does not reveal Himself in any place whatever.

The כִּי which now follows does not give the reason of Job's earnest search after God, but the reason of His not being found by him. He does not allow Himself to be seen anywhere; He conceals Himself from him, lest He should be compelled to acknowledge the right of the sufferer, and to withdraw His chastening hand from him.

10 *For He knoweth the way that is with me :*
   If He should prove me, I should come forth as gold.
11 *My foot held firm to His steps ;*
   His way I kept, and turned not aside.
12 *The command of His lips—I departed not from it ;*
   More than my own determination I kept the words of His
   mouth.
13 *Yet He remaineth by one thing, and who can turn Him ?*
   And He accomplisheth what His soul desireth.

That which is not merely outwardly, but inwardly with

---

[1] In contrast to the extreme north, the abode of the gods, the habitation of life, the extreme south is among the Arians the abode of the prince of death and of demons, *Jama* (*vid.* vol. i. p. 325) with his attendants, and therefore the habitation of death.

(עָם) any one, is that which he thinks and knows (his consciousness), ch. ix. 35, xv. 9, or his willing and acting, ch.
x. 13, xxvii. 11 : he is conscious of it, he intends to do it;
here, ver. 10, עָם is intended in the former sense, in ver. 14 in
the latter. The "way with me" is that which his conscience
(συνείδησις) approves (συμμαρτυρεῖ); comp. *Psychol.* S. 134.
This is known to God, so that he who is now set down as a
criminal would come forth as tried gold, in the event of God
allowing him to appear before Him, and subjecting him to
judicial trial. בְּחָנַנִי is the *prœt. hypotheticum* so often mentioned, which is based upon the paratactic character of the
Hebrew style, as Gen. xliv. 22, Ruth ii. 9, Zech. xiii. 6 ;
Ges. § 155, 4, *a.* His foot has held firmly[1] to the steps of
God (אֲשֻׁרוֹ, together with אַשֻּׁר, ch. xxxi. 7, from אָשַׁר *Piel,* to
go on), so that he was always close behind Him as his predecessor (אָחַז synon. תָּמַךְ, Ps. xvii. 5, Prov. v. 5). He guarded,
i.e. observed His way, and turned not aside (אָט *fut. apoc.
Hiph.* in the intransitive sense of *deflectere,* as *e.g.* Ps. cxxv. 5).

In ver. 12a, מִצְוַת שְׂפָתָיו precedes as *cas. absolutus* (as respects the command of His lips); and what is said in this
respect follows with *Waw apod.* (= Arab. ـِ) without the
retrospective pronoun מִמֶּנָּה (which is omitted for poetic
brevity). On this prominence of a separate notion after the
manner of an antecedent, comp. vol. i. p. 91, note 1. The
Hiph. הֵמִישׁ, like הִטָּה, ver. 11, and הִלְּיז, Prov. iv. 21, is not
causative, but simply active in signification. In ver. 12b the
question arises, whether צָפַן מִן is one expression, as in ch.
xvii. 4, in the sense of "hiding from another," or whether מִן
is comparative. In the former sense Hirz. explains : I removed the divine will from the possible ascendancy of my own.

---

[1] On אָחַז, Carey correctly observes, and it explains the form of the
expression : The oriental foot has a power of grasp and tenacity, because
not shackled with shoes from early childhood, of which we can form but
little idea.

But since צפן is familiar to the poet in the sense of preserving and laying by (צפונים, treasures, ch. xx. 26), it is more natural to explain, according to Ps. cxix. 11 : I kept the words (commands) of Thy mouth, *i.e.* esteemed them high and precious, more than *my* statute, *i.e.* more than what my own will prescribed for me.[1] The meaning is substantially the same ; the LXX., which translates ἐν δὲ κόλπῳ μου (בחקי), which Olsh. considers to be "perhaps correct," destroys the significance of the confession. Hirz. rightly refers to the "law in the members," Rom. vii. 23 : חקי is the expression Job uses for the law of the sinful nature which strives against the law of God, the wilful impulse of selfishness and evil passion, the law which the apostle describes as ἕτερος νόμος, in distinction from the νόμος τοῦ Θεοῦ (*Psychol.* S. 379). Job's conscience can give him this testimony, but He, the God who so studiously avoids him, remains in one mind, viz. to treat him as a criminal ; and who can turn Him from His purpose? (the same question as ch. ix. 12, xi. 10) ; His soul wills it (*stat pro ratione voluntas*), and He accomplishes it. Most expositors explain *permanet in uno* in this sense ; the *Beth* is the usual ב with verbs of entering upon and persisting in anything. Others, however, take the ב as *Beth essentiæ :* He remains one and the same, viz. in His conduct towards me (Umbr., Vaih.), or : He is one, is alone, viz. in absolute majesty (Targ. Jer. ; Schult., Ew., Hlgst., Schlottm.), which is admissible, since this *Beth* occurs not only in the comple-

---

[1] Wetzstein arranges the significations of צפן as follows :—1. (Beduin) *intr. fut. i*, to contain one's self, to keep still (hence in Hebr. to lie in wait), to be rapt in thought; conjug. II. *c. acc. pers.* to make any one thoughtful, irresolute. 2. (Hebr.) *trans. fut. o*, to keep anything to one's self, to hold back, to keep to one's self ; *Niph.* to be held back, *i.e.* either concealed or reserved for future use. Thus we see how, on the one hand, צפן is related to טמן, *e.g.* ch. xx. 26 (Arab. *itmaanna*, to be still) ; and, on the other, can interchange with צפה in the signification *designare* (comp. ch. xv. 22 with xv. 20, xxi. 19), and to spy, lie in wait (comp. Ps. x. 8, lvi. 7, Prov. i. 11, 18, with Ps. xxxvii. 32).

ments of a sentence (Ps. xxxix. 7, like a shadow ; Isa. xlviii.
10, after the manner of silver; Ps. lv. 19, in great number;
Ps. xxxv. 2, as my help), but also with the predicate of a
simple sentence, be it verbal (ch. xxiv. 13; Prov. iii. 26) or
substantival (Ex. xviii. 4; Ps. cxviii. 7). The same construction is found also in Arabic, where, however, it is more
frequent in simple negative clauses than in affirmative (vid.
Psalter, i. 272). The assertion : He is one (as in the primary
monotheistic confession, Deut. vi. 4), is, however, an expression
for the absoluteness of God, which is not suited to this connection ; and if הוא באחד is intended to be understood of the
unchangeable uniformity of His purpose concerning Job, the
explanation : versatur (perstat) in uno, Arab. hua fi wâhidin, is
not only equally, but more natural, and we therefore prefer it.

Here again God appears to Job to be his enemy. His
confidence towards God is again overrun by all kinds of
evil, suspicious thoughts. He seems to him to be a God of
absolute caprice, who punishes where there is no ground for
punishment. There is indeed a phase of the abiding fact
which he considers superior to God and himself, both being
conceived of as contending parties; and this phase God
avoids, He will not hear it. Into this vortex of thoughts, as
terrible as they are puerile, Job is hurried forward by the
persuasion that his affliction is a decree of divine justice.
The friends have greatly confirmed him in this persuasion;
so that his consciousness of innocence, and the idea of God
as inflicting punishment, are become widely opposite extremes,
between which his faith is hardly able to maintain itself.
It is not his affliction in itself, but this persuasion, which pre-
cipitates him into such a depth of conflict, as the following
strophe shows.

14 *For He accomplisheth that which is appointed for me,*
   And much of a like kind is with Him.

15 *Therefore I am troubled at His presence;*
If I consider it, I am afraid of Him.
16 *And God hath caused my heart to be dejected,*
And the Almighty hath put me to confusion ;
17 *For I have not been destroyed before darkness,*
And before my countenance, which thick darkness covereth.

Now it is the will of God, the absolute, which has all at
once turned against him, the innocent (ver. 13); for what He
has decreed against him (חֹקִּי) He also brings to a complete
fulfilment (הִשְׁלִים, as *e.g.* Isa. xliv. 26); and the same troubles
as those which he already suffers, God has still more abundantly decreed for him, in order to torture him gradually,
but surely, to death. Job intends ver. 14*b* in reference to
himself, not as a general assertion: it is, in general, God's way
of acting. Hahn's objection to the other explanation, that
Job's affliction, according to his own previous assertions, has
already attained its highest degree, does not refute it; for
Job certainly has a term of life before him, though it be
but short, in which the wondrously inventive (ch. x. 16)
hostility of God can heap up ever new troubles for him.
On the other hand, the interpretation of the expression in a
general sense is opposed by the form of the expression itself,
which is not that God delights to do this, but that He purposes (עִמּוֹ) to do it. It is a conclusion from the present
concerning the future, such as Job is able to make with
reference to himself; while he, moreover, abides by the reality
in respect to the mysterious distribution of the fortunes of
men. Therefore, because he is a mark for the enmity of
God, without having merited it, he is confounded before His
countenance, which is so angrily turned upon him (comp.
פָּנִים, Ps. xxi. 10, Lam. iv. 16); if he considers it (according to the sense *fut. hypothet.*, as ver. 9*b*), he trembles
before Him, who recompenses faithful attachment by such

torturing pain. The following connection with ‍ and the mention of God twice at the beginning of the affirmations, is intended to mean : (I tremble before Him), and He it is who has made me faint-hearted (הֵרַךְ *Hiph.* from the *Kal,* Deut. xx. 3, and freq., to be tender, soft, disconcerted), and has troubled me ; which is then supported in ver. 17.

His suffering which draws him on to ruin he perceives, but it is not the proper ground of his inward destruction ; it is not the encircling darkness of affliction, not the mysterious form of his suffering which disconcerts him, but God's hostile conduct towards him, His angry countenance as he seems to see it, and which he is nevertheless unable to explain. Thus also Ew., Hirz., Vaih., Hlgst., and Schlottm. explain the passage. The only other explanation worthy of mention is that which finds in ver. 17 the thought already expressed in ch. iii. 10 : For I was not then destroyed, in order that I might experience such mysterious suffering ; an interpretation with which most of the old expositors were satisfied, and which has been revived by Rosenm., Stick., and Hahn. We translate : for I have not been destroyed before darkness (in order to be taken away from it before it came upon me), and He has not hidden darkness before my face ; or as an exclamation : that I have not been destroyed! which is to be equivalent to : Had I but been . . . ! Apart from this rendering of the *quod non = utinam,* which cannot be supported, (1) It is doubly hazardous thus to carry the לֹא forward to the second line in connection with verbs of different persons. (2) The darkness in ver. 17*b* appears (at least according to the usual interpret. *caliginem*) as that which is being covered, whereas it is naturally that which covers something else ; wherefore Blumenfeld explains : and darkness has not hidden, viz. such pain as I must now endure, from my face. (3) The whole thought which is thus gained is without point, and meaningless, in this connection. On the other hand, the antithesis

between מִפָּנָיו and מִפָּנַי, מִמֶּנּוּ and מִפְּנֵי־חֹשֶׁךְ, is at once obvious;
and this antithesis, which forces itself upon the attention,
also furnishes the thought which might be expected from the
context. It is unnecessary to take נִצְמַת in a different signification from ch. vi. 17; in Arabic ﺻﻤﺖ signifies *conticescere;*
the idea of the root, however, is in general a constraining de-
priving of free movement. חֹשֶׁךְ is intended as in the question
of Eliphaz, ch. xxii. 11: "Or seest thou not the darkness?"
to which it perhaps refers. It is impossible, with Schlottm.,
to translate ver. 17*b*: and before that darkness covers my
face; מִן is never other than a *præp.*, not a conjunction with
power over a whole clause. It must be translated: *et a facie
mea quam obtegit caligo.* As the absolute פָּנִים, ch. ix. 27,
signifies the appearance of the countenance under pain, so
here by it Job means his countenance distorted by pain, his
deformed appearance, which, as the attributive clause affirms,
is thoroughly darkened by suffering (comp. ch. xxx. 30).
But it is not this darkness which stares him in the face, and
threatens to swallow him up (comp. מִפְּנֵי־חֹשֶׁךְ, ch. xvii. 12);
not this his miserable form, which the extremest darkness
covers (on אֹפֶל, *vid.* ch. x. 22), that destroys his inmost
nature; but the thought that God stands forth in hostility
against him, which makes his affliction so terrific, and
doubly so in connection with the inalienable consciousness
of his innocence. From the incomprehensible punishment
which, without reason, is passing over him, he now again
comes to speak of the incomprehensible connivance of God,
which permits the godlessness of the world to go on unpunished.

Ch. xxiv. 1 *Wherefore are not bounds reserved by the Almighty,*
  And they who honour Him see not His days?
 2 *They remove the landmarks,*
  They steal flocks and shepherd them.

3 *They carry away the ass of the orphan,*
  And distrain the ox of the widow.
4 *They thrust the needy out of the way,*
  The poor of the land are obliged to slink away together.

The supposition that the text originally stood מַדּוּעַ לָרְשָׁעִים מְשַׁדַּי is natural; but it is at once destroyed by the fact that ver. 1a becomes thereby disproportionately long, and yet cannot be divided into two lines of comparatively independent contents. In fact, לרשעים is by no means absolutely necessary. The usage of the language assumes it, according to which עֵת followed by the genitive signifies the point of time at which any one's fate is decided, Isa. xiii. 22, Jer. xxvii. 7, Ezek. xxii. 3, xxx. 3; the period when reckoning is made, or even the *terminus ad quem*, Eccl. ix. 12; and יום followed by the gen. of a man, the day of his end, ch. xv. 32, xviii. 20, Ezek. xxi. 30, and freq.; or with יהוה, the day when God's judgment is revealed, Joel i. 15, and freq. The boldness of poetic language goes beyond this usage, by using עִתִּים directly of the period of punishment, as is almost universally acknowledged since Schultens' day, and יְמֵי of God's days of judgment or of vengeance;[1] and it is the less ambiguous, since צָפֻן, in the sense of the divine predetermination of what is future, ch. xv. 20, especially of God's storing up merited

---

[1] On עִתִּים, in the sense of times of retribution, Wetzstein compares the Arab. عدات, which signifies predetermined reward or punishment; moreover, עֵת is derived from עֶדֶת (from וְעֶד), and עִתִּים is equivalent to עֶדְתִּים, according to the same law of assimilation, by which now-a-days they say לְתִּי instead of לְדְתִּי (one who is born on the same day with me, from لدة, *lida*), and רִתִּי instead of רְדְתִּי (my drinking-time), since the assimilation of the ד takes place everywhere where ת is pronounced. The ת of the feminine termination in עִתִּים, as in שִׁקְתוֹת and the like, perhaps also in בתים (*bâttim*), is amalgamated with the root.

punishment, ch. xxi. 19, is an acknowledged word of our poet. On מִן with the passive, vid. Ew. § 295, c (where, however, ch. xxviii. 4 is erroneously cited in its favour); it is never more than equivalent to ἀπό, for to use מִן directly as ὑπό with the passive is admissible neither in Hebrew nor in Arabic. יֹדְעוּ (Keri יֹדְעָיו, for which the Targ. unsuitably reads יֹדְעֵי) are, as in Ps. xxxvi. 11, lxxxvii. 4, comp. supra, ch. xviii. 21, those who know God, not merely superficially, but from experience of His ways, consequently those who are in fellowship with Him. לֹא חָזוּ is to be written with Zinnorith over the לֹא, and Mercha by the first syllable of חָזוּ. The Zinnorith necessitates the retreat of the tone of חָזוּ to its first syllable, as in בְּי־חָרָה, Ps. xviii. 8 (Bär's Psalterium, p. xiii.); for if חָזוּ remained Milra, לֹא ought to be connected with it by Makkeph, and consequently remain toneless (Psalter, ii. 507).

Next follows the description of the moral abhorrence which, while the friends (ch. xxii. 19) maintain a divine retribution everywhere manifest, is painfully conscious of the absence of any determination of the periods and days of judicial punishment. Fearlessly and unpunished, the oppression of the helpless and defenceless, though deserving of a curse, rages in every form. They remove the landmarks; comp. Deut. xxvii. 17, "Cursed is he who removeth his neighbour's landmark" (מַסִּיג, here once written with שׂ, while otherwise הִשִּׂיג from נָשַׂג signifies assequi, on the other hand הִסִּיג from סוּג signifies dimovere). They steal flocks, וַיִּרְעוּ, i.e. they are so barefaced, that after they have stolen them they pasture them openly. The ass of the orphans, the one that is their whole possession, and their only beast for labour, they carry away as prey (נָהַג, as e.g. Isa. xx. 4); they distrain, i.e. take away with them as a pledge (on חָבַל, to bind by a pledge, obstringere, and also to take as a pledge, vid. on ch. xxii. 6, and Köhler on Zech. xi. 7), the yoke-ox of the widow (this is the exact meaning of

שׁוֹר, as of the Arab. *thôr*). They turn the needy aside from the way which they are going, so that they are obliged to wander hither and thither without home or right: the poor of the land are obliged to hide themselves altogether. The *Hiph.* הִטָּה, with אֶבְיוֹנִים as its obj., is used as in Amos v. 12; there it is used of turning away from a right that belongs to them, here of turning out of the way into trackless regions. אֶבְיוֹן (*vid.* on ch. xxix. 16) here, as frequently, is the parallel word with עָנָו, the humble one, the patient sufferer; instead of which the *Keri* is עָנִי, the humbled, bowed down with suffering (*vid.* on Ps. ix. 13). עֲנִיֵּי־אָרֶץ occurs without any *Keri* in Ps. lxxvi. 10, Zeph. ii. 3, and might less suitably appear here, where it is not so much the moral attribute as the outward condition that is intended to be described. The *Pual* חֻבָּאוּ describes that which they are forced to do.

The description of these unfortunate ones is now continued; and by a comparison with ch. xxx. 1–8, it is probable that aborigines who are turned out of their original possessions and dwellings are intended (comp. ch. xv. 19, according to which the poet takes his stand in an age in which the original relations of the races had been already disturbed by the calamities of war and the incursions of aliens). If the central point of the narrative lies in Haurân, or, more exactly, in the Nukra, it is natural, with Wetzstein, to think of the

اهل الوكر or عرب الحجر, *i.e.* the (perhaps Ituræan) "races of the caves" in Trachonitis.

> 5 *Behold, as wild asses in the desert,*
> *They go forth in their work seeking for prey,*
> *The steppe is food to them for the children.*
> 6 *In the field they reap the fodder for his cattle,*
> *And they glean the vineyard of the evil-doer.*
> 7 *They pass the night in nakedness without a garment,*

And have no covering in the cold.
8 *They are wet with the torrents of rain upon the mountains,*
And they hug the rocks for want of shelter.

The poet could only draw such a picture as this, after having himself seen the home of his hero, and the calamitous fate of such as were driven forth from their original abodes to live a vagrant, poverty-stricken gipsy life. By ver. 5, one is reminded of Ps. civ. 21-23, especially since in ver. 11 of this Psalm the פְּרָאִים, *onagri* (Kulans), are mentioned,— those beautiful animals[1] which, while young, are difficult to be broken in, and when grown up are difficult to be caught; which in their love of freedom are an image of the Beduin, Gen. xvi. 12; their untractableness an image of that which cannot be bound, ch. xi. 12; and from their roaming about in herds in waste regions, are here an image of a gregarious, vagrant, and freebooter kind of life. The old expositors, as also Rosenm., Umbr., Arnh., and Vaih., are mistaken in thinking that *aliud hominum sceleratorum genus* is described in vers. 5 sqq. Ewald and Hirz. were the first to perceive that vers. 5-8 is the further development of ver. 4*b*, and that here, as in ch. xxx. 1 sqq., those who are driven back into the wastes and caves, and a remnant of the ejected and oppressed aborigines who drag out a miserable existence, are described.

The accentuation rightly connects פראים במדבר; by the omission of the *Caph similit.*, as *e.g.* Isa. li. 12, the comparison (like a wild ass) becomes an equalization (as a wild ass). The *perf.* יָצְאוּ is a general uncoloured expression of that which is usual: they go forth בְּפָעֳלָם, in their work (not: to

---

[1] Layard, *New Discoveries*, p. 270, describes these wild asses' colts. The Arabic name is like the Hebrew, *el-ferâ*, or also *himâr el-wahsh*, *i.e.* wild ass, as we have translated, whose home is on the steppe. For fuller particulars, *vid.* Wetzstein's note on ch. xxxix. 5 sqq.

their work, as the Psalmist, in Ps. civ. 23, expresses himself,
exchanging בְּ for לְ). מְשַׁחֲרֵי לַטָּרֶף, searching after prey, *i.e.* to
satisfy their hunger (Ps. civ. 21), from טָרַף, in the primary
signification *decerpere* (*vid.* Hupfeld on Ps. vii. 3), describes
that which in general forms their daily occupation as they
roam about; the *constructivus* is used here, without any
proper genitive relation, as a form of connection, according
to Ges. § 116, 1.   The idea of waylaying is not to be
connected with the expression. Job describes those who are
perishing in want and misery, not so much as those who
themselves are guilty of evil practices, as those who have
been brought down to poverty by the wrongdoing of others.
As is implied in משחרי (comp. the morning Psalm, lxiii. 2,
Isa. xxvi. 9), Job describes their going forth in the early
morning; the children (נְעָרִים, as ch. i. 19, xxix. 5) are those
who first feel the pangs of hunger. לֹו refers individually to
the father in the company : the steppe (with its scant supply
of roots and herbs) is to him food for the children ; he
snatches it from it, it must furnish it for him. The idea is
not: for himself and his family (Hirz., Hahn, and others);
for ver. 6, which has been much misunderstood, describes how
they, particularly the adults, obtain their necessary subsistence.   There is no MS. authority for reading בְּלִי-לֹו instead of
בְּלִיל ; the translation " what is not to him " (LXX., Targ.,
and partially also the Syriac version) is therefore to be rejected. Raschi correctly interprets יבולו as a general explanation, and Ralbag תבואתו : it is, as in ch. vi. 5, mixed fodder
for cattle, *farrago*, consisting of oats or barley sown among
vetches and beans, that is intended. The meaning is not,
however, as most expositors explain it, that they seek to
satisfy their hunger with the food for cattle grown in the
fields of the rich evil-doer ; for קָצַר does not signify to sweep
together, but to reap in an orderly manner; and if they
meant to steal, why did they not seize the better portion of

the produce? It is correct to take the suff. as referring to the רִשָׁע which is mentioned in the next clause, but it is not to be understood that they plunder his fields *per nefas;* on the contrary, that he hires them to cut the fodder for his cattle, but does not like to entrust the reaping of the better kinds of corn to them. It is impracticable to press the *Hiph.* יקצירו of the *Chethib* to favour this rendering; on the contrary, הקציר stands to קצר in like (not causative) signification as הנחה to נחה (*vid.* on ch. xxxi. 18). In like manner, ver. 6*b* is to be understood of hired labour. The rich man prudently hesitates to employ these poor people as vintagers; but he makes use of their labour (whilst his own men are fully employed at the wine-vats) to gather the straggling grapes which ripen late, and were therefore left at the vintage season. The older expositors are reminded of לֶקֶשׁ, late hay, and explain יְלַקֵּשׁוּ as *denom.* by יכרתו לקשו (Aben-Ezra, Immanuel, and others) or יאכלו לקשו (Parchon); but how unnatural to think of the second mowing, or even of eating the after-growth of grass, where the vineyard is the subject referred to! On the contrary, לָקֵשׁ signifies, as it were, *serotinare, i.e. serotinos fructus colligere* (Rosenm.):[1] this is the work which the rich man assigns to them, because he gains by it, and even in the worst case can lose but little.

Vers. 7 sq. tell how miserably they are obliged to shift for themselves during this autumnal season of labour, and also at other times. Naked (עָרוֹם, whether an adverbial form or not, is conceived of after the manner of an accusative : in

---

[1] In the idiom of Hauran, לָקַשׁ, *fut. i*, signifies to be late, to come late ; in *Piel*, to delay, *e.g.* the evening meal, return, etc.; in *Hithpa. telaqqas*, to arrive too late. Hence *laqîs* לָקִישׁ and *loqsî* לֻקְשִׁי, delayed, of any matter, *e.g.* לָקִישׁ and לְקִישִׁי זֶרַע, late seed (= לֶקֶשׁ, Amos vii. 1, in connection with which the late rain in April, which often fails, is reckoned on), וְלֶד לְקִישִׁי, a child born late (*i.e.* in old age) ; *bakîr* בָּכִיר and *bekrî* בְּכִרִי are the opposites in every signification.—WETZST.

a naked, stripped condition, Arabic *'urjânan*) they pass the
night, without having anything on the body (on לְבִישׁ, *vid.* on
Ps. xxii. 19), and they have no (אֵין supply לָהֶם) covering or
veil (corresponding to the notion of בֶּגֶד) in the cold.[1]   They
become thoroughly drenched by the frequent and continuous
storms that visit the mountains, and for want of other shelter
are obliged to shelter themselves under the overhanging
rocks, lying close up to them, and clinging to them,—an idea
which is expressed here by חֻבָּקוּ, as in Lam. iv. 5, where, of
those who were luxuriously brought up on purple cushions,
it is said that they "embrace dunghills;" for in Palestine
and Syria, the forlorn one, who, being afflicted with some
loathsome disease, is not allowed to enter the habitations of
men, lies on the dunghill (*mezâbil*), asking alms by day of the
passers-by, and at night hiding himself among the ashes which
the sun has warmed.[2]   The usual accentuation, מזרם with *Dechî*,
הרים with *Munach*, after which it should be translated *ab in-*

---

[1] All the Beduins sleep naked at night.   I once asked why they do
this, since they are often disturbed by attacks at night, and I was told
that it is a very ancient custom.   Their clothing (*kiswe*, כְּסוּה), both of
the nomads of the steppe (*bedû*) and of the caves (*wa'r*), is the same,
summer and winter; many perish on the pastures when overtaken by
snow-storms, or by cold and want, when their tents and stores are taken
from them in the winter time by an enemy.—WETZST.

[2] Wetzstein observes on this passage: In the mind of the speaker, מחסה
is the house made of stone, from which localities not unfrequently derive
their names, as *El-hasa*, on the east of the Dead Sea; the well-known
commercial town *El-hasâ*, on the east of the Arabian peninsula, which
is generally called *Lahsâ*; the town of *El-hasja* (אֶלְחַסְיָה), north-east of
Damascus, etc.: so that חבקו צור forms the antithesis to the comfortable
dwellings of the حَضَرِى, *hadarî*, *i.e.* one who is firmly settled.   The
roots חבק, חבך, seem, in the desert, to be only dialectically distinct,
and like the root עבק, to signify to be pressed close upon one another.
Thus חֲבָקָה (pronounced hibtsha), a crowd = *zahme*, and *ásâbi' mahbûke*
(מַחבּוּכָה), the closed fingers, etc.   The locality, *hibikke* (Beduin pronunciation for *habáka*, חֲבָכָה with the Beduin *Dag. euphonicum*), de-

undatione montes humectantur, is false ; in correct Codd. מזרם
has also *Munach ;* the other *Munach* is, as in ch. xxiii. 5*a*, 9*a*,
xxiv. 6*b*, and freq., a substitute for *Dechî.* Having sketched
this special class of the oppressed, and those who are abandoned to the bitterest want, Job proceeds with his description
of the many forms of wrong which prevail unpunished on
the earth :

   9 *They tear the fatherless from the breast,*
      And defraud the poor.
   10 *Naked, they slink away without clothes,*
      And hungering they bear the sheaves.
   11 *Between their walls they squeeze out the oil;*
      They tread the wine-presses, and suffer thirst.
   12 *In the city vassals groan,*
      And the soul of the oppressed crieth out—
      And Eloah heedeth not the anomaly.

The accentuation of ver. 9*a* (יְגֹ֑זְלוּ with *Dechî*, מִשֹּׁ֖ד with

scribed in my *Reisebericht,* has its name from this circumstance alone,
that the houses have been attached to (fastened into) the rocks. Hence
חָבַק in this passage signifies to press into the fissure of a rock, to seek
out a corner which may defend one (*dherwe*) against the cold winds and
rain-torrents (which are far heavier among the mountains than on the
plain). The *dherwe* (from دَرَا, to afford protection, shelter, a word frequently used in the desert) plays a prominent part among the nomads ;
and in the month of March, as it is proverbially said the *dherwe* is better
than the *ferwe* (the skin), they seek to place their tents for protection
under the rocks or high banks of the wadys, on account of the cold
strong winds, for the sake of the young of the flocks, to which the cold
storms are often very destructive. When the sudden storms come on, it
is a general thing for the shepherds and flocks to hasten to take shelter
under overhanging rocks, and the caverns (*mughr* مَغَر) which belong to
the troglodyte age, and are *e.g.* common in the mountains of Hauran ;
so that, therefore, ver. 8 can as well refer to concealing themselves only
for a time (from rain and storm) in the clefts as to troglodytes, who
constantly dwell in caverns, or to those dwelling in tents who, during
the storms, seek the *dherwe* of rock sides.

Munach) makes the relation of שׁד יתוֹם genitival. Heidenheim
(in a MS. annotation to Kimchi's *Lex.*) accordingly badly interprets: they plunder from the spoil of the orphan; Ramban
better: from the ruin, *i.e.* the shattered patrimony; both
appeal to the Targum, which translates מביזת יתום, like the
Syriac version, *men bezto de-jatme* (comp. Jerome: *vim fece-
runt deprædantes pupillos*). The original reading, however, is
perhaps (*vid.* Buxtorf, *Lex.* col. 295) מפיאַ, ἀπὸ βυζίου, from
the mother's breast, as it is also, with LXX. (ἀπὸ μαστοῦ),
to be translated contrary to the accentuation. Inhuman
creditors take the fatherless and still tender orphan away
from its mother, in order to bring it up as a slave, and so to
obtain payment. If this is the meaning of the passage, it is
natural to understand יחְבֹּלוּ, ver. 9*b*, of distraining; but (1)
the poet would then repeat himself tautologically, *vid.* ver. 3,
where the same thing is far more evidently said; (2) חָבַל,
to distrain, would be construed with עַל, contrary to the logic
of the word. Certainly the phrase חבל עַל may be in some
degree explained by the interpretation, "to impose a fine"
(Ew., Hahn), or "to distrain" (Hirz., Welte), or "to oppress
with fines" (Schlottm.); but violence is thus done to the
usage of the language, which is better satisfied by the explanation of Ralbag (among modern expositors, Ges., Arnh.,
Vaih., Stick., Hlgst.): and what the unfortunate one possesses they seize; but this עַל = עַל אֲשֶׁר directly as object is
impossible. The passage, Deut. vii. 25, cited by Schultens in
its favour, is of a totally different kind.

But throughout the Semitic dialects the verb חָבַל also
signifies "to destroy, to treat injuriously" (*e.g.* Arab. *el-
châbil*, a by-name of Satan); it occurs in this signification in
ch. xxxiv. 31, and according to the analogy of הֵרַע עַל, 1 Kings
xvii. 20, can be construed with עַל as well as with לְ. The poet,
therefore, by this construction will have intended to distinguish the one חבל from the other, ch. xxii. 6, xxiv. 3; and it

is with Umbreit to be translated: they bring destruction upon the poor; or better: they take undue advantage of those who otherwise are placed in trying circumstances.

The subjects of ver. 10 are these עֲנִיִּים, who are made serfs, and become objects of merciless oppression, and the poet here in ver. 10a indeed repeats what he has already said almost word for word in ver. 7a (comp. ch. xxxi. 19); but there the nakedness was the general calamity of a race oppressed by subjugation, here it is the consequence of the sin of *merces retenta laborum*, which cries aloud to heaven, practised on those of their own race: they slink away (הִלֵּךְ, as ch. xxx. 28) naked (*nude*), without (בְּלִי = מִבְּלִי, as perhaps *sine = absque*) clothing, and while suffering hunger they carry the sheaves (since their masters deny them what, according to Deut. xxv. 4, shall not be withheld even from the beasts). Between their walls (שׁוּרֹת like שָׁרוֹת, Jer. v. 10, Chaldee שׁוּרַיָּא), *i.e.* the walls of their masters who have made them slaves, therefore under strict oversight, they press out the oil (יַצְהִירוּ, ἅπ. γεγρ.), they tread the wine-vats (יְקָבִים, *lacus*), and suffer thirst withal (*fut. consec.* according to Ew. § 342, *a*), without being allowed to quench their thirst from the must which runs out of the presses (גִּתּוֹת, *torcularia*, from which the verb דָּרַךְ is here transferred to the vats). Böttch. translates: between their rows of trees, without being able to reach out right or left; but that is least of all suitable with the olives. Carey correctly explains: "the factories or the garden enclosures of these cruel slaveholders." This reference of the word to the wall of the enclosure is more suitable than to walls of the press-house in particular. From tyrannical oppression in the country,[1] Job now passes over to the abominations of discord and war in the cities.

Ver. 12a. It is natural, with Umbr., Ew., Hirz., and others,

---

[1] Brentius here remarks: *Quantum igitur judicium in eos futurum est, qui in homines ejusdem carnis, ejusdem patriæ, ejusdem fidei, ejusdem Christi*

to read מֵתִים like the Peschito; but as *mite* in Syriac, so also
מתים in Hebrew as a noun everywhere signifies the dead
(Arab. *mauta*), not the dying, mortals (Arab. *maītûna*); wherefore Ephrem interprets the *præs.* "they groan" by the *perf.*
"they have groaned." The pointing מְתִים, therefore, is quite
correct; but the accentuation which, by giving *Mehupach Zinnorith* to מְעִיר, and *Asla legarmeh* to מתים, places the two words
in a genitival relation, is hardly correct: in the city of men,
i.e. the inhabited, thickly-populated city, they groan; not: men
(as Rosenm. explains, according to Gen. ix. 6, Prov. xi. 6)
groan; for just because מְתִים appeared to be too inexpressive
as a subject, this accentuation seems to have been preferred.
It is also possible that the signification fierce anger (Hos. xi.
9), or anguish (Jer. xv. 8), was combined with עִיר, comp.

غَيِر, jealousy, fury (= קִנְאָה), of which, however, no trace is
anywhere visible.[1]   With Jer., Symm., and Theod., we take
מתים as the sighing ones themselves; the feebleness of the
subject disappears if we explain the passage according to
such passages as Deut. ii. 34, iii. 6, comp. Judg. xx. 48: it

---

*committunt quod nec in bruta animalia committendum est, quod malum in
Germania frequentissimum est.   Væ igitur Germaniæ!*
[1] Wetzstein translates Hos. xi. 9: I will not come as a raging foe, with

בְּ of the attribute = الغَيِور بِصفَة (comp. Jer. xv. 8, עִיר, parall. שֹׁדֵד)

after the form קִים, to which, if not this עִיר, certainly the עִיר, ἐγρήγορος,
occurring in Dan. iv. 10, and freq., corresponds. What we remarked
above, vol. i. p. 440, on the form קִים, is cleared up by the following
observation of Wetzstein: "The form קִים belongs to the numerous class of
segolate forms of the form פַּעְל, which, as belonging to the earliest period
of the formation of the Semitic languages, take neither plural nor feminine
terminations; they have often a collective meaning, and are not originally

abstracta, but *concreta* in the sense of the Arabic *part. act.* مِفَاعَل.   This

inflexible primitive formation is frequently found in the present day in the

is the male inhabitants that are intended, whom any conqueror would put to the sword; we have therefore translated
men (men of war), although "people" (ch. xi. 3) also would
not have been unsuitable according to the ancient use of the
word. נָאַק is intended of the groans of the dying, as Jer. li.
52, Ezek. xxx. 24, as ver. 12*b* also shows: the soul of those
that are mortally wounded cries out. חֲלָלִים signifies not
merely the slain and already dead, but, according to its etymon, those who are pierced through, those who have received
their death-blow; their soul cries out, since it does not leave
the body without a struggle. Such things happen without
God preventing them. לֹא־יָשִׂים תִּפְלָה, He observeth not the
abomination, either = לֹא יָשִׂים בלבו, ch. xxii. 22 (He layeth it
not to heart), or, since the phrase occurs nowhere elliptically,
= לֹא יָשִׂים לבו על, ch. i. 8, xxxiv. 23 (He does not direct His
heart, His attention to it), here as elliptical, as in ch. iv. 20,
Isa. xli. 20. True, the latter phrase is never joined with the
acc. of the object; but if we translate after שִׂים בְּ, ch. iv. 18:
non imputat, He does not reckon such תפלה, *i.e.* does not
punish it, בָּם (בָּהֶם) ought to be supplied, which is still somewhat liable to misconstruction, since the preceding subject

idiom of the steppe, which shows that the Hebrew is essentially of primeval antiquity (*urall*). Thus the Beduin says: *hû qitlî* (הוּא קְטְלִי), he
is my opponent in a hand-to-hand combat; *nîthî* (נְמְחִי), my opponent
in the tournament with lances; *chilfî* (חִלְפִי) and *dîddî* (צִדִּי), my adversary; thus a step-mother is called *dîr* (צִיר), as the oppressor of
the step-children, and a concubine *dirr* (צְרְר), as the oppressor of her
rival. The Kamus also furnishes several words which belong here, as *tilb*
(טִלְב), a persecutor." Accordingly, קִים is derived from קוּם, as also עִיר,
a city, from עוּר (whence, according to a prevalent law of the change of
letters, we have עִיר first of all, *plur.* עָיָרִים, Judg. x. 4), and signifies the
rebelling one, *i.e.* the enemy (who is now in the idiom of the steppe
called *qômânî*, from *qôm*, a state of war, a feud), as עִיר, a keeper,
and צִיר, a messenger; עִיר (קִיר) is also originally concrete, a wall
(enclosure).

is not the oppressors, but those who suffer oppression. תִּפְלָה
is properly insipidity (comp. Arab. *tafila*, to stink), absurdity,
self-contradiction, here the immorality which sets at nought
the moral order of the world, and remains nevertheless
unpunished. The Syriac version reads תְּפִלָּה, and translates,
like Louis Bridel (1818): *et Dieu ne, fait aucune attention à
leur prière.*

> 13 *Others are those that rebel against the light,*
> *They will know nothing of its ways,*
> *And abide not in its paths.*
> 14 *The murderer riseth up at dawn,*
> *He slayeth the sufferer and the poor,*
> *And in the night he acteth like a thief.*
> 15 *And the eye of the adulterer watcheth for the twilight;*
> *He thinks: " no eye shall recognise me,"*
> *And he putteth a veil before his face.*

With הֵמָּה begins a new turn in the description of the moral
confusion which has escaped God's observation; it is to be
translated neither as retrospective, " since they" (Ewald), nor
as distinctive, " they even" (Böttch.), *i.e.* the powerful in distinction from the oppressed, but "those" (for המה corresponds
to our use of " those," אֵלֶּה to " these"), by which Job passes
on to another class of evil-disposed and wicked men. Their
general characteristic is, that they shun the light. Those
who are described in vers. 14 sq. are described according to
their general characteristic in ver. 13; accordingly it is not
to be interpreted: those belong to the enemies of the light,
but: those are, according to their very nature, enemies of the
light. The *Beth* is the so-called *Beth essent.;* הָיוּ (comp. Prov.
iii. 26) affirms what they are become by their own inclination,
or as what they are fashioned, viz. as ἀποστάται φωτός
(Symm.); מָרַד (on the root מר, *vid.* on ch. xxiii. 2) signifies
properly to push one's self against anything, to lean upon, to

rebel ; מֹרֵד therefore signifies one who strives against another, one who is obstinate (like the Arabic *mârid, merîd*, comp. *mumâri*, not conformable to the will of another). The improvement מֹרְדֵי אוֹר (not with *Makkeph*, but with *Mahpach* of *Mercha mahpach*. placed between the two words, *vid.* Bär's *Psalterium*, p. x.) assumes the possibility of the construction with the *acc.*, which occurs at least once, Josh. xxii. 19. They are hostile to the light, they have no familiarity with its ways (הִכִּיר, as ver. 17, Ps. cxlii. 5, Ruth ii. 19, to take knowledge of anything, to interest one's self in its favour), and do not dwell (יָשְׁבוּ, Jer. *reversi sunt*, according to the false reading יָשֻׁבוּ) in its paths, *i.e.* they neither make nor feel themselves at home there, they have no peace therein. The light is the light of day, which, however, stands in deeper, closer relation to the higher light, for the vicious man hateth τὸ φῶς, John iii. 20, in every sense ; and the works which are concealed in the darkness of the night are also ἔργα τοῦ σκότους, Rom. xiii. 12 (comp. Isa. xxix. 15), in the sense in which light and darkness are two opposite principles of the spiritual world. It need not seem strange that the more minute description of the conduct of these enemies of the light now begins with לָאוֹר. It is impossible that this should mean : still in the darkness of the night (Stick.), prop. towards the light, when it is not yet light. Moreover, in biblical Hebrew, אוֹר does not signify evening, in which sense it occurs in Talmudic Hebrew (*Pesachim* 1a, *Seder olam rabba*, c. 5, אור שביעי, *vespera septima*), like אוֹרְתָּא (= נֶשֶׁף) in Talmudic Aramaic. The meaning, on the contrary, is that towards daybreak (comp. הבקר אור, Gen. xliv. 3), therefore with early morning, the murderer rises up, to go about his work, which veils itself in darkness (Ps. x. 8–10) by day, viz. to slay (comp. on יָקוּם . . . יִקְטֹל, Ges. § 142, 3, *c*) the unfortunate and the poor, who pass by defenceless and alone. One has to supply the idea of the ambush in which the waylayer lies in wait; and it is certainly inconvenient that it is not expressed. The antithesis וּבַלַּיְלָה, ver. 14c, shows that nothing but *primo mane* is meant by לָאוֹר. He who in the day-time goes forth to murder and plunder, at night commits petty thefts, where no one whom he could attack passes by. Stickel translates: to slay the poor and wretched, and in the night to play the thief; but then the *subjunctivus* וִיהִי ought to precede (*vid. e.g.* ch. xiii. 5), and in general it cannot be proved without straining it, that the voluntative form of the future everywhere has a modal signification. Moreover, here יְהִי does not differ from ch. xviii. 12, xx. 23, but is only a poetic shorter form for יִהְיֶה: in the night he is like a thief, *i.e.* plays the part of the thief. And the adulterer's eye observes the darkness of evening (*vid.* Prov. vii. 9), *i.e.* watches closely for its coming on (שָׁמַר, in the usual signification *observare*, to be on the watch, to take care, observe anxiously), since he hopes to render himself invisible; and that he may not be recognised even if seen, he puts on a mask. סֵתֶר פָּנִים is something by which his countenance is rendered unrecognisable (LXX. ἀποκρυβὴ προσώπου), like the Arab. *sitr*, *sitâreh*, a curtain, veil, therefore a veil for the face, or, as we say in one word borrowed from the Arabic

سِخَارة, a farce (masquerade): the mask, but not in the proper sense.[1]

> 16 *In the dark they dig through houses,*
> *By day they shut themselves up,*
> *They will know nothing of the light.*

[1] The mask was perhaps never known in Palestine and Syria; סתר פנים is the *mendîl* or women's veil, which in the present day (in *Hauran* exclusively) is called *sitr*, and is worn over the face by all married women in the towns, while in the country it is worn hanging down the back, and is only drawn over the face in the presence of a stranger. If this explanation is correct, the poet means to say that the adulterer, in order to

17 *For the depth of night is to them even as the dawn of the*
    morning,
    For they know the terrors of the depth of night.

The handiwork of the thief, which is but slightly referred
to in ver. 14c, is here more particularly described. The
indefinite subj. of חָתַר, as is manifest from what follows, is
the band ' of thieves. The בְּ, which is elsewhere joined with
חתר (to break into anything), is here followed by the *acc.*
בָּתִּים (to be pronounced *bâttim,* not *bottim*),[1] as in the Talmudic, שִׁנּוֹ חָתַר, to pick one's teeth (and thereby to make
them loose), *b. Kidduschin,* 24 *b.* According to the Talmud,
Ralbag, and the ancient Jewish interpretation in general,
ver. 16*b* is closely connected to בתים : houses which they
have marked by day for breaking into, and the mode of its
accomplishment ; but חָתַם nowhere signifies *designare,* always
obsignare, to seal up, to put under lock and key, ch. xiv. 17,
ix. 7, xxxvii. 7 ; according to which the *Piel,* which occurs
only here, is to be explained : by day they seal up, *i.e.* shut
themselves up for their safety (לָמוֹ is not to be accented with
Athnach, but with *Rebia mugrasch*) : they know not the light,
i.e. as Schlottm. well explains : they have no fellowship with
it ; for the biblical יָדַע, γινώσκειν, mostly signifies a knowledge which enters into the subject, and intimately unites

remain undiscovered, wears women's clothes [comp. Deut. xxii. 5] ; and,
in fact, in the Syrian towns (the figure is taken from town-life) women's
clothing is always chosen for that kind of forbidden nocturnal undertaking, *i.e.* the man disguises himself in an *izâr,* which covers him from head
to foot, takes the *mendîl,* and goes with a lantern (without which at night
every person is seized by the street watchman as a suspicious person) un-
hindered into a strange house.—WETZST.

[1] *Vid.* Aben-Ezra on Ex. xii. 7. The main proof that it is to be pronounced *bâttim* is, that written exactly it is בָּתִּים, and that the *Metheg,*
according to circumstances, is changed into an accent, as Ex. viii. 7, xii. 7,
Jer. xviii. 22, Ezek. xlv. 4, which can only happen by *Kametz,* not by
Kometz (*K. chatûph*); comp. Köhler on Zech. xiv. 2.

itself with it. In ver. 17 one confirmation follows another. Umbr. and Hirz. explain : for the morning is to them at once the shadow of death ; but יַחְדָּו, in the signification at the same time, as we have taken יַחַד in ch. xvii. 16 (nevertheless of simultaneousness of time), is unsupportable : it signifies together, ch. ii. 11, ix. 32 ; and the arrangement of the words יַחְדָּו . . . לָמוֹ (to them together) is like Isa. ix. 20, xxxi. 3, Jer. xlvi. 12. Also, apart from the erroneous translation of the יחדו, which is easily set aside, Hirzel's rendering of ver. 17 is forced : the morning, *i.e.* the bright day, is to them all as the shadow of death, for each and every one of them knows the terrors of the daylight, which is to them as the shadow of death, viz. the danger of being discovered and condemned. The interpretation, which is also preferred by Olshausen, is far more natural : the depth of night is to them as the dawn of the morning (on the precedence of the predicate, comp. Amos iv. 13 and v. 8 : walking in the darkness of the early morning), for they are acquainted with the terrors of the depth of night, *i.e.* they are not surprised by them, but know how to anticipate and to escape them. Ch. xxxviii. 15 also, where the night, which vanishes before the rising of the sun, is called the "light" of the evil-doer, favours this interpretation (not the other, as Olsh. thinks). The accentuation also favours it ; for if בקר had been the subj., and were to be translated : the morning is to them the shadow of death, it ought to have been accented בקר למו צלמות, *Dechî*, *Mercha*, *Athnach*. It is, however, accented *Munach*, *Munach*, *Athnach*, and the second *Munach* stands as the deputy of *Dechî*, whose value in the interpunction it represents ; therefore בקר למו is the predicate : the shadow of death is morning to them. From the *plur.* the description now, with יַכִּיר, passes into the *sing.*, as individualizing it. בַּלְהוֹת, constr. of בַּלָּהוֹת, is without a *Dagesh* in the second consonant. Mercier admirably remarks here : *sunt ei familiares et noti nocturni terrores, neque eos timet aut curat, quasi sibi cum illis necessitudo et familiaritas intercederet et cum illis ne noceant fœdus aut pactum inierit.* Thus by their skill and contrivance they escape danger, and divine justice allows them to remain undiscovered and unpunished,—a fact which is most incomprehensible.

It is now time that this thought was once again definitely expressed, that one may not forget what these accumulated illustrations are designed to prove. But what now follows in vers. 18–21 seems to express not Job's opinion, but that of his opponents. Ew., Hirz., and Hlgst. regard vers. 18–21, 22–25, as thesis and antithesis. To the question, What is the lot that befalls all these evil-doers? Job is thought to give a twofold answer: first, to ver. 21, an ironical answer in the sense of the friends, that those men are overtaken by the merited punishment; then from ver. 22 is his own serious answer, which stands in direct contrast to the former. But (1) in vers. 18–21 there is not the slightest trace observable that Job does not express his own view: a consideration which is also against Schlottman, who regards vers. 18–21 as expressive of the view of an opponent. (2) There is no such decided contrast between vers. 18–21 and 22–25, for vers. 19 and 24 both affirm substantially the same thing concerning the end of the evil-doer. In like manner, it is also not to be supposed, with Stick., Löwenth., Böttch., Welte, and Hahn, that Job, outstripping the friends, as far as ver. 21, describes how the evil-doer certainly often comes to a terrible end, and in vers. 22 sqq. how the very opposite of this, however, is often witnessed; so that this consequently furnishes no evidence in support of the exclusive assertion of the friends. Moreover, ver. 24 compared with ver. 19, where there is nothing to indicate a direct contrast, is opposed to it; and ver. 22, which has no appearance of referring to a direct contrast with what has been previously said, is opposed to such an antithetical rendering of the two final strophes. Ver. 22 might more readily be regarded as a transition to the antithesis, if vers. 18-21 could, with Eichh., Schnurr., Dathe, Umbr., and Vaih., after the LXX., Syriac, and Jerome, be understood as optative: "Let such an one be light on the surface of the water, let . . . be cursed, let him not turn towards," etc., but ver. 18a is not of the optative form ; and 18c, where in that case אל־יִפֶנה would be expected, instead of לֹא־יִפֶנה, shows that 18b, where, according to the syntax, the optative rendering is natural, is nevertheless not to be so rendered. The right interpretation is that which regards both vers. 18-21 and 22 sqq. as Job's own view, without allowing him absolutely to contradict himself. Thus it is interpreted, *e.g.* by Rosenmüller, who, however, as also Renan, errs in connecting ver. 18 with the description of the thieves, and understands ver. 18a of their slipping away, 18b of their dwelling in horrible places, and 18c of their avoidance of the vicinity of towns.

18 *For he is light upon the surface of the water ;*
   Their heritage is cursed upon the earth ;
   He turneth no more in the way of the vineyard.
19 *Drought, also heat, snatch away snow water—*
   So doth Sheôl those who have sinned.
20 *The womb forgetteth him, worms shall feast on him,*
   He is no more remembered ;
   So the desire of the wicked is broken as a tree—
21 *He who hath plundered the barren that bare not,*
   And did no good to the widow.

The point of comparison in ver. 18a is the swiftness of the disappearing : he is carried swiftly past, as any light substance on the surface of the water is hurried along by the swiftness of the current, and can scarcely be seen ; comp. ch. ix. 26 : "My days shoot by as ships of reeds, as an eagle

which dasheth upon its prey," and Hos. x. 7, "Samaria's
king is destroyed like a bundle of brushwood (LXX.,
Theod., φρύγανον) on the face of the water," which is
quickly drawn into the whirlpool, or buried by the approaching wave.[1] But here the idea is not that of being swallowed
up by the waters, as in the passage in Hosea, but, on the
contrary, of vanishing from sight, by being carried rapidly
past by the rush of the waters. If, then, the evil-doer dies
a quick, easy death, his heritage (חֶלְקָה, from חָלַק, to divide)
is cursed by men, since no one will dwell in it or use it,
because it is appointed by God to desolation on account of
the sin which is connected with it (vid. on ch. xv. 28);
even he, the evil-doer, no more turns the way of the vineyard (פָּנָה, with דֶּרֶךְ, not an acc. of the obj., but as indicating
the direction = אֶל־דֶּרֶךְ; comp. 1 Sam. xiii. 18 with ver. 17 of
the same chapter), proudly to inspect his wide extended domain, and overlook the labourers. The curse therefore does
not come upon him, nor can one any longer lie in wait for
him to take vengeance on him; it is useless to think of venting upon him the rage which his conduct during life pro-
voked; he is long since out of reach in Sheôl.

That which Job says figuratively in ver. 18a, and in ch.
xxi. 13 without a figure: "in a moment they go down to
Sheôl," he expresses in ver. 19 under a new figure, and,
moreover, in the form of an emblematic proverb (vid.
Herzog's *Real-Encyklopädie*, xiv. 696), according to the
peculiarity of which, not כֵּן, but either only the copulative
Waw (Prov. xxv. 25) or nothing whatever (Prov. xi. 22), is

---

[1] The translation: like foam (*spuma* or *bulla*), is also very suitable here.
Thus Targ., Symm., Jerome, and others; but the signification to foam
cannot be etymologically proved, whereas קָצַף in the signification *confrin-*
gere is established by קְצָפָה, breaking, Joel i. 7, and قصف; so that consequently קֶצֶף, as synon. of אַף, signifies properly the breaking forth, and
is then allied to עֶבְרָה.

to be supplied before חַטְאוּ שְׁאוֹל. חָטָאוּ is virtually an object: *eos qui peccarunt*. Ver. 19*b* is a model-example of extreme brevity of ·expression, Ges. § 155, 4, *b*. Sandy ground (צִיָּה, arid land, without natural moisture), added to it (גַּם, not: likewise) the heat of the sun—these two, working simultaneously from beneath and above, snatch away (גָּזְלוּ, cogn. גָּזַר, root גָּז, to cut, cut away, tear away; Arab. جَزَر, *fut. i*, used of sinking, decreasing water) מֵימֵי שֶׁלֶג, water of (melted) snow (which is fed from no fountain, and therefore is quickly absorbed), and Sheôl snatches away those who have sinned (= גָּזְלָה אֶת־אֲשֶׁר חָטָאוּ). The two incidents are alike: the death of those whose life has been a life of sin, follows as a consequence easily and unobserved, without any painful and protracted struggle. The sinner disappears suddenly; the womb, *i.e.* the mother that bare him, forgets him (רֶחֶם, *matrix = mater;* according to Ralbag: friendship, from רֶחֶם, to love tenderly; others: relationship, in which sense رَحِم = רֶחֶם is used), worms suck at him (מְתָקוֹ for מְתָקַתּוּ, according to Ges. § 147, *a, sugit eum*, from which primary notion of sucking comes the signification to be sweet, ch. xxi. 33: Syriac, *metkat ennun remto;* Ar. *imtasahum*, from the synonymous مَصَّ = מָצַץ, מָצָה, מָזָה), he is no more thought of, and thus then is mischief (*abstr. pro concr.* as ch. v. 16) broken like a tree (not: a staff, which עֵץ never, not even in Hos. iv. 12, directly, like the Arabic 'asa, 'asât, signifies). Since עַוְלָה is used personally, רֹעֶה וגו', ver. 21, can be connected with it as an appositional permutative. His want of compassion (as is still too often seen in the present day in connection with the tyrannical conduct of the executive in Syria and Palestine, · especially on the part of those who collect the taxes) goes the length of eating up, *i.e.* entirely plundering, the·barren, childless (Gen. xi. 30; Isa. liv. 1), and therefore helpless woman, who has no sons to protect and defend her, and never showing favour to the widow, but, on the contrary, thrusting her away from him. There is as little need for regarding the verb רָעָה here, with Rosenm. after the Targ., in the signification *con-fringere*, as cognate with רָעַע, רָצַץ, as conversely to change תִּרֹעֵם, Ps. ii. 9, into תִּרְעֵם; it signifies *depascere*, as in ch. xx. 26, here in the sense of *depopulari*. On the form יֵיטִיב for יֵטִיב, *vid.* Ges. § 70, 2, rem.; and on the transition from the *part.* to the *v. fin.*, *vid.* Ges. § 134, rem. 2. Certainly the memory of such an one is not affectionately cherished; this is equally true with what Job maintains in ch. xxi. 32, that the memory of the evil-doer is immortalized by monuments. Here the allusion is to the remembrance of a mother's love and sympathetic feeling. The fundamental thought of the strophe is this, that neither in life nor in death had he suffered the punishment of his evil-doing. The figure of the broken tree (broken in its full vigour) also corresponds to this thought; comp. on the other hand what Bildad says, ch. xviii. 16: "his roots dry up beneath, and above his branch is lopped off" (or: withered). The severity of his oppression is not manifest till after his death.

In the next strophe Job goes somewhat further. But after having, in vers. 22, 23, said that the life of the ungodly passes away as if they were the favoured of God, he returns to their death, which the friends, contrary to experience, have so fearfully described, whilst it is only now and then distinguished from the death of other men by coming on late and painlessly.

22 *And He preserveth the mighty by His strength;*
   Such an one riseth again, though he despaired of life.
23 *He giveth him rest, and he is sustained,*
   And His eyes are over their ways.

24 *They are exalted—a little while,—then they are no more,*
   And they are sunken away, snatched away like all others,
   And as the top of the stalk they are cut off.—
25 *And if it is not so, who will charge me with lying,*
   And make my assertion worthless?

Though it becomes manifest after their death how little
the ungodly, who were only feared by men, were beloved,
the form of their death itself is by no means such as to reveal
the retributive justice of God. And does it become at all
manifest during their life? The *Waw*, with which the
strophe begins, is, according to our rendering, not adversative,
but progressive. God is the subject. מָשַׁךְ, to extend in
length, used elsewhere of love, Ps. xxxvi. 11, cix. 12, and
anger, Ps. lxxxv. 6, is here transferred to persons : to prolong, preserve long in life. אַבִּירִים are the strong, who bid
defiance not only to every danger (Ps. lxxvi. 6), but also to
all divine influences and noble impulses (Isa. xlvi. 12).
These, whose trust in their own strength God might smite
down by His almighty power, He preserves alive even in
critical positions by that very power : he (the אַבִּיר) stands up
(again), whilst he does not trust to life, *i.e.* whilst he believes
that he must succumb to death (הָאֲמִין as Ps. xxvii. 13, comp.
Genesis, S. 368; חַיִּין, Aramaic form, like מִלִּין, ch. iv. 2,
xii. 11 ; the whole is a contracted circumstantial clause for
וְהוּא לֹא וגו'). He (God) grants him לְבֶטַח, in security, viz.
to live, or even directly : a secure peaceful existence, since
לבטח is virtually an object, and the לְ is that of condition
(comp. לָרֹב, ch. xxvi. 3). Thus Hahn, who, however, here is
only to be followed in this one particular, takes it correctly :
and that he can support himself, which would only be possible
if an *inf.* with לְ had preceded. Therefore : and he is supported, or he can support himself, *i.e.* be comforted, though
this absolute use of נִשְׁעַן cannot be supported ; in this instance

we miss עַל־טוּבוֹ, or some such expression (ch. viii. 15). God
sustains him and raises him up again : His eyes (עֵינָיו = עֵינֵיהוּ)
are (rest) on the ways of these men, they stand as it were
beneath His special protection, or, as it is expressed in ch.
x. 3 : He causes light to shine from above upon the doings of
the wicked. "They are risen up, and are conscious of the
height (of prosperity)—a little while, and they are no more."
Thus ver. 24a is to be explained. The accentuation רוֹמּוּ
with *Mahpach,* מְעַט with *Asla legarmeh* (according to which
it would have to be translated : they stand on high a short
time), is erroneous. The verb רוּם signifies not merely to be
high, but also to rise up, raise one's self, *e.g.* Prov. xi. 11,
and to show one's self exalted, here *extulerunt se in altum* or
exaltati sunt; according to the form of writing רוּם רוֹמּוּ, is
treated as an *Ayin Waw* verb *med. O,* and the *Dagesh* is a
so-called *Dag. affectuosum* (Olsh. § 83, *b*), while רֹמּוּ (like רֹבּוּ,
Gen. xlix. 23) appears to assume the form of a double *Ayin*
verb *med. O,* consequently רָמֲמוּ (Ges. § 67, rem. 1). מְעַט,
followed by *Waw* of the conclusion, forms a clause of itself,
as more frequently עוֹד מְעַט וְ (yet a little while, then . . .),
as, *e.g.* in an exactly similar connection in Ps. xxxvii. 10;
here, however, not expressive of the sudden judgment of the
ungodly, but of their easy death without a struggle (εὐθα-
νασία) : a little, then he is not (again a transition from the
plur. to the distributive or individualizing *sing.*). They are,
viz. as ver. 24b further describes, bowed down all at once (an
idea which is expressed by the *perf.*), are snatched off like all
other men. הֻמְּכוּ is an Aramaizing *Hophal-*form, approaching
the *Hoph.* of strong verbs, for הוּמֲכוּ (Ges. § 67, rem. 8), from
מָכַךְ, to bow one's self (Ps. cvi. 43), to be brought low (Eccl.
x. 18); comp. مَكَّ, to cause to vanish, to annul. יִקָּפְצוּן (for
which it is unnecessary with Olsh. to read יִקָּבְצוּן, after Ezek.
xxix. 5) signifies, according to the primary signification of

קפץ, *comprehendere, constringere, contrahere* (cogn. קמץ, קבץ, קמט, comp. *supra*, i. 437): they are hurried together, or snatched off, *i.e.* deprived of life, like the Arabic تبضه اللّٰه (קפצו אלהים) and passive قُبِض, equivalent to, he has died. There is no reference in the phrase to the *componere artus*, Gen. xlix. 33; it is rather the figure of housing (gathering into the barn) that underlies it; the word, however, only implies seizing and drawing in. Thus the figure which follows is also naturally (comp. קמץ, قَبْضَة, *manipulus*) con-nected with what precedes, and, like the head of an ear of corn, *i.e.* the corn-bearing head of the wheat-stalk, they are cut off (by which one must bear in mind that the ears are reaped higher up than with us, and the standing stalk is usually burnt to make dressing for the field; *vid.* Ges. *Thes.* *s.v.* קש[1]).

On יִמָּלוּ (*fut. Niph.* = יִמָּלוּ), *vid.* on ch. xiv. 2, xviii. 16; the signification *præciduntur*, as observed above, is more suitable here than *marcescunt* (in connection with which sig-nification ch. v. 26 ought to be compared, and the form regarded as *fut. Kal*). Assured of the truth, in conformity with experience, of that which has been said, he appeals finally to the friends: if it be not so (on אֵפוֹ = אֵפוֹא in con-ditional clauses, *vid.* ch. ix. 24), who (by proving the oppo-site) is able to charge me with lying and bring to nought

---

[1] Another figure is also presented here. It is a common thing for the Arabs (Beduins) in harvest-time to come down upon the fields of standing corn—especially barley, because during summer and autumn this grain is indispensable to them as food for their horses—of a district, chiefly at night, and not unfrequently hundreds of camels are laden at one time. As they have no sickles, they cut off the upper part of the stalk with the 'aqfe (a knife very similar to the Roman *sica*) and with sabres, whence this theft is called *qard* קֶרֶץ, *sabring off*; and that which is cut off, as well as the uneven stubble that is left standing, is called *qarid*.— WETZST.

(לְאֵי = לְאֵין, Ew. § 321, *b*, perhaps by אַל being conceived of as originally *infin.* from אָלַל (comp. אֱלִיל), in the sense of non-existence, العَدَم) my assertion?

The bold accusations in the speech of Eliphaz, in which the uncharitableness of the friends attains its height, must penetrate most deeply into Job's spirit. But Job does not answer like by like. Even in this speech in opposition to the friends, he maintains the passionless repose which has once been gained. Although the misjudgment of his character has attained its height in the speech of Eliphaz, his answer does not contain a single bitter personal word. In general, he does not address them, not as though he did not wish to show respect to them, but because he has nothing to say concerning their unjust and wrong conduct that he would not already have said, and because he has lost all hope of his reproof taking effect, all hope of sympathy with his entreaty that they would spare him, all hope of understanding and information on their part.

In the first part of the speech (ch. xxiii.) he occupies himself with the mystery of his own suffering lot, and in the second part (ch. xxiv.) with the reverse of this mystery, the evil-doers' prosperity and immunity from punishment. How is he to vindicate himself against Eliphaz, since his lament over his sufferings as unmerited is accounted by the friends more and more as defiant obstinacy (מרי), and consequently tends to bring him still deeper into that suspicion which he is trying to remove? His testimony concerning himself is of no avail; for it appears to the friends more self-delusive, hypocritical, and sinful, the more decidedly he maintains it; consequently the judgment of God can alone decide between him and his accusers. But while the friends accuse him by word of mouth, God himself is pronouncing sentence against him by His acts,—his affliction is a *de facto* accusation of

God against him.   Therefore, before the judgment of God
can become a vindication of his affliction against the friends,
he must first of all himself have defended and proved his
innocence in opposition to the Author of his affliction.   Hence
the accusation of the friends, which in the speech of Eliphaz
is become more direct and cutting than heretofore, must urge
on anew with all its power the desire in Job of being able to
bring his cause before God.

At the outset he is confident of victory, for his consciousness does not deceive him; and God, although He is both
one party in the cause and judge, is influenced by the irresistible force of the truth.   Herein the want of harmony
in Job's conception of God, the elevation of which into a
higher unity is the goal of the development of the drama,
again shows itself.   He is not able to think of the God who
pursues him, the innocent one, at the present time with suffering, as the just God; on the other hand, the justice of the
God who will permit him to approach His judgment throne,
is to him indisputably sure: He will attend to him, and for
ever acquit him.   Now Job yields to the arbitrary power of
God, but then he will rise by virtue of the justice and truth
of God.   His longing is, therefore, that the God who now
afflicts him may condescend to hear him: this seems to him
the only way of convincing God, and indirectly the friends,
of his innocence, and himself of God's justice.   The basis of
this longing is the desire of being free from the painful conception of God which he is obliged to give way to.   For it is
not the darkness of affliction that enshrouds him which causes
Job the intensest suffering, but the darkness in which it has
enshrouded God to him,—the angry countenance of God
which is turned to him.   But if this is sin, that he is engaged
in a conflict concerning the justice of the Author of his
affliction, it is still greater that he indulges evil thoughts
respecting the Judge towards whose throne of judgment he

presses forward. He thinks that God designedly avoids him, because He is well aware of his innocence; now, however, he will admit no other thought but that of suffering him to endure to the end the affliction decreed. Job's suspicion / against God is as dreadful as it is childish. This is a pro- ' foundly tragic stroke. It is not to be understood as the sarcasm of defiance; on the contrary, as one of the childish thoughts into which melancholy bordering on madness falls. From the bright height of faith to which Job soars in ch. xix. 25 sqq. he is here again drawn down into the most terrible depth of conflict, in which, like a blind man, he gropes after God, and because he cannot find Him thinks that He flees before him lest He should be overcome by him. The God of the present, Job accounts his enemy; and the God of the future, to whom his faith clings, who will and must vindicate him so soon as He only allows himself to be found and seen—this God is not to be found! He cannot get free either from his suffering or from his ignominy. The future for him is again veiled in a twofold darkness.

Thus Job does not so much answer Eliphaz as himself, concerning the cutting rebukes he has brought against him. He is not able to put them aside, for his consciousness does not help him; and God, whose judgment he desires to have, leaves him still in difficulty. But the mystery of his lot of affliction, which thereby becomes constantly more torturing, becomes still more mysterious from a consideration of the reverse side, which he is urged by Eliphaz more closely to consider, terrible as it may be to him. He, the innocent one, is being tortured to death by an angry God, while for the ungodly there come no times of punishment, no days of vengeance: greedy conquerors, merciless rulers, oppress the poor to the last drop of blood, who are obliged to yield to them, and must serve them, without wrong being helped by the right; murderers, who shun the light, thieves, and adulterers, carry on their evil courses unpunished; and swiftly and easily, without punishment overtaking them, or being able to overtake them, Sheôl snatches them away, as heat does the melted snow; even God himself preserves the oppressors long in the midst of extreme danger, and after a long life, free from care and laden with honour, permits them to die a natural death, as a ripe ear of corn is cut off. Bold in the certainty of the truth of his assertion, Job meets the friends: if it is not so, who will convict me as a liar?! What answer will they give? They cannot long disown the mystery, for experience outstrips them. Will they therefore solve it? They might, had they but the key of the future state to do it with! But neither they nor Job were in possession of that, and we shall therefore see how the mystery, without a knowledge of the future state, struggled through towards solution; or even if this were impossible, how the doubts which it excites are changed to faith, and so are conquered.

Bildad's Third Speech.—Chap. xxv.

Schema: 10.

[Then began Bildad the Shuhite, and said :]

2 *Dominion and terror are with Him,*
  He maketh peace in His high places.

3 *Is there any number to His armies,*
  And whom doth not His light surpass?

4 *How could a mortal be just with God,*
  And how could one born of woman be pure?

5 *Behold, even the moon, it shineth not brightly,*
  And the stars are not pure in His eyes.

6 *How much less mortal man, a worm,*
  And the son of man, a worm!

Ultimum hocce classicum, observes Schultens, *quod a parte triumvirorum sonuit, magis receptui canentis videtur, quam prælium renovantis.* Bildad only repeats the two common-places, that man cannot possibly maintain his supposedly per-verted right before God, the all-just and all-controlling One, to whom, even in heaven above, all things cheerfully submit, and that man cannot possibly be accounted spotlessly pure, and consequently exalted above all punishment before Him, the most holy One, before whom even the brightest stars do not appear absolutely pure. הַמְשֵׁל is an *inf. abs.* made into a substantive, like הַשְׁקֵט; the *Hiph.* (to cause to rule), which is otherwise causative, can also, like *Kal*, signify to rule, or properly, without destroying the *Hiphil*-signification, to exer-cise authority (*vid.* on ch. xxxi. 18); המשל therefore signifies sovereign rule. עֹשֶׂה, with הוא to be supplied, which is not unfrequently omitted both in participial principal clauses (ch. xii. 17 sqq., Ps. xxii. 29, Isa. xxvi. 3, xxix. 8, xl. 19, comp. Zech. ix. 12, where אני is to be supplied) and in partic. subor-dinate clauses (Ps. vii. 10, lv. 20, Hab. ii. 10), is an expression of the simple *præs.*, which is represented by the *partic.* used thus absolutely (including the personal pronoun) as a proper tense-form (Ew. § 168, *c*, 306, *d*). Schlottman refers עֹשֶׂה to המשל ופחד; but the analogy of such attributive descriptions of God is against it. Umbreit and Hahn connect בִּמְרוֹמָיו with the subject: He in His heights, *i.e.* down from His throne in the heavens. But most expositors rightly take it as descriptive of the place and object of the action expressed: He establishes peace in His heights, *i.e.* among the celestial beings immediately surrounding Him. This, only assuming the abstract possibility of discord, might mean : *facit majestate sua ut in summa pace et promptissima obedientia ipsi ministrent angeli ipsius in excelsis* (Schmid). But although from ch. iv. 18, xv. 15, nothing more than that even the holy ones above are neither removed from the possibility of sin nor the necessity of a judicial authority which is high above them, can be inferred; yet, on the other hand, from ch. iii. 8, ix. 13 (comp. xxvi. 12 sq.), it is clear that the poet, in whose conception, as in Scripture generally, the angels and the stars stand in the closest relation, knows of actual, and not merely past, but possibly recurring, instances of hostile dissension and titanic rebellion among the celestial powers; so that עֹשֶׂה שָׁלוֹם, therefore, is intended not merely of a harmonizing reconciliation among creatures which have been contending one against another, but of an actual restoration of the equilibrium that had been disturbed through self-will, by an act of mediation and the exercise of judicial authority on the part of God.

Ver. 3. Instead of the appellation מְרֹומָיו, which reminds one of Isa. xxiv. 21,—where a like peacemaking act of judgment on the part of God is promised in reference to the spirit-host of the heights that have been working seductively among the nations on earth,—גְּדוּדָיו, of similar meaning to צְבָאָיו, used elsewhere, occurs in this verse. The stars, according to biblical representation, are like an army arrayed for battle, but not as after the Persian representation—as an army divided into troops of the *Ahuramazdâ* and *Angramainyus* (Ahriman), but a standing army of the children of light, clad in the armour of light, under the guidance of the one God the Creator (Isa. xl. 26, comp. the anti-dualistic assertion in Isa. xlv. 7). The one God is the Lord among these numberless legions, who commands their reverence, and maintains unity among them; and over whom does not His light arise? Umbr. explains: who does not His light, which He communicates to the hosts of heaven, vanquish (קוּם עַל in the usual warlike meaning: to rise against any one); but this is a thought that is devoid of purpose in this connection. אוֹרֵהוּ with the emphatic suff. *êhu* (as ch. xxiv. 23, עֵינֵיהוּ) at any rate refers directly to God: *His* light in distinction from the derived light of the hosts of heaven. This distinction is better brought out if we interpret (Merc., Hirz., Hahn,

Schlottm., and others) : over whom does (would) not His
light arise? *i.e.* all receive their light from His, and do but
reflect it back. But יָרֵחַ = יָקוּם cannot be justified by ch.
xi. 17. Therefore we interpret with Ew. and Hlgst. thus :
whom does not His light surpass, or, literally, over whom
(*i.e.* which of these beings of light) does it not rise, leaving
it behind and exceeding it in brightness (יָקוּם as synon. of
יָרוּם)? How then could a mortal be just with God, *i.e.* at
His side or standing up before Him ; and how could one of
woman born be spotless! How could he (which is hereby
indirectly said) enter into a controversy with God, who is
infinitely exalted above him, and maintain before Him a
moral character faultless, and therefore absolutely free from
condemnation! In the heights of heaven God's decision is
revered ; and should man, the feeble one, and born flesh of
flesh (*vid.* ch. xiv. 1), dare to contend with God? Behold,
עַד־יָרֵחַ (עַד, as usually when preceded by a negation, *adeo, ne*
... *quidem*, *e.g.* Ex. xiv. 28, comp. Nah. i. 10, where J. H.
Michaelis correctly renders: *adeo ut spinas perplexitate æquent*,
and אַף used in the same way, ch. v. 5, Ew. § 219, *c*), even
as to the moon, it does not (ולא with *Waw apod.*, Ges. § 145,
2, although there is a reading לֹא without ו) shine bright,
יַהֵל = יַאֲהִיל, from הָלַל = אָהַל.[1] Thus LXX., Targ. Jer., and
Gecatilia translate; whereas Saadia translates: it turns not in
(لا يحل), or properly, it does not pitch its tent, fix its habitation. But to pitch one's tent is אָהַל or אֵהֶל, whence יַהֵל, Isa.
xiii. 20, = יַאֲהֵל; and what is still more decisive, one would
naturally expect יַאֲהִיל שָׁם in connection with this thought.
We therefore render אהל as a form for once boldly used in
the scriptural language for הלל, as in Isa. xxviii. 28 אָדַשׁ once
occurs for הִדַּשׁ. Even the moon is only a feeble light before

---

[1] It is worthy of observation, that *hilâl* signifies in Arabic the new
moon (comp. *Genesis*, S. 307); and the Hiphil *ahalla*, like the Kal *halla*,
is used of the appearing and shining of the new moon.

God, and the stars are not clean in His eyes; there is a vast distance between Him and His highest and most glorious creatures—how much more between Him and man, the worm of the dust!

The friends, as was to be expected, are unable to furnish any solution of the mystery, why the ungodly often live and die happily; and yet they ought to be able to give this solution, if the language which they employ against Job were authorized. Bildad alone speaks in the above speech, Zophar is silent. But Bildad does not utter a word that affects the question. This designed omission shows the inability of the friends to solve it, as much as the tenacity with which they firmly maintain their dogma; and the breach that has been made in it, either they will not perceive or yet not acknowledge, because they think that thereby they are approaching too near to the honour of God. Moreover, it must be observed with what delicate tact, and how directly to the purpose in the structure of the whole, this short speech of Bildad's closes the opposition of the friends. Two things are manifest from this last speech of the friends: First, that they know nothing new to bring forward against Job, and nothing just to Job's advantage; that all their darts bound back from Job; and that, though not according to their judgment, yet in reality, they are beaten. This is evident from the fact that Bildad is unable to give any answer to Job's questions, but can only take up the one idea in Job's speech, that he confidently and boldly thinks of being able to approach God's throne of judgment; he repeats with slight variation what Eliphaz has said twice already, concerning the infinite distance between man and God, ch. iv. 17–21, xv. 14–16, and is not even denied by Job himself, ch. ix. 2, xiv. 4. But, secondly, the poet cannot allow us to part from the friends with too great repugnance; for they are Job's friends notwithstanding, and at the close we see them willingly obedient to God's instruction, to go to

Job that he may pray for them and make sacrifice on their behalf. For this reason he does not make Bildad at last repeat those unjust incriminations which were put prominently forward in the speech of Eliphaz, ch. xxii. 5-11. Bildad only reminds Job of the universal sinfulness of the human race once again, without direct accusation, in order that Job may himself derive from it the admonition to humble himself; and this admonition Job really needs, for his speeches are in many ways contrary to that humility which is still the duty of sinful man, even in connection with the best justified consciousness of right thoughts and actions towards the holy God.

Job's Second Answer.—Chap. xxvi.

Schema: 6. 6. 6. 6. 3.

[Then Job began, and said :]
2 *How hast thou helped him that is without power,*
  Raised the arm that hath no strength!
3 *How hast thou counselled him that hath no wisdom,*
  And fully declared the essence of the matter!
4 *To whom hast thou uttered words,*
  And whose breath proceeded from thee?

Bildad is the person addressed, and the exclamations in vers. 2, 3 are ironical : how thy speech contains nothing whatever that might help me, the supposedly feeble one, in conquering my affliction and my temptation ; me, the supposedly ignorant one, in comprehending man's mysterious lot, and mine! לְלֹא־כֹחַ, according to the idea, is only equivalent to לְאֲשֶׁר לֹא (אֵין) כֹּחַ לוֹ, and זְרֹעַ לֹא־עֹז equivalent to זְרֹעַ בְּלֹא־עֹז (לֹא עֹז לוֹ) ; the former is the *abstr. pro concreto*, the latter the genitival connection—the arm of the no-power, *i.e.* powerless (Ges. § 152, 1). The powerless one is Job himself, not God (Merc., Schlottm.), as even the choice of the verbs, vers.

50   THE BOOK OF JOB.

2*b*, 3*a*, shows. Respecting תּוּשִׁיָה, which we have translated
essentiality, duration, completion, we said, on ch. v. 12, that
it is formed from יֵשׁ (*vid.* Prov. viii. 21), not directly indeed,
but by means of a verb יָשַׁ (יָשָׁה), in the signification *sub-
sistere* (comp. كان, and Syriac קוּם¹); it is a *Hophal*-formation
(like תּוּגָה), and signifies, so to speak, durability, *subsistentia,
substantia,* ὑπόστασις, so that the comparison of יֵשׁ with אָשִׁישׁ

اسّ (whence אֶשְׁישׁ, Arab. *asîs, asâs,* etc., *fundamentum*) is
forced upon one, and the relationship to the Sanskrit *as
(asmi = εἰμί)* can remain undecided.   The observation of
J. D. Michaelis² to the contrary, *Supplem.* p. 1167 : *non
placent in linguis ejusmodi etyma metaphysica nimis a vulgari
sensu remota; philosophi in scholis ejusmodi vocabula condunt,
non plebs,* is removed by the consideration that תּוּשִׁיה, which
out of Prov. and Job occurs only in Isa. xxviii. 29, Mic. vi. 9,
is a Chokma-word : it signifies here, as frequently, *vera et
realis sapientia* (J. H. Michaelis).   The speech of Bildad is
a proof of poverty of thought, of which he himself gives the
evidence.   His words—such is the thought of ver. 4—are
altogether inappropriate, inasmuch as they have no reference
whatever to the chief point of Job's speech; and they are,
moreover, not his own, but the suggestion of another, and
.that not God, but Eliphaz, from whom Bildad has borrowed
the substance of his brief declamation.   Since this is the
meaning of ver. 4*b*, it might seem as though אָתְּ־מִי were

¹ Comp. also Spiegel, *Grammatik der Huzvâresch-Sprache,* S. 103.
² Against the comparison of the Arab. والسى, *solari,* by Michaelis, Ges.,
and others (who assume the primary significations *solatium, auxilium*),
Lagarde (*Anmerkungen zur griech. Uebersetzung der Proverbien,* 1863,
S. 57 f.) correctly remarks that وأسى is only a change of letters of the
common language for الأسى; but وشى, to finish painting (whence
توشية, decoration), or אשה as a transposition from שוה, to be level,
simple (Hitzig on Prov. iii. 21), leads to no suitable sense.

intended to signify by whose assistance (Arnh., Hahn); but as the poet also, in ch. xxxi. 37, comp. Ezek. xliii. 10, uses הִגִּיד *seq. acc.*, in the sense of explaining anything to any one, to instruct him concerning anything, it is to be interpreted: to whom hast thou divulged the words (LXX., τίνι ἀνήγγειλας ῥήματα), *i.e.* thinking and designing thereby to affect him?

In what follows, Job now continues the description of God's exalted rule, which Bildad had attempted, by tracing it through every department of creation; and thus proves by fact, that he is wanting neither in a recognition nor reverence of God the almighty Ruler.

> 5 —*The shades are put to pain*
>   *Deep under the waters and their inhabitants.*
> 6 *Sheôl is naked before him,*
>   *And the abyss hath no covering.*
> 7 *He stretched the northern sky over the emptiness;*
>   *He hung the earth upon nothing.*

Bildad has extolled God's majestic, awe-inspiring rule in the heights of heaven, His immediate surrounding; Job continues the strain, and celebrates the extension of this rule, even to the depths of the lower world. The operation of the majesty of the heavenly Ruler extends even to the realm of shades; the sea with the multitude of its inhabitants forms no barrier between God and the realm of shades; the marrowless, bloodless phantoms or shades below writhe like a woman in travail as often as this majesty is felt by them, as, perhaps, by the raging of the sea or the quaking of the earth. On רְפָאִים, which also occurs in Phœnician inscriptions, *vid. Psychol.* S. 409; the book of Job corresponds with Ps. lxxxviii. 11 in the use of this appellation. The *sing.* is not רְפָאִי (whence רפאים, as the name of a people), but רָפָא (רָפָה), which signifies both giants or heroes of colossal stature (from רפה = رَفَ, to be high), and the relaxed (from רפה, to be loose, like رَفَ, to soften, to soothe), *i.e.* those who are bodiless in the state after death (comp. חָלָה, Isa. xiv. 10, to be weakened, *i.e.* placed in the condition of a *rapha*). It is a question whether יְחוֹלָלוּ be *Pilel* (Ges.) or *Pulal* (Olsh.); the *Pul.*, indeed, signifies elsewhere to be brought forth with writhing (ch. xv. 7); it can, however, just as well signify to be put in pain. On account of the reference implied in it to a higher causation here at the commencement of the speech, the *Pul.* is more appropriate than the *Pil.;* and the pausal *â*, which is often found elsewhere with *Hithpael* (*Hithpal.*), ver. 14, ch. xxxiii. 5, but never with *Piel* (*Pil.*), proves that the form is intended to be regarded as passive.

Ver. 6*a.* שְׁאוֹל is seemingly used as *fem.*, as in Isa. xiv. 9*b;* but in reality the *adj.* precedes in the primitive form, without being changed by the gender of שְׁאוֹל. אֲבַדּוֹן alternates with שְׁאוֹל, like קֶבֶר in Ps. lxxxviii. 12. As Ps. cxxxix. 8 testifies to the presence of God in Sheôl, so here Job (comp. ch. xxxviii. 17, and especially Prov. xv. 11) that Sheôl is present to God, that He possesses a knowledge which extends into the depths of the realm of the dead, before whom all things are γυμνὰ καὶ τετραχηλισμένα (Heb. iv. 13). The following *partt.*, ver. 7, depending logically upon the chief subject which precedes, are to be determined according to ch. xxv. 2; they are conceived as present, and indeed of God's primeval act of creation, but intended of the acts which continue by virtue of His creative power.

Ver. 7. By צָפוֹן many modern expositors understand the northern part of the earth, where the highest mountains and rocks rise aloft (accordingly, in Isa. xiv. 13, ירכתי צפון are mentioned parallel with the starry heights), and consequently the earth is the heaviest (Hirz., Ew., Hlgst., Welte, Schlottm., and others). But (1) it is not probable that the poet would first

have mentioned the northern part of the earth, and then in
ver. 7b the earth itself—first the part, and then the whole;
(2) נטה is never said of the earth, always of the heavens,
for the expansion of which it is the stereotype word (נֹטֶה,
ch. ix. 8, Isa. xl. 22, xliv. 24, li. 13, Zech. xiv. 1, Ps. civ. 2;
נוֹטֵיהֶם, Isa. xlii. 5; נטה, Jer. x. 12, li. 15; נָטוּ יָדִי, Isa.
xlv. 12); (3) one expects some mention of the sky in connection with the mention of the earth; and thus is צָפוֹן,[1] with
Rosenm., Ges., Umbr., Vaih., Hahn, and Olsh., to be understood of the northern sky, which is prominently mentioned,
because there is the pole of the vault of heaven, which is
marked by the Pole-star, there the constellation of the Greater
Bear (עָשׁ, ch. ix. 9) formed by the seven bright stars, there
(in the back of the bull, one of the northern constellations
of the ecliptic) the group of the Pleiades (כִּימָה), there also,
below the bull and the twins, Orion (כְּסִיל). On the derivation, notion, and synonyms of תֹּהוּ, vid. Genesis, S. 93; here
(where it may be compared with the Arab. tehîj-un, empty,
and tîh, desert) it signifies nothing more than the unmeasur-
able vacuum of space, parall. בְּלִימָה, not anything = nothing
(comp. modern Arabic lâsh, or even mâsh, compounded of ﻻ

or ﻻ and شَيْ a thing, e.g. bilâs, for nothing, ragul mâsh,
useless men). The sky which vaults the earth from the
arctic pole, and the earth itself, hang free without support in
space. That which is elsewhere (e.g. ch. ix. 6) said of the
pillars and foundations of the earth, is intended of the internal support of the body of the earth, which is, as it were,
fastened together by the mountains, with their roots extend-

[1] The name צָפוֹן signifies the northern sky as it appears by day, from
its beclouded side in contrast with the brighter and more rainless south;
comp. old Persian apâkhtara, if this name of the north really denotes the
"starless" region, Greek ζόφος, the north-west, from the root skap,
σκεπᾶν, σκεπανός (Curtius, Griech. Etymologie, ii. 274), aquilo, the north
wind, as that which brings black clouds with it.

ing into the innermost part of the earth; for the idea that
the earth rests upon the bases of the mountains would be,
indeed, as Löwenthal correctly observes, an absurd inversion.
On the other side, we are also not justified in inferring from
Job's expression the laws of the mechanism of the heavens,
which were unknown to the ancients, especially the law of
attraction or gravitation. The knowledge of nature on the
part of the Israelitish Chokma, expressed in ver. 7, however,
remains still worthy of respect. On the ground of similar
passages of the book of Job, Keppler says of the yet un-
solved problems of astronomy: *Hæc et cetera hujusmodi
latent in Pandectis ævi sequentis, non antea discenda, quam
librum hunc Deus arbiter seculorum recluserit mortalibus.*
From the starry heavens and the earth Job turns to the
celestial and sub-celestial waters.

> 8 *He bindeth up the waters in His clouds,*
>   *Without the clouds being rent under their burden.*
> 9 *He enshroudeth the face of His throne,*
>   *Spreading His clouds upon it.*
> 10 *He compasseth the face of the waters with bounds,*
>   *To the boundary between light and darkness.*

. The clouds consist of masses of water rolled together,
which, if they were suddenly set free, would deluge the
ground; but the omnipotence of God holds the waters together in the hollow of the clouds (צְרַר, *Milel*, according to a
recognised law, although it is also found in Codd. accented
as *Milra*, but contrary to the Masora), so that they do not
burst asunder under the burden of the waters (תַּחְתָּם); by
which nothing more nor less is meant, than that the physical
and meteorological laws of rain are of God's appointment.
Ver. 9 describes the dark and thickly-clouded sky that showers
down the rain in the appointed rainy season. אָחַז signifies to
take hold of, in architecture to hold together by means of

beams, or to fasten together (vid. Thenius on 1 Kings vi. 10,
comp. 2 Chron. ix. 18, מֵאֲחִזִּים, coagmentata), then also, as
usually in Chald. and Syr., to shut (by means of cross-bars,
Neh. vii. 3), here to shut off by surrounding with clouds:
He shuts off פְּנֵי־כִסֵּה, the front of God's throne, which is
turned towards the earth, so that it is hidden by storm-clouds
as by a סֻכָּה, ch. xxxvi. 29, Ps. xviii. 12. God's throne,
which is here, as in 1 Kings x. 19, written כִּסֵּה instead of
כִּסֵּא (comp. Arab. cursi, of the throne of God the Judge, in
distinction from العَرْش, the throne of God who rules over
the world[1]), is indeed in other respects invisible, but the
cloudless blue of heaven is His reflected splendour (Ex.
xxiv. 10) which is cast over the earth. God veils this His
radiance which shines forth towards the earth, פַּרְשֵׁז עָלָיו עֲנָנוֹ,
by spreading over it the clouds which are led forth by Him.
פַּרְשֵׁז is commonly regarded as a Chaldaism for פֵּרֵשׂ (Ges.
§ 56, Olsh. § 276), but without any similar instance in favour
of this vocalization of the 3 pr. Piel (Pil.). Although רַעֲנַן and
שַׁאֲנַן, ch. xv. 32, iii. 18, have given up the i of the Pil., it
has been under the influence of the following guttural; and
although, moreover, i before Resh sometimes passes into a,
e.g. וַיֵּרָא, it is more reliable to regard פַּרְשֵׂז as inf. absol. (Ew.
§ 141, c): expandendo. Ges. and others regard this פַּרְשֵׂז as
a mixed form, composed from פָּרַשׂ and פְרַז; but the verb פָּרַשׂ
(with Shin) has not the signification to expand, which is
assumed in connection with this derivation; it signifies to
separate (also Ezek. xxxiv. 12, vid. Hitzig on that passage),

---

[1] According to the more recent interpretation, under Aristotelian influence, العَرْش is the outermost sphere, which God as πρῶτον κινοῦν
having set in motion, communicates light, heat, life, and motion to the
other revolving spheres; for the causæ mediæ gradually descend from God
the Author of being (muhejji) from the highest heaven into the sub-
lunary world.

whereas פרש certainly signifies to expand (ch. xxxvi. 29, 30);
wherefore the reading פֶּרְשֵׂ (with *Sin*), which some Codd.
give, is preferred by Bär, and in agreement with him by
Luzzatto (*vid.* Bär's *Leket zebi*, p. 244), and it seems to
underlie the interpretation where פרשׂו עליו is translated by
עליו (פָּרַשׂ) פרש, He spreadeth over it (*e.g.* by Aben-Ezra,
Kimchi, Ralbag). But the Talmud, *b. Sabbath*, 88 *b* (פירש
שׁרי מזיו שכינתי וענני עליו, the Almighty separated part of the
splendour of His Shechina and His cloud, and laid it upon
him, *i.e.* Moses, as the passage is applied in the Haggada),
follows the reading פֶּרְשֵׁ (with *Shin*), which is to be retained
on account of the want of naturalness in the consonantal
combination שׁ; but the word is not to be regarded as a
mixed formation (although we do not deny the possibility of
such forms in themselves, *vid. supra*, i. 411), but as an intensive form of פרש formed by Prosthesis and an Arabic change
of *Sin* into *Shin*, like فرشم, فرشد, فرشط, which, being formed
from فرش = פָּרַשׂ (פָּרְשֵׁ), to expand, signifies to spread out
(the legs).

Ver. 10 passes from the waters above to the lower waters.
תַּכְלִית signifies, as in ch. xi. 7, xxviii. 3, Neh. iii. 21, the
extremity, the extreme boundary; and the connection of
תַּכְלִית אוֹר is genitival, as the *Tarcha* by the first word correctly
indicates, whereas אוֹר with *Munach*, the substitute for *Rebia
mugrasch* in this instance (according to *Psalter*, ii. 503, § 2),
is a mistake. God has marked out (חג, LXX. ἐγύρωσεν) a
law, *i.e.* here according to the sense : a fixed bound (comp.
Prov. viii. 29 with Ps. civ. 9), over the surface of the waters
(*i.e.* describing a circle over them which defines their circuit)
unto the extreme point of light by darkness, *i.e.* where the
light is touched by the darkness. Most expositors (Rosenm.,
Hirz., Hahn, Schlottm., and others) take עד־תכלית adverbially:
most accurately, and refer חג to אור as a second object, which
is contrary to the usage of the language, and doubtful and

unnecessary. Pareau has correctly interpreted: *ad lucis usque tenebrarumque confinia;* עַד in the local sense, not *æque ac*, although it might also have this meaning, as *e.g.* Eccl. ii. 16. The idea is, that God has appointed a fixed limit to the waters, as far as to the point at which they wash the *terra firma* of the extreme horizon, and where the boundary line of the realms of light and darkness is; and the basis of the expression, as Bouillier, by reference to Virgil's *Georg.* i. 240 sq., has shown, is the conception of the ancients, that the earth is surrounded by the ocean, on the other side of which the region of darkness begins.

11 *The pillars of heaven tremble* ˙
    And are astonished at His threatening.
12 *By His power He rouseth up the sea,*
    And by His understanding He breaketh Rahab in pieces.
13 *By His breath the heavens become cheerful;*
    His hand hath formed the fugitive dragon.

The mountains towering up to the sky, which seem to support the vault of the sky, are called poetically "the pillars of heaven." יְרוֹפְפוּ is *Pulal*, like יְחוֹלֵל, ver. 5; the signification of violent and quick motion backwards and forwards is secured to the verb רוּף by the Targ. הִתְפַּלֵּף = אִתְרוֹפַף, ch. ix. 6, and the Talm. רִפְרֵף of churned milk, blinking eyes (comp. הֶרֶף עַיִן, the twinkling of the eye, and رَفَّ, *fut. i. o. nictare*), flapping wings (comp. رَفَّ and رَفْرَفَ, *movere, motitare alas*), of wavering thinking. וְגַעֲרָה is the divine command which looses or binds the powers of nature; the astonishment of the supports of heaven is, according to the radical signification of תָּמַהּ (cogn. שָׁמֵם), to be conceived of as a torpidity which follows the divine impulse, without offering any resistance whatever. That רָגַע, ver. 12*a*, is to be understood transitively, not like ch. vii. 5, intransitively, is proved by the

dependent (borrowed) passages, Isa. li. 15, Jer. xxxi. 35,
from which it is also evident that רגע cannot with the LXX.
be translated κατέπαυσεν. The verb combines in itself the
opposite significations of starting up, *i.e.* entering into an
excited state, and of being startled, from which the significations of stilling (*Niph.*, *Hiph.*), and of standing back or
retreat (جر), branch off. The conjecture גָּעַר after the
Syriac version (which translates, *go'ar b'jamo*) is superfluous.
רַהַב, which here also is translated by the LXX. τὸ κῆτος, has
been discussed already on ch. ix. 13. It is not meant of the
turbulence of the sea, to which מָחַץ is not appropriate, but of
a sea monster, which, like the crocodile and the dragon, are
become an emblem of Pharaoh and his power, as Isa. li. 9 sq.
has applied this primary passage: the writer of the book of
Job purposely abstains from such references to the history of
Israel. Without doubt, רהב denotes a demoniacal monster,
like the demons that shall be destroyed at the end of the
world, one of which is called by the Persians *akomano*, evil
thought, another *taromaiti*, pride. This view is supported by
ver. 13, where one is not at liberty to determine the meaning
by Isa. li. 9, and to understand נָחָשׁ בָּרִחַ, like תַּנִּין in that passage, of Egypt. But this dependent passage is an important
indication for the correct rendering of חֹלֲלָה. One thing is
certain at the outset, that שִׁפְּרָה is not *perf. Piel =* שִׁפְּרָה, and
for this reason, that the *Dagesh* which characterizes *Piel*
cannot be omitted from any of the six *mutæ* ; the translation
of Jerome, *spiritus ejus ornavit cœlos*, and all similar ones,
are therefore false. But it is possible to translate: "by His
spirit (creative spirit) the heavens are beauty, His hand has
formed the flying dragon." Thus, in the signification to
bring forth (as Prov. xxv. 23, viii. 24 sq.), חללה is rendered
by Rosenm., Arnh., Vaih., Welte, Renan, and others, of
whom Vaih. and Renan, however, do not understand ver. 13*a*
of the creation of the heavens, but of their illumination. By

this rendering vers. 13*a* and 13*b* are severed, as being without connection; in general, however, the course of thought in the description does not favour the reference of the whole or half of ver. 13 to the creation. Accordingly, חֹלְלָה is not to be taken as *Pilel* from חוּל (חִיל), but after Isa. lvii. 9, as *Poel* from חלל, according to which the idea of ver. 13*a* is determined, since both lines of the verse are most closely connected. נָחָשׁ בָּרִחַ (בָּרִיחַ) is, to wit, the constellation of the Dragon,[1] one of the most straggling constellations, which winds itself between the Greater and Lesser Bears almost half through the polar circle.

> " *Maximus hic plexu sinuoso elabitur Anguis*
> *Circum perque duas in morem fluminis Arctos.*"
> VIRGIL, *Georg.* i. 244 sq.

Aratus in Cicero, *de nat. Deorum*, ii. 42, describes it more graphically, both in general, and in regard to the many stars of different magnitudes which form its body from head to tail. Among the Arabs it is called *el-hajje*, the serpent, *e.g.* in Firuzabâdi: the *hajje* is a constellation between the Lesser Bear (*farqadân*, the two calves) and the Greater Bear (*benât en-na'sch*, the daughters of the bier), "or *et-tanîn*, the dragon, *e.g.* in one of the authors quoted by Hyde on Ulugh Beigh's *Tables of the Stars*, p. 18: the *tanîn* lies round about the north pole in the form of a long serpent, with many bends and windings." Thus far the testimony of the old expositors is found in Rosenmüller. The Hebrew name תְּלִי (the quiver) is perhaps to be distinguished from טְלִי and דְּלִי, the Zodiac constellations Aries and Aquarius.[2] It is questionable how בָּרִחַ is to be understood. The LXX. translates δράκοντα ἀποστάτην in this passage, which is certainly in-

---

[1] Ralbag, without any ground for it, understands it of the milky way (הֶעָגוֹל הֶחָלָבִי), which, according to Rapoport, Pref. to Slonimski's *Toledoth ha-schamajim* (1838), was already known to the Talmud *b. Berachoth*, 58*b*, under the name of נְהַר דִּנוּר.

[2] Vid. *Wissenschaft, Kunst, Judenthum* (1838), S. 220 f.

correct, since בְּרִיחַ beside נָחָשׁ may naturally be assumed to be an attributive word referring to the motion or form of the serpent. Accordingly, Isa. xxvii. 1, ὄφιν φεύγοντα is more correct, where the Syr. version is חִוְיָא חַרְמָנָא, the fierce serpent, which is devoid of support in the language; in the passage before us the Syr. also has חִוְיָא דַעֲרֵק, the fleeing serpent, but this translation does not satisfy the more neuter signification of the adjective. Aquila in Isaiah translates ὄφιν μόχλον, as Jerome translates the same passage *serpentem vectem* (whereas he translates *coluber tortuosus* in our passage), as though it were בְּרִיחַ; Symm. is better, and without doubt a substantially similar thought, ὄφιν συγκλείοντα, the serpent that joins by a bolt, which agrees with the traditional Jewish explanation, for the dragon in Aben-Ezra and Kimchi (in *Lex.*)—after the example of the learned Babylonian teacher of astronomy, Mar-Samuel (died 257), who says of himself that the paths of the heavens are as familiar to him as the places of Nehardea[1]—is called נחש עקלתון, because it is as though it were wounded, and בריח, because it forms a bar (מבריח) from one end of the sky to the other; or as Sabbatai Donolo (about 940), the Italian astronomer,[2] expresses it: "When God created the two lights (the sun and moon) and the five stars (planets) and the twelve מזלות (the constellations of the Zodiac), He also created the תלי (dragon), to unite these heavenly bodies as by a weaver's beam (מנור אורגים), and made it stretch itself on the firmament from one end to another as a bar (כבריח), like a wounded serpent furnished with head and tail." By this explanation בְּרִיחַ is either taken directly as בְּרִיחַ, *vectis*, in which signification it does not, however, occur elsewhere, or the signification *transversus* (*transversarius*) is

---

[1] *Vid.* Grätz, *Geschichte der Juden*, iv. 324. On Isa. xxvii. 1 Kimchi interprets the מבריח differently : he scares (pushes away).

[2] *Vid.* extracts from his ספר המזלות in Joseph Kara's *Comm. on Job*, contributed by S. D. Luzzatto in *Kerem Chemed*, 7th year, S. 57 ff.

assigned to the בָּרִיחַ (=barrîah) with an unchangeable *Kametz*, —a signification which it might have, for ברח בָּ signifies properly to go through, to go slanting across, of which the meanings to unite slanting and to slip away are only variations. בָּרִיחַ, notwithstanding, has in the language, so far as it is preserved to us, everywhere the signification *fugitivus*, and we will also keep to this: the dragon in the heavens is so called, as having the appearance of fleeing and hastening away. But in what sense is it said of God, that He pierces or slays it? In Isa. li. 9, where the תנין is the emblem of Egypt (Pharaoh), and xxvii. 1, where נחש בריח is the emblem of Assyria, the empire of the Tigris, the idea of destruction by the sword of Jehovah is clear. The present passage is to be explained according to ch. iii. 8, where לִוְיָתָן is only another name for נחש בריח (comp. Isa. xxvii. 1). It is the dragon in the heavens which produces the eclipse of the sun, by winding itself round about the sun; and God must continually wound it anew, and thus weaken it, if the sun is to be set free again. That it is God who disperses the clouds of heaven by the breath of His spirit, the representative of which in the elements is the wind, so that the azure becomes visible again; and that it is He who causes the darkening of the sun to cease, so that the earth can again rejoice in the full brightness of that great light,—these two contemplations of the almighty working of God in nature are so expressed by the poet, that he clothes the second in the mythological garb of the popular conception.

In the closing words which now follow, Job concludes his illustrative description : it must indeed, notwithstanding, come infinitely short of the reality.

14 *Behold, these are the edges of His ways,*
   And how do we hear only a whisper thereof!
   But the thunder of His might—who comprehendeth it?

These (אֵלֶּה retrospective, as in ch. xviii. 21) are only קְצוֹת,
the extremest end-points or outlines of the ways of God,
which Job has depicted; the wondrous fulness of His might,
which extends through the whole creation, transcends human
comprehension; it is only שֵׁמֶץ דָּבָר therefrom that becomes
audible to us men. שֵׁמֶץ (שֶׁמֶץ) is translated by Symm. here

ψιθύρισμα, ch. iv. 12, ψιθυρισμός; the Arab. شمص (to speak

very quickly, mutter) confirms this idea of the word; Jerome's
translation, *vix parvam stillam sermonis ejus* (comp. ch. iv. 12,
venas, tropical for parts), is doubly erroneous: the rendering
of the שמץ has the antithesis of רַעַם against it, and דָּבָר is not
to be understood here otherwise than in עֶרְוַת דָּבָר, Deut. xxiii.
15, xxiv. 1: shame of something = something that excites a
feeling of shame, a whisper of something = some whisper.
The notion "somewhat," which the old expositors attribute to
שמץ, lies therefore in דבר. מה is exclamatory in a similar
manner as in Ps. lxxxix. 48: how we hear (נִשְׁמַע, not נִשְׁמַע)
only some whisper thereof (בּ partitive, as *e.g.* Isa. x. 22),
i.e. how little therefrom is audible to us, only as the murmur
of a word, not loud and distinct, which reaches us!

As in the speech of Bildad the poet makes the opposition
of the friends to fade away and cease altogether, as incapable
of any further counsel, and hence as conquered, so in Job's
closing speech, which consists of three parts, ch. xxvi., xxvii.-
xxviii., xxix.-xxxi., he shows how Job in every respect, as
victor, maintains the field against the friends. The friends
have neither been able to loose the knot of Job's lot of suffering, nor the universal distribution of prosperity and misfortune. Instead of loosing the knot of Job's lot of suffering,
they have cut it, by adding to Job's heavy affliction the invention of heinous guilt as its ground of explanation; and
the knot of the contradictions of human life in general with
divine justice they have ignored, in order that they may not

be compelled to abandon their dogma, that suffering everywhere necessarily presupposes sin, and sin is everywhere
necessarily followed by suffering. Even Job, indeed, is not
at present able to solve either one or other of the mysteries;
but while the friends' treatment of these mysteries is untrue,
he honours the truth, and keenly perceives that which is
mysterious. Then he proves by testimony and an appeal to
facts, that the mystery may be acknowledged without therefore being compelled to abandon the fear of God. Job
firmly holds to the objective reality and the testimony of his
consciousness; in the fear of God he places himself above
all those contradictions which are unsolvable by and perplexing to human reason; his faith triumphs over the rational-
ism of the friends, which is devoid of truth, of justice, and
of love.

Job first answers Bildad, ch. xxvi. He characterizes his
poor reply as what it is: as useless, and not pertinent in
regard to the questions before them: it is of no service to
him, it does not affect him, and is, moreover, a borrowed
weapon. For he also is conscious of and can praise God's
exalted and awe-inspiring majesty. He has already shown
this twice, ch. ix. 4–10, xii. 13–25, and shows here for the
third time: its operation is not confined merely to those
creatures that immediately surround God in the heavens;
it extends, without being restrained by the sea, even down
to the lower world; and as it makes the angels above to
tremble, so there it sets the shades in consternation. From
the lower world, Job's contemplation rises to the earth, as a
body suspended in space without support; to the clouds above,
which contain the upper waters without bursting, and veil the
divine throne, of which the sapphire blue of heaven is the reflection; and then he speaks of the sea lying between Sheôl
and heaven, which is confined within fixed bounds, at the
extreme boundaries of which light passes over into darkness;

—he celebrates all this as proof of the creative might of
God. Then he describes the sovereign power of God in the
realm of His creation, how He shakes the pillars of heaven,
rouses the sea, breaks the monster in pieces, lights up the
heavens by chasing away the clouds and piercing the serpent, and thus setting free the sun. But all these—thus he
closes—are only meagre outlines of the divine rule, only a
faint whisper, which is heard by us as coming from the far
distance. Who has the comprehension necessary to take in
and speak exhaustively of all the wonders of His infinite
nature, which extends throughout the whole creation? From
such a profound recognition and so glorious a description of
the exaltation of God, the infinite distance between God and
man is most clearly proved. Job has adequately shown that
his whole soul is full of that which Bildad is anxious to
teach him; a soul that only requires a slight impulse to
make it overflow with such praise of God, as is not wanting
in an universal perception of God, nor is it full of wicked
devices. When therefore Bildad maintains against Job that
no man is righteous before such an exalted God, Job ought
indeed to take it as a warning against such unbecoming
utterances concerning God as those which have escaped him;
but the universal sinfulness of man is no ground of explanation for his sufferings, for there is a righteousness which
avails before God; and of this, Job, the suffering servant of
God, has a consciousness that cannot be shaken.

THIRD PART.—THE TRANSITION TO THE UNRAVELMENT.

Cπap. XXVII.–XXXI.

Job's Final Speech to the Friends.—Chap. xxvii. xxviii.

Schema: 12. 10. 12. 10. | 10. 8. 8. 8. 8. 8. 10.

[Then Job continued to take up his proverb, and said :]

2 *As God liveth, who hath deprived me of my right,*
  And the Almighty, who hath sorely saddened my soul —
3 *For still all my breath is in me,*
  And the breath of Eloah in my nostrils—
4 *My lips do not speak what is false,*
  And my tongue uttereth not deceit!
5 *Far be it from me, to grant that you are in the right :*
  Till I die I will not remove my innocence from me.
6 *My righteousness I hold fast, and let it not go :*
  My heart reproacheth not any of my days.
7 *Mine enemy must appear as an evil-doer,*
  And he who riseth up against me as unrighteous.

The friends are silent, Job remains master of the discourse, and his continued speech is introduced as a continued שְׂאֵת מְשָׁלוֹ (after the analogy of the phrase נָשָׂא קוֹל), as in Num. xxiii. 7 and further on, the oracles of Balaam. מָשָׁל is speech of a more elevated tone and more figurative character; here, as frequently, the unaffected outgrowth of an elevated solemn mood. The introduction of the ultimatum, as מָשָׁל, reminds one of "the proverb (*el-methel*) seals it" in the mouth of the Arab, since in common life it is customary to use a pithy saying as the final proof at the conclusion of a speech.

Job begins with an asseveration of his truthfulness (*i.e.*

the agreement of his confession with his consciousness) by
the life of God. From this oath, which in the form *bi-hajât
allâh* has become later on a common formula of assurance,
R. Josua, in his tractate *Sota*, infers that Job served God
from love to Him, for we only swear by the life of that which
we honour and love; it is more natural to conclude that the
God by whom, on the one hand, he believes himself to be so
unjustly treated, still appears to him, on the other hand, to
be the highest manifestation of truth. The interjectional
clause: living is God! is equivalent to, as true as God liveth.
That which is affirmed is not what immediately follows: He
has set aside my right, and the Almighty has sorely grieved
my soul (Raschi); but הסיר משפטי and המר נפשי are attributive
clauses, by which what is denied in the form of an oath introduced by אם (as Gen. xlii. 15, 1 Sam. xiv. 45, 2 Sam. xi. 11,
Ges. § 155, 2, *f*) is contained in ver. 4; his special reference
to the false semblance of an evil-doer shows that semblance
which suffering casts upon him, but which he constantly
repudiates as surely not lying, as that God liveth. Among
moderns, Schlottm. (comp. Ges. § 150, 3), like most of the
old expositors, translates: so long as my breath is in me, . . .
my lips shall speak no wrong, so that vers. 3 and 4 together
contain what is affirmed. But (1) כִּי indeed sometimes introduces that which shall happen as affirmed by oath, Jer. xxii. 5,
xlix. 13; but here that which shall not take place is affirmed,
which would be introduced first in a general form by כִּי
explic. s. recitativum, then according to its special negative
contents by אם,—a construction which is perhaps possible
according to syntax, but it is nevertheless perplexing; (2) it
may perhaps be thought that "the whole continuance of my
breath in me" is conceived as accusative and adverbial, and is
equivalent to, so long as my breath may remain in me (כל עוד,
as long as ever, like the Arab. *cullama*, as often as ever); but
the usage of the language does not favour this explanation,

for 2 Sam. i. 9, בִּי נַפְשִׁי כְּל־עוֹד, signifies my whole soul (my full life) is still in me; and we have a third instance of this prominently placed כֹּל per hypallagen in Hos. xiv. 3, כְּל־תִּשָּׂא עָוֹן, omnem auferas iniquitatem, Ew. § 289, a (comp. Ges. § 114, rem. 1). Accordingly, with Ew., Hirz., Hahn, and most modern expositors, we take ver. 3 as a parenthetical confirmatory clause, by which Job gives the ground of his solemn affirmation that he is still in possession of his full consciousness, and cannot help feeling and expressing the contradiction between his lot of suffering, which brands him as an evil-doer, and his moral integrity. The נִשְׁמָתִי which precedes the רוּח signifies, according to the prevailing usage of the language, the intellectual, and therefore self-conscious, soul of man (Psychol. S. 76f). This is in man and in his nostrils, inasmuch as the breath which passes in and out by these is the outward and visible form of its being, which is in every respect the condition of life (ib. S. 82f.). The suff. of נשמתי is unaccented; on account of the word which follows being a monosyllable, the tone has retreated (נסוג אחור, to use a technical grammatical expression), as e.g. also in ch. xix. 25, xx. 2, Ps. xxii. 20. Because he lives, and, living, cannot deny his own existence, he swears that his own testimony, which is suspected by the friends, and on account of which they charge him with falsehood, is perfect truth.

Ver. 4 is not to be translated: "my lips shall never speak what is false;" for it is not a resolve which Job thus strongly makes, after the manner of a vow, but the agreement of his confession, which he has now so frequently made, and which remains unalterable, with the abiding fact. Far be from me —he continues in ver. 5—to admit that you are right (חָלִילָה לִּי with unaccented ah, not of the fem., comp. ch. xxxiv. 10, but of direction: for a profanation to me, i.e. let it be profane to me, Ew. § 329, a, Arab. hâshâ li, in a like sense); until I expire (prop.: sink together), I will not put my innocence

(תֻּמָּה, perfection, in the sense of purity of character) away
from me, *i.e.* I will not cease from asserting it. I will hold
fast (as ever) my righteousness, and leave it not, *i.e.* let it
not go or fall away; my heart does not reproach even one of
my days. מִיָּמָי is virtually an obj. in a partitive sense : *mon
cœur ne me reproche pas un seul de mes jours* (Renan). The
heart is used here as the seat of the conscience, which is the
knowledge possessed by the heart, by which it excuses or ac-
cuses a man (*Psychol.* S. 134) ; חָרַף (whence חֹרֶף, the season
in which the fruits are gathered) signifies *carpere*, to pluck =
to pinch, lash, inveigh against. Jos. Kimchi and Ralbag
explain : my heart draws not back (from the confession of
my innocence) my whole life long (as Maimonides explains
נֶחֱרֶפֶת, Lev. xix. 20, of the female slave who is inclined to,
i.e. stands near to, the position of a free woman), by compari-

son with the Arabic اِنْحَرَفَ, *deflectere;* it is not, however,

حَرَفَ, but خَرَفَ, *decerpere*, that is to be compared in the
tropical sense of the prevailing usage of the Hebrew speci-
fied. The old expositors were all misled by the misunderstood partitive מִימֵי, which they translated *ex* (= *inde a*) *diebus
meis*. There is in ver. 7 no ground for taking יְהִי, with
Hahn, as a strong affirmative, as supposed in ch. xviii. 12,
and not as expressive of desire ; but the meaning is not : let
my opponents be evil-doers, I at least am not one (Hirz.).
The voluntative expresses far more emotion : the relation
must be reversed ; he who will brand me as an evil-doer,
must by that very act brand himself as such, inasmuch as·
the מַרְשִׁיעַ of a צַדִּיק really shows himself to be a רָשָׁע, and by
recklessly judging the righteous, is bringing down upon himself a like well-merited judgment. The כ is the so-called
Caph veritatis, since כ, *instar*, signifies not only similarity, but
also equality. Instead of קִימֵי, the less manageable, primitive
form, which the poet used in ch. xxii. 20 (comp. vol. i. 440),

and beside which קָם (קִים, 2 Kings xvi. 7) does not occur in the book, we here find the more usual form מְתְקוֹמְמִי (comp. ch. xx. 27).[1]

The description of the misfortune of the ungodly which now follows, beginning with כִּי, requires no connecting thought, as for instance : My enemy must be accounted as ungodly, on account of his hostility ; I abhor ungodliness, for, etc. ; but that he who regards him as a רָשָׁע is himself a רָשָׁע, Job shows from the fact of the רָשָׁע having no hope in death, whilst, when dying, he can give no confident hope of a divine vindication of his innocence.

8 *For what is the hope of the godless, when He cutteth off,*
  When Eloah taketh away his soul?

9 *Will God hear his cry*
  When distress cometh upon him?

10 *Or can he delight himself in the Almighty,*
   Can he call upon Eloah at all times?

11 *I will teach you concerning the hand of God,*
   I will not conceal the dealings of the Almighty.

12 *Behold, ye have all seen it,*
   Why then do ye cherish foolish notions?

In comparing himself with the רָשָׁע, Job is conscious that he has a God who does not leave him unheard, in whom he delights himself, and to whom he can at all times draw near; as, in fact, Job's fellowship with God rests upon the freedom of the most intimate confidence. He is not one of the godless; for what is the hope of one who is estranged from God, when he comes to die? He has no God on whom his hope

---

[1] In Beduin the enemy is called *qômâni* (*vid. supra*, on ch. xxiv. 12, p. 26), a denominative from *qôm* قوم, war, feud; but *qôm* has also the signification of a collective of *qômâni*, and one can also say: *entum waijânâ qôm*, you and we are enemies, and *bênâtna qôm*, there is war between us.—WETZST.

might establish itself, to whom it could cling. The old expositors err in many ways respecting ver. 8, by taking בצע, *abscindere* (root בצ), in the sense of (*opes*) *corradere* (thus also more recently Rosenm. after the Targ., Syr., and Jer.), and referring יֵשַׁל to שָׁלָה in the signification *tranquillum esse* (thus even Blumenfeld after Ralbag and others). נַפְשׁוֹ is the object to both verbs, and בצע נפשׁ, *abscindere animam*, to cut off the thread of life, is to be explained according to ch. vi. 9, Isa. xxxviii. 12. שׁלה נפשׁ, *extrahere animam* (from שָׁלָה, whence שִׁלְיָה سَلَا, the after-birth, cogn. שָׁלַל سَلّ נשל نسل, نثل, نشل), is of similar signification, according to another figure, since the body is conceived of as the sheath (נִדְנֶה,

Dan. vii. 15) of the soul[1] (comp. سلّ in the universal signification *evaginare ensem*). The *fut. apoc. Kal* יִשֶׁל (= יֵשַׁל) is therefore in meaning equivalent to the intrans. יִשַּׁל, Deut. xxviii. 40 (according to Ew. § 235, *c*, obtained from this by change of vowel), *decidere;* and Schnurrer's supposition that יֵשַׁל, like the Arab. يسأل, is equivalent to יִשְׁאַל (when God demands it), or such a violent correction as De Lagarde's[2] (when he is in distress יצק, when one demands his soul with a curse יִשָּׁאֵל בְּאָלָה), is unnecessary.

The ungodly man, Job goes on to say, has no God to hear his cry when distress comes upon him; he cannot delight himself (יִתְעַנָּג, pausal form of יתענג, the primary form of יתעננ) in the Almighty; he cannot call upon Eloah at any

---

[1] On the similar idea of the body, as the *kosha* (sheath) of the soul, among the Hindus, *vid. Psychol.* S. 227.

[2] *Anm. zur griech. Uebers. der Proverbien* (1863), S. VI. f., where the first reason given for this improvement of the text is this, that the usual explanation, according to which יֵשַׁל and יבצע have the same subj. and obj. standing after the verb, is altogether contrary to Semitic usage. But this assertion is groundless, as might be supposed from the very beginning. Thus, *e.g.* the same obj. is found after two verbs in ch. xx. 19, and the same subj. and obj. in Neh. iii. 20.

time (*i.e.* in the manifold circumstances of life under which we are called to feel the dependence of our nature). Torn away from God, he cannot be heard, he cannot indeed pray and find any consolation in God. It is most clearly manifest here, since Job compares his condition of suffering with that of a חָנֵף, what comfort, what power of endurance, yea, what spiritual joy in the midst of suffering (הִתְעַנֵּג, as ch. xxii. 26, Ps. xxxvii. 4, 11, Isa. lv. 2, lviii. 13 sq.), which must all remain unknown to the ungodly, he can draw from his fellowship with God; and seizing the very root of the distinction between the man who fears God and one who is utterly godless, his view of the outward appearance of the misfortune of both becomes changed; and after having allowed himself hitherto to be driven from one extreme to another by the friends, as the heat of the controversy gradually cools down, and as, regaining his independence, he stands before them as their teacher, he now experiences the truth of *docendo discimus* in rich abundance. I will instruct you, says he, in the hand, *i.e.* the mode of action, of God (בְּ just as in Ps. xxv. 8, 12, xxxii. 8, Prov. iv. 11, of the province and subject of instruction); I will not conceal אֲשֶׁר עִם־שַׁדַּי, *i.e.* according to the sense of the passage: what are the principles upon which He acts; for that which is with (עִם) any one is the matter of his consciousness and volition (*vid.* on ch. xxiii. 10, p. 10).

Ver. 12*a* is of the greatest importance in the right interpretation of what follows from ver. 13 onwards. The instruction which Job desires to impart to the friends has reference to the lot of the evil-doer; and when he says: Behold, ye yourselves have beheld (learnt) it all,—in connection with which it is to be observed that אַתֶּם כֻּלְּכֶם does not signify merely *vos omnes*, but *vosmet ipsi omnes*,—he grants to them what he appeared hitherto to deny, that the lot of the evil-doer, certainly in the rule, although not without exceptions, is such as they have said. The application, however, which they have made of this abiding fact of ex- perience, is and remains all the more false : Wherefore then (הֵן makes the question sharper) are ye vain (blinded) in vanity (self-delusion), viz. in reference to me, who do not so completely bear about the characteristic marks of a רָשָׁע? The verb הָבַל signifies to think and act vainly (without ground or connection), 2 Kings xvii. 15 (comp. ἐματαιώθησαν, Rom. i. 21) ; the combination הָבֵל הֶבֶל is not to be judged of according to Ges. § 138, rem. 1, as it is also by Ew. § 281, *a*, but הָבֵל may also be taken as the representative of the gerund, as *e.g.* עֶרְיָה, Hab. iii. 9.

In the following strophe Job now begins as Zophar (ch. xx. 29) concluded. He gives back to the friends the doctrine they have fully imparted to him. They have held the lot of the evil-doer before him as a mirror, that he may behold him- self in it and be astounded; he holds it before them, that they may perceive how not only his bearing under suffering, but also the form of his affliction, is of a totally different kind.

13 *This is the lot of the wicked man with God,*
  . *And the heritage of the violent which they receive from the*
    Almighty :
14 *If his children multiply, it is for the sword,*
  And his offspring have not bread enough.
15 *His survivors shall be buried by the pestilence,*
  And his widows shall not weep.
16 *If he heapeth silver together as dust,*
  And prepareth garments for himself as mire :
17 *He prepareth it, and the righteous clothe themselves,*
  And the innocent divide the silver among themselves.
18 *He hath built as a moth his house,*
  And as a hut that a watchman setteth up.

We have already had the combination אָדָם רָשָׁע for אִישׁ
רָשָׁע in ch. xx. 29; it is a favourite expression in Proverbs,
and reminds one of ἄνθρωπος ὁδίτης in Homer, and ἄνθρωπος
σπείρων, ἐχθρός, ἔμπορος, in the parables Matt. xiii. *Psik*
(*Pasek*) stands under רָשׁ, to separate the wicked man and
God, as in Prov. xv. 29 (Norzi). לְמוֹ, exclusively peculiar to
the book of Job in the Old Testament (here and ch. xxix. 21,
xxxviii. 40, xl. 4), is לְ rendered capable of an independent
position by means of מוֹ = מָה, *l.c.* The sword, famine, and
pestilence are the three punishing powers by which the evil-
doer's posterity, however numerous it may be, is blotted out;
these three, חֶרֶב, רָעָב, and מָוֶת, appear also side by side in
Jer. xv. 2; מָוֶת, instead of מְמוֹתֵי, *diris mortibus*, is (as also
Jer. xviii. 21) equivalent to דֶּבֶר in the same trio, Jer. xiv. 12;
the plague is personified (as when it is called by an Arabian
poet *umm el-farit*, the mother of death), and Vavassor correctly observes: *Mors illos sua sepeliet, nihil praeterea honoris
supremi consecuturos.* Böttcher (*de inferis*, § 72) asserts that
במות can only signify *pestilentiae tempore*, or better, *ipso mortis
momento;* but since בְּ occurs by the passive elsewhere in the
sense of *ab* or *per, e.g.* Num. xxxvi. 2, Hos. xiv. 4, it can also
by נקבר denote the efficient cause. Olshausen's correction
במות לֹא יקברו, they will not be buried when dead (Jer. xvi. 4),
is still less required; "to be buried by the pestilence" is equivalent to, not to be interred with the usual solemnities, but
to be buried as hastily as possible. Ver. 15*b* (common to
our poet and the psalm of Asaph, lxxviii. 64, which likewise
belongs to the Salomonic age) is also to be correspondingly
interpreted: the women that he leaves behind do not celebrate the usual mourning rites (comp. Gen. xxiii. 2), because
the decreed punishment which, stroke after stroke, deprives
them of husbands and children, prevents all observance of the
customs of mourning, and because the shock stifles the feeling
of pity. The treasure in gold which his avarice has heaped

up, and in garments which his love of display has gathered together, come into the possession of the righteous and the innocent, who are spared when these three powers of judgment sweep away the evil-doer and his family. Dust and dirt (*i.e.* of the streets, חוצות) are, as in Zech. ix. 3, the emblem of a great abundance that depreciates even that which is valuable. The house of the ungodly man, though a palace, is, as the fate of the fabric shows, as brittle and perishable a thing, and can be as easily destroyed, as the fine spinning of a moth, עָשׁ (according to the Jewish proverb, the brother of the סָס), or even the small case which it makes from remnants of gnawed articles, and drags about with it; it is like a light hut, perhaps for the watchman of a vineyard (Isa. i. 8), which is put together only for the season during which the grapes are ripening.[1]

> 19 *He lieth down rich, and doeth it not again,*
> *He openeth his eyes and—is no more.*
> 20 *Terrors take hold of him as a flood;*
> *By night a tempest stealeth him away.*

---

[1] The watchman's hut, for the protection of the vineyards and melon and maize fields against thieves, herds, or wild beasts, is now called either 'arîshe and mantara (מִנְטָרָה) if it is only slightly put together from branches of trees, or chême (חִימָה) if it is built up high in order that the watcher may see a great distance. The chême is the more frequent; at harvest it stands in the midst of the threshing-floors (bejâdir) of a district, and it is constructed in the following manner:—Four poles ('awâmîd) are set up so as to form the corners of a square, the sides of which are about eight feet in length. Eight feet above the ground, four cross pieces of wood ('awârid) are tightly bound to these with cords, on which planks, if they are to be had, are laid. Here is the watcher's bed, which consists of a litter. Six or seven feet above this, cross-beams are again bound to the four poles, on which boughs, or reeds (qasab), or a mat (hasîra, חִצִירָה) forms a roof (sath, שְׂטַח), from which the chême has its name; for the Piel-forms עָשָׁה, חִים, and שְׂפָּה signify, " to be stretched over anything after the manner of a roof." Between the roof and the bed, three sides of the chême are hung round with a mat, or with

21 *The east wind lifteth him up, that he departeth,*
    And hurleth him forth from his place.
22 *God casteth upon him without sparing,*
    Before His hand he fleeth utterly away.
23 *They clap their hands at him,*
    And hiss him away from his place.

The pointing of the text וְלֹא יֶאֱסֹף is explained by Schnurr., Umbr., and Stick.: He goes rich to bed and nothing is taken as yet, he opens his eyes and nothing more is there; but if this were the thought intended, it ought at least to have been וְאֵין נֶאֱסָף, since לֹא signifies *non*, not *nihil*; and Stickel's translation, "while nothing is carried away," makes the *fut.* instead of the *præt.*, which was to be expected, none the more tolerable; also אסף can indeed signify to gather hastily together, to take away (*e.g.* Isa. xxxiii. 4), when the connection favours it, but not here, where the first impression is that רָשָׁע is the subj. both to וְלֹא יֶאֱסֹף and to וְאֵינֶנּוּ. Böttcher's translation, "He lieth down rich and cannot be displaced," gives the words a meaning that is ridiculed by the usage of the language. On the other hand, וְלֹא יֶאֱסֹף can signify: and he

reeds or straw (*qashsh*, קַשׁ) bound together, in order both to keep off the cold night-winds, and also to keep the thieves in ignorance as to the number of the watchers. A small ladder, *sullem* (סֻלָּם), frequently leads to the bed-chamber. The space between the ground and this chamber is closed only on the west side to keep off the hot afternoon sun, for through the day the watcher sits below with his dog, upon the ground. Here is also his place of reception, if any passers-by visit him ; for, like the village shepherd, the field-watcher has the right of showing a humble hospitality to any acquaintances. When the fruits have been gathered in, the *chême* is removed. The field-watchman is now called *nâtûr* (ناطور), and the verb is *natar*, נָטַר, "to keep watch," instead of which the quadriliteral *nôtar*, נוֹטַר (from the *plur.* نواطير, "the watchers"), has also been formed. In one part of Syria all these forms are written with צ (d) instead of ט, and pronounced accordingly. The נֹצֵר in this passage is similarly related to the נֹטֵר in Cant. i. 6, viii. 11, 12.—WETZST.

is not conveyed away (comp. *e.g.* Jer. viii. 2, Ezek. xxix. 5;
but not Isa. lvii. 1, where it signifies to be swept away, and
also not Num. xx. 26, where it signifies to be gathered to the
fathers), and is probably intended to be explained after the
pointing that we have, as Rosenm. and even Ralbag explain
it: "he is not conveyed away; one opens his eyes, and he is
not;" or even as Schlottm.: "he is not conveyed away; in
one moment he still looks about him, in the next he is no
more;" but the relation of the two parts of the verse in this
interpretation is unsatisfactory, and the preceding strophe
has already referred to his not being buried. Since, therefore, only an unsuitable, and what is more, a badly-expressed
thought, is gained by this reading, it may be that the expression should be regarded with Hahn as interrogative: is he
not swept away? This, however, is only a makeshift, and
therefore we must see whether it may not perhaps be susceptible of another pointing. Jerome transl.: *dives cum dor-
mierit, nihil secum auferet;* the thought is not bad, but מְאַסְפָּה
is wanting, and לֹא alone does not signify *nihil*. Better
LXX. (Ital., Syr.): πλούσιος κοιμηθήσεται καὶ οὐ προσ-
θήσει. This translation follows the form of reading יֹאסִף =
יֹוסִיף, gives a suitable sense, places both parts of the verse in
the right relation, and accords with the style of the poet
(*vid.* ch. xx. 9, xl. 5); and accordingly, with Ew., Hirz., and
Hlgst., we decide in favour of this reading: he lieth down to
sleep rich, and he doeth it no more, since in the night he is
removed from life and also from riches by sudden death; or
also: in the morning he openeth his eyes without imagining
it is the last time, for, overwhelmed by sudden death, he
closes them for ever. Vers. 20*a* and 20*b* are attached cross-
wise (*chiastisch*) to this picture of sudden destruction, be it
by night or by day: the terrors of death seize him (*sing. fem.*
with a *plur.* subj. following it, according to Ges. § 146, 3)
like a flood (comp. the floods of Belial, Ps. xviii. 5), by night

a whirlwind (סוּפָה גְּנָבַתּוּ, as ch. xxi. 18) carrieth him away.
The Syriac and Arabic versions add, as a sort of interpola-
tion : as a fluttering (large white) night-moth,—an addition
which no one can consider beautiful.

Ver. 21 extends the figure of the whirlwind. In Hebrew,
even when the narrative has reference to Egyptian matters
(Gen. xli. 23), the קָדִים which comes from the Arabian desert
is the destructive, devastating, and parching wind κατ'
ἐξοχήν.[1] וַיֵּלַךְ signifies *peribit* (*ut pereat*), as ch. xiv. 20,
xix. 10. שָׂעַר (comp. סֹעֲרָה, O storm-chased one) is connected
with the accus. of the person pursued, as in Ps. lviii. 10.
The subj. of וַיַּשְׁלֵךְ, ver. 22, is God, and the verb stands without an obj. : to cast at any one (shoot), as Num. xxxv. 22 (for
the figure, comp. ch. xvi. 13) ; LXX. correctly : ἐπιρρίψει
(whereas ch. xviii. 7, σφάλαι = וְתַבְשִׁילֵהוּ). The gerundive
with יִבְרָח lays stress upon the idea of the exertion of flight :
whithersoever he may flee before the hand of God, every
attempt is in vain. The suff. *êmo*, ver. 23a, both according
to the syntax and the matter, may be taken as the plural
suff. ; but the fact that בַּפֵּימוֹ can be equivalent to כַּפָּיו (comp.

---

[1] In Syria and Arabia the east wind is no longer called *qadîm*, but exclusively *sharqîja*, *i.e.* the wind that blows from the rising of the sun (*sharq*).
This wind rarely prevails in summer, occurring then only two or three
days a month on an average ; it is more frequent in the winter and early
spring, when, if it continues long, the tender vegetation is parched up,
and a year of famine follows, whence in the Lebanon it is called *semûm*
(שָׂמוּם), which in the present day denotes the "poisonous wind" (= *nesme
musimme*), but originally, by alliance with the Hebr. שָׁמֵם, denoted the
"devastating wind." The east wind is dry ; it excites the blood, con-
tracts the chest, causes restlessness and anxiety, and sleepless nights or
evil dreams. Both man and beast feel weak and sickly while it prevails.
Hence that which is unpleasant and revolting in life is compared to the
east wind. Thus a maid in Hauran, at the sight of one of my Damascus
travelling companions, whose excessive ugliness struck her, cried: *billâh,*
nahâr el-jôm aqshar (أقشر), *wagahetni* (وجهتني) *sharqîja*, " by God,
it is an unhealthy day to-day : an east wind blew upon me." And in a
festive dance song of the *Merg* district, these words occur : *wu rudd*

Ps. xi. 7), עָלֵימוֹ to עָלָיו (comp. ch. xx. 23, xxii. 2), as כְּמוֹ is equivalent to כְּ (vid. Isa. xliv. 15, liii. 8), is established, and there is no reason why the same may not be the case here. The accumulation of the terminations êmo and ômo gives a tone of thunder and a gloomy impress to this conclusion of the description of judgment, as these terminations frequently occur in the book of Psalms, where moral depravity is mourned and divine judgment threatened (e.g. in Ps. xvii. xlix. lviii. lix. lxxiii.). The clapping of hands (שָׂפַק כַּפַּיִם = סָפַק, Lam. ii. 15, comp. תָּקַע, Nah. iii. 19) is a token of malignant joy, and hissing (שָׁרַק, Zeph. ii. 15, Jer. xlix. 17) a token of scorn. The expression in ver. 23b is a pregnant one. Clapping of hands and hissing accompany the evil-doer when merited punishment overtakes him, and chases him forth from the place which he hitherto occupied (comp. ch. viii. 18).

Earlier expositors have thought it exceedingly remarkable that Job, in ch. xxvii. 13–23, should agree with the assertions of the three friends concerning the destiny of the ungodly and his descendants, while he has previously opposed them

li nômet hodênik | seb' lejâli bi-'olija | wa berd wa sherd wa sharqîja . . .
   " And grant me again to slumber on thy bosom,
    Seven nights in an upper chamber,
    And (I will then endure) cold, drifting snow, and east wind."
During the harvest, so long as the east wind lasts, the corn that is al-ready threshed and lying on the threshing-floors cannot be winnowed; a gentle, moderate draught is required for this process, such as is only obtained by a west or south wind. The north wind is much too strong, and the east wind is characterized by constant gusts, which, as the Hau-ranites say, "jôchotâ tibn wa-habb, carries away chaff and corn." When the wind shifts from the west to the east, a whirlwind (zôba'a, זוֹבַעָה) not unfrequently arises, which often in summer does much harm to the threshing-floors and to the cut corn that is lying in swaths (unless it is weighted with stones). Storms are rare during an east wind; they come mostly with a west wind (never with a south or north wind). But if an east wind does bring a storm, it is generally very destructive, on account of its strong gusts; and it will even uproot the largest trees.—WETZST.

on this point, ch. xii. 6, xxi. xxiv. Kennicott thinks the confusion is cleared away by regarding ch. xxvi. 2–xxvii. 12 as
Job's answer to the third speech of Bildad, xxvii. 13 sqq. as
the third speech of Zophar, and xxviii. (to which the super-
scription xxvii. 1 belongs) as Job's reply thereto; but this
reply begins with כִּי, and is specially appropriate as a striking
repartee to the speech of Zophar. Stuhlmann (1804) makes
this third speech of Zophar begin with xxvii. 11, and imagines
a gap between xxvii. 10 and xxvii. 11; but who then are
the persons whom Zophar addresses by "you"? The three
everywhere address themselves to Job, while here Zophar,
contrary to custom, would address himself not to him, but,
according to Stuhlmann's exposition, to the others with reference to Job. Ch. xxviii. Stuhlmann removes and places
after ch. xxv. as a continuation of Bildad's speech; Zophar's
speech therefore remains unanswered, and Zophar may thank
this critic not only for allowing him another opportunity of
speaking, but also for allowing him the last word. Bernstein
(Keil-Tzschirner's *Analekten*, Bd. i. St. 3) removes the contradiction into which Job seems to fall respecting himself in a
more thorough manner, by rejecting the division ch. xxvii. 7–
xxviii. 28, which is certainly indissolubly connected as a
whole, as a later interpolation; but there is no difference of
language and poetic spirit here betraying an interpolator;
and had there been one, even he ought indeed to have proceeded on the assumption that such an insertion should be
appropriate to Job's mouth, so that the task of proving its
relative fitness, from his standpoint at least, remains. Hosse
(1849) goes still further: he puts ch. xxvii. 10, xxxi. 35–37,
xxxviii. 1, etc., together, and leaves out all that comes between
these passages. There is then no transition whatever from
the entanglement to the unravelment. Job's final reply, ch.
xxvii. xxviii., with the monologue ch. xxix.–xxxi., in which
even a feeble perception must recognise one of the most

essential and most beautiful portions of the dramatic whole, forms this transition.

Eichhorn (in his translation of Job, 1824), who formerly (*Allgem. Bibliothek der bibl. Lit.* Bd. 2) inclined to Kennicott's view, and Böckel (2d edition, 1804) seek another explanation of the difficulty, by supposing that in ch. xxvii. 13–23 Job reproduces the view of the friends. But in ver. 11 Job announces the setting forth of his own view ; and the supposition that with זֶה חֵלֶק אָדָם רָשָׁע he does not begin the enunciation of his own view, but that of his opponents, is refuted by the consideration that there is nothing by which he indicates this, and that he would not enter so earnestly into the description if it were not the feeling of his heart. Feeling the worthlessness of these attempted solutions, De Wette (*Einleitung*, § 288), with his customary spirit of criticism with which he depreciates the sacred writers, turns against the poet himself. Certainly, says he, the division ch. xxvii. 11–xxviii. 28 is inappropriate and self-contradictory in the mouth of Job; but this want of clearness, not to say inconsistency, must be brought against the poet, who, despite his utmost endeavour, has not been able to liberate himself altogether from the influence of the common doctrine of retribution.

This judgment is erroneous and unjust. Umbreit (2d edition, S. 261 [Clark's edition, 1836, ii. 122]) correctly remarks, that "without this apparent contradiction in Job's speeches, the interchange of words would have been endless ;" in other words : had Job's standpoint been absolutely immoveable, the controversy could not possibly have come to a well-adjusted decision, which the poet must have planned, and which he also really brings about, by causing his hero still to retain an imperturbable consciousness of his innocence, but also allowing his irritation to subside, and his extreme harshness to become moderated. The latter, in reference to the final destiny of the godless, is already indicated in ch. xxiv., but is still more apparent here in ch. xxvii., and indeed in the following line of thought: "As truly as God lives, who afflicts me, the innocent one, I will not incur the guilt of lying, by allowing myself to be persuaded against my conscience to regard myself as an evil-doer. I am not an evil-doer, but my enemy who regards me and treats me as such must be accounted wicked; for how unlike the hopelessness and estrangement from God, in which the evil-doer dies, is my hope and entreaty in the midst of the heaviest affliction! Yea, indeed, the fate of the evil-doer is a different one from mine. I will teach it you; ye have all, indeed, observed it for yourselves, and nevertheless ye cherish such vain thoughts concerning me." What is peculiar in the description that then follows—a description agreeing in its substance with that of the three, and similar in its form—is therefore this, that Job holds up the end of the evil-doer before the friends, that from it they may infer that *he is not an evil-doer*, whereas the friends held it up before Job that he might infer from it that *he is an evil-doer*, and only by a penitent acknowledgment of this can he escape the extreme of the punishment he has merited. Thus in ch. xxvii. Job turns their own weapon against the friends.

But does he not, by doing so, fall into contradiction with himself? Yes; and yet not so. The Job who has become calmer here comes into contradiction with the impassioned Job who had, without modification, placed the exceptional cases in opposition to the exclusive assertion that the evil-doer comes to a fearful end, which the friends advance, as if it were the rule that the prosperity of the evil-doer continues uninterrupted to the very end of his days. But Job does not come into collision with his true view. For how could he deny that in the rule the retributive justice of God is manifest in the case of the evil-doer! We can only perceive.

his true opinion when we compare the views he here expresses
with his earlier extreme antitheses: hitherto, in the heat of
the controversy, he has opposed that which the friends one-
sidedly maintained by the direct opposite; now he has got
upon the right track of thought, in which the fate of the
evil-doer presents itself to him from another and hitherto
mistaken side,—a phase which is also but imperfectly appre-
ciated in ch. xxiv.; so that now at last he involuntarily does
justice to what truth there is in the assertion of his opponent.
Nevertheless, it is not Job's intention to correct himself here,
and to make an admission to the friends which has hitherto
been refused. Hirzel's explanation of this part inclines too
much to this erroneous standpoint. On the contrary, our
rendering accords with that of Ewald, who observes (S. 252 f.
2d edition, 1854) that Job here maintains *in his own favour*,
and against them, what the friends directed *against* him, since
the hope of not experiencing such an evil-doer's fate becomes
strong in him: "Job is here on the right track for more
confidently anticipating his own rescue, or, what is the same
thing, the impossibility of his perishing just as if he were an
evil-doer." Moreover, how well designed is it that the description vers. 13 sqq. is put into Job's mouth! While the poet
allows the friends designedly to interweave lines taken from
Job's misfortunes into their descriptions of the evil-doer's
fate, in Job's description not one single line is found which
coincides with his own lot, whether with that which he has
already experienced, or even with that which his faith presents to him as in prospect. And although the heavy lot
which has befallen him looks like the punitive suffering of
the evil-doer, he cannot acknowledge it as such, and even
denies its bearing the marks of such a character, since even
in the midst of affliction he clings to God, and confidently
hopes for His vindication. With this rendering of ch.
xxvii. 13 sqq. all doubts of its genuineness, which is indeed

admitted by all modern expositors, vanish; and, far from
charging the poet with inconsistency, one is led to admire
the undiminished skill with which he brings the idea of the
drama by concealed ways to its goal.

But the question still comes up, whether ch. xxviii. 1, opening with כִּי, does not militate against this genuineness. Hirzel
and others observe, that this כִּי introduces the confirmation of
ch. xxvii. 12*b* : " But wherefore then do ye cherish such vain
imaginations concerning me ? For human sagacity and perse-
verance can accomplish much, but the depths of divine wisdom
are impenetrable to man." But how is it possible that the כִּי,
ch. xxviii. 1, should introduce the confirmation of ch. xxvii. 12*b*,
passing over ch. xxvii. 13–23 ? If it cannot be explained in
any other way, it appears that ch. xxvii. 13–23 must be rejected. There is the same difficulty in comprehending it by
supplying some suppressed thought, as *e.g.* Ewald explains it:
For, as there may also be much in the divine dealings that is
dark, etc. ; and Hahn : Because evil-doers perish according
to their desert, it does not necessarily follow that every one
who perishes is an evil-doer, and that every prosperous person is godly, *for*—the wisdom of God is unsearchable. This
mode of explanation, which supposes, between the close of
ch. xxvii. and the beginning of ch. xxviii., what is not found
there, is manifestly forced; and in comparison with it, it
would be preferable, with Stickel, to translate כִּי " because,"
and take ch. xxviii. 1, 2 as the antecedent to ver. 3. Then
after ch. xxvii. a dash might be made ; but this dash would indicate an ugly blank, which would be no honour to the poet.
Schlottmann explains it more satisfactorily. He takes ch.
xxvii. 13 sqq. as a warning addressed to the friends, lest they
bring down upon themselves, by their unjust judgment, the evil-
doer's punishment which they have so often proclaimed. If
this rendering of ch. xxvii. 13 sqq. were correct, the description
of the fate of the evil-doer would be influenced by an under-

lying thought, to which the following statement of the exalted nature of the divine wisdom would be suitably connected as a confirmation. We cannot, however, consider this rendering as correct. The picture ought to have been differently drawn, if it had been designed to serve as a warning to the friends.

It has a different design. Job depicts the revelation of the divine justice which is exhibited in the issue of the life of the evil-doer, to teach the friends that they judge him and his lot falsely. To this description of punishment, which is intended thus and not otherwise, ch. xxviii. with its confirmatory כי must be rightly connected. If this were not feasible, one would be disposed, with Pareau, to alter the position of ch. xxviii., as if it were removed from its right place, and put it after ch. xxvi. But we are cautioned against such a violent measure, by the consideration that it is not evident from ch. xxvi. why the course of thought in ch. xxviii., which begins with כי, should assume the exact form in which we find it; whereas, on the other hand, it was said in ch. xxvii. that the ungodly heaps up silver, כסף, like dust, but that the innocent who live to see his fall divide this silver, כסף, among themselves; so that when in ch. xxviii. 1 it continues : כי יש לכסף מוצא, there is a connection of thought for which the way has been previously prepared.

If we further take into consideration the fact of ch. xxviii. being only an amplification of the one closing thought to which everything tends, viz. that the fear of God is man's true wisdom, then ch. xxviii., also in reference to this its special point, is suitably attached to the description of the evil-doer's fate, ch. xxvii. 13 sqq. The miserable end of the ungodly is confirmed by this, that the wisdom of man, which he has despised, consists in the fear of God ; and Job thereby at the same time attains the special aim of his teaching, which is announced at ch. xxvii. 11 by אורה אתכם ביד־אל: viz. he has at the same time proved that he who retains the

fear of God in the midst of his sufferings, though those sufferings are an insoluble mystery, cannot be a רשע. This design
of the confirmation, and that connection of thought, which
should be well noted, prove that ch. xxviii. stands in its original
position. And if we ponder the fact, that Job has depicted
the ungodly as a covetous rich man who is snatched away by
sudden death from his immense possession of silver and other
costly treasures, we see that ch. xxviii. confirms the preceding
picture of punitive judgment in the following manner: silver
and other precious metals come out of the earth, but wisdom,
whose value exceeds all these earthly treasures, is to be found
nowhere within the province of the creature; God alone possesses it, and from God alone it comes; and so as man can
and is to attain to it, it consists in the fear of the LORD, and
the forsaking of evil. This is the close connection of ch.
xxviii. with what immediately precedes, which most expositors
since Schultens have missed, by transferring the central point
to the unsearchableness of the divine wisdom which rules in
the world; whereas Bouiller correctly observes that the whole
of ch. xxviii. treats not so much of the wisdom of God as of
the wisdom of man, which God, the sole possessor of wisdom,
imparts to him: *omnibus divitiis, fluxis et evanidis illis possessio
præponderat sapientiæ, quæ in pio Dei cultu et fuga mali est
posita.* The view of von Hofmann (*Schriftbeweis*, i. 96, 2d
edit.) accords with this: "If ch. xxviii. 1, where a confirmatory
or explanatory כי forms the transition, is taken together with
xxviii. 12, where another part of the speech is introduced with
a *Waw*, and finally with ch. xxviii. 28, where this is rounded
off, as forming the unity of one thought: it thus proves that
the final destruction of the godless, who is happy and prosperous in worldly things, is explained by the fact that man can
obtain every kind of hidden riches by his own exertion and
courage, but not the wisdom which is not indigenous to this
outward world, but is known to God alone, and is to be learned

from Him only; and the teaching concerning it is: behold, the fear of God, that is wisdom, and to depart from evil is understanding."

Before we now pass on to the detailed exposition of ch. xxviii., we may perhaps here, without anticipating, put the question, Whence has the poet obtained the knowledge of the different modes of mining operations which is displayed in ch. xxviii. 1 sqq., and which has every appearance of being the result of personal observation? Since, as we have often remarked already, he is well acquainted with Egypt, it is most natural that he derived this his knowledge from Egypt and the Sinaitic peninsula. The ruins of mines found there show that the Sinaitic peninsula has been worked as a mining district from the earliest times. The first of these mining districts is the *Wadi Nasb*, where Lepsius (*Briefe*, S. 338) found traces of old smelting-places, and where also Graul and his companions, having their attention drawn to it by Wilkinson's work, searched for the remains of a mine, and found at least traces of copper slag, but could see nothing more (*Reise*, ii. 202). E. Rüppell explored the spot at the desire of the Viceroy Mehemed Ali, and Russegger with less successful result (*vid.* the particulars in Ritter's *Erdkunde*, xiv. 784–788).[1] A second mining district is denoted by the ruins of a temple of *Hathor*, on the steep terrace of the rising

[1] The valley is not called *Wadi nahas* (Copper valley), which is only a supposition of Rüppell, but *Wadi nasb*, ﻧﺼﺐ, which, according to Reinaud, signifies valley of statues or columns. Thirty hours' journey from Suez, says a connoisseur in the *Historisch-politische Blätter*, 1863, S. 802 f., lies the *Wadi nesb* [a pronunciation which assumes the form of writing ﻧﺴﺐ]; it is rare that the ore is so easy to get, and found in such abundance, for the blocks containing the copper are in many places 200 feet in diameter, and the ore is almost in a pure state. The mineral (the black earth containing the copper) abounds in the metal. . . . . Besides this, iron-ore, manganese, carbonate of lead, and also the exceeding precious cinnabar, have been discovered on Sinai.

ground *Sarbut* (*Serâbît*) *el-châdim*, which stretches out into a spacious valley. This field of ruins, with its many lofty columns within the still recognisable area of a temple, and round about it, gives the impression of a large burying-ground, and it is described and represented as such by Carsten Niebuhr (*Reise*, 235, Tafel xliv.). In February 1854, Graul (*Reise*, ii. 203) and Tischendorf spent a short time upon this eminence of the desert, which is hard to climb, and abounds in monuments. It produced a strong impression upon us—says the latter (*Aus dem heiligen Lande*, S. 35)—as we tarried in the midst of the grotesque forms of these monuments, while the setting sun cast its deep red gleam over the wild terrific-looking copper rocks that lay around in their varied shades, now light, now dark. That these copper rocks were worked in ancient days, is proved by the large black heaps of slag which Lepsius (*Briefe*, S. 338) discovered to the east and west of the temple. Moreover, in the inscriptions *Hathor* bears the by-name "Queen of *Mafkat*," *i.e.* the copper country (*mafka*, copper, with the feminine post-positive article *t*). It even bears this name on the monuments in the *Wadi maghâra*, one of the side-gorges of the *Wadi mucatteb* (*i.e.* the Written Valley, valley full of inscriptions). These signs of another ancient mining colony belong almost entirely to the earliest Egyptian antiquity, while those on *Sarbut el-châdim* extend back only to *Amenemha* III., consequently to the last dynasty of the old kingdom. Even the second king of the fifth dynasty, *Snefru*, and indeed his predecessor (according to Lepsius, his successor) *Chufu*—that·Χέοψ who built the largest pyramid—appear here as conquerors of foreign peoples, and the mountainous district dedicated to *Hathor* is also called *Mafkat*. The remains of a mine, discovered by J. Wilson, at the eastern end of the north side of the *Wadi mucatteb*, also belongs to this copper country: they lie near the road, but in back gorges; there is a very high wall of rock of granite or porphyry, which is penetrated by dark seams of metal, which have been worked out from above downwards, thus forming artificial caverns, pits, and shafts; and it may be inferred that the yield of ore was very abundant, and, from the simplicity of the manner of working, that it is of very great antiquity. This art of mining thus laid open, as Ritter says,[1] furnishes the most important explanation of Job's remarkable description of mining operations.

As to Egypt itself, it has but few places where iron-ore was obtained, and it was not very plentiful, as iron occurs much more rarely than bronze on the tombs, although Wilkinson has observed important copper mines almost as extensive as the copper country of Sinai: we only, however, possess more exact information concerning the gold mines on the borders of Upper Egypt. Agatharchides mentions them in his *Periplus;* and Diodorus (iii. 11 sqq.) gives a minute description of them, from which it is evident that mining in those days was much the same as it was with us about a hundred years ago: we recognise in it the day and night relays, the structure of shafts, the crushing and washing apparatus, and the smelting-place.[2] There are the gold mines of Nubia, the name of which signifies the gold country, for *NOYB* is the old Egyptian name for gold. From the time of *Sethoshi* I., the father of *Sesostris,* we still possess the plan of a gold mine, which Birch (*Upon a historical tablet of Rameses* II. *of the* XIX. *dynasty, relating to the gold mines of Æthiopia*) has first of all correctly determined. Moreover, on monuments of all ages frequent mention is made of other metals (silver, iron, lead), as of precious stones, with which *e.g.* harps were ornamented; the diamond can also be

---

[1] In the essay on the Sinaitic peninsula in *Piper's Ev. Jahrbuch*, 1852. The mining district that J. Wilson saw (1843–44) is not one that was unknown up to that time, but one of the places of the *Wadi maghâra* recognised as favouring the ancient Egyptian system of excavation.

[2] Thus Klemm, *Allgem. Cultur-Geschichte*, v. 304.

traced. In the *Papyrus Prisse*, which Chabas has worked
up under the title *Le plus ancien livre du monde*, *Phtha-hotep*,
the author of this moral tractate, iv. 14, says: "Esteem my
good word more highly than the (green) emerald, which is
found by slaves under the pebbles." [1] The emerald-hills
near Berenice produced the emerald.

But if the scene of the book of Job is to be sought in
Idumæa proper ('Gebal) or in Hauran, there were certainly
mines that were nearer than the Egyptian. In *Phunon*
(*Phinon*), between Petra and Zoar, there were pits from
which copper (χαλκοῦ μέταλλα, *æris metalla*) was obtained
even to the time of Moses, as may be inferred from the fact
of Moses having erected the brazen serpent there (Num.
xxi. 9 sq., comp. xxxiii. 42 sq.), and whither, during the per-
secutions of the Christians in the time of the emperors, many
witnesses for the faith were banished, that they might fall
victims to the destructive labour of pit life (Athanasius ex-
travagantly says: ἔνθα καὶ φονεὺς καταδικαζόμενος ὀλίγας
ἡμέρας μόγις δύναται ζῆσαι). [2] But Edrîsi also knew of gold
and silver mines in the mountains of Edom, the *'Gebel esh-
Sherâ* (الشَّرَاة), *i.e.* הַר שֵׂעִיר. According to the *Onomasticon*,
דִּי זָהָב, Deut. i. 1 (LXX. καταχρύσεα), indicates such gold
mines in Arabia Petræa; and Jerome (under *Cata ta
chrysea* [3]) observes on that passage: *sed et metallo æris
Phæno, quod nostro tempore corruit, montes venarum auri
plenos olim fuisse vicinos existimant.* Eupolemus' account
(in Euseb. *præp.* ix. 30) of an island Οὐρφῆ, rich in gold, in

[1] According to a contribution from Prof. Lauth of Munich.
[2] *Vid. Genesis,* S. 512; Ritter, *Erdkunde,* xiv. 125–127; as also my
Kirchliches Chronikon des peträischen Arabiens in the *Luth. Zeitschr.*
1840, S. 133.
[3] *Opp. ed. Vallarsi,* iii. 183. The text of Eusebius is to be amended
according to that of Jerome; *vid.* Ugolini, *Thes.* vol. v. col. cxix. sq.
What Ritter says, *Erdkunde,* xiv. 127, is disfigured by mischievous mistakes.

the Red Sea, does not belong here; for by the red sea, ἐρυθρὰ θάλασσα,[1] it is not the Arabian Gulf that is meant; and the reference of the name of the range of hills *Telûl ed-dhahab* in ancient Gilead to gold mines rests only on hearsay up to the present time. But it is all the more worthy of mention that traces of former copper mines are still found on the Lebanon (*vid.* Knobel on Deut. viii. 9); that Edrîsi (*Syria, ed. Rosenm.* p. 12) was acquainted with the existence of a rich iron mine near Beirut; and that, even in the present day, the Jews who dwell in *Deir el-kamar*, on the Lebanon, work the iron on leases, and especially forge horse-shoes from it, which are sent all over Palestine.[2]

The poet of the book of Job might therefore have learned mining in its diversified modes of operation from his own observation, both in the kingdom of Egypt, which he had doubtless visited, and also in Arabia Petræa and in the Lebanon districts, so as to be able to put a description of them into the mouth of his hero. It is unnecessary, with Stickel, to give the preference to the mining of Arabia proper, where iron and lead are still obtained, and where, according to ancient testimony, even gold is said to have been worked at one time. " Since he places his hero in the country east of Jordan, the poet may in ver. 2 have thought chiefly of the mines of the Iron mountain (τὸ σιδηροῦν καλούμενον ὄρος, Jos. *Bell.* iv. 8, 2), which is also called the 'cross mountain,' *el-mi'râd*, because it runs from west to east, while the *'Gebel 'Aglûn* stretches from north to south. It lies between the gorges of the *Wâdî Zerká* and *Wâdî 'Arabûn*, begins at the mouths of the two *Wâdîs* in the *Ghôr*, and ends in the east with a precipitous descent towards the town of *Gerash*, which from its

---

[1] On the meaning of this appellation, *vid. Genesis*, S. 630.

[2] Schwarz, *Das h. Land* (1852), S. 323. The Egyptian monuments mention a district by the name of *Asj*, which paid native iron as tribute; *vid.* Brugsch, *Geogr. der Nachbarländer Ægyptens*, S. 52.

height, and being seen from afar, is called the *Negde* (נֶגְדֶּה).
The ancient worked-out iron mines lie on the south declivity
of the mountain south-west of the village of *Burmâ*, and
about six miles from the level bed of the *Wâdi Zerkâ*. The
material is a brittle, red, brown, and violet sandstone, which
has a strong addition of iron. It also contains here and there
a large number of small shells, where it is then considerably
harder. Of these ancient mines, some which were known in
Syria under the name of the 'rose mines,' *ma'âdin el-ward*,
were worked by Ibrahim Pasha from 1835 till 1839; but
when, in 1840, Syria reverted to Turkey, this mining, which
had been carried on with great success, because there was an
abundance of wood for the smelting furnaces, ceased. A
large forest, without a proprietor, covers the back and the
whole north side of this mountain down to the bed of the
Wâdi 'Arabûn; and as no tree has been cut down in it for
centuries, the thicket, with the fallen and decaying stems,
gives one an idea of a primeval forest. We passed through
the forest from *Kefrengi* to *Burmâ* in June 1860. Except
North Gilead, in which the Iron mountain is situated, no
other province of *Basan* admits of a mine; they are exclusively volcanic, their mountains are slag, lava, and basalt;
and probably the last-mentioned kind of stone owes its name
to the word Βασάλτις, the secondary form of Βασάντις
(= *Basan*)."—WETZST.

Ch. xxviii. 1 *For there is a mine for the silver,*
  And a place for gold which they fine.
 2 *Iron is taken out of the dust,*
  And he poureth forth stone as copper.
 3 *He hath made an end of darkness,*
  And he searcheth all extremities
  For the stone of darkness and of the shadow of
  death.

4 He breaketh away a shaft from those who tarry above :
There, forgotten by every foot,
They hang and swing far from men.[1]

According to the most natural connection demonstrated by
us, Job desires to show that the final lot of the rich man is
well merited, because the treasures which he made the object
of his avarice and pride, though ever so costly, are still
earthy in their nature and origin. Therefore he begins with
the most precious metals, with silver, which has the precedence in reference to ch. xxvii. 16 sq., and with gold. מוֹצָא
without any secondary notion of fulness (Schultens) signifies
the issuing place, *i.e.* the place from which anything naturally
comes forth (ch. xxxviii. 27), or whence it is obtained (1 Kings
x. 28); here in the latter sense of the place where a mineral
is found, or the mine, as the parall. מְקוֹם, the place where the
gold comes forth, therefore a gold mine. According to the
accentuation (*Rebia mugrasch, Mercha, Silluk*), it is not to be
translated: and a place for the gold where they refine it; but:
a place for the gold which they refine. זָקַק, to strain, filter,
is the technical expression for purifying the precious metals
from the rock that is mingled with them (Mal. iii. 3) by
washing. The pure gold or silver thus obtained is called
מְזֻקָּק (Ps. xii. 7; 1 Chron. xxviii. 18, xxix. 4). Diodorus, in
his description of mining in Upper Egypt (iii. 11 sqq.), after
having described the operation of crushing the stone to small

---

[1] Among the expositors of this and the two following strophes, are two
acquainted with mining : The director of mines, von Veltheim, whose
observations J. D. Michaelis has contributed in the *Orient. u. exeg.
Bibliothek*, xxiii. 7–17 ; and the inspector of mines, Rudolf Nasse, in
Studien und Krit. 1863, 105–111. Umbreit's Commentary contains some
observations by von Leonhard ; he understands ver. 4c as referring to
the descent upon a cross bar attached to a rope, ver. 5b of the lighting
up by burning poles, ver. 6 of the lapis lazuli, and ver. 10a of the earliest
mode of " letting off the water."

fragments,[1] proceeds : " Then artificers take the crushed stone and lay it on a broad table, which is slightly inclined, and pour water over it; this washes away the earthy parts, and the gold remains on the slab. This operation is repeated several times, the mass being at first gently rubbed with the hand; then they press it lightly with thin sponges, and thus draw off all that is earthy and light, so that the gold dust is left quite clean. And, finally, other artificers take it up in a mass, shake it in an earthen crucible, and add a proportionate quantity of lead, grains of salt, and a little tin and barley bran; they then place a close-fitting cover over the crucible, and cement it with clay, and leave it five days and nights to seethe constantly in the furnace. After this they allow it to cool, and then finding nothing of the flux in the crucible, they take the pure gold out with only slight diminution." The expression for the first of these operations, the separation of the gold from the quartz by washing, or indeed sifting (straining, *Seihen*), is זָקַק ; and for the other, the separation by exposure to heat, or smelting, is צָרַף.

Ver. 2. From the mention of silver and gold, the description passes on to iron and ore (copper, *cuprum = æs Cyprium*). Iron is called בַּרְזֶל, not with the noun-ending *el* like כַּרְמֶל (thus Ges., Olsh., and others), but probably expanded from בַּזֶּל (Fürst), like שַׁרְבִיט from שַׁבִיט = שֶׁבֶט, סַנְפִּיר from סַפִּיר, βάλσαμον from בֶּשֶׂם, since, as Pliny testifies, the name of basalt (iron-marble) and iron are related,[2] and copper is called נְחֹשֶׁת,

---

[1] *Vid.* the whole account skilfully translated in Klemm's *Allgem. Cultur-Geschichte,* v. 503 f.

[2] *Hist. nat.* xxxvi. 7, 11 : *Invenit eadem Ægyptus in Æthiopia quem vocant basalten (basaniten) ferrei coloris atque duritiæ, unde et nomen ei dedit* (*vid.* von Raumer, *Palästina,* S. 96, 4th edition). Neither Seetzen nor Wetzstein has found proper iron-ore in Basan. Basalt is all the more prevalent there, from which Basan may have its name. For there is no special Semitic word for basalt ; Bocthor calls in the aid of نوع رخام اسود, " a kind of black marble;" but, as Wetzstein informs me, this is

for which the book of Job (ch. xx. 24, xxviii. 2, xl. 18, xli. 19; comp. even Lev. xxvi. 19) always has נְחֻשָׁה (*æreum = æs*, Arab. *nuhâs*). Of the iron it is said that it is procured from the עָפָר, by which the bowels of the earth are meant here, as the surface of the earth in ch. xli. 25; and of copper it is said that they pour out the stone into copper (*vid.* Ges. § 139, 2), *i.e.* smelt copper from it: יָצוּק as ch. xxix. 6, *fundit*, here with a subj. of the most general kind: one pours; on the contrary, ch. xli. 15 sq. *partic.* of יָצַק. Ver. 3 distinctly shows that it is the bowels of the earth from which these metals are obtained: he (man) has made an end of the darkness, since he turns out and lights up the lightless interior of the earth; and לְכָל־תַּכְלִית, to every extremity, *i.e.* to the remotest depths, he searches out the stone of deep darkness and of the shadow of death, *i.e.* hidden in the deepest darkness, far beneath the surface of the earth (*vid.* on ch. x. 22;

only a translation of the phrase of a French dictionary which he had, for the general name of basalt, at least in Syria, is *hagar aswad* (black stone). Iron is called *hadîd* in Arabic (literally a pointed instrument, with the not infrequent transference of the name of the tool to the material from which it is made). בַּרְזֶל (פרזל) is known in Arabic only in the form *firzil*, as the name for iron chains and great smith's shears for cutting iron; but it is remarkable that in Berber, which is related to Egyptian, iron is called even in the present day *wazzâl; vid. Lex. geographicum* ed. *Juynboll*, tom. iv. (*adnot.*) p. 64, l. 16, and Marcel, *Vocabulaire Français-arabe de dialectes vulgaires africains*, p. 249: "*Fer* حَدِيد, *hadyd* (en berbere وَزَّال, *ouezzâl*; أَوْزَال, *ôouzzâl*)." The Coptic name of iron is *benipi* (dialect. *penipe*), according to Prof. Lauth perhaps, as also *barôt*, ore, connected with *ba*, the hieroglyph name of a very hard mineral; the black basalt of an obelisk in the British Museum is called *bechenen* in the inscription. If it really be so, that iron and basalt are homonymous in Semitic, the reason could only be sought for in the dark iron-black colour of basalt, in its hardness, and perhaps also its weight (which, however, is only about half the specific gravity of pure iron), not in the magnetic iron, which has only in more modern times been discovered to be a substantial component part of basalt, the grains of which cannot be seen by the naked eye, and are only detected with the magnetic needle, or by chemical analysis.

and comp. Pliny, *h. n.* xxxiii. *proœm.* of mining: *imus in viscera ejus* [*terræ*] *et in sede Manium opes quærimus*). Most expositors (Hirz., Ew., Hahn, Schlottm., and others) take לבל־תכלית adverbially, "to the utmost" or "most closely," but *vid.* on ch. xxvi. 10; לתכלית might be used thus adverbially, but לבל־תכלית is to be explained according to לבל־רוח, Ezek. v. 10 (to all the winds).

Ver. 4. Job now describes the operation of mining more minutely; and it is worthy of observation that the last-mentioned metal, with which the description is closely connected, is copper. נַחַל, which signifies elsewhere a valley, the bed of a river, and the river itself, like the Arab. وَإِل (not from נָחַל = נָהַל, to flow on, as Ges. *Thes.* and Fürst, but from נָחַל, root נהל to hollow, whence נְחִילָה = חָלִיל, a flute, as being a hollowed musical instrument), signifies here the excavation made in the earth, and in fact, as what follows shows, in a perpendicular direction, therefore the shaft. Nasse contends for the signification "valley," by which one might very well conceive of "the working of a surface vein:" "By this mode of working, a small shaft is made in the vein (consequently in a perpendicular direction), and the ore is worked from both sides at once. At a short distance from the first shaft a second is formed, and worked in the same way. Since thus the work progresses lengthwise, a cutting becomes formed in the mountain which may well be compared to a deep valley, if, as is generally the case where the stone is firm and the ways are almost perpendicular, the space that is hewn out remains open (that is, not broken in or filled in)." But if נחל everywhere else denotes a valley with its watercourse, it has not necessarily a like signification in mining technology. It signifies, perhaps not without reference to its usual signification, the shafts open above and surrounded by walls of rock (in distinction from the more or less horizontal galleries

or pit-ways, as they were cut through the excavated rocks in
the gold mines of Upper Egypt, often so crooked that, as
Diodorus relates, the miners, provided with lights on their
forehead, were always obliged to vary the posture of the body
according to the windings of the galleries); and מֵעִם־גָּר, away
from him who remains above, shows that one is to imagine these
shafts as being of considerable depth; but what follows even
more clearly indicates this: there forgotten (הַנִּשְׁכָּחִים with the
demonstrative *art.* as ch. xxvi. 5, Ps. xviii. 31, xix. 11, Ges.
§ 109 *ad init.*) of (every) foot (that walks above), they hang
(comp. Rabb. מִדְלְדָּל, *pendulus*[1]) far from men, hang and
swing or are suspended; comp. Pliny, *h. n.* xxxiii. 4, 21, according to Sillig's text: *is qui cœdit funibus pendet, ut procul
intuenti species ne ferarum quidem sed alitum fiat. Pendentes
majori ex parte librant et linias itineri præducunt.* דַלְל has

here the primary signification proper also to the Arab. دَلَّ,

deorsum pendēre; and נוּעַ is related to נוד, as *nuere, νεύειν,* to
nutare. The מני of מִנִּי־רָגֶל, taken strictly, does not correspond
to the Greek *ὑπό,* neither does it form an adverbial secondary
definition standing by itself: far away from the foot; but it
is to be understood, as מן is also used elsewhere after נשכח,
Deut. xxxi. 21, Ps. xxxi. 13: forgotten out of the mouth,
out of the heart; here: forgotten away from the foot, so that
this advances without knowing that there is a man beneath;
therefore: totally vanished from the remembrance of those
who pass by above. מֵאֱנוֹשׁ is not to be connected with נָעוּ
(Hahn, Schlottm.), but with דַלּוּ, for *Munach* is the representative of *Rebia mugrasch,* according to *Psalter,* ii. 503, § 2;
and דלו is regularly *Milel,* whereas Isa. xxxviii. 14 is *Milra*

---

[1] *Vid.* Luzzatto on Isa. xviii. 5, where וּלְזַלְזַלִּים, of the trembling and
quivering twigs, is correctly traced to זָלַל = דָלַל; on the other hand, Isa.
xiv. 19, אַבְנֵי־בוּר is wrongly translated *fundo della fossa,* by comparison
with Job xxviii. 3. אֶבֶן does not signify a shaft, still less the lowest
shaft, but stone (rock).

without any evident reason. The accentuation here follows no fixed law with equally regulated exceptions (*vid.* Olsh. § 233, *c*).

Moreover, the perception that ver. 4 speaks of the shaft of the mine, and the descent of the miners by a rope, is due to modern exegesis; even Schultens, who here exclaims : *Cimmeriæ tenebræ, quas me exsuperaturum vix sperare ausim,* perceived the right thing, but only imperfectly as yet. By נחל he understands the course or vein of the metal, where it is embedded; and, since he understands גר after the Arab. *'garr,* foot of the mountain, he translates : *rumpit (homo) alveum de pede montis.* Rosenm., on the other hand, correctly translates : *canalem deorsum actum ex loco quo versatur homo.* Schlottm. understands by גר the miner himself dwelling as a stranger in his loneliness; and if we imagine to ourselves the mining districts of the peninsula of Sinai, we might certainly at once conceive the miners' dwellings themselves which are found in the neighbourhood of the shaft in connection with מעם־גר. But in and for itself גר signifies only those settled (above), without the secondary idea of strangers.

    5 *The earth—from it cometh forth bread,*
       And beneath it is turned up like fire.
    6 *The place of the sapphire are its stones,*
       And it containeth gold ore.
    7 *The way, that no bird of prey knoweth,*
       And the eye of the hawk hath not gazed at,
    8 *Which the proud beast of prey hath not trodden,*
       Over which the lion hath not walked.

Ver. 5 is not to be construed as Rosenm. : *ad terram quod attinet, ex qua egreditur panis, quod subtus est subvertitur quasi igne;* nor with Schlottm. : (they swing) in the earth, out of which comes bread, which beneath one turns about with fire ;

for ver. 5a is not formed so that the *Waw* of וְתַחְתֶּיהָ could be *Waw apod.*, and אֶרֶץ cannot signify "in the interior of the earth" as *locativus;* on the contrary, it stands in opposition to תחתיה, that which is beneath the earth, as denoting the surface of the earth (the proper name of which is אֲדָמָה, from the root דם, with the primary notion of a flat covering). They are two grammatically independent predicates, the first of which is only the foil of the other: the earth, out of it cometh forth bread (לֶחֶם as Ps. civ. 14), and beneath it (the surface of the earth) = that which lies beneath it (ותחתיה only virtually a subj. in the sense of וְתַחְתִּיתֶיהָ, since תַּחְתֵּי occurs only as a preposition), is turned about (comp. the construction of the *sing.* of the verb with the *plur.* subj., ch. xxx. 15) as (by) fire *(instar ignis, scil. subvertentis)* ; *i.e.* the earth above furnishes nourishment to man, but that not satisfying him, he also digs out its inward parts (comp. Pliny, *h. n.* xxxiii. *proœm.: in sede Manium opes quærimus, tanquam parum benigna fertilique quaqua calcatur)*, since this is turned or tossed about (comp. מַהְפֵּכָה, the special word for the overthrow of Sodom by fire) by mining work, as when fire breaks out in a house, or even as when a volcanic fire rumbles within a mountain (Castalio: *agunt per magna spatia cuniculos et terram subeunt non secus ac ignis facet ut in Ætna et Vesuvio).* The reading בְּמוֹ (Schlottm.) instead of כמו is natural, since fire is really used to blast the rock, and to separate the ore from the stone ; but, with the exception of Jerome, who has arbitrarily altered the text *(terra, de qua oriebatur panis in loco suo, igni subversa est)*, all the old translations reproduce כמו, which even Nasse, in opposition to von Veltheim, thinks suitable: Man's restless search, which rummages everything through, is compared to the unrestrainable ravaging fire.

Ver. 6 also consists of two grammatically independent assertions: the place (bed) of the sapphire is its rock. Must we refer לוֹ to סַפִּיר, and translate: "and it contains fine dust of gold" (Hirz., Umbr., Stick., Nasse)? It is possible, for Theophrastus (p. 692, *ed. Schneider*) says of the sapphire it is ὥσπερ χρυσόπαστος, as it were covered with gold dust or grains of gold; and Pliny, *h. n.* xxxvii. 9, 38 sq.: *Inest ei (cyano) aliquando et aureus pulvis qualis in sapphiris, in iis enim aurum punctis conlucet,* which nevertheless does not hold good of the proper sapphire, but of the azure stone (*lapis lazuli*) which is confounded with it, a variegated species of which, with gold, or rather with iron pyrites glittering like gold, is specially valued.[1] But Schultens rightly observes: *vix crediderim, illum auratilem pulvisculum sapphiri peculiari mentione dignum;* and Schlottm.: such a collateral definition to ספיר, expressed in a special clause (not a relative one), has something awkward about it. On the other hand, עֲפָרֹת זָהָב is a perfectly suitable appellation of gold ore. "The earth, which is in itself black," says Diodorus in the passage quoted before, "is interspersed with veins of marble, which is of such pre-eminent whiteness, that its brilliance surpasses everything that glitters, and from it the overseers of the mine prepare gold with a large number of workmen." And further on, of the heating of this gold ore he says: "the hardest auriferous earth they burn thoroughly in a large fire; thus they make it soft, so that it can be worked by the hand." עפרת זהב is a still more suitable expression for such auriferous earth and ore than for the nuggets of ἄπυρος χρυσός (*i.e.* unsmelted) of the size of a chestnut, which, according to Diodorus, ii. 50, are obtained in mines in Arabia (μεταλλεύεται). But it is inadmissible to refer לֹו to man, for the clause would then require to be translated: and gold ore is to him = he has, while it is the rather intended to be said that the interior of the earth has gold ore. לֹו is therefore, with Hahn and Schlottm., to be referred to מָקֹום: and this place of the

[1] Comp. Quenstedt, *Handbuch der Mineralogie* (1863), S. 355 and 302.

sapphire, it contains gold. The poet might have written הֹ֥ל,
but וֹ implies that where the sapphire is found, gold is also
found. The following נְתִיב (with *Dechî*), together with the
following relative clause, is connected with אֲבָנֶיהָ, or even
with מָקוֹם, which through ver. 6*b* is become the chief subj.:
the place of the sapphire and of the gold is the rock of the
bowels of the earth,—a way, which, etc., *i.e.* such a place is
the interior of the earth, accessible to no living being of the
earth's surface except to man alone. The sight of the bird
of prey, the עַיִט, ἀετός, and of the אַיָּה, *i.e.* the hawk or
kite, reaches from above far and wide beneath;[1] the sons of

pride, שָׁחַץ (also Talmud. arrogance, *ferocia*, from שָׁחַץ = شَخَصَ,

to raise one's self, not: fatness, as Meier, after شَخَصَ, to be
fat, thick), *i.e.* the beasts of prey, especially the lion, שַׁחַל (*vid.*
on ch. iv. 10, from שַׁחַל, سَحَلَ, to roar, Arab. of the ass, comp.
the Lat. *rudere* used both of the lion and of the ass), seek
the most secret retreat, and shun no danger; but the way by
which man presses forward to the treasures of the earth is
imperceptible and inaccessible to them.

> 9 *He layeth his hand upon the pebbles;*
>   *He turneth up the mountains from the root.*
> 10 *He cutteth canals through the rocks;*
>   *And his eye seeth all kinds of precious things.*
> 11 *That they may not leak, he dammeth up rivers;*
>   *And that which is hidden he bringeth to light.*
> 12 *But wisdom, whence is it obtained?*
>   *And where is the place of understanding?*

Beneath, whither no other being of the upper world pene-
trates, man puts his hand upon the quartz or rock. חַלָּמִישׁ
(perhaps from חלם, to be strong, firm; Arabic, with the re-

---

[1] The אַיָּה—says the Talmud *b. Chullin*, 63*b*—is in Babylon, and seeth
a carcase in the land of Israel.

duplication resolved, *chalnubûs*, like עֲבָבִישׁ, Arab. *'ancabûth*, *vid. Jesurun*, p. 229) signifies here the quartz, and in general the hard stone; שָׁלַח יָד בְּ something like our "to take in hand" of an undertaking requiring strong determination and courage, which here consists in blasting and clearing away the rock that contains no ore, as Pliny, *h. n.* xxxiii. 4, 21, describes it: *Occursant . . . silices; hos igne et aceto rumpunt, sæpius vero, quoniam id cuniculos vapore et fumo strangulat, cædunt fractariis CL libras ferri habentibus egeruntque umeris noctibus ac diebus per tenebras proxumis tradentes; lucem novissimi cernunt.* Further: he (man, devoted to mining) overturns (*subvertit* according to the primary signification of הָפַךְ, أَفَكَ, أَفَتَ, to turn, twist) mountains from the roots. The accentuation הָפַךְ with *Rebia mugrasch*, מִשֹּׁרֶשׁ with *Mercha*, is false; it is, according to Codd. and old editions, to be accented הָפַךְ with *Tarcha*, מִשֹּׁרֶשׁ with *Munach*, and to be translated accordingly: *subvertit a radice montes* (for *Munach* is the transformation of a *Rebia mugrasch*), not *a radice montium*. Blasting in mining which lays bare the roots (the lowest parts) of the mountains is intended, the conclusion of which—the signal for the flight of the workmen, and the effective crash—is so graphically described by Pliny in the passage cited above : *Peracto opere cervices fornicum ab ultumo cadunt; dat signum ruina eamque solus intellegit in cacumine ejus montis vigil. Hic voce, nutu evocari jubet operas pariterque ipse devolat. Mons fractus cadit ab sese longe fragore qui concipi humana mente non possit eque efflatu incredibili spectant victores ruinam naturæ.*

The meaning of ver. 10 depends upon the signification of the יְאֹרִים. It is certainly the most natural that it should signify canals. The word is Egyptian; *aur* in the language of the hieroglyphs signifies a river, and especially the Nile; wherefore at the close of the Laterculus of Eratosthenes the name of the king, Φρονορῶ (Φουορῶ), is explained by ἤτοι Νεῖλος. If water-canals are intended, they may be either

such as go in or come away. In the first case it may mean
water let in like a cataract over the ruins of the blasted auriferous rock, the *corrugi* of Pliny: *Alius par labor ac vel
majoris impendi: flumina ad lavandam hanc ruinam jugis
montium obiter duxere a centesimo plerumque lapide; corrugos
vocant, a corrivatione credo; mille et hic labores.* But יבקע is
not a suitable word for such an extensive and powerful flood-
ing with water for the purpose of washing the gold. It suits
far better to understand the expression of galleries or ways
cut horizontally in the rock to carry the water away. Thus
von Veltheim explains it: "The miner makes ways through
the hard rock into his section [in which the perpendicular
shaft terminates], guides the water which is found in abundance at that depth through it [*i.e.* the water at the bottom
of the pit that hinders the progress of the work], and is able
[thus ver. 10*b* naturally is connected with what precedes] to
judge of the ore and fragments that are at the bottom, and
bring them to the light. This mode of mining by constantly
forming one gallery under the other [so that a new gallery is
made under the pit that is worked out by extending the shaft,
and also freeing this from water by making another outlet
below the previous one] is the oldest of all, of which anything
certain is known in the history of mining, and the most
natural in the days when they had no notion of hydraulics."
This explanation is far more satisfactory than that of Herm.
Sam. Reimarus, of the "Wolfenbütteler Fragmente" (in his
edition of the *Neue Erkl. des B. Hiob,* by John Ad. Hoffmann, 1734, iv. S. 772): "*He breaks open watercourses in the
rocks.* What the miners call coming upon water, is when
they break into a fissure from which strong streams of water
gush forth. The miner not only knows how to turn such
water to good account, but it is also a sign that there are rich
veins of ore near at hand, as there is the most water by these
courses and fissures. Hence follows: *and then his eye sees*

all kinds of precious things." But there is no ground for saying that water indicates rich veins of ore, and בֶּקַע is much
more appropriate to describe the designed formation of courses
to carry off the water than an accidental discovery of water
in course of the work; moreover, יְאֹרִים is as appropriate to the
former as it is inappropriate to the latter explanation, for it
signifies elsewhere the arms of the Nile, into which the Nile
is artificially divided; and therefore it may easily be transferred to the horizontal canals of the mine cut through the
hard rock (or through the upper earth). Nevertheless,
although the water plays an important part in mining operations, by giving rise to the greatest difficulties, as it frequently
happens that a pit is deluged with water, and must be abandoned because no one can get down to it: it is improbable
that ver. 10 as well as ver. 11 refers to this; we therefore
prefer to understand יְאֹרִים as meaning the (horizontal) courses
(galleries or drifts) in which the ore is dug,—a rendering
which is all the more possible, since, on the one hand, in Coptic
jaro (Sahidic *jero*) signifies the Nile of Egypt (*phiaro ente
chêmi*); on the other, *ior* (*eioor*) signifies a ditch, διῶρυξ
(comp. Isa. xxxiii. 21, יְאֹרִים, LXX. διώρυχες), *vid.* Ges.
Thes. Thus also ver. 10*b* is consistently connected with
what precedes, since by cutting these *cuniculi* the courses
of the ore (veins), and any precious stones that may also be
embedded there, are laid bare.

Ver. 11*a*. Contrary to the correct indication of the accentuation, Hahn translates: he stops up the droppings of the
watercourses; מִבְּכִי has *Dechî*, and is therefore not to .be
connected with what follows as a genitive. But Reimarus'
translation: from the drops he connects the streams, is inadmissible. " The trickling water," he observes, "is carefully
caught in channels by the miners for use, and is thus brought
together from several parts to the reservoir and the water-
wheel. What Pliny calls *corrugus, corrivatio.*" On the

contrary, Schlottm. remarks that חבש cannot signify such a
connection, *i.e.* gathering together of watercourses; it occurs
elsewhere only of uniting, *i.e.* binding up wounds. Nevertheless, although חבש cannot directly signify " to collect," the
signification *coercere* (ch. xxxiv. 17), which is not far from

this idea,—as is evident from the Arab. حَبَسَ (حِبْس), a dam

or sluice for collecting water, and مَحْبِس الماءِ, a reservoir,

cistern,—is easily transferable to water, in the sense of binding = catching up and accumulating. But it is contrary to
the form of the expression that מִבְּכִי, with this use of חבש,
should denote the *materia ex qua*, and that נְהָרוֹת should be
referred to the miry ditches in which " the crushed ore is
washed, for the purpose of separating the good from the
worthless." On the contrary, from the form of the expression,
it is to be translated: *a fletu* (not *e fletu*) *flumina obligat,*
whether it be that *a fletu* is equivalent to *ne flent s. stillent*
(Simeon Duran: שֶׁלֹּא יֵילוּ), or *obligat* equivalent to *cohibet*
(Ralbag: מֵהַגְּלָה). Thus von Veltheim explains the passage,
since he here, as in ver. 10, understands the channels for
carrying off the water. " The miner covers the bottom with
mire, and fills up the crevices so exactly [*i.e.* he besmears it,
where the channel is broken through, with some water-tight
substance, *e.g.* clay], that it may entirely carry off the water
that is caught by it out of the pit [in which the shaft termi-
nates], and not let it fall through the fissures [crevices] to
the company of miners below [to the vein that lies farther
down]; then the miner can descend still deeper [since the
water runs outwards and does not soak through], and bring
forth the ore that lies below the channel." This explanation
overlooks the fact that יְאֹרִים is used in ver. 10, whereas ver. 11
has נהרות. It is not probable that these are only interchange-
able expressions for the channels that carry off the water.

יארים is an appropriate expression for it, but not נהרות, which
as appropriately describes the conflux of water in the mine
itself.

The meaning of ver. 11a is, that he (the miner) binds or
stops the watercourses which his working out of the pit has
interfered with and injured, so that they may not leak, i.e.
that they may not in the least ooze through, whether by building up a wall or by collecting the water that streams forth in
reservoirs (Arab. mahbas) or in the channels which carry it
outwards,—all these modes of draining off the water may be
included in ver. 11a, only the channel itself is not, with von
Veltheim, to be understood by נהרות, but the concourse of the
water which, in one way or the other, is rendered harmless to
the pit-work, so that he (the miner), as ver. 11b says, can
bring to light (לְאוֹר = אוֹר) whatever precious things the bowels
of the earth conceals (תַּעֲלֻמָה, according to Kimchi and others,
with euphonic Mappik, as according to the Masora כבכורה
Isa. xxviii. 4, נִשְׁמָה Ezek. xxii. 24, and also וגלָהּ Zech. iv. 2,
only לתפארת הקריאה ולא לכינוי, i.e. they have Mappik only for
euphony, not as the expression of the suff.).

With the question in ver. 12 the description of mining
attains the end designed: man can search after and find out
silver, gold, and other metals and precious stones, by making
the foundations of the earth accessible to him; but wisdom,
whence shall he obtain it, and which (וְאֵי־זֶה, according to
another reading וְאֵיזֶה) is the place of understanding? הַחָכְמָה
has the art. to give prominence to its transcendency over the
other attainable things. חכמה is the principal name, and בִּינָה
interchanges with it, as תְּבוּנָה, Prov. viii. 1, and other synonyms in which the Chokma literature abounds elsewhere in
Prov. i.–ix. בינה is properly the faculty of seeing through
that which is distinguishable, consisting of the possession
of the right criteria; חכמה, however, is the perception, in
general, of things in their true nature and their final causes.

13 *A mortal knoweth not its price,*
   And it is not found in the land of the living.
14 *The abyss saith: It is not in me,*
   And the sea saith: It is not with me.
15 *Pure gold cannot be given for it,*
   And silver cannot be weighed as its price;
16 *And it is not outweighed with the fine gold of Ophir,*
   With the precious onyx and the sapphire.

It is self-evident that wisdom is found nowhere directly present and within a limited space, as at the bottom of the sea, and cannot be obtained by a direct exchange by means of earthly treasures. It is, moreover, not this self-evident fact that is denied here; but the meaning is, that even if a man should search in every direction through the land of the living, *i.e.* (as *e.g.* Ps. lii. 7) the world—if he should search through the תְּהוֹם, *i.e.* the subterranean waters that feed the visible waters (*vid.* Gen. xlix. 25)—if he should search through the sea, the largest bounded expanse of this water that wells up from beneath—yea, even if he would offer all riches and precious things to put himself in possession of the means and instruments for the acquirement of wisdom,—wisdom, *i.e.* the profoundest perception of the nature of things, would still be beyond him, and unattainable. עֵרֶךְ, ver. 13, an equivalent (from עָרַךְ, to range beside, to place at the side of), inter-changes with מְחִיר (from מָחַר, cogn. מָכַר, מֵחַר, *mercari*). סְגוֹר is זָהָב סָגוּר, 1 Kings vi. 20 and freq., which hardly signifies gold shut up = carefully preserved, rather : closed = com-pressed, unmixed; Targ. סְנִין דְּהַב, *aurum colatum* (*purgatum*). Ewald compares سَخِن, to seethe, heat; therefore : heated, gained by smelting. On the other hand, כֶּתֶם from כָּתַם, كَتَم, *occulere*, seems originally to denote that which is precious, then precious gold in particular, LXX. χρυσίῳ Ωφείρ, *Cod.*

Vat. and *Cod. Sinaiticus,* Σωφίρ (Egyptized by prefixing the Egyptian *sa,* part, district, side, whence *e.g. sa-rēs,* the upper country, and *sa-hēt,* the lower country, therefore = *sa-ofir,* land of Ophir). שֹׁהַם is translated here by the LXX. ὄνυξ (elsewhere σαρδόνυξ or σάρδιος), of which Pliny, *h. n.* xxxvii. 6, 24, appealing to Sudines, says, *in gemma esse candorem unguis humani similitudinem;* wherefore Knobel, Rödiger, and others, compare the Arab. سَاهِم, which, however, does not signify pale, but lean, and parched by the heat, with which, in hot countries at least, not pallor, but, on the contrary, a dark brown-black colour, is identified (Fl.). مُسَهَّم, striped (Mich.), would be more appropriate, since the onyx is marked through by white veins; but this is a *denom.* from *sahm,* a dart, prop. darted, and is therefore wide of the mark. On the etymology of סַפִּיר, *vid. Jesurun,* p. 61. Nevertheless both שֹׁהַם and סַפִּיר are perhaps foreign names, as the name of the emerald (*vid. ib.* p. 108), which is Indian (Sanskr. *marakata,* or even *marakta*); and, on the other hand, it is called in hieroglyph (determined by the stone) *uot,* the green stone (in Coptic *p. auannēse,* the green colour) (Lauth).

The transcendent excellence of wisdom above the most precious earthly treasures, which the author of the introduction to the book of Proverbs briefly describes, ch. iii. 14 sq., is now drawn out in detail.

17 *Gold and glass are not equal to it,*
    Nor is it exchanged for jewels of gold.
18 *Pearls and crystal are not to be mentioned,*
    And the acquisition of wisdom is beyond corals.
19 *The topaz of Ethiopia is not equal to it,*
    It is not outweighed by pure fine gold.

20 *Whence, then, cometh wisdom,*
    And which is the place of understanding?

Among the separate חפצים, Prov. iii. 15, which are here
detailed, apart from זהב, glass has the transparent name
זְכוּכִית, or, as it is pointed in Codd., in old editions, and by
Kimchi, זְכוֹכִית with *Cholem* (in the dialects with ג instead of
כ). Symm. indeed translates crystal, and in fact the ancient
languages have common names for glass and crystal; but the
crystal is here called גָּבִישׁ, which signifies prop., like the Arab.
'gibs, ice; κρύσταλλος also signifies prop. ice, and this only in
Homer, then crystal, exactly as the cognate קֶרַח unites both
significations in itself. The reason of this homonymy lies
deeper than in the outward similarity,—the ancients really
thought the crystal was a product of the cold; Pliny, xxxvii.
2, 9, says: *non alibi certe reperitur quam ubi maxume hibernæ
nives rigent, glaciemque esse certum est, unde nomen Græci
dedere.* The Targ. translates גביש by בֵּירוּלִין, certainly in the
sense of the Arabico-Persic *bullûr* (*bulâr*), which signifies
crystal, or even glass, and moreover is the primary word for
βήρυλλος, although the identical Sanskrit word, according to
the laws of sound, *vaidurja* (Pali, *velurija*), is, according to
the lexicons, a name of the *lapis lazuli* (Persic, *lagurd*).
Of the two words רָאמוֹת and פְּנִינִים, the one appears to mean
pearls and the other corals; the ancient appellations of these
precious things which belong to the sea are also blended; the
Persic *mergân* (Sanskr. *mangara*) unites the signification
pearl and coral in itself. The root פן, نِيَ, which has the
primary notion of pushing, especially of vegetation (whence نِيَ,
a branch, shoot, prop. motion; French, *jet*), and Lam. iv. 7,
where snow and milk, as figures of whiteness (purity), are
placed in contrast with פנינים as a figure of redness, favour
the signification corals for פנינים. The Coptic *b'nôni*, which

signifies *gemma*, favours (so far as it may be compared) corals
rather than pearls. And the fact that רָאמוֹת, Ezek. xxvii. 16,
appear as an Aramæan article of commerce in the market of
Tyre, is more favourable to the signification pearls than
corals; for the Babylonians sailed far into the Indian Ocean,
and brought pearls from the fisheries of Bahrein, perhaps
even from Ceylon, into the home markets (*vid.* Layard, *New
Discoveries,* 536). The name is perhaps, from the Western
Asiatic name of the pearl,[1] mutilated and Hebraized.[2]

The name of the פִּטְדָה of Ethiopia appears to be derived
from *τοπαζ* by transposition; Pliny says of the topaz, xxxvii.
8, 32, among other passages : *Juba Topazum insulam in rubro
mari a continenti stadiis CCC abesse dicit, nebulosam et ideo
quæsitam sæpius navigantibus ; ex ea causa nomen accepisse :*

---

[1] *Vid. Zeitschr. für d. Kunde des Morgenlandes,* iv. 40f. The recently
attempted explanation of κοράλλιον from גּוֹרָל (to which κλῆρος the rather
belongs), in the primary signification *lapillus* (Arab. *'garal*), is without
support.

[2] Two reasons for פְּנִינִים = pearls (in favour of which Bochart compares the name of the pearl-oyster, πίννα) and רָאמוֹת = corals, which
are maintained by Carey, are worthy of remark. (1.) That פְּנִינִים does
not signify corals, he infers from Lam. iv. 7, for the redness of corals
cannot be a mark of bodily beauty; " but when I find that there are some
pearls of a slightly reddish tinge, then I can understand and appreciate
the comparison." (2.) That רָאמוֹת signifies corals, is shown by the origin
of the word, which properly signifies *reêm-* (wild oxen) horns, which is
favoured by a mention of Pliny, *h. n.* xiii. 51 : (*Tradidere*) *juncos quoque
lapideos perquam similes veris per litora, et in alto quasdam arbusculas
colore bubuli cornus ramosas et cacuminibus rubentes.* Although
Pliny there speaks of marine petrified plants of the Indian Ocean (not,
at least in his sense, of corals), this hint of a possible derivation of
רָאמוֹת is certainly surprising. But as to Lam. iv. 7, this passage is to
be understood according to Cant. v. 10 (my friend is צַח וְאָדוֹם). The
white and red are intended to be conceived of as mixed and overlapping
one another, as our [Germ.] popular poetry speaks of cheeks which
" shine with milk and purple;" and as in Homer, *Il.* iv. 141–146, the
colour of the beautifully formed limbs of Menelaus is represented by the
figure (which appears hideous to us): ὡς δ᾽ ὅτε τίς τ᾽ ἐλέφαντα γυνὴ Φοίνικι
μιήνη (ebony stained with purple).

topazin enim Troglodytarum lingua significationem habere quœ-rendi. This topaz, however, which is said to be named after an island of the same name, the Isle of Serpents in Agathar-chides and Diodorus, is, according to Pliny, yellowish green, and therefore distinct from the otherwise so-called topaz. To make a candid confession, we grope about everywhere in the dark here, and the ancient versions are not able to help us out of our difficulty.[1] The poet lays everything under contribution to illustrate the thought, that the worth of wis-dom exceeds the worth of the most valuable earthly thing; beside which, in מֶשֶׁךְ חָכְמָה מִפְּנִינִים, "the acquisition or posses-sion (from מָשַׁךְ, مسك, to draw to one's self, to take hold of) of wisdom is above corals," there is an indication that, although not by the precious things of the earth, still in some way or other, wisdom can be possessed, so that consequently the question repeated at the end of the strophe will not remain unanswered. This is its meaning: now if wisdom is not to be found in any of the places named, and is not to be attained by any of the means mentioned, whence can man hope to attain it, and whither must he turn to find it? for its exist-ence is certain, and it is an indisputable need of man that he should partake of it.

> 21 *It is veiled from the eyes of all living,*
>   *And concealed from the fowls of heaven.*
> 22 *Destruction and death say :*
>   *With our ears we heard a report of it.—*
> 23 *Elohim understandeth the way to it,*

---

[1] The Targ. translates שֹׁהַם by בֵּירוּלִין, βήουλλος; סַפִּיר by שַׁבְזִיזָא (سبج, vid. Pott in the *Zeitschr. f. K. d. M.* iv. 275); פּוּ by אוֹבְרִיזִין, ὄβρυζον; ראמות by סַנְדַּלְכִין, σανδαράχη, red gold-pigment (*vid.* Rödiger-Pott, as just quoted, S. 267) ; נְבִישׁ again by בֵּירוּלִין in the sense of the Arabico-Persic *bullûr*, Kurd. *bellûr*, crystal ; פְּנִינִים by מַרְגָּלִין, μαργαρῖται; פִּטְדָה by מַרְגְּלָא יָרְקָא (the green pearl); כֶּתֶם by פְּטָלוֹן (perhaps פְּטְלוֹן, πέταλον, in the sense of *lamina auri*).

And He—He knoweth its place.
24 *For He looketh to the ends of the earth,*
  Under the whole heaven He seeth.

No living created being (כָּל־חָי, as ch. xii. 10, xxx. 23) is
able to answer the question; even the birds that fly aloft,
that have keener and farther-seeing eyes than man, can give
us no information concerning wisdom; and the world at least
proclaims its existence in a rich variety of its operations, but
in the realm of Abaddon and of death below (comp. the combination שְׁאוֹל ואבדין, Prov. xv. 11, ᾅδου καὶ τοῦ θανάτου, Apoc.
i. 18) it is known only by an indistinct hearsay, and from
confused impressions. Therefore: no creature, whether in
the realm of the living or the dead, can help us to get wisdom. There is but One who possesses a perfect knowledge
concerning wisdom, namely Elohim, whose gaze extends to
the ends of the earth, and who sees under the whole heaven,
i.e. is everywhere present (תַּחַת, definition of place, not equivalent to אֲשֶׁר תַּחַת; comp. on ch. xxiv. 9*b*), who therefore,
after the removal of everything earthly (sub-celestial), alone
remains. And why should He with His knowledge, which
embraces everything, not also know the way and place of
wisdom? Wisdom is indeed the ideal, according to which
He has created the world.

25 *When He appointed to the wind its weight,*
  And weighed the water according to a measure,
26 *When He appointed to the rain its law,*
  And the course to the lightning of the thunder:
27 *Then He saw it and declared it,*
  Took it as a pattern and tested it also,
28 *And said to man: Behold, the fear of the Lord is wisdom,*
  And to depart from evil is understanding.

It is impracticable to attach the *inf.* לַעֲשׂוֹת to ver. 24 as the purpose, because it is contrary to the meaning; but it is impossible, according to the syntax, to refer it to ver. 27 as the purpose placed in advance, or to take it in the sense of *perfecturus*, because in both instances it ought to have been יְתֵּן instead of חֻקּן, or at least וְיִתֵּן with the verb placed first (*vid.* ch. xxxvii. 15). But even the temporal use of לְ in לִפְנוֹת at the turn (of morning, of evening, *e.g.* Gen. xxiv. 63) cannot be compared, but לַעֲשׂוֹת signifies *perficiendo = quum perficeret* (as *e.g.* 2 Sam. xviii. 29, *mittendo = quum mitteret*), it is a gerundival *inf.* (Nägelsb. S. 197f, 2d edition); and because it is the past that is spoken of, the modal *inf.* can be continued in the *perf.*, Ges. § 132, rem. 2. The thought that God, when He created the world, appointed fixed laws of equable and salutary duration, he particularizes by examples: He appointed to the wind its weight, *i.e.* the measure of its force or feebleness; distributed the masses of water by measure; appointed to the rain its law, *i.e.* the conditions of its development and of its beginning; appointed the way, *i.e.* origin and course, to the lightning (חֲזִיז from חָזַז, خَزّ, *secare*). When He thus created the world, and regulated what was created by laws, then He perceived (רָאָהּ with *He Mappic.* according to the testimony of the Masora) it, wisdom, viz. as the ideal of all things; then He declared it, *enarravit*, viz. by creating the world, which is the development and realization of its substance; then He gave it a place הֱכִינָהּ (for which Döderl. and Ewald unnecessarily read הֲבִינָהּ), viz. to create the world after its pattern, and to commit the arrangement of the world as a whole to its supreme protection and guidance; then He also searched it out or tested it, viz. its demiurgic powers, by setting them in motion to realize itself.

If we compare Prov. viii. 22–31 with this passage, we may say: the חבמה is the divine ideal-world, the divine imagination of all things before their creation, the complex unity of all the ideas, which are the essence of created things and the end of their development. "Wisdom," says one of the old theologians,[1] "is a divine imagination, in which the ideas of the angels and souls and all things were seen from eternity, not as already actual creatures, but as a man beholds himself in a mirror." It is not directly one with the Logos, but the Logos is the demiurg by which God has called the world into existence according to that ideal which was in the divine mind. Wisdom is the impersonal model, the Logos the personal master-builder according to that model. Nevertheless the notions, here or in the later cognate portion of Scripture, Prov. viii. 22–31, are not as yet so distinct as the New Testament revelation of God has first of all rendered possible. In those days, when God realized the substance of the חכמה, this eternal mirror of the world, in the creation of the world, He also gave man the law, corresponding to which he corresponds to His idea and participates in wisdom. Fearing the supreme Lord (אֲדֹנָי only here in the book of Job, one of the 134 וראין, *i.e.* passages, where אדני is not merely to be read instead of יהוה, but is actually written[2]), and renouncing evil (סוּר מֵרָע, according to another less authorized mode of writing מֵרָע),—this is man's share of wisdom, this is his relative wisdom, by which he remains in connection with the absolute. This is true human φιλοσοφία, in contrast to all high-flown and profound speculations; comp. Prov. iii. 7, where, in like manner, "fear Jehovah" is placed side by side with "depart from evil," and Prov. xvi. 6, according to which it is rendered possible סור מרע, to escape the evil of sin and its punishment by fearing God. "The fear of God is the beginning of wisdom" (Prov. i. 7; comp. Ps. cxi. 10) is the *symbolum*, the motto and uppermost principle, of that Israelitish Chokma, whose greatest achievement is the book of Job. The whole

[1] *Vid.* Jul. Hamberger, *Lehre Jak. Böhme's*, S. 55.
[2] *Vid.* Buxtorf's *Tiberias*, p. 245 ; comp. Bär's *Psalterium*, p. 133.

of ch. xxviii. is a minute panegyric of this principle, the
materials of which are taken from the far-distant past; and
it is very characteristic, that, in the structure of the book,
this twenty-eighth chapter is the clasp which unites the half
of the δέσις with the half of the λύσις, and that the poet has
inscribed upon this clasp that sentence, "The fear of God
is the beginning of wisdom." But, moreover, Job's closing
speech, which ends in this celebration of the praise of the
חכמה, also occupies an important position, which must now
be determined, in the structure of the whole.

After Job has refuted Bildad, and, continuing his description, has celebrated in such lofty strains the majesty of God,
it can hardly be expected that the poet will allow Zophar
to speak for the third time. Bildad is unable to advance
anything new, and Zophar has already tried his utmost to
terrify Job for the second time; besides, Job's speech furnishes no material for a reply (a motive which is generally
overlooked), unless the controversy were designed to ramble
on into mere personalities. Accordingly the poet allows Job
to address the friends once more, but no longer in the extreme
and excited tone of the previous dialogue, but, since the silence
of the friends must produce a soothing impression on Job,
tempering him to gentleness and forbearance, in a tone of
confession conscious of victory, yet altogether devoid of
haughty triumph,—a confession in which only one single
word of reproach (ch. xxvii. 12b) escapes him. Ch. xxvii.
xxviii. contain this confession—Job's final address to his
friends.

Job once again most solemnly asserts his innocence before
the friends; all attempts on the part of the friends to entice
or to extort from him a confession which is against his conscience, have therefore been in vain : joyous and victorious
he raises his head, invincible, even to death, in the conviction
of that which is a fact of his consciousness that cannot be

got rid of by denial. He is not an evil-doer; accordingly he must stand convicted as an evil-doer who treats him as such. For although he is not far from death, and is in sore vexation, he has not manifested the hopelessness and defection from God in which the evil-doer passes away. Job has indeed even expressed himself despondingly, and complained of God's wrath; but the true essence of his relation to God came to light in such words as ch. xvi. 19–21, xvii. 9, xix. 25–27. If the friends had not been blind to such brilliant aspirations of his life in God, how could they regard him as a godless man, and his affliction as the punishment of such an one! His affliction has, indeed, no connection with the terrible end of the evil-doer. Job here comes before the friends with the very doctrine they have so frequently advanced, but infatuated with the foolish notion that it is suited to his case. He here gives it back to them, to show them that it is not suited to him. He also does not deny, that in the rule the evil-doer meets a terrible end, although he has hitherto disputed the assertion of the friends, because of the exclusiveness with which it was maintained by them. His counter-assertion respecting the prosperity of the evil-doer, which from the beginning was not meant by him so exclusively as the friends meant theirs respecting the misfortune of the evil-doer, is here indirectly freed from the extreme appearance of exclusiveness by Job himself, and receives the necessary modification. Job does not deny, yea, he here brings it under the notice of the friends, that the sword, famine, and pestilence carry off the descendants of the evil-doer, and even himself; that his possessions at length fall into the hands of the righteous, and contain within themselves the germ of destruction from the very first; that God's curse pursues, and suddenly destroys, the godless rich man himself. Thus it comes to pass; for while silver and other precious things come from the depths of the earth, wisdom, whose

worth far transcends all earthly treasures, is to be found with
no created being, but is with God alone; and the fear of God,
to avoid evil, is the share of wisdom to which man is directed
according to God's primeval decree.

The object of the section, ch. xxviii., is primarily to confirm
the assertion concerning the judgment that befalls the evil-
doer, ch. xxvii. 13–23 ; the confirmation is, however, at the
same time, according to the delicately laid plan of the poet,
a glorious general confession, in which Job's dialogue with the
friends comes to a close.   This panegyric of wisdom (similar
to Paul's panegyric of charity, 1 Cor. xiii.) is the presentation
of Job's predominant principle, and as such, is like a song
of triumph, with which, without vain-glory, he closes the
dialogue in the most appropriate manner.   If Job's life has
such a basis, it is not possible that his affliction should be the
punishment of an ungodly man.   And if the fear of God is
the wisdom appointed to man, he also teaches himself that,
though unable to see through the mystery of his affliction,
he must still hold on to the fear of God, and teaches the
friends that they must do the same, and not lay themselves
open to the charge of injustice and uncharitableness towards
him, the suffering one, in order to solve the mystery.   Job's
conclusion, which is first intended to show that he who does
not fear God is overtaken by the merited fate of a fool who
rebels against God's moral government, shows at the same
time that the afflictive lot of those who fear God must be
judged of in an essentially different manner from that of the
ungodly.

We may imagine what impression these last words of Job
to the friends must have made upon them.   Since they were
obliged to be silent, they will not have admitted that they
are vanquished, although the drying up of their thoughts, and
their involuntary silence, is an actual proof of it.   But does
Job make them feel this oppressively?   Now that they are

become so insignificant, does he read them a severe lecture?
does he in general act towards them as vanquished? No
indeed, but solemnly, and without vaunting himself over his
accusers, he affirms his innocence; earnestly, but in a winning
manner, he admonishes them, by tempering and modifying
what was vehement and extreme in his previous replies. He
humbly submits himself to the divine wisdom, by setting the
fear of God, as man's true wisdom, before himself and the
friends as their common aim. Thus he utters "the loftiest
words, which must surprise the opponents as they exhibit
him as the not merely mighty, but also wonderfully calm
and modest conqueror, who here for the first time wears the
crown of true victory, when, in outward victory conquering
himself, he struggles on towards a more exalted clearness of
perception."

Job's Monologue.—Chap. xxix.-xxxi.

FIRST PART.—CHAP. XXIX.

Schema : 10. 8. 8. 6. 6. 11.

[Then Job continued to take up his proverb, and said :]
2 *O that I had months like the times of yore,*
   Like the days when Eloah protected me,
3 *When He, when His lamp, shone above my head,*
   By His light I went about in the darkness;
4 *As I was in the days of my vintage,*
   When the secret of Eloah was over my tent,
5 *When the Almighty was still with me,*
   My children round about me;
6 *When my steps were bathed in cream,*
   And the rock beside me poured forth streams of oil.

Since the optative מִי־יִתֵּן (comp. on ch. xxiii. 3) is connected
with the acc. of the object desired, ch. xiv. 4, xxxi. 31, or of

that respecting which anything is desired, ch. xi. 5, it is in itself possible to explain: who gives (makes) me like the months of yore; but since, when מִרְיִתְּנֵנִי occurs elsewhere, Isa. xxvii. 4, Jer. ix. 1, the *suff.* is meant as the dative (= מִרְיִתֵן לִי, ch. xxxi. 35), it is also here to be explained: who gives me (= O that one would give me, O that I had) like (*instar*) the months of yore, *i.e.* months like those of the past, and indeed those that lie far back in the past; for יַרְחֵי־קֶדֶם means more than יְרָחִים (אֲשֶׁר) עָבְרוּ. Job begins to describe the olden times, that he wishes back, with the virtually genitive relative clause: "when Eloah protected me" (Ges. § 116, 3). It is impossible to take בְּהִלּוֹ as *Hiph.:* when He caused to shine (Targ. בְּאַנְהָרוּתֵיהּ); either בְּהַהֲלוֹ (Olsh.) or even בְּהָלּוֹ (Ew. in his *Comm.*) ought to be read then. On the other hand, הִלּוֹ can be justified as the form for *inf. Kal* of הָלַל (to shine, *vid.* ch. xxv. 5) with a weakening of the *a* to *i* (Ew. § 255, *a*), and the *suff.* may, according to the syntax, be taken as an anticipatory statement of the object: when it, viz. His light, shone above my head; comp. Ex. ii. 6 (him, the boy), Isa. xvii. 6 (its, the fruit-tree's, branches), also xxix. 23 (he, his children); and Ew. § 309, *c*, also decides in its favour. Nevertheless it commends itself still more to refer the *suff.* of בהלו to אֱלוֹהַּ (comp. Isa. lx. 2, Ps. l. 2), and to take נֵרוֹ as a corrective, explanatory per-mutative: when He, His lamp, shone above my head, as we have translated. One is at any rate reminded of Isa. lx. in connection with ver. 3; for as בהלו corresponds to יורח there, so לאורו corresponds to לְאוֹרֵךְ in the 3d ver. of the same: by His light I walked in darkness (חֹשֶׁךְ locative = בַּחֹשֶׁךְ), *i.e.* rejoicing in His light, which preserved me from its dangers (straying and falling).

In ver. 4 כַּאֲשֶׁר is not a particle of time, but of comparison, which was obliged here to stand in the place of the כְּ, which is used only as a preposition. And חָרְפִּי (to be written thus, not חָרְפִּי with an aspirated פ) may not be translated " (in the days) of my spring," as Symm. ἐν ἡμέραις νεότητός μου, Jer. *diebus adolescentiæ meæ*, and Targ. בְּיוֹמֵי חֲרִיפוּתִי, whether it be that חריפות here signifies the point, ἀκμή (from חרף, حَرَف, *acuere*), or the early time (spring time, from חרף, خَرَف, *carpere*). For in reference to agriculture חֹרֶף can certainly signify the early half of the year (on this, *vid. Genesis*, S. 270), inasmuch as sowing and ploughing time in Palestine and Syria is in November and December; wherefore خَرِيف signifies the early rain or autumn rain; and in Talmudic, חָרֵף, premature (ripe too early), is the opposite of אָפֵל, late, but the derivatives of חרף only obtain this signification *connotative*, for, according to its proper signification, חֹרֶף (خَرِيف with other forms) is the gathering time, *i.e.* the time of the fruit harvest (syn. אָסִיף), while the Hebr. אָבִיב (אָב) corresponds to the spring in our sense. If Job meant his youth, he would have said בִּימֵי אָבִּי, or something similar; but as ver. 5*b* shows, he meant his manhood, and this he calls his autumn as the season of maturity, or rather of the abundance of fruits (Schult.: *ætatem virilem suis fructibus fœtum et exuberantum*),[1] which, according to Olympiodorus, also with ὅτε ἤμην ἐπιβρίθων ὁδούς (perhaps καρπούς) of the LXX., is what is intended. Then the blessed fellowship of Eloah (סוֹד, familiarity, confiding, unreserved intercourse, Ps. lv. 15, Prov. iii. 32, comp. Ps. xxv. 14) ruled over his tent; the Almighty

---

[1] The fresh vegetation, indeed, in hotter districts (*e.g.* in the valley of the Jordan and Euphrates) begins with the arrival of the autumnal rains, but the real spring (comp. Cant. ii. 11–13) only begins about the vernal equinox, and still later on the mountains. On the contrary, the late summer, קָיִץ, which passes over into the autumn, חֹרֶף, is the season for gathering the fruit. The produce of the fields, garden fruit, and grapes ripen before the commencement of the proper autumn; some (when the land can be irrigated) summer fruits, *e.g. Dhura* (maize) and melons, in like manner olives and dates, ripen in autumn. Therefore the translation, in the days of my autumn ("of my harvest"), is the only

was still with him (protecting and blessing him), His נְעָרִים
were round about him. It certainly does not mean servants
(Raschi: מְשָׁרְתִי), but children (as ch. i. 19, xxiv. 5); for one
expects the mention of the blessing of children first of all
(Ps. cxxvii. 3 sqq., cxxviii. 3).   His steps (הֲלִיךְ, ἅπ λεγ.) bathed
then בְּחֵמָה = בְּחֵמְאָה, ch. xx. 17 (as שֵׁלָה = שְׁאֵלָה, 1 Sam. i. 17,
and possibly גֵּוֶה = גְּאֵוֶה), and the rocks poured forth, close by
him, streams of oil (a figure which reminds one of Deut.
xxxii. 13).   A rich blessing surrounded him wherever he
tarried or went, and flowed to him wonderfully beyond
desire and comprehension.

> 7 *When I went forth to the gate of the city,*
>   *Prepared my seat in the market,*
> 8 *Then the young men hid themselves as soon as they saw me,*
>   *And the aged rose up, remained standing.*
> 9 *Princes refrained from speaking,*
>   *And laid their hand on their mouth.*
> 10 *The voice of the nobles was hidden,*
>   *And their tongue clave to their palate.*

When he left the bounds of his domain, and came into the
city, he was everywhere received with the profoundest respect.   From the facts of the case, it is inadmissible to translate *quum egrederer portam* after Gen. xxxiv. 24, comp.
infra, ch. xxxi. 34, for the district where Job dwelt is to be

correct one. If חָרְפִּי were intended here in a sense not used elsewhere,
it might signify, according to the Arabic with ح, "(in the days) of my
prosperity," or "my power," or even with خ, "(in the days) of my youthful vigour;" for *charâfât* are rash words and deeds, *charfân* one who
says or does anything rash from lightness, the feebleness of old age, etc·
(according to Wetzst., very common words in Syria); חָרֶף or חֹרֶף, therefore, the thoughtlessness of youth, جهل, *i.e.* the rash desire of doing
something great, which חָרֵף הַנֶּפֶשׁ לְמוּת (Judg. v. 18). But it is most
secure to go back to חרף, خرف, *carpere,* viz. *fructus.*

thought of as being without a gate. True, he did not dwell
with his family in tents, *i.e.* pavilions of hair, but in houses ;
he was not a nomad (a wandering herdsman), or what is the
same thing, a Beduin, otherwise his children would not have
been slain in a stone house, ch. i. 19. "The daughter of the
duck," says an Arabian proverb, "is a swimmer," and the son
of a Beduin never dwells in a stone house. He was, however, also, not a citizen, but a *hadari* (חֲצָרִי), *i.e.* a permanent
resident, a large landowner and husbandman. Thus therefore שַׁעַר (for which Ew. after the LXX. reads שַׁחַר : "when
I went up early in the morning to the city") is locative, for
שַׁעְרָה (comp. צֵא הַשָּׂדֶה, go out into the field, Gen. xxvii. 3) :
when he went forth to the gate above the city ; or even, since
it is natural to imagine the city as situated on an eminence :
up to the city (so that צֵאת includes in itself by implication
the notion of עֲלוֹת) ; not, however : to the gate near the city
(Stick., Hahn), since the gate of a city is not situated near
the city, but is part of the city itself. The gates of cities
and large houses in Western Asia are vaulted entrances,
with large recesses on either side, where people congregate
for business and negotiations.[1] The open space at the gate,
which here, as in Neh. viii. 1, 3, 16, is called רְחוֹב, *i.e.* the
open space within the gate and by the gate, was the forum
(ch. v. 4).

Ver. 8. When Job came hither to the meeting of the
tribunal, or the council of the elders of the city, within
which he had a seat and a voice, the young men hid themselves, conscious of his presence (which εἰρομένῃ λέξει, or, is
expressed paratactically instead of as a period), *i.e.* they
retired into the background, since they feared his look of
salutation ;[2] and old men (hoary heads) stood up, remained

---

[1] *Vid.* Layard, *New Discoveries*, p. 57.

[2] Comp. *jer. Schekalim* ii. 5 (in Pinner's *Compendium des Thalmud*,
S. 58) : "R. Jochanan was walking and leaning upon R. Chija bar-Abba,

standing (ἀσυνδέτως, as ch. xx. 19, xxviii. 4). קוּם signifies
to stand up, עָמַד to advance towards any one and remain
standing (comp. vol. i. 357, note 1). They rose in order not
to seat themselves until he was seated. שָׂרִים are magnates
(*proceres*) of the city. These בְמִלִּים עָצְרוּ, *cohibebant verba* (עצר
with *Beth* of the obj., as ch. iv. 2, xii. 15), and keeping a
respectful silence, they laid their hand on their mouth (comp.
xxi. 5). All stepped back and desisted from speaking before
him: The speech of illustrious men (נְגִידִים from נגד, نجد, to
be visible, pleasant to the sight, comp. *supra*, p. 91) hid itself
(not daring to be heard), and the tongue of the same clave
(motionless) to their palate. We do not translate: as to the
voice illustrious men hid themselves, for it is only the appearance produced by the attractional construction [Ges. § 148, 1]
that has led to the rendering of קוֹל־נְגִידִים as an *acc.* of closer
definition (Schult., Hahn: *quod ad vocem eminentium, com-
primebantur*). The verb is construed with the second member
of the genitival expression instead of with the first, as with
מספר, ch. xv. 20, xxi. 21, xxxviii. 21, and with רֹאשׁ, ch.
xxii. 12; a construction which occurs with קוֹל not merely in
such exclamatory sentences as Gen. iv. 10, Isa. lii. 8, but
also under other conditions, 1 Kings i. 41, comp. xiv. 6.
This may be best called an attraction by the predicate by the
second member of the compound subject, like the reverse instance, Isa. ii. 11; and it is sometimes found even where this
second member is not logically the more important. Thus
Ew. transl.: "the voice of the nobles hides itself;" whereas
Olsh., wrongly denying that the *partt.* in passages like Gen.
iv. 10, 1 Kings i. 41, are to be taken as predicative, wishes to

R. Eliezer perceived him and hid himself from him (ומטמר לה מקמי).
Then said R. Jochanan: This Babylonian insulted him (R. Chija) by
two things; first that he did not salute him, and then that he hid himself. But R. Jakob bar-Idi answered him, it is the custom with them
for the less not to salute the greater,—a custom which confirms Job's
words: Young men saw me and hid themselves."

read נחבא, which is the more inadmissible, as even the choice
of the verb is determined by the attractional construction.

The strophe which follows tells how it came to pass that
those in authority among the citizens submitted to him, and
that on all sides the people were zealous to show him tokens
of respect.

11 *For an ear heard, and called me happy ;*
    And an eye saw, and bear witness to me :
12 *For I rescued the sufferer who cried for help,*
    And the orphan, and him that had no helper.
13 *The blessing of him that was ready to perish came upon me,*
    And I made the widow's heart rejoice.
14 *I put on justice, and it put me on ;*
    As a robe and turban was my integrity.

Thus imposing was the impression of his personal appearance wherever he appeared; for (כִּי *explic.*) the fulness of
the blessing of the possession of power and of prosperity which
he enjoyed was so extraordinary, that one had only to hear of
it to call him happy, and that, especially if any one saw it
with his own eyes, he was obliged to bear laudatory testimony
to him. The *futt. consec.* affirm what was the inevitable consequence of hearing and seeing; הֵעִיד, *seq. acc.*, is used like
הִזְכִּיר in the signification of laudatory recognition. The expression is not brachylogical for וַתָּעַד לִי (*vid.* on ch. xxxi. 18);
for from 1 Kings xxi. 10, 13, we perceive that העיד with the
acc. of the person signifies to make any one the subject of assertion, whether he be lower or higher in rank (comp. the New
Testament word, especially in Luke, μαρτυρεῖσθαι). It was,
however, not merely the outward manifestation of his unusual
prosperity which called forth such admiration, but his active
benevolence united with the abundant resources at his command. For where there was a sufferer who cried for help,
he relieved him, especially orphans and those who had no

helper. וְלֹא־עֹזֵר לוֹ is either a new third object, or a closer definition of what precedes : the orphan and (in this state of orphanhood) helpless one. The latter is more probable both here and in the Salomonic primary passage, Ps. lxxii. 12; in the other case וַאֲשֶׁר אֵין־עֹזֵר לוֹ might be expected.

Ver. 13. The blessing (בִּרְכַּת with closely closed *penult.*) of those who stood on the brink of destruction (אֹבֵד, *interiturus,* as ch. xxxi. 19, Prov. xxxi. 6), and owed their rescue to him, came upon him; and the heart of the widow to whom he gave assistance, compensating for the assistance of her lost husband, he filled with gladness (הִרְנִין causative, as Ps. lxv. 9). For the primary attribute, the fundamental character of his way of thinking and acting, was צֶדֶק, a holding fast to the will of God, which before everything else calls for sympathizing love (root צדק, صدق, to be hard, firm, stiff, *e.g. rumh-un sadq-un,* according to the Kamus : a hard, firm, straight spear), and מִשְׁפָּט, judgment and decision in favour of right and equity against wrong and injustice. Righteousness is here called the garment which he put on (as Ps. cxxxii. 9, comp. Isa. xi. 5, lix. 17), and right is the robe and turban with which he adorns himself (comp. Isa. lxi. 10); as by Arabian poets noble attributes are also called garments, which God puts on any one, or which any one puts on himself (*albasa*).[1] Right-eousness is compared to the לְבוּשׁ (corresponding to the *thob,* *i.e.* garment, *indusium,* of the nomads) which is worn on the naked body, justice to the צָנִיף, a magnificent turban (corre-sponding to the *kefije,* consisting of a thick cotton cloth, and fastened with a cord made of camel's hair), and the magnificent robe (corresponding to the second principal article of clothing, the *'abá*). The LXX., Jer., Syr., and Arab. wrongly refer

[1] In Beidhâwi, if I remember rightly, this expression occurs once, التدرّع بلباس التّقوى, *i.e.* "clothing one's self in the armour of the fear of God."

וַיִּלְבָּשֵׁנִי to מִשְׁפָּט of the second half of the verse, while, on the
contrary, it is said of צֶדֶק, *per antanaclasin*, that Job put this
on, and this in turn put Job on, *induit;* for וַיִּלְבָּשֵׁנִי, as the
usage of the language, as we have it, elsewhere shows, does
not signify: it (righteousness) clothed me well (Umbr.),
or: adorned me (Ew., Vaih.), also not: it dressed me out
(Schlottm.), but only: it put me on as a garment, *i.e.* it made
me so its own, that my whole appearance was the representation of itself, as in Judg. vi. 34 and twice in the Chronicles, of
the Spirit of Jehovah it is said that He puts on any one, *induit*,
when He makes any one the organ of His own manifestation.

> 15 *I was eyes to the blind,*
>   *And feet was I to the lame.*
> 16 *I was a father to the needy,*
>   *And the cause of the unknown I found out,*
> 17 *And broke the teeth of the wicked,*
>   *And I cast the spoil forth out of his teeth.*

The less it is Job's purpose here to vindicate himself before
the friends, the more forcible is the refutation which the
accusations of the most hard-hearted uncharitableness raised
against him by them, especially by Eliphaz, ch. xxii., find
everywhere here. His charity relieved the bodily and spiritual wants of others—eyes to the blind (לַעִוֵּר with *Pathach*),
feet to the lame. A father was he to the needy, which is
expressed by a beautiful play of words, as if it were: the
carer for the care-full ones; or what perhaps corresponds to
the primary significations of אָב and אֶבְיוֹן:[1] the protector of

---

[1] There is an old Arabic defective verb, بَأَى, which signifies " to seek
an asylum for one's self," *e.g. anâ baj*, I come as one seeking protection,
a suppliant, in the usual language synon. of دَخَلَ, and thereby indicating its relationship to the Hebr. בּוֹא, perhaps the root of בַּיִת (בְּתִּים), the
ת of which would then not be a radical letter, but, as according to Ges.

those needing (seeking) protection. The unknown he did not regard as those who were nothing to him, but went unselfishly and impartially into the ground of their cause. לֹא־יְדַעְתִּי is an attributive clause, as ch. xviii. 21, Isa. lv. 5, xli. 3, and freq., with a personal obj. (*eorum*) *quos non noveram*, for the translation *causam quam nesciebam* (Jer.) gives a tame, almost meaningless, thought. With reference to the *suff.* in אֶחְקְרֵהוּ, on the form *ehu* used seldom by *Waw consec.* (ch. xii. 4), and

Thes. in יָיַן, used only in the forming of the word, and the original meaning would be "a refuge." Traced to a secondary verb, אָבָה (properly to take up the fugitive, *qabila-l-bija*) springing from this primitive verb, אָב would originally signify a guardian, protector; and from the fact of this name denoting, according to the form פֹּעֵל, properly in general the protecting power, the ideal *femin.* in אָבוֹת (Arab. *abawât*) and the Arabic dual *abawain* (properly both guardians), which embraces father and mother, would be explained and justified. Thus the rare phenomenon that the same אבה signifies in Hebr. "to be willing," and in Arab. "to refuse," would be solved. The notion of taking up the fugitive would have passed over in the Hebrew, taken according to its positive side, into the notion of being willing, *i.e.* of receiving and accepting (קֵבֵל, *qabila*, *e.g.* 1 Kings xx. 8, לֹא תֹאבֶה == *la taqbal*); in the Arabic, however, taken according to its negative side, as refusing the fugitive to his pursuer, into that of not being willing; and the usage of the language favours this: *abâhu 'aleihi*, he protected him against (عَلَى) the other (refused him to the other); أَبِي == أَبَى, protected, inaccessible to him who longs for it; أَبِيَّة, the protection, *i.e.* the retention of the milk in the udder. Hence أَبِيَن, from the Hebrew signif. of the verb, signifies one who desires anything, or a needy person, but originally (inasmuch as אבה is connected with أَبَى) one who needs protection; from the Arabic signif. of أَبَى, one who restrains himself because he is obliged, one to whom what he wants is denied. To the Arab. *ibja* (defence, being hindered) corresponds in form the Hebr. אָבֶה, according to which אֳנִיּוֹת אֵבֶה, ch. ix. 26, may be understood of ships, which, with all sails set and in all haste, seek the sheltering harbour before the approaching storm. We leave this suggestion for further research to sift and prove. More on ch. xxxiv. 36.—WETZST.

by the *imper.* (ch. xl. 11 sq.), chiefly with a solemn calm tone
of speech, *vid.* Ew. § 250, *c.* Further: He spared not to
render wrong-doers harmless, and snatched from them what
they had taken from others. The cohortative form of the
fut. consec., וָאֲשַׁבְּרָה, has been discussed already on ch. i. 15,
xix. 20. The form מְתַלְּעוֹת is a transposition of מַלְתְּעוֹת, to
render it more convenient for pronunciation, for the Arab.
‏طلع‎, *efferre se,* whence a secondary form, ‏طلى‎, although used
of the appearing of the teeth, furnishes no such appropriate
primary signification as the Arab. ‏لذع‎, *pungere, mordere,*
whence a secondary form, ‏لذى‎; the Æthiopic *maltâht,* jaw-
bone (*maxilla*), also favours מלתעה as the primary form. He
shattered the grinders of the roguish, and by moral indignation against the robber he cast out of his teeth what he had
stolen.

18 *Then I thought: With my nest I shall expire,*
   And like the phœnix, have a long life.
19 *My root will be open for water,*
   And the dew will lodge in my branches.
20 *Mine honour will remain ever fresh to me,*
   And my bow will become young in my hand.

In itself, ver. 18*b* might be translated: "and like to the
sand I shall live many days" (Targ., Syr., Arab., Saad.,
Gecat., Luther, and, among moderns, Umbr., Stick., Vaih.,
Hahn, and others), so that the abundance of days is compared
to the multitude of the grains of sand. The calculation of
the immense total of grains of sand (atoms) in the world was,
as is known, a favourite problem of antiquity; and in the
Old Testament Scriptures, the comprehensive knowledge of
Solomon is compared to "the sand upon the sea-shore,"
1 Kings v. 9,—how much more readily a long life reduced to
days! comp. Ovid, *Metam.* xiv. 136–138: *quot haberet corpora
pulvis, tot mihi natales contingere vana rogavi.* We would

willingly decide in favour of this rendering, which is admissible in itself, although a closer definition like הָיָם is wanting by כחול, if an extensive Jewish tradition did not secure the signification of an immortal bird, or rather one rising ever anew from the dead. The testimony is as follows: (1) *b. Sanhedrin* 108*b*, according to which חול is only another name for the bird אורשׁינא,[1] of which the fable is there recorded, that when Noah fed the beasts in the ark, it sat quite still in its compartment, that it might not give more trouble to the patriarch, who had otherwise plenty to do, and that Noah wished it on this account the reward of immortality (יהא רעוא דלא תמות). (2) That this bird חול is none other than the phœnix, is put beyond all doubt by the Midrashim (collected in the *Jalkut* on Job, § 517). There it is said that Eve gave all the beasts to eat of the fruit of the forbidden tree, and that only one bird, the חול by name, avoided this death-food: "it lives a thousand years, at the expiration of which time fire springs up in its nest, and burns it up to about the size of an egg;" or even : that of itself it diminishes to that size, from which it then grows up again and continues to live (וחוזר ומתגדל איברים וחיה). (3) The Masora observes, that כחול occurs in two different

---

[1] The name is a puzzle, and does not accord with any of the mythical birds mentioned in the Zendavesta (*vid.* Windischmann, *Zoroastrische Studien*, 1863, S. 93). What Lewysohn, *Zoologie des Talmuds*, S. 353, brings forward from the Greek by way of explanation is untenable. The name of the bird, *Vâresha*, in an obscure passage of the Bundehesch in Windischmann, *ib.* S. 80, is similar in sound. Probably, however, אורשׁינא is one and the same word as *Simurg*, which is composed of *si* (= *sin*) and *murg*, a bird (Pehlvi and Parsi *mru*). This *si* (*sin*) corresponds to the Vedic *çjena*, a falcon, and in the Zend form, *çaêna* (*çina*), is the name of a miraculous bird ; so that consequently *Simurg* = *Sinmurg*, Parsi *Cinamru*, signifies the *Si*- or *Cina*-bird (comp. Kuhn, *Herabkunft des Feuers*, 1859, S. 125). In אורשׁינא the two parts of the composition seem to be reversed, and אור to be corrupted from מור. Moreover, the *Simurg* is like the phœnix only in the length of its life ; another mythological bird, *Kuknus*, on the other hand (*vid.* the art. *Phönix* in Ersch u. Gruber), resembles it also in rising out of its own ashes.

significations (בתרי לישני), since in the present passage it does not, as elsewhere, signify sand. (4) Kimchi, in his *Lex.*, says: " in a correct Jerusalem MS. I found the observation : בשורק לנהרדעי ובחלם למערבאי, *i.e.* וְכַחוֹל according to the Nehardean (Babylonian) reading, וְכַחוֹל according to the western (Palestine) reading;" according to which, therefore, the Babylonian Maso-retic school distinguished וכחול in the present passage from וכחול, Gen. xxii. 17, even in the pronunciation. A conclusion respecting the great antiquity of this lexical tradition may be drawn (5) from the LXX., which translates ὥσπερ στέλε-χος φοίνικος, whence the Italic *sicut arbor palmæ*, Jerome *sicut palma.*

If we did not know from the testimonies quoted that חול is the name of the phœnix, one might suppose that the LXX. has explained וכחול according to the Arab. *nachl*, the palm, as Schultens does ; but by a comparison of those testimonies, it is more probable that the translation was ὥσπερ φοῖνιξ originally, and that ὥσπερ στέλεχος φοίνικος is an interpola-tion, for φοῖνιξ signifies both the immortal miraculous bird and the inexhaustibly youthful palm.[1] We have the reverse case in Tertullian, *de resurrectione carnis*, c. xiii., which explains the passage in Psalms, xcii. 13, δίκαιος ὡς φοῖνιξ ἀνθήσει, according to the translation *justus velut phœnix florebit*, of the *ales orientis* or *avis Arabiæ*, which symbolizes

---

[1] According to Ovid, *Metam.* xv. 396, the phœnix makes its nest in the palm, and according to Pliny, *h. n.* xiii. 42, it has its name from the palm : *Phœnix putatur ex hujus palmæ argumento nomen accepisse, iterum mori ac renasci ex se ipsa ;* vid. A. Hahmann, *Die Dattelpalme, ihre Namen und ihre Verehrung in der alten Welt*, in the periodical *Bonplandia*, 1859, Nr. 15, 16. Masius, in his studies of nature, has very beauti-fully described on what ground " the intelligent Greek gave a like name to the fabulous immortal bird that rises again out of its own ashes, and the palm which ever renews its youth." Also comp. (Heimsdörfer's) *Christliche Kunstsymbolik*, S. 26, and Augusti, *Beiträge zur christl. Kunst-Geschichte und Liturgik*, Bd. i. S. 106-108, but especially Piper, *Mythologie der christl. Kunst* (1847), i. 446f.

man's immortality.[1] Both figures, that of the phœnix and
that of the palm, are equally appropriate and pleasing in the
mouth of Job; but apart from the fact- that the palm everywhere, where it otherwise occurs, is called תָּמָר, this would be
the only passage where it occurs in the book of Job, which, in
spite of its richness in figures taken from plants, nowhere mentions the palm,—a fact which is perhaps not accidental.[2] On
the contrary, we must immediately welcome a reference to the
Arabico-Egyptian myth of the phœnix, that can be proved, in
a book which also otherwise thoroughly blends things Egyptian
with Arabian, and the more so since (6) even the Egyptian
language itself supports חֹול or חֻול as a name of the phœnix;
for *ΑΛΛΩΗ*, *ΑΛΛΟΗ* is explained in the Coptico-Arabic
glossaries by *es-semendel* (the Arab. name of the phœnix, or
at least a phœnix-like bird, that, like the salamander, *semendar*,
cannot be burned), and in Kircher by *avis Indica, species
Phœnicis.*[3] חֹול is Hebraized from this Egyptian name of the

---

[1] Not without reference to Clemens Romanus, in his *I. Ep. ad Corinth.*
c. xxv., according to which the phœnix is an Arabian bird, which lives
five hundred years, then dies in a nest which it builds of incense, myrrh,
and spices, and leaves behind it the larva of a young bird, which, when
grown up, brings the nest with the bones of its father and places it upon
the altar of the sun at the Egyptian Heliopolis. The source of this is
Herodotus ii. 73 (who, however, has an egg of myrrh instead of a nest
of myrrh) ; and Tacitus, *Ann.* vi. 28, gives a similar narrative. Lactan-
tius gives a different version in his poem on the phœnix, according to
which this, the only one of its race, "built its nest in a country that
remained untouched by the deluge." The Jewish tragedy writer, Eze-
kiêlos, agrees more nearly with the statement of Arabia being the home
of the phœnix. In his drama 'Εξαγωγή, a spy sent forward before the
pilgrim band of Israel, he states that among other things the phœnix
was also seen ; *vid.* my *Gesch. der jüd. Poesie,* S. 219.

[2] Without attempting thereby to explain the phenomenon observed
above, we nevertheless regard it as worthy of remark, that in general the
palm is not a common tree either in Syria or in Palestine. "At present
there are not in all Syria five hundred palm-trees ; and even in olden
times there was no quantity of palms, except in the valley of the Jordan,
and on the sea-coast."—WETZST.

[3] *Vid.* G. Seyffarth, *Die Phœnix-Periode, Deutsche Morgenländ. Zeitschr.*

phœnix; the word signifies rotation (comp. Arab. *haul*, the year; *haula*, round about), and is a suitable designation of the bird that renews its youth periodically after many centuries of life: *quæ reparat seque ipsa reseminat ales* (Ovid), not merely beginning a new life, but also bringing in a new great year: *conversionem anni magni* (Pliny); in the hieroglyphic representations it has the circle of the sun as a crown. In the full enjoyment of the divine favour and blessing, and in the consciousness of having made a right use of his prosperity, Job hoped φοίνικος ἔτη βιοῦν (Lucian, *Hermot.* 53), to use a Greek expression, and to expire or die עִם־קִנִּי, as the first half of the verse, now brought into the right light, says. Looking to the form of the myth, according to which Ovid sings:

> *Quassa cum fulvâ substravit cinnama myrrhâ,*
> *Se super imponit finitque in odoribus ævum,*

it might be translated: together with my nest (Umbr., Hirz., Hlgst.); but with the wish that he may not see any of his dear ones die before himself, there is at the same time connected the wish, that none of them should survive him, which is in itself unnatural, and diametrically opposed to the character of an Arab, who in the presence of death cherishes the twofold wish, that he may continue to live in his children (a proverb says: *men chalaf el-weled el-fâlih ma mât*, he who leaves a noble child behind him is not dead), and that he may die in the midst of his family. Expressing this latter wish, עִם־קִנִּי signifies: with = in my nest, *i.e.* in the bosom of my family, not without reference to the phœnix, which, according to the form of the myth in Herodotus, Pliny, Clemens, and others, brings the remains of its father in a

iii. (1849) 63 ff., according to which *alloê* (Hierogl. *koli*) is the name of the false phœnix without head-feathers; *bêne* or *bêni* (Hierogl. *bnno*) is the name of the true phœnix with head-feathers, and the name of the palm also. *Alloê*, which accords with חוֹל, is quite secured as a name of the phœnix.

nest or egg of myrrh to Heliopolis, into the sacred precincts
of the temple of the sun, and thus pays him the last and
highest tribute of respect. A different but similar version is
given in Horapollo ii. 57, according to which the young bird
came forth from the blood of its sire, σὺν τῷ πατρὶ πορεύεται
εἰς τὴν Ἡλίου πόλιν τὴν ἐν Αἰγύπτῳ, ὃς καὶ παραγενόμενος
ἐκεῖ ἅμα τῇ ἡλίου ἀνατολῇ τελευτᾷ. The father, therefore,
in death receives the highest tribute of filial respect; and it is
this to which the hope of being able to die with (in) his nest,
expressed by Job, refers.

The following substantival clause, ver. 19a, is to be understood as future, like the similar clause, ver. 16a, as perfect :
my root—so I hoped—will remain open (unclosed) towards
the water, i.e. it will never be deficient of water in its vicinity,
that it may plentifully supply the stem and branches with
nourishment, and dew will lodge on my branches, i.e. will
descend nightly, and remain upon them to nourish them.
אֱלֵי (corresponding to the Arab. ila, originally ilai) occurs
only in the book of Job, and here for the fourth and last
time (comp. ch. iii. 22, v. 26, xv. 22). קָצִיר does not signify
harvest here, as the ancient expositors render it, but, like ch.
xiv. 9, xviii. 16, a branch, or the intertwined branches. The
figure of the root and branch, the flow of vitality downwards
and upwards, is the counterpart of ch. xviii. 16. In ver. 20
a substantival clause also comes first, as in vers. 19, 16 (for
the established reading is חָדָשׁ, not חָדַשׁ), and a verbal clause
follows : his honour—so he hoped—should continue fresh by
him, i.e. should abide with him in undiminished value and
splendour. It is his honour before God and men that is
intended, not his soul (Hahn); כָּבוֹד, δόξα, certainly is an
appellation of the נֶפֶשׁ (Psychol. S. 98), but חָדָשׁ is not appropriate to it as predicate. By the side of honour stands man-
liness, or the capability of self-defence, whose symbol is the
bow : and my bow should become young again in my hand,

i.e. gain ever new strength and elasticity. It is unnecessary to supply פֹּה (Hirz., Schlottm., and others). The verb חלף, خَلَفَ, signifies, as the Arab. shows, properly to turn the back, then to go forth, exchange ; the *Hiph.* to make progress, to cause something new to come into the place of the old, to grow young again. These hopes introduced with וָאֹמַר were themselves an element of his former happiness. Its description can therefore be continued in connection with the ואמר without any fresh indication.

> 21 *They hearkened to me and waited,*
> *And remained silent at my decision.*
> 22 *After my utterance they spake not again,*
> *And my speech distilled upon them.*
> 23 *And they waited for me as for the rain,*
> *And they opened their mouth wide for the latter rain.*
> 24 *I smiled to them in their hopelessness,*
> *And the light of my countenance they cast not down.*
> 25 *I chose the way for them, and sat as chief,*
> *And dwelt as a king in the army,*
> *As one that comforteth the mourners.*

Attentive, patient, and ready to be instructed, they hearkened to him (this is the force of שָׁמַע לְ), and waited, without interrupting, for what he should say. וַיְחֵלּוּ, the pausal pronunciation with a reduplication of the last radical, as Judg. v. 7, חָדֵלּוּ (according to correct texts), Ges. § 20, 2, *c ;* the reading of Kimchi, וַיְחֵלוּ, is the reading of Ben-Naphtali, the former the reading of Ben-Ascher (*vid.* Norzi). If he gave counsel, they waited in strictest silence : this is the meaning of יִדְּמוּ (*fut. Kal* of דָּמַם); לָמוֹ, poetic for לְ, refers the silence to its outward cause (*vid.* on Hab. iii. 16). After his words *non iterabant, i.e.* as Jerome explanatorily translates: *addere nihil audebant,* and his speech came down upon them relieving, rejoicing, and enlivening them. The figure indi-

cated in תְּשֻׁאֹף is expanded in ver. 23 after Deut. xxxii. 2: they
waited on his word, which penetrated deeply, even to the
heart, as for rain, מָטָר, by which, as ver. 23*b*, the so-called
(autumnal) early rain which moistens the seed is prominently
thought of.   They open their mouth for the late rain, כְמַלְקוֹשׁ
(*vid.* on ch. xxiv. 6), *i.e.* they thirsted after his words, which
were like the March or April rain, which helps to bring to
maturity the corn that is soon to be reaped; this rain frequently fails, and is therefore the more longed for.   פָּעֲרוּ פֵה
is to be understood according to Ps. cxix. 131, comp. lxxxi. 11;
and one must consider, in connection with it, what raptures
the beginning of the periodical rains produces everywhere,
where, as *e.g.* in Jerusalem, the people have been obliged
for some time to content themselves with cisterns that are
almost dried to a marsh, and how the old and young dance
for joy at their arrival !

    In ver. 24*a* a thought as suited to the syntax as to the fact
is gained if we translate : " I smiled to them—they believed
it not," *i.e.* they considered such condescension as scarcely
possible (Saad., Raschi, Rosenm., De Wette, Schlottm., and
others) ; אֶשְׂחַק is then *fut. hypotheticum*, as ch. x. 16, xx. 24,
xxii. 27 sq., Ew. § 357, *b*.   But it does not succeed in putting
ver. 24*b* in a consistent relation to this thought; for, with Aben-
Ezra, to explain: they did not esteem my favour the less on that
account, my respect suffered thereby no loss among them, is
not possible in connection with the biblical idea of "the light
of the countenance ;" and with Schlottm. to explain : they let
not the light of my countenance, *i.e.* token of my favour, fall
away, *i.e.* be in vain, is contrary to the usage of the language,
according to which הִפִּיל פָּנִים signifies : to cause the countenance to sink (gloomily, Gen. iv. 5), whether one's own, Jer.
iii. 12, or that of another.   Instead of פָּנַי we have a more
pictorial and poetical expression here, אוֹר פָּנַי : light of my
countenance, *i.e.* my cheerfulness (as Prov. xvi. 15).   More-

over, the אִשְׁחַק אֲלֵיהֶם, therefore, furnishes the thought that he
laughed, and did not allow anything to dispossess him of his
easy and contented disposition. Thus, therefore, those to
whom Job laughed are to be thought of as in a condition
and mood which his cheerfulness might easily sadden, but
still did not sadden ; and this their condition is described by
לֹא יַאֲמִינוּ (a various reading in Codd. and editions is וְלֹא), a
phrase which occurred before (ch. xxiv. 22) in the signification of being without faith or hope, despairing (comp. הֶאֱמִין,
to gain faith, Ps. cxvi. 10),—a clause which is not to be taken
as attributive (Umbr., Vaih.: who had not confidence), but as
a neutral or circumstantial subordinate clause (Ew. § 341, a).
Therefore translate : I smiled to them, if they believed not,
i.e. despaired; and however despondent their position appeared,
the cheerfulness of my countenance they could not cause to
pass away. However gloomy they were, they could not make
me gloomy and off my guard. Thus also ver. 25a is now
suitably attached to the preceding: I chose their way, *i.e.* I
made the way plain, which they should take in order to get
out of their hopeless and miserable state, and sat as chief, as
a king who is surrounded by an armed host as a defence and
as a guard of honour, attentive to the motion of his eye ; not,
however, as a sovereign ruler, but as one who condescended to
the mourners, and comforted them (נִחַם *Piel*, properly to cause
to breathe freely). This peaceful figure of a king brings
to mind the warlike one, ch. xv. 24. כַּאֲשֶׁר is not a conj.
here, but equivalent to כְּאִישׁ אֲשֶׁר, *ut* (*quis*) *qui;* consequently
not : as one comforts, but : as he who comforts; LXX. correctly : ὃν τρόπον παθεινοὺς παρακαλῶν. The accentuation
(כַּאֲשֶׁר *Tarcha*, אבלים *Munach*, ינחם *Silluk*) is erroneous ; כַּאֲשֶׁר
should be marked with *Rebia mugrasch*, and אבלים with *Mercha-Zinnorith.*

From the prosperous and happy past, absolutely passed, Job
now turns to the present, which contrasts so harshly with it.

1 *And now they who are younger than I have me in derision,*
   Those whose fathers I disdained
   To set with the dogs of my flock.
2 *Yea, the strength of their hands, what should it profit me?*
   They have lost vigour and strength.
3 *They are benumbed from want and hunger,*
   They who gnaw the steppe,
   The darkness of the wilderness and waste;
4 *They who pluck mallows in the thicket,*
   And the root of the broom is their bread.

With וְעַתָּה, which also elsewhere expresses the turning-
point from the premises to the conclusion, from accusation to
the threat of punishment, and such like, Job here begins to
bewail the sad turn which his former prosperity has taken.
The first line of the verse, which is marked off by *Mercha-
Mahpach*, is intentionally so disproportionately long, to form
a deep and long breathed beginning to the lamentation which
is now begun. Formerly, as he has related in the first part
of the monologue, an object of reverential fear to the respect-
able youth of the city (ch. xxix. 8), he is now an object of
derision (עַל שָׂחַק, to laugh at, distinct from אֶל שָׂחַק, ch. xxix. 24,
to laugh to, smile upon) to the young good-for-nothing vaga-
bonds of a miserable class of men. They are just the same
עֲנִיֵּי אֶרֶץ, whose sorrowful lot he reckons among the mysteries
of divine providence, so difficult of solution (ch. xxiv. 4*b*–8).
The less he belongs to the merciless ones, who take advantage of the calamities of the poor for their own selfish ends,
instead of relieving their distress as far as is in their power,

the more unjustifiable is the rude treatment which he now
experiences from them, when they who meanly hated him
before because he was rich, now rejoice at the destruction of
his prosperity. Younger than he in days (לְיָמִים as ch. xxxii. 4,
with לְ of closer definition, instead of which the simple *acc.*
was inadmissible here, comp. on ch. xi. 9) laugh at him, sons
of those fathers who were so useless and abandoned that he
scorned (לְ מָאַס, comp. מִי מָאַס מִי, 1 Sam. xv. 26) to entrust to
them even a service so menial as that of the shepherd dogs.
Schult., Rosenm., and Schlottm. take עַם שִׁית for עַל שִׁית, *præ-
ficere*, but that ought to be just simply עַל שִׁית; עַם שִׁית signifies to range beside, *i.e.* to place alike, to associate; moreover,
the *oversight* of the shepherd dogs is no such menial post,
while Job intends to say that he did not once consider them
fit to render such a subordinate service as is that of the dogs
which help the shepherds. And even the strength of their
(these youths') hands (בָּם is referable to the *suff.* of יְדֵיהֶם:
even; not: now entirely, completely, as Hahn translates), of
what use should it be to him? (לְמָה not *cur*, but *ad quid*,
quorsum, as Gen. xxv. 32, xxvii. 46.) They are enervated,
good-for-nothing fellows: כֶּלַח is lost to them (עָלֵימוֹ trebly
emphatic: it is placed in a prominent position, has a pathetic
suff., and is עַל for לְ, 1 Sam. ix. 3). The signif. *senectus*, which
suits ch. v. 26, is here inapplicable, since it is not the aged
that are spoken of, but the young; for that "old age is lost to
them" would be a forced expression for the thought—which,
moreover, does not accord with the connection—that they die
off early. One does not here expect the idea of *senectus* or
senectus vegeta, but *vigor*, as the Syriac ('*ushino*) and Arabic
also translate it. May not כֶּלַח perhaps be related to כֹּחַ, as
שִׁלְאָנַן to שַׁאֲנָן, the latter being a mixed form from שָׁאֵן and
שִׁלְו, the former from כֹּחַ and לֵחַ, fresh juicy vigour, or as we
say: pith and marrow (*Saft and Kraft*)? At all events, if
this is somewhat the idea of the word, it may be derived from

בֶּלַה = בָּלָה (LXX. συντέλεια), or some other way (*vid.* on ch. v. 26) : it signifies full strength or maturity.[1]

With ver. 3*a* begins a new clause. It is גַּלְמוּד, not גַּלְמוּדִים, because the book of Job does not inflect this Hebræo-Arabic word, which is peculiar to it (besides only Isa. xlix. 21, נֻלְמוּדָה). It is also in Arab. more a substantive (stone, a mass) than an adj. (hard as stone, massive, *e.g. Hist. Tamerlani* in Schultens : الصَّخْر الجَلْمُود, the hardest rock) ; and, similar to the Greek χέρσος (*vid.* Passow), it denotes the condition or attribute of rigidity, *i.e.* sterility, ch. iii. 7 ; or stiff as death, ch. xv. 34 ; or, as here, extreme weakness and incapability of

[1] From the root كَل (on its primary notion, *vid.* my review of Bern-stein's edition of Kirsch's *Syr. Chrestomathie, Ergänzungsblatt der A.L.Z.* 1843, Nr. 16 and 17) other derivatives, as كَلَّا, كَلْب, كَلْت, كُلْث, كَلْس, كَلْز, كَلَد, etc., develop in general the significations to bring, take, or hold together, enclose, and the like ; but كَلْح in particular the signification to draw together, distort violently, viz. the muscles of the face in grinning and showing the teeth, or even sardonic laughing, and draw-ing the lips apart. The general signification of drawing together, شَدّ, resolves itself, however, from that special reference to the muscles of the face, and is manifest in the IV. form كَالَح, to show one's self strict and firm (against any one) ; also more sensuously : to remain firm in one's place ; of the moon, which remains as though motionless in one of its twenty-eight halting-places. Hence دَهْر كَالِح, a hard season, زَمَان شَدِيد and كَلْح, كَلَاح (the latter as a kind of *n. propr.* invariably ending in *i*, and always without the article), a hard year, *i.e.* a year of failure of the crops, and of scarcity and want. If it is possible to apply this to בֶּלַח without the hazardous comparison of قَلِح, قَلْحَم, etc. [so *supra*, i. 103], the primary signification might perhaps be that of hard-ness, unbroken strength ; ch. v. 26, " Thou wilt go to the grave with unbroken strength," *i.e.* full of days indeed, but without having thyself experienced the infirmities and burdens of the *ætas decrepita*, as also a shock brought in " in its season" is at the highest point of ripeness ; xxx. 2 : " What (should) the strength of their hands profit me ? as for them, their vigour is departed."—FL.

working. The subj.: such are *they*, is wanting; it is ranged
line upon line in the manner of a mere sketch, participles
with the demonstrative article follow the elliptical substantival
clause.   The *part.* הָעֹרְקִים is explained by LXX., Targ.,
Saad. (فَارٍ), and most of the old expositors, after עָרַק, عرق,
fut. يَعْرُقُ، *fugere, abire,* which, however, gives a tame and—
since the desert is to be thought of as the proper habitation
of these people, be they the Seir remnant of the displaced
Horites, or the Hauran "races of the clefts"—even an inappropriate sense.   On the contrary, عرق in Arab. (also *Pael*
ʿ*arreq* in Syriac) signifies to gnaw; and this Arabic signification of a word exclusively peculiar to the book of Job (here
and ch. xxx. 17) is perfectly suitable.   We do not, however,
with Jerome, translate: *qui rodebant in solitudine* (which is
doubly false), but *qui rodunt solitudinem,* they gnaw the sun-
burnt parched ground of the steppe, stretched out there more
like beasts than men (what Gecatilia also means by his عَلَيْهِمْ,
adhærent), and derive from it their scanty food.   אֶמֶשׁ שׁוֹאָה
וּמְשֹׁאָה is added as an explanatory, or rather further descriptive,
permutative to צִיָּה.   The same alliterative union of substan-
tives of the same root occurs in ch. xxxviii. 27, Zeph. i. 15,
and a similar one in Nah. ii. 11 (בוקה ומבוקה), Ezek. vi. 14,
xxxiii. 29 (שמה ומשמה); on this expression of the superlative
by heaping up similar words, comp. Ew. § 313, *c.*   The verb
שָׁאָה has the primary notion of wild confused din (*e.g.* Isa.
xvii. 12 sq.), which does not pass over to the idea of desolation and destruction by means of the intermediate notion of
ruins that come together with a crash, but by the transfer of
what is confusing to the ear to confusing impressions and
conditions of all kinds; the desert is accordingly called also
תֹּהוּ, Deut. xxxii. 10, from תָּהָה = שָׁאָה (*vid. Genesis,* S. 93).
The noun אֶמֶשׁ signifies elsewhere adverbially, in the past
night, to grow night-like, and in general yesterday, according

to which it is translated: the yesterday of waste and desolation; or, retaining the adverbial form: waste and desolation
are of yesterday = long since. It is undeniable that מֵאֶתְמוּל
and אֶתְמוּל, Isa. xxx. 33, Mic. ii. 8, are used in 'the sense
pridem (not only to-day, but even yesterday); but our poet
uses תְּמוֹל, ch. viii. 9, in the opposite sense, *non pridem* (not
long since, but only of yesterday); and it is more natural to
ask whether אֶמֶשׁ then has not here the substantival signification from which it has become an adverb, in the signification
nightly or yesterday. Since it originally signifies yesterday
evening or night, then yesterday, it must have the primary
signification darkness, as the Arab. اَمْسِ is also traceable
to the primary notion of the sinking of the sun towards the
horizon; so that, consequently, although the usage of Arabic
does not allow this sense,[1] it can be translated (comp. צַלְמָוֶת,
Jer. ii. 6), "the evening darkness (gloominess) of the waste
and wilderness" (אֶמֶשׁ as *regens*, Ew. § 286, *a*). The Targ.

---

[1] اَمْسِ is manifestly connected with مَسَى, مَسَى, first by means of the
IV. form اَمْسَى; it has, however, like this, nothing to do with "darkness."
مَسَاءٌ is, according to the original sources of information, properly the
whole afternoon until sunset; and this time is so called, because in
it the sun تَمَسُّ or تَمَسِّي, touches, *i.e.* sinks towards the horizon
(from the root مَسَّ with the primary notion *stringere, terere, tergere,
trahere, prehendere, capere*). Just so they say تَدَلَّكَ الشَّمْسُ, properly
the sun rubs; تَضَيَّفَ, connects itself; تَشَغَّرَ, goes to the brink (شَفَرَ,
شَفِير), all in the same signification. Used as a substantive, اَمْسِ
followed by the genitive is *la veille de . . .* , the evening before . . . ,
and then generally, the day before . . . , the opposite of غَد with the
same construction, *le lendemain de —*. It is absolutely impossible that it

also translates similarly, but takes אֹמֶשׁ as a special attribute : חֲשׁוֹכָא הֵיךְ רוּמְשָׁא, "darkness like the late evening."
Olshausen's conjecture of אֶרֶץ makes it easier, but puts a
word that affirms nothing in the place of an expressive one.

Ver. 4 tells what the scanty nourishment is which the
chill, desolate, and gloomy desert, with its steppes and gorges,
furnishes them. מַלּוּחַ (also Talmudic, Syriac, and Arabic) is
the orach, and indeed the tall shrubby orach, the so-called
sea-purslain, the buds and young leaves of which are gathered
and eaten by the poor. That it is not merely a coast plant,
but grows also in the desert, is manifest from the narrative
b. Kidduschin, 66a : "King Jannai approached כוחלית in the
desert, and conquered sixty towns there [Ges. translates
wrongly, captis LX talentis]; and on his return with great
joy, he called all the orphans of Israel to him, and said : Our
fathers ate מלוחים in their time when they were engaged with
the building of the temple (according to Raschi : the second
temple ; according to Aruch : the tabernacle in the wilder-

should refer to a far distant past. On the contrary, it is always used like
our " yesterday," in a general sense, for a comparatively near past, or

a past time thought of as near, as غَدٌ is used of a comparatively near
future, or a future time thought of as near. Zamachschari in the *Kes-
schâf* on *Sur.* xvii. 25 : It is a duty of children to take care of their aged
parents, " because they are so aged, and to-day (*el-jauma*) require those
who even yesterday (*bi-l-emsi*) were the most dependent on them of all
God's creatures." It never means absolutely *evening* or *night*. What
Gesenius, *Thes.*, cites as a proof for it from *Vita Timuri*, ii. 428—a sup-

posed أَمْسَى, *vespertinus*—is falsely read and explained (as in general
Manger's translation of those verses abounds in mistakes) ;—both line 1
and line 9, أَمْسَى, IV. form of لَمَسَ, is rhetorically and poetically (as
" sister of كَانَ ") of like signification with the general كَانَ or صَارَ. An
Arab would not be able to understand that אֶמֶשׁ שׁוֹאָה וּמְשֹׁאָה otherwise than : " on the eve of destruction and ruin," *i.e.* at the breaking in
of destruction and ruin which is just at hand or has actually followed
rapidly upon something else.—FL.

ness); we will also eat מַלּוּחִים in remembrance of our fathers!
And מַלּוּחִים were served up on golden tables, and they ate."
The LXX. translates, ἅλιμα (not: ἄλιμα); as in Athenæus,
poor Pythagoreans are once called ἅλιμα τρώγοντες καὶ κακὰ
τοιαῦτα συλλέγοντες.[1] The place where they seek for and
find this kind of edible plant is indicated by עֲלֵי־שִׂיחַ. שִׂיחַ is
a shrub in general, but certainly pre-eminently the شِيح,
that perennial, branchy, woody plant of uncultivated ground,
about two-thirds of a yard high, and the same in diameter,
which is one of the greatest blessings of Syria and of the
steppe, since, with the exception of cow and camel's dung, it
is often the only fuel of the peasants and nomads,—the principal, and often in a day's journey the only, vegetation of the
steppe, in the shade of which, when everything else is parched,
a scanty vegetation is still preserved.[2] The poor in search of
the purslain surround this شِيح (shîh), and as ver. 4b continues: the broom-root is their bread. Ges. understands לַחְמָם
according to Isa. xlvii. 14, where it is certainly the pausal
form for לְחֻמָּם ("there is not a coal to warm one's self"), and
that because the broom-root is not eatable. But why should
broom-root and not broom brushwood be mentioned as fuel?
The root of the steppe that serves as fuel, together with the
shîh, is called gizl (from גָּזַל, to tear out), not retem, which is
the broom (and is extraordinarily frequent in the Belka).
The Arabs, however, not only call Genista monosperma so,
but also Chamærops humilis, a degenerate kind of which produces a kind of arrow-root which the Indians in Florida use.[3]

---

[1] Huldrich Zwingli, in the Greek Aldine of 1518 (edited by Andrea of
Asola), which he has annotated throughout in the margin, one of the
choicest treasures of the Zurich town library, explains ἅλιμα by θαλάσσια,
which was natural by the side of the preceding περικυκλοῦντες. We shall
mention these marginal notes of Zwingli now and again.

[2] Thus Wetzstein in his Reise in den beiden Trachonen und um das
Haurangebirge.

[3] The description of these eaters of the steppe plants corresponds exactly

לְחָמָם in the signification *cibus eorum* is consequently not incomprehensible. LXX. (which throws vers. 4–6 into sad confusion): οἳ καὶ ῥίζας ξύλων ἐμασσῶντο.[1] All the ancient versions translate similarly. One is here reminded of what Agatharchides says in Strabo concerning the Egyptio-Ethiopian eaters of the rush root and herb.[2]

to the reality, especially if that race, bodily so inferior, is contrasted with the agricultural peasant, and some allowance is made for the figure of speech مُبَالَغَة (*i.e.* a description in colours, strongly brought out), without which poetic diction would be flat and devoid of vividness in the eye of an Oriental. The peasant is large and strong, with a magnificent beard and an expressive countenance, while *e.g.* the Trachonites of the present day (*i.e.* the race of the *W'ar*, יְעָר), both men and women, are a small, unpleasant-looking, weakly race. It is certain that bodily perfection is a plant that only thrives in a comfortable house, and needs good nourishment, viz. bread, which the Trachonite of the present day very rarely obtains, although he levies heavy contributions on the harvest of the villagers. Therefore the roots of plants often serve as food. Two such plants, the *gahh* (נֵח) and the *rubbe halîle* (רִבָּה חֲלִילָה), are described in my *Reisebericht*. A Beduin once told me that it should be properly called *rubh lêle* (רִבַּח לֵילָה), "the gain of a supper," inasmuch as it often takes the place of this, the chief meal of the day. To the genus *rubbe* belongs also the *holêwâ* (חֲלֵיוָא); in like manner they eat the bulbous plant, *qotên* (קְטֵין); of another, the *mesha'* (מָשַׁע), they eat leaves, stem, and root. I often saw the poor villagers (never Beduins) eat the broad thick fleshy leaves of a kind of thistle (the thistle is called شُوك, *shôk*), the name of which is '*aqqub* (עַקּוּב); these leaves are a handbreadth and a half in length, and half a handbreadth in width. They gather them before the thorns on the innumerable points of the serrated leaves become strong and woody; they boil them in salt and water, and serve them up with a little butter. Whole tribes of the people of the *Ruwala* live upon the small brown seed (resembling mustard-seed) of the *semh* (שֶׂמַח). The seeds are boiled to a pulp.—WETZST.

[1] Zwingli observes here: Sigma only once. *Codd. Alex. and Sinait.* have the reading ἐμασωντο, which he prefers.

[2] *Vid.* Meyer, *Botanische Erläuterungen zu Strabons Geographie*, S. 108 ff.

5 *They are driven forth from society,*
   They cry after them as after a thief.
6 *In the most dismal valleys they must dwell,*
   In holes of the earth and in rocks.
7 *Among the bushes they croak,*
   Under nettles are they poured forth,
8 *Sons of fools, yea sons of base men :*
   They are driven forth out of the land !—

If, coming forth from their lurking-places, they allow
themselves to be seen in the villages of the plain or in the
towns, they are driven forth from among men, *e medio pellun-
tur* (to use a Ciceronian phrase). גֵּו (Syr. *gau*, Arab. *gaww,
guww*) is that which is internal, here the circle of social
life, the organized human community. This expression also
is Hebræo-Arabic; for if one contrasts a house or district
with what is outside, he says in Arabic, جَوًّا وَبَرًّا, *guwwâ
wa-berrâ*, within and without, or الجَوَانِى وَالبَرَانِى, *el-guwwâni
wa'l-berrâni*, the inside and the outside. In ver. 5*b*, בְּמוֹ,
like the thief, is equivalent to, as after the thief, or since this
generic *Art.* is not usual with us [Germ. and Engl.]: after
a thief; French, *on crie après eux comme après le voleur.* In
ver. 6*a*, לִשְׁכֹּן is, according to Ges. § 132, rem. 1 (comp. on
Hab. i. 17), equivalent to הָיוּ לִשְׁכֹּן, "they are to dwell" =
they must dwell; it might also signify, according to the still
more frequent usage of the language, *habitaturi sunt;* it here,
however, signifies *habitandum est eis*, as לִבְלוֹם, Ps. xxxii. 9,
obturanda sunt. Instead of בַּעֲרוּץ with *Shurek*, the reading
בַּעֲרוֹץ with *Cholem* (after the form סְגוֹר, Hos. xiii. 8) is also
found, but it is without support. עֲרוּץ is either a substantive
after the form גְּבוּל (Ges., as Kimchi), or the construct of
עֲרוּץ = נֶעֱרָץ, feared = fearful, so that the connection of the
words, which we prefer, is a superlative one: *in horridissima*

vallium, in the most terrible valleys, as ch. xli. 22, *acutissimæ testarum* (Ew., according to § 313, *c*). The further description of the habitation of this race of men: in holes (בְּחֹרֵי = חֹרֵי) of the earth (עָפָר, earth with respect to its constituent parts) and rocks (LXX. τρῶγλαι πετρῶν), may seem to indicate the aborigines of the mountains of the district of Seir, who are called הַחֹרִים, τρωγλοδύται (*vid. Genesis*, S. 507); but why not, which is equally natural, חַוְּרָן, Ezek. xlvii. 16, 18, the "district of caverns," the broad country about *Bosra*, with the two Trachônes (τράχωνες), of which the smaller western, the *Legâ*, is the ancient Trachonitis, and with Ituræa (the mountains of the Druses)?[1]

As ch. vi. 5 shows, there underlies ver. 7a a comparison of this people with the wild ass. The פֶּרֶא, *ferâ*, goes about in herds under the guidance of a so-called leader (*vid*. on ch. xxxix. 5), with which the poet in ch. xxiv. 5 compares the bands that go forth for forage; here the point of comparison, according to ch. vi. 5, is their bitter want, which urges from them the cry of pain; for יִנְהָקוּ, although not too strong, would nevertheless be an inadequate expression for their *sermo*

---

[1] Wetzstein also inclines to refer the description to the Iturœans, who, according to Apuleius, were *frugum pauperes*, and according to others, freebooters, and are perhaps distinguished from the *Arabes Trachonitæ* (if they were not these themselves), as the troglodytes are from the Arabs who dwell in tents (on the troglodytes in Eastern Hauran, *vid. Reisebericht*, S. 44, 126). "The troglodyte was very often able to go without nourishment and the necessaries of life. Their habitations are not unfrequently found where no cultivation of the land was possible, *e.g.* in *Safa*. They were therefore either rearers of cattle or marauders. The cattle-rearing troglodyte, because he cannot wander about from one pasture to another like the nomads who dwell in tents, often loses his herds by a failure of pasture, heavy falls of snow (which often produce great devastation, *e.g.* in Hauran), epidemics, etc. Losses may also arise from marauding attacks from the nomads. Still less is this marauding, which is at enmity with all the world, likely to make a race prosperous, which, like the troglodyte, being bound to a fixed habitation, cannot escape the revenge of those whom it has injured."—WETZST.

barbarus (Pineda), in favour of which Schlottmann calls to
mind Herodotus' (iv. 183) comparison of the language of
the Troglodyte Ethiopians with the screech of the night-owl
(τετρίγασι κατάπερ αἱ νυκτερίδες). Among bushes (especially
the bushes of the *shih*, which affords them some nourishment
and shade, and a green resting-place) one hears them, and
hears from their words, although he cannot understand them
more closely, discontent and lamentation over their desperate
condition: there, under nettles (חָרוּל, root חר, خَر, as *urtica*
from *urere*), *i.e.* useless weeds of the desert, they are poured
forth, *i.e.* spread about in disorder. Thus most moderns
take ספח = שָׁפַךְ, سفح, comp. סָרוּחַ, *profusus*, Amos vi. 4, 7,
although one might also abide by the usual Hebrew meaning of the verb ספח (hardened from ספה), *adjungere, associare*
(*vid. Habak.* S. 88), and with Hahn explain: under nettles
they are united together, *i.e.* they huddle together. But
neither the *fut.* nor the *Pual* (instead of which one would
expect the *Niph.* or *Hithpa.*) is favourable to the latter interpretation; wherefore we decide in favour of the former, and
find sufficient support for a Hebr.-Arabic ספה in the signification *effundere* from a comparison of ch. xiv. 19 and the
present passage. Ver. 8, by dividing the hitherto latent subject, tells what sort of people they are: sons of fools, profane,
insane persons (*vid.* on Ps. xiv. 1); moreover, or of the like
kind (גַּם, not אַף), sons of the nameless, *ignobilium* or *in-
famium*, since בְּלִי־שֵׁם is here an adj. which stands in dependence, not *filii infamiæ = infames* (Hirz. and others), by which
the second בְּנֵי is rendered unlike the first. The assertion
ver. 8*b* may be taken as an attributive clause: who are
driven forth . . . ; but the shortness of the line and the
prominence of the verb are in favour of the independence
of the clause like an exclamation in its abrupt and halting
form. נִכְּאוּ is *Niph.* of נָכָא = נָכָה (נָבָה), root נך, to hew, pierce,

strike.¹ On הָאָרֶץ, of arable land in opposition to the steppe,
vid. on ch. xviii. 17.

9 *And now I am become their song,*
  And a by-word to them.
10 *They avoid me, they flee far from me,*
  And spare not my face with spitting.
11 *For my cord of life He hath loosed, and afflicted me,*
  Therefore they let loose the bridle recklessly.
12 *The rabble presses upon my right hand,*
  They thrust my feet away,
  And cast up against me their destructive ways.

The men of whom Job complains in this strophe are none
other than those in the preceding strophe, described from the
side of their coarse and degenerate behaviour, as ch. xxiv. 4–8
described them from the side of the wrong which was practised against them. This rabble, constitutionally as well as
morally degraded, when it comes upon Job's domain in its
marauding expeditions, makes sport of the sufferer, whose
former earnest admonitions, given from sympathizing anxiety
for them, seemed to them as insults for which they revenge
themselves. He is become their song of derision (נְגִינָתָם) to
be understood according to the dependent passage, Lam.
iii. 14, and Ps. lxix. 13), and is לְמִלָּה to them, their θρύλλημα

---

¹ The root نَكَ is developed in Hebr. נָכָה, הִכָּה, in Arab. نَكَا and
نَكَى, first to the idea of outward injury by striking, hewing, etc.; but
it is then also transferred to other modes of inflicting injury, and in
نَوْك, to being injured in mind. The root shows itself in its most sensuous development in the reduplicated form نَكْنَكَ, to strike one with
repeated blows, fig. for: to press any one hard with claims. According
to another phase, the obscene نَالَ *fut. i*, and the decent نَكَح, signify
properly to pierce.—FL.

148　　THE BOOK OF JOB.

(LXX.), the subject of their foolish talk (מִלָּה = Arab. *mille*, not = *melle*, according to which Schultens inteprets it, *sum iis fastidio*). Avoiding him, and standing at a distance from him, they make their remarks upon him; and if they come up to him, it is only for the sake of showing him still deeper scorn : *a facie ejus non cohibent sputam.* The expositors who explain that, contrary to all decent bearing, they spit in his presence (Eichh., Justi, Hirz., Vaih., Hlgst.), or with Fie! spit out before him (Umbr., Hahn, Schlottm.), overlook the fact of its being מִפָּנַי, not לְפָנָי. The expression as it stands can only affirm that they do not spare his face with spitting (Jer. correctly : *conspuere non veruntur*), so that consequently he is become, as he has complained in ch. xvii. 6, a תֹּפֶת, an object of spitting (comp. also the declaration of the servant of Jehovah, Isa. l. 6, which stands in close connection with this declaration of Job, according to previous explanations).

It now becomes a question, Who is the subj. in ver. 11*a*? The *Chethib* יִתְרוֹ demands an attempt to retain the previous subj. Accordingly, most moderns explain : *solvit unusquisque eorum funem suum, i.e. frenum suum, quo continebatur antea a me* (Rosenm., Umbr., Stick., Vaih., Hlgst., and others), but it is to be doubted whether יתר can mean *frenum;* it signifies a cord, the string of a bow, and of a harp. The reconciliation of the signification *redundantia*, ch. xxii. 20, and *funis*, is, in the idea of the root, to be stretched tight and long.[1] Hirz. therefore imagines the loosing of the cord

---

[1] The verb وَتَرَ shows its sensuous primary signification in وَتَّرَ, יתר, cord, bow-string, harp-string (Engl. *string*) : to stretch tight, to extend, so that the thing continues in one line. Hence then وَتَّرَ, وَتَرَ, separate, unequal, *singulus, impar*, opp. شَفْع, *bini, par*, just as *fard*, single, separate, unequal (*opp. zaug*, a pair, equal number), is derived from *farada*, properly, so to strain or stretch out, that the thing has no bends or folds; Greek ἐξαπλοῦν (as in the *Shepherd* of Hermas : ἐπάνω λεντίου ἐξηπλω-

round the body, which served them as a girdle, in order to strike Job with it. But whether one decides in favour of the *Chethib* יתרו or of the *Keri* יתרי, the persons who insult Job cannot in any case be intended. The isolated *sing.* form of the assertion, while the rabble is everywhere spoken of in the *plur.*, is against it; and also the כִּי, which introduces it, and after which Job here allows the reason to come in, why he is abandoned without any means of defence to such brutal misconduct. The subj. of ver. 11*a* is God. If יתרו is read, it may not be interpreted: He hath opened = taken off the covering of His string (= bow) (Ew., Hahn, and similarly even LXX., Jer.), for יתר does not signify the bow, but the string (Arab. *muwattar*, stretched, of a bow); and while פָּתַח, Ezek. xxi. 33 (usually שָׁלַף or הֵרִיק), can certainly be said of drawing a sword from its sheath, עֵרָה is the appropriate and usual word (*vid. Hab.* S. 164) for making bare the bow and shield. Used of the bow-string, פִּתֵּחַ signifies to loose what is

μένον λίνον καρπάσινον), an original transitive signification still retained in low Arabic (*vid.* Bocthor under *Étendre* and *Déployer*). Then from وَتَّرَ spring the secondary roots تَنَّرَ and تَرَّى, which proceed from the VIII. form (*ittatara*). The former (*tatara*) appears only in the adverb تَنَّرَا and تَّرَى, *sigillatim*, *alii post alios*, singly one after another, so that several persons or things form a row interrupted by intervals of space or time; the latter (*tara*) and its IV. form (*atra*) are equivalent to *wâtara*, to be active at intervals, with pauses between, as the Arabs explain: " We say أَتْرَى of a man when he so performs several acts which do not directly follow one another, that there is always a فَنَرَة, *intermissio*, between two acts." Hence also תְּרֵין, תְּרֵתֵּין, duals of an assumed *sing.* תַּר, *singulus* (*um*), תַּרְתְּ *singula*, therefore prop. *duo singuli* (*a*), *duæ singulæ*, altogether parallel to the like meaning *thinâni* (*ithnâni*), *thinaini* (*ithnaini*), שְׁנַיִם; fem. *thintâni* (*ithnatâni*), *thintaini* (*ithnataini*), שְׁתֵּים instead of שְׁנְתַּיִם, from an assumed *sing. thin-un* (*ithn-un*), *thint-un*

strained, by sending the arrow swiftly forth from it, according
to which, *e.g.* Elizabeth Smith translates: Because He hath
let go His bow-string and afflicted me. One cannot, however, avoid feeling that וַיְעַנֵּנִי is not a right description of the
effect of shooting with arrows, whereas an idea is easily gained
from the *Keri* יתרי, to which the description of the effect corresponds. It has been interpreted: He has loosed my rein
or bridle, by means of which I hitherto bound them and held
them in check; but יתר in the signification rein or bridle is,
as already observed, not practicable. Better Capellus: *meta-
phora ducta est ab exarmato milite, cujus arcûs solvitur nervus
sicque inermis redditur;* but it is more secure, and still more
appropriate to the ויענני which follows, when it is interpreted
according to ch. iv. 21: He has untied (loosened) my cord
of life, *i.e.* the cord which stretched out and held up my tent
(the body) (Targ. similarly: my chain and the threads of my
cord, *i.e.* surely: my outward and inward stay of life), and

(*ithnat-un*), from ثِنًى, שָׁנָה, like *bin* (*ibn*), *bint* (*ibnat*), בֵּן, בַּת (= בְּנָת,

hence בַּתִּי) from بِنًى, בָּנָה.

The significations of *watara* which Freytag arranges under 1, 2, 3, 4,
proceed from the transitive application of יָתַר, as the Italian *soperchiare*,
soverchiare, from *supra*, to offend, insult; *oltraggiare*, *outrager*, from
ultra; ὑβρίζειν from ὑπέρ. Similarly, تطاول علیه and علیه استطال
(form VI. and X. from طال), to act haughtily towards any one, to make
him feel one's superiority, properly to stretch one's self out over or
against any one.

But in another direction the signif. to be stretched out goes into:
overhanging, surpassing, projecting, to be superfluous, and to be left over,
περιττόν εἶναι, to exceed a number or bulk, *superare* (comp. Italian *soperchiare* as intrans.), περισσεῖναι, ὑπερισσεῖναι; to prove, as result, gain, etc.,
περισσεῖναι, etc. Similar is the development of the meaning of فَضَل and
of طائِل, gain, use, from طال, to be stretched out. In like manner, the
German *reich*, *reichlich* [rich, abundant], comes from the root *reichen*,
recken [to stretch, extend].—FL.

bowed me down, *i.e.* deprived me of strength (comp. Ps. cii. 24); or also: humbled me. Even in this his feebleness he is the butt of unbridled arrogance: and they let go the bridle before me (not לְפָנַי, in my presence, but מִפָּנַי, before me, before whom previously they had respect; מפני the same as Lev. xix. 32), they cast or shake it off (שִׁלַּח as ch. xxxix. 3, synon. of הִשְׁלִיךְ; comp. 1 Kings ix. 7 with 2 Chron. vii. 20).

Is it now possible that in this connection פִּרְחָה can denote any else but the rabble of these good-for-nothing fellows? Ewald nevertheless understands by it Job's sufferings, which as a rank evil swarm rise up out of the ground to seize upon him; Hahn follows Ew., and makes these sufferings the subj., as even in ver. 11*b*. But if we consider how Ew. translates: "they hung a bridle from my head;" and Hahn: "they have cast a bit before my face," this might make us tired of all taste for this allegorical mode of interpretation. The stump over which they must stumble is ver. 13*c*, where all climax must be abandoned in order to make the words לֹא עֹזֵר לָמוֹ intelligible in this allegorical connection. No indeed; פִּרְחָה (instead of which פַּרְחַח might be expected, as *supra*, ch. iii. 5, כְּמִרִירֵי for כְּמִרִירֵי) is the offspring or rabble of those fathers devoid of morals and honour, those צְעִירִים of ver. 1, whose laughing-stock Job is now, as the children of priests are called in Talmudic פִּרְחֵי כְהֻנָּה, and in Arabic فَرْخ denotes not only the young of animals, but also a rascal or vagabond. This young rabble rises עַל־יָמִין, on Job's right hand, which is the place of an accuser (Ps. cix. 6), and generally one who follows him up closely and oppresses him; and they press him continually further and further, contending one foot's-breadth after another with him: רַגְלַי שִׁלֵּחוּ, my feet thrust them forth, *protrudunt* (שִׁלַּח the same as ch. xiv. 20). By this pressing from one place to another, a way is prepared for the description of their hostile conduct, which begins in ver. 12*c* under

the figure of a siege. The *fut. consec.* וַיִּסֹּלּוּ, ver. 12c, is not
meant retrospectively like וַיְעַנֵּנִי, but places present with present in the connection of cause and effect (comp. Ew. 343, a).
We must not be misled by the fact that וַיָּסֹלּוּ, ch. xix. 12
(which see), was said of the host of sufferings which come
against Job; here it is those young people who cast up the
ramparts of misfortune or burdensome suffering (אֵיד) against
Job, which they wish to make him feel. The tradition, supported by the LXX., that Job had his seat outside his
domain ἐπὶ τῆς κοπρίας, *i.e.* upon the *mezbele*, is excellently
suited to this and the following figures. Before each village
in Hauran there is a place where the households heap up the
sweepings of their stalls, and it gradually reaches a great
circumference, and a height which rises above the highest
buildings of the village.[1] Notwithstanding, everything is intelligible without this thoroughly Hauranitish conception of
the scene of the history. Bereft of the protection of his children and servants, become an object of disgust to his wife,
and an abhorrence to his brethren, forsaken by every attention of true affection, ch. xix. 13–19, Job lies out of doors;
and in this condition, shelterless and defenceless, he is aban-

---

[1] One ought to have a correct idea of a Hauranitish *mezbele*. The
dung which is heaped up there is not mixed with straw, because in warm,
dry countries no litter is required for the cattle, and comes mostly from
single-hoofed animals, since small cattle and oxen often pass the nights
on the pastures. It is brought in a dry state in baskets to the place
before the village, and is generally burnt once every month. Moreover,
they choose days on which the wind is favourable, *i.e.* does not cast the
smoke over the village. The ashes remain. The fertile volcanic ground
does not need manure, for it would make the seed in rainy years too luxuriant at the expense of the grain, and when rain fails, burn it up. If
a village has been inhabited for a century, the *mezbele* reaches a height
which far surpasses it. The winter rains make the ash-heaps into a
compact mass, and gradually change the *mezbele* into a firm mound of
earth, in the interior of which those remarkable granaries, *biâr el-ghalle*,
are laid out, in which the wheat can be completely preserved against
heat and mice, garnered up for years. The *mezbele* serves the inhabitants

doned to the hideous malignant joy of those gipsy hordes which wander hither and thither.

13 *They tear down my path,*
   They minister to my overthrow,
   They who themselves are helpless.

14 *As through a wide breach they approach,*
   Under the crash they roll onwards.

15 *Terrors are turned against me,*
   They pursue my nobility like the wind,
   And like a cloud my prosperity passed away.—

They make all freedom of motion and any escape impossible to him, by pulling down, *diruunt*, the way which he might go. Thus is נֶחֱסוּ (cogn. form of נתין, נתע נתה, נחש) to be translated, not: they tear open (*proscindunt*), which is contrary to the primary signification and the usage of the language. They, who have no helper, who themselves are so miserable and despised, and yet so feelingless and overbearing, contribute to his ruin. הוֹעִיל, to be useful, to do any good, to furnish anything effective (*e.g.* Isa. xlvii. 12), is here united with לְ of the purpose; comp. לְ עֲזֻר, to help towards anything, Zech. i. 15.

of the district as a watch-tower, and on close oppressive evenings as a place of assembly, because there is a current of air on the height. There the children play about the whole day long ; there the forsaken one lies, who, having been seized by some horrible malady, is not allowed to enter the dwellings of men, by day asking alms of the passers-by, and at night hiding himself among the ashes which the sun has warmed. There the dogs of the village lie, perhaps gnawing at a decaying carcase that is frequently thrown there. Many a village of Hauran has lost its original name, and is called *umm el-mezâbil* from the greatness and number of these mounds, which always indicate a primitive and extensive cultivation for the villages. And many a more modern village is built upon an ancient *mezbele*, because there is then a stronger current of air, which renders the position more healthy. The Arabic signification of the root זבל seems to be similarly related to the Hebrew as that of the old Beduin *seken* (שָׁכֵן), "ashes," to the Hebrew and Arabic מִשְׁכָּן, "a dwelling."— WETZST.

הַוָּה (for which the *Keri* substitutes the primary form הַיָּה), as
was already said on ch. vi. 2, is prop. *hiatus*, and then *bara-
thrum, pernicies*, like הַוָּה in the signification *cupiditas*, prop.
inhiatio. The verb הָוָה, هوى, also signifies *delabi*, whence it
may be extended (*vid.* on ch. xxxvii. 6) in like manner to the
signification abyss (rapid downfall); but a suitable medium
for the two significations, strong passion (Arab. *hawa*) and
abyss (Arab. *hâwije, huwwe, mahwa*), is offered only by the
signification of the root *flare* (whence *hawâ*, air). לֹא עֹזֵר לָמוֹ
is a genuine Arabic description of these Idumæan or Hauranite pariahs. Schultens compares a passage of the *Hamâsa*:
"We behold you ignoble, poor, *laisa lakum min sâir-in-nâsi
nasirun, i.e.* without a helper among the rest of men." The
interpretations of those who take לָמוֹ for לֹו, and this again
for לֹי (Eichh., Justi), condemn themselves. It might more
readily be explained, with Stick.: without any one helping
them, *i.e.* with their own strong hand; but the thought thus
obtained is not only aimless and tame, but also halting and
even untrue (*vid.* ch. xix. 13 sqq.).

Ver. 14. The figure of a siege, which is begun with ver.
12*c* and continued in ver. 13, leaves us in no doubt concerning פֶּרֶץ רָחָב and שֹׁאָה. The Targ. translates: like the force
of the far-extending waves of the sea, not as though פֶּרֶץ could
in itself signify a stream of water, but taking it as = פֶּרֶץ מַיִם,
2 Sam. v. 20 (synon. *diffusio aquarum*). Hitzig's translation:[1]
"like a broad forest stream they come, like a rapid brook
they roll on," gives unheard-of significations to the doubtful
words. In ch. xvi. 14 we heard Job complain: He (Eloah)
brake through me פָּרַץ עַל־פְּנֵי־פָרֶץ, breach upon breach,—by
the divine decrees of sufferings, which are completed in this
ill-treatment which he receives from good-for-nothing fellows,
he is become as a wall with a wide-gaping breach, through

---

[1] *Vid. Deutsche Morgenländ. Zeitschr.* ix. (1855), S. 741, and *Proverbs*,
S. 11.

which they rush in upon him (*instar rupturæ*, a concise mode
of comparison instead of *tanquam per rupt.*), in order to get
him entirely into their power as a plaything for their coarse
passions. שֹׁאָה is the crash of the wall with the wide breaches,
and תַּחַת שֹׁאָה signifies *sub fragore* in a local sense: through
the wall which is broken through and crashes above the
assailants. There is no ground in ver. 15a for dividing, with
Umbreit, thus: He hath turned against me! Terrors drove
away, etc., although this would not be impossible according
to the syntax (comp. Gen. xlix. 22, בָּנוֹת צָעֲדָה). It is translated: terrors are turned against me; so that the predicate
stands first in the most natural, but still indefinite, personal
form, Ges. § 147, a, although בַּלָּהוֹת might also be taken as
the accus. of the object after a passive, Ges. § 143, 1. The
subj. of ver. 15b remains the same: they (these terrors) drive
away my dignity like the wind; the construction is like ch.
xxvii. 20, xiv. 19; on the matter, comp. ch. xviii. 11. Hirz.
makes כָּרוּחַ the subj.: *quasi ventus aufert nobilitatem meam*,
in which case the subj. would be not so much *ventus* as *simili-
tudo venti*, as when one says in Arabic, *'gâani kazeidin*, there
came to me one of Zeid's equals, for in the Semitic languages
כְּ has the manner of an indeclinable noun in the signification
instar. But the reference to בלהות is more natural; and
Hahn's objection, that calamity does not first, if it is there,
drive away prosperity, but takes the place of that which is
driven away, is sophisticated and inadequate, since the object
of the driving away here is not Job's prosperity, but Job's
נְדִיבָה, appearance and dignity, by which he hitherto commanded the respect of others (Targ. רַבְּנוּתִי). The storms of
suffering which pass over him take this nobility away to the
last fragment, and his salvation—or rather, since this word
in the mouth of an extra-Israelitish hero has not the meaning
it usually otherwise has, his prosperous condition (from ﻳﺴﻊ,

amplum esse)—is as a cloud, so rapidly and without trace (ch. vii. 9; Isa. xliv. 22), passed away and vanished. Observe the music of the expression בְּעָב עֲבָרָה, which cannot be reproduced in translation.

> 16 *And now my soul is poured out within me,*
> *Days of suffering hold me fast.*
> 17 *The night rendeth my bones from me,*
> *And my gnawers sleep not.*
> 18 *By great force my garment is distorted,*
> *As the collar of my shirt it encompasseth me.*
> 19 *He hath cast me into the mire,*
> *And I am in appearance as dust and ashes.*

With this third וְעַתָּה (vers. 1, 9) the elegiac lament over the harsh contrast between the present and the past begins for the third time. The dash after our translation of the second and fourth strophes will indicate that a division of the elegy ends there, after which it begins as it were anew. The soul is poured out within a man (עַל as ch. x. 1, *Psychol.* S. 152), when, "yielding itself without resistance to sadness, it is dejected to the very bottom, and all its organization flows together, and it is dissolved in the one condition of sorrow" —a figure which is not, however, come about by water being regarded as the symbol of the soul (thus Hitzig on Ps. xlii. 5), but rather by the intimate resemblance of the representation of a flood of tears (Lam. ii. 19): the life of the soul flows in the blood, and the anguish of the soul in tears and lamentations; and since the outward man is as it were dissolved in the gently flowing tears (Isa. xv. 3), his soul flows away as it were in itself, for the outward incident is but the manifestation and result of an inward action. יְמֵי־עֹנִי we have translated days of suffering, for עֹנִי, with its verb and the rest of its derivatives, is the proper word for suffering, and especially the passion of the Servant of Jehovah. Days of suffering

—Job complains—hold him fast ; אֲחָזוּ unites in itself, like הֶחֱזִיק, the significations *prehendere* and *prehensum tenere*. In ver. 17*a* we must not, with Arnh. and others, translate : by night it (affliction) pierces . . . , for עֲנִי does not stand sufficiently in the foreground to be the subject of what follows; it might sooner be rendered : by night it is pierced through (Targ., Rosenm., Hahn) ; but why is not לַיְלָה to be the subject, and נִקַּר consequently *Piel* (not *Niph.*)? The night has been personified already, ch. iii. 2 ; and in general, as Herder once said, Job is the brother of Ossian for personifications : Night (the restless night, ch. vii. 3 sq., in which every malady, or at least the painful feeling of it, increases) pierces his bones from him, *i.e.* roots out his limbs (synon. בַּדִּים, ch. xviii. 13) so inwardly and completely. The *lepra Arabica* (البرص, *el-baras*) terminates, like syphilis, with an eating away of the limbs, and the disease has its name جُذَام from جذم, *truncare, mutilare* : it feeds on the bones, and destroys the body in such a manner that single limbs are completely detached.

In ver. 17*b*, LXX. (νεῦρα), Parchon, Kimchi, and others translate עֹרְקַי according to the Targum. עֶרְקִין (= גִּידִים), and the Arab. عروق, veins, after which Blumenf. : my veins are in constant motion. But עֹרְקַי in the sense of ch. xxx. 3 : my gnawers (Jer. *qui me comedunt*, Targ. דִּמְעַסָן יָתִי, *qui me conculcant, conterunt*), is far more in accordance with the predicate and the parallelism, whether it be gnawing pains that are thought of—pains are unnatural to man, they come upon him against his will, he separates them from himself as wild beasts—or, which we prefer, those worms (רִמָּה, ch. vii. 5) which were formed in Job's ulcers (comp. Aruch, עַרְקָא, a leech, *plur.* עַרְקָתָא, worms, *e.g.* in the liver), and which in the extra-biblical tradition of Job's decease are such a standing feature, that the pilgrims to Job's monastery even now-a-days take away with them thence these supposedly petrified worms of Job.[1]

Ver. 18a would be closely and naturally connected with what precedes if לְבוּשִׁי could be understood of the skin and explained : By omnipotence (viz. divine, as ch. xxiii. 6, Ew. § 270a) the covering of my body is distorted, as even Raschi: מִשְׁתַּנֶּה גִּלֶד אַחַר גִּלֶד, it is changed, by one skin or crust being formed after another. But even Schultens rightly thinks it remarkable that לְבוּשׁ, ver. 18a, is not meant to signify the proper upper garment but the covering of the skin, but כֻּתָּנְתִּי, ver. 18b, the under garment in a proper sense. The astonishment is increased by the fact that הִתְחַפֵּשׂ signifies to disguise one's self, and thereby render one's self unrecognisable, which leads to the proper idea of לְבוּשׁ, to a clothing which looks like a disguise. It cannot be cited in favour of this unusual meaning that לְבוּשׁ is used in ch. xli. 5 of the scaly skin of the crocodile : an animal has no other לְבוּשׁ but its skin. Therefore, with Ew., Hirz., and Hlgst., we take לְבוּשׁ strictly : "by (divine) omnipotence my garment is distorted (becomes unlike itself), like the collar of my shirt it fits close to me." It is unnecessary to take כְּפִי as a compound præp. : according to

---

[1] In Mugir ed-dîn's large history of Jerusalem and Hebron (kitâb el-ins el-gelîl), in an article on Job, we read: God had so visited him in his body, that he got the disease that devours the limbs (tegedhdhem), and worms were produced (dawwad) in the wounds, while he lay on a dunghill (mezbele), and except his wife, who tended him, no one ventured to come too near him. In a beautiful Kurdic ballad "on the basket dealer" (zembilfrosh), which I have obtained from the Kurds in Salihîje, are these words : Veki Gergis beshara beri | Jusuf veki abdan keri | bikesr' Ejub kurman deri | toh anin ser sultaneti | to men chalaski 'j zahmeti.

"When they divided Gergis with a saw
And sold Joseph like a slave,
When worms fed themselves in Job's body,
Then Thou didst guide them by a sure way :
Thou wilt also deliver me from need."

More concerning these worms of Job in the description of the monastery of Job.—WETZST.

(comp. Zech. ii. 4, Mal. ii. 9 : "according as"), in the sense of
כְּמוֹ, as ch. xxxiii. 6, since פִּי כֻתָּנְתִּי is, according to the nature of
the thing mentioned, a designation of the upper opening, by
means of which the shirt, otherwise only provided with arm-
holes (distinct from the Beduin shirt *thôb*, which has wide and
long sleeves), is put on.   Also, Ps. cxxxiii. 2, פִּי מִדּוֹתָיו signifies
not the lower edge, but the opening at the head (פִּי הָרֹאשׁ, Ex.
xxviii. 32) or the collar of the high priest's vestment (*vid.* the
passage cited).   Thus even LXX. ὥσπερ τὸ περιστόμιον
τοῦ χιτῶνός μου, and Jer.: *velut capitio tunicæ meæ.*   True,
Schlottm. observes against this rendering of ver. 18, that it is
unnatural according to substance, since on a wasted body it is
not the outer garment that assumes the appearance of a narrow
under one, but on the contrary the under garment assumes the
appearance of a wide outer one.   But this objection is not to
the point.   If the body is wasted away to a skeleton, there is
an end to the rich appearance and beautiful flow which the
outer garment gains by the full and rounded forms of the
limbs : it falls down straight and in perpendicular folds upon
the wasted body, and contributes in no small degree to make
him whom one formerly saw in all the fulness of health still
less recognisable than he otherwise is.   יְאַזְּרֵנִי, *cingit me,* is not
merely the falling together of the outer garment which was
formerly filled out by the members of the body, but its
appearance when the sick man wraps himself in it : then it
girds him, fits close to him like his shirt-collar, lying round
about the shrivelled figure like the other about a thin neck.
On the terrible wasting away which is combined with hyper-
trophical formations in elephantiasis, *vid.* ch. vii. 15, and
especially xix. 20.   The subject of ver. 19 is God, whom
ver. 18 also describes as efficient cause : He has cast me into,
or daubed[1] me with, mud, and I am become as (כְּ instead of
the *dat.,* Ew. § 221, *a*) dust and ashes.   This is also intended

[1] The reading wavers between הֹרָנִי and הֹרְנִי, for the latter form of

pathologically: the skin of the sufferer with elephantiasis becomes first an intense red, then assumes a black colour; scales like fishes' scales are formed upon it, and the brittle, dark-coloured surface of the body is like a lump of earth.

20 *I cry to Thee for help, and Thou answerest not;*
  I stand there, and Thou lookest fixedly at me.
21 *Thou changest Thyself to a cruel being towards me,*
  With the strength of Thy hand Thou makest war upon me.
22 *Thou raisest me upon the stormy wind, Thou causest me*
  to drive along
  And vanish in the roaring of the storm.
23 *For I know: Thou wilt bring me back to death,*
  Into the house of assembly for all living.

If he cries for help, his cry remains unanswered; if he stands there looking up reverentially to God (perhaps עמד, with מִשֻּׁעַ to be supplied, has the sense of desisting or restraining, as Gen. xxix. 35, xxx. 9), the troubling, fixed look of God, who looks fixedly and hostilely upon him, anything but ready to help (comp. ch. vii. 20, xvi. 9), meets his up-turned eye. הִתְבֹּנֵן, to look consideringly upon anything, is elsewhere joined with אֶל, עַל, עַד, or even with the *acc.*; here, where a motionless fixed look is intended, with בְּ (= ڢ). It is impossible to draw the לֹא, ver. 20*a*, over to וַתִּתְבֹּנֵן (Jer., Saad., Umbr., Welte, and others), both on account of the *Waw consec.* (Ew. § 351*a*), and on account of the separation by the new antecedent עֲמַדְתִּי. On the reading of two Codd. ותתכנן ("Thou settest Thyself against me"), which Houbigant and Ew. prefer, Rosenm. has correctly pronounced judgment: *est potius pro mendo habenda.* Instead of consolingly answering his prayer, and instead of showing Himself willing to help, God, who was formerly so kind towards him, changes

writing is sometimes found even out of pause by conjunctive accents, *e.g.* 1 Sam. xxviii. 15, Ps. cxviii. 5.

towards him, His creature, into a cruel being, *sævum* (אַכְזָר) in the book of Job only here and ch. xli. 2, where it signifies "foolhardy;" comp. לְאֹיֵב in the dependent passage, Isa. lxiii. 10), and makes war upon him (שָׂטַם as ch. xvi. 9) by causing him to feel the strength of His omnipotent hand (עֹצֶם יָד as Deut. viii. 17, synon. חֹזֶק).

It is not necessary in ver. 22*a* to forsake the accentuation, and to translate : Thou raisest me up, Thou causest me go in the wind (Ew., Hirz., and others) ; the accentuation of רוח is indeed not a disjunctive *Dechî*, but a conjunctive *Tarcha*, but preceded by *Munach*, which, according to the rule, *Psalter* ii. 500, § 5, here, where two conjunctives come together, has a smaller conjunctive value. Therefore : *elevas me in ventum, equitare facis me*, viz. *super ventum* (Dachselt), for one does not only say הִרְכִּיב עַל, 1 Chron. xiii. 7, or לְ, Ps. lxvi. 12, but also אֶל, 2 Sam. vi. 3 ; and accordingly תִּשָּׂאֵנִי אֶל־רוּחַ is also not to be translated : Thou snatchest me into the wind or storm (Hahn, Schlottm.), but : Thou raisest me up to the wind or storm, as upon an animal for riding (Umbr., Olsh.). According to Oriental tradition, Solomon rode upon the east wind, and in Arabic they say of one who hurries rapidly by, *racab al-genáhai er-rîh*, he rides upon the wings of the wind ; in the present passage, the point of comparison is the being absolutely passively hurried forth from the enjoyment of a healthy and happy life to a dizzy height, whence a sudden overthrow threatens him who is unwillingly removed (comp. Ps. cii. 11, Thou hast lifted me up and hurled me forth).

The lot which threatens him from this painful suspense Job expresses (ver. 22*b*) in the puzzling words : וּתְמֹגְגֵנִי תֻּשִׁיָּה. Thus the *Keri*, after which LXX. transl. (if it has not read מִישׁוּעָה), καὶ ἀπέρριψάς με ἀπὸ σωτηρίας. The modern expositors who follow the *Keri*, by taking ותמגנני for ותמנג לי (according to Ges. § 121, 4), translate : Thou causest counsel and understanding (Welte), happiness (Blumenf.), and the like, to vanish from me; continuance, existence, duration would be better (vid. ch. vi. 13, and especially on ch. xxvi. 3). The thought is appropriate, but the expression is halting. Jerome, who translates *valide*, points to the correct thing, and Buxtorf (*Lex.* col. 2342 sq.) by interpreting the not less puzzling Targum translation *in fundamento = funditus* or *in essentia = essentialiter*, has, without intending it, hit upon the idea of the Hebr. *Keri*; תְּשֻׁיָּה is intended as a closer defining, or adverbial, accusative: Thou causest me to vanish as to existence, *ita ut tota essentia pereat h.e. totaliter et omnino*. Perhaps this was really the meaning of the poet: most completely, most thoroughly, altogether, like the Arab. جِدّ. But it is un-favourable to this *Keri*, that חוּשִׁיָה (from the verb יֵשׁ), as might be expected, is always written *plene* elsewhere; the correction of the תִּשֻׁוֶה is violent, and moreover this form, cor-rectly read, gives a sense far more consistent with the figure, ver. 22*a*. Ges., Umbr., and Carey falsely read תִּשֶׁוָּה, *terres me*; this verb is unknown in Hebr., and even in Chaldee is only used in *Ithpeal*, אֶשְׁתְּוִי (= Hebr. חֲרַד); for a similar reason Böttcher's תִּשֶׁוֶּה (which is intended to mean: in de-spair) is also not to be used. Even Stuhlmann perceived that תִּשֻׁוֶה is equivalent to תְּשׁוּאָה; it is, with Ew. and Olsh., to be read תִּשֻׁוֶה (not with Pareau and Hirz. תְּשֻׁוֶה without the *Dag.*), and this form signifies, as הַשֻׁוָּאָה, ch. xxxvi. 29, from שָׁוְא = שָׁאָה, from which it is derived by change of consonants, the crash of thunder, or even the rumbling or roar as of a storm or a falling in (*procellæ sive ruinæ*). The meaning is hardly, that he who rides away upon the stormy wind melts and trickles down like drops of rain among the pealing of the thunder, when the thunder-storm, whose harbinger is the stormy wind, gathers; but that in the storm itself, which increases in fury to the howling of a tempest, he dissolves away. תִּשֻׁוֶה for בִּתְשֻׁוֶה, comp. Ps. cvii. 26: their soul melted

away (dissolved) בְּרָעָה. The compulsory journey in the air,
therefore, passes into nothing or nearly nothing, as Job is
well aware, ver. 23 : " for I know: (without כִּי, as ch. xix. 25,
Ps. ix. 21) Thou wilt bring me back to death" (acc. of the
goal, or locative without any sign). If תְּשִׁיבֵנִי is taken in its
most natural signification reduces, death is represented as
essentially one with the dust of death (comp. ch. i. 21 with
Gen. iii. 19), or even with non-existence, out of which man
is come into being; nevertheless הֵשִׁיב can also, by obliterating
the notion of return, like redigere, have only the signification
of the turn of destiny and change of condition that is effected.
The assertion that שׁוּב always includes an " again," and retains
it inexorably (vid. Köhler on Zech. xiii. 7, S. 239), is untenable.   In post-biblical Hebrew, at least, it is certain that
שׁוּב signifies not only " to become again," but also " to
become," as عاد is used as synon. of جاء, devenir.[1] With
מָוֶת, the designation of the condition, is coupled the designation of the place : Hades (under the notion of which that of
the grave is included) is the great involuntary rendezvous of
all who live in this world.

24 *Doth one not, however, stretch out the hand in falling,*
   Doth he not raise a cry for help on that account in his ruin?
· 25 *Or have I not wept for him that was in trouble,*
   Hath not my soul grieved for the needy?—
26 *For I hoped for good, then evil came ;*
   I waited for light, and darkness came.
27 *My bowels boiled without ceasing,*
   Days of misery met me.

Most of the ancient versions indulge themselves in strange
fancies respecting ver. 24 to make a translatable text, or find
their fancies in the text before them. The translation of the

[1] Vid. my Anekdota der mittelalterlichen Scholastik unter Juden und
Moslemen, S. 347.

Targum follows the fancies of the Midrash, and places itself beyond the range of criticism. The LXX. reads בּי instead of בְּעִי, and finds in ver. 24 a longing for suicide, or death by the hand of another. The Syriac likewise reads בּי, although it avoids this absurdity. Jerome makes an address of the assertion, and, moreover, also moulds the text under the influence of the Midrash. Aq., Symm., and Theod. strive after a better rendering than the LXX., but (to judge from the fragments in the *Hexapla*) without success. Saadia and Gecatilia wring a sense out of ver. 24a, but at the expense of the syntax, and by dragging ver. 24b after it, contrary to the tenor of the words. The old expositors also advance nothing available. They mostly interpret it as though it were not לָהֶן, but לָהֶם (a reading which has been forced into the Midrash texts and some Codd. instead of the reading of the text that is handed down to us). Even Rosenm. thinks לָהֶן might, like the Aram. לְהֵן, be equivalent to לָהֶם; and Carey explains the *enallage generis* from the perhaps existing secondary idea of womanly fear, as 2 Sam. iv. 6, הֵנָּה instead of הֵמָּה is used of the two assassins to describe them as cowards. But the Hebr. לָהֶן is *fem.;* and often as the *enallage masc. pro fem.* occurs, the *enallage fem. pro masc.* is unknown; הֵנָּה, 2 Sam. iv. 6, is an adv. of place (*vid.*, moreover, Thenius *in loc.*). It is just as absolutely inadmissible when the old expositors combine שׁוּעַ with שַׁע (וֶשַׁע), or as *e.g.* Raschi with עֲשֵׁעַ, and translate, "welfare" or "exhilaration" (refreshing). The signif. "wealth" would be more readily admissible, so that שׁוּעַ, as Aben-Ezra observes, would be the subst. to שׁוֹעַ, ch. xxxiv. 19; but in ch. xxxvi. 19 (which see), שׁוּעַ (as שֹׁעַ Isa. xxii. 5) signifies a cry of distress (= שֶׁוַע), and an attempt must be made here with this meaning before every other.

On the other hand comes the question whether בְּעִי is not perhaps to be referred to the verb בָּעָה, whether it be as subst. after the form מְרִי (Ralbag after the Targ.) or as *part.*

pass. (Saad. غيرانه ليس المبتغى, "only that it is not desired"). The verb does not, indeed, occur elsewhere in the
book of Job, but is very consistent with its style, which so
abounds in Aramaisms, and is at the same time so coloured
with Arabic that we should almost say, its Hauranitish style.[1]
Thus taking בעי as one word, Ralbag transl.: prayer stretches
not forth the hand, which is intended to mean: is not able to
do anything, cannot cause the will of God to miscarry. This
meaning is only obtained by great·violence; but when Renan
(together with Böckel and Carey, after Rosenm.) translates:
*Vaines prières ! . . . il étend sa main ; à quoi bon protester
contre ses coups ?* the one may be measured with the other.
If בעי is to be derived from בעה, it must be translated either:
shall He, however, without prayer (*sine imploratione*), or:
shall He, however, unimplored (*non imploratus*), stretch out
His hand ? The thought remains the same by both renderings of בעי, and suits as a vindication of the cry for help in
the context. But בָּעָה, in the specific signification *implorare,
deprecari,* is indeed the usage of the Targum, although strange
to the Hebr., which is here so rich in synonyms; then, in the
former case, לא for בלא is harsh, and in the other, בעי as *part.
pass.* is too strong an Aramaism. We must therefore consider whether בְּעִי as עִי with the *præp.* בְּ gives a suitable
sense. Since שָׁלַח יָד בְּ, *e.g.* ch. xxviii. 9 and elsewhere, most
commonly means "to lay the hand on anything, stretch out
the hand to anything," it is most natural to take בעי in de-

---

[1] The verb بغا is still extensively used in Syria, and that in two forms:
بغا يبغى and بغا يبغا. In Damascus the *fut. i* is alone used; whereas in Hauran and the steppe I have only found *fut. a.* Thus *e.g.* the
Hauranite poet *Kâsim el-Chinn* says: "The gracious God encompass thee
with His favour and whatever thy soul desires (*wa-l-nefsu ma tebghâ*), it
must obtain its desire" (*tanûlu munâhâ*, in connection with which it is to
be observed that نال *fut. u* is used here in the signification *adipisci,*
comp. Fleischer on ch. xv. 29 [*supra* i. 270, note]).—WETZST.

pendence upon יָדוֹ יִשְׁלַח, and we really gain an impressive
thought, if we translate : Only may He not stretch out His
hand (to continue His work of destruction) to a heap of
rubbish (which I am already become) ; but by this translation
of ver. 24a, ver. 24b remains a glaring puzzle, insoluble in
itself and in respect of the further course of the thought, for
Schlottmann's interpretation, "Only one does not touch ruins,
or the ruin of one is the salvation of another," which is itself
puzzling, is no solution. The reproach against the friends
which is said to lie in ver. 24a is contrary to the character of
this monologue, which is turned away from his human opponents; then שׁוּעַ does not signify salvation, and there is no "one"
and "another" to be found in the text. We must therefore,
against our inclination, give up this dependent relation of בְּעִי,
so that בְּעִי signifies either, upon a heap of rubbish, or, since this
ought to be עֲלֵי־עִי : by the falling in ; עִי (from עָוָה = 'iwj) can
mean both : a falling in or overthrow (bouleversement) as an
event, and ruins or rubbish as its result. Accordingly Hirz.
translates : Only upon the ruins (more correctly at least : upon
ruins) one will not stretch out his hand, and Ew.: Only—
does not one stretch out one's hand by one's overthrow ? But
this "only" is awkward. Hahn is of opinion that אַךְ לֹא may
be taken in the signification not once, and translates : may
one not for once raise one's hand by one's downfall ; but even
this is lame, because then all connection with what precedes
is wanting ; besides, אַךְ לֹא does not signify ne quidem. The
originally affirmative אַךְ has certainly for the most part a
restrictive signification, which, as we observed on ch. xviii. 21,
is blended with the affirmative in Hebr., but it is also, as
more frequently אָכֵן, used adversatively, e.g. ch. xvi. 7, and
in the combination אַךְ לֹא this adversative signification coincides with the restrictive, for this double particle signifies
everywhere else : only not, however not, Gen. xx. 12, 1 Kings
xi. 39, 2 Kings xii. 14, xiii. 6, xxiii. 9, 26. It would be more

natural to translate, as we have stated above: only may he not, etc., but ver. 24*b* puts in its veto against this. If, as Hirz., Ew., and Hahn also suppose, לֹא, ver. 24*a*, is equivalent to הֲלֹא, so that the sentence is to be spoken with an interrogative accent, we must translate אַךְ as Jer. has done, by *veruntamen*. He knows that he is being hurried forth to meet death; he knows it, and has also already made himself so familiar with this thought, that the sooner he sees an end put to this his sorrowful life the better—nevertheless does one not stretch out one's hand when one is falling? This involuntary reaction against destruction is the inevitable result of man's instinct of self-preservation. It needs no proof that שָׁלַח יָד can signify "to stretch out one's hand for help;" יִשְׁלַח is used with a general subj.: one stretches out, as ch. xvii. 5, xxi. 22. With this determination of the idea of ver. 24*a*, 24*b* is now also naturally connected with what precedes. It is not, however, to be translated, as Ew. and Hirz.: if one is in distress, is not a cry for help heard on account of it? If אִם were intended hypothetically, a continuation of the power of the interrogative לֹא from ver. 24*a* would be altogether impossible. Hahn and Loch-Reischl rightly take אִם in the sense of *an*. It introduces another turn of the question: Does one, however, not stretch out one's hand to hasten the fall, or in his downfall (raise) a cry for help, or a wail, on that account? Döderlein's conjecture, לְחֵן for לְהֶן (praying "for favour"), deserves respectful mention, but it is not needed: לְהֶן signifies neutrally: in (under) such circumstances (comp. בָּהֶם, ch. xxii. 21, Isa. lxiv. 5), or is directly equivalent to לְהֵן, which (Ruth i. 13) signifies *propterea*, and even in biblical Chaldee, beside the Chaldee signif. *sed, nisi*, retains this Hebrew signif. (Dan. ii. 6, 9, iv. 24). פִּיד, which signifies dying and destruction (Talmud. in the peculiar signif.: that which is hewn or pecked open), synon. of אֵיד, has been already discussed on ch. xii. 5.

Ver. 25. The further progress of the thoughts seems to be well carried out only by our rendering of ver. 24. The manifestation of feeling—Job means to say—which he himself felt at the misfortune of others, will be still permitted to him in his own misfortune, the seeking of compassion from the sympathising: or have I not wept for the hard of day? *i.e.* him whose lot in life is hard (comp. قَسِى, *durus, miser*); did not my soul grieve for the needy? Here, also, לֹא from ver. 25a continues its effect (comp. ch. iii. 10, xxviii. 17); עָנֵם is ἄπ. γεγρ., of like signification with אָגֵם, whence אָגְמֵי Isa. xix. 10, אֲגֻמָּה (sadness) *b. Moëd katan* 14*b*, Arab. *agima*, to feel disgust. If the relation of ver. 25 to ver. 24 is confirmatory, ver. 26 and what follows refers directly to ver. 24: he who felt sympathy with the sufferings of others will nevertheless dare in his own affliction to stretch out his hand for help in the face of certain ruin, and pour forth his pain in lamentation; for his affliction is in reality inexpressibly great: he hoped for good (for the future from his prosperous condition, in which he rejoiced),[1] then came evil; and if I waited for light, deep darkness came.   Ewald (§ 232, *h*) regards וָאֲיַחֵלָה as contracted from וָאֲיִחֵלָה, but this shortening of the vowel is a pure impossibility. The former signifies rather καὶ ἤλπιζον or ἐβουλόμην ἐλπίζειν, the latter καὶ ἤλπισα, and that cohortative *fut.* logically forms a hypothetical antecedent, exactly like ch. xix. 18, if I desire to rise (אָקוּמָה), they speak against me (*vid.* Ew. § 357, *b*). In feverish heat and anxiety his bowels were set boiling (רָתַח as ch. xli. 23, comp. Talmud. רְתָחָן, a hot-headed fellow), and rested not (from this boiling). The accentuation *Tarcha, Mercha,* and *Athnach* is here incorrect; instead of *Athnach, Rebia mugrasch* is required. Days of affliction came upon him (קָדֵם as Ps. xviii. 6), viz.

---

[1] LXX. *Aldina: ἐγὼ δὲ ἀπίχων ἀγαθοῖς,* which Zwingli rightly corrects ἐπίχων (*Codd. Vat., Alex.,* and *Sinait.*).

as a hostile power cutting off the previous way of his prosperity.

28 *I wandered about in mourning without the sun ;*
   I rose in the assembly, I gave free course to my complaint.
29 *I am become a brother of the jackals*
   And a companion of ostriches.
30 *My skin having become black, peels off from me,*
   And my bones are parched with dryness.
31 *My harp was turned to mourning,*
   And my pipe to tones of sorrow.

Several expositors (Umbr., Vaih., Hlgst.) understand קֹדֵר
of the dirty-black skin of the leper, but contrary to the usage
of the language, according to which, in similar utterances (Ps.
xxxv. 14, xxxviii. 7, xlii. 10, xliii. 2, comp. *supra*, ch. v. 11),

it rather denotes the dirty-black dress of mourners (comp. قَذَّرَ,

conspurcare vestem); to understand it of the dirty-black skin
as *quasi sordida veste* (Welte) is inadmissible, since this dis-
tortion of the skin which Job bewails in ver. 30 would hardly
be spoken of thus tautologically.   קדר therefore means in the
black of the שַׂק, or mourning-linen, ch. xvi. 15, by which, however, also the interpretation of בְּלֹא חַמָּה, "without sunburn"
(Ew., Hirz.), which has gained ground since Raschi's day (לֹא
שְׁשׁוּפַתְנִי הַשֶּׁמֶשׁ), is disposed of ; for "one can perhaps say of the
blackness of the skin that it does not proceed from the sun,
but not of the blackness of mourning attire" (Hahn). קדר
also refutes the reading בלא חֵמָה in LXX. *Complut.* (ἄνευ
θυμοῦ),[1] Syr., Jer. (*sine furore*), which ought to be understood
of the deposition of the gall-pigment on the skin, and therefore
of jaundice, which turns it (especially in tropical regions) not
merely yellow, but a dark-brown.   Hahn and a few others

---

[1] Whereas *Codd. Alex., Vat.,* and *Sinait.,* ἄνευ φιμοῦ, which is correctly explained by κημοῦ in Zwingli's *Aldine,* but gives no sense.

170   THE BOOK OF JOB.

render בלא חמה correctly in the sense of בחשך, "without the sun
having shone on him." Bereft of all his possessions, and finally
also of his children, he wanders about in mourning (הֵלֵּךְ as ch.
xxiv. 10, Ps. xxxviii. 7), and even the sun had clothed itself
in black to him (which is what קֹדֵר הַשֶּׁמֶשׁ means, Joel ii. 10
and freq.); the celestial light, which otherwise brightened his
path, ch. xxix. 3, was become invisible. We must not forget
that Job here reviews the whole chain of afflictions which have
come upon him, so that by ver. 28a we have not to think
exclusively, and also not prominently, of the leprosy, since
הלכתי indeed represents him as still able to move about freely.
In ver. 28b the accentuation wavers between Dechî, Munach,
Silluk, according to which בַּקָּהָל אֲשַׁוֵּעַ belong together, which
is favoured by the Dagesh in the Beth, and Tarcha, Munach,
Silluk, according to which (because Munach, according to
Psalter ii. 503, § 2, is a transformation of Rebia mugrasch)
קַמְתִּי בַּקָּהָל belong together. The latter mode of accentuation,
according to which בקהל must be written without the Dag.
instead of בַּקָּהָל (vid. Norzi), is the only correct one (because
Dechî cannot come in the last member of the sentence before
Silluk), and is also more pleasing as to matter: I rose (and
stood) in the assembly, crying for help, or more generally:
wailing. The assembly is not to be thought of as an assembly
of the people, or even tribunal (Ew.: "before the tribunal
seeking a judge, with lamentations"), but as the public; for
the thought that Job sought help against his unmerited sufferings before a human tribunal is absurd; and, moreover,
the thought that he cried for help before an assembly of the
people called together to take counsel and pronounce decisions
is equally absurd. Welte, however, who interprets: I was as
one who, before an assembled tribunal, etc., introduces a
quasi of which there is no trace in the text. בַּקָּהָל must
therefore, without pressing it further, be taken in the sense
of publice, before all the world (Hirz.: comp. בְּקָהָל, ἐν

φανερῷ, Prov. xxvi. 26); אִשֶּׁוַע, however, is a circumstantial clause declaring the purpose (Ew. § 337, *b;* comp. De Sacy, *Gramm. Arabe* ii. § 357), as is frequently the case after קוּם, ch. xvi. 8, Ps. lxxxviii. 11, cii. 14: *surrexi in publico ut lamentarer,* or *lamentaturus,* or *lamentando.* In this lament, extorted by the most intense pain, which he cannot hold back, however many may surround him, he is become a brother of those תַּנִּים, jackals (*canes aurei*), whose dolorous howling produces dejection and shuddering in all who hear it, and a companion of בְּנוֹת יַעֲנָה, whose shrill cry is varied by wailing tones of deep melancholy.[1] The point of comparison is not the insensibility of the hearers (*Sforno*), but the fellowship of wailing and howling together with the accompanying idea of the desert in which it is heard, which is connected with the idea itself (comp. Mic. i. 8).

Ver. 30. Now for the first time he speaks of his disfigurement by leprosy in particular: my skin (עוֹרִי, *masc.,* as it is also used in ch. xix. 26, only apparently as *fem.*) is become black (*nigruit*) from me, *i.e.* being become black, has peeled from me, and my bones (עַצְמִי, construed as *fem.* like ch. xix. 20, Ps. cii. 6) are consumed, or put in a glow (חָרָה, *Milel,*

---

[1] It is worth while to cite a passage from Shaw's *Travels in Barbary,* ii. 348 (transl.), here: "When the ostriches are running and fighting, they sometimes make a wild, hideous, hissing noise with their throats distended and beaks open ; at another time, if they meet with a slight opposition, they have a glucking or cackling voice like our domestic fowls : they seem to rejoice and laugh at the terror of their adversary. During the loneliness of the night however, as if their voice had a totally different tone, they often set up a dolorous, hideous moan, which at one time resembles the roar of the lion, and at another is more like the hoarser voice of other quadrupeds, especially the bull and cow. I have often heard them groan as if they were in the greatest agonies." In General Doumas' book on the *Horse of the Sahara,* I have read that the male ostrich (*delim*), when it is killed, especially if its young ones are near, sends forth a dolorous note, while the female (*remda*), on the other hand, does not utter a sound; and so, when the ostrich digs out its nest, one hears a languishing and dolorous tone all day long, and when it has laid its egg, its usual cry is again heard, only about three o'clock in the afternoon.

from חָרֵר, as Ezek. xxiv. 11) by a parching heat. Thus, then, his harp became mournful, and his pipe (וְעֻגָּבִי with ג raphatum) the cry of the weepers; the cheerful music (comp. ch. xxi. 12) has been turned into gloomy weeping and sobbing (comp. Lam. v. 15). Thus the second part of the monologue closes. It is somewhat lengthened and tedious; it is Job's last sorrow-ful lament before the catastrophe. What a delicate touch of the poet is it that he makes this lament, ver. 31, die away so melodiously! One hears the prolonged vibration of its elegiac strains. The festive and joyous music is hushed; the only tones are tones of sadness and lament, *mesto, flebile*.

THE THIRD PART OF THE MONOLOGUE.—CHAP. XXXI.

Schema: 8. 9. 8. 6. 6. 10. 10. 4. 4. 5. 7. 6.

1 *I have made a covenant with mine eyes,*
   And how should I fix my gaze upon a maiden!
2 *What then would be the dispensation of Eloah from above,*
   And the inheritance of the Almighty from the heights—
3 *Doth not calamity overtake the wicked,*
   And misfortune the workers of evil?
4 *Doth He not see my ways*
   And count all my steps?

After Job has described and bewailed the harsh contrast between the former days and the present, he gives us a picture of his moral life and endeavour, in connection with the character of which the explanation of his present affliction as a divinely decreed punishment becomes impossible, and the sudden overthrow of his prosperity into this abyss of suffer-ing becomes to him, for the same reason, the most painful mystery. Job is not an Israelite, he is without the pale of the positive, Sinaitic revelation; his religion is the old patri-archal religion, which even in the present day is called *dîn Ibrâhîm* (the religion of Abraham), or *dîn el-bedu* (the

religion of the steppe) as the religion of those Arabs who are
not Moslem, or at least influenced by the penetrating Islamism,
and is called by Mejânîshî *el-hanîfîje* (*vid. supra*, i. p. 216,
note) as the patriarchally orthodox religion.[1] As little as
this religion, even in the present day, is acquainted with the
specific Mohammedan commandments, so little knew Job of
the specifically Israelitish. On the contrary, his confession,
which he lays down in this third monologue, coincides remarkably with the ten commandments of piety (*el-felâh*)
peculiar to the *dîn Ibrâhîm*, although it differs in this respect,
that it does not give the prominence to submission to the
dispensations of God, that *teslîm* which, as the whole of this
didactic poem teaches by its issue, is the duty of the perfectly pious; also bravery in defence of holy property and
rights is wanting, which among the wandering tribes is
accounted as an essential part of the *hebbet er-rîh* (inspiration
of the Divine Being), *i.e.* active piety, and to which it is
similarly related, as to the binding notion of "honour" which
was coined by the western chivalry of the middle ages.

Job begins with the duty of chastity. Consistently with the
prologue, which the drama itself nowhere belies, he is living in
monogamy, as at the present day the orthodox Arabs, averse to
Islamism, are not addicted to Moslem polygamy. With the

---

[1] Also in the *Merg* district east of Damascus, which is peopled by
an ancient unmixed race, because the fever which prevails there kills
strangers, remnants of the *dîn Ibrâhîm* have been preserved despite the
penetrating Islamism.   There the *mulaqqin* (Souffleur), who says the
creed into the grave as a farewell to the buried one, adds the following
words : "The *muslim* is my brother, the *muslima* my sister, Abraham is
my father (*abî*), his religion (*dînuh*) is mine, and his confession (*medh-
hebuh*) mine."   It is indisputable that the words *muslim* (one who is submissive to God) and *islâm* (submission to God) have originally belonged
to the *dîn Ibrâhîm*.   It is also remarkable that the Moslem salutation
selâm occurs only as a sign in war among the wandering tribes, and that
the guest parts from his host with the words: *dâimâ besât el-Chalîl, lâ
maqtû' walâ memnû'*, *i.e.* mayest thou always have Abraham's table, and
plenty of provisions and guests.—WETZST.

confession of having maintained this marriage (although, to
infer from the prologue, it was not an over-happy, deeply
sympathetic one) sacred, and restrained himself not only from
every adulterous act, but also from adulterous desires, his
confessions begin. Here, in the middle of the Old Testament, without the pale of the Old Testament νόμος, we meet
just that moral strictness and depth with which the Preacher
on the mount, Matt. v. 27 sq., opposes the spirit to the letter
of the seventh commandment. It is לְעֵינַי, not עַם־עֵינַי (comp.
ch. xl. 28), designedly ; כרת ברית עם or אֶת is the usual phrase
where two equals are concerned ; on the contrary, כרת ברית לְ
where the superior—Jehovah, or a king, or conqueror—binds
himself to another under prescribed conditions, or the covenant is made not so much by a mutual advance as by the one
taking the initiative. In this latter case, the secondary notions
of a promise given (e.g. Isa. lv. 3), or even, as here, of a law
prescribed, are combined with כרת ברית : "as lord of my
senses I prescribed this law for my eyes " (Ew.). The eyes,
says a Talmudic proverb, are the procuresses of sin (סרסורי
דחטאה נינהו) ; " to close his eyes, that they may not feast on
evil," is, in Isa. xxxiii. 15, a clearly defined line in the picture
of him on whom the everlasting burnings can have no hold.
The exclamation, ver. 1b, is spoken with self-conscious indignation : Why should I . . . (comp. Joseph's exclamation,
Gen. xxxix. 9) ; Schultens correctly : est indignatio repellens
vehementissime et negans tale quicquam committi par esse ; the
transition of the מה, ﻻ, to the expression of negation, which
is complete in Arabic, is here in its incipient state, Ew.
§ 325, b. הִתְבּוֹנֵן עַל is intended to express a fixed and inspect-
ing (comp. אֶל, 1 Kings iii. 21) gaze upon an object, combined
with a lascivious imagination (comp. Sir. ix. 5, παρθένον μὴ
καταμάνθανε, and ix. 8, ἀπόστρεψον ὀφθαλμὸν ἀπὸ γυναικὸς
εὐμόρφου καὶ μὴ καταμάνθανε κάλλος ἀλλότριον), a βλέπειν
which issues in ἐπιθυμῆσαι αὐτήν, Matt. v. 28. Adulterium

reale, and in fact two-sided, is first spoken of in the third strophe, here it is *adulterium mentale* and one-sided ; the object named is not any maiden whatever, but any בְּתוּלָה, because virginity is ever to be revered, a most sacred thing, the holy purity of which Job acknowledges himself to have guarded against profanation from any lascivious gaze by keeping a strict watch over his eyes. The *Waw* of וּמָה is, as in ver. 14, copulative : and if I had done it, what punishment might I have looked for ?

The question, ver. 2, is proposed in order that it may be answered in ver. 3 again in the form of a question : in consideration of the just punishment which the injurer of female innocence meets, Job disavows every unchaste look. On חֵלֶק and נַחֲלָה used of allotted, adjudged punishment, comp. ch. xx. 29, xxvii. 13 ; on נֵכֶר, which alternates with אֵיד (burden of suffering, misfortune), comp. Obad. ver. 12, where in its stead נָכְרִי occurs, as Arab. *nukr*, properly *id quod patienti paradoxum, insuetum, intolerabile videtur, omne ingratum* (Reiske). Conscious of the just punishment of the unchaste, and, as he adds in ver. 4, of the omniscience of the heavenly Judge, Job has made dominion over sin, even in its first beginnings and motions, his principle.

The הוּא, which gives prominence to the subject, means Him who punishes the unchaste. By Him who observes his walk on every side, and counts (יִסְפּוֹר, *plene*, according to Ew. § 138, *a*, on account of the pause, but *vid.* the similar form of writing, ch. xxxix. 2, xviii. 15) all his steps, Job has been kept back from sin, and to Him Job can appeal as a witness.

> 5 *If I had intercourse with falsehood,*
> *And my foot hastened after deceit :*
> 6 *Let Him weigh me in the balances of justice,*
> *And let Eloah know my innocence.*

7 *If my steps turned aside from the way,*
   And my heart followed mine eyes,
   And any spot hath cleaved to my hands:
8 *May I sow and another eat,*
   And let my shoots be rooted out.

We have translated שָׁוְא (on the form *vid.* on ch. xv. 31, and the idea on ch. xi. 11) falsehood, for it signifies desolateness and hollowness under a concealing mask, therefore the contradiction between what is without and within, lying and deceit, parall. מִרְמָה, deceit, delusion, imposition. The phrase הָלַךְ עִם־שָׁוְא is based on the personification of deceit, or on thinking of it in connection with the מְתֵי־שָׁוְא (ch. xi. 11). The form וַתַּחַשׁ cannot be derived from חוּשׁ, from which it ought to be וַתֵּחַשׁ, like וַיֵּסַר Judg. iv. 18 and freq., וַיֵּשַׁר (*serravit*) 1 Chron. xx. 3, וַיֵּעַם (*increpavit*) 1 Sam. xxv. 14. Many grammarians (Ges. § 72, rem. 9; Olsh. 257, *g*) explain the *Pathach* instead of *Kametz* as arising from the virtual doubling of the guttural (*Dagesh forte implicitum*), for which, however, no ground exists here; Ewald (§ 232, *b*) explains it by "the hastening of the tone towards the beginning," which explains nothing, since the retreat of the tone has not this effect anywhere else. We must content ourselves with the supposition that וַתַּחַשׁ is formed from a חָשָׁה having a similar meaning to חוּשׁ (חִישׁ), as also וַיֵּעַט, 1 Sam. xv. 19, comp. xiv. 32, is from a עָטָה of similar signification with עִיט. The hypothetical antecedent, ver. 5, is followed by the conclusion, ver. 6: If he have done this, may God not spare him. He has, however, not done it; and if God puts him to an impartial trial, He will learn his תֻּמָּה, *integritas*, purity of character. The "balance of justice" is the balance of the final judgment, which the Arabs call ميزان الاعمال, "the balance of actions (works)."[1]

[1] The manual of ethics by Ghazzâli is entitled *mîzân el-aʿmâl* in the

Ver. 7 also begins hypothetically: if my steps (אֲשֻׁרִי from אָשֻׁר, which is used alternately with אָשׁוּר without distinction, contrary to Ew. § 260, *b*) swerve (תִּטֶּה, the predicate to the *plur.* which follows, designating a thing, according to Ges. § 146, 3) from the way (*i.e.* the one right way), and my heart went after my eyes, *i.e.* if it followed the drawing of the lust of the eye, viz. to obtain by deceit or extortion the property of another, and if a spot (מְאוּם, *macula*, as Dan. i. 4, = מוּם, ch. xi. 15; according to Ew., equivalent to מְחוּם, what is blackened and blackens, then a blemish, and according to Olsh., in מְאוּמָה . . . לֹא, like the French *ne . . . point*) clave to my hands: I will sow, and let another eat, and let my shoots be rooted out. The poet uses צֶאֱצָאִים elsewhere of off-spring of the body or posterity, ch. v. 25, xxi. 8, xxvii. 14; here, however, as in Isaiah, with whom he has this word in common, ch. xxxiv. 2, xlii. 5, the produce of the ground is meant. Ver. 8*a* is, according to John iv. 37, a λόγος, proverb. In so far as he may have acted thus, Job calls down upon himself the curse of Deut. xxviii. 30 sq.: what he sows, let strangers reap and eat; and even when that which is sown does not fall into the hands of strangers, let it be uprooted.

> 9 *If my heart has been befooled about a woman,*
>   *And if I lay in wait at my neighbour's door:*
> 10 *Let my wife grind unto another,*
>   *And let others bow down over her.*
> 11 *For this is an infamous act,*
>   *And this is a crime [to be brought before] judges;*
> 12 *Yea, it is a fire that consumeth to the abyss,*
>   *And should root out all my increase.*

As he has guarded himself against defiling virgin innocence

original, מֹאזְנֵי צֶדֶק in Bar-Chisdai's translation, *vid.* Gosche on Ghazzâli's life and works, S. 261 of the volume of the *Berliner Akademie d. Wissensch.* for 1858.

'by lascivious glances, so is he also conscious of having made
no attempt to trespass upon the marriage relationship of his
neighbour (עֵ֫ as in the Decalogue, Ex. xx. 17) : his heart
was not persuaded, or he did not allow his heart to be persuaded (נִפְתָּה like πείθεσθαι), *i.e.* misled, on account of a
woman (אִשָּׁה as אִ֫ישׁ אֵ֫שֶׁת אֵ֫שֶׁת, in post-bibl. usage, of another's
wife), and he lay not in wait (according to the manner of
adulterous lovers described at ch. xxiv. 15, which see) at his
neighbour's door. We may here, with Wetzstein, compare the
like-minded confession in a poem of Muhâdi ibn-Muhammel :

ما نَبّ كَلبُ الجّارِ مِنّا ولا عَوَى, *i.e.* "The neighbour's dog

never barked (נَב, Beduin equivalent to נבח in the Syrian
towns and villages) on our account (because we had gone by
night with an evil design to his tent), and it never howled
(being beaten by us, to make it cease its barking lest it should
betray us)." In ver. 10 follows the punishment which he
wishes might overtake him in case he had acted thus : " may
my wife grind to another," *i.e.* may she become his "maid
behind the mill," Ex. xi. 5, comp. Isa. xlvii. 2, who must
allow herself to be used for everything; ἀλετρίς and a
common low woman (comp. Plutarch, *non posse suav. viv.*
c. 21, καὶ παχυσκελὴς ἀλετρὶς πρὸς μύλην κινουμένη) are
almost one and the same. On the other hand, the Targ.
(*coeat cum alio*), LXX. (euphemistically ἀρέσαι ἑτέρῳ, not,
as the Syr. Hexapl. shows, ἀλέσαι), and Jer. (*scortum sit
alterius*), and in like manner Saad., Gecat., understand תִּטְחַן
directly of carnal surrender ; and, in fact, according to the
traditional opinion, *b. Sota* 10a : אֵין טחינה אלא לשון עבירה, *i.e.*
"טחן everywhere in Scripture is intended of (carnal) trespass."
With reference to Judg. xvi. 21 and Lam. v. 13 (where טְחוֹן,

like طَاحُون, signifies the upper mill-stone, or in gen. the mill),

this is certainly incorrect; the parallel, as well as Deut.

xxviii. 30, favours this rendering of the word in the obscene
sense of μύλλειν, *molere*, in this passage, which also is seen
under the Arab. synon. of grinding, دَكَّ (*trudere*); according to which it would have to be interpreted: let her grind
to another, *i.e.* serve him as it were as a nether mill-stone.
The verb טָחַן, used elsewhere (in Talmud.) of the man, would
here be transferred to the woman, like as it is used of the mill
itself as that which grinds. This rendering is therefore not
refuted by its being תִּטְחַן and not תִּטְחֶה. Moreover, the word
thus understood is not unworthy of the poet, since he designedly makes Job seize the strongest expressions. Among
moderns, תטחן is thus tropically explained by Ew., Umbr.,
Hahn, and a few others, but most expositors prefer the proper
sense, in connection with which *molat* certainly, especially
with respect to ver. 9*b*, is also equivalent to *fiat pellex*. It is
hard to decide; nevertheless the preponderance of reasons
seems to us to be on the side of the traditional tropical rendering, by the side of which ver. 10*b* is not attached in progressive,
but in synonymous parallelism: *et super ea incurvent se alii,* יִכְרְעוּן
of the man, as in the phrase كرعت المرأة الى الرجل (*curvat
se mulier ad virum*) of the acquiescence of the woman; אַחֵרִין
is a poetical Aramaism, Ew. § 177, *a*. The sin of adultery,
in case he had committed it, ought to be punished by another
taking possession of his own wife, for that (הוּא a neutral *masc.*,
Keri הִיא in accordance with the *fem.* of the following predicate, comp. Lev. xviii. 17) is an infamous act, and that (הִיא
referring back to זִמָּה, *Keri* הוּא in accordance with the *masc.*
of the following predicate) is a crime for the judges. On
this wavering between הוּא and הִיא *vid.* Gesenius, *Handwörterbuch*, 1863, *s. v.* הוּא, S. 225. זִמָּה is the usual Thora-word
for the shameless subtle encroachments of sensual desires
(*vid.* Saalschütz, *Mosaisches Recht*, S. 791 f.), and עָוֹן פְּלִילִים
(not עָוֹן), according to the usual view equivalent to *crimen et*

crimen quidem judicum (however, on the form of connection
intentionally avoided here, where the genitival relation might
easily give an erroneous sense, *vid.* Ges. § 116, rem.), signifies
a crime which falls within the province of the penal code, for
which in ver. 28 it is less harshly פְּלִילִי עָוֹן: a judicial, *i.e.*
criminal offence. פְּלִילִים is, moreover, not the *plur.* of פְּלִילִי
(Kimchi), but of פָּלִיל, an arbitrator (root פַּל, *findere, dirimere*).

The confirmatory clause, ver. 12, is co-ordinate with the
preceding: for it (this criminal, adulterous enterprise) is a
fire, a fire consuming him who allows the sparks of sinful
desire to rise up within him (Prov. vi. 27 sq.; Sir. ix. 8),
which devours even to the bottom of the abyss, not resting
before it has dragged him whom it has seized down with it
into the deepest depth of ruin, and as it were melted him
away, and which ought to root out all my produce (all the
fruit of my labour).[1] The function of בְּ is questionable.
Ew. (§ 217, *f*) explains it as local: in my whole revenue, *i.e.*
throughout my whole domain. But it can also be *Beth objecti*,
whether it be that the obj. is conceived as the means of the
action (*vid.* on ch. xvi. 4, 5, 10, xx. 20), or that, "corresponding to the Greek genitive, it does not express an entire full
coincidence, but an action about and upon the object" (Ew.
§ 217, S. 557). We take it as *Beth obj.* in the latter sense,
after the analogy of the so-called pleonastic Arab. ـب (*e.g.*
qaraa bi-suwari, he has practised the act of reading upon the
Suras of the Koran): and which ought to undertake the act
of outrooting upon my whole produce.[2]

---

[1] It is something characteristically Semitic to express the notion of
destruction by the figure of burning up with fire [*vid. supra*, i. 377, note],
and it is so much used in the present day as a natural inalienable form of
thought, that in curses and imprecations everything, without distinction
of the object, is to be burned; *e.g. juhrik*, may (God) burn up, or *juhrak*,
ought to burn, *biláduh*, his native country, *bedenuh*, his body, *'ênuh*, his
eye, *shawâribuh*, his moustache (*i.e.* his honour), *nefesuh*, his breath,
'omruh, his life, etc.—WETZST.

[2] On this pleonastic *Beth obj.* (*el-Bâ el-mezîde*) *vid.* Samachschari's

13 *If I despised the cause of my servant and my maid,*
  When they contended with me:
14 *What should I do, if God should rise up,*
  And if He should make search, what should I answer Him?
15 *Hath not He who formed me in the womb formed him also,*
  And hath not One fashioned us in the belly?

It might happen, as ver. 13 assumes, that his servant or

his maid (אָמָה, اَمَة, denotes a maid who is not necessarily a

slave, 'abde, as ch. xix. 15, whereas שִׁפְחָה does not occur in
the book) contended with him, and in fact so that they on
their part began the dispute (for, as the Talmud correctly
points out, it is not בְּרִיבִי עִמָּם, but בְּרִיבָם עִמָּדִי), but he did not
then treat them as a despot; they were not accounted as *res*
but *personæ* by him, he allowed them to maintain their personal right in opposition to him. Christopher Scultetus observes here: *Gentiles quidem non concedebant jus servo contra
dominum, cui etiam vitæ necisque potestas in ipsum erat; sed
Iob amore justitiæ libere se demisit, ut vel per alios judices aut
arbitros litem talem curaret decidi vel sibi ipsi sit moderatus,
ut juste pronuntiaret.* If he were one who despised (אֶמְאַס,
not מָאַסְתִּי) his servants' cause: what should he do if God
arose and entered into judgment; and if He should appoint
an examination (thus Hahn correctly, for the conclusion
shows that פקד is here a synon. of בחן Ps. xvii. 3, and חקר Ps.
xliv. 22, فقَّد, V., VIII., *accurate inspicere*), what should he
answer?

Mufassal, ed. Broch, pp. 125, 132 (according to which it serves " to give
intensity and speciality "), and Beidhâwi's observation on *Sur.* ii. 191.
The most usual example for it is *alqa bi-jedeihi ila et-tahlike,* he has
plunged his hands, *i.e.* himself, into ruin. The *Bâ el-megâz* (the metaphorical *Beth obj.*) is similar; it is used where the verb has not its most
natural signification but a metaphorical one, *e.g. ashada bidhikrihi,* he
has strengthened his memory: comp. De Sacy, *Chrestomathie Arabe,* i. 397.

THE BOOK OF JOB.

Ver. 15. The same manner of birth, by the same divine
creative power and the same human agency, makes both
master and servant substantially brethren with equal claims:
Has not He who brought me forth in my mother's womb
(also) brought forth him (this my servant or my maid), and
has not One fashioned us in our mother's belly? אֶחָד, *unus*,
viz. God, is the subj., as Mal. ii. 10, אֶחָד (אָב) אֶל (for the
thought comp. Eph. vi. 9), as it is also translated by the
Targ., Jer., Saad., and Gecat.; whereas the LXX. (ἐν τῇ
αὐτῇ κοιλίᾳ), Syr., Symm. (as it appears from his translation
ἐν ὁμοίῳ τρόπῳ), construe אחד as the adj. to בְּרֶחֶם, which is
also the idea of the accentuation (*Rebia mugrasch, Mercha,
Silluk*). On the other hand, it has been observed (also
Norzi) that it ought to be הָאֶחָד according to this meaning;
but it was not absolutely necessary, vid. Ges. § 111, 2, *b*. אחד
also would not be unsuitable in this combination; it would, as
e.g. in חלום אחד, not affirm identity of number, but of character.
But אחד is far more significant, and as the final word of the
strophe more expressive, when referred to God. The form
וַיְכֻנֶנּוּ is to be judged of just like וַהֲמֻגֶנּוּ, Isa. lxiv. 6; either
they are forms of an exceptionally transitive (as שׁוּב, Ps.
lxxxv. 5, and in שׁוּב שְׁבוּת) use of the *Kal* of these verbs (*vid.
e.g.* Parchon and Kimchi), or they are syncopated forms of
the *Pilel* for וַיְכוֹנְנֵנּוּ וַתְּמוֹגְנֵנוּ, syncopated on account of the same
letters coming together, especially in ויכננו (Ew. § 81, *a*, and
most others); but this coincidence is sought elsewhere (*e.g.*
Ps. l. 23, Prov. i. 28), and not avoided in this manner (*e.g.* Ps.
cxix. 73). Beside this syncope וַיְכוֹנֵנּוּ might also be expected,
while according to express testimony the first *Nun* is *raphatum*:
we therefore prefer to derive these forms from *Kal*, without
regarding them, with Olsh., as errors in writing. The *suff*.
is rightly taken by LXX., Targ., Abulwalid, and almost all
expositors,[1] not as singular (*ennu* = *êhu*), but as plural (*ennu*

---

[1] Also in the Jerusalem Talmud, where R. Johanan, eating nothing

= énu) ; the Babylonian school pointed וַיְכוֹנֵנוּ, like מִמֶּנּוּ where it signifies a nobis, מִמֶּנּוּ (Psalter ii. 459, and further informa-tion in Pinsker's works, Zur Geschichte des Karaismus, and Ueber das sogen. assyrische Punktationssystem). Therefore: One, i.e. one and the same God, has fashioned us in the womb without our co-operation, in an equally animal way, which smites down all pride, in like absolute conditionedness.

16 If I held back the poor from what they desired,
  And caused the eyes of the widow to languish,
17 And ate my morsel alone
  Without letting the fatherless eat thereof:—
18 No indeed, from my youth he grew up to me as to a father,
  And from my mother's womb I guided her—

The whole strophe is the hypothetical antecedent of the imprecative conclusion, ver. 22 sq., which closes the following strophe. Since מָנַע דְּבָר מִמֶּנּוּ, cohibere aliquid ab aliquo (ch. xxii. 7), is said as much in accordance with the usage of the language as מָנַע מִדְּבָר, cohibere aliquem ab aliquo (Num. xxiv. 11, Eccl. ii. 10), in the sense of denegare alicui aliquid, there is no reason for taking מֵחֵפֶץ דַּלִּים together as a geni-tival clause (a voto tenuium), as the accentuation requires it. On חֵפֶץ, vid. on ch. xxi. 21; it signifies solicitude (what is ardently desired) and business, here the former: what is ever the interest and want of the poor (the reduced or those without means). From such like things he does not keep the poor back, i.e. does not refuse them; and the eyes of the widow

which he did not also share with his slave, refers to these words of Job. Comp. also the story from the Midrash in Guiseppe Levi's Parabeln Legenden und Ged. aus Thalmud und Midrasch, S. 141 (Germ. transl. 1863): The wife of R. Jose began a dispute with her maid. Her husband came up and asked the cause, and when he saw that his wife was in the wrong, told her so in the presence of the maid. The wife said in a rage: Thou sayest I am wrong in the presence of my maid? The Rabbi answered: I do as Job did.

he did not cause or allow to languish (כִּלָּה, to bring to an end, *i.e.* cause to languish, of the eyes, as Lev. xxvi. 16, 1 Sam. ii. 33); he let not their longing for assistance be consumed of itself, let not the fountain of their tears become dry without effect. If he had done the opposite, if he had eaten his bread (פַּת = פַּת לֶחֶם) alone, and not allowed the orphan to eat of it with him—but no, he had not acted thus; on the contrary (כִּי as Ps. cxxx. 4 and frequently), he (the parentless one) grew up to him (גְּדֵלַנִי = גָּדֵל לִי, Ges. § 121, 4, according to Ew. § 315, *b*, " by the interweaving of the dialects of the people into the ancient form of the declining language;" perhaps it is more correct to say it is by virtue of a poetic, forced, and rare brevity of expression) as to a father (= כְּמוֹ לְאָב), and from his mother's womb he guided her, the helpless and defenceless widow, like a faithful child leading its sick or aged mother. The hyperbolical expression מִבֶּטֶן אִמִּי dates this sympathizing and active charity back to the very beginning of Job's life. He means to say that it is in-born to him, and he has exercised it ever since he was first able to do so. The brevity of the form גְּדֵלַנִי, brief to incorrectness, might be removed by the pointing גִּדְּלַנִי (Olsh.): from my youth up he (the fatherless one) honoured me as a father; and גִּדְּלַנִי instead of כִּבְּדַנִי would be explained by the consideration, that a veneration is meant that attributed a dignity which exceeds his age to the נער who was not yet old enough to be a father. But גִּדֵּל signifies " to cause to grow" in such a connection elsewhere (parall. רוֹמֵם, to raise), wherefore LXX. translates ἐξέτρεφον (גִּדַּלְתִּי); and גְּדֵלַנִי has similar examples of the construction of intransitives with the *acc.* instead of the *dat.* (especially Zech. vii. 5) in its favour: they became me great, *i.e.* became great in respect of me. Other ways of getting over the difficulty are hardly worth mentioning: the Syriac version reads כְּאֵב (pain) and אֲנָחוֹת; Raschi makes ver. 18*a*, the idea of benevolence, the subj., and ver. 18*b* (as מִדָּה, attribute) the obj. The *suff.* of אֲנַחֲנָּה Schlottm. refers to the female orphan; but Job refers again to the orphan in the following strophe, and the reference to the widow, more natural here on account of the gender, has nothing against it. The choice of the verb (comp. ch. xxxviii. 32) also corresponds to such a reference, since the *Hiph.* has an intensified *Kal*-signification here.[1] From earliest youth, so far back as he can remember, he was wont to behave like a father to the orphan, and like a child to the widow.

19 *If I saw one perishing without clothing,*
   And that the needy had no covering;
20 *If his loins blessed me not,*
   And he did not warm himself from the hide of my lambs;
21 *If I have lifted up my hand over the orphan,*
   Because I saw my help in the gate:
22 *Let my shoulder fall out of its shoulder-blade,*
   And mine arm be broken from its bone;
23 *For terror would come upon me, the destruction of God,*
   And before His majesty I should not be able to stand.

On אוֹבֵד comp. on ch. iv. 11, xxix. 13; he who is come down from his right place and is perishing (root בד, to separate, still perfectly visible through the Arab. *bâda, ba'ida,* to perish), or also he who is already perished, *periens* and *perditus.* The clause, ver. 19*b*, forms the second obj. to אִם אֶרְאֶה, which otherwise signifies *si video,* but here, in accordance

---

[1] זכר and הַזְכִּיר, to remember; זרע and הִזְרִיע, to sow, to cover with seed; חרש and הֶחֱרִישׁ, both in the signification *silere* and *fabricari*; לענ and הֶלְעִינ, to mock, ch. xxi. 3; מָשַׁל and הִמְשִׁיל, *dominari,* ch. xxv. 2; נטה and הַטָּה, to extend, to bow; קנה and הִקְנָה (to obtain by purchase); קצר and הִקְצִיר, to reap, ch. xxiv. 6, are all similar. In Arab. the *Kal nahaituhu* signifies I put him aside by going on one side (*nahw* or *nâhije*), the *Hiph. anhaituhu,* I put him aside by bringing him to the side (comp. יְנַחֵם, ch. xii. 23).

with the connection, signifies *si videbam*. The blessing of the thankful (ch. xxix. 13) is transferred from the person to the limbs in ver. 20*a*, which need and are benefited by the warmth imparted. אִם־לֹא here is not an expression of an affirmative asseveration, but a negative turn to the continuation of the hypothetical antecedents. The shaking, הֲנִיף, of the hand, ver. 21*a*, is intended, like Isa. xi. 15, xix. 16 (comp. the *Pilel*, ch. x. 32), Zech. ii. 13, as a preparation for a crushing stroke. Job refrained himself from such designs upon the defenceless orphan, even when he saw his help in the gate, *i.e.* before the tribunal (ch. xxix. 7), *i.e.* even when he had a certain prospect of powerful assistance there. If he has acted otherwise, his כָּתֵף, *i.e.* his upper arm together with the shoulder, must fall out from its שְׁכֶם, *i.e.* the back which bears it together with the shoulder-blades, and his אֶזְרֹעַ, upper and lower arm, which is considered here according to its outward flesh, must be broken out of its קָנֶה, tube, *i.e.* the reed-like hollow bone which gives support to it, *i.e.* be broken asunder from its basis (Syr. *a radice sua*), this sinning arm, which did not compassionate the naked, and mercilessly threatened the defenceless and helpless. The ה *raphatum* which follows in both cases, and the express testimony of the Masora, show that מִשִּׁכְמָה and מִקָּנָה have no *Mappik*. The *He quiescens*, however, is in both instances softened from the *He mappic.* of the *suff.*, Ew. § 21, *f.* פַּחַד in ver. 23 is taken by most expositors as predicate : for terror is (was) to me evil as God, the righteous judge, decrees it. But אֵלַי is not favourable to this. It establishes the particular thing which he imprecates upon himself, and that consequently which, according to his own conviction and perception, ought justly to overtake him out of the general mass, viz. that terror ought to come upon him, a divinely decreed weight of affliction. אֵיד אֵל is a permutative of פַּחַד אֱלֹהִים = פַּחַד, and אֵלַי with *Dechî* equivalent to אֵלַי (יָבֹא) יִהְיֶה, comp. Jer. ii. 19 (where it is to be interpreted : and that thou lettest no fear before me

come over thee). Thus also ver. 23*b* is suitably connected
with the preceding : and I should not overcome His majesty,
i.e. I should succumb to it. The מִן corresponds to the *præ*
in *prævalerem;* שְׂאֵת (LXX. falsely, λῆμμα, judgment, decision = מַשָּׂא, Jer. *pondus*) is not intended otherwise than ch.
xiii. 11 (parall. פַּחַד as here).

24 *If I made gold my confidence,*
   And said to the fine gold : O my trust;
25 *If I rejoiced that my wealth was great,*
   And that my hand had gained much ;—
26 *If I saw the sunlight when it shone,*
   And the moon walking in splendour,
27 *And my heart was secretly enticed,*
   And I threw them a kiss by my hand:
28 *This also would be a punishable crime,*
   For I should have played the hypocrite to God above.

Not only from covetous extortion of another's goods was he
conscious of being clear, but also from an excessive delight in
earthly possessions. He has not made gold his כֶּסֶל, confidence
(*vid.* on בִּסְלָתֶךְ, ch. iv. 6) ; he has not said to כֶּתֶם, fine gold
(pure, ch. xxviii. 19, of Ophir, xxviii. 16), מִבְטַחִי (with *Dag.
forte implicitum* as ch. viii. 14, xviii. 14) : object (ground) of
my trust ! He has not rejoiced that his wealth is great (רַב,
adj.), and that his hand has attained כַּבִּיר, something great
(neutral *masc.* Ew. § 172, *b*). His joy was the fear of God,
which ennobles man, not earthly things, which are not worthy
to be accounted as man's highest good. He indeed avoided
πλεονεξία as εἰδωλολατρεία (Col. iii. 5), how much more
the heathenish deification of the stars ! אוֹר is here, as ch.
xxxvii. 21 and φάος in Homer, the sun as the great light of
the earth. יָרֵחַ is the moon as a wanderer (from רח = ארה),
i.e. night-wanderer (*noctivaga*), as the Arab. *tárik* in a like
sense is the name of the morning-star. The two words

יְקָר הֹלֵךְ, describe with exceeding beauty the solemn majestic wandering of the moon; יָקָר is *acc.* of closer definition, like תמים, Ps. xv. 2, and this "brilliantly rolling on" is the *acc.* of the predicate to אֶרְאֶה, corresponding to the כִּי יָהֵל, "that (or how) it shoots forth rays" (*Hiph.* of הָלַל, distinct from יֵחַל Isa. xiii. 20), or even: that it shot forth rays (*fut.* in signif. of an imperf. as Gen. xlviii. 17).

Ver. 27 proceeds with *futt. consec.* in order to express the effect which this imposing spectacle of the luminaries of the day and of the night might have produced on him, but has not. The *Kal* וַיִּפְתְּ is to be understood as in Deut. xi. 16 (comp. *ib.* iv. 19, נִדַּח): it was enticed, gave way to the seducing influence. Kissing is called נָשַׁק as being a joining of lip to lip. Accordingly the kiss by hand can be described by נָשְׁקָה יָד לְפֶּה; the kiss which the mouth gives the hand is to a certain extent also a kiss which the hand gives the mouth, since the hand joins itself to the mouth. Thus to kiss the hand in the direction of the object of veneration, or also to turn to it the kissed hand and at the same time the kiss which fastens on it (as compensation for the direct kiss, 1 Kings xix. 18, Hos. xiii. 2), is the proper gesture of the προσκύνησις and *adoratio* mentioned; comp. Pliny, *h. n.* xxviii. 2, 5: *Inter adorandum dexteram ad osculum referimus et totum corpus circumagimus.* Tacitus, *Hist.* iii. 24, says that in Syria they salute the rising sun; and that this was done by kissing the hand (τὴν χεῖρα κύσαντες) in Western Asia as in Greece, is to be inferred from Lucian's Περὶ ὀρχήσεως, c. xvii.[1] In the passage before us Ew. finds an indication of the spread of the Zoroaster doctrine in the beginning of the seventh century B.C., at which period he is of opinion the book of Job was composed, but without any ground. The ancient Persian

---

[1] *Vid.* Freund's *Lat. Wörterbuch s. v. adorare*, and K. Fr. Hermann's *Gottesdienstliche Alterth. der Griechen*, c. xxi. 16, but especially *Excursus* 123 in Dougtæus' *Analecta*.

worship has no knowledge of the act of adoration by throwing a kiss; and the Avesta recognises in the sun and moon exalted genii, but created by Ahuramazda, and consequently not such as are to be worshipped as gods. On the other hand, star-worship is everywhere the oldest and also comparatively the purest form of heathenism. That the ancient Arabs, especially the Himjarites, adored the sun, שֶׁמֶשׁ, and the moon, שִׂין (סִן, whence סִינַי, the mountain dedicated to the moon), as divine, we know from the ancient testimonies,[1] and many inscriptions[2] which confirm and supplement them; and the general result of Chwolsohn's[3] researches is unimpeachable, that the so-called Sabians (صابِوُن with or without *Hamza* of the *Jê*), of whom a section bore the name of worshippers of the sun, *shemsije*, were the remnant of the ancient heathenism of Western Asia, which lasted into the middle ages. This heathenism, which consisted, according to its basis, in the worship of the stars, was also spread over Syria, and its name, usually combined with צְבָא הַשָּׁמַיִם (Deut. iv. 19), perhaps is not wholly devoid of connection with the name of a district of Syria, אֲרַם צוֹבָה; certainly our poet found it already there, where he heard the tradition about Job, and in his hero presents to us a true adherent of the patriarchal religion, who had kept himself free from the influence of the worship of the stars, which was even in his time forcing its way among the tribes.

It is questionable whether ver. 28 is to be regarded as a conclusion, with Umbr. and others, or as a parenthesis, with Ew., Hahn, Schlottm., and others. We take it as a conclusion, against which there is no objection according to the syntax,

---

[1] *Vid.* the collection in Lud. Krehl's *Religion der vorislamischen Araber*, 1863.

[2] *Vid.* Osiander in the *Deutsche Morgenl. Zeitschr.* xvii. (1863) 795.

[3] In his great work, *Ueber die Ssabier und den Ssabismus*, 2 Bdd. Petersburg, 1856.

although strictly it is only a confirmation (*vid.* vers. 11, 23)
of an implied imprecatory conclusion: therefore it is (would
be) also a judicial misdeed, *i.e.* one to be severely punished,
for I should have played the hypocrite to God above (לְאֵל
מִמַּעַל, recalling the universal Arabic expression *allah ta'âla,*
God, the Exalted One) by making gold and silver, the sun
and moon my idols. By פְּלִילִי both the sins belonging to the
judgment-seat of God, as in ἔνοχος τῷ συνεδρίῳ, Matt. v. 22,
are not referred to a human tribunal, but only described κατ'
ἄνθρωπον as punishable transgressions of the highest grade.
כִּחֵשׁ לְ signifies to play the hypocrite to any one, whereas to
disown any one is expressed by כֹּחֵשׁ בְּ. His worship of God
would have been hypocrisy, if he had disowned in secret the
God whom he acknowledged openly and outwardly.

Now follow strophes to which the conclusion is wanting.
The single imprecatory conclusion which yet follows (ver. 40),
is not so worded that it might avail for all the preceding
hypothetical antecedents. There are therefore in these
strophes no conclusions that correspond to the other clauses.
The inward emotion of the confessor, which constantly increases in fervour the more he feels himself superior to his
accusers in the exemplariness of his life hitherto, struggles
against this rounding off of the periods. A "yea then — !"
is easily supplied in thought to these strophes which *per
aposiopesin* are devoid of conclusions.

> 29 *If I rejoiced over the destruction of him who hated me,*
>   *And became excited when evil came upon him—*
> 30 *Yet I did not allow my palate to sin*
>   *By calling down a curse upon his life.*

The aposiopesis is here manifest, for ver. 29 is evidently
equal to a solemn denial, to which ver. 30 is then attached as
a simple negative. He did not rejoice at the destruction

(פִיד, Arab. فَيْد, *fêd*,[1] as ch. xii. 5, xxx. 24) of his enemy who
was full of hatred towards him (מְשַׂנְאִי, elsewhere also שֹׂנְאִי),
and was not excited with delight (הִתְעֹרֵר, to excite one's self,
a description of emotion, whether it be pleasure, or as ch.
xvii. 8, displeasure, as a not merely passive but moral incident)
if calamity came upon him, and he did not allow his palate
(חֵךְ as the instrument of speech, like ch. vi. 30) to sin by
asking God that he might die as a curse. Love towards an
enemy is enjoined by the Thora, Ex. xxiii. 4, but it is more
or less with a national limitation, Lev. xix. 18, because the
Thora is the law of a people shut out from the rest of the
world, and in a state of war against it (according to which
Matt. v. 43 is to be understood); the books of the Chokma,
however (comp. Prov. xxiv. 17, xxv. 21), remove every limit
from the love of enemies, and recognise no difference, but
enjoin love towards man as man. With ver. 30 this strophe
closes. Among modern expositors, only Arnh. takes in ver.
31 as belonging to it: "Would not the people of my tent
then have said: Would that we had of his flesh?! we have
not had enough of it," *i.e.* we would eat him up both skin
and hair. Of course it does not mean after the manner of
cannibals, but figuratively, as ch. xix. 22; but in a figurative
sense "to eat any one's flesh" in Semitic is equivalent to
lacerare, vellicare, obtrectare (*vid.* on ch. xix. 22, and comp.
also *Sur.* xlix. 12 of the Koran, and Schultens' *Erpenius*,
pp. 592 sq.), which is not suitable here, as in general this
drawing of ver. 31 to ver. 29 sq. is in every respect, and

---

[1] Gesenius derives the noun פִיד from the verb פִיד, but the Arabic,
which is the test here, has not only the verb *fâda* as *med. u* and as *med. i*
in the signification to die, but also in connection with *el-feid* (*fêd*) the
substantival form *el-fîd* (= *el-môt*), which (= *fiwd*, comp. p. 26, *note*) is
referable to *fâda, med. u.* Thus *Neshwân*, who in his *Lexicon* (vol. ii.
fol. 119) even only knows *fâda, med. u*, in the signif. to die (comp. *infra*
on ch. xxxix. 18, *note*).

especially that of the syntax, inadmissible. It is the duty of beneficence, which Job acknowledges having practised, in ver. 31 sq.

31 *If the people of my tent were not obliged to say :*
   Where would there be one who has not been satisfied with
   his flesh? !—
32 *The stranger did not lodge out of doors,*
   I opened my door towards the street.

Instead of אָמְרוּ, it might also be יֹאמְרוּ (*dicebant*) ; the *perf.*, however, better denotes not merely what happens in a general way, but what must come to pass. The " people of the tent" are all who belong to it, like the Arab. *ahl* (tent, metonym. dwellers in the tent), here pre-eminently the servants, but without the expression in itself excluding wife, children, and relations. The optative מִי־יִתֵּן, so often spoken of already, is here, as in ver. 35, ch. xiv. 4, xxix. 2, followed by the *acc. objecti*, for נִשְׂבָּע is *part.* with the long accented *â* (*quis exhibebit* or *exhibeat non saturatum*), and מִבְּשָׂרוֹ is not meant of the flesh of the person (as even the LXX. in bad taste renders : that his maids would have willingly eaten him, their kind master, up from love to him), but of the flesh of the cattle of the host. Our translation follows the accentuation, which, however, perhaps proceeds from an interpretation like that of Arnheim given above. His constant and ready hospitality is connected with the mention of his abundant care and provision for his own household. It is unnecessary to take אֹרַח, with the ancient versions, for אָרַח, or so to read it ; לָאֹרַח signifies towards the street, where travellers are to be expected, comp. *Pirke aboth* i. 5 : " May thy house be open into the broad place (לָרְוָחָה), and may the poor be thy guests." The Arabs pride themselves on the exercise of hospitality. " To open a guest-chamber" is the same as to establish one's own household in Arabic. Stories of judgments by which the

want of hospitality has been visited, form an important element of the popular traditions of the Arabs.[1]

33 *If I have hidden my wickedness like Adam,*
   Concealing my guilt in my bosom,
34 *Because I feared the great multitude*
   And the contempt of families affrighted me,
   So that I acted secretly, went not out of the door.—

Most expositors translate כְּאָדָם : after the manner of men;
but appropriate as this meaning of the expression is in Ps.
lxxxii. 7, in accordance with the antithesis and the parallelism
(which see), it would be as tame here, and altogether expres-
sionless in the parallel passage Hos. vi. 7[2]—the passage which
comes mainly under consideration here—since the force of
the prophetic utterance: "they have כְאָדָם transgressed the
covenant," consists in this, "that Israel is accused of a trans-

---

[1] In the spring of 1860—relates Wetzstein—as I came out of the
forest of *Gôlan,* I saw the water of *Râm* lying before us, that beautiful
round crater in which a brook that runs both summer and winter forms
a clear but fishless lake, the outflow of which underground is recognised
as the fountain of the Jordan, which breaks forth below in the valley
out of the crater *Tell el-Kadi;* and I remarked to my companion, the
physician *Regeb,* the unusual form of the crater, when my Beduins, full
of astonishment, turned upon me with the question, "What have you
Franks heard of the origin of this lake?" On being asked what they
knew about it, they related how that many centuries ago a flourishing
village once stood here, the fields of which were the plain lying between
the water and the village of *Megdel Shems.* One evening a poor traveller
came while the men were sitting together in the open place in the middle
of the village, and begged for a supper and a resting-place for the night,
which they refused him. When he assured them that he had eaten nothing
since the day before, an old woman amidst general laughter reached out
a *gelle* (a cake of dried cow-dung, which is used for fuel), and drove him
out of the village. Thereupon the man went to the village of *Nimra*
(still standing, south of the lake), where he related his misfortune, and
was taken in by them. The next morning, when the inhabitants of Nimra
woke, they found a lake where the neighbouring village had stood.
[2] Pusey also (*The Minor Prophets with Commentary,* P. i. 1861) im-
proves "like men" by translating "like Adam."

gression which is only to be compared to that of the first
man created : here, as there, a like transgression of the expressed will of God" (von Hofmann, *Schriftbeweis*, i. 412f.);
as also, according to Rom. v. 14, Israel's transgression is that
fact in the historical development of redemption which stands
by the side of Adam's transgression. And the mention of
Adam in Hosea cannot surprise one, since he also shows himself in other respects to be familiar with the contents of
Genesis, and to refer back to it (*vid.* *Genesis*, S. 11-13).
Still much less surprising is such a reference to primeval
history in a book that belongs to the literature of the Chokma
(*vid.* Introduction, § 2). The descent of the human race from
a single pair, and the fall of those first created, are, moreover,
elements in all the ancient traditions ; and it is questionable
whether the designation of men by *beni Adama* (children of
Adam), among the Moslems, first sprang from the contact of
Judaism and Christianity, or whether it was not rather an
old Arabic expression. Therefore we translate with Targ.,
Schult., Bouillier, Rosenm., Hitz., Kurtz, and von Hofm. :
if I have hidden (disowned) like Adam my transgression.
The point of comparison is only the sinner's dread of the
light, which became prominent as the prototype for every
succeeding age in Adam's hiding himself. The לִטְמוֹן which
follows is meant not so much as indicating the aim, as gerundive (*abscondendo*) ; on this use of the *inf. constr.* with לְ, *vid.*
Ew. § 280, *d.* חֹב, bosom, is ἀπ. γεγρ. ; Ges. connects it with
the Arab. *habba*, to love ; it is, however, to be derived from
the חב, *occulere*, whence *chabîbe*, that which is deep within,
a deep valley (comp. חֲבָא, *chabaa*, with their derivatives) ; in
Aramaic it is the common word for the Hebr. חֵיק.

Ver. 34a. With כִּי follows the motive which Job might
have had for hiding himself with his sin : he has been neither
an open sinner, nor from fear of men and a feeling of honour
a secret sinner. He cherished within him no secret accursed

thing, and had no need for playing the hypocrite, because he dreaded (עָרַץ only here with the *acc.* of the obj. feared) the great multitude of the people (רַבָּה not adv. but adj.; הָמוֹן with *Mercha-Zinnorith*, consequently *fem.*, as עַם sometimes, Ew. § 174, *b*), and consequently the moral judgment of the people; and because he feared the stigma of the families, - and therefore the loss of honour in the higher circles of society, so that as a consequence he should have kept himself quiet and retired, without going out of the door. One might think of that abhorrence of voluptuousness, with which, in the consciousness of its condemnatory nature, a man shuts himself up in deep darkness; but according to ver. 33 it is in general deeds that are intended, which Job would have ground for studiously concealing, because if they had become known he would have appeared a person to be scouted and despised: he could frankly and freely meet any person's gaze, and had no occasion to fear the judgment of men, because he feared sin. He did nothing which he should have cause for carefully keeping from the light of publicity. And yet his affliction is to be accounted as the punishment of hidden sin! as proof that he has committed punishable sin, which, however, he will not confess!

35 *O that I had one who would hear me!*
   Behold my signature—the Almighty will answer me—
   And the writing which my opponent hath written!
36 *Truly I will carry it upon my shoulder,*
   I will wind it about me as a crown.
37 *The number of my steps I will recount to Him,*
   As a prince will I draw near to Him.

The wish that he might find a ready willing hearer is put forth in a general way, but, as is clear in itself, and as it becomes manifest from what follows, refers to Him who, because it treats of a contradiction between the outward

appearance and the true but veiled fact, as searcher of the
heart, is the only competent judge. It may not be translated: *et libellum* (the indictment, or even: the reply to Job's
self-defence) *scribat meus adversarius* (Dachselt, Rosenm.,
Welte)—the accentuation seems to proceed from this rendering, but it ought to be וְכָתַב סֵפֶר; if כָּתַב governed by יַעֲנֵנִי were
intended to be equivalent to יִכְתֹּב, and referred to God, the
longing would be, as it runs, an unworthy and foolish one—
nor: (O that I had one who would hear me . . .) and had
the indictment, which my adversary has written (Ew., Hirz.,
Schlottm.)—for וספר is too much separated from מִי יִתֵּן by
what intervenes—in addition to which comes the consideration that the wish, as it is expressed, cannot be referred to
God, but only to the human opponent, whose accusations
Job has no occasion to wish to hear, since he has already
heard amply sufficient even in detail. Therefore הֵן (instead
of הֶן with a conjunctive accent, as otherwise with *Makkeph*)
will point not merely to תָוִי, but also to *liber quem scripsit
adversarius meus* as now lying before them, and the parenthetical שַׁדַּי יַעֲנֵנִי will express a desire for the divine decision
in the cause now formally prepared for trial, ripe for discussion. By תָוִי, my sign, *i.e.* my signature (comp. Ezek. ix. 4,
and Arab. *tiwa*, a branded sign in the form of a cross), Job
intends the last word to his defence which he has just spoken,
ch. xxxi.; it is related to all his former confessions as a confirmatory mark set below them; it is his ultimatum, as it were,
the letter and seal to all that he has hitherto said about his
innocence in opposition to the friends and God. Moreover,
he also has the indictment of the triumvirate which has come
forward as his opponent in his hands. Their so frequently
repeated verbal accusations are fixed as if written; both—their
accusation and his defence—lie before him, as it were, in the
documentary form of legal writings. Thus, then, he wishes
an observant impartial hearer for this his defence; or more

exactly: he wishes that the Almighty may answer, *i.e.* decide. Hahn interprets just as much according to the syntax, but understanding by תוי the witness which Job carries in his breast, and by ספר וגו׳ the testimony to his innocence written by God in his own consciousness; which is inadmissible, because, as we have often remarked already, איש ריבי (comp. ch. xvi. 21) cannot be God himself.

In ver. 36 Job now says how he will appear before Him with this indictment of his opponent, if God will only condescend to speak the decisive word. He will wear it upon his shoulder as a mark of his dignity (comp. Isa. xxii. 22, ix. 5), and wind it about him as a magnificent crown of diadems intertwined and heaped up one above another (Apoc. xix. 12, comp. Köhler on Zech. vi. 11)—confident of his victory at the outset; for he will give Him, the heart-searcher, an account of all his steps, and in the exalted consciousness of his innocence, he will approach Him as a prince (קָרֵב intensive of *Kal*). How totally different from Adam, who was obliged to be drawn out of his hiding-place, and tremblingly, because conscious of guilt, underwent the examination of the omniscient God! Job is not conscious of cowardly and slyly hidden sins; no secret accursed thing is cherished in the inmost recesses of his heart and home.

> 38 *If my field cry out against me,*
> *And all together its furrows weep;*
> 39 *If I have devoured its strength without payment,*
> *And caused the soul of its possessor to expire:*
> 40 *May thistles spring up instead of wheat,*
> *And darnel instead of barley.*

The field which he tills has no reason to cry out on account of violent treatment, nor its furrows to weep over wrong done to them by their lord.[1] אֲדָמָה, according to its radical signifi-

---

[1] In a similar figure a Rabbinic proverb says (with reference to Mal.

cation, is the covering of earth which fits close upon the body of the earth as its skin, and is drawn flat over it, and therefore especially the arable land; חֶלֶם (Arab. *telem*, not however directly referable to an Arab. root, but as also other words used in agriculture, probably borrowed from the North Semitic, first of all the Aramaic or Nabataic), according to the explanation of the Turkish Kamus, the " ditch-like crack which the iron of the ploughman tears in the field," not the ridge thrown up between every two furrows (*vid.* on Ps. lxv. 11). He has not unlawfully used (which would be the reason of the crying and weeping) the usufruct of the field (כֹּחַ meton., as Gen. iv. 12, of the produce, proportioned to its capability of production) without having paid its value, by causing the life to expire from the rightful owner, whether slowly or all at once (Jer. xv. 9). The wish in ver. 40 is still stronger than in vers. 8, 12 : there the loss and rooting out of the produce of the field is desired, here the change of the nature of the land itself ; the curse shall and must come upon it, if its present possessor has been guilty of the sin of unmerciful covetousness, which Eliphaz lays to his charge in ch. xxii. 6-9.

According to the view of the Capuchin Bolducius (1637), this last strophe, vers. 38-40, stood originally after ver. 8, according to Kennicott and Eichhorn after ver. 25, according to Stuhlmann after ver. 34. The modern expositors retain it in its present position. Hirzel maintains the counter arguments: (1) that none of the texts preserved to us favour the change of position ; (2) that it lay in the plan of the poet not to allow the speeches of Job to be rounded off, as would be the case by vers. 35-37 being the concluding strophe, but to break off suddenly without a rhetorical conclusion. If now we imagine the speeches of Elihu as removed, God interrupts

ii. 13), that the altar of God weeps over him who separates himself from the wife of his youth.

Job, and he must cease without having come to an end with what he had to say. But these counter arguments are an insufficient defence: for (1) there is a number of admitted misplacements in the Old Testament which exceed the Masora (*e.g.* 1 Sam. xiii. 1, Jer. xxvii. 1), and also the LXX. (*e.g.* 1 Sam. xvii. 12, באנשים, LXX. ἐν ἀνδράσιν, instead of בשנים); (2) Job's speech would gain a rhetorical conclusion by vers. 38–40, if, as Hirzel in contradiction of himself supposes, vers. 35–37 ought to be considered as a parenthesis, and ver. 40 as a grammatical conclusion to the hypothetical clauses from ver. 24 onwards. But if this strange view is abandoned, it must be supposed that with ver. 38 Job intends to begin the assertion of his innocence anew, and is interrupted in this course of thought now begun, by Jehovah. But it is improbable that one has to imagine this in the mind of such a careful poet. Also the first word of Jehovah, " Who is this that darkeneth counsel with words without knowledge? " ch. xxxviii. 2, is much more appropriate to follow directly on ch. xxxi. 37 than ch. xxxi. 40 ; for a new course of thought, which Jehovah's appearing interrupts, begins with ver. 35; and the rash utterance, ver. 37, is really a " darkening of the divine decree." For by declaring he will give an account to God, his judge, concerning each of his steps, and approach Him like a prince, Job does not merely express the injustice of the accusations raised by his human opponents, but he casts a reflection of injustice upon the divine decree itself, inasmuch as it appears to him to be a *de facto* accusation of God.

Nevertheless, whether Elihu's speeches are to be put aside as not forming an original portion of the book, or not, the impression that vers. 38–40 follow as stragglers, and that vers. 35–37 would form a more appropriate close, and a more appropriate connection for the remonstrance that follows, whether it be Jehovah's or Elihu's, remains. For the assertion in vers. 38–40 cannot in itself be considered to be a justifiable boldness; but in vers. 35–37 the whole condition of Job's inner nature is once more mirrored forth : his longing after God, by which Satan's prediction is destroyed; and his over-stepping the bounds of humility, on account of which his affliction, so far as it is of a tentative character, cannot end before it is also become a refining fire to him. Therefore we cannot refrain from the supposition that it is with vers. 38–40 just as with Isa. xxxviii. 21 sq. The LXX. also found these two verses in this position ; they belong, however, after Isa. xxxviii. 6, as is clear in itself, and as is evident from 2 Kings xx. 7 sq. There they are accidentally omitted, and are now added at the close of the narration as a supplement. If the change of position, which is there an oversight, is considered as too hazardous here, vers. 35–37 must be put in the special and close relation to the preceding strophe indicated by us in the exposition, and vers. 38–40 must be regarded as a final round-ing off (not as the beginning of a fresh course of thought); for instead of the previous aposiopeses, this concluding strophe dies away, and with it the whole confession, in a particularly vigorous, imprecative conclusion.

Let us once more take a review of the contents of the three sharply-defined monologues. After Job, in ch. xxvii. xxviii., has closed the controversy with the friends, in the first part of this trilogy, ch. xxix., he wishes himself back in the months of the past, and describes the prosperity, the activity, for the good of his fellow-men, and the respect in which he at that time rejoiced, when God was with him. It is to be observed here, how, among all the good things of the past which he longs to have back, Job gives the pre-eminence to the fellow-ship and blessing of God as the highest good, the spring and fountain of every other. Five times at the beginning of ch. xxix. in diversified expressions he describes the former days as a time when God was with him. Look still further from the beginning of the monologue to its close, to the likewise very

expressive כאשר אבלים ינחם. The activity which won every
heart to Job, and toward which he now looks back so long-
ingly, consisted of works of that charity which weeps with
them that weep, and rejoices not in injustice, ch. xxix. 12–17.
The righteousness of life with which Job was enamoured, and
which manifested itself in him, was therefore charity arising
from faith (*Liebe aus Glauben*). He knew and felt himself
to be in fellowship with God; and from the fulness of this
state of being apprehended of God, he practised charity.
He, however, is blessed who knows himself to be in favour
with God, and in return loves his fellow-men, especially the
poor and needy, with the love with which he himself is loved
of God. Therefore does Job wish himself back in that past,
for now God has withdrawn from him; and the prosperity,
the power, and the important position which were to him the
means for the exercise of his charity, are taken from him.

This contrast of the past and present is described in
ch. xxx., which begins with ועתה. Men who have become
completely animalized, rough hordes driven into the mountains, with whom he sympathized, but without being able to
help them as he had wished, on account of their degeneracy,
—these mock at him by their words and acts. Now scorn
and persecution for the sake of God is the greatest honour of
which a man can be accounted worthy; but, apart from the
consideration that this idea could not yet attain its rightful
expression in connection with the present, temporal character
of the Old Testament, it was not further from any one than
from him who in the midst of his sufferings for God's sake
regards himself, as Job does now, as rejected of God. That
scorn and his painful and loathsome disease are to him a decree
of divine wrath; God has, according to his idea, changed to
a tyrant; He will not hear his cry for help. Accordingly,
Job can say that his welfare as a cloud is passed away. He
is conscious of having had pity on those who needed help, and

yet he himself finds no pity now, when he implores pity
like one who, seated upon a heap of rubbish, involuntarily
stretches forth his hand for deliverance. In this gloomy
picture of the present there is not even a single gleam of
light; for the mysterious darkness of his affliction has not
been in the slightest degree lighted up for Job by the treatment the friends have adopted. Also he is as little able as the
friends to think of suffering and sin as unconnected, for which
very reason his affliction appears to him as the effect of divine
wrath; and the sting of his affliction is, that he cannot consider this wrath just. From the demand made by his faith,
which here and there breaks through his conflict, that God
cannot allow him to die the death of a sinner without testifying to his innocence, Job nowhere attains the conscious conclusion that the motive of his affliction is love, and not wrath.

   In the third part of the speech (ch. xxxi.), which begins
with the words, "I had made a covenant," etc., without everywhere going into the detail of the visible conjunction of the
thought, Job asserts his earnest struggle after sanctification,
by delivering himself up to just divine punishment in case
his conduct had been the opposite. The poet allows us to
gain a clear insight into that state of his hero's heart, and
also of his house, which was well-pleasing to God. Not
merely outward adultery, even the adulterous look; not
merely the unjust acquisition of property and goods, but
even the confidence of the heart in such things; not merely
the share in an open adoration of idols, but even the side-
glance of the heart after them, is accounted by him as condemnatory. He has not merely guarded himself from using
sinful curses against his enemies, but he has also not rejoiced
when misfortune overtook them. As to his servants, even
when he has had a dispute with any of them, he has not forgotten that master and servant, without distinction of birth,
are creatures of one God. Towards orphans, from early

youth onwards, he has practised such tender love as if he were their father; towards widows, as if he were their son. With the hungry he has shared his bread, with the naked his clothes; his subordinates had no reason to complain of niggardly sustenance; his house always stood open hospitably to the stranger; and, as the two final strophes affirm: he has not hedged in any secret sin, anxious only not to appear as a sinner openly, and has not drawn forth wailings and tears from the ground which he cultivated by avarice and oppressive injustice. Who does not here recognise a righteousness of life and endeavour, the final aim of which is purity of heart, and which, in its relation to man, flows forth in that love which is the fulfilling of the law? The righteousness of which Job (ch. xxix. 14) says, he has put it on like a garment, and it has put him on, is essentially the same as that which the New Testament Preacher on the mount enjoins. As the work of an Israelitish poet, ch. xxxi. is a most important evidence in favour of the assertion, that a life well-pleasing to God is not, even in the Old Testament, absolutely limited to the Israelitish nation, and that it enjoins a love which includes man as man within itself, and knows of no distinction.

If, now, Job can lay down the triumphant testimony of such a genuine righteousness of life concerning himself, in opposition to men's misconstruction, the contrast of his past and present becomes for the first time mysterious; but we are also standing upon the extreme boundary where the knot that has been tied must be untied. The injustice done to Job in the accusations which the friends bring against him must be laid bare by the appearance of accusation on the part of God, which his affliction casts upon him, being destroyed. With the highest confidence in a triumphant issue, even before the trial of his cause, Job longs, in the concluding words, vers. 35-37, for the judicial decision of God. As a prince he will go before the Judge, and bind his indictment like a costly diadem upon his brow. For he is certain that he has not merited his affliction, that neither human nor divine accusation can do anything against him, and that he will remain conqueror—as over men, so over God Himself.

Thus has the poet, in this threefold monologue of Job, prepared the way for the *catastrophe*, the unravelment of the knot of the drama. But will God enter into a controversy respecting His cause with Job? This is contrary to the honour of God; and that Job desires it, is contrary to the lowliness which becomes him towards God. On this very account God will not at once acknowledge Job as His servant: Job will require first of all to be freed from the sinful presumption concerning God with which he has handled the problem of his sufferings. But he has proved himself to be a servant of God, in spite of the folly into which he has fallen; the design of Satan to tear him away from God is completely frustrated. Thus, therefore, after he has purified himself from his sin into which, both in word and thought, he has allowed himself to be drawn by the conflict of temptation, Job must be proved to be the servant of God in opposition to the friends.

But before God Himself appears in order to bring about the unravelment, there follow still four speeches, ch. xxxii.–xxxvii., of a speaker, for whose appearance the former part of the drama has in no way prepared us. It is also remarkable that they are marked off from the book of Job, as far as we have hitherto read, by the formula תַּמּוּ דִּבְרֵי אִיּוֹב, *are ended the words of Job.* Carey is of the opinion that these three words may possibly be Job's own closing *dixi*. According to Hahn, the poet means to imply by them that Job has now said all that he intended to say, so that it would now have been the friends' turn to speak. These views involve a perplexity like that of those who think that Ps. lxxii. 20 must be regarded as a constituent part of the Psalm. As in that position the words, "The prayers of David the son of Jesse are finished," are as a memorial-stone between the original collection and its later extensions, so this תמו דברי איוב, which is transferred by the LXX. (καὶ ἐπαύσατο Ἰὼβ ῥήμασιν) to the historical introduction of the Elihu section, seems to be an important hint in reference to the origin of the book of Job in its present form. Since Job has come to an end with his speeches, and is silent at the four speeches of a new speaker, although they strongly enough provoke him to reply; according to the idea of the poet, Elihu's appearance is to be regarded as belonging to the catastrophe itself. And since a hasty glance at the speeches of Jehovah shows that they do not say anything concerning the motive and object of Job's affliction, these speeches of Elihu, in so far as they seem to be an integral part of the whole, as they cast light upon this dark point, will therefore prove in the midst of the action of the drama, what we know already from the prologue, that Job's affliction has not the wrath of God as its motive power, nor the punishment of Job as ungodly for its object. If the four speeches really furnish this, it is still not absolutely decisive in favour of their forming originally a part of the book. For it would be even possible that a second poet might have added a part, in harmony with its idea, to the work of the first. What we expect, moreover, is the mark of the same high poetic genius which we have hitherto regarded with amazement. But since we are now passing on to the exposition of these speeches, it must be with the assumption that they have a like origin with the whole, and that they also really belong to this whole with which they are embodied, in the place where they now stand. We shall only be able to form a conclusive judgment concerning the character of their form, the solution of their problem, and the manner of their composition, after the exposition is completed, by then taking a comprehensive and critical review of the impressions produced, and our observations.

FOURTH PART.—THE UNRAVELMENT.

CHAP. XXXII.–XLII.

THE SPEECHES OF ELIHU WHICH PREPARE THE WAY FOR
THE UNRAVELMENT.—CHAP. XXXII.–XXXVII.

Historical Introduction to the Section.—Chap. xxxii. 1–6a.

A short introduction in historical prose, which introduces
the speaker and justifies his appearance, opens the section.
It is not, like the prologue and epilogue, accented as prose;
but, like the introductions to the speeches and the clause, ch.
xxxi. 40 *extra*, is taken up in the network of the poetical
mode of accentuation, because a change of the mode of
accentuation in the middle of the book, and especially in a
piece of such small compass, appeared awkward. The opposition of the three has exhausted itself, so that in that respect
Job seems to have come forth out of the controversy as
conqueror.

Vers. 1–3. *So these three men ceased to answer Job, because*
he was righteous in his own eyes. And the wrath of
Elihu, the son of Barachel the Buzite, of the family of
Ram, was kindled: against Job was his wrath kindled,
because he justified himself at the expense of God. And
against his three friends was his wrath kindled, because
they found no answer, and condemned Job.

The name of the speaker is אֱלִיהוּא (with *Mahpach*), son of
בָּרַכְאֵל (with *Munach*) the בּוּזִי (with *Zarka*). The name *Elihu*
signifies " my God is He," and occurs also as an Israelitish
name, although it is not specifically Israelitish, like *Elijah*
(my God is Jehovah). *Barach'el* (for which the mode of
writing בַּרַכְאֵל with *Dag. implic.* is also found) signifies " may

God bless!" (Olsh. § 277, S. 618); for proper names, as the Arabian grammarians observe, can be formed both into the form of assertory clauses (*ichbár*), and also into the form of modal (*inshá*); the name בְּרְכְאֵל is in this respect distinguished from the specifically Israelitish name בְּרֶכְיָה (Jehovah blesseth). The accompanying national name defines the scene; for on the one side בּוּז and עוּץ, according to Gen. xxii. 21, are the sons of Nahor, Abraham's brother, who removed with him (though not at the same time) from Ur Casdim to Haran, therefore by family Aramæans; on the other side, בּוּז, Jer. xxv. 23, appears as an Arab race, belonging to ·the קְצוּצֵי פֵאָה (comp. Jer. ix. 25, xlix. 32), *i.e.* to the Arabs proper, who cut the hair of their heads short all round (περιτρόχαλα, Herodotus iii. 8), because wearing it long was accounted as dis-graceful (*vid.* Tebrîzi on the *Hamása*, p. ۳٥٩, l. 10 sqq.). Within the Buzite race, Elihu sprang from the family of רָם. Since רם is the name of the family, not the race, it cannot be equivalent to אֲרָם (like רָמִים, 2 Chron. xxii. 5, = אֲרָמִים), and it is therefore useless to derive the Aramaic colouring of Elihu's speeches from design on the part of the poet. But by making him a Buzite, he certainly appears to make him an Aramæan Arab, as Aristeas in Euseb. *præp.* ix. 25 calls him Ἐλιοῦν τὸν Βαραχιὴλ τὸν Ζωβίτην (from אֲרָם צוֹבָה). It is remarkable that Elihu's origin is given so exactly, while the three are described only according to their country, without any statement of father or family. It would indeed be possible, as Lightfoot and Rosenm. suppose, for the poet to conceal his own name in that of Elihu, or to make allusion to it; but an instance of this later custom of Oriental poets is found nowhere else in Old Testament literature.

The three friends are silenced, because all their attempts to move Job to a penitent confession that his affliction is the punishment of his sins, have rebounded against this fact, that he was righteous in his own eyes, *i.e.* that he imagined him-

self righteous; and because they now (שָׁבַּת of persons, in
distinction from חדל, has the secondary notion of involuntari-
ness) know of nothing more to say. Then Elihu's indignation breaks forth in two directions. First, concerning Job,
that he justified himself מֵאֱלֹהִים, *i.e.* not a *Deo* (so that He
would be obliged to account him righteous, as ch. iv. 17),
but *præ Deo*. Elihu rightly does not find it censurable in
Job, that as a more commonly self-righteous man he in
general does not consider himself a sinner, which the three
insinuate of him (ch. xv. 14, xxv. 4), but that, declaring himself to be righteous, he brings upon God the appearance of
injustice, or, as Jehovah also says further on, ch. xl. 8, that
he condemns God in order that he may be able to maintain
his own righteousness. Secondly, concerning the three, that
they have found no answer by which they might have been
able to disarm Job in his maintenance of his own righteousness at the expense of the divine justice, and that in consequence of this they have condemned Job. Hahn translates:
so that they should have represented Job as guilty; but that
they have not succeeded in stamping the servant of God as a
רָשָׁע, would wrongly excite Elihu's displeasure. And Ewald
translates: and that they had nevertheless condemned him
(§. 345, *a*); but even this was not the real main defect of
their opposition. The *fut. consec.* describes the condemnation
as the result of their inability to hit upon the right answer;
it was a miserable expedient to which they had recourse.
According to the Jewish view, וַיַּרְשִׁיעוּ אֶת־אִיּוֹב is one of the
eighteen תקוני סופרים (*correctiones scribarum*), since it should
be וירשיעו את־האלהים. But it is not the friends who have been
guilty of this sin of הַרְשִׁיעַ against God, but Job, ch. xl. 8, to
whom Elihu opposes the sentence אֵל לֹא־יִרְשִׁיעַ, ch. xxxiv. 12.
Our judgment of another such *tiqqûn*, ch. vii. 20, was more
favourable. That Elihu, notwithstanding the inward conviction to the contrary by which he is followed during the

course of the controversial dialogue, now speaks for the first time, is explained by what follows.

Vers. 4–6. *And Elihu had waited for Job with words, for they were older than he in days. And Elihu saw that there was no answer in the mouth of the three men, then his wrath was kindled. And Elihu the son of Barachel the Buzite began, and said.*

He had waited (*perf.* in the sense of the *plusquamperf.*, Ew. § 135, *a*) for Job with words (בִּדְבָרִים as elsewhere בְּמִלִּים, בְּמִלִּין), *i.e.* until Job should have spoken his last word in the controversial dialogue. Thus he considered it becoming on his part, for they (הֵמָּה, *illi*, whereas אֵלֶּה according to the usage of the language is *hi*) were older (*seniores*) than he in days (לְיָמִים as ver. 6, less harsh here, instead of the *acc.* of closer definition, ch. xv. 10, comp. xi. 9). As it now became manifest that the friends made no reply to Job's last speeches for want of the right solution of problem, and therefore also Job had nothing further to say, he believes that he may venture, without any seeming want of courtesy, to give utterance to his long-restrained indignation; and Elihu (with *Mahpach*) the son of Barach'el (*Mercha*) the Buzite (with *Rebia parvum*) began and spoke (וַיֹּאמַר not with *Silluk*, but *Mercha mahpach.*, and in fact with *Mercha* on the accented *penult.*, as ch. iii. 2, and further).

Elihu's First Speech.—Chap. xxxii. 6*b*–xxxiii.

Schema: 5. 6. 10. 6. 10. | 6. 8. 10. 13. 8. 6. 10. 10.

Ch. xxxii. 6*b* *I am young in days, and ye are hoary,*
Therefore I stood back and was afraid
To show you my knowledge.
7 *I thought: Let age speak,*
And the multitude of years teach wisdom.

210

It becomes manifest even here that the Elihu section has in part a peculiar usage of the language. יָחַל in the signi-fication of جَحَلِ, cogn. with جَحَلِ, יָחַל, to frighten back;[1] and יֵעַ for דֵעָה (here and vers. 10, 17, ch. xxxvi. 3, xxxvii. 16) occurs nowhere else in the Old Testament; עַל־בֵּן (comp. לֵב, ch. xlii. 3) is used only by Elihu within the book of Job. יָמִים, days = fulness of days, is equivalent to advanced age, old age with its rich experience. רֹב with its plural genitive is followed (as כֹל usually is) by the predicate in the plur.; it is the attraction already described by מִסְפַּר, ch. xv. 10, xxi. 21, Ges. § 148, 1.

8 *Still the spirit, it is in mortal man,*
   And the breath of the Almighty, that giveth them under-
   standing.

9 *Not the great in years are wise,*
   And the aged do not understand what is right.

10 *Therefore I say: O hearken to me,*
   I will declare my knowledge, even I.

The originally affirmative and then (like אוּלָם) adversative אָכֵן also does not occur elsewhere in the book of Job. In contradiction to biblical psychology, Rosenm. and others take ver. 8 as antithetical: Certainly there is spirit in man, but . . .

---

[1] The lexicographers explain the Arab. جَحَلِ by *zâla* (זוּל), to stand away from, back, to retreat, or *tanahha*, to step aside; *Piel*, *Hiph.*, to push any one aside, place anything back; *Hithpa.*, to keep one's self on one side; adj. זָחֵל, זָחִיל, זָחֻל, זָחֵל, etc., standing back. Thus the town of *Zahla* in the plain of the Lebanon takes its name from the fact that it does not stand out in the plain, but is built close at the foot of the mountain in a corner, and consequently retreats. And *zuhale* (according to the *Kamus*) is an animal that creeps backwards into its hole, *e.g.* the scorpion; and hence, improperly, a man who, as we say with a similar figure, never comes out of his hole, always keeps in his hole, *i.e.* never leaves his dwelling, as *zuhal* in general signifies a man who retires or keeps far from active life; in connection with which also the planet Saturn is called *Zuhal*, the retreating one, on account of its great distance

The two halves of the verse are, on the contrary, a synonymous ("the spirit, it is in man, viz. that is and acts") or progressive parallelism (thus according to the accents: "the spirit, even that which is in man, and . . ."). It is the Spirit of God to which man owes his life as a living being, according to ch. xxxiii. 4; the spirit of man is the principle of life creatively wrought, and indeed breathed into him, by the Spirit of God; so that with regard to the author it can be just as much God's רוּחַ or נְשָׁמָה, ch. xxxiv. 14, as in respect of the possessor: man's רוח or נשמה. All man's life, his thinking as well as his bodily life, is effected by this inwrought principle of life which he bears within him, and all true understanding, without being confined to any special age of life, comes solely from this divinely originated and divinely living spirit, so far as he acts according to his divine origin and basis of life. רַבִּים are here (as the opposite of צעירים, Gen. xxv. 23) *grandes* = *grandævi* (LXX. πολυχρόνιοι). לֹא governs both members of the verse, as ch. iii. 10, xxviii. 17, xxx. 24 sq. Understanding or ability to form a judgment is not limited to old age, but only by our allowing the πνεῦμα to rule in us in its connection with the divine. Elihu begs a favourable hearing for that of which he is conscious. דֵּעַ, and the Hebr.-Aramaic חִוָּה, which likewise belong to his favourite words, recur here.

from the rest. Slippery (of ground) is זַחֲלֹגֹל, because it draws the foot backwards (*muzhil*) by its smoothness, and thus causes the walker to fall. A further formation is זחלק, to be slippery, and to slip in a slippery place; beside which, זלק, a word of similar meaning, is no longer used in Syria. According to this Arabic primary notion of زَحَل, it appears זחלי ארץ, Mic. vii. 17, is intended to describe the serpents not as creeping upon the earth, but as creeping into the earth (comp. the name of the serpent, *achbi' at el-ard*, those that hide themselves in the earth); but in Talmud. and Aram. זחל used of animals has the general signification to creep, and of water, to glide (flow gently down). The primary notion, to *glide* (to slip, creep, flow gently, *labi*), is combined both in the derivatives of the root זחל and in those of the root זל with the notion of a departing and retreating motion.—WETZST. and FL.

11 *Behold, I waited upon your words,*
   ╱   *Hearkened to your perceptions,*
       While ye searched out replies.
12 *And I attended closely to you,*
       Yet behold: there was no one who refuted Job,
       Who answered his sentences, from you.
13 *Lest ye should say : " We found wisdom,*
       God is able to smite him, not man !"
14 *Now he hath not arranged his words against me,*
       And with your sentences I will not reply to him.

He has waited for their words, viz. that they might give
utterance to such words as should tend to refute and silence
Job.   In what follows, עַד still more emphatically than לְ
refers this aim to that to which Elihu had paid great attention: I hearkened to your understandings, *i.e.* explanations
of the matter, that, or whether, they came forth, (I hearkened)
to see if you searched or found out words, *i.e.* appropriate
words.   Such abbreviated forms as אָזִין = אַאֲזִין (comp. מֵזִין =
מֵיזִין for מְאֲזִין, Prov. xvii. 4, Ges. § 68, rem. 1, if it does not
signify *nutriens*, from זן) we shall frequently meet with in
this Elihu section.   In ver. 12, 12*a* evidently is related as an
antecedent to what follows: and I paid attention to you
(עָרֵיכֶם contrary to the analogy of the cognate *præp.* instead of
עֲדֵיכֶם, moreover for אֲלֵיכֶם, with the accompanying notion :
intently, or, according to Aben-Duran: thoroughly, without
allowing a word to escape me), and behold, intently as I paid
attention : no one came forward to refute Job ; there was no
one from or among you who answered (met successfully) his
assertions.   Every unbiassed reader will have an impression
of the remarkable expressions and constructions here, similar
to that which one has in passing from the book of the Kings
to the characteristic sections of the Chronicles.   The three,
Elihu goes on to say, shall not indeed think that in Job a

wisdom has opposed them—a false wisdom, indeed—which only God and not any man can drive out of the field (נָדַף, ـجـۮ, *discutere, dispellere*, as the wind drives away chaff or dry leaves); while he has not, however (וְלֹא followed directly by a *v. fin.* forming a subordinate clause, as ch. xlii. 3, Ps. xliv. 18, and freq., Ew. § 341, *a*), arrayed (עָרַךְ in a military sense, ch. xxxiii. 5; or forensic, xxiii. 4; or even as ch. xxxvii. 19, in the general sense of *proponere*) words against him (Elihu), *i.e.* utterances before which he would be compelled to confess himself affected and overcome. He will not then also answer him with such opinions as those so frequently repeated by them, *i.e.* he will take a totally different course from theirs in order to refute him.

> 15 *They are amazed, they answer no more,*
> *Words have fled from them.*
> 16 *And I waited, for they spake not,*
> *For they stand still, they answer no more.*
> 17 *Therefore I also will answer for my part,*
> *I will declare my knowledge, even I.*

In order to give a more rapid movement and an emotional force to the speech, the figure asyndeton is introduced in ver. 15, as perhaps in Jer. xv. 7, Ew. § 349, *a*. Most expositors render הֶעְתִּיקוּ passively, according to the sense: they have removed from them, *i.e.* are removed from them; but why may העתיק not signify, like Gen. xii. 8, xxvi. 22, to move away, viz. the tent = to wander on (Schlottm.)? The figure: words are moved away (as it were according to an encampment broken up) from them, *i.e.* as we say: they have left them, is quite in accordance with the figurative style of this section. It is unnecessary to take וְהוֹחַלְתִּי, ver. 16*a*, with Ew. (§ 342, *c*) and Hirz. as *perf. consec.* and interrogative: and should I wait, because they speak no more? Certainly the interrog. part. sometimes disappears after the *Waw* of consequence, *e.g.* Ezek. xviii. 13, 24 (and will he live?); but by what would וְהוֹחַלְתִּי be distinguished as *perf. consec.* here? Hahn's interpretation: I have waited, until they do not speak, for they stand . . ., also does not commend itself; the poet would have expressed this by עַד לֹא יְדַבְּרוּ, while the two כִּי, especially with the poet's predilection for repetition, appear to be co-ordinate. Elihu means to say that he has waited a long time, surprised that the three did not speak further, and that they stand still without speaking again. Therefore he thinks the time is come for him also to answer Job. אַעֲנֶה cannot be *fut. Kal*, since where the 1 *fut. Kal* and *Hiph.* cannot be distinguished by the vowel within the word (as in the *Ayin Waw* and double *Ayin* verbs), the former has an inalienable *Segol*; it is therefore 1 *fut. Hiph.*, but not as in Eccl. v. 19 in the signification to employ labour upon anything (LXX. περισπᾶν), but in an intensive *Kal* signification (as הֵזְעִיק for זָעַק, ch. xxxv. 9, comp. on ch. xxxi. 18): to answer, to give any one an answer when called upon. Ewald's supposedly proverbial: I also plough my field! (§ 192, *c*, Anm. 2) does unnecessary violence to the usage of the language, which is unacquainted with this הֶעֱנָה, to plough. It is perfectly consistent with Elihu's diction, that חֶלְקִי beside אֲנִי as permutative signifies, "I, my part," although it might also be an *acc.* of closer definition (as *pro parte mea*, for my part), or even—which is, however, less probable—*acc.* of the obj. (my part). Elihu speaks more in the scholastic tone of controversy than the three.

18 *For I am full of words,*
The spirit of my inner nature constraineth me.

19 *Behold, my interior is like wine which is not opened,*
Like new bottles it is ready to burst.

20 *I will speak, that I may gain air,*
I will open my lips and reply.

21 *No, indeed, I will accept no man's person,*
   And I will flatter no man.
22 *For I understand not how to flatter;*
   My Maker would easily snatch me away.

The young speaker continues still further his declaration, promising so much. He has a rich store of מִלִּים, words, *i.e.* for replying. מִלֵּתִי defective for מִלֵּאתִי, like יָצְתִי for יָצָאתִי, ch. i. 21; whereas מָלוּ, Ezek. xxviii. 6, is not only written defectively, but is also conjugated after the manner of a *Lamed He* verb, Ges. §§ 23, 3, 74, rem. 4, 75, 21, *c*. The spirit of his inner nature constrains him, since, on account of its intensity and the fulness of this interior, it struggles to break through as through a space that is too narrow for it. בֶּטֶן, as ch. xv. 2, 35, not from the curved appearance of the belly, but from the interior of the body with its organs, which serve the spirit life as the strings of a harp; comp. Arab. *batn*, the middle or interior; *bâtin*, inwardly (opposite of *zâhir*, outwardly). His interior is like wine לֹא יִפָּתֵחַ, which, or (as an adverbial dependent clause) when it is not opened, *i.e.* is kept closed, so that the accumulated gas has no vent, LXX. δεδεμένος (bound up), Jer. *absque spiraculo*; it will burst like new bottles. יִבָּקֵעַ is not a relative clause referring distributively to each single one of these bottles (Hirz. and others), and not an adverbial subordinate clause (Hahn: when it will explode), but predicate to בְּטֻנִי: his interior is near bursting like new bottles (אֹבוֹת *masc.* like נֹאדוֹת, Josh. ix. 13), *i.e.* not such as are themselves new (ἀσκοὶ καινοί, Matt. ix. 17, for these do not burst so easily), but like bottles of new wine, which has to undergo the action of fermentation, LXX. ὥσπερ φυσητὴρ (*Cod. Sinait.*[1] φυσητής) χαλκέως, *i.e.* חֲרָשִׁים (whence it is evident that a bottle and also a pair of bellows were called אוֹב). Since he will now yield to his irresistible impulse, in order that he may obtain air or free space, *i.e.*

disburdening and ease (וִירוַח לִי), he intends to accept no man's person, *i.e.* to show partiality to no one (*vid.* on ch. xiii. 8), and he will flatter no one. כִּנָּה signifies in all three dialects to call any one by an honourable name, to give a surname, here with אֶל, to speak fine words to any one, to flatter him. This Elihu is determined he will not do; for לֹא יָדַעְתִּי אֲכַנֶּה, I know not how to flatter (French, *je ne sais point flatter*), for כַּנּוֹת or לְכַנּוֹת; comp. the similar constructions, ch. xxiii. 3 (as Esth. viii. 6), x. 16, 1 Sam. ii. 3, Isa. xlii. 21, lii. 1, Ges. 142, 3, *c;* also in Arabic similar verbs, as "to be able" and "to prepare one's self," are thus connected with the *fut.* without a particle between (*e.g. anshaa jef'alu*, he began to act). Without partiality he will speak, flattery is not his forte. If by flattery he should deny the truth, his Maker would quickly carry him off. כִּמְעַט followed by subjunct. *fut.:* for a little (with disjunctive accent, because equivalent to *haud multum abest quin*), *i.e.* very soon indeed, or easily would or might . . . ; יִשָּׂאֵנִי (as ch. xxvii. 21) seems designedly to harmonize with עֹשֵׂנִי.

Ch. xxxiii. 1 *But nevertheless, O Job, hear my speeches,*
And hearken to all my words.

2 *Behold now, I have opened my mouth,*
My tongue speaketh in my palate.

3 *Sincere as my heart are my utterances,*
And knowledge that is pure my lips declare.

The issue of the impartial discussion which Elihu designs to effect, is subject to this one condition, that Job listens to it, and observes not merely this or that, but the whole of its connected contents; and in this sense וְאוּלָם, which is used just as in ch. i. 11, xi. 5, xii. 7, xiii. 4, xiv. 18, xvii. 10, in the signification *verumtamen*, stands at the head of this new turn in his speech. Elihu addresses Job, as none of the previous speakers have done, by name. With הִנֵּה־נָא (as ch. xiii. 18), he directs Job's observation to that which he is about to say: he has already opened his mouth, his tongue is already in motion,—circumstantial statements, which solemnly inaugurate what follows with a consciousness of its importance. Job has felt the absence of אִמְרֵי־יֹשֶׁר, ch. vi. 25, in the speeches of the three; but Elihu can at the outset ensure his word being "the sincerity of his heart," *i.e.* altogether heartily well meant: and—thus it would be to be translated according to the accentuation—the knowledge of my lips, they (my lips) utter purely. But "the knowledge of the lips" is a notion that seems strange with this translation, and בָּרוּר is hardly intended thus adverbially. דַעַת, contrary to the accentuation, is either taken as the accusative of the obj., and בָּרוּר as the acc. of the predicate (*masc.* as Prov. ii. 10, xiv. 6): knowledge my lips utter pure; or interpreted, if one is not willing to depart from the accentuation, with Seb. Schmid: *scientiam labiorum meorum quod attinet* (the knowledge proceeding from my lips), *puram loquentur sc. labia mea.* The notions of purity and choice coincide in ברור (comp. Arab. *ibtarra*, to separate one's self; *asfa*, to prove one's self pure, and to select). The *perff.*, vers. 2 sq., describe what is begun, and so, as relatively past, extending into the present.

4 *The Spirit of God hath made me,*
  And the breath of the Almighty hath given me life.
5 *If thou canst, answer me,*
  Prepare in my presence, take thy stand!
6 *Behold, I am like thyself, of God,*
  Formed out of clay am I also.
7 *Behold, my terror shall not affright thee,*
  And my pressure shall not be heavy upon thee.

He has both in common with Job: the spirituality as well as the earthliness of man's nature; but by virtue of the former he does not, indeed, feel himself exalted above Job's

person, but above the present standpoint taken up by Job ;
and in consideration of this, Job need not fear any unequal
contest, nor as before God, ch. ix. 34, xiii. 21, in order that
he may be able to defend himself against Him, make it a
stipulation that His majesty may not terrify him. It is man's
twofold origin which Elihu, vers. 4, 6, gives utterance to in
harmony with Gen. ii. 7 : the mode of man's origin, which is
exalted above that of all other earthly beings that have life ;
for the life of the animal is only the individualizing of the
breath of the Divine Spirit already existing in matter. The
spirit of man, on the contrary (for which the language has
reserved the name נְשָׁמָה)), is an inspiration directly coming
forth from God the personal being, transferred into the bodily
frame, and therefore forming a person.[1] In the exalted consciousness of having been originated by the Spirit of God,
and being endowed with life from the inbreathed breath of
the Almighty, Elihu stands invincible before Job : if thou
canst, refute me (הָשִׁיב with acc. of the person, as ch. xxxiii. 32) ;
array thyself (עֶרְכָה for עֶרְכָה, according to Ges. 63, rem. 1)
before me (here with the additional thought of מִלְחָמָה, as
ch. xxiii. 4, in a forensic sense with מִשְׁפָּט)), place thyself in
position, or take thy post (imper. Hithpa. with the ah less
frequent by longer forms, Ew. § 228, a).

On the other side, he also, like Job, belongs to God, i.e. is
dependent and conditioned. הֵן־אֲנִי is to be written with Segol
(not Ssere) ; לְאֵל is intended like לְ, ch. xii. 16 ; and כְּפִיךָ signifies properly, according to thine utterance, i.e. standard, in
accordance with, i.e. like thee, and is used even in the Pentateuch (e.g. Ex. xvi. 21) in this sense pro ratione ; כפי, ch.
xxx. 18, we took differently. He, Elihu, is also nipped from
the clay, i.e. taken from the earth, as when the potter nips off

---

[1] God took a small piece of His own life—says the tradition among the
Karens, a scattered tribe of Eastern India—blew into the nostrils of His
son and daughter, and they became living beings, and were really human.

a piece of his clay (comp. Aram. קְרָץ, a piece, Arab. *qurs*, a bread-cake, or a dung-cake, *vid. supra*, vol. i. p. 377, from *qarasa*, to pinch off, take off, cogn. *qarada*, to gnaw off, cut off, ii. p. 40). Thus, therefore, no terribleness in his appearing will disconcert Job, and his pressure will not be a burden upon him. By a comparison of ch. xiii. 21*a*, it might seem that אַכְפִּי is equivalent to כַּפִּי (LXX. ἡ χείρ μου), but כְּבֵד is everywhere connected only with יָד, never with כַּף; and the ἀπ. γεγρ. is explained according to Prov. xvi. 26, where אָכַף signifies to oppress, drive (Jer. *compulit*), and from the dialects differently, for in Syr. *ecaf* signifies to be anxious about anything (*ecaf li*, it causes me anxiety, *curæ mihi est*), and in Arab. *accafa*, to saddle, *ucáf*, Talmud. אוּכָּף, a saddle, so that consequently the Targ. translation of אַכְפִּי by טוּנִי, my burden, and the Syr. by אוכפני, my pressing forward (Arabic version *iqbáli*, my touch), are supported, since אֶכֶף signifies pressure, heavy weight, load, and burden; according to which it is also translated by Saad. (my constraint), Gecat. (my might). It is therefore not an opponent who is not on an equality with him by nature, with whom Job has to do. If he is not able to answer him, he will have to be considered as beaten.

8 *Verily thou hast said in mine ears,*
   And I heard the sound of thy words:
9 " *I am pure, without transgression;*
   " *Spotless am I, and I have no guilt.*
10 " *Behold, He findeth malicious things against me,*
   " *He regardeth me as His enemy;*
11 " *He putteth my feet in the stocks,*
   " *He observeth all my paths.*"
12 *Behold, therein thou art not right, I will answer thee,*
   For Eloah is too exalted for man.

With אַף אָמַרְתָּ Elihu establishes the undeniable fact,

whether it be that אַךְ is intended as restrictive (only thou hast said, it is not otherwise than that thou . . .), or as we have translated, according to its primary meaning, affirmative (forsooth, it is undeniable). To say anything בְּאָזְנֵי of another is in Hebrew equivalent to not saying it secretly, and so as to be liable to misconstruction, but aloud and distinctly. In ver. 9, Elihu falls back on Job's own utterances, as ch. ix. 21, חַם אָנִי; xvi. 17, תְּפִלָּתִי זָכָה; xii. 4, where he calls himself צַדִּיק תָּמִים, comp. x. 7, xiii. 18, 23, xxiii. 10 sqq., xxvii. 5 sq., ch. xxix. xxxi. The expression חַף, *tersus*, did not occur in the mouth of Job; Geiger connects חַף with the Arab. hanîf (*vid.* on ch. xiii. 16); it is, however, the adj. of the Semitic verb חַף, حَفّ, to rub off, scrape off; Arab. to make smooth by scraping off the hair; Targ., Talm., Syr., to make smooth by washing and rubbing (after which Targ. שְׁזָיִן, *lotus*).[1] אָנֹכִי has here, as an exception, retained its accentuation of the final syllable in pause. In ver. 10 Elihu also makes use of a word that does not occur in Job's mouth, viz. תְּנוּאוֹת, which, according to Num. xiv. 34, signifies "alienation," from נוּא (הֲנִיא), to hinder, restrain, turn aside, *abalienare*, Num. xxxii. 7; and according to the Arab. نَاءَ (to rise heavily),[2] III. to lean one's self upon, to oppose any one; it might also signify directly, "hostile risings;" but according to the Hebr. it signifies grounds and occasions for hostile aversion. Moreover, Elihu here recapitulates what Job has in reality often in meaning

---

[1] *Vid.* Nöldecke in *Benfey's Zeitschrift*, 1863, S. 383.

[2] Nevertheless Zamachschari does not derive نَاوَى, to treat with enmity, from نَأَ, but from نَوَى, so that *nâwa fulânan* signifies "to have evil designs against any one, to meditate evil against one." The phrases *iluh 'alêji nijât*, he has evil intentions (wicked designs) against me, *nijetuh zertje aleik*, he has evil intentions against thee, and similar, are very common.—WETZST.

said, *e.g.* ch. x. 13–17 ; and ver. 10*b* are his own words, ch.
xiii. 24, וּתַחְשְׁבֵנִי לְאוֹיֵב לָךְ ; xix. 11, וַיַּחְשְׁבֵנִי לוֹ כְצָרָיו ; xxx. 21,
תֵּהָפֵךְ לְאַכְזָר לִי. In like manner, ver. 11 is a *verbatim* quotation from ch. xiii. 27 ; יָשֵׂם is a poetic contracted *fut.* for
יָשִׂים. It is a principal trait of Job's speeches which Elihu
here makes prominent: his maintenance of his own righteousness at the expense of the divine justice. In ver. 12 he first
of all refutes this צָדַק נַפְשׁוֹ מֵאֱלֹהִים in general. The verb צָדַק
does not here signify to be righteous, but to be in the right
(as ch. xi. 2, xiii. 18)—the prevailing signification in Arabic
(*sadaqa,* to speak the truth, be truthful). זֹאת (with *Munach,*
not *Dechî*) is *acc. adv.:* herein, in this case, comp. on ch.
xix. 26. רָבָה מִן is like Deut. xiv. 24 (of the length of the
way exceeding any one's strength), but used, as nowhere else,
of God's superhuman greatness; the Arabic version has the
preposition عَنْ in this instance for מִן. God is too exalted to
enter into a defence of Himself against such vaingloring
interwoven with accusations against Him. And for this
reason Elihu will enter the lists for God.

13 *Why hast thou contended against Him,*
    That He answereth not concerning all His doings?
14 *Yet no—in one way God speaketh,*
    And in two, only one perceiveth it not.
15 *In the dream, in a vision of the night,*
    When deep sleep falleth upon men,
    In slumberings upon the bed:
16 *Then He openeth the ear of men,*
    And sealeth admonition for them,
17 *That He may withdraw man from mischief,*
    And hide pride from man;
18 *That He may keep back his soul from the pit,*
    And his life from the overthrow of the sword.

Knowing himself to be righteous, and still considering
himself treated as an enemy by God, Job has frequently
inquired of God, Why then does He treat him thus with
enmity, ch. vii. 20, and why has He brought him into being
to be the mark of His attack? ch. x. 18.   He has longed for
God's answer to these questions; and because God has veiled
Himself in silence, he has fallen into complaint against Him,
as a ruler who governs according to His own sovereign
arbitrary will.   This is what Elihu has before his mind in
ver. 13.   רִיב (elsewhere in the book of Job with עִם or the
acc. of the person with whom one contends) is here, as Jer.
xii. 1 and freq., joined with אֶל and conjugated as a contracted
Hiph. (רִיבוֹתָ instead of רַבְתָּ, Ges. § 73, 1); and עָנָה with the *acc.*
signifies here : to answer anything (comp. ch. xxxii. 12, xl. 2,
and especially ix. 3); the *suff.* does not refer back to אֱנוֹשׁ of
the preceding strophe (Hirz., Hahn), but to God.   דְּבָרָיו are
the things, *i.e.* facts and circumstances of His rule; all those
things which are mysterious in it He answers not, *i.e.* He
answers concerning nothing in this respect (comp. כֹּל לֹא, ch.
xxxiv. 27), He gives no kind of account of them (Schnurr.,
Ges., and others).   כִּי, ver. 14*a*, in the sense of *imo*, is
attached to this negative thought, which has become a ground
of contention for Job : yet no, God does really speak with
men, although not as Job desires when challenged and in His
own defence.   Many expositors take בְּאַחַת and בִּשְׁתַּיִם after
LXX., Syr., and Jer., in the signification *semel, secundo*
(thus also Hahn, Schlottm.); but *semel* is אַחַת, whereas בְּאַחַת
is nowhere equivalent to בְּפַעַם אַחַת, for in Num. x. 4 it signifies with one, viz. trumpet; Prov. xxviii. 18, on one, viz. of
the many ways; Jer. x. 8, in one, *i.e.* in like folly (not:
altogether, at once, which בְּאֶחָד, Syr. *bachdo*, signifies); then
further on it is not twice, but two different modes or means
of divine attestation, viz. dreams and sicknesses, that are
spoken of; wherefore it is rightly translated by the Targ.

una loquela, by Pagn. *uno modo,* by Vatabl., Merc., *una via.*
The form of the declaration : by one—by two, is that of the
so-called number-proverbs, like ch. v. 19. In diverse ways
or by different means God speaks to mortal man—he does
not believe it, it is *his own* fault if he does perceive it. לֹא
יְשׁוּרֶנָּה, which is correctly denoted as a separate clause by
Rebia mugrasch, is neither with Schlottm. to be regarded as a
circumstantial clause (without one's . . .), nor with Vatablus
and Hahn as a conditional clause (if one does not attend to
it), nor with Montanus and Piscator as a relative clause (to
him who does not observe it), but with Tremellius as a co-
ordinate second predicative clause without a particle (one
might expect אַף): he (mortal man) or one observes it not
(שׁוּר with neut. *suff.* exactly like ch. xxxv. 13).

Vers. 15 sqq. Elihu now describes the first mode in which
God speaks to man : He Himself comes forward as a witness
in man's sleep, He makes use of dreams or dream-like visions,
which come upon one suddenly within the realm of nocturnal
thought (*vid. Psychol.* S. 282 sq.), as a medium of revelation
—a usual form of divine revelation, especially in the heathen
world, to which positive revelation is wanting. The reading
בְּחֶזְיוֹן (Codd., LXX., Syr., Symm., Jer.), as also the accentuation of the בחלום with *Mehupach Legarme,* proceeds from the
correct assumption, that vision of the night and dream are
not coincident notions; moreover, the detailing ver. 15, is
formed according to ch. iv. 13. In this condition of deep or
half sleep, *revelat aurem hominum,* a phrase used of the preparation of the ear for the purpose of hearing by the removal
of hindrances, and, in general, of confidential communication,
therefore : He opens the ear of men, and seals their admonition, *i.e.* the admonition that is wholesome and necessary for
them. Elihu uses בְּ חָתַם here and ch. xxxvii. 7 as בְּעַד חָתַם
is used in ch. ix. 7 : to seal anything (to seal up), comp. حَتَم,
σφραγίζειν, in the sense of infallible attestation and confirma-

tion (John vi. 27), especially (with ـب) of divine revelation or inspiration, distinct in meaning from خَتَم, σφραγίζειν, in the proper sense. Elihu means that by such dreams and visions, as rare overpowering facts not to be forgotten, God puts the seal upon the warning directed to them which, sent forth in any other way, would make no such impression. Most ancient versions (also Luther) translate as though it were יְחַתֵּם (LXX. ἐξεφόβησεν αὐτούς). סֹר is a secondary form to מוּסָר, ch. xxxvi. 10, which occurs only here. Next comes the fuller statement of the object of the admonition or warning delivered in such an impressive manner. According to the text before us, it is to be explained: in order that man may remove (put from himself) mischief from himself (Ges. § 133, 3); but this inconvenient change of subject is avoided, if we supply a מ to the second, and read אדם ממעשׂה, as LXX. ἀποστρέψαι ἄνθρωπον ἀπὸ ἀδικίας αὐτοῦ (which does not necessarily presuppose the reading ממעשׂהו), Targ. ab opere malo; Jer. not so good: ab his quæ fecit. מַעֲשֶׂה signifies facinus, an evil deed, as 1 Sam. xx. 19, and פֹּעַל, ch. xxxvi. 9, evil-doing. The infin. constr. now passes into the v. fin., which would be very liable to misconstruction with different subjects: and in order that He (God) may conceal arrogance from man, i.e. altogether remove from him, unaccustom him to, render him weary of, the sin of pride (גֵּוָה from גֵּוָה = גֵּאָה, as ch. xxii. 29, according to Ges., Ew., Olsh., for גַּאֲוָה = גַּאֲוָה). Here everything in thought and expression is peculiar. Also חַיָּה, ver. 18b (as vers. 22, 28), for חַיִּים (ver. 30) does not occur elsewhere in the book of Job, and the phrase עָבַר בַּשֶּׁלַח here and ch. xxxvi. 12 (comp. עָבַר בַּשַּׁחַת, ver. 28) nowhere else in the Old Testament. שֶׁלַח (Arab. silâh, a weapon of offence, opp. metâ', a weapon of defence) is the engine for shooting, from שָׁלַח, emittere, to shoot; and עבר בשלח is equivalent to נפל בעד השלח, Joel ii. 8, to pass away by (precipitate one's self into) the weapon for shooting. To deliver man from sin, viz. sins of carnal security and imaginary self-importance, and at the same time from an early death, whether natural or violent, this is the disciplinary design which God has in view in connection with this first mode of speaking to him ; but there is also a second mode.

> 19 *He is chastened also with pain upon his bed,*
> *And with the unceasing conflict of his limbs ;*
> 20 *And his life causeth him to loathe bread,*
> *And his soul dainty meat.*
> 21 *His flesh consumeth away to uncomeliness,*
> *And his deranged limbs are scarcely to be seen.*
> 22 *Then his soul draweth near to the grave,*
> *And his life to the destroyers.*

Another and severer lesson which God teaches man is by painful sickness: he is chastened with pain (בְּ of the means) on his bed, he and the vigorous number of his limbs, *i.e.* he with this hitherto vigorous (Raschi), or : while the multitude of his limbs is still vigorous (Ew.). Thus is the *Keri* וְרֹב to be understood, for the interpretation : and the multitude of his limbs with unceasing pain (Arnh. after Aben-Ezra), is unnatural. But the *Chethib* is far more commendable : and with a constant tumult of his limbs (Hirz. and others). Ver. 19*b* might also be taken as a substantival clause : and the tumult of his limbs is unceasing (Umbr., Welte); but that taking over of בְּ from בְמַכְאוֹב is simpler and more pleasing. רִיב (opposite of שָׁלוֹם, *e.g.* Ps. xxxviii. 4) is an excellent description of disease which consists in a disturbance of the equilibrium of the powers, in the dissolution of their harmony, in the excitement of one against another (*Psychol.* S. 287). אֶתָן for אֵיתָן belongs to the many defective forms of writing of this section. In ver. 20 we again meet a Hebræo-Arabic *hapaxlegomenon*, זִהֵם from זָהַם. In Arab. *zahuma* signifies to stink, like the Aram. זִהֵם (whence זוּהֲמָא, dirt and stench), *zahama* to thrust back, restrain, after which Abu Suleiman Daûd Alfâsi, in his

Arabic *Lexicon* of the Hebrew, interprets: "his soul thrusts back (נפסה חוהם) food and every means of life,"[1] beside which the *suff.* of וְהִהֲמָתּוּ is taken as an anticipation of the following object (*vid.* on ch. xxix. 3): his life feels disgust at it, at bread, and his soul at dainty meat. The *Piel* has then only the intensive signification of *Kal* (synon. תִּעֵב, Ps. cvii. 18), according to which it is translated by Hahn with many before him. But if the poet had wished to be so understood, he would have made use of a less ambiguous arrangement of the words, וזהמתו לחם חיתו. We take וְהֵם with Ew. § 122, *b*, as causative of *Kal*, in which signification the *Piel*, it is true, occurs but rarely, yet it does sometimes, instead of *Hiph.*; but without translating, with Hirz., חיה by hunger and נפס by appetite, which gives a confused thought. Schlottm. appropriately remarks: "It is very clearly expressed, as the proper vital power, the proper ψυχή, when it is inwardly consumed by disease, gives one a loathing for that which it otherwise likes as being a necessary condition of its own existence." Thus it is: health produces an appetite, sickness causes nausea; the soul that is in an uninjured normal state longs for food, that which is severely weakened by sickness turns the desire for dainties into loathing and aversion.

·Ver. 21*a*. The contracted future form יִכֶל, again, like יִשֶׁם, ver. 11*a*, is poetic instead of the full form: his flesh vanishes מֵרֹאִי, from sight, *i.e.* so that it is seen no longer; or from comeliness, *i.e.* so that it becomes unsightly; the latter (comp. 1 Sam. xvi. 12 with Isa. liii. 2, ולא־מראה) might be preferred. In ver. 21*b* the *Keri* corrects the text to וְשֻׁפּוּ, *et contrita sunt*, whereas the *Chethib* is to be read וְשֻׁפִּי, *et contritio*. The verb שָׁפָה, which has been explained by Saadia from the Talmudic,[2] signifies *conterere, comminuere;* Abulwalid (in Ges.

---

[1] *Vid.* Pinsker's *Likkute Kadmoniot*, p. קמג.

[2] He refers to *b. Aboda zara* 42*a*: If a heathen have broken an idol to pieces (שִׁפָּה) to derive advantage from the pieces, both the (shattered)

Thes.) interprets it here by *suhifet wa-baradet*, they are consumed and wasted away, and explains it by בְּתְתוֹ. The radical
notion is that of scraping, scratching, rubbing away (not to
be interchanged with سفه ,ספה, which, starting from the radical
notion of sweeping away, vanishing, comes to have that of
wasting away; cognate, however, with the above سكف,
whence *suhâf*, consumption, prop. a rasure of the plumpness
of the body). According to the *Keri*, ver. 21*b* runs: and his
bones (limbs) are shattered (fallen away), they are not seen,
i.e. in their wasting away and shrivelling up they have lost
their former pleasing form. Others, taking the bones in their
strict sense, and שׁפה in the signification to scrape away = lay
bare, take לא ראו as a relative clause, as Jer. has done: *ossa
quæ tecta fuerant nudabuntur* (rather *nudata sunt*), but this
ought with a change of mood to be וַיִּשְׁפוּ . . . לא ראו. To the
former interpretation corresponds the unexceptionable *Chethib:*
and the falling away of his limbs are not seen, *i.e.* (*per
attractionem*) his wasting limbs are diminished until they are
become invisible. רֻאּוֹ is one of the four Old Testament words
(Gen. xliii. 26, Ezra viii. 18, Lev. xxiii. 17) which have a
Dagesh in the *Aleph;* in all four the *Aleph* stands between
two vowels, and the dageshing (probably the remains of a
custom in the system of pointing which has become the prevailing one, which, with these few exceptions, has been suffered to fall away) is intended to indicate that the *Aleph* is
here to be carefully pronounced as a guttural (to use an
Arabic expression, as *Hamza*), therefore in this passage *ru-'û*.[1]
Thus, then, the soul (the bearer of the life of the body) of the

idol and the fragments (שְׁפוּיָיו) are permitted (since both are deprived of
their heathenish character).

[1] *Vid.* Luzzatto's *Grammatica della Lingua Ebraica* (1853), § 54.
Ewald's (§ 21) view, that in these instances the pointed *Aleph* is to be
read as *j* (therefore *ruju*), is unfounded; moreover, the point over the
Aleph is certainly only improperly called *Dagesh*, it might at least just as
suitably be called *Mappik*.

sick man, at last succumbing to this process of decay, comes
near to the pit, and his life to the מְמִתִים, destroying angels
(comp. Ps. lxxviii. 49, 2 Sam. xxiv. 16), *i.e.* the angels who
are commissioned by God to slay the man, if he does not
anticipate the decree of death by penitence.   To understand
the powers of death in general, with Rosenm., or the pains of
death, with Schlottm. and others, does not commend itself,
because the Elihu section has a strong angelological colouring
in common with the book of Job.   The following strophe,
indeed, in contrast to the מְמִיתִים, speaks of an angel that
effects deliverance from death.

> 23 *If there is an angel as mediator for him,*
>   *One of a thousand,*
>   *To declare to man what is for his profit:*
> 24 *He is gracious to him, and saith:*
>   *Deliver him, that he go not down to the pit—*
>   *I have found a ransom.*

The former case, vers. 15–18, was the easier; there a
strengthening of the testimony of man's conscience by a
divine warning, given under remarkable circumstances, suf-
fices.   This second case, which the LXX. correctly distinguishes from the former (it translates ver. 19, πάλιν δὲ
ἤλεγξεν αὐτὸν ἐν μαλακίᾳ ἐπὶ κοίτης), is the more difficult:
it treats not merely of a warning against sin and its wages of
death, but of a deliverance from the death itself, to which the
man is almost abandoned in consequence of sin.   This deliverance, as Elihu says, requires a mediator.   This course of
thought does not admit of our understanding the מַלְאָךְ of a
human messenger of God, such as Job has before him in
Elihu (Schult., Schnurr., Boullier, Eichh., Rosenm., Welte),
an " interpreter of the divine will, such as one finds one man
among a thousand to be, a God-commissioned speaker, in one
word: a prophet" (von Hofmann in *Schriftbew.* i. 336f.).   The

מלאך appears not merely as a declarer of the conditions of
the deliverance, but as a mediator of this deliverance itself.
And if the מְמִתִים, ver. 22*b*, are angels by whom the man is
threatened with the execution of death, the מלאך who comes
forward here for him who is upon the brink of the abyss
cannot be a man. We must therefore understand מלאך not
as in ch. i. 14, but as in ch. iv. 18 ; and the more surely so,
since we are within the extra-Israelitish circle of a patriarchal
history. In the extra-Israelitish world a far more developed
doctrine of angels and demons is everywhere found than in
Israel, which is to be understood not only subjectively, but
also objectively; and within the patriarchal history after
Gen. xvi., that מלאך יהוה (אלהים) appears, who is instrumental in effecting the progress of the history of redemption,
and has so much the appearance of the God of revelation,
that He even calls himself God, and is called God. He it is
whom Jacob means, when (Gen. xlviii. 15 sq.), blessing Joseph,
he distinguishes God the Invisible, God the Shepherd, *i.e.*
Leader and Ruler, and " the Angel who delivered (הַגֹּאֵל) me
from all evil;" it is the Angel who, according to Ps. xxxiv. 8,
encampeth round about them that fear God, and delivereth
them ; " the Angel of the presence" whom Isaiah in the
Thephilla, ch. lxiii. 7 sqq., places beside Jehovah and His
Holy Spirit as a third *hypostasis*. Taking up this perception,
Elihu demands for the deliverance of man from the death
which he has incurred by his sins, a superhuman angelic
mediator. The "Angel of Jehovah" of primeval history is
the oldest prefigurement in the history of redemption of the
future incarnation, without which the Old Testament history
would be a confused *quodlibet* of premises and radii, without
a conclusion and a centre; and the angelic form is accordingly
the oldest form which gives the hope of a deliverer, and to
which it recurs, in conformity to the law of the circular connection between the beginning and end, in Mal. iii. 1.

The strophe begins without any indication of connection with the preceding: one would expect וְאִם or אִם אָם, as we felt the absence of אַף in ver. 14, and לְכֵן in ch. xxxii. 17. We might take מַלְאָךְ מֵלִיץ together as substantive and *epitheton;* the accentuation, however, which marks both מלאך and מליץ with *Rebia magnum* (in which case, according to Bär's *Psalterium,* p. xiv., the second distinctive has somewhat less value than the first), takes מלאך as subj., and מליץ as predicate : If there is then for him (עליו, *pro eo,* Ew. § 217, *i*) an angel as מליץ, *i.e.* mediator; for מליץ signifies elsewhere an interpreter, Gen. xlii. 23; a negotiator, 2 Chron. xxxii. 31; a God-commissioned speaker, *i.e.* prophet, Isa. xliii. 27;—everywhere (if it is not used as in ch. xvi. 20, *in malam parte*) the shades of the notion of this word are summarized under the general notion of *internuncius,* and therefore of mediator (as the Jewish name of the mediating angel מטטרון, probably equivalent to *mediator,* not μετάθρονος, which is no usable Greek word). The Targ. translates by פרקליטא, παράκλητος (*opp.* קטיגור, κατήγορος, κατήγωρ). Therefore : if an angel undertakes the mediatorial office for the man, and indeed one of a thousand, *i.e.* not any one whatever of the thousands of the angels (Deut. xxxiii. 2, Ps. lxviii. 18, Dan. vii. 10, comp. Tobit xii. 15, εἶς ἐκ τῶν ἑπτά), but one who soars above the thousands, and has not his equal among them (as Eccl. vii. 28). Hirz. and Hahn altogether falsely combine: one of the thousands, whose business it is to announce . . . The accentuation is correct, and that forced mode of connection is without reason or occasion. It is the function of the מלאך itself as מליץ, which the clause which expresses the purpose affirms : if an angel appears for the good of the man as a mediator, to declare to him יָשְׁרוֹ, his uprightness, *i.e.* the right, straight way (comp. Prov. xiv. 2), in one word : the way of salvation, which he has to take to get free of sin and death, viz. the way of repentance and of faith (trust in God): God takes pity on the man . . . Here the conclusion begins; Rosenm. and others erroneously continue the antecedent here, so that what follows is the intercession of the angel; the angel, however, is just as a mediator who brings about the favour of God, and therefore not the חֵן himself. He renders pardon possible, and brings the man into the state for receiving it.

Therefore: then God pardons, and says to His angel: Deliver him from the descent to the pit, I have found a ransom. ✓ Instead of פְּדָעֵהוּ, it would be admissible to read פְּרָעֵהוּ, let him free (from פרע, غرف), if the angel to whom the command is given were the angel of death. פָּדַע is a cognate form, perhaps dialectic, with פָּדָה, root פד (as יפה, יפע, وفع, وفى, from the common root יך, וף).[1] The verb מָצָא (מְטָא) signifies to come at, ch. xi. 7, to attain something, and has its first signification here, starting from which it signifies the finding on the part of the seeker, and then when weakened finding without seeking. One is here reminded of Heb. ix. 12, αἰωνίαν λύτρωσιν εὑράμενος. כֹּפֶר (on this word, vid. Hebräerbrief, S. 385, 740), according to its primary notion, is not a covering = making good, more readily a covering = cancelling (from כָּפַר, Talmud. to wipe out, away), but, as the usual combination with עַל shows, a covering of sin and guilt before wrath, punishment, or execution on account of guilt, and in this sense λύτρον, a means of getting free, ransom-money. The connection is satisfied if the repentance of the chastened one (thus e.g. also von Hofm.) is understood by this ransom, or better, his affliction, inasmuch as it has brought him to repentance. But wherefore should the mediatorship of the angel be excluded from the notion of the כֹּפֶר? Just this mediatorship is meant, inasmuch as it puts to right him who by his

---

[1] Wetzstein is inclined to regard פרע as a metathesis of רפע, رفع: thrust (tear, hold) him back from the grave. A proper name, fed'ân, which often occurs among the Beduins, is of uncertain signification; perhaps it would serve as an explanation of פְּדָעֵהוּ.

sins had worked death, *i.e.* places him in a condition in which
no further hindrance stands in the way of the divine pardon.
If we connect the mediating angel, like the angel of Jehovah
of the primeval history, with God Himself, as then the logos
of this mediating angel to man can be God's own logos communicated by him, and he therefore as מליץ, God's speaker
(if we consider Elihu's disclosure in the light of the New
Testament), can be the divine Logos himself, we shall here
readily recognise a presage of the mystery which is unveiled
in the New Testament: "God was in Christ, and recon-
ciled the world unto Himself." A presage of this mystery,
flashing through the darkness, we have already read in ch.
xvii. 3 (comp. ch. xvi. 21; and, on the other hand, in order
to see how this anticipation is kindled by the thought of the
opposite, ch. ix. 33). The presage which meets us here is
like another in Ps. cvii.—a psalm which has many points of
coincidence with the book of Job—where in ver. 20 we find,
"He sent His word, and healed them."[1] At any rate, Elihu
expresses it as a postulate, that the deliverance of man can
only be effected by a superhuman being, as it is in reality
accomplished by the man who is at the same time God, and
from all eternity the Lord of the angels of light.

The following strophe now describes the results of the
favour wrought out for man by the מלאך מליץ.

25 *His flesh swelleth with the freshness of youth,*
   He returneth to the days of his youth.
26 *If he prayeth to Eloah, He showeth him favour,*
   So that he seeth His face with joy,
   And thus He recompenseth to man his uprightness.

---

[1] In his introduction, p. 76, Schlottmann says: "The conceptions of
Wisdom and of the Revealing Angel were already united in that of the
Eternal Word in the ante-Christian, Jewish theology. Therein the fact
of the divine revelation in Christ found the forms in which it could
accommodate itself to the understanding, and stimulate succeeding ages

27 *He singeth to men and saith:*

" *I had sinned and perverted what was straight,*

" *And it was not recompensed to me.*

28 " *He hath delivered my soul from going down into the pit,*

" *And my life rejoiceth in the light.*"

Misled by the change of the *perf.* and *fut.* in ver. 25, Jer. translates 25a: *consumta est caro ejus a suppliciis;* Targ.: His flesh had been weakened (אִתְחֲלִישׁ), or made thin (אִתְקְלִישׁ), more than the flesh of a child; Raschi: it had become burst (French אשקושא, in connection with which only פּשׂ appears to have been in his mind, in the sense of springing up, *prendre son escousse*) from the shaking (of disease). All these interpretations are worthless; נֹעַר, peculiar to the Elihu section in the book of Job (here and ch. xxxvi. 14), does not signify shaking, but is equivalent to נְעֻרִים (ch. xiii. 26, xxxi. 18); and רֻטֲפַשׁ is in the *perf.* only because the passive quadriliteral would not so easily accommodate itself to inflexion (by which all those asserted significations, which suit only the *perf.* sense, fall to the ground). The *Chateph* instead of the simple *Shevâ* is only in order to give greater importance to the passive *u*. But as to the origin of the quadriliteral (on the four modes of the origin of roots of more than three radicals, *vid. Jesurun,* pp. 160–166), there is no reason for regarding it as a mixed form derived from two different verbs: it is formed just like פַּרְשֵׁז (from פָּרַשׂ, by Arabizing = פָּרַשׁ) with a sibilant termination from רָטַף = רֻטַב, and therefore signifies to be (to have been made) over moist or juicy. However, there is yet another almost more commendable explanation possible. In Arab. طرفش signifies to further thought and penetration." Thus it is: between the Chokma of the canonical books and the post-biblical development of the philosophy of religion (dogmatism) which culminates in Philo, there is an historical connection, and, indeed, one that has to do with the development of redemption. *Vid. Luth. Zeitschrift,* 1863, S. 219 ff.

to recover, prop. to grow green, become fresh (perhaps from *tarufa*, as in the signification to blink, from *tarafa*). From this Arab. *tarfasha*, or even from a Hebr. טָרַף,[1] *pinguefacere* (which may with Fürst be regarded as springing from טָפַשׁ, to be fleshy, like כִּרְבֵּל, כִּרְסֵם), רְטַפַּשׁ might have sprung by transposition. In a remarkable manner one and the same idea is attained by all these ways: whether we regard רטפשׁ as a mixed form from רטב and טפשׁ, or as an extended root-form from one or other of these verbs, it is always according to the idea: a superabundance of fresh healthfulness. The מִן of מִנֹּעַר is chiefly regarded as comparative: more than youth, *i.e.* leaving this behind, or exceeding it, Ew. § 221, *a*; but ver. 25*b*, according to which he who was hitherto sick unto death actually renews his youth, makes it more natural to take the מִן as causal: it swells from youth or youthfulness. In this description of the renovation which the man experiences, it is everywhere assumed that he has taken the right way announced to him by the mediating angel. Accordingly, ver. 26*a* is not intended of prayer that is heard, which resulted in pardon, but of prayer that may be heard continually, which results from the pardon: if he prays to Eloah (*fut. hypotheticum* as ch. xxii. 27, *vid.* on xxix. 24),

He receives him favourably (רָצָה, رضِيَ, with בּ, بِ, to have pleasure in any one, with the acc. *eum gratum vel acceptum habere*), and he (whose state of favour is now established anew) sees God's countenance (which has been hitherto veiled

---

[1] The Talmud. טרפשׁא דליבא (*Chullin*, 49*b*) signifies, according to the customary rendering, the pericardium, and טרפשׁא דכבדא (*ib.* 46*a*) the diaphragm, or rather the little net (*omentum minus*). Originally, however, the former signified the cushion of fat under the pericardium on which the heart rests, especially in the crossing of the furrows; the latter the accumulation of fat on the porta (πύλη) and between the laminæ of the little net. For טרפשׁ is correctly explained by שׁוּמָן, fat. It has nothing to do with τράπεζα (an old name for a part of the liver), with which Ges. after Buxtorf connects it.

from him, ch. xxxiv. 29) with rejoicing (as Ps. xxxiii. 3 and
freq.), and He (God) recompenses to the man his uprightness (in his prolonged course of life), or prop., since it is not
וַיְשַׁלֵּם, but וַיָּשֶׁב, He restores on His part his relation in accordance with the order of redemption, for that is the idea of
צדקה; the word has either a legal or a so-to-speak evangeli-
cal meaning, in which latter, used of God (as so frequently
in Isaiah II.), it describes His rule in accordance with His
counsel and order of redemption; the primary notion is strict
observance of a given rule.

In ver. 27a the favoured one is again the subj. This
change of person, without any indication of the same, belongs
to the peculiarities of the Hebrew, and, in general, of the
Oriental style, described in the *Geschichte der jüd. Poesie*,
S. 189 [*History of Jewish Poetry*]; the reference of וַיַּרְא, as
Hiph., to God, which is preferred by most expositors, is consequently unnecessary. Moreover, the interpretation: He
causes his (the favoured one's) countenance to behold joy
(Umbr., Ew.), is improbable as regards the phrase (נראה) ראה
פְּנֵי ה׳, and also syntactically lame; and the interpretation:
He causes (him, the favoured one) to behold His (the divine)
countenance with joy (Hirz., Hahn, Schlottm., and others),
halts in like manner, since this would be expressed by וַיַּרְאֵהוּ
(וַיַּרְאֶנּוּ). By the reference to psalmody which follows in
ver. 27 (comp. ch. xxxvi. 24), it becomes natural that we
should understand ver. 26b according to such passages in the
Psalms as xcv. 2, lxvii. 2, xvii. 15. יָשֹׁר is a poetically contracted *fut.* after the manner of a jussive, for יָשׁוּר; and perhaps it is a dialectic form, for the *Kal* שׁוּר = שִׁיר occurs only
besides in 1 Sam. xviii. 6 as *Chethîb*. With עַל (comp. Prov.
xxv. 20) it signifies to address a song to any one, to sing to
him. Now follows the psalm of the favoured one in outline;
ver. 28 also belongs to it, where the *Keri* (Targ. Jer.), without
any evident reason whatever, gets rid of the 1 *pers.* (LXX.,

Syr.). I had sinned—he says, as he looks back ashamed and thankful—and perverted what was straight (comp. the confession of the penitent, Ps. cvi. 6), וְלֹא שָׁוָה לִי, *et non æquale factum s. non æquatum est mihi*,[1] *i.e.* it has not been recompensed to me according to my deserts, favour instead of right is come upon me. שָׁוָה (سوى) is intended neutrally, not so that God would be the subj. (LXX. καὶ οὐκ ἄξια ἥτασέ με ὧν ἥμαρτον). Now follows, ver. 28, the positive expression of the favour experienced. The phrase עָבַר בִּשַּׁחַת, after the analogy of עָבַר בַּשֶּׁלַח above, and also חָיָה for חַיִּים, are characteristic of the Elihu section. Beautiful is the close of this psalm *in nuce*: "and my life refreshes itself (בְּ ראה as ch. xx. 17 and freq.) in the light," viz. in the light of the divine countenance, which has again risen upon me, *i.e.* in the gracious presence of God, which I am again become fully conscious of.

> 29 *Behold, God doeth all*
> *Twice, thrice with man,*
> 30 *To bring back his soul from the pit,*
> *That it may become light in the light of life.*
> 31 *Listen, O Job, hearken to me;*
> *Be silent and let me speak on.*
> 32 *Yet if thou hast words, answer me;*
> *Speak, for I desire thy justification.*
> 33 *If not, hearken thou to me;*
> *Be silent and I will teach thee wisdom.*

After having described two prominent modes of divine in-

---

[1] In Arabic سوى (*sawa*) is the most general expression for "to be worth, to cost," usually with the *acc.* of price, but also with *li*, *e.g.* in the proverb *hal ka'ke mâ tiswe li-hal da'ke*, this (wretched) bite of bread (of subsistence) is not worth this (excessive) pressure after it. Accordingly וְלֹא שָׁוָה לִי would signify: it (what I suffered) came not equal to me (did not balance me), which at any rate is equivalent to "it did not cost my life" (Wetzst.), but would be indistinctly expressed.

terposition for the moral restoration and welfare of man, he
adds, vers. 29 sq., that God undertakes (observe the want of
parallelism in the distich, ver. 29) everything with a man
twice or thrice (asyndeton, as *e.g.* Isa. xvii. 6, in the sense of *bis
terve*) in order to bring back his soul from the pit (שַׁחַת, here
for the fifth time in this speech, without being anywhere interchanged with שְׁאוֹל or another synonym, which is remarkable),
that it, having hitherto been encompassed by the darkness of
death, may be, or become, light (לְאוֹר, *inf. Niph.*, syncopated
from לְהֵאוֹר, Ew. § 244, *b*) in the light of life (as it were bask
in the new and restored light of life)—it does not always
happen, for these are experiences of no ordinary kind, which
interrupt the daily course of life; and it is not even repeated
again and again constantly, for if it is without effect the first
time, it is repeated a second or third time, but it has an end
if the man trifles constantly with the disciplinary work of
grace which designs his good. Finally, Elihu calls upon
Job quietly to ponder this, that he may proceed; nevertheless, if he has words, *i.e.* if he thinks he is able to advance
any appropriate objections, he is continually to answer him
(הָשִׁיב with *acc.* of the person, as ver. 5), for he (Elihu) would
willingly justify him, *i.e.* he would gladly be in the position
to be able to acknowledge Job to be right, and to have the
accusation dispensed with. Hirz. and others render falsely:
I wish thy justification, *i.e.* thou shouldst justify thyself; in
this case נַפְשְׁךָ ought to be supplied, which is unnecessary:
חָפֵץ, without a change of subject, has the *inf. constr.* here
without לְ, as it has the *inf. absol.* in ch. xiii. 3, and צַדֵּק signifies to vindicate (as ch. xxxii. 2), or acknowledge to be in the
right (as the *Piel* of צָדֵק, ver. 12), both of which are blended
here. The LXX., which translates θέλω γὰρ δικαιωθῆναί
σε, has probably read צִדְקֶךָ (Ps. xxxv. 27). If it is not so
(אִם־אַיִן as Gen. xxx. 1), viz. that he does not intend to defend
himself with reference to his expostulation with God on

account of the affliction decreed for him, he shall on his part (אֶתְּ‎) listen, shall be silent and be further taught wisdom.

Quasi hac ratione Heliu sanctum Iob convicerit! exclaims Beda, after a complete exposition of this speech. He regards Elihu as the type of the false wisdom of the heathen, which fails to recognise and persecutes the servant of God: *Sunt alii extra ecclesiam, qui Christo ejusque ecclesiæ similiter adversantur, quorum imaginem prætulit Balaam ille ariolus, qui et Elieu sicut patrum traditio habet* (Balaam and Elihu, one person—a worthless conceit repeated in the Talmud and Midrash), *qui contra ipsum sanctum Iob multa improbe et injuriose locutus est, in tantum ut etiam displiceret in una ejus et indisciplinata loquacitas.*[1] Gregory the Great, in his *Moralia*, expresses himself no less unfavourably at the conclusion of this speech:[2] *Magna Eliu ac valde fortia protulit, sed hoc unusquisque arrogans habere proprium solet, quod dum vera ac mystica loquitur subito per tumorem cordis quædam inania et superba permiscet.* He also regards Elihu as an emblem of confident arrogance, yet not as a type of a heathen philosopher, but of a believing yet vain and arrogant teacher. This tone in judging of Elihu, first started by Jerome, has spread somewhat extensively in the Western Church. In the age of the Reformation, *e.g.*, Victorin Strigel takes this side: Elihu is regarded by him as *exemplum ambitiosi oratoris qui plenus sit ostentatione et audacia inusitata sine mente.* Also in the Greek Eastern Church such views are not wanting. Elihu says much that is good, and excels the friends in this, that he does not condemn Job; Olympiodorus adds, πλὴν οὐκ ἐνόησε τοῦ δικαίου τὴν διάνοιαν, but he has not understood the true idea of the servant of God![3]

---

[1] *Bedæ Opp. ed. Basil.* iii. col. 602 sq. 786. The commentary also bears the false name of Jerome [Hieronymus], and as a writing attributed to him is contained in *tom.* v. *Opp. ed. Vallarsi.*

[2] *Opp. ed. Paris*, i. col. 777.

[3] *Catena in Job. Londin.* p. 484, where it is further said, Ὅθεν λογιζό-

In modern times, Herder entertains the same judgment. Elihu's speech, in comparison with the short, majestic, solemn language of the Creator, he calls "the weak rambling speech of a boy." "Elihu, a young prophet"—he says further on in his *Geist der Ebr. Poesie,* where he expounds the book of Job as a composition—"arrogant, bold, alone wise, draws fine pictures without end or aim; hence no one answers him, and he stands there merely as a shadow."[1] Among the latest expositors, Umbreit (Edition 2, 1832) consider's Elihu's appearance as "an uncalled-for stumbling in of a, conceited young philosopher into the conflict that is already properly ended; the silent contempt with which one allows him to speak is the merited reward of a babbler." In later years Umbreit gave up this depreciation of Elihu.[2] Nevertheless Hahn, in his *Comm. zu Iob* (1850), has sought anew to prove that Elihu's speeches are meant indeed to furnish a solution, but do not really do so : on the contrary, the poet intentionally represents the character of Elihu as that "of a most conceited and arrogant young man, boastful and officious in his undeniable knowingness." The unfavourable judgments have been carried still further, inasmuch as an attempt has even been made to regard Elihu as a disguise for Satan in the organism of the drama;[3] but it may be more suitable to break off this unpleasant subject than to continue it.

In fact this dogmatic criticism of Elihu's character and speeches produces a painful impression. For, granted that it might be otherwise, and the poet really had designed to bring forward in these speeches of Elihu respecting God's

---

μεθα καὶ τὸν θεὸν μήτε ἐπαινέσαι τὸν Ελιοὺς, ἐπειδὴ μὴ νενόηκε τοῦ Ἰὼβ τοὺς λόγους, μήτε μὴν καταδικάσαι, ἐπειδὴ μὴ ἀσεβείας αὐτὸν κατέκρινε.

[1] Edition 1805, S. 101, 142.

[2] *Vid.* Riehm, *Blätter der Erinnerung an F. W. C. Umbreit* (1862), S. 58.

[3] Thus the writer of a treatise in the 3d vol. of Bernstein's *Analekten,* entitled : *Der Satan als Irrgeist und Engel des Lichts.*

own appearing an incontrovertible apology for His holy love, as a love which is at work even in such dispensations of affliction as that of Job: what offence against the deep earnestness of this portion of Holy Scripture would there be in this degradation of Elihu to an absurd character, in that depreciation of him to a babbler promising much and performing little! But that the poet is really in earnest in everything he puts into Elihu's mouth, is at once shown by the description, ch. xxxiii. 13–30, which forms the kernel of the contents of the first speech. This description of the manifold ways of the divine communication to man, upon a contrite attention to which his rescue from destruction depends, belongs to the most comprehensive passages of the Old Testament; and I know instances of the powerful effect which it can produce in arousing from the sleep of security and awakening penitence. If one, further, casts a glance at the historical introduction of Elihu, ch. xxxii. 1–5, the poet there gives no indication that he intends in Elihu to bring the odd character of a young poltroon before us. The motive and aim of his coming forward, as they are there given, are fully authorized. If one considers, further, that the poet makes Job keep silence at the speeches of Elihu, it may also be inferred therefrom that he believes he has put answers into Elihu's mouth by which he must feel himself most deeply smitten; such truths as ch. xxxii. 13–30, drawn from the depths of moral experience, could not have been put forth if Job's silence were intended to be the punishment of contempt.

These counter-considerations also really affect another possible and milder apprehension of the young speaker, inasmuch as, with von Hofmann, the gravitating point of the book of Job is transferred to the fact of the Theophany as the only satisfactory practical solution of the mystery of affliction: it is solved by God Himself coming down and acknowledging Job

as His servant. Elihu—thus one can say from this point of
view—is not one of Job's friends, whose duty it was to comfort him; but the moral judgment of man's perception of
God is made known by this teacher, but without any other
effect than that Job is silent. There is one duty towards
Job which he has not violated, for he has not to fulfil the
duty of friendship: The only art of correct theorizing is to
put an opponent to silence, and to have spoken to the wind is
the one punishment appropriate to it. This milder rendering
also does not satisfy; for, in the idea of the poet, Elihu's
speeches are not only a thus negative, but the positive preparation for Jehovah's appearing. In the idea of the poet,
Job is silent because he does not know how to answer Elihu,
and therefore feels himself overcome.[1] And, in fact, what
answer should he give to this first speech? Elihu wishes to
dispute Job's self-justification, which places God's justice in
the shade, but not indeed in the friends' judging, condemnatory manner: he wishes to dispute Job's notion that his
affliction proceeds from a hostile purpose on the part of God,
and sets himself here, as there, a perfectly correct task, which
he seeks to accomplish by directing Job to regard his affliction, not indeed as a punishment from the angry God, but as
a chastisement of the God who desires his highest good, as
disciplinary affliction which is intended to secure him against
hurtful temptation to sin, especially to pride, by salutary
humiliation, and will have a glorious issue, as soon as it has
in itself accomplished that at which it aims.

It is true one must listen very closely to discover the difference between the tone which Elihu takes and the tone in

---

[1] The preparation is negative only so far as Elihu causes Job to be
silent and to cease to murmur; but Jehovah draws from him a confession
of penitence on account of his murmuring. This positive relation of the
appearing of Jehovah to that for which Elihu negatively prepares the way,
is rightly emphasized by Schlottm., Rübiger (*De l. Iobi sententia primaria*,
1860, 4), and others, as favourable to the authenticity.

which Eliphaz began his first speech. But there is a difference notwithstanding: both designate Job's affliction as a
chastisement (מוּסָר), which will end gloriously, if he receives
it without murmuring; but Eliphaz at once demands of him
humiliation under the mighty hand of God; Elihu, on the
contrary, makes this humiliation lighter to him, by setting
over against his longing for God to answer him, the pleasing
teaching that his affliction in itself is already the speech of
God to him,—a speech designed to educate him, and to bring
about his spiritual well-being. What objection could Job,
who has hitherto maintained his own righteousness in opposition to affliction as a hostile decree, now raise, when it is
represented to him as a wholesome medicine reached forth to
him by the holy God of love? What objection could Job
now raise, without, in common, offensive self-righteousness,
falling into contradiction with his own confession that he is
a sinful man, ch. xiv. 4, comp. xiii. 26? Therefore Elihu
has not spoken to the wind, and it cannot have been the
design of the poet to represent the feebleness of theory and
rhetoric in contrast with the convincing power which there is
in the fact of Jehovah's appearing.

But would it be possible, that from the earliest times one
could form such a condemnatory, depreciating judgment concerning Elihu's speeches, if it had not been a matter of
certainty with them? If of two such enlightened men as
Augustine and Jerome, the former can say of Elihu: *ut
primas partes modestiæ habuit, ita et sapientiæ*, while the
latter, and after his example Bede, can consider him as a
type of a heathen philosophy hostile to the faith, or of a
selfishly perverted spirit of prophecy: they must surely have
two sides which make it possible to form directly opposite
opinions concerning them. Thus is it also in reality. On
the one side, they express great, earnest, humiliating truths,
which even the holiest man in his affliction must suffer him-

self to be told, especially if he has fallen into such vainglorying and such murmuring against God as Job did; on
the other side, they do not give such sharply-defined expression to that which is intended characteristically to distinguish
them from the speeches of the friends, viz. that they regard
Job not as רשע, and his affliction not as just retribution,
but as a wholesome means of discipline, that all misunderstanding would be excluded, as all the expositors who acknowledge themselves unable to perceive an essential difference
between Elihu's standpoint and the original standpoint of
the friends, show. But the most surprising thing is, that
the peculiar, true aim of Job's affliction, viz. his being proved
as God's servant, is by no means thoroughly clear in them.
From the prologue we know that Job's affliction is designed ·
to show that there is a piety which also retains its hold on
God amid the loss of all earthly goods, and even in the face
of death in the midst of the darkest night of affliction; that
it is designed to justify God's choice before Satan, and bring
the latter to ruin; that it is a part of the conflict with the
serpent, whose head cannot be crushed without its sting being
felt in the heel of the conqueror; in fine, expressed in New
Testament language, that it falls under the point of view of
the cross ($\sigma\tau\alpha\nu\rho\acute{o}\varsigma$), which has its ground not so much in the
sinfulness of the sufferer, as in the share which is assigned to
him in the conflict of good with evil that exists in the world.
It cannot be supposed that the poet would, in the speeches of
Elihu, set another design in opposition to the design of Job's
affliction expressed in the prologue; on the contrary, he
started from the assumption that the one design does not
exclude the other, and in connection with the imperfectness
of the righteousness even of the holiest man, the one is easily
added to the other; but it was not in his power to give
expression to both grounds of explanation of Job's affliction
side by side, and thus to make this intermediate section "the

beating heart"[1] of the whole. The aspect of the affliction as
a chastisement so greatly preponderates, that the other, viz. as
a trial or proving, is as it were swallowed up by it. One of
the old writers[2] says, "Elihu proves that it can indeed be
that a man may fear and honour God from the heart, and consequently be in favour with God, and still be heavily visited
by God, either for a trial of faith, hope, and patience, or for
the revelation and improvement of the sinful blemishes which
now and then are also hidden from the pious." According
to this, both aspects are found united in Elihu's speeches;
but in this first speech, at least, we cannot find it.

There is another poet, whose *charisma* does not come up
to that of the older poet, who in this speech pursues the well-
authorized purpose not only of moderating what is extreme in
Job's speeches, but also of bringing out what is true in the
speeches of the friends.[3] While the book of Job, apart from
these speeches, presents in the Old Testament way the great
truth which Paul, Rom. viii. 1, expresses in the words, οὐδέν
κατάκριμα τοῖς ἐν Χριστῷ Ἰησοῦ, this other poet has given
expression at the same time, in the connection of the drama,
to the great truth, 1 Cor. xi. 32, κρινόμενοι ὑπὸ τοῦ κυρίου
παιδευόμεθα, ἵνα μὴ σὺν τῷ κόσμῳ κατακριθῶμεν. That it
is another poet, is already manifest from his inferior, or if it
is preferred, different, poetic gift. True, A. B. Davidson has
again recently asserted, that by supporting it by such observations, the critical question is made "a question of subjective
taste." But if these speeches and the other parts of the book
are said to have been written by one poet, there is an end to
all critical judgment in such questions generally. One cannot

[1] *Vid.* Hengstenberg, *Lecture on the Book of Job.*
[2] Jacob Hoffmann (of St Gallen), *Gedult Iobs*, Basel, 1663 (a rare little
book which I became acquainted with in the town library of St Gallen).
[3] On this subject see my Art. *Hiob* in Herzog's *Real-Encyklopädie*,
vi. 116–119, and comp. Kahnis, *Dogmatik*, i. 306–309, and my *Für und
wider Kahnis* (1863), S. 19–21.

avoid the impression of the distance between them; and if it be suppressed for a time, it will nevertheless make itself constantly felt. But do the prophecies of Malachi stand lower in the scale of the historical development of revelation, because the Salomonic glory of prophetic speech which we admire in Isaiah is wanting in them? Just as little do we depreciate the spiritual glory of these speeches, when we find the outward glory of the rest of the book wanting in them. They occupy a position of the highest worth in the historical development of revelation and redemption. They are a perfecting part of the canonical Scriptures. In their origin, also, they are not much later;[1] indeed, I venture to assert that they are by a cotemporary member even of the Chokma-fellowship from which the book of Job has its rise. For they stand in like intimate relation with the rest of the book to the two Ezrahite Psalms, lxxxviii., lxxxix.; they have, as to their doctrinal contents, the fundamental features of the Israelitish Chokma in common; they speak another and still similar Aramaizing and Arabizing language (*hebraicum arabicumque sermonem et interdum syrum*, as Jerome expresses it in his *Præf. in l. Iobi*); in fact, we shall further on meet with linguistic signs that the poet who wrote this addition has lived together with the poet of the book of Job in one spot beyond the Holy Land, and speaks a Hebrew bearing traces of a like dialectic influence.

---

[1] Seinecke (*Der Grundgedanke des B. Hiob*, 1863) places it, with Ewald, 100–200 years later; and, moreover, asserts that the book of Job has no foundation whatever in oral tradition—Job is the Israel of the exile, Uz is Judæa, etc.

Elihu's Second Speech.—Chap. xxxiv.

Schema: 6. 10. 5. 8. 12. 6. 10. 9. 13.

[Then began Elihu and said :]
2 *Hear, ye wise men, my words,*
   And ye experienced ones, give ear to me!
3 *For the ear trieth words,*
   As the palate tasteth by eating.
4 *Let us find out what is right,*
   Let us explore among ourselves what is good.

After his first speech Elihu has made a brief pause; now since Job is silent, he begins anew. ויען ויאמר, LXX. correctly, here as in all other instances where the phrase occurs : ὑπολαβὼν λέγει, taking up the word he said. The wise and the knowing (Arab. *'ulamâ*), whose attention he bespeaks, are not Job and the three (Umbr., Hahn), who are indeed a party, and as such a subject for the arbitrative appearance of Elihu; also not every one capable of forming a judgment (Hirz.); but those in the circle of spectators and listeners which, as is assumed, has assembled round the disputants (Schlottm.). In ver. 3 Elihu does not expressly mean his own ear, but that of the persons addressed : he establishes his summons to prove what he says by the general thought brought over from ch. xii. 11, and as there (comp. ch. v. 7, xi. 12), clothed in the form of the emblematic proverb,—that as there is a bodily, so there is also a mental organ of sense which tries its perceptions. לֶאֱכֹל is not intended as expressing a purpose (*ad vescendum*), but as gerundive (*vescendo*). The phrase בָּחַר־מִשְׁפָּט, occurring only here, signifies neither to institute a search for the purpose of decision (Schult. and others), since בחר does not signify to decide upon anything, nor to investigate a cause (Hahn), which would be נבחנה, but to test and choose what is right, δοκιμάζειν καὶ τὸ καλὸν κατέχειν, 1 Thess. v. 21, after which the parallel runs: *cognoscamus inter nos* (*i.e.* in common) *quid bonum.*

5 *For Job hath said:* "*I am guiltless,*
  "*And God hath put aside my right.*
6 "*Shall I lie in spite of my right,*
  "*Incurable is mine arrow without transgression.*"
7 *Where is there a man like Job,*
  Who drinketh scorning like water,
8 *And keepeth company with the workers of iniquity,*
  And walketh with wicked men,
9 *So that he saith:* "*A man hath no profit*
  "*From entering into fellowship with God*"?!

That in relation to God, thinking of Him as a punishing judge, he is righteous or in the right, *i.e.* guiltless (צָדְקְתִּי with *Pathach* in pause, according to Ew. § 93, *c*, from צָדֵק = צָדֵק, but perhaps, comp. Prov. xxiv. 30, Ps. cii. 26, because the *Athnach* is taken only as of the value of *Zakeph*), Job has said *verbatim* in ch. xiii. 18, and according to meaning, ch. xxiii. 10, xxvii. 7, and throughout; that He puts aside his right (the right of the guiltless, and therefore not of one coming under punishment): ch. xxvii. 2. That in spite of his right (עַל, to be interpreted, according to Schultens' example, just like ch. x. 7, xvi. 17), *i.e.* although right is on his side, yet he must be accounted a liar, since his own testimony is belied by the wrathful form of his affliction, that therefore the appearance of wrong remains inalienably attached to him, we find in idea in ch. ix. 20 and freq. Elihu makes Job call his affliction חִצִּי, *i.e.* an arrow sticking in him, viz. the arrow of the wrath of God (on the objective *suff.* comp. on ch. xxiii. 2), after ch. vi. 4, xvi. 9, xix. 11; and that this his arrow, *i.e.* the pain which it causes him, is incurably bad, desperately malignant without (בְּלִי as ch. viii. 11) פֶּשַׁע, *i.e.* sins existing as the ground of it, from which he would be

obliged to suppose they had thrust him out of the condition
of favour, is Job's constant complaint (*vid. e.g.* ch. xiii. 23 sq.).
Another utterance of Job closely connected with it has so
roused Elihu's indignation, that he prefaces it with the exclamation of astonishment: Who is a man like Job, *i.e.* where
in all the world (מִי as 2 Sam. vii. 23) has this Job his equal,
who . . . The attributive clause refers to Job; "to drink
scorn (here: blasphemy) like water," is, according to ch.
xv. 16, equivalent to to give one's self up to mockery with
delight, and to find satisfaction in it. אָרַח לְחֶבְרָה, to go over
to any one's side, looks like a poeticized prose expression.
לָלֶכֶת is a continuation of the אָרַח, according to Ew. § 351, *c*,
but not directly in the sense "and he goes," but, as in the
similar examples, Jer. xvii. 10, xliv. 19, 2 Chron. vii. 17, and
freq., in the sense of: "he is in the act of going;" comp. on
ch. xxxvi. 20 and Hab. i. 17. The utterance runs: a man
does not profit, viz. himself (on the use of סָכַן of persons as
well as of things, *vid.* on ch. xxii. 2), by his having joyous
and familiar intercourse (בִּרְצֹתוֹ, as little equivalent to בְּרוּן as
in Ps. l. 18) with God. Job has nowhere expressly said this,
but certainly the declaration in ch. ix. 22, in connection with
the repeated complaints concerning the anomalous distribution
of human destinies (*vid.* especially ch. xxi. 7 sqq., xxiv. 1 sqq.),
are the premises for such a conclusion. That Elihu, in vers.
7 sq., is more harsh against Job than the friends ever were
(comp. *e.g.* the well-measured reproach of Eliphaz, ch. xv. 4),
and that he puts words into Job's mouth which occur nowhere
verbatim in his speeches, is worked up by the Latin fathers
(Jer., Philippus Presbyter, Beda,[1] Gregory) in favour of their

---

[1] Philippus Presbyter was a disciple of Jerome. His *Comm. in Iobum*
is extant in many forms, partly epitomized, partly interpolated (on this
subject, *vid. Hieronymi Opp. ed. Vallarsi*, iii. 895 sqq.). The commentary
of Beda, dedicated to a certain Nectarius (Vectcrius), is fundamentally
that of this Philippus.

unfavourable judgment of Elihu; the Greek fathers, however, are deprived of all opportunity of understanding him
by the translation of the LXX. (in which μυκτηρισμόν
signifies the scorn of others which Job must swallow down,
comp. Prov. xxvi. 6), which here perverts everything.

10 *Therefore, men of understanding, hearken to me!*
   Far be it from God to do evil,
   And the Almighty to act wrongfully.
11 *No indeed, man's work He recompenseth to him,*
   And according to man's walk He causeth it to be with him.

" Men of heart," according to *Psychol.* S. 249, comp. 254,
is equivalent to νοήμονες or νοηροί (LXX. συνετοὶ καρδίας).
The clause which Elihu makes prominent in the following
reply is the very axiom which the three defend, perfectly true
in itself, but falsely applied by them : evil, wrong, are incon-
ceivable on the part of God; instead of וּלְשַׁדַּי it is only וְשַׁדַּי
in the second member of the verse, with the omission of the
præp.—a frequent form of ellipsis, particularly in Isaiah (ch.
xv. 8, xxviii. 6, xlviii. 14, lxi. 7, comp. Ezek. xxv. 15). Far
removed from acting wickedly and wrongfully, on the contrary He practises recompense exactly apportioned to man's
deeds, and ever according to the walk of each one (אֹרַח like
דֶּרֶךְ or דִּרְבֵי, *e.g.* Jer. xxxii. 19, in an ethical sense) He causes
it to overtake him, *i.e.* to happen to him (הִמְצִיא only here
and ch. xxxvii. 13). The general assertion brought forward
against Job is now proved.

12 *Yea verily God acteth not wickedly,*
   And the Almighty perverteth not the right.
13 *Who hath given the earth in charge to Him?*
   And who hath disposed the whole globe?
14 *If He only set His heart upon Himself,*
   If He took back His breath and His inspiration to Himself:

15 *All flesh would expire together,*
And man would return to dust.

With אַף אָמְנָם (Yea verily, as ch. xix. 4, "and really")
the counter-assertion of ver. 11 is repeated, but negatively
expressed (comp. ch. viii. 3). הִרְשִׁיעַ signifies sometimes to
act as רָשָׁע, and at others to be set forth and condemned as a
רָשִׁע; here, as the connection requires, it is the former. Ver.
13 begins the proof. Ewald's interpretation: who searcheth,
and Hahn's: who careth for the earth beside Him, are
hazardous and unnecessary. פָּקַד with עַל of the person and
the *acc.* of the thing signifies: to enjoin anything as a duty
on any one, to entrust anything to any one, ch. xxxvi. 23,
Num. iv. 27, 2 Chron. xxxvi. 23; therefore: who has made
the earth, *i.e.* the care of it, a duty to Him? אָרְצָה (*Milel*) is
not to be refined into the meaning "to the earth" (as here
by Schultens and a few others, Isa. viii. 23 by Luzzatto: he
hath smitten down, better: dishonoured, to the earth with a
light stroke), but is poetically equivalent to אֶרֶץ, as לַיְלָה (comp.
modern Greek ἡ νύχθα) is in prose equivalent to לַיִל. Ver.
13*b* is by no means, with Ew. and Hahn, to be translated:
who observes (considers) the whole globe, שִׂים as ver. 23, ch.
iv. 20, xxiv. 12—the expression would be too contracted to
affirm that no one but God bestowed providential attention
upon the earth; and if we have understood ver. 13*a* correctly,
the thought is also inappropriate. A more appropriate thought
is gained, if עָלָיו is supplied from ver. 13*a*: who has enjoined
upon Him the whole circle of the earth (Saad., Gecat., Hirz.,
Schlottm.); but this continued force of the עליו into the second
independent question is improbable in connection with the repetition of מִי. Therefore: who has appointed, *i.e.* established
(שָׂם as ch. xxxviii. 5, Isa. xliv. 7),—a still somewhat more
suitable thought, going logically further, since the one giving
the charge ought to be the lord of him who receives the com-

mission, and therefore the Creator of the world. This is just God alone, by whose רוּחַ and נְשָׁמָה the animal world as well as the world of men (vid. xxxii. 8, xxxiii. 4) has its life, ver. 14: if He should direct His heart, i.e. His attention (שִׂים לֵב אֶל as ch. ii. 3), to Himself (emphatic: Himself alone), draw in (אָסַף as Ps. civ. 29; comp. for the matter Eccl. xii. 7, Psychol. S. 406) to Himself His inspiration and breath (which emanated from Him or was effected by Him), all flesh would sink together, i.e. die off at once (this, as it appears, has reference to the taking back of the animal life, רוּחַ), and man would return (this has reference to the taking back of the human spirit, נשׁמה) to dust (עַל instead of אֶל, perhaps with reference to the usual use of the עַל־עָפָר, ch. xvii. 16, xx. 11, xxi. 26).

Only a few modern expositors refer אֵלָיו, as Targ. Jer. and Syr., to man instead of reflexively to God; the majority rightly decide in favour of the idea which even Grotius perceived: si sibi ipsi tantum bonus esse (sui unius curam habere) vellet. אִם followed by the fut. signifies either si velit (LXX. εἰ βούλοιτο), as here, or as more frequently, si vellet, Ps. l. 12, cxxxix. 8, Obad. ver. 4, Isa. x. 22, Amos ix. 2–4. It is worthy of remark that, according to Norzi's statement, the Babylonian texts presented יָשִׁיב, ver. 14a, as Chethîb, ישׁים as Kerî (like our Palestine text, Dan. xi. 18), which a MS. of De Rossi, with a Persian translation, confirms; the reading gives a fine idea: that God's heart is turned towards the world, and is unclosed; its ethical condition of life would then be like its physical ground of life, that God's spirit dwells in it; the drawing back of the heart, and the taking back to Himself of the spirit, would be equivalent to the exclusion of the world from God's love and life. However, ישׁים implies the same; for a reference of God's thinking and willing to Himself, with the exclusion of the world, would be just a removal of His love. Elihu's proof is this: God does

not act wrongly, for the government of the world is not a
duty imposed upon Him from without, but a relation entered
into freely by Him : the world is not the property of another,
but of His free creative appointment; and how unselfishly,
how devoid of self-seeking He governs it, is clear from the
fact, that by the impartation of His living creative breath He
sustains every living thing, and does not, as He easily might,
allow them to fall away into nothingness. There is therefore
a divine love which has called the world into being and keeps
it in being; and this love, as the perfect opposite of sovereign
caprice, is a pledge for the absolute righteousness of the
divine rule.

16 *And oh understand now, hear this;*
   Hearken to the sound of my words.
17 *Would one who hateth right also be able to subdue?*
   Or wilt thou condemn the All-just?
18 *Is it becoming to say to a king: Worthless One!?*
   Thou evil-doer! to princes?
19 *To Him who accepteth not the person of rulers,*
   And regardeth not the noble before the poor:
   For they are all the work of His hands.
20 *In a moment they die, and at midnight*
   The people are overthrown and perish,
   And they put aside the mighty—not by the hand of man.

This strophe contains several grammatical rarities. At
first sight it appears that ver. 16*a* ought to be translated:
" and if there is understanding (viz. to thee = if thou hast),
then hear this.". But בִּינָה is accented as *Milel* and with
Mercha, and can therefore not be a substantive (Hirz., Hahn,
and others); for the retreat of the accent would be absolutely
incomprehensible, and instead of a conjunctive, a distinctive,
viz. *Dechî*, ought to be expected. Several of the old expositors, therefore, interpret with Nolde: *quod quum ita sit,*

intellige; but this elliptical וְאִם, well as it might also be used for ch. xxi. 4, is unsupportable; the *Makkeph* between the two words is also against it, which rather arises from the assumption that בִּינָה is the *imperat.*, and אִם as an exception, like Gen. xxiii. 13, is an optative particle joined to the *imper.* instead of to the *fut.*: "and if thou shouldst observe" (= וְאִם־תָּבִין). To translate ver. 17*a* with Schultens: *num iram osor judicii frenabit*, is impracticable on account of the order of the words, and gives a thought that is inappropriate here. אַף is a particle, and the *fut.* is *potentialis:* is it also possible that an enemy of right should govern? (חָבַשׁ, *imperio coercere,* as עָצַר 1 Sam. ix. 17, אָסַר Ps. cv. 22); right and government are indeed mutually conditioned, without right everything would fall into anarchy and confusion. In ver. 17*b* this is applied to the Ruler of the world: or (וְאִם, *an,* as ch. viii. 3, xxi. 4, xl. 9) wilt thou condemn the mighty just One, *i.e.* the All-just? As Elihu calls God שַׂגִּיא כֹחַ, ch. xxxvii. 23, as the Almighty, and as the Omniscient One, תְּמִים דֵּעִים, ch. xxxvii. 16, so here as the All-just One, צַדִּיק כַּבִּיר. The two adjectives are put side by side ἀσυνδέτως, as is frequently the case in Arabic, and form one compound idea, Ew. § 270, *d.*

Ver. 18*a.* The interrogative הֲ is joined to the *inf.,* not, however, as ch. xl. 2 (*num litigare cum Deo castigator, scil. vult*), with the *inf. absol.,* but with the *inf. constr.;* the form אֲמֹר for אָמֹר occurs also in Prov. xxv. 7, and is also otherwise not rare, especially in combination with particles, *e.g.* בֶּאֱכֹל, Num. xxvi. 10, Olsh. § 160, *b.*[1] It is unnecessary to suppose that the *inf. constr.,* which sometimes, although rarely, does occur (Ges. § 131, rem. 2), is used here instead of the *inf. absol.;* it is thus, as after טוֹב, *e.g.* Judg. ix. 2 (הַמְשֹׁל), Prov. xxv. 7, Ps. cxxxiii. 1, and Ps. xl. 6 after אֵין, used as *n.*

---

[1] Ezek. xxv. 8 is also to be read אֱמֹר according to the Masora and old editions (as אֱבֹד Deut. vii. 20, אֱבֹל xii. 23, אֱחֹז 1 Kings vi. 6), for distinction from the imperatives, which have *Chateph-Segol.*

actionis, since הֲ in a pregnant sense is equivalent to *num licet* (הֲטוֹב), if one does not prefer, with Olsh., to suppose an aposiopesis: "(dare one be so bold as) to say to a king: Thou worthless one! Thou evil-doer! to princes?" The reading הָאֹמֵר is an unnecessary lightening of the difficulty. It were a *crimen læsæ,* if one reproached a king with being unjust, and therefore thereby denied him the most essential requisite of a ruler; and now even Him (Merc. correctly supplies *tanto minus ei*) who does not give the preference to the person (נָשָׂא פְנֵי as ch. xiii. 8, xxxii. 21) of princes, and does not (with preference) regard (on נִכַּר *vid.* on ch. xxi. 29, also here *Piel,* and according to the statement of the Masora, *Milel,* for an acknowledged reason which can be maintained even in remarkable instances, like Deut. x. 5 in וְיִהְיוּ, Ezek. xxxii. 26 in מְחֹלְלֵי, whereas 1 Sam. xxiii. 7 is *Milra*) the rich before (לִפְנֵי in the sense of *præ*) the poor! therefore the King of kings, who makes no partial distinction, because the king and the beggar are the work of His hands: they stand equally near to Him as being His creatures, and He is exalted above both alike as their Creator, this order and partiality are excluded;—what a *nota bene* against the doctrine of the *decretum absolutum,* which makes the love of the Creator a partial love, and turns this love, which in its very nature is perfect love, into caprice! In ver. 20 Elihu appeals to human history in favour of this impartiality of the Ruler of the world. It may there appear as though God with partiality suffered rulers and peoples in authority in the world to do as they please; but suddenly they die away, and in fact in the middle of the night (here *Mercha-mahpach*), the individuals of a great people (thus must עָם be understood in accordance with the prominently-placed plur. predicate, Ges. § 146, 1) tremble and perish; and they remove (וְיָסִירוּ instead of the passive, as ch. iv. 20 and frequently) the mighty—לֹא־בְיָד. It is not the hand of man which does this, but an invisible higher power (which, if it is called יָד, only bears this name *per anthropomorphismum*); comp. Dan. ii. 34, בִּידַיִן לָא; Dan. viii. 25, בְּאֶפֶס יָד; and also ch. xx. 26, like the New Testament use of οὐ χειροποίητος. The subj. of ver. 20a are the previously mentioned princes. The division according to the accents may be received with hesitation, since the symmetry of the stichs, which it restores, is not unfrequently wanting in the Elihu section. Ver. 20c refers back to the possessors of power, and in the interval, ver. 20b describes the fate of those who belong to the people which has become subservient to their lust of conquest, for עָם cannot signify "in crowds" (Ew., Hahn); it is therefore, and especially when mentioned as here between princes and rulers, the people, and in fact, in distinction from גּוֹי, the people together forming a state.

21 *For His eyes are upon the ways of each one,*
   And He seeth all his steps.
22 *There is no darkness nor shadow of death*
   Wherein the workers of iniquity might hide themselves.
23 *For He needeth not long to regard a man*
   That he may enter into judgment with God.

As the preceding strophe showed that God's creative order excludes all partiality, so this strophe shows that His omniscience qualifies Him to be an impartial judge. He sees everything, nothing can escape His gaze; He sees through man without being obliged to wait for the result of a judicial investigation. שִׂים with עַל does not here signify: to lay upon (Saad., Gecat.), but as ch. xxxvii. 15, and as with אֶל (ver. 14) or בְּ (ch. xxiii. 6): to direct one's attention (supply לִבּוֹ, ch. i. 8) towards anything; the *fut.* has here a modal signification; עוֹד is used as *e.g.* Gen. xlvi. 29: again and again, continuously; and in the clause expressive of purpose it is אֶל־אֵל (instead of אֵלָיו, a very favourite combination used throughout the whole book, ch. v. 8, viii. 5, xiii. 3, and so on) from

the human standpoint: He, the all-seeing One, needs not to
observe him long that he should enter into judgment with
God—He knows him thoroughly before any investigation
takes place, which is not said without allusion to Job's vehement longing to be able to appear before God's tribunal.

24 *He breaketh the mighty in pieces without investigation*
   And setteth others in their place.
25 *Thus He seeth through their works,*
   And causeth their overthrow by night, thus they are crushed.
26 *He smiteth them after the manner of evil-doers*   .
   In the sight of the public.
27 *For for such purpose are they fallen away from Him*
   And have not considered any of His ways,
28 *To cause the cry of the poor to come up to Him,*
   And that He should hear the cry of the needy.

He makes short work (לֹא־חֵקֶר for בְּלֹא, as ch. xii. 24,
xxxviii. 26: without research, viz. into their conduct, which
is at once manifest to Him; not: in an incomprehensible
manner, which is unsuitable, and still less: *innumerabiles*, as
Jer., Syr.) with the mighty (כַּבִּירִים, Arab. *kibâr, kubarâ*),
and in consequence of this (*fut. consec.*) sets up (*constituit*)
others, *i.e.* better and worthier rulers (comp. אַחֵר, ch. viii. 19,
Isa. lxv. 15), in their stead. The following לָכֵן is not equivalent to לְכֵן אֲשֶׁר, for which no satisfactory instance exists;
on the contrary, לכן here, as more frequently, introduces not
the real consequence (ch. xx. 2), but a logical inference,
something that directly follows in and with what precedes
(corresponding to the Greek ἄρα, just so, consequently),
comp. ch. xlii. 3, Isa. xxvi. 14, lxi. 7, Jer. ii. 33, v. 2, Zech.
xi. 7 (*vid.* Köhler *in loc.*). Thus, then, as He hereby proves,
He is thoroughly acquainted with their actions (מַעְבָּד, nowhere
besides in the book of Job, an Aramaizing expression for
מעשׂה). This abiding fact of divine omniscience, inferred

from the previously-mentioned facts, then serves again in its
turn, in ver. 25b, as the source of facts by which it is verified.
לַיְלָה is by no means an obj. The expositions: *et inducit
noctem* (Jer.), He walks in the night in which He has veiled
Himself (Umbr.), *convertit eos in noctem* (Syr., Arab.), and
such like, all read in the two words what they do not imply.
It is either to be translated: He throws them by night (לִילָה
as ch. xxvii. 20) upon the heaps (הָפַךְ as Prov. xii. 7), or,
since the verb has no objective *suff.*: He maketh a reformation or overthrow during the night, *i.e.* creates during the
night a new order of things, and they who stood at the head
of the former affairs are crushed by the catastrophe.

Ver. 26. The following תַּחַת רְשָׁעִים cannot signify: on the
place of the evil-doers, *i.e.* in the place where evil-doers are
punished (Hirz., Hahn, and others), for תַּחַת (תַּחְתֵּי) only has
this signification with the *suff.* (*vid.* on Hab. iii. 16); but not
otherwise than: in the evil-doers' stead, taking them and
treating them as such, as Jer. has correctly translated: *quasi
impios* (comp. Isa. x. 4, Jerome, *cum interfectis*). The place
first mentioned afterwards is not exactly the usual place of
judgment, but any place whatever where all can see it.
There He smites those who hitherto held positions of eminence, as of unimpeachable honour, like the common criminal;
סָפַק, صفق, *complodere*, and then *ictu resonante percutere*, as
the likewise cognate صفع signifies first to box the ear (as صفن
= صفق), then so to strike that it smacks. As little as לְבֵן,
ver. 25a, was = לָכֵן אֲשֶׁר, just so little is אֲשֶׁר עַל־כֵּן, ver. 27a,
= עַל־כֵּן אֲשֶׁר (*vid.* on the other hand what is said on Gen.
xviii. 5 concerning כִּי־עַל־כֵּן). Elihu wishes to say that they
endure such a destiny of punishment, because they therefore,
i.e. in order to suffer such, have turned aside from following
after God, and have not thought on all His ways, *i.e.* guidings,
by which He manifested Himself to them: they have thus
sought to cause the cry of the poor to come (Jer. well renders:

ut pervenire facerent ad eum) before Him (עָלָיו, perhaps with the idea of urging forward = לְפָנָיו or בְּאָזְנָיו), and that He may hear the cry of the lowly (construction exactly like ch. xxxiii. 17), *i.e.* have sought to bring forth His avenging justice by injustice that cries aloud to heaven.

29 *If He, however, maketh peace, who will then condemn?*
   And if He hideth His countenance—who then can behold Him?—
   Both concerning numbers and individuals together:
30 *That godless men reign not,*
   That they be not nets to the people.
31 *For one, indeed, saith to God,*
   " *I have been proud, I will not do evil;*
32 " *What I see not, show Thou me;*
   " *If I have done wrong, I will do it no more"!?—*

If God makes peace (יַשְׁקִט as Ps. xciv. 13, comp. Isa. xiv. 7, שָׁקְטָה כָּל־הָאָרֶץ, viz. after the overthrow of the tyrant) in connection with such crying oppression of the poor, who will then condemn Him without the rather recognising therein His comprehensive justice? The conjecture יִרְעַשׁ[1] is not required either here or 1 Sam. xiv. 47 (where הִרְשִׁיעַ signi- fies to punish the guilty); יַרְשִׁעַ is also not to be translated *turbabit* (Rosenm.), since רָשַׁע (رَسِع, رَشِغ) according to its primitive notion does not signify "to be restless, to rage," but "to be relaxed, hollow" (opposite of צדק, صدق, to be hard, firm, tight). Further: If God hides His countenance, *i.e.* is angry and punishes, who can then behold Him, *i.e.* make Him, the veiled One, visible and claim back the favour withdrawn? The *Waw* of וּמִי, if one marks off the periods of the paratactic expression, is in both cases the *Waw* of conclusion after hypo- thetical antecedents, and ver. 29*b* refers to Job's impetuous challenging of God. Thus exalted above human controversy

---

[1] *Vid.* Grätz in Frankel's *Monatsschrift*, 1861, i.

and defiance, God rules both over the mass and over individuals alike. יַחַד gives intensity to the equality thus correlatively (*et — et*) expressed (Targ., Syr.) ; to refer it to אדם as generalizing (LXX., Jer. *et super omnes homines*), is forbidden by the antithesis of peoples and individuals. To the thought, that God giveth rest (from oppressors) and hides His countenance (from the oppressors and in general those who act wrongly), two co-ordinate negative final clauses are attached : in order that godless men may not rule (מִמְּלֹךְ, as *e.g.* 2 Kings xxiii. 33, *Keri*), in order that they may no longer be (מ = מְהִיוֹת, under the influence of the notion of putting aside contained in the preceding final clause, therefore like Isa. vii. 8 מעם, xxv. 2 מעיר, Jer. xlviii. 2 מגוי, and the like) snares of the people, *i.e.* those whose evil example and bad government become the ruin of the community.

In ver. 31*a* the view of those who by some jugglery concerning the laws of the vowel sounds explain הֶאָמַר as *imper. Niph.* (= הֵאָמֵר), be it in the sense of לְהֵאָמֵר, *dicendum est* (Rosenm., Schlottm., and others, after Raschi), or even in the unheard-of reflexive signification: express thyself (Stick., Hahn), is to be rejected. The syncopated form of the *infin.* בְּהֻרֻ, Ezek. xxvi. 15, does not serve as a palliation of this adventurous imperative. It is, on the contrary, אָמַר with הַ *interrog.*, as Ezek. xxviii. 9 הֶאָמֹר, and probably also הֶאָמוּר Mic. ii. 7 (*vid.* Hitz.). A direct exhortation to Job to penitence would also not be in place here, although what Elihu says is levelled against Job. The כִּי is confirmatory. Thus God acts with that class of unscrupulous men who abuse their power for the destruction of their subjects: for he (one of them) says (or : has said, from the standpoint of the execution of punishment) to God, etc. Ew.· differently : "for one says thus to God even : I expiate what I do not commit," by understanding the speech quoted of a defiance which reproachfully demands an explanation. It is, however, manifestly

a compendious model confession. And since Elihu with כִּי
establishes the execution of punishment from this, that it
never entered the mind of the אָדָם חָנֵף thus to humble himself
before God, so נָשָׂאתִי here cannot signify : I have repented
(put up with and had to bear what I have deserved); on the
contrary, the confession begins with the avowal : I have
exalted myself (נָשָׂא, se efferre, in Hos. xiii. 1, Ps. lxxxix. 10),
which is then followed by the vow : I will not (in the future)
do evil (חָבַל synon. עָוָה, as Neh. i. 7, and probably also supra,
ch. xxiv. 9), and the entreaty, ver. 32 : beside that which I
behold (elliptical object-clause, Ew. § 333, b), i.e. what lies
beyond my vision (= נִסְתָּרוֹת or עֲלָמִים, Ps. xix. 13, xc. 8,
unacknowledged sins), teach me ; and the present vow has
reference to acknowledged sins and sins that have still to be
acknowledged: if I have done wrong, I will do it no more.
Thus speaking—Elihu means—those high ones might have
anticipated the punishment of the All-just God, for favour
instead of wrath cannot be extorted, it is only reached by
the way of lowly penitence.

33 *Shall He recompense it as thou wilt? For thou hast found*
fault,
So that thou hast to determine, not I,
And what thou knowest speak out !
34 *Men of understanding will say to me,*
And a wise man who listeneth to me :
35 " *Job speaketh without knowledge,*
" *And his words are without intelligence.*"
36 *O would that Job were proved to the extreme*
On account of his answers after the manner of evil men ;
37 *For he addeth transgression to his sin,*
Among us he clappeth
And multiplieth his speeches against God.

The question put to Job, whether then from him or accord-

ing to his idea (עֹם in מֵעִמְּךָ as ch. xxiii. 10, xxvii. 11, which
see) shall God recompense it (viz., as this "it" is to be understood according to ver. 32b : man's evil-doing and actions in
general), Elihu proves from this, that Job has despised
(shown himself discontented with it) the divine mode of
recompense, so that therefore (this second כִּי signifies also
nam, but is, because extending further on account of the
first, according to the sense equivalent to *ita ut*) he has to
choose (seek out) another mode of recompense, not Elihu (who
is perfectly satisfied with the mode with which history furnishes us); which is then followed by the challenge (דַּבֵּר not
infin., but as ch. xxxii. 33) : what (more corresponding to just
retribution) thou knowest, speak out then ! Elihu on his part
knows that he does not stand alone against Job, the censurer
of the divine government of the world, but that men of heart
(understanding) and (every) wise man who listens to him will
coincide with him in the opinion that Job's talk is devoid of
knowledge and intelligence (on the form of writing הַשְׂכֵּיל as
Jer. iii. 15, *vid.* Ges. § 53, rem. 2).

In ver. 36 sq. we will for the present leave the meaning of
אָבִי undecided ; יְבָחֵן is certainly intended as optative : let Job
be tried to the extreme or last, *i.e.* let his trial by affliction
continue until the matter is decided (comp. Hab. i. 4), on
account of the opposition among men of iniquity, *i.e.* after the
manner of such (on this *Beth* of association comp. בְּקֹרְשִׁים, ch.
xxxvi. 14), for to הֵשָׁאת, by which the purpose of his affliction
is to be cleared up, he adds פֶּשַׁע, viz. the wickedness of blas-
phemous speeches: among us (therefore without fear) he
claps (viz. his hands scornfully together, יִסְפּוֹק only here thus
absolute instead of יִשְׂפֹּק כַּפָּיו, ch. xxvii. 23, comp. בִשְׂפֵק ch.
xxxvi. 18 with ספקו xx. 22[1]) and multiplies (יֶרֶב, *fut. apoc.*
Hiph. as ch. x. 17, and instead of the full fut., as יֹשֵׁר, ch.

---

[1] The mode of writing with ס instead of שׂ is limited in the book of
Job, according to the Masora, to ch. xxxiv. 26, 37.

xxxiii. 27) his speeches against God, *i.e.* exceeds himself in speeches which irreverently dictate to and challenge God.

But we now ask, what does that אָבִי, ver. 36*a*, signify? According to the accentuation with *Rebia*, it appears to be intended to signify *pater mi* (Jer.), according to which Saad. (*jâ rabbî*) and Gecat. (*munshiî*, my Creator) translate it. This would be the only passage where an Old Testament saint calls God אבי; elsewhere God is called the Father of Israel, and Israel as a people, or the individual comprehending himself with the nation, calls Him אבינו. Nevertheless this *pater mi* for Elihu would not be inappropriate, for what the writer of the Epistle to the Hebrews, ch. xii. 7, says to believers on the ground of Prov. iii. 11: εἰς παιδείαν ὑπομένετε, ye suffer for the purpose of paternal discipline, is Elihu's fundamental thought; he also calls God in ch. xxxii. 22, xxxvi. 3, with a like reference to himself, עֹשֵׂנִי and פֹּעֲלִי—this ejaculatory "my Father!" especially in conjunction with the following wish, remains none the less objectionable, and only in the absence of a more agreeable interpretation should we, with Hirz., decide in its favour. It would be disproportionately repulsive if ver. 36 sq. still belonged to the assenting language of another, and Elihu represented himself as addressed by.אבי (Wolfson, Maur.). Thus, therefore, אבי must be taken somehow or other interjectionally. It is untenable to compare it with אֲבוֹי, Prov. xxiii. 29, for אוי ואבוי (Arab. *âh wa-âwâh*) is "ah! and alas!" The Aramaic בייא בייא, *væ væ* (Buxtorf, col. 294), compared by Ges. to בִּי, signifies just the same. The Targ. translates צְבֵינָא, I wish; after which Kimchi, among moderns, Umbr., Schlottm., Carey, and others derive אָבִי from אָבָה, a wish (after the form חָזֶה, קָצֶה), but the participial substantival-form badly suits this signification, which is at once improbable according to the usage of the language so far as we at present know it. This interpretation also does not well suit the בִּי, which is to be explained at the same time. Ewald,

§ 358, *a*, regards אָבִי as the fuller form of בִּי, and thinks אבי is dialectic = לְבִי = לְוִי = לֹי, but this is an etymological legerdemain. The two Schultens (died 1750 and 1793) were on the right track when they traced back אבי to בוא, but their interpretation: *rem eo adducam ut* (אבי = אביא, as it is certainly not unfrequently written, *e.g.* 1 Kings xxi. 29, with the assumption of a root בִי cognate with בא), is artificial and without support in the usage of the language and in the syntax. Körber and Simonis opened up the right way, but with inadequate means for following it out, by referring (*vid.* Ges. *Thes. s.v.* בִּי) to the formula of a wish and of respect, *bawwâk allah*, which, however, also is *bajjâk*. The Kamus interprets *bajjâk*, though waveringly, by *bawwâk*, the meaning of which (may he give thee a resting-place) is more transparent. In an annotated Codex of Zamachschari *hajjâk allah wa-bajjâk* is explained: God preserve thy life and grant thee to come to a place of rest, *bawwaaka* (therefore بَوَّى = بَوَّأَ)

menzilan. That אָבִי (as also בִּי) is connected with this *bajjâk* since the latter is the *Piel*-form of an old verb *bajja* (*vid. supra*, p. 125), which with the forms بَاءَ (whence بِيئَة, a sheltering house) and بَوَأ (بَوَى) has one root similar in signification with בוא, the following contributions of Wetzstein will show.

In elucidation of the present passage he observes: The expressions *abî, tebî, jebî; nebî, tebû, jebû*, are so frequent in Damascus, that they very soon struck me, and on my first inquiry I always received the same answer, that they are a mutilation of ابغِي, *abghi*, I desire, etc. [*vid. supra*, p. 165], until one day a fugitive came into the consulate, and with these words, *abî wâlidêk*, seized me in that part of the body where the Arabs wear the girdle (*zunnâr*), a symbolic action by which one seeks some one's protection. Since the word here could not be equivalent to *abghi* ("I desire" thy parents), I turned to the person best acquainted with the idiom of the country, the scribe *Abderrahmân el-Midâni*, whose father had been a wandering minstrel in the camps for twenty years; and he explained to me that *abghi* only signifies "I desire;" on the contrary, *abî*, "I implore importunately, I pray for God's sake," and the latter belongs to a defective verb, بَيْ, from which, except the forms mentioned, only the part. *anâ bâj*, "I come as a suppliant," and its plur. *nahn bâjin*, is used. The poet *Musa Rârâ* from *Krêje* in the south of Hauran, who lived with me six months in Damascus in order to instruct me in the dialect of his district, assured me that among the Beduins also the *perf.* forms *bît, bînâ* (I have, we have entreated), and the *fut.* forms *tabîn* (thou, woman . . .), *jaben* (they, the women . . .), and *taben* (ye women . . .), are used. In the year 1858, in the course of a journey in his native country, I came to *Dimâs*, whither they had brought two strange Beduins who had been robbed of their horses in that desert (Sahra *Dimâs*), and one of them had at the same time received a mortal gunshot-wound. As I came to these men, who were totally forsaken, the wounded man began to express his importunate desire for a surgeon with the words *jâ shêch nebî 'arabak*, "Sir, we claim the protection of thy Arabs," *i.e.* we·adjure thee by thy family. Naturally *abî* occurs most frequently. It generally has its obj. in the *acc.*, often also with the *præpos.* عَلَى, exactly like دَخَل (to enter, to flee anywhere and hide), which is its correct synonym and usual substitute in common life. It is often used without an obj., and, indeed, very variously. With women it is chiefly the introduction to a question prompted by curiosity, as : *abî* (ah, tell me), have you really betrothed your daughter? Or the word is accompanied by a gesture by the five fingers of the right hand, with the tips united, being stretched out towards the hasty or impatient listener, as if one wished to show some costly object, when *abî* signifies as much as: I pray thee wait till I have shown thee this precious thing, *i.e.* allow me to make one more remark to thee in reference to the matter. Moreover, בִּי (probably not corrupted from אָב, but a derived *nomen concretum* in the sense of *dachîl* or *mustagîr*, one seeking protection, protégé, after the form אָי, צָי, from בוח = בוא) still exists unaltered in Hauran and in the steppe. The Beduin introduces an important request with the words *anâ bî ahlak*, I am a protégé of thy family, or *anâ bî 'irdak*, I trust to thine honour, etc.; while in Damascus they say, *anâ dachîl ahlak*, *harîmak*, *aulâdak*, etc. The Beduin women make use of this *bî* in a weakened signification, in order to beg a piece of soap or sugar, and *anâ bî lihjetak*, I pray by thy beard, etc., is often heard.

If now we combine that אָבִי of Elihu with *abghi* (from بَغَى, Hebr. בָּעָה, Aram. בְּעָא, *fut.* יִבְעֶי, as בִּי with בְּעָי) or with *abî* = אָבָא, from the verb *bajja* = בוא (בִי),[1] it always remains a re-markable instance in favour of the Arabic colouring of the Elihu section similar to the rest of the book,—a colouring, so to speak, dialectically Hauranitish; while, on the other hand, even by this second speech, one cannot avoid the impression of a great distance between it and the rest of the book: the language has a lofty tone, without its special harshness, as there, being the necessary consequence of a carefully concentrated fulness of thought; moreover, here in general the usual

---

[1] We cannot in any case, with Wetzst., explain the אָבִי אָבִי, 2 Kings ii. 12, xiii. 14, according to the above, so that the king of Israel adjured the dying prophet by the national army and army of the faithful not to forsake him, as an Arab is now and then adjured in most urgent and straitened circumstances "by the army of Islam;" *vid.* on the other hand, 2 Kings vi. 21, comp. v. 13, viii. 9 (בֶּנֶּךְ). Here rather, if an Arabian parallel be needed, the usual death wail, *bi-abî anta* (thou wast dear as a father to me), *e.g.* in Kosegarten, *Chrestom.* p. 140, 3, is to be compared. אָבִי, 1 Sam. xxiv. 12, might more readily, with Ew. § 101, *c*, be brought in here and regarded as belonging to the North Palestine peculiarities of the book of Kings; but by a comparison of the passages cited, this is also improbable.

regularity of the strophe-lines no longer prevails, and also the usual symmetrical balance of thought in them.

If we confine our attention to the real substance of the speech, apart from the emotional and rough accessories, Elihu casts back the reproach of injustice which Job has raised, first as being contradictory to the being of God, ch. xxxiv. 10 sq. ; then he seeks to refute it as contradicting God's government, and this he does (1) apagogically from the unselfish love with which God's protecting care preserves the breath of every living thing, while He who has created all things might bring back all created things to the former non-existence, ch. xxxiv. 12–15 ; (2) by induction from the impartial judgment which He exercises over princes and peoples, and from which it is inferred that the Ruler of the world is also all-just, ch. xxxiv. 16–20. From this Elihu proves that God can exercise justice, and from that, that He is omniscient, and sees into man's inmost nature without any judicial investigation, ch. xxxiv. 21–28; inaccessible to human accusation and human defiance, He rules over peoples and individuals, even over kings, and nothing turns His just punishment aside but lowly penitence blended with the prayer for the disclosure of unperceived sin, ch. xxxiv. 29–32. For in His retributive rule God does not follow the discontented demands of men arrogant and yet devoid of counsel, ch. xxxiv. 33. It is worthy of recognition, that Elihu does not here coincide with what has been already said (especially ch. xii. 15 sqq.), without applying it to another purpose ; and that his theodicy differs essentially from that proclaimed by the friends. It is not derived from mere appearance, but lays hold of the very principles. It does not attempt the explanation of the many apparent contradictions to retributive justice which outward events manifest, as agreeing with it; it does not solve the question by mere empiricism, but from the idea of the Godhead and its relation to the world, and by such inner necessity guarantees to the

mysteries still remaining to human shortsightedness, their
future solution.

Elihu's Third Speech.—Chap. xxxv.

Schema : 6. 8. 10. 6.

[Then began Elihu, and said:]

2 *Dost thou consider this to be right,*
   Sayest thou : my righteousness exceedeth God's,
3 *That thou sayest, what advantage is it to thee,*
   What doth it profit me more than my sin ?
4 *I will answer thee words,*
   And thy companions with thee.

The neutral זֹאת, ver. 2*a*, refers prospectively to כִּי־תֹאמַר,
ver. 3*a*: this that thou sayest. חָשַׁב with *acc.* of the obj. and
לְ of the predicate, as ch. xxxiii. 10, comp. xiii. 24, and freq.
The second interrogative clause, ver. 2*b*, is co-ordinate with
the first, and the collective thought of this ponderous construction, vers. 2, 3, is this: Considerest thou this to be right,
and thinkest thou on this account to be able to put thy
righteousness above the divine, that, as thou maintainest,
no righteousness on the side of God corresponds to this thy
righteousness, because God makes no distinction between
righteousness and the sin of man, and allows the former to
go unrewarded ? צִדְקִי (for which Olsh. wishes to read צָדַקְתִּי,
as ch. ix. 27 אמרתי for אָמְרִי) forms with מֵאֵל a substantival
clause : *justitia mea est præ Deo (præ divina)*; מִן comparative
as ch. xxxii. 2, comp. on the matter xxxiv. 5, not equivalent
to ἀπό as ch. iv. 17. כִּי־תֹאמַר is first followed by the *oratio
obliqua:* what it (viz. צדקך) advantageth thee, then by the *or.
directa* (on this change *vid.* Ew. § 338, *a*): what profit have I
(viz. בצדקי), *præ peccato meo ;* this מִן is also comparative ; the
constantly ambiguous combination would be allowable from
the fact that, according to the usage of the language, " to

obtain profit from anything" is expressed by בְּ הוֹעִיל, not by
הוֹעִיל מִן. Moreover, *præ peccato meo* is equivalent to *plus
quam inde quod pecco*, comp. Ps. xviii. 24 מֵעֲוֺנִי, Hos. iv. 8
אֶל־עֲוֺנָם. We have already on ch. xxxiv. 9 observed that Job
has not directly said (he cites it, ch. xxi. 15, as the saying of
the ungodly) what Elihu in ver. 3 puts into his mouth, but
as an inference it certainly is implied in such utterances as
ch. ix. 22. Elihu's polemic against Job and his companions
(רֵעֶיךָ are not the three, as LXX. and Jer. translate, but the
אַנְשֵׁי אָוֶן, to whom Job is likened by such words as ch. xxxiv.
8, 36) is therefore not unauthorized; especially since he
assails the conclusion together with its premises. In the
second strophe the vindication of the conclusion is now
refuted.

5 *Look towards heaven and see,*
  And behold the ethereal heights : they are high above thee.
6 *If thou sinnest, what dost thou effect with Him?*
  And if thy transgressions are many, what doest thou to Him?
7 *If thou art righteous, what dost thou give Him,*
  Or what doth He take from thy hand?
8 *To man like thee thy godlessness availeth,*
  . *And to thee, a son of man, thy righteousness.*

Towards heaven he is to direct his gaze, to obtain from the
height of heaven a notion of the exaltation of God who dwells
above the heavens. The combination הַבֵּט וּרְאֵה is like Ps.
lxxx. 15 and freq. שְׁחָקִים (שָׁחַק, سحق, to rub in pieces, make
thin, therefore the opposite of עָבִים) are the thin transparent
strata of the atmosphere above the hanging clouds. מִן after
גָּבַהּ denotes the height that is on the opposite side to the
beholder. From the exaltation of God it is then further
inferred that it is impossible to exercise any human influence
upon Him, by which He might suffer. The pointing wavers
here between תִּפְעַל (the common *fut.* form) and תִּפְעָל (as a con-

traction of תִּפְעָל after the form אָוֶם, Num. xxiii. 8). • Human
wrong or right doing neither diminishes nor increases His
blessedness; injury or advantage is only on the side of man,
from whom it proceeds. Others, whom his conduct affects,
are not included in ver. 8 : righteous or ungodly doing, Elihu
means to say, as such and with its consequences, belongs
solely to the doer himself, the man " like thee" (לְאִישׁ with
Munach, כָּמוֹךָ with *Munach*), the son of man, *i.e.* man, capable
of evil as of good, and who always, after deciding in favour of
the latter or the former, determines his fortune or misfortune,
in distinction from God, who ever remains unchangeably the
same in His perfect righteousness. What Elihu here says we
have already heard from Eliphaz, ch. xxii. 2 sq., and Job
even expresses himself similarly in ch. vii. 20 ; but to Elihu's
mind it all becomes for Job new and powerful motives to
quiet submission, for what objection should Job raise in justification of his complaints concerning his affliction against such
sentiments as these, that goodness bears its reward and evil
its punishment in itself, and that God's reward of goodness
is not a work of indebtedness, nor His punishment of evil
a work of necessity ? Before such truth he must really hold
his peace.

  9 *By reason of the multitude of oppressions they raise a cry,*
     They call for help by reason of the arm of the great,
 10 *But none saith : Where is Eloah my Creator,*
     Who giveth songs of praise in the night,
 11 *Who teacheth us by the beasts of the earth,*
     And maketh us wise by the fowls of heaven ?
 12 *Then they cry, yet He answereth not,*
     Because of the pride of evil men.
 13 *Vanity alone God heareth not,*
     And the Almighty observeth it not.

  In ver. 9*a* the accentuation of מֵרֹב with *Dechî*, according

to which Dachselt interprets: *præ multitudine (oppressionum)*
oppressi clamabunt, is erroneous; it is to be written מֵרֹב, as
everywhere else, and this (according to Codd. and the editions
of Jablonski, Majus, Michaelis, and others) is to be accented
with *Munach,* which is followed by עֲשׁוּקִים with a vicarious
Munach: præ multitudine oppressionum (עֲשׁוּקִים like Eccl.
iv. 1*a,* and probably also Amos iii. 9) *edunt clamorem (Hiph.*
in the intensive *Kal* signification, as *e.g.* הִזְנָה, to commit forni-
cation, Hos. iv. 10, and freq., comp. p. 185, note). On וְזֹרוֹעַ,
ver. 9*b, vid.* vol. i. 432; רַבִּים are the great or lords (Arab.
arbâb). The *plur.* with a general subj. is followed by the
sing. in ver. 10*a:* and no one says (exactly as in הֶאָמַר, ch.
xxxiv. 31). Elihu weakens the doubt expressed by Job in
ch. xxiv. 12, that God allows injustice to prevail, and oppressed innocence remains without vindication. The failure
of the latter arises from the fact of the sufferers complaining,
but not seeking earnestly the only true helper, God their
maker (עֹשִׂים, intensive *plur.,* as Isa. xxii. 11, liv. 5, Ps.
cxlix. 2), who gives (to which may be compared a passage
of the Edda: "Wuodan gives songs to the Scalds") songs
(זְמִרוֹת, from the onomatopoetic זמר) in the night, *i.e.* who in
the night of sorrow puts songs of praise concerning the dawn-
ing light of help into the mouth of the sufferers. The singing
of the glory of the nightly heavens (Stick., Hahn) is to be as
little thought of as the music of the spheres; the night is, as
ch. xxxiv. 20, 25, the time of unexpectedly sudden change.

In ver. 11 most expositors (last of all Schlottm.) take the
two מִ as comparative. Elihu would then, since he feels the
absence of the asking after this God on the part of the sufferers, mean the conscious relation in which He has placed
us to Himself, and in accordance with which the sufferer
should not merely instinctively complain, but humbly bow
himself and earnestly offer up prayer. But according to ch.
xii. 7 (comp. Prov. vi. 6, וחכם), it is to be translated: who

teaches (מִאַלְּפֵנוּ = מַלְּפֵנוּ, comp. 2 Sam. xxii. 40, *Psalter* i. 160) us from the beasts of the earth (so that from them as a means of instruction teaching comes to us), and makes us wise from the birds of heaven. The *fut.* interchanging with the *part.* better accords with this translation, according to which ver. 11 is a continuation of the assertion of a divine instruction, by means of the animal creation; the thought also suits the connection better, for of the many things that may be learned from the animal creation, prayer here comes under consideration,—the lions roar, Ps. civ. 21; the thirsty cattle cry to God, Joel i. 20; the ravens call upon God, Ps. cxlvii. 9. If we now determine the collective thought of vers. 10 sq., that affliction does not drive most men to God the almighty Helper, who will be humbly entreated for help: it is more natural to take שָׁם (*vid.* on ch. xxiii. 7) in the sense of then (τότε), than, with reference to the scene of oppression, in the sense of there (LXX., Jer.: *ibi*). The division of the verse is correct, and H. B. Starcke has correctly interpreted: *Tunc clamabunt (sed non respondebit) propter superbiam (insolentiam) malorum.* מִפְּנֵי is not to be connected with יַעֲנֶה. in the sense of *non exaudiet et servabit*, by which *constr. prægnans* one would expect מִן, Ps. xxii. 22, instead of מפני, nor in the sense of *non exaudiet propter* (Hirz., Schlottm.), for the arrogant רָעִים are not those who complain unheard: but, as the connection shows, those from whom the occasion of complaint proceeds. Therefore: not allowing themselves to be driven to God by oppression, they cry then, without, however, being heard of God, by reason of the arrogance of evil men which they have to endure. Ver. 13 gives the reason of their obtaining no answer: Only emptiness (*i.e.* mere motion of the lips without the true spirit of prayer) God heareth not, and the Almighty observeth it not. Hahn wrongly denies אַךְ the significations *certo* and *verumtamen*; but we prefer the restrictive signification (sheer emptiness or hollowness) which

proceeds from the affirmative primary signification[1] here, to
the adversative (nevertheless emptiness), since the adversative
thought, *verumtamen non exaudit*, has found its expression
already in וְלֹא יַעֲנֶה.

14 *Although thou sayest, thou seest Him not:*
  The cause lieth before Him, and thou mayest wait for Him.
15 *Now, then, if His wrath hath not yet punished,*
  Should He not be well acquainted with sullenness?
16 *While Job openeth his mouth without reason,*
  Without knowledge multiplieth words.

The address is not directed to Job exclusively, for it here
treats first of the acts of injustice which prevail among men
and remain apparently unpunished; but to Job, however,
also, so far as he has, ch. xxiii. 8–10, comp. xix. 7, xxx. 20,
thus complained concerning his prayer being unanswered.
אַף כִּי signifies elsewhere *quanto minus*, ch. iv. 19, or also
quanto magis, Prov. xv. 11, but nowhere *quanto minus si*
(Hirz., Hlgst.) or *quanto magis si* (Hahn), also not Ezek.
xv. 5, where it signifies *etiamne quum*. As it can, however,
naturally signify *etiam quum*, it can also signify *etiamsi*,
etsi, as here and Neh. ix. 18. This *quamvis dicas* (*opineris*)
is followed by the *oratio obliqua*, as ch. xxxv. 3a. The relation of the matter—says the conclusion, ver. 14b—is other
than thou thinkest: the matter to be decided lies before Him,
is therefore well known to Him, and thou mightest only wait
for Him (חוֹלֵל instead of יָחֵל or הוֹחִיל only here, comp. Ps.
xxxvii. 7, וְהִתְחוֹלֵל לוֹ); the decision, though it pass by, will not
fail. In vers. 15 sq., ver. 15 is taken by most modern com-
mentators as antecedent to ver. 16, in which case, apart from
the distortions introduced, two interpretations are possible:
(1) However now, because His (God's) wrath does not
visit . . . Job opens his mouth; (2) However now, because

[1] *Vid.* Hupfeld in the *Zeitschr. für Kunde des Morgenl.* ii. 441 f.

He (God) does not visit his (Job's) wrath (comp. on this reference of the אַפּוֹ to Job, ch. xviii. 4, xxxvi. 13, 18) . . . Job opens, etc. That a clause with a confirmatory כִּי is made to precede its principal clause is not without example, Gen. iii. 14, 17; but in connection with this arrangement the verb is accustomed always, in the principal clause or in the conclusion, to stand prominent (so that consequently we should expect וַיִּפְקֹד אִיּוֹב אֵיוֹב), although in Arabic this position of the words, וְאִיּוֹב יִפְקֹד, and in fact فَأَيُّوبُ instead of وَأَيُّوبُ (in connection with a difference of the subj. in the antecedent and in the conclusion, vid. De Sacy, *Gramm. Arabe*, § 1201, 2), is regular. Therefore for a long time I thought that ver. 15 was to be taken interrogatively: And now (וְעַתָּה as logical inference and conclusion, which is here its most probable function, Ew. § 353, *b*) should His wrath not punish (פָּקַד as absolute as ch. xxxi. 14), and should He not take notice, etc., פִּי interrogative as 1 Sam. xxiv. 20, xxviii. 13, 1 Kings xi. 22, as הֲכִי (is it so that, or: should it be so that), ch. vi. 22, and freq., in connection with which, what is said on Gen. xxi. 7 concerning the modal use of the *præt.* might be compared on the two *prætt.* But by this rendering the connection of ver. 16 with what precedes is awkward. Ewald has given the correct rendering (apart from the misunderstanding of פָּשׁ): Therefore, because His wrath has not yet punished, He does not know much about foolishness! Ver. 15*b* requires to be taken as the conclusion to ver. 15*a*, yet not as an exclamation, but as an interrogative. The interrogative use of וְלֹא is not unusual, 2 Sam. xix. 44, Ezek. xvi. 43, 47, 56, xxxii. 27; and just as here, this interrogative וְלֹא is found after a hypothetical antecedent clause, 1 Sam. xx. 9, Ex. viii. 22.

In connection with this interrogative rendering of ver. 15, it still remains questionable whether it refers to Job's sin, or sin which prevails among men. The theme of this third speech of Elihu requires the latter reference, although perhaps not without a side-glance at Job's own arrogant behaviour. The translation shows how suitably ver. 16 is connected with what precedes: ver. 16 is a circumstantial clause, or, if one is not willing to take it as a subordinate clause, but prefers to take it as standing on a level with ver. 15, an adversative clause attached with *Waw*, as is frequently the case: but (nevertheless) Job . . . ; פֶּה פָּצָה of opening the mouth in derision, as Lam. ii. 16, iii. 46 ; הֶבֶל is the *acc.* of closer definition to it (= בְּהֶבֶל), and the הִכְבִּיר, which occurs only here and ch. xxxvi. 31, signifies without distinction *magnificare* and *multiplicare:* Job multiplies high emotional words. As this יַכְבִּיר is, so to speak, Hebræo-Arabic (Arab. *akbara*), so is ver. 15 full of Arabisms: (1) The combination פָּקַד אֵין, which has not its like in the Hebrew language (whether it be originally intended as relative or not: *non est quod visitaverit*, Ew. § 321, *b*), corresponds to the popular Arabic use of ليس for ﻻ, Ges. *Thes.* i. 82, *b;* probably אֵין has the value of an intensive negation (Carey: not at all). (2) The combination יָדַע בְּ, to know about anything, to take knowledge of anything (differently ch. xii. 9, but comp. ch. xxiv. 12 on the idea), is like the Arab. construction of the verb *'alima* with *bi* (concerning) or *bianna* (because that) of the obj.; מְאֹד (on this *vid.* on Ps. xxxi. 12) belongs not to בַּפַּשׁ (which is indeed possible), but, according to Ps. cxxxix. 14, to ידע. (3) פַּשׁ is especially to be explained from the Arabic. The signification a multitude (Jewish expositors, after פּוֹשׁ, *Niph. se diffundere*, Nah. iii. 18) is not suitable; the signification evil (LXX., Jer., and others : פַּשׁ = פֶּשַׁע) presents a forcibly mutilated word, and moreover one devoid of significance in this connection; whereas the

Arab. فَشّ (but not in its derivatives, *fashsh*, empty-headed;

fâshûsh, empty-headedness, imbecility, with its metaphorical

sense) indicates a development of signification which leads to
the desired end, especially in the Syro-Arabic usage most
natural here.   The verb فَشّ (פּשׁשׁ, cogn. فشر, فرش, to extend, *expandere*) is used originally of water (*fashsh el-mâ*):
to overflow its dam, to overflow its banks, whence a valley by
the lake of *el-Higáne*, into which the waters of the lake flow
after the winter rains, is called *el-mefeshsh*; then of a leathern
bottle: to run out (*tarf mefshûsh*, an emptied bottle), of a
tumour (*waram*): to disperse, disappear, and tropically of
anger (*el-chulq*): to break forth, vent itself on anything,
hence the phrase: dost thou make me a *mefeshshe* (an object
for the venting) of thine anger?   From this فَشّ (distinct
from فاش *med. Waw*, to swim on the surface, trop. to be
above, not to allow one's self to be kept down, and *med. Je*,
comp. פּוּשׁ, Hab. i. 8, Jer. l. 11, Mal. iii. 20, signifies to be
proud) is פָּשׁ, formed after the forms בַּד, מַד, מַם, a synon. of
זָדוֹן, or even of עֶבְרָה in the signification of excessive haughtiness, pride that bursts forth violently.[1]

Thus, even at the close of this third speech of Elihu, the
Arabic, and in fact Syro-Arabic colouring, common to this

[1] The signification *expandere* also underlies the noun *fishshe*, the lungs
(in Egypt.); the signification *discutere* (especially *carminare*, to card
wool), which the Talmud. פִּשְׁפֵּשׁ also has, is only a shade of the same
signification; the origin of the trop. signification *fatuum esse* is clear
from *'gaus fashûsh*, empty nuts.   The rice from the Palestine valley of
Húle, it is somewhere said, is worse than the Egyptian, because (what is
a fault in the East) in cooking *tufeshfish*, *i.e.* it bursts, breaks in pieces
(comp. on the other hand : if the seed for sowing sinks to the bottom
when put into water, it is good ; if it swims on the surface, *jefûsh*, it is
bad).   The *Piel* of this *fashsha* signifies to cause the water to overflow,
trop. *fashshasha qalbahu*, he gave air to his heart, *i.e.* he revealed a secret
which burdened him.   A proverb says : the market (with its life and
changing scenes) is a *feshshâsh* of cares, *i.e.* consoles a troubled heart.   In
the *Iliph.* one says in like manner proverbially, *el-bukâ jufishsh*, weeping
removes the anguish of the soul.—WETZST.

section with the rest of the book, is confirmed; while, on the other hand, we miss the bold, original figures which up to ch. xxxi. followed like waves one upon another, and we perceive a deficiency of skill, as now and then between Koheleth and Solomon. The chief thought of the speech we have also heard already from the three friends and Job himself. That the piety of the pious profits himself without involving God in any obligation to him, Eliphaz has already said, ch. xxii. 2 sq.; and that prayer that is heard in time of need and the unanswered cry of the godly and the ungodly are distinct, Job said, ch. xxvii. 9 sq. Elihu, however, deprives these thoughts of their hitherto erroneous application. If piety gives nothing to God which He ought to reward, Job dare not regard his affliction, mysterious as it is to him, as unjust; and if the godly do not directly experience the avenging wrath of God on the haughtiness of their oppressors, the question, whether then their prayer for help is of the right kind, is more natural than the complaint of a want of justice in God's government of the world. Job is silent also after this speech. It does not contain the right consolation; it contains, however, censure which he ought humbly to receive. It touches his heart. But whether it touches the heart of the idea of the book, is another question.

Elihu's Fourth Speech. — Chap. xxxvi. xxxvii.

Schema: 6. 7. 6. 6. 7. 6. 8. 8. 8. | 11. 11. 8. 6. 8. 11.

[Then Elihu continued and said:]

2 *Suffer me a little, and I will inform thee,*
   For there is something still to be said for Eloah.
3 *I will fetch my knowledge from afar,*
   And to my Creator will I ascribe right.
4 *For truly my words are not lies,*
   One perfect in knowledge stands before thee.

Elihu's preceding three speeches were introduced by וַיַּעַן; this fourth, in honour of the number three, is introduced only as a continuation of the others. Job is to wait yet a little while, for he still has (= לִי עוֹד), or: there still are, words in favour of Eloah; *i.e.* what may be said in vindication of God against Job's complaints and accusations is not yet exhausted. This appears to be the only instance of the Aramaic בַּתַּר being taken up as Hebr.; whereas חָוָה, *nunciare* (Arab. حوى, I. IV.), is a poetic Aramaism occurring even in Ps. xix. 3 (comp. on the construction ch. xxxii. 6); and זְעִיר (a diminutive form, after the manner of the Arab. *zu'air*) belongs in Isa. xxviii. 10, 13 to the popular language (of Jerusalem), but is here used poetically. The verb נָשָׂא, ver. 3*a*, is not to be understood according to נשׂא משׂל, but according to 1 Kings x. 11; and לְמֵרָחוֹק signifies, as also ch. xxxix. 29, Isa. xxxvii. 26, *e longinquo*, viz. out of the wide realm of history and nature. The expression נָתַן צֶדֶק follows the analogy of (עֹז) נתן כבוד. דֵּעָה, ver. 4*b*, interchanges with the דֵּעַ which belongs exclusively to Elihu, since Elihu styles himself תְּמִים דֵּעוֹת, as ch. xxxvii. 16 God תְּמִים דֵּעִים (comp. 1 Sam. ii. 3, אֵל דֵּעוֹת). תמים in this combination with דעות cannot be intended of purity of character; but as Elihu there attributes absolute perfection of knowledge in every direction to God, so here, in reference to the theodicy which he opposes to Job, he claims faultlessness and clearness of perception.

> 5 *Behold, God is mighty, and yet doth not act scornfully,*
> *Mighty in power of understanding.*
> 6 *He preserveth not the life of the ungodly,*
> *And to the afflicted He giveth right.*
> 7 *He withdraweth not His eyes from the righteous,*
> *But with kings on the throne*
> *He establisheth them for ever, and they are exalted.*

The obj. that must be mentally supplied to וְלֹא יִמְאָס is, as in ch. xlii. 6, to be derived from the connection. The idea of the verb is, as in ch. viii. 20 : He is exalted, without however looking down disdainfully (*non despicit*) from His height, or more definitely : without setting Himself above the justice due to even the meanest of His creatures—great in power of heart (comp. ch. xxxiv. 33 לבב אנשׁי, Arab. *úlú-l-elbáb*), *i.e.* understanding (*νοῦς, πνεῦμα*), to see through right and wrong everywhere and altogether. Vers. 6, 7 describe how His rule among men evinces this not merely outward but spiritual superiority coupled with condescension to the lowly. The notion of the object, לַכִּסֵּא וְאֶת־מְלָכִים (as Isa. ix. 11 the subject), becomes the more distinctly prominent by virtue of the *fut. consec.* which follows like a conclusion, and takes it up again. Ewald thinks this explanation contrary to the accents and the structure of the sentence itself; but it is perfectly consistent with the former, and indisputably syntactic (Ges. § 129, 2, *b*, and Ew. himself, § 344, *b*). Ps. ix. 5, comp. cxxxii. 12, Isa. xlvii. 1, shows how לכסא is intended (He causes them to sit upon the throne). Ch. v. 11, 1 Sam. ii. 8, Ps. cxiii. 7 sq. are parallel passages.

> 8 *And if they are bound with chains,*
> *Holden in cords of affliction :*
> 9 *Then He declareth to them their doing*
> *And their transgressions, that they have been vainglorious ;*
> 10 *Then He openeth their ear to warning,*
> *And commandeth them to turn from iniquity.*

The subj. is in no case the רשׁעים (Hahn), but the צדיקים, or those who are as susceptible to discipline as it is needful to them, just as in Ps. cvii., which in general presents many instances for an extensive comparison with the speeches of Elihu. The chains, ver. 8*a*, are meant literally, and the bands, ver. 8*b*, figuratively; the Psalmist couples both in אסירי עֳני וברזל, cvii. 10. The conclusion begins with ver. 9, and is repeated in another application, ver. 10. פֹּעַל in the sense of *maleficium*, as Arab. فَعلَة, recalls מַעֲשֶׂה, *facinus*, ch. xxxiii. 17. כִּי, ver. 9*b*, is, as in ver. 10*b*, an objective *quod*. It is not translated, however, *quod invaluerint* (Rosenm.), which is opposed to the most natural sense of the *Hithpa.*, but according to ch. xv. 25 : *quod sese extulerint.* מוּסָר, παιδεία, *disciplina*, interchanges here with the more rare מֹסֵר used in ch. xxxiii. 16 ; there we have already also met with the phrase גָּלָה אֹזֶן, to uncover the ear, *i.e.* to open. אָמַר כִּי corresponds to the Arab. *amara an* (*bi-an*), to command that. The fundamental thought of Elihu here once again comes unmistakeably to view : the sufferings of the righteous are well-meant chastisements, which are to wean them from the sins into which through carnal security they have fallen—a warning from God to penitence, designed to work their good.

> 11 *If they hear and yield,*
> *They pass their days in prosperity*
> *And their years in pleasure.*
> 12 *And if they hear not,*
> *They pass away by the bow*
> *And expire in lack of knowledge.*

Since a declaration of the divine will has preceded in ver. 10*b*, it is more natural to take וְיַעֲבֹדוּ in the sense of *obsequi*, to do the will of another (as 1 Kings xii. 7, comp. מַעֲבָד from עָבַד in the generalized sense of *facere*), than, with Umbr., in the sense of *colere scil. Deum* (as Isa. xix. 23, Arab. '*âbid*, one who reveres God, a godly person). Instead of יְבַלּוּ, Isa. lxv. 22 (on which the Masora observes לֵית, *i.e.* "nowhere else") and ch. xxi. 13 *Chethîb*, it is here without dispute יְכַלּוּ (Targ. יִשְׁלְמוּן, *peragent*, as Ezek. xliii. 27). נְעִימִים is, as Ps. xvi. 6, a neutral masc.: *amœna*. On עָבַר בִּשְׁלַח, to precipitate one's self into the weapon, *i.e.* to incur peremptory

punishment, comp. ch. xxxiii. 18. On בבלי דעת comp. xxxv.
16, iv. 21. Impenitence changes affliction, which is intended
to be a means of rescue, into total destruction; yet there are
some who will not be warned and affrighted by it.

> 13 *Yet the hypocrites in heart cherish wrath,*
>   *They cry not when He hath chained them.*
> 14 *Thus their soul dieth in the vigour of youth,*
>   *And their life is like that of the unclean.*
> 15 *Yet He delivereth the sufferer by his affliction,*
>   *And openeth their ear by oppression.*

He who is angry with God in his affliction, and does not
humbly pray to Him, shows thereby that he is a חָנֵף, one
estranged from God (on the idea of the root, *vid.* i. 216),
and not a צדיק. This connection renders it natural to understand not the divine wrath by אָף: θησαυρίζουσιν ὀργήν
(Rosenm. after Rom. ii. 5), or: they heap up wrath upon
themselves (Wolfson, who supplies עֲלֵיהֶם), but the impatience, discontent, and murmuring of man himself: they
cherish or harbour wrath, viz. בְּלִבָּם (comp. ch. xxii. 22, where
שִׂים בלב signifies to take to heart, but at the same time to
preserve in the heart). Used thus absolutely, שִׂים signifies
elsewhere in the book, to give attention to, ch. iv. 20, xxiv.
12, xxxiv. 23, or (as وضع) to lay down a pledge; here it
signifies *reponunt s. recondunt* (with an implied *in ipsis*), as
also شام *fut. i,* to conceal with the idea of sinking into
(*immittentem*), *e.g.* the sword in the sheath. With תֶּמֹת, for
וְתָמֹת (Isa. l. 2) or וַתֶּמֶת, the punishment which issues forth
undistinguished from this frustration of the divine purpose
of grace follows ἀσυνδέτως, as *e.g.* Hos. vii. 16. חַיָּה interchanges with נפשׁ, as ch. xxxiii. 22, 28; נֹעַר (likewise a
favourite word with Elihu) is intended just as ch. xxxiii. 25,
and in the Ps. lxxxviii. ver. 16, which resembles both the Elihu
section and the rest of the book. The *Beth* of בַּקְּדֵשִׁים has

the sense of *æque ac* (Targ. הֵיךְ), as ch. xxxiv. 36, comp. תַּחַת, ch. xxxiv. 26. Jer. translates *inter effeminatos*; for קְדֵשִׁים (heathenish, equivalent to קְדֹשִׁים, as כְּמָרִים, heathenish, equivalent to כֹּהֲנִים) are the consecrated men, who yielded themselves up, like the women in honour of the deity, to passive, prematurely-enervating incontinence (*vid.* Keil on Deut. xxiii. 18), a heathenish abomination prevailing now and again even in Israel (1 Kings xiv. 24, xv. 12, xxii. 47), which was connected with the worship of Astarte and Baal that was transferred from Syria, and to which allusion is here made, in accordance with the scene of the book. For the sufferer, on the other hand, who suffers not merely of necessity, but willingly, this his suffering is a means of rescue and moral purification. Observe the play upon the words יְחַלֵּץ and בְּלַחַץ. The *Beth* in both instances is, in accordance with Elihu's fundamental thought, the *Beth instrum.*

16 *And He even bringeth thee out of the jaws of distress*
   To a broad place, whose ground hath no straitness,
   And the adorning of thy table shall be full of fatness.
17 *Yet thou art become full of the judging of the evil-doer :*
   Judging and judgment lay hold on one another !
18 *For let not anger indeed entice thee to scorning,*
   And let not the greatness of the ransom mislead thee.

With ver. 16a Elihu passes over to the application to Job of what he said in the preceding strophe. Since it is usual to place אַף (like גַּם and אָף) at the beginning of the sentence, although not belonging to the member of the sentence which immediately follows, וְהֵסִית אַף אֹתְךָ for וְאַף הֲסִיתְךָ cannot be remarkable. The *præt.* הסיתך is not promissory, but Elihu says with what design God has decreed the present suffering for Job. הֵסִיף מִן is like 2 Chron. xviii. 31: out of distress (צָר for צַר by *Rebia magnum*), which has him in its jaws, and threatens to swallow him, God brings him away to great prosperity; a thought which Elihu expresses in the imagery of the Psalms of a broad place and a bountiful table (comp. *e.g.* Ps. iv. 2, xxiii. 5). רַחַב is locative, and לֹא־מוּצָק תַּחְתֶּיהָ is either a relative clause: whose beneath (ground) is not straitened, no-straitness (in which case מוּצָק would not be *constr.* from the *n. hophal.* מוּצָק, Isa. viii. 23, but *absol.* after the form מֶחֱנַק, ch. vii. 15, Ew. § 160, *c*, Anm. 4), Saad. لا ضيق في موضعها (*cujus in loco non angustiæ*); or it is virtually an adj.: without (לֹא = בְּלֹא, as ch. xxxiv. 24, comp. on ch. xii. 24) straitness of what is beneath them, *eorum quæ sub se habet* (comp. on ch. xxviii. 5). רַחַב is *fem.*, like רְחוֹב, Dan. ix. 25. A special clause takes the place of the locative, ver. 16*c*: and the settling or spreading, *i.e.* the provision (from נוּחַ, to come down gradually, to seat one's self) of thy table shall be full of fatness. מָלֵא (whether it be adj. or verb) is treated by attraction, according to the gender of the governed noun; and it is unnecessary, with Rosenm. and others, to derive נַחַת from נָחַת (Aram. for יָרַד).

In ver 17, דִּין is intended of Job's negative judgment concerning God and His dealings (comp. Ps. lxxvi. 9, where it signifies a judicial decision, and Prov. xxii. 10, where it signifies a wrangling refusal of a fair decision). Ver. 17*a* is not a conditional clause (Hahn), in which case the *præt. hypothet.* would have a prominent position, but an adversative predicative clause: but (nevertheless) thou art full of the judging of the evil-doer (evil judging); after which, just as ἀσυνδέτως as ver. 14*a*, the sad issue in which this judging after the manner of evil-doers results is expressed: such judging and judgment border closely upon one another. Röd., Dietr., and Schlottm. have wrongly reproduced this idea, discerned by Ges., when they translate: judgment and sentence (guilt and punishment) shall seize thee. יִתְמְכוּ, *prehendunt scil. se* (Ebr.: put forth the hand), is used like the Aram. סְמַךְ, to draw nearer, fasten together (Rabb. סָמוּךְ, near at hand), Arab. *tamásaka*

(from لَمَسَ = סמך, as *e.g.* hanash = נִחַשׁ). In ver. 18 we
leave the signification thick milk or cream (חֵמָה = חֶמְאָה,
as ch. xxix. 6) to those who persuade themselves that
cream can be metaphorically equivalent to superfluity (Ew.,
Hirz., Vaih., Hlgst). Renan's translation: *N'espère pas
détourner la colère de Dieu par une amende,* we also leave
as a simple puzzle to its discoverer, who, with this one exception, is destitute of thoughts proper to the book of Job.
In general, the thought, "do not imagine by riches, by a
great ransom, to be able to satisfy the claims of God," is
altogether out of place here. Moreover, חֵמָה, which, as *e.g.*
דְּאָגָה, Prov. xii. 25 (Ew. § 174, *g*), is construed as *masc.*,
cannot be understood of God's wrath, since the poet by הֵסִית
will not at one time have ascribed to God a well-meant
incitation, at another an enticement *in malam partem.* That
which allures is Job's own חֵמָה, and that not the excitement
of his affliction (Hahn), but of his passion; comp. אַף, ver. 13.
שֶׁפֶק is, however, to be explained according to ch. xxxiv. 37,
comp. xxvii. 23 (clapping of hands = derision); and כֹּפֶר
signifies reconciliation or expiation, as ch. xxxiii. 24. Elihu
admonishes Job not to allow himself to be drawn by the heat
of passion into derision, or to deride; nor to be allured from
the right way by the ransom which is required of him as the
price of restoration to happiness, viz. humble submission to
the divine chastisement, as though this ransom were exceeding great. The connection is clear: an adverse verdict
(דִּין) and condemnation (מִשְׁפָּט) are closely connected; for
(כִּי) hastiness of temper, let it not (פֶּן) lead thee astray . . .
thou wouldst not escape the judgment of God!

19 *Shall thy crying place thee beyond distress,*
   And all the efforts of strength?
20 *Long not for the night to come,*
   Which shall remove people from their place!

> 21 *Take heed, incline not to evil;*
> *For this thou hast desired more than affliction.*

Those expositors who found in ver. 18*b* the warning, that Job should not imagine that he would be able to redeem himself from judgment by a large ransom, go on to explain: will He esteem thy riches? (Farisol, Rosenm., Umbr., Carey, Ebr., and others); or: will thy riches suffice? (Hirz., Schlottm.); or some other way (Ew.). But apart from the want of connection of this insinuation, which is otherwise not mentioned in the book, and apart from the violence which must be done to הֲיַעֲרֹךְ to accommodate it to it, שׁוּעַ, although it might, as the abstract of שׁוֹעַ, ch. xxxiv. 19, signify wealth (comp. ﺍﺴﻊ, *amplitudo*), is, however, according to the usage of the language (*vid.* ch. xxx. 24), so far as we can trace it, a secondary form of שֶׁוַע (שַׁוְעָה), a cry for help; and ch. xxxv. 9 sq., ver. 13, and other passages, also point to this signification. What follows is still less appropriate to this thought of ransom; Hirz. translates: Oh, not God and all the treasures of wealth! But בְּצָר is nowhere equivalent to בֶּצֶר, ch. xxii. 24; but צָר, ver. 16, signifies distress; and the expression לֹא בְצָר, in a condition devoid of distress, is like לֹא בחכמה, ch. iv. 21, and לֹא ביד, ch. xxxiv. 20. Finally, אַמִּיץ כֹּחַ signifies mighty in physical strength, ch. ix. 4, 19, and מַאֲמַצֵּי־כֹחַ strong proofs of strength, not "treasures of wealth." Stick. correctly interprets: "Will thy wild raging cry, then, and all thine exertions, as a warrior puts them forth in the tumult of battle to work his way out, put thee where there is an open space?" but the figure of a warrior is, with Hahn, to be rejected; עֲרָךְ is only a nice word for שִׂים, שִׁית, to place, set up, ch. xxxvii. 19.

Ver. 20. Elihu calls upon Job to consider the uselessness of his vehement contending with God, and then warns him against his dreadful provocation of divine judgment : *ne anheles* (ch. vii. 2) *noctem illam* (with the emphatic *art.*) *sublaturam populos loco suo.* לְעָלוֹת is equivalent to *futuram* (הַהֹוָה or הָעֲתִידָה) *ut tollat = sublaturam* (*vid.* on ch. v. 11, לָשׁוּם, *collocaturus ;* xxx. 6, לִשְׁכֹּן, *habitandum est*), syncopated from לְהַעֲלוֹת, in the sense of Ps. cii. 25; and תַּחְתָּם signifies, as ch. xl. 12 (comp. on Hab. iii. 16), nothing but that just where they are, firmly fixed without the possibility of escape, they are deprived of being. If whole peoples are overtaken by such a fate, how much less shall the individual be able to escape it! And yet Job presses forward on to the tribunal of the terrible Judge, instead of humbling himself under His mighty hand. Oh that in time he would shrink back from this absolute wickedness (אָוֶן), for he has given it the preference before עֳנִי, quiet, resigned endurance. בָּחַר עַל signifies, 2 Sam. xix. 39, to choose to lay anything on any one ; here as בחר בְּ, elsewhere to extend one's choice to something, to make something an object of choice; perhaps also under the influence of the phrase הִתְעַנֵּג עַל, and similar phrases. The construction is remarkable, since one would sooner have expected זֶה בחרת עַל־עֳנִי, *hanc elegisti præ toleratione.*

> 22 *Behold, God acteth loftily in His strength ;*
> *Who is a teacher like unto Him?*
> 23 *Who hath appointed Him His way,*
> *And who dare say : Thou doest iniquity !?*
> 24 *Remember that thou magnify His doing,*
> *Which men have sung.*
> 25 *All men delight in it,*
> *Mortal man looketh upon it from afar.*

Most modern expositors, after the LXX. δυνάστης, give מוֹרֶה the signification lord, by comparing the Arab. *mar-un* (*imru-un*), Syr. *mor* (with the art. *moro*) or *more* (with the art. *morjo*), Chald. מָרָא, Talmud. מָר (comp. Philo, ii. 522, *ed.*

Mangey : οὕτως, viz. μάριν, φασὶ τὸν κύριον ὀνομάζεσθαι παρὰ Σύροις), with it; but Rosenm., Arnh., Löwenthal, Wolfson, and Schlottm., after the Targ., Syr., and Jer., rightly abide by the signification : teacher. For (1) מוֹרֶה (from הוֹרָה, ·Ps. xxv. 8, 12, xxxii. 8) has no etymological connection with מוֹר (of מְרָא, مَرَ, *opimum, robustum esse*); (2) it is, moreover, peculiar to Elihu to represent God as a teacher both by dreams and dispensations of affliction, ch. xxxiii. 14 sqq., xxxiv. 32, and by His creatures, xxxv. 11; and (3) the designation of God as an incomparable teacher is also not inappropriate here, after His rule is described in ver. 22*a* as transcendently exalted, which on that very account commands to human research a reverence which esteems itself lightly. Ver. 23*a* is not to be translated : who overlooketh Him in His way ? (פָּקַד with עַל of the personal and *acc.* of the neutral obj.), which is without support in the language; but : who has prescribed to Him (פקד על as ch. xxxiv. 13) His way ? *i.e.* as Rosenm. correctly interprets : *quis ei præscripsit quœ agere deberet*, He is no mandatory, is responsible to no one, and under obligation to no one, and who should dare to say (*quis dixerit;* on the *perf.* comp. on ch. xxxv. 15) : Thou doest evil ?—man shall be a docile learner, not a self-satisfied, conceited censurer of the absolute One, whose rule is not to be judged according to the laws of another, but according to His own laws. Thus, then, shall Job remember (*memento =* *cura ut*) to extol (תַשְׂגִּיא, ch. xii. 23) God's doings, which have been sung (comp. *e.g.* Ps. civ. 33) by אֲנָשִׁים, men of the right order (ch. xxxvii. 24) ; Jer. *de quo cecinerunt viri.* שֹׁרֵר nowhere has the signification *intueri* (Rosenm., Umbr.) ; on the other hand, Elihu is fond of direct (ch. xxxiii. 27, xxxv. 10) and indirect allusions to the Psalms. All men—he continues, with reference to God's פֹּעַל, working—behold it, viz., as בּ implies, with pleasure and astonishment; mortals gaze upon

it (reverentially) from afar,—the same thought as that which
has already (ch. xxvi. 14) found the grandest expression in
Job's mouth.

26 *Behold, God is exalted—we know Him not entirely ;*
    The number of His years, it is unsearchable.
27 *For He draweth down the drops of water,*
    They distil as rain in connection with its mist,
28 *Which the clouds do drop,*
    Distil upon the multitude of men.
29 *Who can altogether understand the spreadings of the clouds,*
    The crash of His tabernacle ?

The *Waw* of the quasi-conclusion in ver. 26*b* corresponds
to the *Waw* of the train of thought in ver. 26*a* (Ges. § 145, 2).
מִסְפַּר שָׁנָיו is, as the subject-notion, conceived as a nominative
(*vid.* on ch. iv. 6, vol. i. 91, note 1), not as in similar quasi-
antecedent clauses, *e.g.* ch. xxiii. 12, as an *acc.* of relation.
שָׁנָיא here and ch. xxxvii. 23 occurs otherwise only in Old
Testament Chaldee. In what follows Elihu describes the
wondrous origin of rain. "If Job had only come," says a
Midrash (*Jalkut*, § 518), "to explain to us the matter of the
race of the deluge (*vid.* especially ch. xxii. 15–18), it had
been sufficient; and if Elihu had only come to explain to us
the matter of the origin of rain (מעשה ירידת גשמים), it had
been enough." In Gesenius' *Handwörterbuch,* ver. 27 is
translated: when He has drawn up the drops of water to
Himself, then, etc. But it is יִגְרַע, not גֵּרַע; and גָּרַע neither in
Hebr. nor in Arab. signifies *attrahere in sublime* (Rosenm.), but
only *attrahere* (root גר) and *detrahere;* the latter signification
is the prevailing one in Hebr. (ch. xv. 8, xxxvi. 7). With
כִּי the transcendent exaltation of the Being who survives all
changes of creation is shown by an example: He draws
away (draws off, as it were) the water-drops, viz. from the
waters that are confined above on the circle of the sky, which

pass over us as mist and cloud (*vid. Genesis*, S. 107); and these water-drops distil down (זָקַק, to ooze, distil, here not in a transitive but an intransitive signification, since the water-drops are the rain itself) as rain, לְאֵדוֹ, with its mist, *i.e.* since a mist produced by it (Gen. ii. 6) fills the expanse (רָקִיעַ), the downfall of which is just this rain, which, as ver. 28 says, the clouds (called שְׁחָקִים on account of its thin strata of air, in distinction from the next mist-circle) cause to flow gently down upon the multitude of men, *i.e.* far and wide over the mass of men who inhabit the district visited by the rain; both verbs are used transitively here, both נָזַל as Isa. xlv. 8, and רָעַף, as evidently Prov. iii. 20. אַף אִם, ver. 29*a*, commences an intensive question: moreover, could one understand = could one completely understand; which certainly, according to the sense, is equivalent to: how much less (אַף כִּי). אִם is, however, the interrogative *an*, and אַף אִם corresponds to הַאַף in the first member of the double question, ch. xxxiv. 17, xl. 8 sq. מִפְרְשֵׂי are not the burstings, from פָּרַשׂ = פָּרַס, *frangere, findere*, but spreadings, as Ezek. xxvii. 7 shows, from פָּרַשׂ, *expandere*, Ps. cv. 39, comp. *supra* on ch. xxvi. 9. It is the growth of the storm-clouds, which collect often from a beginning "small as a man's hand" (1 Kings xviii. 44), that is intended; majestic omnipotence conceals itself behind these as in a סֻכָּה (Ps. xviii. 12) woven out of thick branches; and the rolling thunder is here called the crash (תְּשֻׁאוֹת, as ch. xxxix. 7, is formed from שׁוֹא, to rumble, whence also שׁוֹאָה, if it is not after the form גּוֹלָה, migration, exile, from שָׁאָה, *vid.* on ch. xxx. 3) of this pavilion of clouds in which the Thunderer works.

> 30 *Behold, He spreadeth His light over Himself,*
> 　　*And the roots of the sea He covereth.*
> 31 *For thereby He judgeth peoples,*
> 　　*He giveth food in abundance.*

32 *Both hands He covereth over with light,*
   And directeth it as one who hitteth the mark.
33 *His noise announceth Him,*
   The cattle even that He is approaching.

A few expositors (Hirz., Hahn, Schlottm.) understand the celestial ocean, or the sea of the upper waters, by יָם, ver. 30*b*; but it is more than questionable (*vid.* on ch. ix. 8) whether יָם is used anywhere in this sense. Others as (Umbr., Ew.) the masses of water drawn up to the sky out of the depths of the sea, on which a Persian passage cited by Stick. (who, however, regards the *Waw* of וְשָׁרְשֵׁי as *Waw adæquationis*) from Schebisteri may be compared : " an exhalation rises up out of the sea, and comes down at God's command upon the deserts." In both cases כִּפָּה would be equivalent to כסה עָלָיו, *obtegit se,* which in and of itself is possible. But he who has once witnessed a storm in the neighbourhood of the sea, will decide in favour of one of the three following explanations : (1.) He covereth the uprooted ground of the sea (comp. Ps. xviii. 15 sq.) with the subsiding waves (Blumenf.) ; but then ver. 30*a* would require to be understood of the light of the brightening sky following the darkness of the storm, which is improbable in respect of ver. 32*a*. (2.) While the sky is brilliantly lighted up by the lightning, the abysses of the ocean are veiled in a so much deeper darkness; the observation is correct, but not less so another, that the lightning by a thunder-storm, especially when occurring at night, descends into the depths of the sea like snares that are cast down (פַּחִים, Ps. xi. 6), and the water is momentarily changed as it were into a sea of flame; accordingly it may be explained, (3.) Behold, He spreadeth over Himself His light (viz. the light which incessantly illumines the world), and the roots of the sea, *i.e.* the sea down to its depths, He covers with it, since He makes it light through and through (Stuhlm., Wolfs.). Thus, as it appears, Jerome also interprets: *Et (si voluerit) fulgurare lumine suo desuper, cardines quoque maris operiet.*[1]

This, that He makes the light of the lightning His manifestation (פָּרַשׂ עָלָיו), and that He covers the earth down to the roots of the sea beneath with this light, is established in ver. 31 from the design, partly judicial, partly beneficial, which exists in connection with it. בָּם refers as neuter (like בָּהֶם, ch. xxii. 21) to the phenomena of the storm; מַכְבִּיר (with the adverbial לְ like לָרֹב, ch. xxvi. 3), what makes great = a making great, abundance (only here), is *n. hiphil.* after the form מַשְׁחִית, *perdens = perditio.* In ver. 32 God is represented under a military figure as a slinger of lightnings: He covers light over both hands, *i.e.* arms both completely with light

(comp. סִכְסֵךְ and شكّ, *totum se operire armis*), and directs it

(עָלֶיהָ referring to אוֹר as *fem.* like Jer. xiii. 16, and sometimes in the Talmud). But what is the meaning of בְּמַפְגִּיעַ? Hahn takes מפגיע as *n. hiphil.* like מכביר: an object of attack; but what then becomes of the original *Hiphil* signification? It ought to be בְּמִפְגָּע (ch. vii. 20), as Olsh. wishes to read it. Ew., Hirz., and others, after the example of Theod. (LXX.), Syr., Jer., translate: against the adversary; מפגיע signifies indeed the opposite in Isa. lix. 16: *intercessor* (properly, one who assails with prayers); however, it would be possible for this word, just as פגע *c. acc.* (which signifies usually a hostile meeting, Ex. v. 3 and freq., but sometimes also a friendly, Isa. xlvii. 3, lxiv. 4), to be an ἐναντιόσημον. We prefer to abide by the usage of the language as we have it, according

---

[1] The Targ. translates אוֹר, vers. 30, 32, by מְטְרָא, *pluvia*, according to the erroneous opinion of R. Jochanan: כל אורה שנאמר באליהוא אינו אלא בירידת גשמים. Aben-Ezra and Kimchi explain even עֲלֵי־אוֹר, Isa. xviii. 4, according to this passage. The LXX. translates ver. 30a: ἰδοὺ ἐκτείνει ἐπ᾽ αὐτὸν ἠδώ (*Cod. Alex.* επ αυτον το τοξον; *Cod. Sinait.* επ αυτην ηωδη with the corrections ηδω and τοξον), probably according to the reading אֵידוֹ for אוֹרוֹ. But what connection have ἠδώ and rainbow?

to which הפגיע signifies *facere ut quid incurset s. petat,* Isa.
liii. 6 ; מפגיע therefore is one who hits, in opposition to one who
misses the mark. The *Beth* is the *Beth essentiæ* (*vid.* on ch.
xxiii. 13), used here like Ex. vi. 3, Ps. lv. 19, Isa. xl. 10.
With both hands He seizes the substance of the lightning, fills
them with it so that they are completely covered by it, and
gives it the command (appoints it its goal), a sure aimer!

Ver. 33*a.* Targ., Syr., Symm., Theod. (from which ver.
32 sq. is supplied in the LXX.[1]), Jer., Luther, and others
destroy the idea, since they translate רֵעוֹ = רֵעֵהוּ, " his friend
(companion)." Among moderns, only Umbr. and Schlottm.
adopt this signification ; Böttch. and Welte, after the example
of Cocceius, Tingstad, and others, attempt it with the signification "thought = determination;" but most expositors, from
Ew. to Hahn, decide in favour of the rendering as simple as
it is consistent with the usage of the language and the connection : His noise (רֵעוֹ as Ex. xxxii. 17) gives tidings concerning Him (announces Him). In ver. 33*b* Theod. (LXX.),
Syr., and Jer. point מקנה like our text, but translate *possessio,*
with which we can do nothing. It seems that in the three
attempts of the Targ. to translate ver. 33, the translators had
קִנְאָה and קְנָא before their mind, according to which Hahn
translates : the arousing of anger (announces) the comer,
which assumes מקְנֶה instead of מקְנֶה ; and Schlottm. : fierce
wrath (goes forth) over evil (according to Symm. ζῆλον περὶ
ἀδικίας), which assumes the reading עָוְלָה (עֹלָה), ἀδικία, adopted
also by Syr., Theod. (LXX.). Schultens even renders similarly : *rubedinem flammantem nasi contra elatum,* and Tingstad : *zelum iræ in iniquitatem.* But it is not probable that the
language was acquainted with a subst. מִקְנֶה, exciting, although
in Ezek. viii. 3 הַמַּקְנֶה is equivalent to הַמַּקְנִיא, so that one might

---

[1] *Vid.* Bickel, *De indole ac ratione versionis Alex. in interpretando l.
Iobi,* p. 50. *Cod. Sinait.* has, like *Cod. Vat.:* αναγγελει περι αυτου Φιλον
(corr. Φιλοσ) αυτου κσ κτησισ και περι αδικιασ.

more readily be tempted (*vid.* Hitz. *in loc.*) to read מַקְנֶה אַף,
" one who excites anger against evil," if one is not willing to
decide with Berg, and recently Bleek, in favour of (מִקַּנֵּה) מְקַנֵּא
אַף בְּעַוְלָה, *excandescens* (*zelans*) *irâ contra iniquitatem*. But
does the text as it stands really not give an appropriate idea?
Aben-Ezra and Duran have understood it of the foreboding
of an approaching thunder-storm which is manifested by
cattle, מִקְנֶה. Accordingly Ew. translates: His thunder announces Him, the cattle even, that He is approaching; and
peculiarly new (understanding יגיד not of a foreboding but of
a thankful lowing) is Ebrard's rendering: also the cattle at
fresh sprouting grass. But such a change of the position of
אף is without precedent. Hirz. and Ges.: His rumble (rumble
of thunder) announces Him to the herds, Him, and indeed as
Him who rises up (approaches). But this new interpunction
destroys the division of the verse and the syntax. Better
Rosenm. like Duran: *pecus non tantum pluviam proximam,
sed et antequam nubes in sublime adscenderint adscensuras
præsagit*, according to Virgil, *Georg.* i. 374 sq.:

> *illum* (*imbrem*) *surgentem vallibus imis
> Aeriæ fugere grues.*

But עָלָיו refers to God, and therefore עַל־עוֹלָה also, viz. Him who
leads forth the storm-clouds (Jer. x. 13, li. 16, Ps. cxxxv. 7),
and Himself rising up in them; or, what עָלָה frequently signifies, coming on as to battle. It is to be interpreted: His
thunder-clap announces Him (who is about to reveal Himself
as a merciful judge), the cattle even (announce) Him at His
first rising up, since at the approach of a storm they herd
together affrighted and seek shelter. The speakers are
Arabian, and the scene is laid in the country: Elihu also
refers to the animal world in ch. xxxv. 11; this feature of
the picture, therefore, cannot be surprising.

Ch. xxxvii. 1 *Yea, at this my heart trembleth*
   And tottereth from its place.
   2 *Hear, O hear the roar of His voice,*
   And the murmur that goeth out of His mouth.
   3 *He sendeth it forth under the whole heaven,*
   And His lightning unto the ends of the earth.
   4 *After it roareth the voice of the thunder,*
   He thundereth with the voice of His majesty,
   And spareth not the lightnings, when His voice is heard.
   5 *God thundereth with His voice marvellously,*
   Doing great things, incomprehensible to us.

Louis Bridel is perhaps right when he inserts after ch.
xxxvi. the observation: *L'éclair brille, la tonnerre gronde.*
לְזֹאת does not refer to the phenomenon of the storm which is
represented in the mind, but to that which is now to be perceived by the senses. The combination שְׁמְעוּ שָׁמוֹעַ can signify
both hear constantly, Isa. vi. 9, and hear attentively, ch.
xiii. 17; here it is the latter. רֹגֶז of thunder corresponds to
the verbs رحز and رجس, which can be similarly used. The
repetition of קוֹל five times calls to mind the seven קוֹלוֹת (ἑπτὰ
βρονταί) in Ps. xxix. The parallel is הֶגֶה, ver. 2*b*, a murmuring, as elsewhere of the roar of the lion and the cooing
of the dove. The *suff.* of יְשָׁרֵהוּ refers to the thunder which
rolls through the immeasurable breadth under heaven; it is
not *perf. Piel* of יָשַׁר (Schlottm.), for " to give definite direction" (2 Chron. xxxii. 30) is not appropriate to thunder, but
fut. Kal of שָׁרָה, to free, to unbind (Ew., Hirz., and most
others). What ver. 3*a* says of thunder, ver. 3*b* says of light,
i.e. the lightning: God sends it forth to the edges, πτέρυγες,
i.e. ends, of the earth. אַחֲרָיו, ver. 4*a*, naturally refers to the
lightning, which is followed by the roar of the thunder; and
יְעַקְּבֵם to the flashes, which, when once its rumble is heard, God
does not restrain (עַקֵּב = עָכַב of the Targ., and Arab. ʿaqqaba,
to leave behind, postpone), but causes to flash forth in quick

succession. Ewald's translation : should He not find (prop. *non investigaverit*) them (the men that are to be punished), gives a thought that has no support in this connection. In ver. 5a נִפְלָאוֹת, *mirabilia*, is equivalent to *mirabiliter*, as Dan. viii. 24, comp. Ps. lxv. 6, cxxxix. 14. וְלֹא נֵדַע is intended to say that God's mighty acts, with respect to the connection between cause and effect and the employment of means, transcend our comprehension.

> 6 *For He saith to the snow : Fall towards the earth,*
> *And to the rain-shower*
> *And the showers of His mighty rain.*
> 7 *He putteth a seal on the hand of every man,*
> *That all men may come to a knowledge of His creative work.*
> 8 *The wild beast creepeth into a hiding-place,*
> *And in its resting-place it remaineth.*
> 9 *Out of the remote part cometh the whirlwind,*
> *And cold from the cloud-sweepers.*
> 10 *From the breath of God cometh ice,*
> *And the breadth of the waters is straitened.*

Like אֱבִי, ch. xxxiv. 36, and פֶּשׁ, ch. xxxv. 15, הֱוֵא, ver. 6a (is falsely translated "be earthwards" by LXX., Targ., and Syr.), also belongs to the most striking Arabisms of the Elihu section : it signifies *delabere* (Jer. *ut descendat*), a signification which the Arab. هَوَى does not gain from the radical signification placed first in Gesenius-Dietrich's *Handwörterbuch*, to breathe, blow, but from the radical signification, to gape, yawn, by means of the development of the meaning which also decides in favour of the primary notion of the Hebr. הָוָּה, according to which, what was said on ch. vi. 2, xxx. 13 is to be corrected.[1] The לְ of לְפֶלֶג influences ver. 6bc also. The

---

[1] هَوَى is originally χαίνειν, to gape, yawn, *hiare, e.g. hawat et-ta'natu*, the stab gapes (imperf. *tahwî*, inf. *huwîjun*), " when it opens its mouth "

Hebr. name for rain, גֶּשֶׁם (cogn. with Chald. גִּשְׁם, Arab. *'gism*, a body), denotes the rain collectively. The expression ver. 6*b* is exceeded in ver. 6*c*, where מְטָרוֹת does not signify rain-drops (Ew.), but, like the Arab. *amtár*, rain-showers. The wonders of nature during the rough season (סְתָיו, חֹרֶף, Cant. ii. 11, comp. p. 119), between the autumnal and vernal equinoxes, are meant; the rains after the autumnal equinox (the early rain), which begin the season, and the rains before the vernal equinox (the late rain, Zech. x. 1), which close it, with the falls of snow between, which frequently produce great desolation, especially the proper winter with its frosty winds and heavy showers, when the business of the husbandmen as of the nomads is brought to a stand-still, and every one retreats to his house or seeks a sheltering corner (*vid.* p. 23, note). This is the meaning of ver. 7: He sealeth up (בְּ חָתַם as

—the Turkish Kamus adds, to complete the picture: like a tulip. Thence next *hâwijatun*, χαίνουσα, χαῖνον, i.e. χάσμα = *hûwatun*, *uhwijatun*, *huwâatun*, *mahwâtun*, a cleft, yawning deep, chasm, abyss, βάραθρον, *vorago*; *hawijatun* and *hauhâtun* (a reduplicated form), especially a very deep pit or well. But these same words, *hâwijatun*, *hûwatun*, *uhwîjatun*,

mahwâtun, also signify, like the usual هَوَاءٌ, the χάσμα between heaven and earth, *i.e.* the wide, empty space, the same as *'gauwun*. The wider significations, or rather applications and references of *hawâ*: air set in motion, a current of air, wind, weather, are all secondary, and related to that primary signification as *samâ*, rain-clouds, rain, grass produced by the rain, to the prim. signification height, heaven, *vid.* Mehren, *Rhetorik d. Araber*, S. 107, Z. 14 ff. This *hawâ*, however, also signifies in general: a broad, empty space, and by transferring the notion of "empty" to mind and heart, as the reduplicated forms *hûhatun* and *hauhâtun*: devoid of understanding and devoid of courage, *e.g.* Koran xiv. 44: *wa-af'i-datuhum hawâun*, where Beidhâwi first explains *hawâ* directly by *chalâ*, emptiness, empty space, *i.e.*, as he adds, *châlijetun 'an el-fahm*, as one says of one without mind and courage *qalbuhu hawâun*. Thence also *hauwun*, emptiness, a hole, *i.e.* in a wall or roof, a dormar-window (*kauwe*, *kûwe*), but also with the genit. of a person or thing: their hole, *i.e.* the space left empty by them, the side not taken up by them, *e.g. qa'ada fi hauwihi*, he set himself beside him. From the signification to be empty then comes, (1) *hawat el-mar'atu, i.e. vacua fuit mulier = orba liberis*, as χήρα, ch. xxxiii. 16) the hand of all men that they cannot, viz. on account of the cold out of doors, be opened for work, that all people of His work (*i.e.* thanking Him for their origin as His handiwork, ch. xxxiv. 19) may come to the perception (of Him who doeth all things). The expression is remarkable, and by the insertion of a מ may be as easily cleared up as ch. xxxiii. 17: לָדַעַת כָּל־אֲנָשִׁים מַעֲשֵׂהוּ, in order that each and every one may acknowledge His work; after which even Jer. translates: *ut noverint singuli opera sua.* The conjecture אנשים עֹשֵׂהוּ (Schultens junior, Reiske, Hirz.) is inferior to the former (Olsh.) by its awkward *synecdoche num.* The *fut. consec.* in ver. 8 continues the description of what happens in consequence of the cold rainy season; the expression calls to mind Ps. civ. 22, as ch. xxxiv. 14 sq. does Ps. civ. 29. The winter is also the time of the stormy and raw winds. In ver. 9*a* Elihu means the storms which come across from the great wide desert, ch. i. 19, therefore the south (Isa. xxi. 1,

vidua, properly empty, French *vide*; (2) *hawâ er-ragulu*, *i.e. vacuus, inanis factus est vir = exanimatus* (comp. فرغ, he became empty, euphemistic for he died).

From this variously applied primary signification is developed the generally known and usual هوى, loose and free, without being held or holding to anything one's self, to pass away, fly, swing, etc., *libere ferri, labi*, in general in every direction, as the wind, or what is driven hither and thither by the wind, especially however from above downwards, *labi, delabi, cadere, deorsum ruere.* From this point, like many similar, the word first passes into the signification of sound (as certainly also שָׁאָה, שָׁא): as anything falling has a dull noise, and so on, δουπεῖν, *rumorem, fragorem edere* (*fragor* from *frangi*), hence *hawat udhnuhu hawijan* of a singing in the ears.

Finally, the mental هوى (perf. *hawija*, imperf. *jahwâ* with the acc.), *animo ad* or *in aliquid ferri*, is attached to the notion of passing and falling through space (though by no means to *hiare*, or the supposed meaning "to breathe, blow"). It is used both emotionally of desire, lust, appetites, passions, and strong love, and intellectually of free opinions or assertions springing from mere self-willed preference, caprices of the understanding.—FL.

Zech. ix. 14), or rather (*vid.* p. 77, note) south-east winds (Hos. xiii. 15), increasing in violence to storms. הַחֶדֶר (properly the surrounded, enclosed space, never the storehouse,—so that Ps. cxxxv. 7 should be compared,—but *adytum, penetrale,* as Arab. *chidr, e.g.* in *Vita Timuri* ii. 904 : after the removal of the superincumbent earth, they drew away *sitr chidrihâ,* the curtain of its innermost part, *i.e.* uncovered its lowest depth) is here the innermost part of the south (south-east),—comp. ch. ix. 9 חדרי תימן, and xxiii. 9 ימין יעטף (so far as יעטף there signifies *si operiat se*),—especially of the great desert lying to the south (south-east), according to which אֶרֶץ חַדְרָךְ, Zech. ix. 1, is translated by the Targ. ארעא דרומא. In opposition to the south-east wind, מְזָרִים, ver. 9*b,* seems to mean the north winds; in and of itself, however, the word signifies the scattering ·or driving, as also in the Koran the winds are called the scatterers, *dhârijât, Sur.* li. 1.[1] In מזרים, Reiske, without any ground for it, traces the Arab. *mirzam* (a name of two stars, from which north wind, rain, and cold are derived); the Targ. also has one of the constellations in view : מִבַּח מְזָרִים (from the window, *i.e.* the window of the vault of heaven, of the *mezarim*) ; Aq., Theod. ἀπὸ μαζούρ (= מזרות, ch. xxxviii. 32) ; LXX. ἀπὸ δὲ τῶν ἀκρωτηρίων, we know not wherefore. Concerning מִנְּשָׁמַת־אֵל (with causal מִן) with reference to the wind, *vid.* on ch. iv. 15. יֻתֵּן, it gives, *i.e.* comes to light, is used as in Gen. xxxviii. 28, Prov. xiii. 10. The idea of מוּצָק (not *fusum* from יָצַק, but *coarctatum* from צוּק) cannot be doubtful in connection with the antithesis of רֹחַב, comp. ch. xxxvi. 16, the idea is like ch. xxxviii. 30 (comp. Mutenebbi : "the flood is bound by bands of ice") ; the בְּ of בְּמוּצָק is, as ch. xxxvi. 32, the *Beth essentiæ,* used far more extensively in Hebr. than in Arab. as an exponent of the

---

[1] This *dhârijât* is also differently explained ; but the first explanation in Beidhâwi (ii. 183, Fleischer's edition) is, "the winds which scatter (blow away) the dust and other things."

predicate: the breadth of the water is (becomes) straitened
(forcibly drawn together).

> 11 *Also He loadeth the clouds with water,*
> *He spreadeth far and wide the cloud of His light,*
> 12 *And these turn themselves round about,*
> *Directed by Him, that they execute*
> *All that He hath commanded them*
> *Over the wide earth.*
> 13 *Whether for a scourge, or for the good of His earth,*
> *Or for mercy, He causeth it to discharge itself.*

With אַף extending the description, Elihu, in the presence
of the storm that is in the sky, continually returns to this one
marvel of nature. The old versions connect בְּרִי partly with
בַּר, *electus* (LXX., Syr., Theod.) or *frumentum* (Symm.,
Jer.), partly with בָּרָה = בְּרִי in the signification *puritas,
serenitas* (Targ.); but בְּרִי is, as Schultens has already perceived, the Hebr.-Arabic רִי, رِيّ, *rij-un* (from רוה = *riwj*),
abundant irrigation, with בְּ; and יַטְרִיחַ does not signify, according to the Arab. *atraha*, "to hurl down," so that what is
spoken of would be the bursting of the clouds (Stick.),[1] but,
according to טָרַח, a burden (comp. Arab. *taraha ala*, to load),
"to burden;" with fluidity (Ew., Hirz., Hahn, Schlottm.),
better: fulness of water, He burdens the clouds (comp. *rawij-
un* as a designation of cloud as the place of rain). עֲנַן אוֹרוֹ,
His cloud of light, is that that is charged with lightning, and
הֵפִיץ has here its Hebr.-Arab. radical signification *effundere,
diffundere*, with a preponderance of the idea not of scattering,
but of spreading out wide (Arab. *faid*, abundance). וְהוּא, ver.
12a, refers to the cloud pregnant with lightning; this turns

---

[1] This "*atraha*" is, moreover, a pure invention of our ordinary Arabic
lexicons instead of *ittaraha* (VIII. form): (1) to throw one's self, (2) to
throw anything from one's self, with an *acc.* of the thing.—FL.

round about (מְסִבּוֹת, adv. as מֵסַב, round about, 1 Kings vi. 29) seeking a place, where it shall unburden itself by virtue of His (God's) direction or disposing (תַחְבּוּלֹת, a word belonging to the book of Proverbs; LXX., *Cod. Vat.* and *Alex.*, untranslated: εν θεεβουλαθωθ, *Cod. Sinait.* still more monstrous), in order that they (the clouds full of lightning) may accomplish everything that He commands them over the surface of the earth; אָרְצָה as ch. xxxiv. 13, and the combination תֵּבֵל אָרְצָה as Prov. viii. 31, comp. אֶרֶץ וְתֵבֵל, Ps. xc. 2. The reference of the pronominal *suff.* to men is as inadmissible here as in ver. 4c. In ver. 13 two אִם have certainly, as. ch. xxxiv. 29, two וְ, the correlative signification *sive . . . sive* (Arab. *in . . . wa-in*), and a third, as appears, a conditional, but which? According to Ew., Hirz., Hahn, Schlottm., and others, the middle one: if it (the rod) belongs to His land, *i.e.* if it has deserved it. But even the possessive *suff.* of לְאַרְצוֹ shows that the לְ is to be taken as *dat. commodi*: be it for a rod, be it for the good of His land; which is then followed by a conditional verbal clause: in case He mercifully causes it (the storm) to come, *i.e.* causes this His land to be overtaken by it (הִמְצִיאָ here with the *acc.*, the thing coming, whereas in ch. xxxiv. 11 of the thing to be overtaken). The accentuation, indeed, appears to assume a threefold *sive*: [whether He causeth it to discharge itself upon] man for punishment, man for mercy, or His earth for good with reference to man. Then Elihu would think of the uninhabited steppe in connection with אִם לְאַרְצוֹ. Since a conditional אִם by the side of two correlatives is hazardous, we decide finally with the LXX., Targ., and all the old versions, in favour of the same rendering of the threefold אִם, especially since it corresponds to the circumstances of the case.

14 *Hearken unto this, O Job;*
   Stand still and consider the wonderful works of God!

15 *Dost thou know when God designeth*
   To cause the light of His clouds to shine?
16 *Dost thou understand the balancings of the clouds,*
   The wondrous things of Him who is perfect in knowledge?

Job is to stand still, instead of dictating to God, in order
to draw from His wondrous acts in nature a conclusion with
reference to his mystery of suffering. In ver. 15*a* בְּ יָדַע does
not, as ch. xxxv. 15 (Ew. § 217, S. 557), belong together,
but בְּ is the temporal *Beth.* שׂוּם is equivalent to לְבוֹ שִׂים (*vid.*
on ch. xxxiv. 23); עֲלֵיהֶם does not refer to נִפְלָאוֹת (Hirz.) or
the phenomena of the storm (Ew.), but is intended as neuter
(as בָּם ch. xxxvi. 31, בָּהֶם xxii. 21), and finds in ver. 15*b* its
distinctive development: "the light of His clouds" is their
effulgent splendour. Without further support, עַל יָדַע is to
have knowledge concerning anything, ver. 16*a;* מִפְלְשֵׂי is also
ἀπ. γεγρ. It is unnecessary to consider it as wrongly written
from מִפְרְשֵׂי, ch. xxxvi. 29, or as from it by change of letter (as
אַרְמְנוֹת = אַלְמְנוֹת, Isa. xiii. 22). The verb פָּלַּס signifies to make
level, prepare (viz. a way, also weakened: to take a certain
way, Prov. v. 6), once: to weigh, Ps. lviii. 3, as *denom.* from
פֶּלֶס, a balance (and indeed a steelyard, *statera*), which is
thus mentioned as the means of adjustment. מִפְלְשֵׂי accordingly signifies either, as synon. of מִשְׁקְלֵי (thus the Midrash,
vid. Jalkut, § 522), weights (the relations of weight), or even
equipoised balancings (Aben-Ezra, Kimchi, and others), Lat.
quomodo librentur nubes in aëre.[1] מִפְלָאוֹת is also a word that
does not occur elsewhere; in like manner דֵּעַ belongs exclu-

---

[1] The word is therefore a metaphor taken from the balance, and it may
be observed that the Syro-Arabic, on account of the most extensive application of the balance, is unusually rich in such metaphors. Moreover, the
Arabic has no corresponding noun: the *teflis* (a balance) brought forward
by Ges. in his *Thes.* and *Handwörterbuch* from Schindler's *Pentaglotton,*
is a word devoid of all evidence from original sources and from the
modern usage of the language, in this signification.

sively to Elihu. God is called תְּמִים דֵּעִים (comp. ch. xxxvi. 4) as the Omniscient One, whose knowledge is absolute as to its depth as well as its circumference.

> 17 *Thou whose garments become hot,*
> *When the land is sultry from the south:*
> 18 *Dost thou with Him spread out the sky,*
> *The strong, as it were molten, mirror?*
> 19 *Let us know what we shall say to Him!—*
> *We can arrange nothing by reason of darkness.*
> 20 *Shall it be told Him that I speak,*
> *Or shall one wish to be destroyed?*

Most expositors connect ver. 17a with ver. 16: (Dost thou know) how it comes to pass that . . . ; but אֲשֶׁר after יָדַע signifies *quod*, Ex. xi. 7, not *quomodo*, as it sometimes occurs in a comparing antecedent clause, instead of כַּאֲשֶׁר, Ex. xiv. 13, Jer. xxxiii. 22. We therefore translate: thou whose . . .,—connecting this, however, not with ver. 16 (*vid. e.g.* Carey), but as Bolduc. and Ew., with ver. 18 (where הֲ before תַּרְקִיעַ is then the less missed): thou who, when the land (the part of the earth where thou art) keeps rest, *i.e.* in sultriness, when oppressive heat comes (on this *Hiph. vid.* Ges. § 53, 2) from the south (*i.e.* by means of the currents of air which come thence, without דָּרוֹם signifying directly the south wind),—thou who, when this happens, canst endure so little, that on the contrary the heat from without becomes perceptible to thee through thy clothes: dost thou now and then with Him keep the sky spread out, which for firmness is like a molten mirror? Elsewhere the hemispheric firmament, which spans the earth with its sub-celestial waters, is likened to a clear sapphire Ex. xxiv. 10, a covering Ps. civ. 2, a gauze Isa. xl. 22; the comparison with a metallic mirror (מוּצָק here not from צוּק, ver. 10, ch. xxxvi. 16, but from יָצַק) is therefore to be understood according to Petavius: *Cœlum aëreum* στερίωμα *dicitur non a naturæ propria conditione, sed ab effectu, quod perinde aquas separet, ac si murus esset solidissimus.* Also in תרקיע lies the notion both of firmness and thinness; the primary notion (root רק) is to beat, make thick, *stipare* (رَقَّ, to stop up in the sense of *resarcire, e.g.* to mend stockings), to make thick by pressure. The ל joined with תרקיע is *nota acc.;* we must not comp. ch. viii. 8, xxi. 22, as well as ch. v. 2, xix. 3.

Therefore: As God is the only Creator (ch. ix. 8), so He is the all-provident Preserver of the world—make us know (הֹורִיעֶנוּ, according to the text of the Babylonians, *Keri* of הֹורִיעֵנִי) what we shall say to Him, viz. in order to show that we can cope with Him! We cannot arrange, viz. anything whatever (to be explained according to עֲרָךְ מִלִּין, ch. xxxii. 14, comp. "to place," ch. xxxvi. 19), by reason of darkness, viz. the darkness of our understanding, σκότος τῆς διανοίας; מִפְּנֵי is much the same as ch. xxiii. 17, but different from ch. xvii. 12, and חֹשֶׁךְ different from both passages, viz. as it is often used in the New Testament, of intellectual darkness (comp. Eccl. ii. 14, Isa. lx. 2). The meaning of ver. 20 cannot now be mistaken, if, with Hirz., Hahn, and Schlottm., we call to mind ch. xxxvi. 10 in connection with אָמַר כִּי: can I, a short-sighted man, enshrouded in darkness, wish that what I have arrogantly said concerning and against Him may be told to God, or should one earnestly desire (אָמַר, a modal *perf.,* as ch. xxxv. 15*b*) that (*an jusserit s. dixerit quis ut*) he may be swallowed up, *i.e.* destroyed (comp. לְבַלַּע, ch. ii. 3)? He would, by challenging a recognition of his unbecoming arguing about God, desire a tribunal that would be destructive to himself.

> 21 *Although one seeth not now the sunlight*
>   *That is bright in the ethereal heights:*
>   *A wind passeth by and cleareth them up.*

22   *Gold is brought from the north,—*
      Above Eloah is terrible majesty.
23   *The Almighty, whom we cannot find out,*
      The excellent in strength,
      And right and justice He perverteth not.
24   *Therefore men regard Him with reverence,*
      He hath no regard for all the wise of heart.

He who censures God's actions, and murmurs against God, injures himself—how, on the contrary, would a patiently submissive waiting on Him be rewarded! This is the connection of thought, by which this final strophe is attached to what precedes. If we have drawn the correct conclusion from ch. xxxvii. 1, that Elihu's description of a storm is accompanied by a storm which was coming over the sky, וְעַתָּה, with which the speech, as ch. xxxv. 15, draws towards the close, is not to be understood as purely conclusive, but temporal: And at present one does not see the light (אוֹר of the sun, as ch. xxxi. 26) which is bright in the ethereal heights (בָּהִיר again a Hebr.-Arab. word, comp. *bâhir*, outshining, surpassing, especially of the moon, when it dazzles with its brightness); yet it only requires a breath of wind to pass over it, and it clears it, *i.e.* brings the ethereal sky with the sunlight to view. Elihu hereby means to say that the God who is hidden only for a time, respecting whom one runs the risk of being in perplexity, can suddenly unveil Himself, to our surprise and confusion, and that therefore it becomes us to bow humbly and quietly to His present mysterious visitation. With respect to the removal of the clouds from the beclouded sun, to which ver. 21 refers, זָהָב, ver. 22*a*, seems to signify the gold of the sun; *esh-shemsu bi-tibrin*, the sun is gold, says Abulola. Oriental and Classic literature furnishes a large number of instances in support of this calling the sunshine gold; and it should not perplex us here, where we have an Arabizing Hebrew poet before us, that not a single passage can be brought forward from the Old Testament literature. But מִצָּפוֹן is against this figurative rendering of the זָהָב (LXX. νέφη χρυσαυγοῦντα). In Ezek. i. 4 there is good reason for the storm-clouds, which unfold from their midst the glory of the heavenly Judge, who rideth upon the cherubim, coming from the north; but wherefore should Elihu represent the sun's golden light as breaking through from the north? On the other hand, in the conception of the ancients, the north is the proper region for gold: there griffins (γρυπές) guard the gold-pits of the Arimaspian mountains (Herod. iii. 116); there, from the narrow pass of the Caucasus along the Gordyæan mountains, gold is dug by barbarous races (Pliny, *h. n.* vi. 11), and among the Scythians it is brought to light by the ants (*ib.* xxxiii. 4). Egypt could indeed provide itself with gold from Ethiopia, and the Phœnicians brought the gold of Ophir, already mentioned in the book of Job, from India; but the north was regarded as the fabulously most productive chief mine of gold; to speak more definitely: Northern Asia, with the Altai mountains.[1] Thus therefore ch. xxviii. 1, 6 is to be compared here.

What Job describes so grandly and minutely in ch. xxviii., viz. that man lays bare the hidden treasures of the earth's interior, but that the wisdom of God still transcends him, is here expressed no less grandly and compendiously: From the north cometh gold, which man wrests from the darkness of the gloomy unknown region of the north (צָפוֹן, ζόφος, from צָפַן, cogn. טמן, טמר,[2] *vid.* p. 53, note, comp. p. 11, note); upon

---

[1] *Vid.* the art. *Gold*, S. 91, 101, in Ersch and Gruber. The Indian traditions concerning *Uttaraguru* (the "High Mountain"), and concerning the northern seat of the god of wealth *Kuvêra*, have no connection here; on their origin comp. Lassen, *Indische Alterthumskunde*, i. 848.

[2] The verb צָפָה, *obducere*, does not belong here, but to צפח, and signifies properly to flatten (as רקע, to make thin and thick by striking),

Eloah, on the contrary, is terrible majesty (not genitival: terror of majesty, Ew. § 293, *c*), *i.e.* it covers Him like a garment (Ps. civ. 1), making Him inaccessible (הוֹד, glory as resounding praise, *vid.* on ch. xxxix. 20, like כבוד as imposing dignity). The beclouded sun, ver. 21 said, has lost none of the intensity of its light, although man has to wait for the removing of the clouds to behold it again. So, when God's doings are mysterious to us, we have to wait, without murmuring, for His solution of the mystery. While from the north comes gold—ver. 22 continues—which is obtained by laying bare the interior of the northern mountains, God, on the other hand, is surrounded by inaccessibly terrible glory: the Almighty—thus ver. 23 completes the thought towards which ver. 22 tends—we cannot reach, the Great in power, *i.e.* the nature of the Absolute One remains beyond us, the counsel of the Almighty impenetrable; still we can at all times be certain of this, that what He does is right and good: " Right and the fulness of justice (וְרֹב־ according to the Masora, not וְרָב־) He perverteth not." The expression is remarkable: עָנָה מִשְׁפָּט is, like the Talmudic עָנָה דִין, equivalent elsewhere to הִטָּה משפט; and that He does not pervert רֹב־צְדָקָה, affirms that justice in its whole compass is not perverted by Him; His acts are therefore perfectly and in every way consistent with it: רֹב־צְדָקָה is the *abstract.* to צַדִּיק כַּבִּיר, ch. xxxiv. 17, therefore *summa justitia.* One may feel tempted to draw שֹׂגִיא כֹח to ומשפט, and to read וְרָב according to Prov. xiv. 29 instead of וְרֹב, but the expression gained by so doing is still more difficult than the combination ומשפט . . . לֹא יְעַנֶּה; not merely difficult, however, but putting a false point in place of a correct one, is the reading לֹא יַעֲנֶה (LXX., Syr., Jer.),

comp. صفح, to strike on something flat (whence *el-musâfaha*, the salutation by striking the hand), and صفح, to strike with the flat hand on anything, therefore *diducendo obducere.*

according to which Hirz. translates: He answers not, *i.e.*
gives no account to man. The accentuation rightly divides
ver. 23 into two halves, the second of which begins with
וּמִשְׁפָּט—a significant *Waw*, on which J. H. Michaelis observes:
*Placide invicem in Deo conspirant infinita ejus potentia et
justitia quæ in hominibus sæpe disjuncta sunt.*

Elihu closes with the practical inference: Therefore men,
viz. of the right sort, of sound heart, uncorrupted and unaffected, fear Him (יִרְאֻהוּ *verentur eum*, not יִרְאֻהוּ *veremini
eum*); He does not see (regard) the wise of heart, *i.e.* those
who imagine themselves such and are proud of their לֵב, their
understanding. The *qui sibi videntur* (Jer.) does not lie in
לֵב (comp. Isa. v. 21), but in the antithesis. Stick. and others
render falsely: Whom the aggregate of the over-wise beholds
not, which would be יִרְאֶנּוּ. God is the subj. as in ch. xxviii. 24,
xxxiv. 21, comp. xli. 26. The assonance of יראהו and יראה,
which also occurs frequently elsewhere (*e.g.* ch. vi. 21), we
have sought to reproduce in the translation.

In this last speech also Elihu's chief aim (ch. xxxvi. 2-4)
is to defend God against Job's charge of injustice. He shows
how omnipotence, love, and justice are all found in God.
When judging of God's omnipotence, we are to beware of
censuring Him who is absolutely exalted above us and our
comprehension; when judging of God's love, we are to beware
of interpreting His afflictive dispensations, which are designed
for our well-being, as the persecution of an enemy; when
judging of His justice, we are to beware of maintaining our
own righteousness at the cost of the Divine, and of thus
avoiding the penitent humbling of one's self under His well-
meant chastisement. The twofold peculiarity of Elihu's
speeches comes out in this fourth as prominently as in the
first: (1) They demand of Job penitential submission, not by
accusing him of coarse common sins as the three have done,
but because even the best of men suffer for hidden moral

defects, which must be perceived by them in order not to perish on account of them. Elihu here does for Job just what in Bunyan (*Pilgrim's Progress*) the man in the Interpreter's house does, when he sweeps the room, so that Christian had been almost choked with the dust that flew about. Then (2) they teach that God makes use of just such sufferings, as Job's now are, in order to bring man to a knowledge of his hidden defects, and to bless him the more abundantly if he will be saved from them; that thus the sufferings of those who fear God are a wholesome medicine, disciplinary chastenings, and saving warnings; and that therefore true, not merely feigned, piety must be proved in the school of affliction by earnest self-examination, remorseful self-accusation, and humble submission.

Elihu therefore in this agrees with the rest of the book, that he frees Job's affliction from the view which accounts it the evil-doer's punishment (*vid.* ch. xxxii. 3). On the other hand, however, he nevertheless takes up a position apart from the rest of the book, by making Job's sin the cause of his affliction; while in the idea of the rest of the book Job's affliction has nothing whatever to do with Job's sin, except in so far as he allows himself to be drawn into sinful language concerning God by the conflict of temptation into which the affliction plunges him. For after Jehovah has brought Job over this his sin, He acknowledges His servant (ch. xlii. 7) to be in the right, against the three friends: his affliction is really not a merited affliction, it is not a result of retributive justice; it also had not chastisement as its design, it was an enigma, under which Job should have bowed humbly without striking against it—a decree, into the purpose of which the prologue permits us an insight, which however remains unexplained to Job, or is only explained to him so far as the issue teaches him that it should be to him the way to a so much the more glorious testimony on the part of God Himself.

With that criticism of Job, which the speeches of Jehovah consummate, the criticism which lies before us in the speeches of Elihu is irreconcilable. The older poet, in contrast with the false doctrine of retribution, entirely separates sin and punishment or chastisement in the affliction of Job, and teaches that there is an affliction of the righteous, which is solely designed to prove and test them. His thema, not Elihu's (as Simson[1] with Hengstenberg thinks), is *the mystery of the Cross.* For the Cross according to its proper notion is suffering ἕνεκεν δικαιοσύνης (or what in New Testament language is the same, ἕνεκεν Χριστοῦ). Elihu, however, leaves sin and suffering together as inseparable, and opposes the false doctrine of retribution by the distinction between disciplinary chastisement and judicial retribution. The Elihu section, as I have shown elsewhere,[2] has sprung from the endeavour to moderate the bewildering boldness with which the older poet puts forth his idea. The writer has felt in connection with the book of Job what every Christian must feel. Such a maintaining of his own righteousness in the face of friendly exhortations to penitence, as we perceive it in Job's speeches, is certainly not possible where " the dust of the room has flown about." The friends have only failed in this, that they made Job more and more an evil-doer deservedly undergoing punishment. Elihu points him to vainglorying, to carnal security, and in the main to those defects from which the most godly cannot and dare not claim exemption. It is not contrary to the spirit of the drama that Job holds his peace at these exhortations to penitence. The similarly expressed admonition to penitence with which Eliphaz, ch. iv. sq., begins, has not effected it. In the meanwhile, however, Job is become more softened and composed, and in remembrance of his unbecoming language concerning God,

---

[1] *Zur Kritik des B. Hiob*, 1861, S. 34.
[2] *Vid.* Herzog's *Real-Encyklopädie*, art. *Hiob*, S. 119.

he must feel that he has forfeited the right of defending himself. Nevertheless this silent Job is not altogether the same as the Job who, in ch. xl. and xlii., forces himself to keep silence, whose former testimony concerning himself; and whose former refusal of a theodicy which links sin and calamity together, Jehovah finally sets His seal to.

On the other hand, however, it must be acknowledged, that what the introduction to Elihu's speeches, ch. xxxii. 1–5, sets before us, is consistent with the idea of the whole, and that such a section as the introduction leads one to expect, may be easily understood really as a member of the whole, which carries forward the dramatic development of this idea; for this very reason one feels urged to constantly new endeavours, if possible, to understand these speeches as a part of the original form. But they are without result, and, moreover, many other considerations stand in our way to the desired goal; especially, that Elihu is not mentioned in the epilogue, and that his speeches are far behind the artistic perfection of the rest of the book. It is true the writer of these speeches has, in common with the rest of the book, a like Hebræo-Arabic, and indeed Hauranitish style, and like mutual relations to earlier and later writings; but this is explained from the consideration that he has completely blended the older book with himself (as the points of contact of the fourth speech with ch. xxviii. and the speeches of Jehovah, show), and that to all appearance he is a fellow-countryman of the older poet. There are neither linguistic nor any other valid reasons in favour of assigning it to a much later period. He is the second issuer of the book, possibly the first, who brought to light the hitherto hidden treasure, enriched by his own insertion, which is inestimable in its relation to the history of the perception of the plan of redemption.

We now call to mind that in the last (according to our

view) strophe of Job's last speech, ch. xxxi. 35–37, Job desires, yea challenges, the divine decision between himself and
his opponents. His opponents have explained his affliction
as the punishment of the just God; he, however, is himself so
certain of his innocence, and of his victory over divine and
human accusation, that he will bind the indictment of his
opponents as a crown upon his brow, and to God, whose hand
of punishment supposedly rests upon him, will he render an
account of all his steps, and go forth as a prince to meet
Him. That he considers himself a צדיק is in itself not censurable, for he is such: but that he is מצדק נפשו מאלהים, *i.e.*
considers himself to be righteous in opposition to God, who
is now angry with him and punishes him; that he maintains
his own righteousness to the prejudice of the Divine; and
that by maintaining his own right, places the Divine in the
shade,—all this is explainable as the result of the false idea
which he entertains of his affliction, and in which he is
strengthened by the friends; but there is need of censure and
penitence. For since by His nature God can never do wrong,
all human wrangling before God is a sinful advance against
the mystery of divine guidance, under which he should rather
humbly bow. But we have seen that Job's false idea of God
as his enemy, whose conduct he cannot acknowledge as just,
does not fill his whole soul. The night of temptation in which
he is enshrouded, is broken in upon by gleams of faith, in
connection with which God appears to him as his Vindicator
and Redeemer. Flesh and spirit, nature and grace, delusion
and faith, are at war within him. These two elements are
constantly more definitely separated in the course of the controversy; but it is not yet come to the victory of faith over
delusion, the two lines of conception go unreconciled side by
side in Job's soul. The last monologues issue on the one side
in the humble confession that God's wisdom is unsearchable,
and the fear of God is the share of wisdom appointed to man;

on the other side, in the defiant demand that God may answer
for his defence of himself, and the vaunting offer to give Him
an account of all his steps, and also then to enter His presence
with the high feeling of a prince. If now the issue of the
drama is to be this, that God really reveals Himself as Job's
Vindicator and Redeemer, Job's defiance and boldness must
be previously punished in order that lowliness and submission
may attain the victory over them. God cannot acknowledge
Job as His servant before he penitently acknowledges as such
the sinful weakness under which he has proved himself to be
God's servant, and so exhibits himself anew in his true character which cherishes no known sin. This takes place when
Jehovah appears, and in language not of wrath but of loving
condescension, and yet earnest reproof, He makes the Titan
quite puny in his own eyes, in order then to exalt him who is
outwardly and inwardly humbled.

THE UNRAVELMENT IN THE CONSCIOUSNESS.—
CHAP. XXXVIII.–XLII. 6.

The First Speech of Jehovah, and Job's Answer.—
Chap. xxxviii.–xl. 5.

Schema : 4. 8. 8. 8. 12. 12. 6. 6. 10. 7. | 8. 8. 8. 12. 15. 10. | 2. 4.

[Then Jehovah answered Job out of the storm, and said:]
2 *Who then darkeneth counsel*
With words without knowledge ?
3 *Gird up now thy loins as a man :*
I will question thee, and inform thou me !

" May the Almighty answer me!" Job has said, ch. xxxi. 35;
He now really answers, and indeed out of the storm (*Chethib*,
according to a mode of writing occurring only here and ch.
xl. 6, מנהסערה, arranged in two words by the *Keri*), which

is generally the forerunner of His self-manifestation in the
world, of that at least by which He reveals Himself in His
absolute awe-inspiring greatness and judicial grandeur. The
art. is to be understood generically, but, with respect to
Elihu's speeches, refers to the storm which has risen up in
the meanwhile. It is not to be translated: Who is he who
. . . , which ought to be הַמַּחְשִׁיךְ, but: Who then is darkening; זֶה makes the interrogative מִי more vivid and demonstrative, Ges. § 122, 2; the *part.* מַחְשִׁיךְ (instead of which it
might also be יַחְשִׁיךְ) favours the assumption that Job has
uttered such words immediately before, and is interrupted
by Jehovah, without an intervening speaker having come
forward. It is intentionally עֵצָה for עֲצָתִי (comp. עַם for עַמִּי,
Isa. xxvi. 11), to describe that which is spoken of according
to its quality: it is nothing less than a decree or plan full
of purpose and connection which Job darkens, *i.e.* distorts
by judging it falsely, or, as we say: places in a false light,
and in fact by meaningless words.[1]

When now Jehovah condescends to negotiate with Job
by question and answer, He does not do exactly what Job
wished (ch. xiii. 22), but something different, of which Job
never thought. He surprises him with questions which are
intended to bring him indirectly to the consciousness of the
wrong and absurdity of his challenge—questions among
which "there are many which the natural philosophy of the
present day can frame more scientifically, but cannot satisfactorily solve."[2] Instead of כְּנָבֵר (the received reading of
Ben-Ascher), Ben-Naphtali's text offered כְּנ (as Ezek. xvii.
10), in order not to allow two so similar, aspirated *mutæ* to
come together.

---

[1] The correct accentuation is מחשׁיך with *Mercha*, עצה with *Athnach*,
במלין with *Rebia mugrasch*, בלי (without *Makkeph*) with *Munach*.

[2] Alex. v. Humboldt, *Kosmos*, ii. 48 (1st edition), comp. Tholuck,
Vermischte Schriften, i. 354.

4 *Where wast thou when I established the earth?*
Say, if thou art capable of judging!
5 *Who hath determined its measure, if thou knowest it,*
Or who hath stretched the measuring line over it?
6 *Upon what are the bases of its pillars sunk in,*
Or who hath laid its corner-stone,
7 *When the morning stars sang together*
And all the sons of God shouted for joy?

The examination begins similarly to ch. xv. 7 sq. In opposition to the censurer of God as such the friends were right,
although only negatively, since their conduct was based on
self-delusion, as though they were in possession of the key
to the mystery of the divine government of the world. יָדַע
בִּינָה signifies to understand how to judge, to possess a competent understanding, 1 Chron. xii. 32, 2 Chron. ii. 12, or
(יְדַע taken not in the sense of *novisse*, but *cognoscere*) to
appropriate to one's self, Prov. iv. 1, Isa. xxix. 24. כִּי, ver.
5a, interchanges with אִם (comp. ver. 18b), for כִּי תֵדַע signifies: suppose that thou knowest it, and this *si forte scias* is
almost equivalent to *an forte scis*, Prov. xxx. 4. The founding of the earth is likened altogether to that of a building
constructed by man. The question: upon what are the
bases of its pillars or foundations sunk (טבע, طبع, according
to its radical signification, to press with something flat upon
something, comp. طبق, to lay two flat things on one another,
then both to form or stamp by pressure, vid. i. 377, note,
and to press into soft pliant stuff, or let down into, *immergere*,
or to sink into, *immergi*), points to the fact of the earth
hanging free in space, ch. xxvi. 7. Then no human being
was present, for man was not yet created; the angels, however, beheld with rejoicing the founding of the place of the
future human family, and the mighty acts of God in accordance with the decree of His love (as at the building of

the temple, the laying of the foundation, Ezra iii. 10, and
the setting of the head-stone, Zech. iv. 7, were celebrated),
for the angels were created before the visible world (*Psychol.*
S. 63; *Genesis*, S. 105), as is indeed not taught here, but
still (*vid.* on the other hand, Hofmann, *Schriftbew.* i. 400)
is assumed. For בְּנֵי אֱלֹהִים are, as in ch. i. ii., the angels, who
proceeded from God by a mode of creation which is likened
to begetting, and who with Him form one πατριά (*Genesis*,
S. 121). The "morning stars," however, are mentioned in
connection with them, because between the stars and the
angels, which are both comprehended in צְבָא הַשָּׁמַיִם (*Genesis*,
S. 128), a mysterious connection exists, which is manifoldly
attested in Holy Scripture (*vid.* on the other hand, Hofm. *ib.*
S. 318). כּוֹכַב בֹּקֶר is the morning star which in Isa. xiv. 12
is called הֵילֵל (as extra-bibl. נֹגַהּ) from its dazzling light, which
exceeds all other stars in brightness, and בֶּן־שַׁחַר, son of the
dawn, because it swims in the dawn as though it were born
from it. It was just the dawn of the world coming into being,
which is the subject spoken of, that gave rise to the mention
of the morning star; the *plur.*, however, does not mean the
stars which came into being on that morning of the world
collectively (Hofm., Schlottm.), but Lucifer with the stars
his peers, as כְּסִילִים, Isa. xiii. 10, Orion and the stars his peers.

سُهَيْل (Canopus) is used similarly as a generic name for
stars of remarkable brilliancy, and in general *suhêl* is to the
nomads and the Hauranites the symbol of what is brilliant,
glorious, and beautiful;[1] so that even the beings of light of
the first rank among the celestial spirits might be understood
by כוכבי בקר. But if this ought to be the meaning, ver. 7*a*

---

[1] A man or woman of great beauty is called *suhêli, suhelije.* Thus I
heard a Hauranitish woman say to her companion: *nahâr el-jôm nedâ,
shuft ledsch* (لَكِ) *wâhid Suhêli,* To-day is dew, I saw a *Suhêli, i.e.* a
very handsome man, for thee.—WETZST.

and 7*b* would be in an inverted order. They are actual stars, whether it is intended of the sphere belonging to the earth or to the higher sphere comprehended in השׁמים, Gen. i. 1. Joy and light are reciprocal notions, and the scale of the tones of joy is likened to the scale of light and colours; therefore the fulness of light, in which the morning stars shone forth all together at the founding of the earth, may symbolize one grandly harmonious song of joy.

> 8 *And* [*who*] *shut up the sea with doors,*
>   *When it broke through, issued from the womb,*
> 9 *When I put clouds round it as a garment,*
>   *And thick mist as its swaddling clothes,*
> 10 *And I broke for it my bound,*
>   *And set bars and doors,*
> 11 *And said: Hitherto come, and no further,*
>   *And here be thy proud waves stayed!?*

The state of תהו ובהו was the first half, and the state of תהום the second half of the primeval condition of the forming earth. The question does not, however, refer to the תהום, in which the waters of the sky and the waters of the earth were as yet not separated, but, passing over this intermediate condition of the forming earth, to the sea, the waters of which God shut up as by means of a door and bolt, when, first enshrouded in thick mist (which has remained from that time one of its natural peculiarities), and again and again manifesting its individuality, it broke forth (גיח of the fœtus, as Ps. xxii. 10) from the bowels of the, as yet, chaotic earth. That the sea, in spite of the flatness of its banks, does not flow over the land, is a work of omnipotence which broke over it, *i.e.* restraining it, a fixed bound (חק as ch. xxvi. 10, Prov. viii. 29, Jer. v. 22, = גבול, Ps. civ. 9), viz. the steep and rugged walls of the basin of the sea, and which thereby established a firm barrier behind which it should be kept.

Instead of וּפֹה, Josh. xviii. 8, ver. 11*b* has the *Chethib* וּפֹא. חֹק is to be understood with יָשִׁית, and "one set" is equivalent to the passive (Ges. § 137*): let a bound be set (comp. שָׁת, Hos. vi. 11, which is used directly so) against the proud rising of thy waves.

> 12 *Hast thou in thy life commanded a morning,*
>   *Caused the dawn to know its place,*
> 13 *That it may take hold of the ends of the earth,*
>   *So that the evil-doers are shaken under it?*
> 14 *That it changeth like the clay of a signet-ring,*
>   *And everything fashioneth itself as a garment.*
> 15 *Their light is removed from the evil-doers,*
>   *And the out-stretched arm is broken.*

The dawn of the morning, spreading out from one point, takes hold of the carpet of the earth as it were by the edges, and shakes off from it the evil-doers, who had laid themselves to rest upon it the night before. נָעַר, combining in itself the significations to thrust and to shake, has the latter here, as in the Arab. *nâ'ûra*, a water-wheel, which fills its compartments below in the river, to empty them out above. Instead of יָדַעְתָּ שַׁחַר with *He otians*, the *Keri* substitutes יָדַעְתָּ הַשַּׁחַר. The earth is the subj. to ver. 14*a*: the dawn is like the signet-ring, which stamps a definite impress on the earth as the clay, the forms which floated in the darkness of the night become visible and distinguishable. The subj. to ver. 14*b* are not morning and dawn (Schult.), still less the ends of the earth (Ew. with the conjecture: יתיבצו, "they become dazzlingly white"), but the single objects on the earth: the light of morning gives to everything its peculiar garb of light, so that, hitherto overlaid by a uniform darkness, they now come forth independently, they gradually appear in their variegated diversity of form and hue. In לבוש כְּמוֹ לְבֻשׁ, לבוש is conceived as accusative (Arab. *kemâ* *libâsan*, or *thauban*), while in כלבוש (Ps. civ. 6, *instar vestis*) it would be genitive. To the end of the strophe everything is under the logical government of the ל of purpose in ver. 13*a*. The light of the evil-doers is, according to ch. xxiv. 17, the darkness of the night, which is for them in connection with their works what the light of day is for other men. The sunrise deprives them, the enemies of light in the true sense (ch. xxiv. 13), of this light *per antiphrasin*, and the carrying out of their evil work, already prepared for, is frustrated. The ע of רשעים, vers. 13 and 15, is עין תלויה [*Ayin suspensum*], which is explained according to the Midrash thus: the רשעים, now עשירים (rich), become at a future time רשים (poor); or: God deprives them of the עין (light of the eye), by abandoning them to the darkness which they loved.

16 *Hast thou reached the fountains of the sea,*
   And hast thou gone into the foundation of the deep?

17 *Were the gates of death unveiled to thee,*
   And didst thou see the gates of the realm of shades?

18 *Hast thou comprehended the breadth of the earth?*
   Speak, in so far as thou knowest all this!

19 *Which is the way to where the light dwelleth,*
   And darkness, where is its place,

20 *That thou mightest bring it to its bound,*
   And that thou mightest know the paths of its house?

21 *Thou knowest it, for then wast thou born,*
   And the number of thy days is great!—

The root נב has the primary notion of obtruding itself upon the senses (*vid. Genesis*, S. 635), whence נבך in Arabic of a rising country that pleases the eye (*nabaka*, a hill, a hillside), and here (cognate in root and meaning נבע, Syr. Talmud. נְבַּג, نبع, نبط, *scaturire*) of gushing and bubbling water. Hitzig's conjecture, approved by Olsh., נבלי, sets aside a word

that is perfectly clear so far as the language is concerned.
On חֵקֶר *vid.* on ch. xi. 7. The question put to Job in ver. 17,
he must, according to his own confession, ch. xxvi. 6, answer
in the negative. In order to avoid the collision of two
aspirates, the interrogative הַ is wanting before הִתְבֹּנַנְתָּ, Ew.
§ 324, *b;* עַד הִתְבֹּנֵן signifies, according to ch. xxxii. 12, to
observe anything carefully; the meaning of the question
therefore is, whether Job has given special attention to the
breadth of the earth, and whether he consequently has a
comprehensive and thorough knowledge of it. כֻּלָּהּ refers
not to the earth (Hahn, Olsh., and others), but, as neuter, to
the preceding points of interrogation. The questions, ver. 19,
refer to the principles of light and darkness, *i.e.* their final
causes, whence they come forth as cosmical phenomena.
יִשְׁכָּן־אוֹר is a relative clause, Ges. § 123, 3, *c;* the noun that
governs (the *Regens*) this virtual genitive, which ought in
Arabic to be without the *art.* as being determined by the
regens, is, according to the Hebrew syntax, which is freer in
this respect, הַדֶּרֶךְ (comp. Ges. § 110, 2). That which is said
of the bound of darkness, *i.e.* the furthest point at which
darkness passes away, and the paths to its house, applies also
to the light, which the poet perhaps has even prominently
(comp. ch. xxiv. 13) before his mind: light and darkness
have a first cause which is inaccessible to man, and beyond
his power of searching out. The admission in ver. 21 is
ironical: Verily! thou art as old as the beginning of creation, when light and darkness, as powers of nature which are
distinguished and bounded the one by the other (*vid.* ch.
xxvi. 10), were introduced into the rising world; thou art as
old as the world, so that thou hast an exact knowledge of its
and thine own cotemporaneous origin (*vid.* ch. xv. 7). On
the *fut.* joined with אָז regularly in the signification of the
aorist, *vid.* Ew. § 134, *b.* The attraction in connection
with מִסְפַּר is like ch. xv. 20, xxi. 21.

22 *Hast thou reached the treasures of the snow,*
   And didst thou see the treasures of the hail,
23 *Which I have reserved for a time of trouble,*
   For the day of battle and war?
24 *Which is the way where the light is divided,*
   Where the east wind is scattered over the earth?
25 *Who divideth a course for the rain-flood*
   And the way of the lightning of thunder,
26 *That it raineth on the land where no one dwelleth,*
   On the tenantless steppe,
27 *To satisfy the desolate and the waste,*
   And to cause the tender shoot of the grass to spring forth?

The idea in ver. 22 is not that—as for instance the peasants of *Menîn*, four hours' journey from Damascus, garner up the winter snow in a cleft of the rock, in order to convey it to Damascus and the towns of the coast in the hot months—God treasures up the snow and hail above to cause it to descend according to opportunity. אֹצְרוֹת (comp. Ps. cxxxv. 7) are the final causes of these phenomena which God has created—the form of the question, the design of which (which must not be forgotten) is ethical, not scientific, is regulated according to the infancy of the perception of natural phenomena among the ancients; but at the same time in accordance with the poet's task, and even, as here, in the choice of the agents of destruction, not merely hail, but also snow, according to the scene of the incident. Wetzstein has in his possession a writing of Muhammed el-Chatîb el-Bosrâwi, in which he describes a fearful fall of snow in Hauran, by which, in February 1860, innumerable herds of sheep, goats, and camels, and also many human beings perished.[1] עֵת־צָר might, according to ch.

---

[1] Since the Hauranites say of snow as of fire : *jahrik*, it burns (*brûlant* in French is also used of extreme cold), ch. i. 16 might also be understood of a fall of snow ; but the tenor of the words there requires it to be understood of actual fire.

xxiv. 1, xix. 11, signify a time of judgment for the oppressor, *i.e.* adversary; but it is better to be understood according to ch. xxxvi. 16, xxi. 30, a time of distress: heavy falls of snow and tempestuous hail-storms bring hard times for men and cattle, and sometimes decide a war as by a divine decree (Josh. x. 11, comp. Isa. xxviii. 17, xxx. 30, Ezek. xiii. 13).

In ver. 24*a* it is not, as in ver. 19*a*, the place whence light issues, but the mode of the distribution of light over the earth, that is intended; as in ver. 24*b*, the laws according to which the east wind flows forth, *i.e.* spreads over the earth. אוֹר is not lightning (Schlottm.), but light in general: light and wind (instead of which the east wind is particularized, *vid.* p. 77) stand together as being alike untraceable in their courses. הֵפִיץ, *se diffundere*, as Ex. v. 12, 1 Sam. xiii. 8, Ges. § 53, 2. In ver. 25*a* the descent of torrents of rain inundating certain regions of the earth is intended—this earthward direction assigned to the water-spouts is likened to an aqueduct coming downwards from the sky—and it is only in ver. 25*b*, as in ch. xxviii. 26, that the words have reference to the lightning, which to man is untraceable, flashing now here, now there. This guiding of the rain to chosen parts of the earth extends also to the tenantless steppe. לֹא־אִישׁ (for בְּלֹא) is virtually an adj. (*vid.* on ch. xii. 24). The superlative combination שֹׁאָה וּמְשֹׁאָה (from שׁוֹא = שָׁאָה, to be desolate, and to give forth a heavy dull sound, *i.e.* to sound desolate, *vid.* on ch. xxxvii. 6), as ch. xxx. 3 (which see). Not merely for the purposes of His rule among men does God direct the changes of the weather contrary to human foresight; His care extends also to regions where no human habitations are found.

28 *Hath the rain a father,*
   Or who begetteth the drops of dew?
29 *Out of whose womb cometh the ice forth,*

> *And who bringeth forth the hoar-frost of heaven?*
> 30 *The waters become hard like stone,*
>   *And the face of the deep is rolled together.*

Rain and dew have no created father, ice and hoar-frost no created mother. The parallelism in both instances shows that מִי הוֹלִיד asks after the one who begets, and מִי יָלַד the one who bears (*vid.* Hupfeld on Ps. ii. 7). בֶּטֶן is *uterus*, and meton. (at least in Arabic) *progenies uteri; ex utero cujus* is מִבֶּטֶן מִי, in distinction from מֵאֵי־זֶה בֶטֶן, *ex quo utero.* אֶגְלֵי־טָל is excellently translated by the LXX., *Codd. Vat.* and *Sin.*, βώλους (with *Omega*) δρόσου; Ges. and Schlottm. correct to βόλους, but βῶλος signifies not merely a clod, but also a lump and a ball. It is the particles of the dew holding together (LXX., *Cod. Alex.*: συνοχὰς καὶ βω. δρ.) in a globular form, from אָגַל, which does not belong to גָּלַל, but to اجل, *retinere*, II. *colligere* (whence *agîl*, standing water, *ma"gal*, a pool, pond); אֶגְלֵי is *constr.*, like עֶגְלֵי from עֵגֶל. The waters "hide themselves," by vanishing as fluid, therefore: freeze. The surface of the deep (LXX. ἀσεβοῦς, for which Zwingli has *in marg.* ἀβύσσου) "takes hold of itself," or presses together (comp. Arab. *lekda*, crowding, synon. *hugûm*, a striking against) by forming itself into a firm solid mass (*continuum*, ch. xli. 9, comp. xxxvii. 10). Moreover, the questions all refer not merely to the analysis of the visible origin of the phenomena, but to their final causes.

> 31 *Canst thou join the twistings of the Pleiades,*
>   *Or loose the bands of Orion?*
> 32 *Canst thou bring forth the signs of the Zodiac at the right time,*
>   *And canst thou guide the Bear with its children?*
> 33 *Knowest thou the laws of heaven,*
>   *Or dost thou define its influence on the earth?*

That מְעַדַנּוֹת here signifies the bindings or twistings (from עָדַן = עָנַד, ch. xxxi. 36) is placed beyond question by the unanimous translations of the LXX. (δεσμόν) and the Targ. (שִׁירֵי = σειράς), the testimony of the Masora, according to which the word here has a different signification from 1 Sam. xv. 32, and the language of the Talmud, in which מערנין, *Kêlim*, c. 20, signifies the knots at the end of a mat, by loosing which it comes to pieces, and *Succa*, 13*b*, the bands (formed of rushes) with which willow-branches are fastened together above in order to form a booth (*succa*); but מדאני, *Sabbat*, 33*a*, signifies a bunch of myrtle (to smell on the Sabbath). מעדנות כִּימָה is therefore explained according to the Persian comparison of the Pleiades with a bouquet of jewels, mentioned on ch. ix. 9, and according to the comparison with a necklace ('iqd-eth-thurajja), *e.g.* in Sadi in his *Gulistan*, p. 8 of Graf's translation: "as though the tops of the trees were encircled by the necklace of the Pleiades." The Arabic name *thurajja* (diminutive feminine of *tharwân*) probably signifies the richly-adorned, clustered constellation. But כִּימָה signifies without doubt the clustered group,[1] and Beigel (in Ideler, *Sternnamen*, S. 147) does not translate badly: "Canst thou not arrange together the rosette of

---

[1] The verb כום is still in general use in the *Piel* (to heap up, form a heap, *part. mukauwam*, heaped up) and *Hithpa.* (to accumulate) in Syria, and *kôm* is any village desolated in days of yore whose stones form a desolate heap [comp. Fleischer, *De Glossis Habichtianis*, p. 41 sq.]. If, according to Kamus, in old Jemanic *kîm* in the sense of *mukâwim* signifies a confederate (synon. *chilt*, *gils*), the כִּימָה would be a confederation, or a heap, assemblage (coetus) of confederates. Perhaps the בימה was regarded as a troop of camels; the Beduins at least call the star directly before the seven-starred constellation of the Pleiades the *hâdi, i.e.* the singer riding before the procession, who cheers the camels by the sound of the *hadwa* (חִדְוָה), and thereby urges them on.—WETZST.

On πλειάδες, which perhaps also bear this name as a compressed group (figuratively βότρυς) of several stars (ὅτι πλείους ὁμοῦ κατὰ συναγωγήν εἰσι), vid. Kuhn's *Zeitschr.* vi. 282–285.

diamonds (chain would be better) of the Pleiades?" As to
כְּסִיל, we firmly hold that it denotes Orion (according to which
the Greek versions translate Ὠρίων, the Syriac gaboro, the
Targ. נְפִלָא or נְפִילָא, the Giant). Orion and the Pleiades are
visible in the Syrian sky longer in the year than with us, and
there they come about 17° higher above the horizon than
with us. Nevertheless the figure of a giant chained to the
heavens cannot be rightly shown to be Semitic, and it is
questionable whether כסיל is not rather, with Saad., Gecat.,
Abulwalid, and others, to be regarded as the *Suhêl, i.e.* Canopus, especially as this is placed as a sluggish helper (כסיל,
Hebr. a fool, Arab. the slothful one, *ignavus*) in mythical
relation to the constellation of the Bear, which here is called
עָיִשׁ, as ch. ix. 9 עָשׁ, and is regarded as a bier, נַעֲשׁ (even in
the present day this is the name in the towns and villages of
Syria), with the sons and daughters forming the attendants
upon the corpse of their father, slain by *Gedi*, the Pole-star.
Understood of Orion, מֹשְׁכוֹת (with which مسك, *tenere, de-*
tinere, is certainly to be compared) are the chains (مسكة,
compes), with which he is chained to the sky; understood of
Suhêl, the restraints which prevent his breaking away too
soon and reaching the goal.[1] מְזָרוֹת is not distinct from מַזָּלוֹת,

---

[1] In June 1860 I witnessed a quarrel in an encampment of *Mo'gil-*
Beduins, in which one accused the others of having rendered it possible
for the enemy to carry off his camels through their negligence; and when
the accused assured him they had gone forth in pursuit of the marauders
soon after the raid, and only turned back at sunset, the man exclaimed:
Ye came indeed to my assistance as *Suhêl* to *Gedi* (פֿוֹעַ סהיל לִי פֿוֹעַ פֿוֹעַתֿם
לְלֹנְדִי). I asked my neighbour what the words meant, and was informed
they are a proverb which is very often used, and has its origin as follows:
The *Gedi* (*i.e.* the Pole-star, called *mismâr*, מִשְׁמָר, in Damascus) slew
the *Na'sh* (נַעֲשׁ), and is accordingly encompassed every night by the
children of the slain *Na'sh*, who are determined to take vengeance on the
murderer. The sons (on which account poets usually say *benî* instead of
benât Na'sh) go first with the corpse of their father, and the daughters
follow. One of the latter is called *waldâne*, a lying-in woman; she has

2 Kings xxiii. 5 (comp. מַזָּרֹת, "Thy star of fortune," on Cilician coins), and denotes not the twenty-eight *menâzil* (from نَزَلَ, to descend, turn in, lodge) of the moon,[1] but the twelve signs of the Zodiac, which were likewise imagined as *menâzil, i.e.* lodging-houses or *burûg*, strongholds, in which one after another the sun lodges as it describes the circle of the year.[2] The usage of the language transferred מַזָּל also to the planets, which, because they lie in the equatorial plane of the sun, as the sun (although more irregularly), run through the constellations of the Zodiac. The question in ver. 32*a* therefore means: canst thou bring forth the appointed zodiacal sign for each month, so that (of course with the variation which is limited to about two moon's diameters by the daily progress of the sun through the Zodiac) it becomes visible after sunset and is visible before sunset? On ver. 33 *vid.* on Gen. i. 14–19. מִשְׁטָר is construed after the analogy of רְדֵה בְּ, עָצֵר, מָשַׁל; and שָׁמַיִם, as *sing.* (Ew. § 318, *b*).

only recently given birth to a child, and carries her child in her bosom, and she is still pale from her lying-in. (The clear atmosphere of the Syrian sky admits of the child in the bosom of the *waldâne* being distinctly seen.) In order to give help to the *Gedi* in this danger, the *Suhêl* appears in the south, and struggles towards the north with a twinkling brightness, but he has risen too late; the night passes away ere he reaches his goal. Later I frequently heard this story, which is generally known among the Hauranites.—WETZST.

We add the following by way of explanation. The Pleiades encircle the Pole-star as do all stars, since it stands at the axis of the sky, but they are nearer to it than to Canopus by more than half the distance. This star of the first magnitude culminates about three hours later than the Pleiades, and rises, at the highest, only ten moon's diameters above the horizon of Damascus—a significant figure, therefore, of ineffectual endeavour.

[1] Thus A. Weber in his *Abh. über die vedischen Nachrichten von den naxatra* (halting-places of the moon), 1860 (comp. *Lit. Centralbl.* 1859, col. 665), refuted by Steinschneider, *Hebr. Bibliographie*, 1861, Nr. 22, S. 93 f.

[2] The names "the Ram, the Bull," etc., are, according to Epiphanius, *Opp.* i. p. 34 sq. (*ed. Petav.*), transferred from the Greek into the Jewish astrology, *vid. Wissenschaft Kunst Judenthum*, S. 220 f.

34 *Dost thou raise thy voice to the clouds*
   That an overflow of waters may cover thee?
35 *Dost thou send forth lightnings, and they go,*
   And say to thee: Here we are?
36 *Who hath put wisdom in the reins,*
   Or who hath given understanding to the cock?
37 *Who numbereth the strata of the clouds with wisdom,*
   And the bottles of heaven, who emptieth them,
38 *When the dust flows together into a mass,*
   And the clods cleave together?

As ver. 25*b* was worded like ch. xxviii. 26, so ver. 34*b* is worded like ch. xxii. 11; the ך of תכסך is dageshed in both passages, as ch. xxxvi. 2, 18, Hab. ii. 17. What Jehovah here denies to the natural power of man is possible to the power which man has by faith, as the history of Elijah shows: this, however, does not come under consideration here. In proof of divine omnipotence and human feebleness, Elihu constantly recurs to the rain and the thunder-storm with the lightning, which is at the bidding of God. Most moderns since Schultens therefore endeavour, with great violence, to make טֻחוֹת and שֶׂכְוִי mean meteors and celestial phenomena. Eichh. (Hirz., Hahn) compares the Arabic name for the clouds, *tachá* (*tachwa*), Ew. ضَحَا, sunshine, with the former; the latter, whose root is שָׂכָה (סְכָה), *spectare*, is meant to be something that is remarkable in the heavens: an atmospheric phenomenon, a meteor (Hirz.), or a phenomenon caused by light (Ew., Hahn), so that *e.g.* Umbr. translates: "Who hath put wisdom in the dark clouds, and given understanding to the meteor?" But the meaning which is thus extorted from the words in favour of the connection borders closely upon absurdity. Why, then, shall טֻחוֹת, from טוּחַ, طَيَّخَ, *oblinere, adipe obducere*, not signify here, as in Ps. li. 8, the

reins (embedded in a cushion of fat), and in fact as the seat
of the predictive faculty, like כְּלָיוֹת, ch. xix. 27, as the seat of
the innermost longing for the future; and particularly since
here, after the constellations and the influences of the stars
have just been spoken of, the mention of the gift of divination is not devoid of connection; and, moreover, as a glance
at the next strophe shows, the connection which has been
hitherto firmly kept to is already in process of being resolved?

If טֻחוֹת signifies the reins, it is natural to interpret שֶׂכְוִי also
psychologically, and to translate the intellect (Targ. I., Syr.,
Arab.), or similarly (Saad., Gecat.), as Ges., Carey, Renan,
Schlottm. But there is another rendering handed down
which is worthy of attention, although not once mentioned
by Rosenm., Hirz., Schlottm., or Hahn, according to which
שֶׂכְוִי signifies a cock, *gallum*. We read in *b. Rosch ha-Schana*,
26a: "When I came to Techûm-Kên-Nishraja, R. Simeon
b. Lakish relates, the bride was there called נינפי and the
cock שֶׂכְוִי, according to which Job xxxviii. 36 is to be interpreted: שֶׂכְוִי = תרנגול." The Midrash interprets in the same
way, *Jalkut*, § 905, beginning: "R. Levi says: In Arabic
the cock is called סְכְוָא." We compare with this, *Wajikra
rabba*, c. 1: "סוכו is Arabic; in Arabia a prophet is called
סַכְיָא;" whence it is to be inferred that שֶׂכְוִי, as is assumed,
describes the cock as a seer, as a prophet.

As to the formation of the word, it would certainly be
without parallel (Ew., Olsh.) if the word had the tone on
the *penult.*, but Codd. and the best old editions have the
Munach by the final syllable; Norzi, who has overlooked
this, at least notes שֶׂכְוִי with the accent on the *ult.* as a various
reading. It is a secondary noun, Ges. § 86, 5, a so-called
relative noun (De Sacy, *Gramm. Arabe*, § 768): שֶׂכְוִי, *speculator*, from שָׂכָה (שָׂכוּ, שָׂכָה), *speculatio*, as פִּלְאִי, Judg. xiii. 18
(comp. Ps. cxxxix. 6), *miraculosus*, from פֶּלֶא, a cognate form
to the Chald. סָכְוִי (סָכְוָאה), of similar meaning. In connection

with this primary signification, *speculator*, it is intelligible
how סכוי in Samaritan (*vid.* Lagarde on Proverbs, S. 62) can
signify the eye; here, however, in a Hebrew poet, the cock,
of which *e.g.* Gregory says: *Speculator semper in altitudine
stat, ut quidquid venturum sit longe prospiciat.* That this
signification *speculator = gallus*[1] was generally accepted at
least in the Talmudic age, the *Beracha* prescribed to him who
hears the cock crow: "Blessed be He who giveth the cock
(שֶׂכְוִי) knowledge to distinguish between day and night!"
shows. In accordance with this, Targ. II. translates: who
has given understanding לְתַרְנְגוֹל בְּרָא, *gallo sylvestri* (whereas
Targ. I. לְלִבָּא, *cordi, scil. hominis*), to praise his Lord? and
Jer.: (*quis posuit in visceribus hominis sapientiam) et quis
dedit gallo intelligentiam.* This traditional rendering, condemned as *talmudicum commentum* (Ges.), we follow rather
than the "phenomenon" of the moderns who guess at a
meaning. What is questioned in Cicero, *de divin.* ii. 26:
*Quid in mentem venit Callistheni dicere, Deos gallis signum
dedisse cantandi, quum id vel natura vel casus efficere potuisset,*
Jehovah here claims for Himself. The weather-prophet κατ᾽
ἐξοχήν among animals appropriately appears in this astro-
logico-meteorological connection by the side of the reins as,
according to the Semitic view, a medium of augury (*Psychol.*
S. 268 f.). The Koran also makes the cock the watchman
who wakes up the heavenly hosts to their duty; and Masius,
in his *Studies of Nature,* has shown how high the cock is
placed as being prophetically (for divination) gifted. Moreover, the worship of cocks in the idolatry of the Semites was
a service rendered to the stars: the Sabians offered cocks,
probably (*vid.* Chwolsohn, ii. 87) as the white cock of Jezides,

---

[1] No Arab. word offers itself here for comparison: *tuchaj*, a cock, has
different consonants, and if شَكَا in the sense of شَالَ, *fortem esse,* were
to be supposed, שֶׂכְוִי would be a synon. of גֶּבֶר, which is likewise a name
of the cock.

regarded by them as a symbol of the sun (*Deutsch. Morgenländ. Zeitschr.* 1862, S. 365 f.).

In ver. 37*b* Jerome translates: *et concentum cælorum quis
dormire faciet;* נִבְלֵי, however, does not here signify harps,
but bottles; and הִשְׁכִּיב is not: to lay to rest, but to lay down
= to empty, pour out, which the *Kal* also, like the Arab.
sakaba, directly signifies. בְּצֶקֶת might be taken actively:
when it pours, but according to 1 Kings xxii. 35 the intransitive rendering is also possible: when the dust pours forth,
i.e. flows together, לְמוּצָק, to what is poured out, *i.e.* not: to
the fluid, but in contrast: to a molten mass, *i.e.* as cast metal
(to be explained not according to ch. xxii. 16, but according
to ch. xxxvii. 18), for the dry, sandy, dusty earth is made

firm by the downfall of the rain (Arab. رصدت, *firmata est*

terra imbre, comp. لغد, *pluviam emisit donec arena cohæreret*).
רְגָבִים, *glebæ,* as ch. xxi. 33, from רֶגֶב, رجب, in the primary
signification, which as it seems must be supposed: to bring
together, from which the significations branch off, to thicken,
become firm (*muraggab,* supported), and to be seized with
terror.

> 39 *Dost thou hunt for the prey of the lioness*
>   *And still the desire of the young lions,*
> 40 *When they couch in the dens,*
>   *Sit in the thicket lying in wait for prey?*
> 41 *Who provideth for the raven its food,*
>   *When its young ones cry to God,*
>   *They wander about without food?*

On the wealth of the Old Testament language in names
for the lion, *vid.* on ch. iv. 10 sq. לְבִיא can be used of the
lioness; the more exact name of the lioness is לְבִיָּה, for לְבִיא
is = לְבִי, whence לְבָאִים, lions, and לְבָאוֹת, lionesses. The lioness
is mentioned first, because she has to provide for her young

ones (גּוּרִים); then the lions that are still young, but yet are left to themselves, כְּפִירִים. The phrase מְלֹא חַיָּה (comp. חַיָּה of life that needs nourishment, ch. xxxiii. 20) is equivalent to מְלֹא נֶפֶשׁ, Prov. vi. 30 (*Psychol.* S. 204 *ad fin.*). The book of Psalms here furnishes parallels to every word: comp. on ver. 39*b*, Ps. civ. 21; on יִשָּׁחוּ, Ps. x. 10;[1] on מְעוֹנוֹת, *lustra*, Ps. civ. 22 (compared on ch. xxxvii. 8 already); on סֹךְ, סֻכָּה, which is used just in the same way, Ps. x. 9, Jer. xxv. 38. The picture of the crying ravens has its parallel in Ps. cxlvii. 9. כִּי, *quum*, is followed by the *fut.* in the signif. of the *præs.*, as Ps. xi. 3. As here, in the Sermon on the Mount in Luke xii. 24 the ravens, which by their hoarse croaking make themselves most observed everywhere among birds that seek their food, are mentioned instead of the fowls of heaven.

Ch. xxxix. 1 *Dost thou know the bearing time of the wild goats*
 of the rock?
 Observest thou the circles of the hinds?
 2 *Dost thou number the months which they fulfil,*
 And knowest thou the time of their bringing forth?
 3 *They bow down, they let their young break through,*
 They cast off their pains.
 4 *Their young ones gain strength, grow up in the*
 desert,
 They run away and do not return.

The strophe treats of the female chamois or steinbocks, *ibices* (perhaps including the certainly different kinds of chamois), and stags. The former are called יְעֵלִים, from יָעֵל,

[1] The Semitic is rich in such words as describe the couching posture of beasts of prey lying in wait for their prey, which then in general signify to lie in wait, lurk, wait (רָצַד, רָבַץ, رَبَصَ, رَبَضَ, لَبَدَ, وَكَدَ) ; تَعَدَ لَهُ, *subsedit ei*, i.e. *insidiatus est ei*, which corresponds to יִשְׁבֹּן, ver. 40*b*, also belongs here, comp. *Psalter*, i. 500, note.

وعل‎ (a secondary formation from עלה‎, علا‎), to mount, therefore: rock-climbers. חוֹלֵל‎ is *inf. Pil.*: τὸ ὠδίνειν, comp. the
Pul. ch. xv. 7. שָׁמַר‎, to observe, exactly as Eccl. xi. 4, 1 Sam.
i. 12, Zech. xi. 11.   In ver. 2 the question as to the expiration
of the time of bearing is connected with that as to the time of
bringing forth. תִּסְפּוֹר‎, *plene,* as ch. xiv. 16; לְדִתְּנָה‎ (*littána,* like
עֵת = עֲדְת‎, *vid.* p. 16, note) with an euphonic termination for
לְדִתֵּן‎, as Gen. xlii. 36, xxi. 29, and also out of pause, Ruth
i. 19, Ges. § 91, 1, rem. 2.   Instead of תִּפַלַּחְנָה‎ Olsh. wishes
to read תִּפַלַּטְנָה‎, but this (synon. תמלטנה‎) would be: they let
slip away; the former (synon. תבקענה‎): they cause to divide,
i.e. to break through (comp. Arab. *feláh,* the act of breaking
through, freedom, prosperity).   On כָּרַע‎, to kneel down as
the posture of one in travail, *vid.* 1 Sam. iv. 19.   "They
cast off their pains" is not meant of an easy working off of
the after-pains (Hirz., Schlottm.), but חֶבֶל‎ signifies in this
phrase, as Schultens has first shown, meton. directly the

fœtus, as Arab. حَبَل‎, plur. ahbál, and ὠδίν, even of a child

already grown up, as being the fruit of earlier travail, *e.g.*
in Æschylus, *Agam.* 1417 sq.; even the like phrase, ῥίψαι
ὠδῖνα = *edere fœtum,* is found in Euripides, *Ion* 45.   Thus
born with ease, the young animals grow rapidly to maturity
(חָלַם‎, *pinguescere, pubescere,* whence חֲלוֹם‎, a dream as the result
of puberty, *vid. Psychol.* S. 282), grow in the desert (בַּבָּר‎,
Targ. = בַּחוּר‎, *vid.* i. 329, note), seek the plain, and return
not again לָמוֹ‎, *sibi h. e. sui juris esse volentes* (Schult.),
although it might also signify *ad eas,* for the Hebr. is rather
confused on the question of the distinction of gender, and
even in חבליהם‎ and בניהם‎ the *masc.* is used ἐπικοίνως.   We,
however, prefer to interpret according to ch. vi. 19, xxiv. 16.
Moreover, Bochart is right: *Non hic agitur de otiosa et mere
speculativa cognitione, sed de ea cognitione, quæ Deo propria
est, qua res omnes non solum novit, sed et dirigit atque gubernat.*

5 *Who hath sent forth the wild ass free,*
   And who loosed the bands of the wild ass,
6 *Whose house I made the steppe,*
   And his dwelling the salt country?
7 *He scorneth the tumult of the city,*
   He heareth not the noise of the driver.
8 *That which is seen upon the mountains is his pasture,*
   And he sniffeth after every green thing.

On the wild ass (not: ass of the forest), *vid.* p. 19, note.[1]
In Hebr. and Arab. it is פֶּרֶא (*ferâ* or *himâr el-wahsh, i.e.*
asinus ferus), and Aram. עֲרוֹד; the former describes it as a
swift-footed animal, the latter as an animal shy and difficult
to be tamed by the hand of man; "Kulan" is its Eastern
Asiatic name. LXX. correctly translates: τίς δέ ἐστιν ὁ
ἀφεὶς ὄνον ἄγριον ἐλεύθερον. חָפְשִׁי is the *acc.* of the predi-

---

[1] It is a dirty yellow with a white belly, single-hoofed and long-eared;
its hornless head somewhat resembles that of the gazelle, but is much
larger; its hair has the dryness of the hair of the deer, and the animal forms
the transition from the stag and deer genus to the ass. It is entirely
distinct from the *mahâ* or *baqar el-wahsh*, wild ox, whose large soft eyes
are so much celebrated by the poets of the steppe. This latter is horned
and double-hoofed, and forms the transition from the stag to the ox
[distinct from the *ri'm*, רְאֵם, therefore perhaps an antelope of the kind
of the Indian *nîlgau*, blue ox, *Portax tragocamelus*]. I have not seen
both kinds of animals alive, but I have often seen their skins in the tents
of the *Ruwalâ*. Both kinds are remarkable for their very swift running,
and it is especially affirmed of the *ferâ* that no rider can overtake it.
The poets compare a troop of horsemen that come rushing up and vanish
in the next moment to a herd of *ferâ*. In spite of its difficulty and
hazardousness, the nomads are passionately given to hunting the wild ass,
and the proverb cited by the Kâmûs: *kull es-sêd bigôf el-ferâ* (every
hunt sticks in the belly of the *ferâ, i.e.* compared with that, every other
hunt is nothing), is perfectly correct. When the approach of a herd, which
always consists of several hundred, is betrayed by a cloud of dust which
can be seen many miles off, so many horsemen rise up from all sides in
pursuit that the animals are usually scattered, and single ones are obtained
by the dogs and by shots. The herd is called *gemîle*, and its leader is
called '*anûd* (עָנוּד), as with gazelles.—WETZST.

cate (comp. Gen. xxxiii. 2, Jer. xxii. 30). Parallel with עֲרָבָה (according to its etymon perhaps, land of darkness, *terra incognita*) is מְלֵחָה, salt [*adj.*] or (*sc.* אֶרֶץ) a salt land, *i.e.* therefore unfruitful and incapable of culture, as the country round the Salt Sea of Palestine: that the wild ass even gladly licks the salt or natron of the desert, is a matter of fact, and may be assumed, since all wild animals that feed on plants have a partiality, which is based on chemical laws of life, for licking salt. On ver. 8*a* Ew. observes, to render יְתוּר as "what is espied" is insecure, "on account of the structure of the verse" (*Gramm.* S. 419, Anm.). This reason is unintelligible; and in general there is no reason for rendering יְתוּר, after LXX., Targ., Jer., and others, as an Aramaic 3 *fut.* with a mere half vowel instead of Kametz before the tone = יְתוּר, which is without example in Old Testament Hebrew (for יְהוּא, Eccl. xi. 3, follows the analogy of יְהִי), but יְתוּר signifies either *abundantia* (after the form לְחוּם יְבוּל ch. xx. 23, from יתר, وَتَر, p. 148) or *investigabile*, what can be searched out (after the form יְקוּם, that which exists, from תּוּר, طَار, to go about, look about), which, with Olsh. § 212, and most expositors, we prefer.

> 9 *Will the oryx be willing to serve thee,*
>   *Or will he lodge in thy crib?*
>
> 10 *Canst thou bind the oryx in the furrow with a leading rein,*
>   *Or will he harrow the valleys, following thee?*
>
> 11 *Wilt thou trust him because his strength is great,*
>   *And leave thy labour to him?*
>
> 12 *Wilt thou confide in him to bring in thy sowing,*
>   *And to garner thy threshing-floor?*

In correct texts רֵים has a *Dagesh* in the *Resh*, and הֲיֹאבֶה the accent on the *penult.*, as Prov. xi. 21 יִנָּקֶה רָע, and Jer. xxxix. 12 מְאוּמָה רָע. The tone retreats according to the rule, Ges. § 29, 3, *b*; and the *Dagesh* is, as also when the second word begins with an aspirate,[1] *Dag. forte conj.*, which the *Resh* also takes, Prov. xv. 1 מַעֲנֶה־רַּךְ, exceptionally, according to the rule, Ges. § 20, 2, *a*. In all, it occurs thirteen times with *Dagesh* in the Old Testament—a relic of a mode of pointing which treated the ר (as in Arabic) as a letter capable of being doubled (Ges. § 22, 5), that has been supplanted in the system of pointing that gained the ascendency. רִים (Ps. xxii. 22, רֵם) is contracted from רְאָם (Ps. xcii. 11, *plene*, רְאִים),

which (= רְאָם) is of like form with رِمْ (Olsh. § 154, *a*).[2]

Such, in the present day in Syria, is the name of the gazelle that is for the most part white with a yellow back and yellow stripes in the face (*Antilope leucoryx*, in distinction from عَفْرَى, *'ifrî*, the earth-coloured, dirty-yellow *Antilope oryx*, and حَمَرَى, himrî, the deer-coloured *Antilope dorcas*); the Talmud also (*b. Zebachim*, 113*b*; *Bathra*, 74*b*) combines ראימא and אורילא

or ארוילא, a gazelle (غَزال), and therefore reckons the *reêm* to the antelope genus, of which the gazelle is a species; and

---

[1] The National Grammarians call this exception to the rule, that the *muta* is aspirated when the preceding word ends with a vowel, אתי מרחיק (*veniens e longinquo*), *i.e.* the case, where the word ending with a vowel is *Milel*, whether from the very first, or, when the second word is a monosyllable or has the tone on the *penult.*, on account of the accent that has retreated (in order to avoid two syllables with the chief tone coming together); in this case the aspirate, and in general the initial letter (if capable of being doubled) of the second monosyllabic or *penultima*-accented word, takes a *Dagesh;* but this is not without exceptions that are quite as regular. Regularly, the second word is not dageshed if it begins with וּ, כְ, לְ, בְ, or if the first word is only a bare verb, *e.g.* עָשָׂה לֹּ, or one that has only וּ before it, *e.g.* וְעָשָׂה פֶּסַח ; the tone of the first word in both these examples retreats, but without the initial of the second being doubled. This is supplementary, and as far as necessary a correction, to what is said in *Psalter*, i. 392, Anm.

[2] Since *ra'ima*, inf. *ri'mân*, has the signification *assuescere*, רים, ראם, רימנא (Targ.) might describe the oryx as a gregarious animal, although all ruminants have this characteristic in common. On ראם, رِئْم, *vid.* Seetzen's *Reise*, iii. S. 393, Z 9ff., and also iv. 496.

the question, ver. 10*b*, shows that an animal whose home is on the mountains is intended, viz., as Bochart, and recently Schlottm. (making use of an academic treatise of Lichtenstein on the antelopes, 1824), has proved, the oryx, which the LXX. also probably understands when it translates μονόκερως; for the Talmud. קרש, mutilated from it, is, according to *Chullin*, 59*b*, a one-horned animal, and is more closely defined as טביא דבי עילאי, "gazelle (antelope) of Be (Beth)-Illâi" (comp. Lewysohn, *Zoologie des Talmuds*, 1858, § 146). The oryx also appears on Egyptian monuments sometimes with two horns, but mostly with one variously curled; and both Aristotle[1] and Pliny describe it as a one-horned cloven-hoof; so that one must assent to the supposition of a one-horned variety of the oryx (although as a fact of natural history it is not yet fully established), as then there is really tolerably certain information of a one-horned antelope both in Upper Asia and in Central Africa;[2] and therefore there is sufficient ground for seeking the origin of the tradition of the unicorn in an antelope,—perhaps rather like a horse,—with one horn rising out of the two points of ossification over the frontal suture. The proper buffalo, *Bos bubalus*, cannot therefore

[1] *Vid.* Sundevall, *Die Thierarten des Aristoteles* (Stockholm, 1863), S. 64 f.

[2] J. W. von Müller (*Das Einhorn von gesch. u. naturwiss. Standpunkte betrachtet*, 1852) believed that in a horn in the Ambras Collection at Vienna he recognised a horn of the Monocerôs (comp. Fechner's *Central-blatt*, 1854, Nr. 2), but he is hardly right. J. W. von Müller, Francis Galton (*Narrative of an Explorer in Tropical South Africa*, 1853), and other travellers have heard the natives speak ingenuously of the unicorn, but without seeing it themselves. On the other hand, Huc and Gabet (*Journeyings through Mongolia and Thibet*, Germ. edition) tell us "a horn of this animal was sent to Calcutta: it was 50 centimetres long and 11 in circumference; from the root it ran up to a gradually diminishing point. It was almost straight, black, etc. . . . Hodgson, when English consul at Nepal, had the good fortune to obtain an unicorn. . . . It is a kind of antelope, which in southern Thibet, that borders on Nepal, is called *Tschiru*. Hodgson sent a skin and horn to Calcutta; they came from an unicorn that died in the menagerie of the Raja of Nepal." The

be intended, because it only came from India to Western Asia and Europe at a more recent date, but also not any other species whatever of this animal (Carey and others), which is recognisable by its flat horns, which are also near together, and its forbidding, staring, bloodshot eyes; for it is tameable, and is (even in modern Syria) used as a domestic animal. On the other hand there are antelopes which somewhat resemble the horse, others the ox (whence βού-βαλος, βούβαλις, is a name for the antelope), others the deer and the ass. Schultens erroneously considers ראם to be the buffalo, being misled by a passage in the Divan of the Hudheilites, which gives the *rīm* the by-name of *dhu chadam*, *i.e.* oxen-like white-footed, which exactly applies to the *A. oryx* or even the *A. leucoryx*; for the former has white feet and legs striped lengthwise with black stripes, the latter white feet and legs. Just as little reason is there for imagining the rhinoceros after Aquila (and in part Jerome); ῥινοκέρως is nothing but an unhappy rendering of the μονοκέρως of the LXX. The question in ver. 10*b*, as already observed, requires an animal that inhabits the mountains.

On אבה, to be willing = to take up, receive, *vid.* p. 125, detailed description follows, and the suggestion is advanced that this *Antilope Hodgsonii*, as it has been proposed to call the *Tschiru*, is the one-horned oryx of the ancients. The existence of one-horned wild sheep (not antelopes), attested by R. von Schlagintweit (*Zoologischer Garten*, 1st year, S. 72), the horn of which consists of two parts gradually growing together, covered by one horn-sheath, does not depreciate the credibility of the account given by Huc-Gabet (to which Prof. Will has called my attention as being the most weighty testimony of the time). Another less minute account is to be found in the Arabic description of a journey (communicated to me by Prof. Fleischer) by Selim Bisteris (Beirût, 1856): In the menagerie of the Viceroy of Egypt he saw an animal of the colour of a gazelle, but the size and form of an ass, with a long straight horn between the ears, and (what, as he says, seldom go together) with hoofs, viz.—and as the expression حافر, horse's hoof (not خف, a camel's hoof), also implies—proper, uncloven hoofs,—therefore an one-horned and at the same time one-hoofed antelope.

note. The "furrow (תֶּלֶם, *sulcus*, not *porca*, the ridge between the furrows, *vid.* p. 198) of his cord" is that which it is said to break up by means of the ploughshare, being led by a rein. אַחֲרֶיךָ refers to the leader, who goes just before or at the side; according to Hahn, to one who has finished the sowing which precedes the harrowing; but it is more natural to imagine the leader of the animal that is harrowing, which is certainly not left to itself. On כִּי, ver. 12*a*, as an exponent of the obj., *vid.* Ew. § 336, *b.* The *Chethib* here uses the *Kal* שׁוּב transitively: to bring back (viz. that which was sown as harvested), which is possible (*vid.* ch. xlii. 10). גָּרְנְךָ, ver. 12*b*, is either a locative (into thy threshing-floor) or *acc.* of the obj. *per synecd. continentis pro contento*, as Ruth iii. 2, Matt. iii. 12. The position of the question from beginning to end assumes an animal outwardly resembling the yoke-ox, as the ראם is also elsewhere put with the ox, Deut. xxxiii. 17, Ps. xxix. 6, Isa. xxxiv. 7. But the conclusion at length arrived at by Hahn and in Gesenius' *Handwörterbuch*, that on this very account the buffalo is to be understood, is a mistake: *A*. *oryx* and *leucoryx* are both (for this very reason not distinguished by the ancients) entirely similar to the ox; they are not only ruminants, like the ox, with a like form of the hoof, but also of a plump form, which makes them appear to be of the ox tribe.

13 *The wing of the ostrich vibrates joyously,*
   Is she pious, wing and feather?
14 *No, she leaveth her eggs in the earth*
   And broodeth over the dust,
15 *Forgetting that a foot may crush them,*
   And the beast of the field trample them.
16 *She treateth her young ones harshly as if they were not hers;*
   In vain is her labour, without her being distressed.
17 *For Eloah hath caused her to forget wisdom,*
   And gave her no share of understanding.

18 *At the time when she lasheth herself aloft,*
   She derideth the horse and horseman.

As the wild ass and the ox-like oryx cannot be tamed by
man, and employed in his service like the domestic ass and
ox, so the ostrich, although resembling the stork in its stilt-
like structure, the colour of its feathers, and its gregarious life,
still has characteristics totally different from those one ought
to look for according to this similarity. רְנָנִים, a wail, prop.
a tremulous shrill sound (*vid.* ver. 23), is a name of the female
ostrich, whose peculiar cry (*vid.* p. 171) is called in Arabic
zimâr (וְמָר). נֶעֱלָס (from עָלַס, which in comparison with עָלַץ,
עָלַז, rarely occurs) signifies to make gestures of joy. אִם,
ver. 13*b*, is an interrogative *an;* חֲסִידָה, *pia*, is a play upon
the name of the stork, which is so called: *pia instar ciconiæ*
(on this figure of speech, comp. Mehren's *Rhetorik der Araber,*
S. 178). כִּי, ver. 14*a*, establishes the negation implied in the
question, as *e.g.* Isa. xxviii. 28. The idea is not that the hen-
ostrich abandons the hatching of her eggs to the earth (עָזַב לְ
as Ps. xvi. 10), and makes them "glow over the dust"
(Schlottm.), for the maturing energy compensating for the
sitting of the parent bird proceeds from the sun's heat, which
ought to have been mentioned; one would also expect a *Hiph.*
instead of the *Piel* תְּחַמֵּם, which can be understood only of hatching by her own warmth. The hen-ostrich also really broods herself, although from time to time she abandons the חַמֵּם to the
sun.[1] That which contrasts with the φιλοστοργία of the stork,
which is here made prominent, is that she lays her eggs in a
hole in the ground, and partly, when the nest is full, above
round about it, while חסידה ברושים ביתה, Ps. civ. 17. רננים is

---

[1] It does, however, as it appears, actually occur, that the female leaves
the work of hatching to the sun by day, and to the male at night, and
does not sit at all herself; *vid.* Funke's *Naturgeschichte,* revised by
Taschenberg (1864), S. 243 f.

construed in accordance with its meaning as *fem. sing.*, Ew.
§ 318, *a*. Since she acts thus, what next happens consistently
therewith is told by the not aoristic but only consecutive
וַתִּשְׁכַּח: and so she forgets that the foot may crush (זוּר, to
press together, break by pressure, as הַזּוּרֶה, Isa. lix. 5 = הַזּוּרָה,
that which is crushed, comp. לָנֶה = לְנֶה, Zech. v. 4) them (*i.e.*
the eggs, Ges. § 146, 3), and the beast of the field may
trample them down, crush them (הִישׁ as كاسي, to crush by
treading upon anything, to tread out).

Ver. 16. The difficulty of הִקְשִׁיחַ (from קָשַׁח, قسم, hardened
from קָשָׁה, قسا) being used of the hen-ostrich in the *masc.*,
may be removed by the pointing הִקְשִׁיחַ (Ew.); but this
alteration is unnecessary, since the Hebr. also uses the *masc.*
for the *fem.* where it might be regarded as impossible (*vid.*
ver. 3*b*, and comp. *e.g.* Isa. xxxii. 11 sq.). Jer. translates
correctly according to the sense: *quasi non sint sui*, but לְ is
not directly equivalent to כְ (*vid.* vol. i. pp. 325, 398, note 1);
what is meant is, that by the harshness of her conduct she
treats her young as not belonging to her, so that they become
strange to her, Ew. § 217, *d*. In ver. 16*b* the accentuation
varies·: in vain (לְרִיק with *Rebia mugrasch*) is her labour
that is devoid of anxiety; or: in vain is her labour (לריק with
Tarcha, יְגִיעָהּ with *Munach vicarium*) without anxiety (on her
part); or: in vain is her labour (לריק with *Mercha*, יגיעה with
Rebia mugrasch), yet she is without anxiety. The middle of
these renderings (לְרִיק in all of them, like Isa. xlix. 4 = לְרִיק, Isa.
lxv. 23 and freq.) seems to us the most pleasing: the labour
of birth and of the brooding undertaken in places where the
eggs are put beyond the danger of being crushed, is without
result, without the want of success distressing her, since she
does not anticipate it, and therefore also takes no measures to
prevent it. The eggs that are only just covered with earth,
or that lie round about the nest, actually become a prey to
the jackals, wild-cats, and other animals; and men can get

them for themselves one by one, if they only take care to prevent their footprints being recognised; for if the ostrich observes that its nest is discovered, it tramples upon its own eggs, and makes its nest elsewhere (Schlottm., according to Lichtenstein's *Südafrik. Reise*). That it thus abandons its eggs to the danger of being crushed and to plunder, arises, according to ver. 17, from the fact that God has caused it to forget wisdom, *i.e.* as ver. 17*b* explains, has extinguished in it, deprived it of, the share thereof (בְּ as Isa. liii. 12*a*, LXX. ἐν, as Acts viii. 21) which it might have had. It is only one of the stupidities of the ostrich that is made prominent here; the proverbial *ahmaq min en-na'âme*, "more foolish than the ostrich," has its origin in more such characteristics. But if the care with which other animals guard their young ones is denied to it, it has in its stead another remarkable characteristic: at the time when (כְּעֵת here followed by an elliptical relative clause, which is clearly possible, just as with בְּעֵת, ch. vi. 17) it stretches (itself) on high, *i.e.* it starts up with alacrity from its ease (on the radical signification of הִמְרִיא = הִמְרָה, *vid.* p. 2, note), and hurries forth with a powerful flapping of its wings, half running half flying, it derides the horse and its rider—they do not overtake it, it is the swiftest of all animals; wherefore اعدى من الظليم (*zalîm*, equivalent to *delîm* according to a less exact pronunciation, *supra*, p. 171, note) and انفر من النعامة, fleeter than the ostrich, is just as proverbial as the above احمق من النعامة; and "on ostrich's wings" is equivalent to driving along with incomparable swiftness. Moreover, on תַּמְרִיא and תִּשְׂחַק, which refer to the female, it is to be observed that she is very anxious, and deserts everything in her fright, while the male ostrich does not forsake his young, and flees no danger.[1]

---

[1] We take this remark from Doumas, *Horse of the Sahara*. The following contribution from Wetzstein only came to hand after the exposition was completed: "The female ostriches are called רְנָנִים not from

19 *Dost thou give to the horse strength ?*
   Dost thou clothe his neck with flowing hair ?

20 *Dost thou cause him to leap about like the grasshopper?*
   The noise of his snorting is a terror !

21 *He paweth the ground in the plain, and boundeth about with*
      strength.
   He advanceth to meet an armed host.

22 *He laugheth at fear, and is not affrighted,*
   And turneth not back from the sword.

23 *The quiver rattleth over him,*
   The glittering lance and spear.

24 *With fierceness and rage he swalloweth the ground,*
   And standeth not still, when the trumpet soundeth.

the whirring of their wings when flapped about, but from their piercing screeching cry when defending their eggs against beasts of prey (chiefly hyænas), or when searching for the male bird. Now they are called *rubd*, from sing. *rubda* (instead of *rabdâ*), from the black colour of their long wing-feathers; for only the male, which is called חָיִץ (pronounce hêtsh), has white. The ostrich-tribe has the name of בַּת הַיְעֵנָה (بِنْت الْوَعْنَة), 'inhabitant of the desert,' because it is only at home in the most lonely parts of the steppe, in perfectly barren deserts. *Neshwân* the Himjarite, in his ' *Shems el-'olâm* ' (MSS. in the Royal Library at Berlin, *sectio Wetzst. I.* No. 149, Bd. i. f. 110b), defines the word *el-wa'na* by: אֶרֶץ בִּיצָא לֹא תִנְבַּת שִׂיא, a white (chalky or sandy) district, which brings forth nothing; and the Kâmûs explains it by אֶרֶץ צַלְבָּה, a hard (unfruitful) district. In perfect analogy with the Hebr. the Arabic calls the ostrich *abu* (and *umm*) *es-sahârâ*, ' possessor of the sterile deserts.' The name יְעֵנִים, Lam. iv. 3, is perfectly correct, and corresponds to the form

יְעֵלִים (steinbocks); the form פֶּעֵל (نَعِل) is frequently the *Nisbe* of פֶּעֵל and פֶּעְלָה, according to which יַעֵן = יַעֲנָה = בַּת הַיְעֵנָה and יַעֵל = הַיְעֵלָה = בַּת הַיְעֵלָה, 'inhabitant of the inaccessible rocks.' Hence, says *Neshwân* (against the non-Semite *Firûzâbâdî*), *wa'l* (יַעֵל and *wa'la*) is exclusively the high place of the rocks, and *wa'il* (יַעֵל) exclusively the steinbock. The most common Arabic name of the ostrich is *na'âme*, נַעֲמָה, collective *na'âm*, from the softness (*nu'âma*, נְעוּמָה) of its feathers, with which the Arab women (in Damascus frequently) stuff cushions and pillows. *Umm*

25 *He saith at every blast of the trumpet: Ha, ha !*
And from afar he scenteth the battle,
The thundering of the captains and the shout of war.

After the ostrich, which, as the Arabs say, is composed of
the nature of a bird and a camel, comes the horse in its
heroic beauty, and impetuous lust for the battle, which is
likewise an evidence of the wisdom of the Ruler of the world
—a wisdom which demands the admiration of men. This
passage of the book of Job, says K. Löffler, in his *Gesch.
des Pferdes* (1863), is the oldest and most beautiful description of the horse. It may be compared to the praise of the
horse in Hammer-Purgstall's *Duftkörner ;* it deserves more

thelâthin, 'mother of thirty,' is the name of the female ostrich, because as
a rule she lays thirty eggs. The ostrich egg is called in the steppe *dahwa,*
דַּחְוָה (coll. *dahû*), a word that is certainly very ancient. Nevertheless the
Hauranites prefer the word *medha,* מֻדְחָה. A place hollowed out in the
ground serves as a nest, which the ostrich likes best to dig in the hot
sand, on which account they are very common in the sandy tracts of *Ard
ed-Dehânâ* (דְּהֲנָא), between the *Shemmar* mountains and the *Sawâd*
(Chaldæa). Thence at the end of April come the ostrich hunters with
their spoil, the hides of the birds together with the feathers, to Syria.
Such an unplucked hide is called *gizze* (גִּוָּה). The hunters inform us that
the female sits alone on the nest from early in the day until evening, and
from evening until early in the morning with the male, which wanders
about throughout the day. The statement that the ostrich does not sit
on its eggs, is perhaps based on the fact that the female frequently, and
always before the hunters, forsakes the eggs during the first period of
brooding. Even vers. 14 and 15 do not say more than this. But when
the time of hatching (called *el-faqs,* פֶּקֶץ) is near, the hen no longer
leaves the eggs. The same observation is also made with regard to the
partridge of Palestine (*el-ḥagel,* חָגֵל), which has many other characteristics in common with the ostrich. That the ostrich is accounted stupid
(ver. 17) may arise from the fact, that when the female has been
frightened from the eggs she always seeks out the male with a loud cry ;
she then, as the hunters unanimously assert, brings him forcibly back to
the nest (hence its Arabic name *zalīm,* ' the violent one'). During the
interval the hunter has buried himself in the sand, and on their arrival,
by a good shot often kills both together in the nest. It may also be

than this latter the praise of majestic simplicity, which is
the first feature of classic superiority. Jer. falsely renders
ver. 19b: *aut circumdabis collo ejus hinnitum;* as Schlottm., who
also wishes to be so understood : Dost thou adorn his neck
with the voice of thunder? The neck (צַוָּאר, prop. the twister,
as Persic *gerdân, gerdan,* from צוּר, صار, to twist by pressure,
to turn, bend, as Pers. from *gerdîden,* to turn one's self,
twist) has nothing to do with the voice of neighing. But
רַעְמָה also does not signify dignity (Ew. 113, *d*), but the
mane, and is not from רָעַם = רָאַם = רָם, the hair of the mane,
as being above, like λοφιά, but from רָעַם, *tremere,* the mane
as quivering, trembling (Eliz. Smith : the shaking mane) ;

accounted as stupidity, that, when the wind is calm, instead of flying
before the riding hunters, the bird tries to hide itself behind a mound or
in the hollows of the ground. But that, when escape is impossible, it is
said to try to hide its head in the sand, the hunters regard as an absurdity.
If the wind aids it, the fleeing ostrich spreads out the feathers of its tail
like a sail, and by constantly steering itself with its extended wings, it
escapes its pursuers with ease. The word הַמְרִיא, ver. 18, appears to be
a hunting expression, and (without an *accus. objecti*) to describe this
spreading out of the feathers, therefore to be perfectly synonymous with
the תַּעְרִישׁ (تعريش) of the ostrich hunters of the present day. Thus
sings the poet *Râshid* of the hunting race of the Suhubât: ' And the
head (of the bride with its loosened locks) resembles the (soft and black)
feathers of the ostrich-hen, when she spreads them out (*'arrashannâ*). |
They saw the hunter coming upon them where there was no hiding-place,
| And stretched their legs as they fled.' The prohibition to eat the
ostrich in the Thora (Lev. xi. 16 ; Deut. xiv. 15) is perhaps based upon
the cruelty of the hunt ; for it is with the rarest exceptions always killed
only on its eggs. The female, which, as has been said already, does not
flee towards the end of the time of brooding, stoops on the approach of
the hunter, inclines the head on one side and looks motionless at her
enemy. Several Beduins have said to me, that a man must have a hard
heart to fire under such circumstances. If the bird is killed, the hunter
covers the blood with sand, puts the female again upon the eggs, buries
himself at some distance in the sand, and waits till evening, when the
male comes, which is now shot likewise, beside the female. The Mosaic
law might accordingly have forbidden the hunting of the ostrich from
the same feeling of humanity which unmistakeably regulated it in other
decisions (as Ex. xxiii. 19, Deut. xxii. 6 sq., Lev. xxii. 28, and freq.).

like φόβη, according to Kuhn, cogn. with σόβη, the tail, from φοβεῖν (σοβεῖν), to wag, shake, scare, comp. ἀΐσσεσθαι of the mane, *Il.* vi. 510.

Ver. 20*a*. The motion of the horse, which is intended by תַּרְעִישֶׁנּוּ (רְעַשׁ, رعس, رعش, *tremere, trepidare*), is determined according to the comparison with the grasshopper: what is intended is a curved motion forwards in leaps, now to the right, now to the left, which is called the caracol, a word used in horsemanship, borrowed from the Arab. *hargala-l-farasu* (comp. חַרְגֹּל), by means of the Moorish Spanish; moreover, رعس is used of the run of the ostrich and the flight of the dove in such "successive lateral and oblique motions" (Carey). נַחַר, ver. 20*b*, is not the neighing of the horse, but its snorting through the nostrils (comp. Arab. *nachîr*, snoring, a rattling in the throat), Greek φρύαγμα, Lat. *fremitus* (comp. Æschylus, *Septem c. Th.* 374, according to the text of Hermann: ἵππος χαλινῶν δ'ὡς κατασθμαίνων βρέμει); הוֹד, however, might signify pomp (his pompous snorting), but perhaps has its radical signification, according to which it corresponds to the Arab. *hawîd*, and signifies a loud strong sound, as the peal of thunder (*hawîd er-ra'd*), the howling of the stormy wind (*hawîd er-rijâh*), and the like.[1] The substantival clause is intended to affirm that its dull-toned snort causes or spreads terror. In ver. 21*a* the

---

[1] A verse of a poem of Ibn-Dûchi in honour of Dôkân ibn-Gendel runs: Before the crowding (*lekdata*) of Taijâr the horses fled repulsed, | And thou mightest hear the sound of the bell-carriers (*hawîda mubershemât*) of the warriors (*el-menâir*, prop. one who thrusts with the lance). Here *hawîd* signifies the sound of the bells which those who wish to announce themselves as warriors hang about their horses, to draw the attention of the enemy to them. *Mubershemât* are the mares that carry the *burêshimân*, *i.e.* the bells. The meaning therefore is: thou couldst hear this sound, which ought only to be heard in the fray, in flight, when the warriors consecrated to death fled as cowards. Taijâr (Têjâr) is Sâlih the son of Cana'an (died about 1815), mentioned in vol. i. p. 390, note 1, a great warrior of the wandering tribe of the 'Aneze.—WETZST.

plur. alternates with the *sing.*, since, as it appears, the representation of the many pawing hoofs is blended with that of the pawing horse, according to the well-known line,

> Quadrupedante putrem sonitu quatit ungula campum
> (VIRGIL, *Æn.* viii. 596) ;

or, since this is said of the galloping horse, according to the likewise Virgilian line,

> Cavatque
> Tellurem, et solido graviter sonat ungula cornu
> (*Georg.* iii. 87 sq.).

חָפַר is, as the Arab. *háfir*, hoof, shows, the proper word for the horse's impatient pawing of the ground (whence it then, as in ver. 29, signifies *rimari, scrutari*). עֵמֶק is the plain as the place of contest ; for the description, as now becomes still more evident, refers to the war-horse. The verb יָשִׂישׂ (שׂוּשׂ) has its radical signification *exsultare* (comp. شام, σκιρτᾶν, of the fœtus) here ; and since בְּכֹחַ, not בַּכֹּחַ, is added to it, it is not to be translated : it rejoices in its strength, but : it prances or is joyous with strength, LXX. γαυριᾷ ἐν ἰσχύϊ. The difference between the two renderings is, however, scarcely perceptible. נֶשֶׁק, armament, ver. 21*b*, is meton. the armed host of the enemy ; אַשְׁפָּה, "the quiver," is, however, not used metonymically for the arrows of the enemy whizzing about the horse (Schult.), but ver. 23 is the concluding description of the horse that rushes on fearlessly, proudly, and impetuously in pursuit, under the rattle and glare of the equipment of its rider (Schlottm. and others). רָנָה (cogn. of רָנַן), of the rattling of the quiver, as Arab. *ranna, ranima*, of the whirring of the bow when the arrow is despatched ; to point it תִּרְנֶה (Prov. i. 20, viii. 3), instead of תִּרְנֶה, would be to deprive the language of a word supported by the dialects (*vid.* Ges. *Thes.*). On ver. 24*a* we may compare the Arab. *iltahama-l-farasu-l-arda*, the horse swallows up the ground, whence *lahimm, lahîm*, a swallower

= swift-runner; so here: with boisterous fierceness and angry impatience (בְּרַעַשׁ וְרֹגֶז) it swallows up the ground, *i.e.* passes so swiftly over it that long pieces vanish so rapidly before it, as though it greedily sucked them up (יְגַמֵּא intensive of גָּמָא, whence גֹּמֶא, the water-sucking papyrus); a somewhat differently applied figure is *nahab-el-arda*, *i.e.* according to Silius' expression, *rapuit campum.* The meaning of ver. 24*b* is, as in Virgil, *Georg.* iii. 83 sq. :

> *Tum si qua sonum procul arma dedere,*
> *Stare loco nescit ;*

and in Æschylus, *Septem*, 375 : ὅστις βοὴν σάλπιγγος ὁρμαίνει (Hermann, ὀργαίνει) μένων (impatiently awaiting the call of the trumpet). הֶאֱמִין signifies here to show stability (*vid. Genesis,* S. 367f.) in the first physical sense (Bochart, Rosenm., and others) : it does not stand still, *i.e.* will not be held, when (כִּי, *quum*) the sound of the war-trumpet, *i.e.* when it sounds. שׁוֹפָר is the signal-trumpet when the army was called together, *e.g.* Judg. iii. 27; to gather the army that is in pursuit of the enemy, 2 Sam. ii. 28; when the people rebelled, 2 Sam. xx. 1; when the army was dismissed at the end of the war, 2 Sam. xx. 22; when forming for defence and for assault, *e.g.* Amos iii. 6; and in general the signal of war, Jer. iv. 19. As often as this is heard (בְּדֵי, in sufficiency, *i.e.* happening at any time = *quotiescunque*), it makes known its lust of war by a joyous neigh, even from afar, before the collision has taken place; it scents (*præsagit* according to Pliny's expression) the approaching conflict, (scents even in anticipation) the thundering command of the chiefs that may soon be heard, and the cry of battle giving loose to the assault. "Although," says Layard (*New Discoveries*, p. 330), "docile as a lamb, and requiring no other guide than the halter, when the Arab mare hears the war-cry of the tribe, and sees the quivering spear of her rider, her eyes glitter with fire, her blood-red nostrils open wide, her neck is nobly arched, and her tail and mane are raised and spread out to the wind. The Bedouin proverb says, that a high-bred mare when at full speed should hide her rider between her neck and her tail."

26 *Doth the hawk fly by thy wisdom,*
   Doth it spread its wings towards the south?
27 *Or is it at thy command that the eagle soareth aloft,*
   And buildeth its nest on high?
28 *It inhabiteth the rock, and buildeth its nest*
   Upon the crag of the rock and fastness.
29 *From thence it seeketh food,*
   Its eyes see afar off.
30 *And its young ones suck up blood;*
   And where the slain are, there is it.

The ancient versions are unanimous in testifying that, according to the signification of the root, נֵץ signifies the hawk (which is significant in the Hieroglyphics): the soaring one, the high-flyer (comp. نَضَ, to rise, struggle forwards, and نَضَ, to raise the wings for flight). The *Hiph.* יַאֲבֶר (jussive form in the question, as ch. xiii. 27) might signify: to get feathers, *plumescere* (Targ., Jer.), but that gives a tame question; wherefore Gregory understands the *plumescit* of the Vulgate of moulting, for which purpose the hawk seeks the sunny side. But הַאֲבִיר alone, by itself, cannot signify "to get new feathers;" moreover, an annual moulting is common to all birds, and prominence is alone given to the new feathering of the eagle in the Old Testament, Ps. ciii. 5, Mic. i. 16, comp. Isa. xl. 31 (LXX. πτεροφυήσουσιν ὡς ἀετοί).[1] Thus, then, the point of the question will lie in לְתֵימָן: the hawk is

---

[1] Less unfavourable to this rendering is the following, that אֶבְרָה signifies the long feathers, and אֵבֶר the wing that is composed of them

a bird of passage, God has endowed it with instinct to migrate
to the south as the winter season is approaching.

In vers. 27 sqq. the circle of the native figures taken from
animal life, which began with the lion, the king of quadrupeds, is now closed with the eagle, the king of birds. It is
called נֶשֶׁר, from נָשַׁר ,نسر, *vellere;* as also *vultur* (by virtue of a
strong power of assimilation = *vultor*) is derived from *vellere,*
—a common name of the golden eagle, the lamb's vulture, the
carrion-kite (*Cathartes percnopterus*), and indeed also of other
kinds of kites and falcons. There is nothing to prevent our
understanding the eagle κατ' ἐξοχήν, viz. the golden eagle
(*Aquila chrysaëtos*), in the present passage ; for even to this,
corpses, though not already putrified, are a welcome prey.
In ver. 27b we must translate either: and is it at thy command that . . . ? or: is it so that (as in הֲכִי) at thy command
. . . ? The former is more natural here. מְצוּדָה, ver. 28b,
signifies prop. *specula* (from צוּד, to spy) ; then, however, as
Arab. *masâd* (referred by the original lexicons to *masada*),
the high hill, and the mountain-top. The rare form יְעַלְעוּ, for
which Ges., Olsh., and others wish to read לַעְלְעוּ or יְלַעְלְעוּ
(from לוּעַ, *deglutire*), is to be derived from עָלַע, a likewise
secondary form out of עָלַל (from עוּל, to suck, to give suck[1]),

like שָׁרַשׁ out of שִׁרְשֵׁר (from שָׁרַר ,سرّ, to make firm), Ew.
§ 118, *a*, comp. Fürst, *Handwörterbuch, sub* עַל, since instances

(perhaps, since the Talm. אֲבָרִים signifies wings and limbs, *artus,* from
אָבַר = חָבַר ,ابر, to divide, furnish with joints), although נוֹצָה (from
נָצָה, to fly) is the more general designation of the feathers of birds.

[1] The Arab. *'alla* does not belong here: it gains the signification *iterum
libere* from the primary signification of " coming over or upon anything,"
which branches out in various ways: to take a second, third, etc., drink
after the first. More on this point on Isa. iii. 4.

Supplementary note : The quadriliteral עַלְעַל to be supposed, is not to
be derived from עָלַל, and is not, as it recently has been, to be compared
with عَلّ, "to drink." This Arab. verb does not signify "to drink" at all,

are wanting in favour of עֵלַע being formed out of לְעֵלַע (*Jesurun*, p. 164). Schult. not inappropriately compares even נלֹב = נִגְלֹל in אֶגְלְתָא, Γολγοθᾶ = גָּלְגָּלְתָּא. The concluding words, ver. 30*b*, are perhaps echoed in Matt. xxiv. 28. High up on a mountain-peak the eagle builds its eyrie, and God has given it a remarkably sharp vision, to see far into the depth below the food that is there for it and its young ones. Not merely from the valley in the neighbourhood of its eyrie, but often from distant plains, which lie deep below on the other side of the mountain range, it seizes its prey, and rises with it even to the clouds, and bears it home to its nest.[1] Thus does God work exceeding strangely, but wondrously, apparently by contradictions, but in truth most harmoniously and wisely, in the natural world.

[Then Jehovah answered Job, and said :]
Ch. xl. 2 *Will now the censurer contend with the Almighty?*
    Let the instructor of Eloah answer it!

With ver. 1, ch. xxxviii. 1 is again taken up, because the speech of Jehovah has now in some measure attained the end which was assigned to it as an answer to Job's outburst of censure. רֹב is *inf. abs.*, as Judg. xi. 25; it is left to the hearer to give to the simple verbal notion its syntactic rela-tion in accordance with the connection ; here it stands in the sense of the *fut.* (comp. 2 Kings iv. 43) : *num litigabit*, Ges. § 131, 4, *b*. The *inf. abs.* is followed by יִסּוֹר as subj., which

but, among many other branchings out of its general primary significa-tion, related to עֲלַה, ﻼ, also signifies: "to take a second, third, etc., drink after the first," concerning which more details will be given elsewhere. עֲלְעֵל goes back to עוּל, *lactare*, with the middle vowel, whence also עֵיל, ch. xvi. 11, xii. 18, xxi. 11 (which see). The Hauran dialect has '*âlâl* (plur. '*awâlîl*), like the Hebr. עֲוֵיל (עֲוֵיל = מְעֵיל), in the signification *juvenis*, and especially *juvencus* (comp. *infra*, p. 359, note 1, "but they are heifers," Arab. *illâ 'awâlîl*).

[1] *Vid.* the beautiful description in Charles Boner's *Forest Creatures*, 1861.

(after the form שׁוֹבָב) signifies a censurer and fault-finder, μωμητής. The question means, will Job persist in this contending with God? He who sets God right, as though he knew everything better than He, shall answer the questions put before him.

[Then Job answered Jehovah, and said:]

4 *Behold, I am too mean: what shall I answer Thee?*
   I lay my hand upon my mouth.
5 *Once have I spoken, and will not begin again;*
   And twice—I will do it no more.

He is small, *i.e.* not equal to the task imposed, therefore he keeps his mouth firmly closed (comp. ch. xxi. 5, xxix. 9), for whatever he might say would still not be to the point. Once he has dared to criticise God's doings; a second time (שְׁתַּיִם = שְׁנֵית, Ges. § 120, 5) he ventures it no more, for God's wondrous wisdom and all-careful love dazzle him, and he gladly bows.

But how? Is not the divine speech altogether different from what one ought to expect? One expects to hear from the mouth of Jehovah something unheard of in the previous course of the drama, and in this expectation we find ourselves disappointed at the outset. For one need only look back and read ch. ix. 4–10, where Job acknowledges and describes God as a wise and mighty Lord over the natural world, especially as an irresistible Ruler over everything great in it; ch. xii. 7–10, where he refers to the creatures of the sky and deep as proofs of God's creative power; ch. xii. 11–25, where he sketches the grandest picture of God's terrible doings in nature and among men; ch. xxvi. 5–14, where he praises God as the Creator and Lord of all things, and describes what he says concerning Him as only a faint echo of the thunder of His might; ch. xxviii. 23 sqq., where he ascribes absolute wisdom to Him as the Creator and Ruler of the world. If one ponders these passages of Job's speeches, he will not be able to say that the speech of Jehovah, in the exhibition of the creative power and wisdom of God, which is its theme, would make Job conscious of anything which was previously unknown to him; and it is accordingly asked, What, then, is there that is new in the speech of Jehovah by which the great effect is brought about, that Job humbles himself in penitence, and becomes ready for the act of redemption which follows?

It has indeed never occurred to Job to desire to enter into a controversy with God concerning the works of creation; he is far from the delusion of being able to stand such a test; he knows in general, that if God were willing to contend with him, he would not be able to answer God one in a thousand, ch. ix. 3. And yet God closely questioned him, and thereby Job comes to the perception of his sin—how comes it to pass? Has the plot of the drama perhaps failed in this point? Has the poet made use of means unsuited to the connection of the whole, to bring about the needful effect, viz. the repentance of Job,—because, perhaps, the store of his thoughts was exhausted? But this poet is not so poor, and we shall therefore be obliged to try and understand the disposition of the speech of Jehovah before we censure it.

When one of Job's last words before the appearing of Jehovah was the word שַׁדַּי יַעֲנֵנִי, Job thereby desired God's decision concerning the testimony of his innocence. This wish is in itself not sinful; yea, it is even a fruit of his hidden faith, when he casts the look of hope away from his affliction and the accusation of the friends, into the future to God as his Vindicator and Redeemer. But that wish becomes sinful when he looks upon his affliction as a *de facto* accusation on the part of God, because he cannot think of suffering and sin as separable, and because he is conscious of his innocence, looks upon it as a decree of God, his opponent and his enemy,

which is irreconcilable with the divine justice. This Job's
condition of conflict and temptation is the prevailing one;
his faith is beclouded, and breaks through the night which
hangs over him only in single rays. The result of this condition of conflict is the sinful character which that wish
assumes: it becomes a challenge to God, since Job directs
against God Himself the accusation which the friends have
directed against him, and asserts his ability to carry through
his good cause even if God would enter with him into a
judicial contention; he becomes a יסור and מוכיח אלוה, and
raises himself above God, because he thinks he has Him for
an enemy who is his best friend. This defiance is, however,
not common godlessness; on the contrary, Job is really the
innocent servant of God, and his defiant tone is only the
result of a false conception which the tempted one indulges
respecting the Author of his affliction. So, then, this defiance
has not taken full possession of Job's mind; on the contrary,
the faith which lays firm hold on confidence in the God
whom he does not comprehend, is in conflict against it; and
this conflict tends in the course of the drama, the nearer it
comes to the catastrophe, still nearer to the victory, which
only awaits a decisive stroke in order to be complete. Therefore Jehovah yields to Job's longing שדי יענני, in as far as He
really answers Job; and even that this takes place, and that,
although out of the storm, it nevertheless takes place, not in
a way to crush and destroy, but to instruct and convince, and
displaying a loving condescension, is an indirect manifestation
that Job is not regarded by God as an evil-doer mature for
judgment. But that folly and temerity by which the servant
of God is become unlike himself must notwithstanding be
destroyed; and before Job can realize God as his Witness
and Redeemer, in which character his faith in its brighter
moments has foreseen Him, his sinful censuring and blaming
of God must be blotted out by penitence; and with it at the

same time his foolish imagination, by which his faith has been almost overwhelmed, must be destroyed, viz. the imagination that his affliction is a *hostile* dispensation of God.

And by what means is Job brought to the penitent recognition of his gloomy judgment concerning the divine decree, and of his contending with God? Is it, perhaps, by God's admitting to him what really is the case: that he does not suffer as a sinner the punishment of his sin, but showing at the same time that the decree of suffering is not an unjust one, because its design is not hostile? No, indeed, for Job is not worthy that his cause should be acknowledged on the part of God before he has come to a penitent recognition of the wrong by which he has sinned against God. God would be encouraging self-righteousness if He should give Job the testimony of his innocence, before the sin of vainglory, into which Job has fallen in the consciousness of his innocence, is changed to *humility*, by which all uprightness that is acceptable with God is tested. Therefore, contrary to expectation, God begins to speak with Job about totally different matters from His justice or injustice in reference to his affliction. Therein already lies a deep humiliation for Job. But a still deeper one in God's turning, as it were, to the *abecedarium naturæ*, and putting the censurer of His doings to the blush. That God is the almighty and all-wise Creator and Ruler of the world, that the natural world is exalted above human knowledge and power, and is full of marvellous divine creations and arrangements, full of things mysterious and incomprehensible to ignorant and feeble man, Job knows even before God speaks, and yet he must now hear it, because he does not know it rightly; for the nature with which he is acquainted as the herald of the creative and governing power of God, is also the preacher of humility; and exalted as God the Creator and Ruler of the natural world is above Job's censure, so is He also as the Author of his affliction. That which is new, therefore, in the speech of Jehovah, is not the proof of God's exaltation in itself, but the relation to the mystery of his affliction, and to his conduct towards God in this his affliction, in which Job is necessitated to place perceptions not in themselves strange to him. He who cannot answer a single one of those questions taken from the natural kingdom, but, on the contrary, must everywhere admire and adore the power and wisdom of God— he must appear as an insignificant fool, if he applies them to his limited judgment concerning the Author of • his affliction.

The fundamental tone of the divine speech is the thought, that the divine working in nature is infinitely exalted above human knowledge and power, and that consequently man must renounce all claim to better knowledge and right of contention in the presence of the divine dispensations. But at the same time, within the range of this general thought, it is also in particular shown how nature reflects the goodness of God as well as His wisdom (He has restrained the destructive power of the waters, He also sendeth rain upon the steppe, though untenanted by man); how that which accomplishes the purposes for which it was in itself designed, serves higher purposes in the moral order of the world (the dawn of day puts an end to the works of darkness, snow and hail serve as instruments of divine judgments); how divine providence extends to all creatures, and always according to their need (He provides the lion its prey, He satisfies the ravens that cry to Him); and how He has distributed His manifold gifts in a way often paradoxical to man, but in truth worthy of admiration (to the steinbock ease in bringing forth and growth without toil, to the wild ass freedom, to the antelope untameable fleetness, to the ostrich freedom from anxiety about its young and swiftness, to the horse heroic and proud lust for the battle, to the hawk the instinct of

354   THE BOOK OF JOB.

migration, to the eagle a lofty nest and a piercing sight).
Everywhere the wonders of God's power and wisdom, and
in fact of His goodness abounding in power, and His providence abounding in wisdom, infinitely transcend Job's knowledge and capacity. Job cannot answer one of all these
questions, but yet he feels to what end they are put to him.
The God who sets bounds to the sea, who refreshes the
desert, who feeds the ravens, who cares for the gazelle in
the wilderness and the eagle in its eyrie, is the same God
who now causes him seemingly thus unjustly to suffer. But
if the former is worthy of adoration, the latter will also be so.
Therefore Job confesses that he will henceforth keep silence,
and solemnly promises that he will now no longer contend
with Him. From the marvellous in nature he divines that
which is marvellous in his affliction. His humiliation under
the mysteries of nature is at the same time humiliation
under the mystery of his affliction; and only now, when he
penitently reveres the mystery he has hitherto censured, is
it time that its inner glory should be unveiled to him. The
bud is mature, and can now burst forth, in order to disclose
the blended colours of its matured beauty.

*The Second Speech of Jehovah, and Job's Second Penitent
Answer.*—Chap. xl. 6–xlii. 6.

Schema: 6. 10. 9. 12. 10. 9. | 4. 6. 6. 8. 8. 8. 10. | 6. 6.

[Then Jehovah answered Job out of the storm, and said:]
This second time also Jehovah speaks to Job out of the
storm; not, however, in wrath, but in the profound condescension of His majesty, in order to deliver His servant
from dark imaginings, and to bring him to free and joyous
knowledge. He does not demand blind subjection, but free
submission; He does not extort an acknowledgment of His
greatness, but it is effected by persuasion. It becomes manifest

that God is much more forbearing and compassionate than men. Observe the friends, the defenders of the divine honour, these sticklers for their own orthodoxy, how they rave against Job! How much better is it to fall into the hands of the living God, than into the hands of man! For God is truth and love; but men have at one time love without truth, at another truth without love, since they either connive at one or anathematize him. When a man who, moreover, like Job, is a servant of God, fails in one point, or sins, men at once condemn him altogether, and admit nothing good in him; God, however, discerns between good and evil, and makes the good a means of freeing the man from the evil. He also does not go rashly to work, but waits, like an instructor, until the time of action arrives. How long He listens to Job's bold challenging, and keeps silence! And then, when He does begin to speak, He does not cast Job to the ground by His authoritative utterances, but deals with him as a child; He examines him from the catechism of nature, and allows him to say for himself that he fails in this examination. In this second speech He acts with him as in the well-known poem of Hans Sachs with St Peter: He offers him to take the government of the world for once instead of Himself. Here also He produces conviction; here also His mode of action is a deep lowering of Himself. It is Jehovah, the God, who at length begets Himself in humanity, in order to convince men of His love.

7 *Gird up thy loins manfully:*
  I will question thee, and do thou answer me!
8 *Wilt thou altogether annul my right,*
  Condemn me, that thou mayest be righteous?
9 *And hast thou then an arm like God,*
  And canst thou with the voice thunder like Him?

The question with הַאַף stands to ch. xl. 2 in the relation of

a climax: Job contended not alone with God, which is in
itself wrong, let it be whatsoever it may; he went so far as
to lose sight of the divine justice in the government of the
world, and in order not to be obliged to give up his own
righteousness, so far as to doubt the divine. וְאִם, ver. 9*a*,
is also interrogative, as ch. viii. 3, xxi. 4, xxxiv. 17, comp.
xxxix. 13, not expressive of a wish, as ch. xxxiv. 16. In the
government of the world, God shows His arm, He raises His
voice of thunder: canst thou perhaps—asks Jehovah—do
the like, thou who seemest to imagine thou couldst govern the
world more justly, if thou hadst to govern it? וּבְקוֹל כָּמֹהוּ are
to be combined: of like voice to Him; the translation follows
the accents (וּבְקוֹל with *Rebia mugrasch*).

10 *Deck thyself then with pomp and dignity,*
    And in glory and majesty clothe thyself!
11 *Let the overflowings of thy wrath pour forth,*
    And behold all pride, and abase it!
12 *Behold all pride, bring it low,*
    And cast down the evil-doers in their place;
13 *Hide them in the dust together,*
    Bind their faces in secret:
14 *Then I also will praise thee,*
    That thy right hand obtaineth thee help.

He is for once to put on the robes of the King of kings
(עָדָה, comp. עָטָה, to wrap round, Ps. civ. 2), and send forth
his wrath over pride and evil-doing, for their complete removal. הֵפִיץ, *effundere, diffundere*, as Arab. *afáda, vid.* ch.
xxxvii. 11. עֶבְרוֹת, or rather, according to the reading of Ben-
Ascher, עֲבָרוֹת, in its prop. signif. oversteppings, *i.e.* overflowings. In connection with vers. 11–13, one is directly reminded
of the judgment on everything that is high and exalted
in Isa. ii., where טָמְנֵם בֶּעָפָר also has its parallel (Isa. ii. 10).
Not less, however, does ver. 14*b* recall Isa. lix. 16, lxiii. 5

(comp. Ps. xcviii. 1); Isaiah I. and II. have similar descriptions to the book of Job. The ἀπ λεγ. הָדַךְ is Hebræo-Arab.; *hadaka* signifies, like *hadama*, to tear, pull to the ground. In connection with טָמוּן (from טָמַן; Aram., Arab., טמר), the lower world, including the grave, is thought of (comp. Arab. *mat-murát*, subterranean places); חָבַשׁ signifies, like حبس IV., to chain and to imprison. Try it only for once—this is the collective thought—to act like Me in the execution of penal justice, I would praise thee. · That he cannot do it, and yet ventures with his short-sightedness and feebleness to charge God's rule with injustice, the following pictures of foreign animals are now further intended to make evident to him :—

15 *Behold now the behêmôth,*
    Which I have made with thee :
    He eateth grass like an ox.
16 *Behold now, his strength is in his loins,*
    And his force in the sinews of his belly.
17 *He bendeth his tail like a cedar branch,*
    The sinews of his legs are firmly interwoven.
18 *His bones are like tubes of brass,*
    His bones like bars of iron.

בְּהֵמוֹת (after the manner of the intensive *plur.* הוֹלֵלוֹת, חָכְמוֹת, which play the part of the abstract termination), which sounds like a *plur.*, but without the numerical plural signification, considered as Hebrew, denotes the beast κατ' ἐξοχήν, or the giant of beasts, is however Hebraized from the Egyptian *p-ehe-mau*, (*muau*), *i.e.* the (*p*) ox (*ehe*) of the water (*mau* as in the Hebraized proper name מֹשֶׁה). It is, as Bochart has first of all shown, the so-called river or Nile horse, *Hippopotamus amphibius* (in Isa. xxx. 6, בְּהֵמוֹת נֶגֶב, as emblem of Egypt, which extends its power, and still is active in the interest of others), found in the rivers of Africa, but no longer found in the Nile, which is not inappropriately called a horse; the Arab. water-

hog is better, Italian *bomarino*, Engl. sea-cow [?], like the
Egyptian *p-ehe-mau*. The change of *p* and *b* in the exchange
of Egyptian and Semitic words occurs also elsewhere, *e.g.*
pug' and בּוּץ, *harpu* and חֶרֶב (ἅρπη), *Apriu* and עֲבָרִים (according to Lauth). Nevertheless *p-ehe-mau* (not *mau-t*, for
what should the post-positive fem. art. do here?) is first of
all only the בהמות translated back again into the Egyptian
by Jablonsky; an instance in favour of this is still wanting.
In Hieroglyph the Nile-horse is called *apet;* it was honoured
as divine. Brugsch dwelt in Thebes in the temple of the
Apet.[1]　In ver. 15*b* עִמָּךְ signifies nothing but "with thee," so
that thou hast it before thee. This water-ox eats חָצִיר, green
grass, like an ox. That it prefers to plunder the produce of
the fields—in Arab. *chadîr* signifies, in particular, green
barley—is accordingly self-evident. Nevertheless, it has
gigantic strength, viz. in its plump loins and in the sinews
(שְׂרִירֵי, properly the firm constituent parts,[2] therefore: liga-
ments and muscles) of its clumsy belly. The brush of a tail,
short in comparison with the monster itself, is compared to a
cedar (a branch of it), *ratione glabritiei, rotunditatis, spissi-*

---

[1] In the astronomical representations the hippopotamus is in the neighbourhood of the North Pole in the place of the dragon of the present
day, and bears the name of *hes-mut*, in which *mut* = *t. mau*, "the mother."
Hes however is obscure ; Birch explains it by : raging.

[2] Starting from its primary signification (made firm, fast), سَرَّ,
שְׂרִירָא can signify *e.g.* also things put together from wood : a throne, a
hand-barrow, bedstead and cradle, metaphor. the foundation. Wetzst.
otherwise : "The שְׂרִירֵי הבטן are not the sinews and muscles, still less
'the private parts' of others, but the four bearers of the animal body
= *arkân el-batn*, viz. the bones of the מתנים, ver. 16*a*, together with the
two shoulder-blades. The Arab. *sarîr* is that on which a thing is supported or rests, on which it stands firmly, or moves about. *Neshwân*
(i. 280) says : '*sarîr* is the substratum on which a thing rests,' and
the *sarîr er-ra's*, says the same, is the place where the head rests upon the
nape of the neck. The Kâmûs gives the same signification *primo loco*,
which shows that it is general ; then follows in gen. مَضْطَجِع, "the
support of a thing."

tudinis et firmitatis (Bochart); since the beast is in general almost without hair, it looks like a stiff, naked bone, and yet it can bend it like an elastic cedar branch; חָפֵץ is Hebræo-Arab., حفض‎ [1] is a word used directly of the bending of wood (*el-'ûd*). Since this description, like the whole book of Job, is so strongly Arabized, פחד, ver. 17*b*, will also be one word with the Arab. *fachidh*, the thigh; as the Arabic version also translates: *'urûku afchâdhihi* (the veins or strings of its thigh). The Targ., retaining the word of the text here,[2] has פְּחֲדִין in Lev. xxi. 20 for אֶשֶׁךְ, a testicle, prop. *inguina*, the groins; we interpret: the sinews of its thighs or legs[3] are intertwined after the manner of intertwined vine branches, שׂרִיגִים.[4] But

---

[1] Wetzst. otherwise: One may compare the Arab. خفض‎, *fut. i*, to hold, sit, lie motionless (in any place), from which the signification of desiring, longing, has been developed, since in the Semitic languages the figure of fixing (*ta'alluq*) the heart and the eye on any desired object is at the basis of this notion (wherefore such verbs are joined with the *præp.* בְּ). According to this, it is to be explained, "his tail is motionless like (the short and thick stem of) the cedar," for the stunted tail of an animal is a mark of its strength to a Semite. In 1860, as I was visiting the neighbouring mountain fortress of *el*-Hosn with the octogenarian *Fêjâd*, the sheikh of *Fîk* in *Gôlân*, we rode past Fêjâd's ploughmen; and as one of them was letting his team go slowly along, the sheikh cried out to him from a distance: Faster! faster! They (the steers, which thou ploughest) are not oxen weak with age, nor are they the dower of a widow (who at her second marriage receives only a pair of weak wretched oxen from her father or brother); but they are heifers (3–4 year-old steers) with stiffly raised tails (*wadhujûluhin muqashmare*, מְקַשְׁמָר an intensive קָשׁוּר or מְקַשָּׁר [comp. שָׁלָאֵן, ch. xxi. 23]).

[2] Another Targ., which translates נבריה ושׁעבזוותי, *penis et testiculi ejus*, vid. Aruch *s.v.* עזבן.

[3] According to Fleischer, *fachidh* signifies properly the thick-leg (= thigh), from the root *fach*, with the general signification of being puffed out, swollen, thick.

[4] In the choice of the word ישׂרוּ, the *mushâgarat ed-dawâli* (from ישׂרע) = שׂנר), "the interweaving of the vine branches" was undoubtedly before the poet's eye; comp. *Deutsch. Morgenl. Zeitschr.* xi. 477: "On all sides in this delightful corner of the earth (the *Ghûta*) the vine left to itself, in diversified ramifications, often a dozen branches resembling so many huge snakes entangled together, swings to and fro upon the

why is פְּחָדָיו pointed thus, and not פְּחָדָיו (as *e.g.* שְׂעָרָיו)? It is
either an Aramaizing (with אַשְׁרָיו it has another relationship)
pointing of the *plur.*, or rather, as Köhler has perceived, a
regularly-pointed *dual* (like רַגְלָיו), from פְּחָדַיִם (like פַּעֲמַיִם),
which is equally suitable in connection with the signification
femora as *testiculi.* מְטִיל, ver. 18*b*, is also Hebræo-Arab.;
for مَطَل signifies to forge, or properly to extend by forging
(hammering), and to lengthen, undoubtedly a secondary
formation of טול, *tâla*, to be long, as *makuna* of *kâna*, *madana*
of *dâna*, *massara* (to found a fortified city) of *sâra*, chiefly
(if not always) by the intervention of such nouns as *makân*,
medîne, *misr* (= מְצֹור), therefore in the present instance by
the intervention of this *metîl* (= *memtûl*[1]), whence probably
μέταλλον (metal), properly iron in bars or rods, therefore
metal in a wrought state, although not yet finished.[2] Its
bones are like tubes of brass, its bones (גְּרָמָיו, the more Aram.
word) like forged rods of iron—what an appropriate description of the comparatively thin but firm as iron skeleton by
which the plump mass of flesh of the gigantic boar-like grass-
eater is carried!

shining stem of the lofty white poplar." And *ib.* S. 491 : " a' twisted
vine almost the thickness of a man, as though formed of rods of iron
(comp. ver. 18)."

. [1] The noun מְטִיל is also found in the Lexicon of *Neshwân*, i. 63 : " מְטִיל
is equivalent to מַמְטוּל, viz. that which is hammered out in length, used of
iron and other metals; and one says חַדִירָה מְטִילָה of a piece of iron that
has been hammered for the purpose of stretching it." The verb *Neshwân*
explains : " מְטַל said of iron signifies to stretch it that it may become
long." The verb מְטַל can be regarded as a fusion of the root מדד (מטט,
מוט, comp. מוּטָה, and مَوْط Beduin : to take long steps) with the root
טול, to be long.—WETZST. The above explanation of the origin of the
verb מטל seems to us more probable.

[2] Ibn-Koreisch in Pinsker, *Likkute*, p. קנא, explains it without exact-
ness by *sebîkat* hadîd, which signifies a smelted and formed piece of
iron.

19 *He is the firstling of the ways of God;*
    He, his Maker, reached to him his sword.
20 *For the mountains bring forth food for him,*
    And all the beasts of the field play beside him.
21 *Under the lote-trees he lieth down,*
    In covert of reeds and marsh.
22 *Lote-trees cover him as shade,*
    The willows of the brook encompass him.
23 *Behold, if the stream is strong, he doth not quake ;*
    He remaineth cheerful, if a Jordan breaketh forth upon his
    mouth.
24 *Just catch him while he is looking,*
    With snares let one pierce his nose !

God's ways is the name given to God's operations as the
Creator of the world in ver. 19*a* (comp. ch. xxvi. 14, where
His acts as the Ruler of the world are included) ; and the
firstling of these ways is called the Behêmôth, not as one of
the first in point of time, but one of the hugest creatures, *un
chef-d'œuvre de Dieu* (Bochart) ; רֵאשִׁית not as Prov. viii. 22,
Num. xxiv. 20, of the priority of time, but as Amos vi. 1, 6,
of rank.   The *art.* in הָעֹשׂוֹ is, without the pronominal *suff.*
being meant as an accusative (Ew. § 290, *d*), equal to a
demonstrative pronoun (comp. Ges. § 109, *init.*) : this its
Creator (but so that "this" does not refer back so much as
forwards).   It is not meant that He reached His sword to
behêmoth, but (on which account לֹ is intentionally wanting)
that He brought forth, *i.e.* created, its (behêmoth's) peculiar
sword, viz. the gigantic incisors ranged opposite one another,
with which it grazes upon the meadow as with a sickle :
ἀρούρῃσιν κακὴν ἐπιβάλλεται ἅρπην (Nicander, *Theriac.* 566),
ἅρπη is exactly the sickle-shaped Egyptian sword (*harpu =*
חֶרֶב).   Vegetable food (to which its teeth are adapted) is
appointed to the behêmoth : "for the mountains produce

food for him ;" it is the herbage of the hills (which is scanty
in the lower and more abundant in the upper valley of the
Nile) that is intended, after which this uncouth animal climbs
(vid. Schlottm.). בּוּל is neither a contraction of יְבוּל (Ges.),
nor a corruption of it (Ew.), but Hebræo-Arab. = baul, produce, from bâla, to beget, comp. aballa, to bear fruit (prop.
seed, bulal), root בל, to soak, wet, mix.[1] Ver. 20b describes
how harmless, and if unmolested, inoffensive, the animal is;
שָׁם there, viz. while it is grazing.

In ver. 21a Saadia correctly translates: تكسّت الضِّلَال; and

ver. 22a, Abulwalid: يغطيه الضل ظِلُّهُ لَهُ, tegit eum lotus

obumbrans eum, by interpreting الضل, more correctly الضَّال,
with es-sidr el-berrî, i.e. Rhamnus silvestris (Rhamnus Lotus,
Linn.), in connection with which Schultens' observation is to
be noticed: Cave intelligas lotum Ægyptiam s. plantam Niloti-
cam quam Arabes نوفر. The fact that the wild animals of the
steppe seek the shade of the lote-tree, Schultens has supported
by passages from the poets. The lotus is found not only in
Syria, but also in Egypt, and the whole of Africa.[2]   The

---

[1] Whether בְּלִיל, ch. vi. 5, xxiv. 6, signifies mixed provender (farrago),
or perhaps ripe fruit, i.e. grain, so that jabol, Judg. xix. 21, in the signification " he gave dry provender consisting of barley-grain," would be
·the opposite of the jahushsh (יָחֻשׁ) of the present day, " he gives green
provender consisting of green grass or green barley, hashîsh," as Wetzst.
supposes, vid. on Isa. xxx. 24.

[2] The ضال or Dûm-tree, which likes hot and damp valleys, and hence
is found much on the northern, and in great numbers on the eastern, shores
of the Sea of Galilee, is called in the present day sidra, collect. sidr; and
its fruit, a small yellow apple, dûma, collect. dûm, perhaps " the not
ending, perennial," because the fruit of the previous year only falls from
the tree when that of the present year is ripe.   Around Bagdad, as they
told me, the Dûm-tree bears twice a year.   In Egypt its fruit is called
nebq (נֶבֶק, not nibq as in Freytag), and the tree is there far stronger and
taller than in Syria, where it is seldom more than about four and twenty
feet high.   Only in the Wâdî 's-sidr on the mountains of Judæa have I
seen several unusually large trunks.   The Kâmûs places the signification

plur. is formed from the primary form צָאֵל, as שִׁקְמִים from שֶׁקֶם, Olsh. § 148, *b;* the single tree was perhaps called צָאֵלָה (= ظِلّ), as שִׁקְמָה (Ew. § 189, *h*). Ammianus Marc. xxii. 15 coincides with ver. 21*b*: *Inter arundines celsas et squalentes nimia densitate hæc bellua cubilia ponit.* צֶלְלוֹ, ver. 22*a* (resolved from צֵלֹל, as גֶּלְלוֹ, ch. xx. 7, from גֶּלֹל¹), is in apposition with the subj.: Lote-trees cover it as its shade (shading it). The double play of words in ver. 22 is [not] reproduced in the [English] translation. הֵן, ver. 23*a*, pointing to something possible, obtains almost the signification of a conditional particle, as ch. xii. 14, xxiii. 8, Isa. liv. 15. The Arabic version appropriately translates ان طغى النهر, for طغى denotes exactly like עָשַׁק, excessive, insolent behaviour, and is then, as also ظلم, عتا, and other verbs given by Schultens, transferred from the sphere of ethics to the overflow of a river beyond its banks, to the rush of raging waters, to the rising and bursting forth of swollen streams. It does

" the sweet *Dûm*-tree " first of all to ضال, and then " the wild D." In hotter regions there may also be a superior kind with fine fruit, in Syria it is only wild—*Neshwân* (ii. 192) says: "*dâla,* collect. *dâl,* is the wild *Dûm*-tree,"—yet I have always found its fruit sweet and pleasant to the taste.—WETZST.

¹ Forms like גֶּלְלוֹ, צֶלֶל, are unknown to the language, because it was more natural for ease of pronunciation to make the primary form סָבַב into סַב than into סֵבַב; גֶּלְלוֹ (*vid.* i. 377), צֶלְלוֹ, might more readily be referred to גְּלָל, צְלָל (in which the first *a* is a helping vowel, and the second a root vowel); but although the form קָטֹל and the segolate forms completely pass into one another in inflection, still there does not exist a safe example in favour of the change of vowels of קָטֹל into קֶטְלוֹ; wherefore we have also derived אֶגְלֵי, ch. xxxviii. 28, from אָגַל, not from אֵגֶל, although, moreover, *ě* frequently enough alternates with *ĭ* (*e.g.* יִשְׁעֵךְ), and a transition into *ĕ* of the *ĭ* weakened from *ă* (*e.g.* יִדְבַּם) also occurs. But there are no forms like נֶטְפִּי = נִטְפֵּי from נָטֹף in reality, although they would be possible according to the laws of vowels. In Ges. *Handwörterb.* (1863) גֶּלְלוֹ stands under גֵּל (according to the form לֵבַב, which, however, forms לְבָבוֹ) and צֶלְלוֹ under צֵל (a rare noun-form, which does not occur at all form verbs double *Ayin*).

not, however, terrify the behêmoth, which can live as well in
the water as on the land; לֹא יַחְפּוֹז, properly, it does not spring
up before it, is not disturbed by it. Instead of the Jordan,
ver. 23*b*, especially in connection with יָגִיחַ, the 'Gaïhûn (the
Oxus) or the 'Gaïhân (the Pyramus) might have been mentioned, which have their names from the growing force with
which they burst forth from their sources (גּוּחַ, גִּיחַ, comp.
'gâcha, to wash away). But in order to express the notion
of a powerful and at times deep-swelling stream, the poet
prefers the יַרְדֵּן of his fatherland, which, moreover, does not
lie so very far from the scene, according to the conception
at least, since all the wadis in its neighbourhood flow directly
or indirectly (as *Wâdi el-Meddân*, the boundary river between
the district of *Suwêt* and the *Nukra* plain) into the Jordan.
For יַרְדֵּן (perhaps from יָרַד[1]) does not here signify a stream
(rising in the mountain) in general; the name is not deprived
of its geographical definiteness, but is a particularizing expression of the notion given above.

The description closes in ver. 24 with the ironical challenge:
in its sight (בְּעֵינָיו as Prov. i. 17) let one (for once) catch
it; let one lay a snare which, when it goes into it, shall
spring together and pierce it in the nose; *i.e.* neither the
open force nor the stratagem, which one employs with effect
with other animals, is sufficient to overpower this monster.
מוֹקְשִׁים is generally rendered as equal to חַתִּים, Isa. xxxvii. 29,
Ezek. xix. 4, or at least to the cords drawn through them, but
contrary to the uniform usage of the language. The description of the hippopotamus[2] is now followed by that of the crocodile, which also elsewhere form a pair, *e.g.* in Achilles Tatius,

---

[1] Certainly one would have expected יַרְדֵּן like פַּרְדֵּן, while יַרְדֵּן like יַעֲבֵץ,
יַעְזֵר, appears formed from רָדָן; nevertheless יַרְדֵּן (with changeable *Ssere*)
can be understood as a change of vowel from יַרְדֵּן (comp. יֵשֵׁב for יָשֵׁב).

[2] *Vid.* Brehm, *Aus dem Leben des Nilpferds*, *Gartenlaube* 1859, Nr.
48, etc.

iv. 2, 19. Behemoth and leviathan, says Herder, are the pillars of Hercules at the end of the book, the *non plus ultra* of another world [distant from the scene]. What the same writer says of the poet, that he does not "mean to furnish any contributions to Pennant's *Zoologie* or to Linnæus' *Animal Kingdom*," the expositor also must assent to.

> 25 *Dost thou draw the crocodile by a hoop-net,*
> *And dost thou sink his tongue into the line?!*
> 26 *Canst thou put a rush-ring into his nose,*
> *And pierce his cheeks with a hook?*
> 27 *Will he make many supplications to thee,*
> *Or speak flatteries to thee?*
> 28 *Will he make a covenant with thee,*
> *To take him as a perpetual slave?*
> 29 *Wilt thou play with him as a little bird,*
> *And bind him for thy maidens?*

In ch. iii. 8, לִוְיָתָן signified the celestial dragon, that causes the eclipses of the sun (according to the Indian mythology, *râhu* the black serpent, and *ketu* the red serpent); in Ps. civ. 26 it does not denote some great sea-saurian after the kind of the hydrarchus of the primeval world,[1] but directly the whale, as in the Talmud (Lewysohn, *Zoologie des Talm.* § 178 sq.). Elsewhere, however, the crocodile is thus named, and in fact as תַּנִּין also, another appellation of this natural wonder of Egypt, as an emblem of the mightiness of Pharaoh (*vid.* on Ps. lxxiv. 13 sq.), as once again the crocodile itself is called in Arab. *el-fir'aunu*. The Old Testament language possesses no proper name for the crocodile; even the Talmudic makes use of קְרוּקְתָּא = κροκόδειλος (Lewysohn, § 271). לִוְיָתָן is the generic name of twisted, and תַּנִּין long-extended monsters. Since the Egyptian name of the crocodile has not been Hebraized, the poet contents himself in תְּמַשֵּׁךְ with

[1] *Vid.* Grässe, *Beiträge*, S. 94 ff.

making a play upon its Egyptian, and in تمساح, *timsâh*,[1]
Arabized name (Ew. § 324, *a*). To wit, it is called in Coptic
temsah, Hierogl. (without the *art*.) *msuh* (*emsuh*), as an animal
that creeps "out of the egg (*suh*)."[2]   In ver. 25*b*, Ges. and
others falsely translate: Canst thou press its tongue down
with a cord; תשקיע does not signify *demergere* = *deprimere*,
but *immergere*: canst thou sink its tongue into the line, *i.e.*
make it bite into the hook on the line, and canst thou thus
draw it up? Ver. 25*b* then refers to what must happen in
order that the מקשיו of the *msuh* may take place. Herodotus
(and after him Aristotle) says, indeed, ii. 68, the crocodile
has no tongue; but it has one, only it cannot stretch it out,
because the protruding part has grown to the bottom of the
mouth, while otherwise the saurians have a long tongue, that
can be stretched out to some length.   In ver. 26 the order of
thought is the same: for first the Nile fishermen put a ring
through the gills or nose of valuable fish; then they draw a
cord made of rushes (σχοῖνον) through it, in order to put
them thus bound into the river. "As a perpetual slave,"
ver. 28*b* is intended to say: like one of the domestic animals.

---

[1] Herodotus was acquainted with this name (χάμψαι = κροκόδειλοι);
thus is the crocodile called also in Palestine, where (as Tobler and Joh.
Roth have shown) it occurs, especially in the river *Damûr* near *Tantûra*.

[2] *Les naturalistes*—says Chabas in his *Papyr. magique*, p. 190—*comptent
cinq espèces de crocodiles vivant dans le Nil, mais les hieroglyphes rapportent
un plus grand nombre de noms déterminés par le signe du crocodile.* Such
is really the case, apart from the so-called land crocodile or σκίγκος
(Arab. *isqanqûr*), the Coptic name of which, *hankelf* (according to Lauth
ha. n. kelf, ruler of the bank), is not as yet indicated on the monuments.
Among the many old Egyptian names for the crocodile, Kircher's *charuki*
is, however, not found, which reminds one of the Coptic *karus*, as κροκόδειλος of κρόκος, for κροκόδειλος is the proper name of the *Lacerta viridis*
(Herod. ii. 69). Lauth is inclined to regard *charuki* as a fiction of
Kircher, as also the name of the phœnix, αλλοη (*vid.* p. 130). The
number of names of the crocodile which remain even without *charuki*,
leads one to infer a great variety of species, and crocodiles, which differ
from all living species, have also actually been found in Egyptian tombs;
vid. Schmarda, *Verbreitung der Thiere*, i. 89.

By צִפּוֹר, ver. 29a, can hardly be meant צִפֹּרֶת הַכְּרָמִים, the little bird of the vineyard, i.e. according to a Talmud. usage of the language, the golden beetle (*Jesurun*, p. 222), or a pretty eatable grasshopper (Lewysohn, § 374), but, according to the words of Catullus, *Passer deliciæ meæ puellæ*, the sparrow, Arab. ʾaṣfûr—an example of a harmless living plaything (שָׂחַק בְּ, to play with anything, different from Ps. civ. 26, where it is not, with Ew., to be translated: to play with it, but: therein).

> 30 *Do fishermen trade with him,*
> *Do they divide him among the Canaanites?*
> 31 *Canst thou fill his skin with darts,*
> *And his head with fish-spears?*
> 32 *Only lay thy hand upon him—*
> *Remember the battle, thou wilt not do it again!*
> Ch. xli. 1 *Behold, every hope becometh disappointment:*
> *Is not one cast down even at the sight of him?*

The fishermen form a guild (صَنْف, *sunf*), the associated members of which are called חַבָּרִים (distinct from חֲבֵרִים). On בָּרָה עַל, *vid.* on ch. vi. 27. "When I came to the towns of the coast," says R. Akiba, *b. Rosch ha-Schana*, 26b, "they called selling, which we call מְכִירָה, בִּירָה, there," according to which, then, Gen. 1. 5 is understood, as by the Syriac; the word is Sanscrito-Semitic, Sanscr. *kri*, Persic *chirîden* (*Jesurun*, p. 178). LXX. ἐνσιτοῦνται, according to 2 Kings vi. 23, to which, however, עָלָיו is not suitable. כְּנַעֲנִים are Phœnicians; and then, because they were the merchant race of the ancient world, directly traders or merchants. The meaning of the question is, whether one sells the crocodile among them, perhaps halved, or in general divided up (*vid.* i. 409). Further, ver. 31: whether one can kill it בְּשֻׂכּוֹת, with pointed missiles (Arab. *shauke*, a thorn, sting, dart), or with fish-spears (צִלְצַל, so called from its whizzing, צָלַל, salla). In ver. 32 the accentuation is the right indication : only seize upon him—remember the battle, i.e. thou wilt be obliged to remember it, and thou wilt have no wish to repeat it. זְכֹר is a so-called imperat. consec.: if thou doest it, thou wilt . . ., Ges. § 130, 2. תּוֹסַף is the pausal form of תּוֹסֵף (once tôsp, Prov. xxx. 6), of which it is the original form.

Ch. xli. 1. The suff. of תּוֹחַלְתּוֹ refers to the assailant, not objectively to the beast (the hope which he indulges concerning it). נִכְזָבָה, ch. xli. 1, is 3 præt., like נֶאֶלְמָה, Isa. liii. 7 (where also the participial accenting as Milra, occurs in Codd.); Fürst's Concord. treats it as part., but the participial form נִקְטָלָה, to be assumed in connection with it, along with נִקְטָלָה and נִקְטָלַת, does not exist. הֲנַם, ver. 1b, is, according to the sense, equivalent to הֲלֹא גַם; vid. on ch. xx. 4. מַרְאָיו (according to Ges., Ew., and Olsh., sing., with the plural suff., without a plur. meaning, which is natural in connection with the primary form מַרְאָי; or what is more probable, from the plur. מַרְאִים with a sing. meaning, as פָּנִים) refers to the crocodile, and יֻטַל (according to a more accredited reading, יֻטַל = יוּטָל) to the hunter to whom it is visible.

What is said in ver. 30 is perfectly true; although the crocodile was held sacred in some parts of Egypt, in Elephantine and Apollonopolis, on the contrary, it was salted and eaten as food. Moreover, that there is a small species of crocodile, with which children can play, does not militate against ver. 29. Everywhere here it is the creature in its primitive strength and vigour that is spoken of. But if they also knew how to catch it in very early times, by fastening a bait, perhaps a duck, on a barb with a line attached, and drew the animal to land, where they put an end to its life with a lance-thrust in the neck (Uhlemann, Thoth, S. 241): this was angling on the largest scale, as is not meant in ver. 25. If, on the other hand, in very early times they harpooned the crocodile, this would certainly be more difficult of reconcilement with ver. 31, than that mode of catching it by means of a fishing-hook of the greatest calibre with ver. 25. But harpooning is generally only of use when the animal can be hit between the neck and head, or in the flank; and it is very questionable whether, in the ancient times, when the race was without doubt of an unmanageable size, that has now died out, the crocodile hunt (ch. vii. 12) was effected with harpoons. On the whole subject we have too little information for distinguishing between the different periods. So far as the questions of Jehovah have reference to man's relation to the two monsters, they concern the men of the present, and are shaped according to the measure of power which they have attained over nature. The strophe which follows shows what Jehovah intends by these questions.

2 *None is so foolhardy that he dare excite him!*
  And who is it who could stand before Me?
3 *Who hath given Me anything first of all, that I must requite it?*
  Whatsoever is under the whole heaven is Mine.

One sees from these concluding inferences, thus applied, what is the design, in the connection of this second speech of Jehovah, of the reference to behêmoth and leviathan, which somewhat abruptly began in ch. xl. 15. If even the strength of one of God's creatures admits no thought of being able to attack it, how much more should the greatness of the Creator deter man from all resistance! For no one has any claim on God, so that he should have the right of appearing before Him with a rude challenge. Every creature under heaven is God's; man, therefore, possesses nothing that was not God's property and gift, and he must humbly yield, whether God gives or takes away. לֹא, ver. 2*a*, is not directly equivalent to אֵין, but the clause is exclamatory. עוּרֵנוּ *Chethib,*

עִירֵנוּ *Keri*, is the Palestine reading, the reverse the Babylonian; the authorized text (chiefly without a *Keri*) is יְעִירֶנּוּ,
from עוּר in a transitive signification (ἐγείρειν), as שׁוּב, ch.
xxxix. 12, comp. xlii. 10. The meaning of הִקְדִּימַנִי is determined according to וַיְאַשְּׁלֵם: to anticipate, viz. by gifts presented as a person is approaching the giver (Arab. *aqdama*).
הוּא, ver. 3*b*, is neutral, as ch. xiii. 16, xv. 9, xxxi. 11, 28.
תַּחַת is virtually a subj.: that which is under . . . After
these apparently epiphonematic verses (2 and 3), one might
now look for Job's answer. But the description of the
leviathan is again taken up, and in fact hitherto it was only
the invincibility of the animal that was spoken of; and yet
it is not so described that this picture might form the exact
pendent of the preceding.

4 *I will not keep silence about his members,*
   The proportion of his power and the comeliness of his struc-
        ture.
5 *Who could raise the front of his coat of mail?*
   Into his double teeth—who cometh therein?
6 *The doors of his face—who openeth them?*
   Round about his teeth is terror.

The *Keri* לֹו authorized by the Masora assumes an interrogative rendering: as to it, should I be silent about its
members (לֹו at the head of the clause, as Lev. vii. 7–9, Isa.
ix. 2),—what perhaps might appear more poetic to many.
הֶחֱרִישׁ (once, ch. xi. 3, to cause to keep silence) here, as
usually: to be silent. בַּדָּיו, as ch. xviii. 13, vol. i. p. 323.
דְּבַר signifies the relation of the matter, a matter of fact, as
דִּבְרֵי, facts, Ps. lxv. 4, cv. 27, cxlv. 5. חִין (compared by Ew.
with הִין, a measure) signifies grace, χάρις (as synon. חֶסֶד),
here delicate regularity, and is made easy of pronunciation
from חֵן, just as the more usual חֵן; the language has avoided
the form חֶנֶן, as observed above. לְבוּשׁ, clothing, we have

translated "coat of mail," which the Arab. *libâs* usually signifies; פְּנֵי לְבֻשׁוֹ is not its face's covering (Schlottm.), which ought to be פְּנֵי לְבֻשׁוֹ; but פְּנֵי is the upper or front side turned to the observer (comp. Isa. xxv. 7), as Arab. وجه (*wag'h*), *si rem desuper spectes, summa ejus pars, si ex adverso, prima* (Fleischer, *Glossæ*, i. 57). That which is the "doubled of its mouth" (רֶסֶן, prop. a bit in the mouth, then the mouth itself) is its upper and lower jaws armed with powerful teeth. The "doors of the face" are the jaws; the jaws are divided back to the ears, the teeth are not covered by lips; the impression of the teeth is therefore the more terrible, which the substantival clause, ver. 6*b* (comp. ch. xxxix. 20), affirms. שִׁנָּיו *gen. subjecti*: the circle, ἕρκος, which is formed by its teeth (Hahn).

> 7 *A pride are the furrows of the shields,*
> *Shut by a rigid seal.*
> 8 *One joineth on to the other,*
> *And no air entereth between them.*
> 9 *One upon another they are arranged,*
> *They hold fast together, inseparably.*

Since the writer uses אָפִיק both in the signif. *robustus*, ch. xii. 12, and *canalis*, ch. xl. 18, it is doubtful whether it must be explained *robusta* (*robora*) *scutorum* (as *e.g.* Ges.), or *canales scutorum* (Hirz., Schlottm., and others). We now prefer the latter, but so that "furrows of the shields" signifies the square shields themselves bounded by these channels; for only thus is the סָגוּר, which refers to these shields, considered, each one for itself, suitably attached to what precedes. חוֹתָם צָר is an *acc.* of closer definition belonging to it: closed is (each single one) by a firmly attached, and therefore firmly closed, seal. LXX. remarkably ὥσπερ σμυρίτης λίθος, *i.e.* emery (*vid.* Krause's *Pyrogeteles*, 1859, S. 228). Six rows of knotty scales and four scales of the neck cover the upper part of the animal's body, in themselves firm, and attached to one another in almost impenetrable layers, as is described in vers. 7 sq. in constantly-varying forms of expression (where יֶעְשׁוֹ with *Pathach* beside *Athnach* is the correct reading),—a גַּאֲוָה, *i.e.* an equipment of which the animal may be proud. Umbr. takes גַּאוּה, with Bochart, = גֵּוָה, the back; but although in the language much is possible, yet not everything.

> 10 *His sneezing sendeth forth light,*
> *And his eyes are like the eyelids of the dawn;*
> 11 *Out of his mouth proceed flames,*
> *Sparks of fire escape from him;*
> 12 *Out of his nostrils goeth forth smoke*
> *Like a seething pot and caldron;*
> 13 *His breath kindleth coals,*
> *And flames go forth out of his mouth.*

That the crocodile delights to sun itself on the land, and then turns its open jaws to the sunny side, most Nile travellers since Herodotus have had an opportunity of observing;[1] and in connection therewith the reflex action of sneezing may occur, since the light of the sun produces an irritation on the retina, and thence on the vagus; and since the sun shines upon the fine particles of watery slime cast forth in the act of sneezing, a meteoric appearance may be produced. This delicate observation of nature is here compressed into three words; in this concentration of whole, grand thoughts and pictures, we recognise the older poet. עֲטִישׁ is the usual

---

[1] Dieterici, *Reisebilder*, i. 194: "We very often saw the animal lying in the sand, its jaws wide open and turned towards the warm sunbeams, while little birds, like the slender white water-wagtail, march quietly about in the deadly abyss, and pick out worms from the watery jaws." Herodotus, ii. 68, tells exactly the same story; as the special friend of the crocodile among little birds, he mentions τὸν τροχῖλον (the sand-piper, *Pluvianus Ægyptius*).

Semitic word for "sneezing" (synon. זֹרֶה, 2 Kings iv. 35). תָּהֵל shortened from תָּהֵל, ch. xxxi. 26, *Hiph.* of הָלַל (comp. p. 47). The comparison of the crocodile's eyes with עַפְעַפֵּי־שָׁחַר (as ch. iii. 9, from עָעַף, to move with quick vibrations, to wink, *i.e.* tremble), or the rendering of the same as εἴδος ἑωσφόρου (LXX.), is the more remarkable, as, according to Horus, i. 68, two crocodile's eyes are the hieroglyph[1] for dawn, ἀνατολή: ἐπειδήπερ (probably to be read ἐπειδὴ πρὸ) παντὸς σώματος ζώου οἱ ὀφθαλμοὶ ἐκ τοῦ βυθοῦ ἀναφαίνονται. There it is the peculiar brilliancy of the eyes of certain animals that is intended, which is occasioned either by the iris being furnished with a so-called lustrous substance, or there being in the pupil of the eye (as *e.g.* in the ostrich) that spot which, shining like metal, is called *tapetum lucidum.* For ἀναφαίνεσθαι of the eyes ἐκ τοῦ βυθοῦ, is the lustre of the pupil in the depth of the eye. The eyes of the crocodile, which are near together, and slanting, glimmer through the water, when it is only a few feet under water, with a red glow. Nevertheless the comparison in ver. 10*b* might also be intended differently. The inner (third) eyelid[2] of the croco-

---

[1] The eyes of the crocodile alone by themselves are no hieroglyph: how could they have been represented by themselves as *crocodile's eyes?* But in the Ramesseum and elsewhere the crocodile appears with a head pointing upwards in company with couching lions, and the *eyes* of the crocodile are rendered specially prominent. Near this group it appears again in a curved position, and quite small, but this time in company with a scorpion which bears a disc of the sun. The former (κροκοδείλου δύο ἰφθαλμοί) seems to me to be a figure of the longest night, the latter (κροκόδειλος κεκυφώς in Horapollo) of the shortest, so that consequently ἀνατολή and δύσις do not refer to the rising and setting of the sun, but to the night as prevailing against or succumbing to the day (communicated by Lauth from his researches on the astronomical monuments). But since the growth of the day begins with the longest night, and *vice versâ*, the notions ἀνατολή and δύσις can, as it seems to me, retain their most natural signification ; and the crocodile's eyes are, notwithstanding, a figure of the light shining forth from the darkness, as the crocodile's tail signifies black darkness (and Egypt as the black land).

[2] Prof. Will refers the figure not to the third eyelid or the *membrana*

dile is itself a rose red; and therefore, considered in themselves, its eyes may also be compared with the "eyelids of
the dawn." What is then said, vers. 11–13, of the crocodile,
Achilles Tatius, iv. 2, says of the hippopotamus: μυκτὴρ ἐπὶ
μέγα κεχηνὼς καὶ πνέων πυρώδη καπνὸν ὡς ἀπὸ πηγῆς πυρός.
Bartram has observed on the alligator, that as it comes on the
land a thick smoke issues from its distended nostrils with a
thundering sound. This thick, hot steam, according to the
credible description which is presented here, produces the impression of a fire existing beneath, and bursting forth. The
subjective truth of this impression is faithfully but poetically
reproduced by the poet. On כּידוֹד (root כד, *escudere*), vid.
i. 408. הִתְמַלֵּט signifies no more than to disentangle one's
self, here therefore: to fly out in small particles. אֲגָמוֹן,
ver. 11b, is rendered by Saad., Gecat., and others, by *qumqum*
(קוּמְקוּם), a caldron; the modern expositors derive it from אגם
= *agama*, to glow, and understand it of a "heated caldron."
But the word signifies either heat or caldron; the latter signification, however, cannot be linguistically established; one
would look for אֵן (Arab. *iggâne*, a copper [Germ. *Wasch-
kessel*]). The noun אֲגְמוֹן signifies, ch. xl. 26, the reed σχοῖνος,
and in the Jerusalem Talmud, *Sota* ix. 12, some menial service (comp. Arab. *ugum*); Ew. rightly retains the former
signification, like a pot blown upon, *i.e.* fired, heated, and
beside it (in combination with it) reeds as fuel, which in
themselves, and especially together with the steaming water,
produce a thick smoke. The *Waw* is to be compared to the
Arabic *Waw concomitantiæ* (which governs the *acc.*).

nictitans, but to that spot on the *choroidea*, glistening with a metallic
lustre, which the crocodile has in common with most animals of the night
or the twilight, therefore to the brilliancy of its eye, which shines by
virtue of its lustrous coating; *vid.* the magnificent head of a crocodile in
Schlegel's *Amphibien-Abbildungen* (1837–44).

14 *Great strength resteth upon his neck,*
    And despair danceth hence before him.
15 *The flanks of his flesh are thickly set,*
    Fitting tightly to him, immoveable.
16 *His heart is firm like stone,*
    And firm like the nether millstone.
17 *The mighty are afraid of his rising up;*
    From alarm they miss their aim.

Overpowering strength lodges on its neck, *i.e.* has its
abiding place there, and before it despair, prop. melting away,
dissolution (דְּאָבָה from דָּאַב, نأب = دּُוב *Hiph.*, نأب II., to
bring into a loose condition, synon. הֵמֵס), dances hence, *i.e.*
springs up and away (יְדֹץ, Arab. *jadisu*, to run away), *i.e.* it
spreads before it a despondency which produces terror, and
deprives of strength. Even the pendulous fleshy parts (מַפְּלֵי),
especially of its belly, hang close together, דָּבְקוּ, *i.e.* they are
not flabby, but fit to it, like a metal casting, without moving,
for the skin is very thick and covered with thick scales;
and because the digestive apparatus of the animal occupies
but little space, and the scales of the back are continued
towards the belly, the tender parts appear smaller, narrower,
and closer together than in other animals. יָצוּק here is not,
as ch. xxviii. 2, xxix. 6, the *fut.* of יָצַק, but the *part.* of יָצַק,
as also ver. 16*ab* : its heart is firm and obdurate, as though
it were of cast brass, hard as stone, and in fact as the nether
millstone (פֶּלַח from פלח, *falacha*, to split, crush in pieces),
which, because it has to bear the weight and friction of the
upper, must be particularly hard. It is not intended of actual
stone-like hardness, but only of its indomitable spirit and
great tenacity of life : the activity of its heart is not so easily
disturbed, and even fatal wounds do not so quickly bring it
to a stand. מִשֵּׂתוֹ (from שֵׂת = שְׂאֵת = שְׂאֵת), primary form
שְׂאָה, is better understood in the active sense : afraid of its
rising, than the passive : of its exaltedness. אֵלִים (according ·

to another reading אֵלִים) is not, with Ew., to be derived from אַיִל (Arab. *ijal*), a ram; but אֵילִים Ex. xv. 15, Ezek. xvii. 13 (comp. גְּיָרִים 2 Chron. ii. 16, גִּירֵי 2 Sam. xxii. 29), אֵלִים Ezek. xxxi. 11, xxxii. 21, and אוּלִים *Cheth.* 2 Kings xxiv. 15, are only alternating forms and modes of writing of the participial adject., derived from אוּל (אֵיל) first of all in the primary form *awil* (as גֵּר = *gawir*). The signif. assigned to the verb אֵל: to be thick = fleshy, which is said then to go over into the signif. to be stupid and strong (Ges. *Handwörterb.*), rests upon a misconception: *âla* is said of fluids "to become thick," because they are condensed, since they go back, *i.e.* sink in or settle (Ges. correctly in *Thes.*: *notio crassitiei a retrocedendo*). The verb *âla*, *ja'ûlu*, unites in itself the significations to go backward, to be forward, and to rule; the last two: *anteriorem* and *superiorem esse*, probably belong together, and אֵל signifies, therefore, a possessor of power, who is before and over others. הִתְחַטֵּא, ver. 17*b*, has the signif., which does not otherwise occur, to miss the mark (from חטא, خَطِئَ, to miss, *opp.* صَابَ, to hit the mark), viz. (which is most natural where אֵילִים is the subject spoken of) since they had designed the slaughter and capture of the monster. שְׂבָרִים is intended subjectively, as תְּבִירָא = פַּחַד Ex. xv. 16, Targ. II., and also as the Arab. *thubûr*, employed more in reference to the mind, can be used of pain.

18 *If one reacheth him with the sword—it doth not hold;*
   Neither spear, nor dart, nor harpoon.
19 *He esteemeth iron as straw,*
   Brass as rotten wood.
20 *The son of the bow doth not cause him to flee,*
   Sling stones are turned to stubble with him.
21 *Clubs are counted as stubble,*
   And he laugheth at the shaking of the spear.

מַשִּׂיגֵהוּ, which stands first as *nom. abs.*, "one reaching him," is equivalent to, if one or whoever reaches him, Ew. § 357, *c*, to which בְּלִי תָקוּם, it does not hold fast (בְּלִי with *v. fin.*, as Hos. viii. 7, ix. 16, *Chethîb*), is the conclusion. חֶרֶב is instrumental, as Ps. xvii. 13. מַסָּע, from נָסַע, ٤ن, to move on, hasten on, signifies a missile, as Arab. *minz'a*, an arrow, *manz'a*, a sling. The Targ. supports this latter signification here (*funda quæ projicit lapidem*); but since קֶלַע, the handsling, is mentioned separately, the word appears to mean missiles in general, or the catapult. In this combination of weapons of attack it is very questionable whether שִׁרְיָה is a cognate form of שִׁרְיוֹן (שִׁרְיָן), a coat of mail; probably it is equivalent to Arab. *sirwe* (*surwe*), an arrow with a long broad edge (comp. *serîje*, a short, round, as it seems, pearshaped arrow-head), therefore either a harpoon or a peculiarly formed dart.[1] "The son of the bow" (and of the אַשְׁפָּה, *pharetra*) is the arrow. That the ἀπ. γεγρ. תּוֹתָח signifies a club (war-club), is supported by the Arab. *watacha*, to beat. כִּידוֹן (*vid.* i. 408), in distinction from חֲנִית (a long lance), is a short spear, or rather, since רַעַשׁ implies a whistling motion, a javelin. Iron the crocodile esteems as תֶּבֶן, *tibn*, chopped straw; sling stones are turned with him into קַשׁ. Such is the name here at least, not for stumps of cut stubble that remain standing, but the straw itself, threshed and easily driven before the wind (ch. xiii. 25), which is cut up for provender (Ex. v. 12), generally dried (and for that reason light) stalks (*e.g.* of grass), or even any remains of plants (*e.g.* splinters of wood).[2] The *plur.* נֶחְשְׁבוּ, ver. 21*a*,

---

[1] On the various kinds of Egyptian arrows, *vid.* Klemm. *Culturgeschichte*, v. 371 f.

[2] The Egyptio-Arabic usage has here more faithfully preserved the ancient signification of the word (*vid.* Fleischer, *Glossæ*, p. 37) than the Syro-Arabic; for in Syria cut but still unthreshed corn, whether lying in swaths out in the field and weighted with stones to protect it against the whirlwinds that are frequent about noon, or corn already

does not seem to be occasioned by תוחח being conceived
collectively, but by the fact that, instead of saying תוחח וכידון,
the poet has formed וכידון into a separate clause. Parchon's
(and Kimchi's) reading תוחה is founded upon an error.

> 22 *His under parts are the sharpest shards,*
> *He spreadeth a threshing sledge upon the mire.*
> 23 *He maketh the deep foam like a caldron,*
> *He maketh the sea like a pot of ointment.*
> 24 *He lighteth up the path behind him,*
> *One taketh the water-flood for hoary hair.*
> 25 *Upon earth there is not his equal,*
> *That is created without fear.*
> 26 *He looketh upon everything high,*
> *He is the king over every proud beast.*

Under it, or, תַּחְתָּיו taken like תַּחַת, ch. xli. 3, as a virtual
subject (*vid.* ch. xxviii. 5, p. 98): its under parts are the
most pointed or sharpest shards, *i.e.* it is furnished with
exceedingly pointed scales. חַדּוּד is the intensive form of חַד
(Arab. hadîd, sharpened = iron, p. 94, note), as חַלּוּק, 1 Sam.
xvii. 40, of חָלָק (smooth),[1] and the combination חַדּוּדֵי חֶרֶשׂ
(equal the combination חֲדוּדֵי הֲחֲרָשִׂים, comp. ch. xxx. 6) is
moreover superlative: in the domain of shards standing prominent as sharp ones, as Arab. *chairu ummatin,* the best
people, prop. *bon en fait de peuple* (Ew. § 313, *c, Gramm.
Arab.* § 532). LXX. ἡ στρωμνὴ αὐτοῦ ὀβελίσκοι ὀξεῖς, by
drawing יִרְפַּד to ver. 22a, and so translating as though it
were רִפְיָדתוֹ (Arab. *rifâde, stratum*). The verb רָפַד (*rafada*),

brought to the threshing-floors but not yet threshed, is called *qashsh.*—
WETZST.

[1] In Arabic also this substantival form is intensive, *e.g. lebbûn,* an
exceedingly large kind of tile, dried in the open air, of which farm-yards
are built, nearly eight times larger than the common tile, which is called
libne (לְבֵנָה).

cogn. רָבַד, signifies *sternere* (ch. xvii. 13), and then also *fulcire;* what is predicated cannot be referred to the belly of the crocodile, the scales of which are smooth, but to the tail with its scales, which more or less strongly protrude, are edged round by a shallow cavity, and therefore are easily and sharply separated when pressed; and the meaning is, that when it presses its under side in the morass, it appears as though a threshing-sledge with its iron teeth had been driven across it.

The pictures in ver. 23 are true to nature; Bartram, who saw two alligators fighting, says that their rapid passage was marked by the surface of the water as it were boiling. With מְצוּלָה, a whirlpool, abyss, depth (from צוּל = צָלַל, to hiss, clash; to whirl, surge), יָם alternates; the Nile even in the present day is called *bahr* (sea) by the Beduins, and also compared, when it overflows its banks, to a sea. The observation that the animal diffuses a strong odour of musk, has perhaps its share in the figure of the pot of ointment (LXX. ὥσπερ ἐξάλειπτρον, which Zwingli falsely translates *spongia*); a double gland in the tail furnishes the Egyptians and Americans their (pseudo) musk. In ver. 24*a* the bright white trail that the crocodile leaves behind it on the surface of the water is intended; in ver. 24*b* the figure is expressed which underlies the descriptions of the foaming sea with πολιός, *canus*, in the classic poets. שֵׂיבָה, hoary hair, was to the ancients the most beautiful, most awe-inspiring whiteness. מָשְׁלוֹ, ver. 25*a*, understood by the Targ., Syr., Arab. version, and most moderns (*e.g.* Hahn: there is not on earth any mastery over it), according to Zech. ix. 10, is certainly, with LXX., Jer., and Umbr., not to be understood differently from the Arab. *mithlahu* (its equal); whether it be an inflexion of מֹשֶׁל, or what is more probable, of מָשָׁל (comp. ch. xvii. 6, where this *nomen actionis* signifies a proverb = word of derision, and הִתְמַשֵּׁל, to compare one's self, be equal, ch. xxx. 19). עַל־עָפָר

is also Hebr.-Arab.; the Arabic uses *turbe*, formed from
turâb (*vid.* on ch. xix. 25), of the surface of the earth, and
et-tarbâ-u as the name of the earth itself. הָעָשׂוּי (for הֶעָשׂוּי,
as עָפִי, ch. xv. 22, *Cheth.* = עָפִי, resolved from עָשׂוּי, *'asûw*,
1 Sam. xxv. 18, *Cheth.*) is the confirmatory predicate of the
logical subj. described in ver. 25a as incomparable; and
לִבְלִי־חָת (from חַת, the *a* of which becomes *t* in inflexion),
absque terrore (comp. ch. xxxviii. 4), is virtually a nom. of the
predicate: the created one (becomes) a terrorless one (a being
that is terrified by nothing). Everything high, as the לְבַל־חַת,
ver. 25a, is more exactly explained, it looketh upon, *i.e.* remains standing before it, without turning away affrighted; in
short, it (the leviathan) is king over all the sons of pride, *i.e.*
every beast of prey that proudly roams about (*vid.* on ch.
xxviii. 8).

[Then Job answered Jehovah, and said:]
Ch. xlii. 2 *Now I know that Thou canst do all things,*
  And no plan is impracticable to Thee.
  3 " *Who then hideth counsel—*
  Without knowledge?"
  Thus have I judged without understanding,
  What was too wonderful for me, without knowing.

He indeed knew previously what he acknowledges in ver. 2,
but now this knowledge has risen upon him in a new divinely-
worked clearness, such as he has not hitherto experienced.
Those strange but wondrous monsters are a proof to him that
God is able to put everything into operation, and that the
plans according to which He acts are beyond the reach of
human comprehension. If even that which is apparently
most contradictory, rightly perceived, is so glorious, his
affliction is also no such monstrous injustice as he thinks; on
the contrary, it is a profoundly elaborated מְזִמָּה, a well-
digested, wise עֵצָה of God. In ver. 3 he repeats to himself the

chastening word of Jehovah, ch. xxxviii. 2, while he chastens himself with it; for he now perceives that his judgment was wrong, and that he consequently has merited the reproof. With לָכֵן 'he draws a conclusion from this confession which the chastening word of Jehovah has presented to him: he has rashly pronounced an opinion upon things that lie beyond his power of comprehension, without possessing the necessary capacity of judging and perception. On the mode of writing יָדַעְתִּ, *Cheth.*, which recalls the Syriac form *jed'et* (with the pronominal *suff.* cast off), *vid.* Ges. § 44, rem. 4; on the expression ver. 2*b*, comp. Gen. xi. 6. The repetition of ch. xxxviii. 2 in ver. 3 is not without some variations according to the custom of authors noticed in *Psalter*, i. 330. הִגַּדְתִּי, "I have affirmed," *i.e.* judged, is, ver. 3*c*, a closed thought, which, however, then receives its object, ver. 3*d*, so that the notion of judging goes over into that of pronouncing a judgment. The clauses with וְלֹא are circumstantial clauses, Ew. § 341, *a*.

> 4 *O hear now, and I will speak:*
> *I will ask Thee, and instruct Thou me.*
> 5 *I had heard of Thee by the hearing of the ear,*
> *And now mine eye hath seen Thee.*
> 6 *Therefore I am sorry, and I repent*
> *In dust and ashes.*

The words employed after the manner of entreaty, in ver. 4, Job also takes from the mouth of Jehovah, ch. xxxviii. 3, xl. 7. Hitherto Jehovah has interrogated him, in order to bring him to a knowledge of his ignorance and weakness. Now, however, after he has thoroughly perceived this, he is anxious to put questions to Jehovah, in order to penetrate deeper and deeper into the knowledge of the divine power and wisdom. Now for the first time with him, the true, living perception of God has its beginning, being no longer

382   THE BOOK OF JOB.

effected by tradition (לְ of the external cause: in consequence of the tidings which came to my ears, comp. Ps.
xviii. 45, comp. Isa. xxiii. 5), but by direct communication
with God. In this new light he can no longer deceive himself concerning God and concerning himself; the delusion
of the conflict now yields to the vision of the truth, and only
penitential sorrow for his sin towards God remains to him.
The object to אֶמְאַס is his previous conduct. נִחַם is the exact
expression for μετανοεῖν, the godly sorrow of repentance not
to be repented of. He repents (sitting) on dust and ashes
after the manner of those in deep grief.

If the second speech of Jehovah no longer has to do with
the exaltation and power of God in general, but is intended
to answer Job's doubt concerning the justice of the divine
government of the world, the long passage about the hippopotamus and the crocodile, ch. xl. 15–xli. 26, in this second
speech seems to be devoid of purpose and connection. Even
Eichhorn and Bertholdt on this account suppose that the
separate portions of the two speeches of Jehovah have fallen
into disorder. Stuhlmann, Bernstein, and De Wette, on the
other hand, explained the second half of the description of the
leviathan, ch. xli. 4–26, as a later interpolation; for this part
is thought to be inflated, and to destroy the connection between
Jehovah's concluding words, ch. xli. 2, 3, and Job's answer,
ch. xlii. 2–6. Ewald forcibly rejected the whole section,
ch. xl. 15–xli. 26, by ascribing it to the writer of Elihu's
speeches,—an opinion which he has again more recently
abandoned. In fact, this section ought to have had a third
poet as its writer. But he would be the double (*Doppel-
gänger*) of the first; for, deducting the somewhat tame לֹא
אַחֲרִישׁ בַּדָּיו, ch. xli. 4,—which, however, is introduced by
the interrupted description being resumed, in order now to
begin in real earnest,—this section stands upon an equally
exalted height with the rest of the book as a poetic production

and lofty description; and since it has not only, as also Elihu's speeches, an Arabizing tinge, but also the poetic genius, the rich fountain of thought, the perfection of technical detail, in common with the rest of the book; and since the writer of the book of Job also betrays elsewhere an acquaintance with Egypt, and an especial interest in things Egyptian, the authenticity of the section is by no means doubted by us, but we freely adopt the originality of its present position.

But before one doubts the originality of its position, he ought, first of all, to make an earnest attempt to comprehend the portion in its present connection, into which it at any rate has not fallen from pure thoughtlessness. The first speech of Jehovah, moreover, was surprisingly different from what was to have been expected, and yet we recognised in it a deep consistency with the plan; perhaps the same thing is also the case in connection with the second.

After Job has answered the first speech of Jehovah by a confession of penitence, the second can have no other purpose but that of strengthening the conviction, which urges to this confession, and of deepening the healthful tone from which it proceeds. The object of censure here is no longer Job's contending with Jehovah in general, but Job's contending with Jehovah on account of the prosperity of the evil-doer, which is irreconcilable with divine justice; that contending by which the sufferer, in spite of the shadow which affliction casts upon him, supported the assertion of his own righteousness. Here also, as a result, the refutation follows in the only way consistent with the dignity of Jehovah, and so that Job must believe in order to perceive, and does not perceive in order not to be obliged to believe. Without arguing the matter with Job, as to why many things in the government of the world are thus and not rather otherwise, Jehovah challenges Job to take the government of the world into his own hand, and to give free course to his wrath, to cast down everything that is exalted, and to render the evil-doer for ever harmless. By thus thinking of himself as the ruler of the world, Job is obliged to recognise the cutting contrast of his feebleness and the divine rule, with which he has ventured to find fault; at the same time, however, he is taught, that—what he would never be able to do —God really punishes the ungodly, and must have wise purposes when, which He indeed might do, He does not allow the floods of His wrath to be poured forth immediately.

Thus far also Simson is agreed; but what is the design of the description of the two Egyptian monsters, which are regarded by him as by Ewald as out of place here? To show Job how little capable he is of governing the world, and how little he would be in a position to execute judgment on the evil-doer, two creatures are described to him, two unslain monsters of gigantic structure and invincible strength, which defy all human attack. These two descriptions are, we think, designed to teach Job how little capable of passing sentence upon the evil-doer he is, who cannot even draw a cord through the nose of the behêmoth, and who, if he once attempted to attack the leviathan, would have reason to remember it so long as he lived, and would henceforth let it alone. It is perhaps an emblem that is not without connection with the book of Job, that these בהמות and לויתן (תנין), in the language of the Prophets and the Psalms, are the symbols of a worldly power at enmity with the God of redemption and His people. And wherefore should Job's confession, ch. xlii. 2, not be suitably attached to the completed description of the leviathan, especially as the description is divided into two parts by the utterances of Jehovah, ch. xli. 2, 3, which retrospectively and prospectively set it in the right light for Job?

THE UNRAVELMENT IN OUTWARD REALITY.—
CHAP. XLII. 7 SQQ.

Job's confession and tone of penitence are now perfected.
He acknowledges the divine omnipotence which acts according to a wisely-devised scheme, in opposition to his total
ignorance and feebleness. A world of divine wisdom, of
wondrous thoughts of God, now lies before him, concerning
which he knows nothing of himself, but would gladly learn
a vast amount by the medium of divine instruction. To
these mysteries his affliction also belongs. He perceives it
now to be a wise decree of God, beneath which he adoringly
bows, but it is nevertheless a mystery to him. Sitting in dust
and ashes, he feels a deep contrition for the violence with
which he has roughly handled and shaken the mystery,—
now will it continue, that he bows beneath the enshrouded
mystery? No, the final teaching of the book is not that
God's rule demands *faith* before everything else; the final
teaching is, that sufferings are for the righteous man the
way to glory, and that his faith is the way to sight. The
most craving desire, for the attainment of which Job hopes
where his faith breaks forth from under the ashes, is this,
that he will once more behold God, even if he should succumb to his affliction. This desire is granted him ere he
yields. For he who hitherto has only heard of Jehovah, can
now say: עתה עיני ראתך; his perception of God has entered
upon an entirely new stage. But first of all God has only
borne witness of Himself to him, to call him to repentance.
Now, however, since the rust of pollution is purged away
from Job's pure soul, He can also appear as his Vindicator
and Redeemer. After all that was sinful in his speeches is
blotted out by repentance, there remains only the truth of
his innocence, which God Himself testifies to him, and the

truth of his holding fast to God in the hot battle of temptation, by which, without his knowing it, he has frustrated the
design of Satan.

> Ver. 7. *And it came to pass, after Jehovah had spoken these
> words to Job, that Jehovah said to Eliphaz the Temanite,
> My wrath is kindled against thee and thy two friends: for
> ye have not spoken what is correct in reference to Me, as
> My servant Job.*

In order that they may only maintain the justice of God,
they have condemned Job against their better knowledge
and conscience; therefore they have abandoned truth in
favour of the justice of God,—a defence which, as Job has
told the friends, God abhors. Nevertheless He is willing to
be gracious.

> Ver. 8. *And now take unto you seven bullocks and seven
> rams, and go to My servant Job, and offer an offering for
> yourselves, and Job My servant shall pray for you; only
> his person will I accept, that I recompense not unto you
> your folly: for ye have not spoken what is correct in
> reference to Me, as My servant Job.*

Schlottm., like Ew., translates נְכוֹנָה what is sincere, and
understands it of Job's inward truthfulness, in opposition to
the words of the friends contrary to their better knowledge
and conscience. But נכון has not this signification anywhere:
it signifies either *directum* = *rectum* or *erectum* = *stabile*, but
not *sincerum*. However, objective truth and subjective truthfulness are here certainly blended in the notion "correct."
The "correct" in Job's speeches consists of his having denied
that affliction is always a punishment of sin, and in his holding fast the consciousness of his innocence, without suffering
himself to be persuaded of the opposite. That denial was
correct; and this truthfulness was more precious to God than

the untruthfulness of the friends, who were zealous for the honour of God.

After Job has penitently acknowledged his error, God decides between him and the friends according to his previous supplicatory wish, ch. xvi. 21. The heavenly Witness makes Himself heard on earth, and calls Job by the sweet name of עַבְדִּי. And the servant of Jehovah is not only favoured himself, but he also becomes the instrument of grace to sinners. As where his faith shone forth he became the prophet of his own and the friends' future, so now he is the priestly mediator between the friends and God. The friends against whom God is angry, but yet not as against רְשָׁעִים, but only as against those who have erred, must bring an offering as their atonement, in connection with which Job shall enter in with a priestly intercession for them, and only him (כִּי אִם, non alium sed = non nisi), whom they regarded as one punished of God, will God accept (comp. Gen. xix. 21)— under what deep shame must it have opened their eyes!

Here also, as in the introduction of the book, it is the עֹלָה which effects the atonement. It is the oldest and, according to its meaning, the most comprehensive of all the blood-offerings. Bullocks and rams are also the animals for the whole burnt-offerings of the Mosaic ritual; the proper animal for the sin-offering, however, is the he-goat together with the she-goat, which do not occur here, because the age and scene are strange to the Israelitish branching off of the חטאת from the עולה. The double seven gives the mark of the profoundest solemnity to the offering that was to be offered. The three also obey the divine direction; for although they have erred, God's will is above everything in their estimation, and they cheerfully subordinate themselves as friends to the friend.[1]

<hr/>

[1] Hence the Talmudic proverb (vid. Fürst's Perlenschnüre, S. 80): או חברא כחברי איוב או מיתותא, either a friend like Job's friends or death!

Ver. 9. *Then Eliphaz of Teman, and Bildad of Shuach,*
[and] Zophar of Naamah, went forth and did as Jehovah
had said to them; and Jehovah accepted the person of Job.

Jehovah has now risen up as a witness for Job, the spiritual
redemption is already accomplished ; and all that is wanting
is, that He who has acknowledged and testified to Job as His
servant should also act outwardly and visibly, and in mercy
show Himself the righteous One.

Ver. 10. *And Jehovah turned the captivity of Job, when he*
prayed for his friends; and Jehovah increased everything
that Job had possessed to the double.

רֵעֵהוּ is to be understood generally, as ch. xvi. 21, and the בְּ
signifies not " because," but " when." The moment in which
Job prayed for his friends became, as the climax of a life
that is well-pleasing with God, the turning-point of glory to
him. The Talmud has borrowed from here the true proverb :
כל־המתפלל בעד חברו נענה תחלה, *i.e.* he who prays for his fellow-
men always finds acceptance for himself first of all. The
phrase שׁוּב שְׁבוּת (שְׁבִית) signifies properly to turn captivity,
then in general to make an end of misery; also in German,
elend, old High Germ. *elilenti*, originally signified another,
foreign country (*vid. Psalter,* ii. 192), since an involuntary
removal from one's native land is regarded as the emblem of
a lamentable condition. This phrase does not exactly stamp
Job as the *Mashal* of the Israel of the Exile, but it favoured
this interpretation. Now when Job was recovered, and doubly
blessed by God, as is also promised to the Israel of the
Exile, Isa. lxi. 7 and freq., sympathizing friends also appeared
in abundance.

Ver. 11. *Then came to him all his brothers, and all his sisters,*
and all his former acquaintances, and ate bread with him

in his house, and expressed sympathy with him, and com-
forted him concerning all the evil which Jehovah had
brought upon him; and each one gave him a Kesitá, and
each a golden ring.

Prosperity now brought those together again whom calamity
had frightened away; for the love of men is scarcely anything
but a number of coarse or delicate shades of selfishness. Now
they all come and rejoice at Job's prosperity, viz. in order to
bask therein. He, however, does not thrust them back; for
the judge concerning the final motives of human love is God,
and love which is shown to us is certainly more worthy of
thanks than hatred. They are his guests again, and he
leaves them to their own shame. And now their tongues,
that were halting thus far, are all at once become eloquent:
they mingle congratulations and comfort with their expressions of sorrow at his past misfortune. It is now an easy
matter, that no longer demands their faith. They even bring
him each one a present. In everything it is manifest that
Jehovah has restored His servant to honour. Everything is
now subordinated to him, who was accounted as one forsaken
of God. קְשִׂיטָה is a piece of metal weighed out, of greater
value than the shekel, moreover indefinite, since it is nowhere
placed in the order of the Old Testament system of weights
and measures, adapted to the patriarchal age, Gen. xxxiii. 19,
in which Job's history falls.[1] נְזָמִים are rings for the nose
and ear; according to Ex. xxxii. 3, an ornament of the women
and men.

The author now describes the manner of Job's being
blessed.

---

[1] According to *b. Rosch ha-Schana*, 26a, R. Akiba found the word קְשִׂיטָה
in Africa in the signification מָעָה (coin), as a Targ. (*vid.* Aruch, *s.v.*
קְשִׂיטָה) also translates; the Arab. *qist* at least signifies balances and
weight.

Ver. 12. *And Jehovah blessed Job's end more than his begin-ning; and he had fourteen thousand sheep and six thousand camels, and a thousand yoke of oxen and a thousand she-asses.*

The numbers of the stock of cattle, ch. i. 3,[1] now appear doubled, but it is different with the children.

Ver. 13. *And he had seven sons and three daughters.*

Therefore, instead of the seven sons and three daughters which he had, he receives just the same again, which is also so far a doubling, as deceased children also, according to the Old Testament view, are not absolutely lost, 2 Sam. xii. 23. The author of this book, in everything to the most minute thing consistent, here gives us to understand that with men who die and depart from us the relation is different from that with things which we have lost. The pausal שִׁבְעָנָה (instead of שִׁבְעָה), with paragogic *âna*, which otherwise is a *fem. suff.* (Ges. § 91, rem. 2), here, however, standing in a

---

[1] Job, like all the wealthier husbandmen in the present day, kept she-asses, although they are three times dearer than the male, because they are useful for their foals; it is not for the sake of their milk, for the Semites do not milk asses and horses. Moreover, the foals are also only a collateral gain, which the poor husbandman, who is only able to buy a he-ass, must forego. What renders this animal indispensable in husbandry is, that it is the common and (since camels are extremely rare among the husbandmen) almost exclusive means of transport. How would the husbandman, *e.g.*, be able to carry his seed for sowing to a field perhaps six or eight miles distant? Not on the plough, as our farmers do, for the plough is transported on the back of the oxen in Syria. How would he be able to get the corn that was to be ground (*tachne*) to the mill, per-haps a day's journey distant; how carry wood and grass, how get the manure upon the field in districts that require to be manured, if he had not an ass? The camels, on the other hand, serve for harvesting (*ragâd*), and the transport of grain (*ghalle*), chopped straw (*tibn*), fuel (*hatab*), and the like, to the large inland towns, and to the seaports. Those village communities that do not possess camels for this purpose, hire them of the Arabs (nomads).—WETZST.

prominent position, is an embellishment somewhat violently brought over from the style of the primeval histories (Gen. xxi. 29; Ruth i. 19): a septiad of sons. The names of the sons are passed over in silence, but those of the daughters are designedly given.

Ver. 14. *And the one was called Jemîma, and the second Kezia, and the third Keren ha-pûch.*

The subject of וַיִּקְרָא is each and every one, as Isa. ix. 5 (comp. *supra*, ch. xli. 25, *existimaverit quis*). The one was called יְמִימָה (Arab. *jemâme*, a dove) on account of her dove's eyes; the other קְצִיעָה, cassia, because she seemed to be woven out of the odour of cinnamon; and the third קֶרֶן הַפּוּךְ, a horn of paint (LXX. Hellenizing: κέρας ἀμαλθείας), which is not exactly beautiful in itself, but is the principal cosmetic of female beauty (*vid.* Lane, *Manners and Customs of the Modern Egyptians*, transl.): the third was altogether the most beautiful, possessing a beauty heightened by artificial means. They were therefore like three graces. The writer here keeps to the outward appearance, not disowning his Old Testament standpoint. That they were what their names implied, he says in

Ver. 15. *And in all the land there were not found women so fair as the daughters of Job: and their father gave them inheritance among their brothers.*

On וַיִּמָּצֵא, followed by the *acc.*, *vid.* Ges. § 143, 1, *b.* לָהֶם, etc., referring to the daughters, is explained from the deficiency in Hebrew in the distinction of the genders. Ver. 15*b* sounds more Arabian than Israelitish, for the Thora only recognises a daughter as heiress where there are no sons, Num. xxvii. 8 sqq. The writer is conscious that he is writing an extra-Israelitish pre-Mosaic history. The equal distribution of the property again places before our eyes the pleasing picture of family concord in the commencement of the history; at the same time it implies that Job will not have been wanting in sons-in-law for his fair, richly-dowried daughters,—a fact which ver. 16 establishes:

> *And Job lived after this a hundred and forty years, and saw his children and his children's children to four generations.*

In place of יֵרֶא, the *Keri* gives the unusual Aorist form וַיִּרְאֶה, which, however, does also occur elsewhere (*e.g.* 1 Sam. xvii. 42). The style of the primeval histories, which we here everywhere recognise, Gen. l. 23 (comp. Isa. liii. 10), is retained to the last words.

Ver. 17. *And Job died, old, and weary of life.*

In the very same manner Genesis, xxv. 8, xxxv. 29, records the end of the patriarchs. They died satiated of life; for long life is a gift of God, but neither His greatest nor His final gift.

A New Testament poet would have closed the book of Job differently. He would have shown us how, becoming free from his inward conflict of temptation, and being divinely comforted, Job succumbs to his disease, but waves his palm of victory before the throne of God among the innumerable hosts of those who have washed their robes and made them white in the blood of the Lamb. The Old Testament poet, however, could begin his book with a celestial scene, but not end it with the same. True, in some passages, which are like New Testament luminous points in the Old Testament poem, Job dares to believe and to hope that God will indeed acknowledge him after death. But this is a purely individual aspiration of faith—the extreme of hope, which comes forth against the extreme of fear. The unravelment does not correspond to this aspiration. The view of heaven which a Christian poet would have been able to give at the close of the book is only rendered possible by the resurrection and ascension of Christ. So far, what Oehler in his essay on the Old Testament Wisdom (1854, S. 28) says, in opposition to those who think the book of Job is directed against the Mosaic doctrine of retribution, is true: that, on the contrary, the issue of the book sanctions the present life phase of this doctrine anew. But the comfort which this theologically and artistically incomparable book presents to us is substantially none other than that of the New Testament. For the final consolation of every sufferer is not dependent upon the working of good genii in the heavens, but has its seat in God's love, without which even heaven would become a very hell. Therefore the book of Job is also a book of consolation for the New Testament church. From it we learn that we have not only to fight with flesh and blood, but with the prince of this world, and to accomplish our part in the conquest of evil, to which, from Gen. iii. 15 onwards, the history of the world tends; that faith and avenging justice are absolutely distinct opposites; that the right kind of faith clings to divine love in the midst of the feeling of wrath; that the incomprehensible ways of God always lead to a glorious issue; and that the suffering of the present time is far outweighed by the future glory—a glory not always revealed in this life and visibly future, but the final glory above. The nature of faith, the mystery of the cross, the right practice of the care of souls,—this, and much besides, the church learns from this book, the whole teaching of which can never be thoroughly learned and completely exhausted.

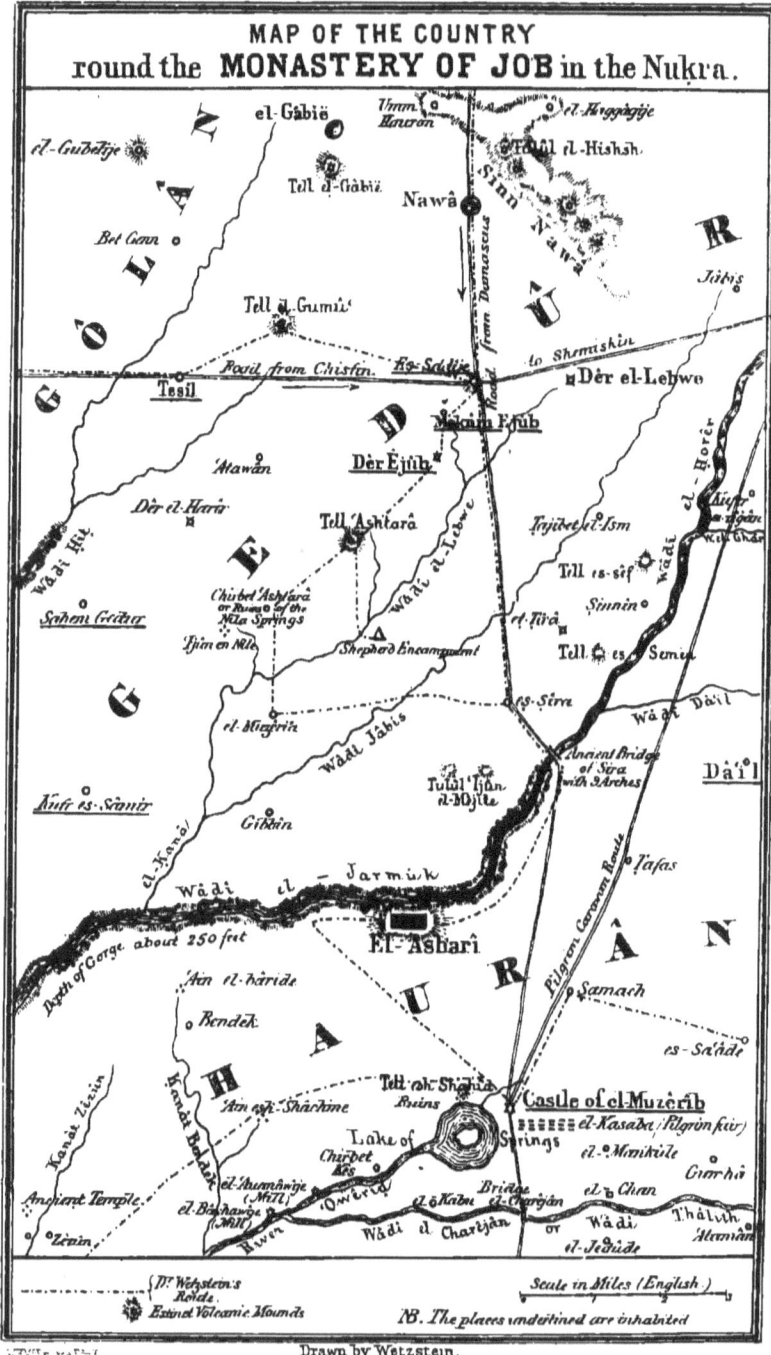

MAP OF THE COUNTRY
round the **MONASTERY OF JOB** in the Nukra.

Drawn by Wetzstein.

APPENDIX.

THE MONASTERY OF JOB IN HAURAN, AND THE TRADITION OF JOB.

(WITH A MAP OF THE DISTRICT.)

BY J. G. WETZSTEIN.

THE oral tradition of a people is in general only of very subordinate value from a scientific point of view when it has reference to an extremely remote past; but that of the Arabs especially, which is always combined with traditions and legends, renders the simplest facts perplexing, and wantonly clothes the images of prominent persons in the most wonderful garbs, and, in general, so rapidly disfigures every object, that after a few generations it is no longer recognisable. So far as it has reference to the personality of Job, whose historical existence is called in question or denied by some expositors, it may be considered as altogether worthless, but one can recognise when it speaks of Job's native country. By the אֶרֶץ עוּץ the writer of the book of Job meant a definite district, which was well known to the people for whom he wrote; but the name has perished, like many others, and all the efforts of archæologists to assign to the land its place in the map of Palestine have been fruitless. Under these circumstances the matter is still open to discussion, and the tradition respecting Job has some things to authorize it.

True, it cannot of itself make up for the want of an historical testimony, but it attains a certain value if it is old, *i.e.* if
it can be traced back about to the time of the destruction of
Jerusalem by the Romans, when reliable information was
still obtainable·respecting that district, although its name was
no longer in use.

In all the larger works of travel on Palestine and Syria,
we find it recorded that Haurân is there called Job's fatherland. In Hauran itself the traveller hears this constantly;
if any one speaks of the fruitfulness of the whole district, or
of the fields around a village, he is always answered: Is it
not the land of Job (*bilâd Êjûb*)? Does it not belong to
the villages of Job (*diâ' Êjûb*)? Thus to Seetzen[1] *Bosrâ*
was pointed out as a city of Job; and to Eli Smith[2] even the
country lying to the east of the mountains was called the
land of Job. In *Kanawat*, a·very spacious building, belonging to the Roman or Byzantine period, situated in the
upper town, was pointed out to me as the summer palace of
Job (the inscription 8799 in *Corp. Inscr. Græc.* is taken from
it). The shepherds of *Dâ'il*, with whom I passed a night on
the *Wâdi el-Lebwe*, called the place of their encampment
Job's pasture-ground. In like manner, the English traveller
Buckingham, when he wandered through the *Nukra*, was
shown in the distance the village of *Gherbi* (*i.e. Chirbet el-
ghazale*, which from its size is called *el-chirbe* κατ' ἐξοχήν)
as the birthplace and residence of Job,[3] and it seems altogether as though Hauran and the Land of Job are
synonymous. But if one inquires particularly for that part
of the country in which Job himself dwelt, he is directed
to the central point of Hauran, the plain of Hauran (*sahl*

---

[1] Seetzen, *Reisen durch Syrien*, etc., i. 66.

[2] Ed. Robinson, *Palästina*, iii. 911 [Germ. edit.].

[3] C. Ritter, *Geogr. von Syr. u. Pal.* ii. 842 [= *Erdkunde*, xv. Pt. 2,
p. 842].

Haurân),[1] and still more exactly to the district between the towns of *Nawâ* and *Edre'ât*, which is accounted the most fertile portion of the country, covered with the ruins of villages, monasteries, and single courts, and is even now comparatively well cultivated. Among the nomads as well as among the native agricultural population, this district is called from its formation *Nukra* or *Nukrat esh-Shâm*,[2] a name by which this highly-favoured plain is known and celebrated by the poets in the whole Syrian desert, as far as 'Irâk and *Higâz*.

But even the national writers are acquainted with and frequently make mention of the Hauranitish tradition of Job; yet they do not call Job's home *Nukra*,—for this word, which belongs only to the idiom of the steppe, is unknown to the literature of the language,—but *Bethenîje* (*Batanœa*). It is so called in a detailed statement of the legends of Job:[3] After the death of his father, Job journeyed into Egypt[4] to marry *Rahme* (רַחְמָה) the daughter of Ephraim, who had inherited from her grandfather Joseph the robe of beauty; and after he had brought her to his own country, he received from God a mission as prophet to his countrymen, viz. to the inhabitants of Haurân and Batanœa (بعثه الله تع رسولا الى قومه وهم اهل حوران والبثنية). The historian of Jerusalem, Mugîr ed-dîn el-*H*ambeli, in the chapter on the legends of the prophets, says: "Job came from *el-'Ês*,

---

[1] Whether the word מִישֹׁר, Deut. iii. 10, only signifies the plain of Hauran or its southern continuation, the eastern *Belkâ*, may be doubtful, because in that passage both the Amorite kingdoms are spoken of. But since it is the "cities" of the plain, of which the eastern Belkâ can have had but few or none, that are spoken of, מִישֹׁר will surely exclude the latter.

[2] On this name, which belongs to the modern geography of the country, comp. my *Reisebericht über Hauran u. d. Trachonen*, S. 87.

[3] Catalogue of Arab. MSS. collected in Damascus by J. G. Wetzstein. Berlin 1863, No. 46, p. 56.

[4] [The connection with Egypt, in which these legends place Job, is worthy of observation.—DEL.]

and the Damascene province of Batanæa was his property."
In like manner, in the *Geography* of Jâkût el-*H*amawi,[1]
under the art. *Bethenîje*, it is said: "and in this land lived
Job (*wakân Êjûb minhâ*)."

Modern exegetes, as is known, do not take the plain of
Hauran, but the mountain range of Hauran with its eastern
slope, as the *Provincia Batanæa*. I have sought elsewhere[2] to
show the error of this view, and may the more readily confine
myself to merely referring to it, as one will be convinced of
the correctness of my position in the course of this article.
One thing, however, is to be observed here, that the supposition
that Basan is so called as being the land of basalt rocks, is an
untenable support of this error. The word basalt may be
derived from Βασάντις, or a secondary formation, Βασάλτις,
because Basan is exclusively volcanic;[3] but we have no more
right to reverse the question, than to say that Damascus may
have received its name from the manufacture of damask.[4]

---

[1] Orient. MSS. in the Royal Library in Berlin, Sect. Sprenger, No.
7-10.

[2] *Reisebericht*, S. 83-87.

[3] *Vid.* vol. ii. p. 91, comp. p. 93, note 2, of the foregoing Commentary.

[4] In the fair at *Muzêrib* we again saw the sheikh of the *Wêsîje*-Beduins,
whose guest we had been a week before at the Springs of Joseph in
western *Gôlân*, where he had pitched his tent on a wild spot of ground
that had been traversed by lava-streams. In answer to our question
whether he still sojourned in that district, he said: "No, indeed! *Nâzilin
el-jôm bi-ard bethêne shêle* (we are now encamped in a district that is
completely *bethêne*)." I had not heard this expression before, and inquired what it meant. The sheikh replied: *bethêne* (بَثَيْنَة) is a stoneless plain covered with rich pasture. I often sought information
respecting this word, since I was interested about it on account of the
Hebrew word בָּשָׁן, and always obtained the same definition. It is a
diminutive form, without having exactly a diminutive signification, for
in the language of the nomads it is an acknowledged fact that such a
form takes the place of the usual form. The usual form is either *bathne*
or *bathane*. The *K*âmûs gives the former signification, "a level country."
That the explanation of the Kamus is too restricted, and that of the
Sheikh of Wêsîje the more complete, may be shown from the Kamus

The home of Job is more definitely described in the following passages. Mu*h*ammed el-Ma*k*deshi[1] says, p. 81 of his
geography: "And in *H*aurân and Batanæa lie the villages
of Job and his home (diá' Êjûb wa-diáruh). The chief place
(of the district) is Nawâ, rich in wheat and other cereals."
The town of Nawâ is still more definitely connected with
Job by Jâkût el-*H*amawi under the article *Nawâ:* "Between Nawa and Damascus is two days' journey; it belongs
to the district of *H*auran,[2] and is, according to some, the

itself. In one place it says, The word moreover signifies (*a*) the thick of
the milk (cream); (*b*) a tender maiden; (*c*) repeated acts of benevolence.
These three significations given are, however, manifestly only figurative
applications, not indeed of the signification which the Kamus places *primo
loco*, but of that which the Sheikh of the Wêsije gave; for the likening
of a "voluptuously formed maiden," or of repeated acts of benevolence,
to a luxurious meadow, is just as natural to a nomad, as it was to the
shepherd Amos (ch. iv. 1) to liken the licentious women of Samaria to
well-nourished cows of the fat pastures of Basan. Then the Kamus

brings forward a collective form *buthun* (بُثُن,) perhaps from the sing.

bathan = בָּשָׁן, like اَسَد from *asad*) in the signification pastures (رِياض);
pastures, however, that are damp and low, with a rich vegetation. That
the word is ancient, may be seen from the following expression of
Châlid ibn el-Weltd, the victor on the Jarmûk: "'Omar made me
governor of Damascus; and when I had made it into a *buthêne*, *i.e.* a
stoneless fertile plain (easy to govern and profitable), he removed me."
Jâkût also mentions this expression under *Bethenîje.* Châlid also uses
the diminutive as the nomads do (he was of the race of Machzûm); probably the whole word belongs only to the steppe, for all the women who
were called *buthêne*, *e.g.* the beloved of the poet Gemîl, and others mentioned in the "Diwân of Love" (*Diwân es-sabâbe*), were Beduin women.
After what has been said, we cannot assign to the Hebr. בָּשָׁן any other
signification than that of a fertile stoneless plain or low country. This
appellation, which was given, properly and originally, only to the heart
of the country, and its most valuable portion, viz. the Nu*k*ra, would then
a potiori be transferred to the whole, and when the kingdom of
Basan was again destroyed, naturally remained to that province, of
which it was the proper designation.

[1] Orient. MSS. in the Royal Library at Berlin; Sect. Sprenger, No. 5.
[2] If writers mention Haurân alone, they mean thereby, according to
the usage of the language of the Damascenes, and certainly also of the

chief town of the same. Nawâ was the residence (*menzil*) of Job;" and Ibn er-Râbi says, p. 62 of his essay on the excellences of Damascus:[1] "To the prophets buried in the region of Damascus belongs also Job, and his tomb is near Nawâ, in the district of Hauran." Such passages prove at the same time the identity of the Nu*k*ra with Batanæa; for if the latter is said to be recognisable from the fact of Job's home being found in it, and we find this sign in connection with the Nu*k*ra in which Nawâ with its surrounding country is situated, both names must denote one and the same district.

That, according to the last citation, Job's tomb is also shown in the Nu*k*ra, has been already observed in my *Reisebericht*, . S. 121. Jâkût, under *Dêr Êjûb*, thus expresses himself: "The Monastery of Job is a locality in Hauran, a Damascene province, in which Job dwelt and was tried of God. There also is the fountain which he made to flow with his foot, and the block of rock on which he leant. There also is his tomb." What *K*azwîni says in his *Wonders of Creation* ('*agâib el-machlûkât*), under *Dêr Êjûb*, accords with it: "The Monastery of Job lies in one of the Damascene provinces, and was the place of Job's residence, in which God tried him. There

prophet Ezekiel (ch. xlvii. 16, 18), the plain of Haurân as far as the borders of the Bel*k*â, including the mountains of Haurân, the Legâ, and Gêdûr ; it is only in the district itself, where special divisions are rendered necessary, that the three last mentioned parts are excluded. If writers mention Haurân and *Bethenîje* together, the context must determine whether the former signifies the whole, and the latter the part, as in the above quotation from Ma*k*deshi, or whether both are to be taken as co-ordinate, as in a passage of Is*t*achri (edited by Möller, Gotha 1839) : "And *H*aurân and Bethenîje are two provinces of Damascus with luxuriant corn-fields." Here the words are related to one another as Auranitis (with the chief town Bostra) to Batanæa (with the chief town Adratum, *i.e.* *Edrê'ât*), or as the *H*aurân of the Beduins and the Nu*k*ra of the same. The boundary between both is the *Wâdi 'Irâ*, which falls into the *Zêdi* south of *Edrê'ât*.

[1] Catalogue of Arab. MSS. collected in Damascus, No. 26.

also is the fountain which sprang forth at the stamping of his foot, when at the end of his trial God commanded him, and said: Strike with thy foot—(thus a fountain will spring forth, and) this shall be to thee a cool bath and a draught (*Korân*, xxxviii. 41 sqq.). There is also the rock on which he sat, and his tomb." Recurring to the passage of the Koran cited, we shall see that the stone of Job, the fountain and the tomb, are not situated in the Monastery itself, but at some little distance from it.

I came with my *cortége* out of Gôlân, to see the remarkable pilgrim fair of *Muzérib*, just when the Mekka caravan was expected; and since the Monastery of Job, never visited by any one now-a-days, could not lie far out of the way, I determined to seek it out, because I deluded myself with the hope of finding an inscription of its founder, 'Amr I., and in fact one with a date, which would have been of the greatest importance in reference to the history of the Ghassanides,—a hope which has remained unfulfilled. In the evening of the 8th of May we came to *Tesîl*. Here the Monastery was for the first time pointed out to us. It was lighted up by the rays of the setting sun,—a stately ruin, which lay in the distance a good hour towards the east. The following morning we left Tesîl. Our way led through luxuriant corn-fields and fields lying fallow, but decked with a rich variety of flowers in gayest blossom, to an isolated volcanic mound, *Tell el-Gumú'*,[1] from which we intended to reconnoitre the surrounding country. From this point, as far as the eye could reach, it swept over fields of wheat belonging to the communities of *Sahm*, *Tell Shihâb*, *Tesîl*, *Nawâ*, and *Sa'dîje*, which covered a region which tradition calls the home of Job. True, the volcanic chaos (*el-wa'r*) extended in the west to the distance

---

1 " Hill of the heaps of riders." The hill is said to have been named after a great engagement which took place there in ancient days. Among the 'Aneze the *geni'*, ﻮ, plur. *gumú'*, is a division of 400-600 horsemen.

of some three miles up the hill on which we stood, and on
the north the plain was bounded partly by *Tell el-Gâbŭa* and
the "tooth of Nawâ" (*sinn Nawâ*), a low ridge with a few
craters; but towards the E. and S. and S.W. the plain was
almost unbounded, for isolated eminences, as *Tell 'Ashtarâ,
T. Ash'arî, T. Shihâb, T. el-Chammân*, and others, rose above
the level of the plain only like mole-hills; and the deep gorges
of the *Meddân, Jarmûk*, Hît, and *Muchébi*, were sudden and
almost perpendicular ravines, either not seen at all, or appeared as dark marks. The plain slopes gently and scarcely
perceptibly towards *Kufr el-mâ, Kufr es-sâmir, Zézûn*, and
Bendek; and the *Naher el-'Owérid*, a river abounding in
water in its level bed, resembles a glistening thread of silver.
If this district had trees, as it once had,—for among the ruins
one often discovers traces of vineyards and garden walls,
which it can have no longer, since the insecurity and injustice
of the country do not admit of men remaining long in one
and the same village, therefore not to take hold upon the soil
and establish one's self, and become at home anywhere,—it
would be an earthly paradise, by reason of its healthy climate
and the fertility of its soil. That even the Romans were
acquainted with the glorious climate of Hauran, is proved by
the name *Palæstina salutaris*, which they gave to the district.[1]
The inhabitants of Damascus say there is no disease whatever
in Haurân; and as often as the plague or any other infectious
disease shows itself in their city, thousands flee to Hauran,
and to the lava-plateau of the Legâ. This healthy condition
may arise from the volcanic formation of the country, and
from the sea-breeze, which it always has in connection with

[1] This appellation is erroneously given to the province of Petra
(*Palæstina tertia*) in Burckhardt's Travels (Gesenius' edition, S. 676).
Böcking also, *Not. dign. or.* pp. 189, 345, and 873, is guilty of this
oversight. Comp. thereon, Mommsen, *Verzeichniss der röm. Provinzen
aufgesetzt um*, 297, in the *Transactions of the Berlin Acad. der Wissensch.*
1862, S. 501 f.

its position, which is open towards the west. Even during the hottest days, when *e.g.* in the *Ghûta* a perfect calm prevails, so that no breeze is felt, this cool and moist sea-breeze blows refreshingly and regularly over the plain; and hence the Hauranitish poet never speaks of his native country without calling it the "cool-blowing Nukra" (*en-nukra el-'adîje*). But as to the fertility of the district, there is indeed much good arable land in the country east of the Jordan, as in *Irbid* and *Suwêt*, of the same kind as between *Salt* and *'Ammân*, but nowhere is the farming, in connection with a small amount of labour (since no manure is used), more productive than in Hauran, or more profitable; for the transparent "Batanæan wheat" (*hinta bethenîje*) is always at least 25 per cent. higher in price than other kinds. Hence the agriculture of that region also, in times of peace and security (during the first six centuries after Christ), produced that fondness for building, some of the magnificent memorials of which are our astonishment in the present day; and, in fact, not unfrequently the inscriptions testify that the buildings themselves owe their origin to the produce of the field. Thus, in the locality of *Nâhite* in the Nukra, I found the following fragment of an inscription: ... Μασαλέμου Ράββου κτίσμα ἐξ ἰδίων κόπων γεωργικῶν ἐν ἔτι σπ, Masalemos son of Rabbos set up (this memorial) out of the produce of his farming in the year 280. Of a like kind is the following remains of two distichs in Murduk: ... δρός τε σαόφρων | ... μεγαρόν | ... ισ ἀνάπαυμα μέγιστον | ... γεωπονίης. In *Shakkâ* the longer inscription of a mausoleum in a state of good preservation begins:

Βάσσος ἐῆς πάτρης μεγακύδεος ἀγλαὸν ὄμμα
'Εκ σφετέρου καμάτοιο γεωπονίης τέ μ' ἔδειμεν.

Bassos, beaming eye of the honourable city of his birth,
Has built me out of the produce of his own tillage.

Similar testimonies are to be found in the inscriptions in Burckhardt.

After a long sojourn on the hill, which was occasioned by the investigation of some interesting plants in the crater of the mound, we set out for *Sa'dĳe*, which is built on the slope of a hill. After a good hour's journey we arrived at the *Makâm Êjûb*, "the favoured tomb of Job," situated at the southern base of the hill, and rendered conspicuous by two white domes, and there we dismounted. The six attendants and alumni of the Makâm, or, as the Arabs thoughtfully call them, "the servants of our master Job" (*châdimîn sêjidna Êjûb*), received us, with some other pilgrims, at the door of the courtyard, and led us to the basin of the fountain of Job, by the side of which they spread out their mantles for us to rest upon under the shade of a walnut tree and a willow. While the rest were engaged in the duties of hospitality, the superior of the Makâm, the Sheikh Sa'îd el-Darfûri (from Darfûr) did not leave us, and made himself in every way obliging. Like him, all the rest of the inhabitants of the place were black, and all unmarried; their celibacy, however, I imagine, was only caused by the want of opportunity of marrying, and the limited accommodation of `the place. Sheikh Sa'îd believed himself to be fifty years of age; he left his home twenty years before to go on pilgrimage to Mekka, where he "studied" four years; the same length of time he sojourned in Medîna, and had held his present office ten years. Besides his mother tongue, he spoke Arabic and a little Turkish, having been in Constantinople a few years before. His judgment of the inhabitants of that city is rather harsh: he charges them with immorality, drunkenness, and avarice. In one year, said he, I could hardly save enough to travel by the steamer to Chôdscha Bêk (Odessa). How different was my experience of the inhabitants of this city! I was there three months, during which time I had nothing to provide for, and left with ninety *Mânôt* (imperials), which just sufficed to set up these dilapidated relics again. A Russian ship brought me to Smyrna, whence I travelled by the *Nemsâwi* (Austrian Lloyd steamer) to Syria.

According to the account given by the inhabitants of Sa'dîje, the Makâm has been from ancient times a negro hospice. These Africans, commonly called '*Abîd* in Damascus, and in the country *Tekârine*, come chiefly from Tekrûr in Sûdân ; they first visit Mekka and Medîna, then Damascus, and finally the Makâm of Job. Here they sojourn from twenty to thirty days, during which time they wash themselves daily in Job's fountain, and pray upon Job's stone; and the rest of the day they either read or assist the dwellers in the Makâm in their tillage of the soil. When they are about to leave, they receive a testimonial, and often return home on foot across the Isthmus of Suez, often by water, chiefly from Jâfâ, by the Austrian Lloyd ship to Egypt, and thence to their native country. These pilgrims, so far as the requirements of their own country are concerned, are *literati;* and it appears as though by this journey they obtained their highest degree. I have frequently met them in my travels. They are known by their clean white turban, and the white broad-sleeved shirt, which reaches to the ankles, their only garment. They carry a small bundle over the shoulder upon a strong staff, which may serve as a weapon of defence in case of need. In this bundle they carry a few books and other effects, and above this their cloak. They are modest, taciturn men, who go nimbly onward on their way, and to whom one always gladly gives a supper and a night's lodging.

We visited the holy places in the company of the Sheikh Sa'îd. The Makâm, and the reservoir, which lies fifty paces to the front of it, are surrounded by a wall. This reservoir is filled by a strong, rapid, and cold stream of water, which comes from the fountain of Job, about 400 paces distant. The fountain itself springs up by the basalt hill on which the village and the Job's stone are situated; and it is covered in as far as the reservoir (called *birke*), in order to keep the water fresh, and to guard against pollution. Between the fountain and the Makâm stand a half-dozen acacias and a pomegranate, which were just then in full bloom. The Makâm itself, on which the wretched habitations for the attendants and pilgrims adjoin, is a one-storey stone building, of old material and moderate circumference. The first thing shown us was the stone trough, called *gurn*, in which Job bathed at the end of his trial. The small space in which this relic stands, and over which, so far as I remember, one of the two domes is raised, is called *wadjet sêjidnâ Êjûb*, "the lavatory of our lord Job." Adjoining this is the part with the tomb, the oblong mound of which is covered with an old torn green cloth. The tomb of *Sa'd* was more carefully tended. Our Damascene travelling companions were divided in their opinions as to the person whose tomb was near that of Job, as in Syria it is hardly possible to find and distinguish the makâms of the many men of God (*rigâl Allâh*) or favoured ones of God (*auliâ*) who bear the same names; but a small white flag standing upon the grave informed us, for it bore the inscription : "This is the military emblem (*râje*) of our lord *Sa'd abû Merzûka.*"

Perhaps the preservation of the Makâm of Job is due to the tomb of Sa'd, as its endowments have long since disappeared, while the tomb of Sa'd still has its revenues. From 'Aglûn it receives tribute of oil and olives yearly. And several large vegetable gardens, which lie round about the Makâm, and are cultivated by its attendants, must also contribute something considerable towards its maintenance. In these gardens they grow *dura* (maize), tobacco, turnips, onions, and other things, for their own use and for sale.

The plants, which can be freely watered from the fountain of Job, are highly esteemed. The government levies no taxes on the Makâm, and the Arabs no tribute; and since, according to the popular belief, the Beduin horse that is watered from the *birke* dies, the Beduins do not even claim the rights of hospitality,—a fortunate circumstance, the removal of which would speedily cause the ruin of the hospice. From nightly thieves, who not unfrequently break through the walls of the stables in the villages of the plain, and carry off the smaller cattle, both the Makâm and the village are secure; for if the night thieves come, they see, as every one in Hauran testifies, a surging sea around the place, which prevents their approach.

From the Makâm we ascended the hill of the village, on the highest part of which is the stone of Job (*Sachrat Êjûb*). It is inside a small Mussulman hall of prayer, which in its present form is of more modern origin, but is undoubtedly built from the material of a Christian chapel, which stood here in the pre-Muhammedan age. It is an unartistic structure, in the usual Hauranitish style, with six or eight arches and a small dome, which is just above the stone of Job. My Mussulman attendants, and a Hauranite Christian from the village of Shemiskîn, who had joined us as we were visiting the *Sachra*, trod the sacred spot with bare feet, and kissed the rock, the basaltic formation of which is unmistakeable. Against this rock, our guide told us, Job leaned "when he was afflicted by his Lord" (*hîn ibtelâ min rabbuh*).[1] While these people were offering up their *'Asr* (afternoon) prayer in this place, Sa'îd brought me a handful of small long round

---

[1] As is generally known, the black stone in Mekka and the *Sachra* in Jerusalem are more celebrated than the stone of Job; but less revered are the *Mebrak en-nâka* in Bosrâ, the thievish stone of Moses in the great mosque at Damascus, the *doset en-nebî* on the mountain of el-Higâne, and others.

stones and slag, which the tradition declares to be the worms
that fell to the ground out of Job's sores, petrified. "Take
them with thee," said he, "as a memento of this place; let
them teach thee not to forget God in prosperity, and in misfortune not to contend with Him." The frequent use of
these words in the mouth of the man might have weakened
them to a set phrase: they were, however, appropriate to the
occasion, and were not without their effect. After my attendants had provided themselves with Job's worms, we left
the *Sachra*. These worms form a substantial part of the
Hauranitish tradition of Job, and they are known and revered
generally in the country. Our Christian attendant from
Shemiskîn bound them carefully in the broad sleeve of his
shirt, and recited to us a few verses from a kasîde, in which
they are mentioned. The poem, which a member of our
company, the dervish *Regeb*, wrote down, is by a Hauranite
Christian, who in it describes his unhappy love in colours as
strong as the bad taste it displays. The lines that are appropriate here are as follows:—

Min 'azma nârî nâra jôm·el-qijâma,
Tûfâna Nûha 'dmû' a 'ênî 'anuh zôd.
Ja' qûba min hoznî hizânuh qisâma
Min belweti Ejûba jertaʿ bihe 'd-dûd.[1]

The fire of hell at the last day will kindle itself from the glow of my pain,
    And stronger than the flood of Noah are the tear-streams of mine eyes.
The grief of Jacob for his son was but a small part of my grief;
    And, visited with my misery, Job was once the prey of worms.[2]

The village, which the peasants call *Shêch Saʿd*, and the
nomads *Saʿdîje*, is, as the name implies, of later origin, and
perhaps was founded by people who fled hither when oppressed elsewhere, for the sake of being able to live more
peacefully under the protection of the two tombs. That the

[1] The metre forms two spondeo-iambics and trochæo-spondaics.
[2] Comp. vol. ii. p. 158 of the foregoing Commentary.

place is not called Êjâbíje, is perhaps in order to distinguish it from the Monastery of Job.

In less than a quarter of an hour we rode up to the *Dér* Êjâb, a square building, standing entirely alone, and not surrounded by ruins. When the Arabian geographers call it a village, they reckon to it the neighbouring Sa'díje with the Ma'kâm. It is very extensive, and built of fine square blocks of dolerite. While my fellow-traveller, M. Dörgens, was engaged in making a ground-plan of the shattered building, which seemed to us on the whole to have had a very simple construction, I took some measurements of its sides and angles, and then searched for inscriptions. Although the ground-floor is now in part hidden in a *mezbele*,[1] which has been heaped up directly against the walls, on the east side, upon the architrave, not of the chief doorway, which is on the south, but of a door of the church, is found a large Greek inscription in a remarkable state of preservation. The architrave consists of a single carefully-worked block of dolerite, and at present rests almost upon the ground, since the rubbish has filled the whole doorway. The writing and sculpture are hollowed out.

In the centre is a circle, and the characters inscribed at each side of this circle are still undeciphered ; the rest of the inscription is easy to be read: αὕτη ἡ πύλη κ(υρίο)υ δίκαιοι εἰσελεύσοντε ἐν αὐτῇ· τοῦτο τὸ ὑπέρθυρον ἐτέθη ἐν χρόνοις Ἡλίου εὐλαβεστ(άτου) ἡγουμ(ένου) μ(ηνί) Ἰουλίῳ κε ἰνδ(ι)κ-(τίωνος) ιε τοῦ ἔτους πηντακοσιοστοῦ τρικοστοῦ ἕκτου κ(υρί)ου Ἰ(ησ)οῦ Χ(ριστ)οῦ βασιλεύοντος. The passage of Scripture, Ps. cxviii. 20, with · which this inscription begins, is frequently found in these districts in the inscriptions on church portals.

This inscription was an interesting discovery ; for, so far as I know, it is the oldest that we possess which reckons

1 On the word and subject, *vid.* vol. ii. 152 of the foregoing Commentary.

according to the Christian era, and in the Roman indiction
(*indictio*)[1] we have an important authority for determining its
date. Now, since there might be a difference of opinion as
to the beginning of the "kingdom of Christ," I was anxious
to have the judgment of an authority in chronology on the
point; and I referred to Prof. Piper of Berlin, who kindly
furnished me with the following communication:—". . . The
inscription therefore furnishes the following data: July 25,
indict. xv., year 536, κυρίου Ἰοῦ Χοῦ βασιλεύοντος. To
begin with the last, the Dionysian era, which was only just
introduced into the West, is certainly not to be assumed here.
But it is also by no means the birth of Christ that is intended. Everything turns upon the expression βασιλεύοντος.
The same expression occurs once in an inscription from
Syria, *Corp. Inscr. Græc.* 8651: βασιλεύοντος Ἰουστινιανοῦ
τῷ ια ἔτει. The following expression, however, occurs later
concerning Christ on Byzantine coins: *Rex regnantium*
and Βασιλεὺς Βασιλέων (after Apoc. xvii. 14, xix. 16), the
latter under John Zimiszes (died 975), in *De Saulcy, Pl.*
xxii. 4. But if the βασιλεία of Christ is employed as the
era, we manifestly cannot refer to the epoch of the birth of
Christ, but must take the epoch of His ascension as our
basis: for with this His βασιλεία first began; just as in the
West we sometimes find the calculation begins *a passione*.
Now the fathers of the Western Church indeed place the
death (and therefore also the ascension) of Christ in the
consulate of the two *Gemini*, 29 A.D. Not so with the
Greek fathers. Eusebius takes the year of His death, according to one supposition, to be the 18th year of Tiberius,
i.e. 785 A.U.C. = 32 A.D. Supposing we take this as the
first year *regnante Jesu Christo*, then the year 536, of the
inscription of the Monastery of Job, is reduced to our era,
after the birth of Christ, by adding 31. Thus we have the

---

[1] *Vid.* Gibbon, ed. Smith, ii. 333.—Tr.

number of the year 567, to which the accompanying xv. *indictio* corresponds, for 567 + 3 = 570 ; and $\frac{570}{15}$ has no re-mainder. XV. is therefore the indiction of the year 567, which more accurately belongs to the year from 1st Sept. 566 to 31st Aug. 567. And since the day of the month is mentioned in the inscription, it is the 25th July 567 that is indicated. For it appears to me undoubted that the indic-tions, according to the usual mode of computation among the Greeks, begin with the 1st Sept. 312. Thus a Sidonian inscription of Dec. 642 A.D. has the I. indiction (*Corp. Inscr. Gr.* 9153). . . ."

Thus far Prof. Piper's communication. According to this satisfactory explanation of its date, this inscription is perhaps not unqualified to furnish a contribution worth notice, even for the chronology of the life of Jesus, since the Ghassinides, under whom not only the inscription, but the Monastery itself 300 years earlier, had its origin, dwelt in Palestine, the land of Christ; and their kings were perhaps the first who professed Christianity.

The "festival of the Monastery of Job," which, according to *Kazwînî's* Syrian Calendar,[1] the Christians of the country celebrated annually on the 23d April, favours the pre-Muhammedan importance of the Monastery. This festival in *Kazwînî's* time, appearing only by name in the calendar, had undoubtedly ceased with the early decline of Christianity in the plain of Hauran, for the historically remarkable exodus of a large portion of the Ghassinides out of the cities of Hauran to the north of Georgia had taken place even under the chalifate of Omar. The Syrian Christians of the present day celebrate the festival of Mâr Gorgius (St George), who slew the dragon (*tennîn*) near Beirût, on the 23d April. A week later (the 1st May, oriental era) the Jews of Damascus have the *sóm Êjûb* (the fast of Job), which lasts twenty-

[1] *Calendarium Syriacum Cazwinii*, ed. Guil. Volck, Lips. 1859, p. 15.

four hours. In *Kazwînî's* calendar it is erroneously set down to the 3d May.

Moreover, with reference to the Monastery, it must be mentioned that, according to the history of *Ibn Kethîr*,[1] the great Greco-Ghassinide army, which, under the leadership of Theodoric, a brother of the Emperor Heraclius, was to have repulsed the attack of the Mussulmans on Syria, revolted in its neighbourhood in the 13th year of the Hegira (*Higra*), while the enemy was encamped on the south bank of the *Meddân*, and was drawn up near *Edre'ât*. After several months had passed came the battle known as the "battle of the *Jarmûk*," the issue of which cost the Byzantines Syria. The volcanic hollows of the ground, which for miles form a complex network of gorges, for the most part inaccessible, offer great advantages in defensive warfare; and here the battle near *Edre'i*, in which 'Og king of Bashan lost his kingdom, was probably fought.

According to the present division of the country, the Monastery of Job and the Makâm are in the southern part of *Gêdûr*, an administrative district, which is bounded on the north by the *Wâdi Bêrût*, on the east by the *W. el-Horêr* and the high road, on the south by the *Jarmûk*, and on the west by the *W. Hit* and by a range of volcanic mounds, which stretch to the south-east corner of the Snow-mountain (*el-Hermôn*); this district, however, has only a nominal existence, for it has no administration of its own. Either it is added to *Haurân*, or its revenues, together with those of Gôlân, are let out to the highest bidder for a number of years. *Gêdûr* is the natural north-western continuation of the plain of *Haurân*; and the flat bed of the *Horêr*, which does not form a gorge until it comes to the bridge of Sîra, forms no boundary proper. Moreover, the word is not found in ancient geography; and the Arabian geographers, even

[1] Comp. A. v. Kremer, *Mittelsyrien*, etc., Vienna 1853, S. 10.

the later ones, who recognised the idea of *Gêdûr*, always
so define the position of a locality situated in Gêdûr, that
they say it is situated in the *Haurân*. Thus Jâkût describes
the town of el-Gâbïa, situated in western Gêdûr, and in like
manner, as we have seen above, Nawâ and the Monastery of
Job, etc.[1] There is no doubt that, as the Gêdûr of the
present day is reckoned in the *Nukra*, so this country also
in ancient days, at least as far as its northern watershed, has
belonged to the tetrarchy of *Batancea*.

The Monastery of Job is at present inhabited. A certain
sheikh, *Ahmed el-Kâdirî*, has settled down here since the
autumn of 1859, as partner of the senior of the Damascene
'Omarîje (the successors of the Chalif 'Omar), to whose
family endowments (*waqf*) the Monastery belongs, and with
his family he inhabits a number of rooms in the inner court,
which have escaped destruction. He showed us the decree
of his partner appointing him to his position, in which he is
styled Sheikh of the *Dêr Êjûb*, *Dêr el-Lebwe*, and *'Ashtarâ*.
Dêr el-Lebwe, "the monastery of the lion,"[2] was built by the
Gefnide *Eihem ibn el-Hârith;* and we shall have occasion to
refer to *'Ashtarâ*, in which Newbold,[3] in the year 1846,
believed he had found the ancient capital of Basan, *'Ashtarôt*,
further on. But the possessor of all these grand things was
a very unhappy man. While we were drinking coffee with
him, he related to us how the inhabitants of Nawâ had left

---

[1] Jâkût says under *Gêdûr*, " It is a Damascene district, it has villages,
and lies in the north of *Haurân*; according to others, it is reckoned
together with *Haurân* as one district." The last words do not signify
that *Gêdûr* and *Haurân* are words to be used without any distinction; on
the contrary, that Gêdûr is a district belonging to *Haurân*, and comprehended in it.

[2] The name of this monastery, which is about a mile and a half north-
east of the Dêr Ejûb, is erroneously called D. el-lebû in Burckhardt's
Travels in Syria (ed. Gesenius, S. 449). The same may be said of D.
en-nubuwwe in *Annales Hamzæ*, ed. Gottwaldt, p. ١١٨.

[3] C. Ritter, *Geogr. v. Syr. u. Pal.* ii. 821 [*Erdk.* xv. Pt. 2, p. 821].

him only two yoke (*feddân*) of arable land from the territory assigned to him, and taken all the rest to themselves. The harvest of that year, after the deduction of the *bedhâr* (the new seed-corn), would hardly suffice to meet the demands of his family, and of hospitality; and for his partner, who had advanced money to him, there would be nothing left. In Damascus he found no redress; and the Sheikh of Nawâ, *Dhiâb el-Medhjeb*, had answered his last representation with the words, "He who desires Job's inheritance must look for trials." Here also, as in Arabia generally, I found that intelligence and energy was on the side of the wife. During our conversation, his wife, with one of her children, had drawn near; and while the child kissed my hand, according to custom, she said: "To-morrow thou wilt arrive at *Muzêrib;* Dhiâb will also be going thither with contributions for the pilgrims. We put our cause in thy hands, arrange it as seems thee best; this old man will accompany thee." And as we were riding, the Sheikh A*h*med was also obliged to mount, and his knowledge of the places did us good service on *Tell Ashtarâ* and *Tell el-Ash'arî.* In Muzêrib, where the pilgrim fair and the arriving caravans for Mekka occupied our attention for five days, we met Dhiâb and the *Ichtiârîje* (elders of the community) of Nawâ; and, after some opposi-tion, the sheikh of the Monastery of Job obtained four *feddân* of land under letter and seal, and returned home satisfied.

The case of this man is no standard of the state of the Hauranites, for there are so many desolated villages that there is no lack of land; only round about *Nawâ* it is insuf-ficient, since this place is obliged to take possession of far outlying fields, by reason of its exceedingly numerous agri-cultural population.[1] The more desolate a land exposed to

---

[1] That the Sheikh A*h*med was permitted to take up his abode in the Monastery, was owing to a religious dread of his ancestor (*gidd*), '*Abdel-Kâdir el-Gilâni*, and out of courteousness towards his partner.

plunder becomes, the more populous must its separate towns become, since the inhabitants of the smaller defenceless villages crowd into them. Thus the inhabitants of the large town of *Kenâkir* at the present time till the fields of twelve neighbouring deserted villages; and S*alt*, the only inhabited place in the *Belkâ*, has its corn-fields even at a distance of fifteen miles away. The poet may also have conceived of Job's domain similarly, for there were five hundred ploughmen employed on it; so that it could not come under the category of ordinary villages, which in Syria rarely have above, mostly under, fifty yoke of oxen. According to the tradition, which speaks of "Job's villages" (di*á*ʿ *Éjûb*), these ploughmen would be distributed over several districts; but the poet, who makes them to be overwhelmed by one ghazwe, therefore as ploughing in one district, will have conceived of them only as dwelling in one locality.

It might not be out of place here to give some illustration of the picture which the poet draws of Job's circumstances and position as a wealthy husbandman. *H*aurân, the scene of the drama (as we here assume), must at that period, as at present, have been without protection from the government of the country, and therefore exposed to the marauding attacks of the tribes of the desert. In such a country there is no private possession; but each person is at liberty to take up his abode in it, and to cultivate the land and rear cattle at his own risk, where and to what extent he may choose. Whoever intends doing so must first of all have a family, or as the Arabs say, "men" (*rigâl*), *i.e.* grown-up sons, cousins, nephews, sons-in-law; for one who stands alone, "the cut off one" (*maktûʿ*), as he is called, can attain no position of eminence among the Semites, nor undertake any important enterprise.[1] Then he has to make treaties with all the nomad

[1] In the present day the household is called ʿ*ashîra*, and all families of importance in Haurân are and call themselves ʿ*ashâir* (عشاير); but the

tribes from which he has reason to fear any attack, *i.e.* to pledge himself to pay a yearly tribute, which is given in native produce (in corn and garments). Thus the community of *el-Higâne*, ten years since, had compacts with 101 tribes; and that Job also did this, seems evident from the fact that the poet represents him as surprised not by neighbouring, but by far distant tribes (Chaldæans and Sabæans), with whom he could have no compact.[1] Next he proceeds to erect a *chirbe*, *i.e.* a village that has been forsaken (for a longer or shorter period), in connection with which, excepting the relations, slaves, and servants of the master, all those whom interest, their calling, and confidence in the good fortune of the master, have drawn thither, set about

---

ancient word *batn* does also occur, and among the Semitic tribes that have migrated to Mauritania it is still in use instead of the Syrian '*ashira*. *Batn*, collect. *butûn*, is the fellowship of all those who are traced back to the בֶּטֶן of one ancestral mother. Thus even in Damascus they say: *nahn ferd batn*, we belong to one family; in like manner in the whole of Syria: this foal is the *batn* of that mare, *i.e.* its young one ; or : I sold my mare without *batn*, or with one, two, three-fourths of her *batn*, *i.e.* without her descendants, or so that the buyer has only 6 or 12 or 18 *kirât* right of possession in the foals she will bear. In all these applications, *batn* is the *progenies uteri*, not the *uterus* itself ; and, according to this, בְּנֵי בִטְנִי, ch. xix. 17, ought to be explained by " all my relations by blood."

[1] These sudden attacks, at any rate, do not say anything in favour of the more southernly position of *Ausitis*. If the Beduin is but once on his horse or *delûl*, it is all the same to him whether a journey is ten days longer or shorter, if he can only find water for himself and his beast. This, however, both bands of marauders found, since the poet distinctly represents the attacks as having been made in the winter. The general ploughing of the fallow-lying *wâgiha* of a community (it is called *shiqâq el-wâgiha*), ready for the sowing in the following autumn, always takes place during January and February, because at this time of the year the earth is softened by the winter rains, and easy to plough. While engaged in this work, the poet represents Job's ploughmen as being surprised and slain. Hence, for the destruction of 500 armed ploughmen—and they were armed, because they could only have been slain with their weapons in their hands in consequence of their resistance—at least 2000 horsemen were necessary. So large a *ghazwe* is, however, not possible in the summer,

the work. Perhaps ch. xv. 28 has reference to Job's settlement.[1]

With reference to the relation of the lord of a village (*ustâd beled*, or *sâhib dé'a*) to his work-people, there are among the dependants two classes. The one is called *zurrâ'*, "sowers," also *fellâhin kism*, "participating husbandmen," because they share the produce of the harvest with the *ustâd* thus: he receives a fourth while they retain three-fourths, from which they live, take the seed for the following season, give their quota towards the demands of the Arabs, the village shepherds, the field watchmen, and the scribe of the community (*chatib*); they have also to provide the farming implements and the yoke-oxen. On the other hand, the *ustâd* has to provide for the dwellings of the people, to pay the land-tax to the government, and, in the event of a failure of the crops, murrain, etc., to make the necessary advances, either in money or in kind at the market price, and without

but only in the winter, because they could not water at a draw-well, only at the pools (*ghudrân*) formed by the winter rains. For one of these raids of the Chaldæans, Haurân, whither marauding bands come even now during the winter from the neighbourhood of Babylon in six or seven days, lay far more convenient than the country around *Ma'ân* and *'Akaba*, which is only reached from the Euphrates, even in winter, by going a long way round, since the *Nufûd* (sandy plains) in the east, and their western continuation the Hâlât, suck in the rain without forming any pools. On the other hand, however, this southern region lay nearer and more convenient for the incursions of the Sabæans, viz. the Keturæan (Gen. xxv. 3), *i.e.* Petræan tribe of this name. The greater or less distance, however, is of little consequence here. Thus, as the *Shemmar* of *Negd* from time to time make raids into the neighbourhood of Damascus, so even the tribes of *Wâdi el-Korâ* might also do the same. Moreover, as we observed above, the poet represents the sudden attacks as perpetrated by the Sabæans and Chaldæans, probably because *they only*, as being foreign and distant races which never had anything to do with Job and his men, and therefore were without any consideration, could practise such unwonted barbarities as the robbery of ploughing heifers, which a *ghazwe* rarely takes, and the murder of the ploughmen.

[1] [Verbally, ch. iii. 14*b*, which we, however, have interpreted differently, accords with this.—DEL.]

any compensation. This relation, which guarantees the maintenance of the family, and is according to the practice of a
patriarchal equity, is greatly esteemed in the country; and
one might unhesitatingly consider it therefore to be that
which existed between Job and his ploughmen, because it
may with ease exist between a single *ustâd* and hundreds,
indeed thousands, of country people, if ch. i. 3 did not neces-
sitate our thinking of another class of country people, viz.
the *murâbi'în*, the "quarterers." They take their name from
their receiving a fourth part of the harvest for their labour,
while they have to give up the other three-fourths to the
ustâd, who must provide for their shelter and board, and in
like manner everything that is required in agriculture. As
Job, according to ch. i. 3 (comp. on ch. xlii. 12), provided
the yoke-oxen and means of transport (asses and camels), so
he also provided the farming implements, and the seed for
sowing. We must not here think of the paid day-labourer
of the Syrian towns, or the servants of our landed pro-
prietors; they are unknown on the borders of the desert.
The hand that toils has there a direct share in the gain ; the
workers belong to the *aulâd*, "children of the house," and
are so called; in the hour of danger they will risk their life
for their lord.

This rustic labour is always undertaken simultaneously by
all the *murâbi'în* (it is so also in the villages of the *zurrá'*)
for the sake of order, since the *ustâd*, or in his absence the
village sheikh, has the general work of the following day
announced from the roof of his house every evening. Thus
it is explained how the 500 ploughmen could be together in
one and the same district, and be slain all together.

The *ustâd* is the sole judge, or, by deputy, the *sheikh*. An
appeal to the government of the country would be useless,
because it has no influence in Hauran ; but the servant who
has been treated unjustly by his master, very frequently

turns as *dachîl fi 'l-haqq* (a suppliant concerning his right) to his powerful neighbour, who is bound, according to the customs of the country, to obtain redress for him (comp. ch. xxix. 12–17). If he does not obtain this by persuasion, he cries for force, and such a demand lies at the root of many a bloody feud.

Powerful and respected also as the position, described in ch. xxix., of such a man is, it must, according to the nature of its basis, fall in under strokes of misfortune, like those mentioned in ch. i. 14–19, and change to the very opposite, as the poet describes it in ch. xxx.

After these observations concerning the agricultural relations of Hauran, we return to the tradition of Job. As we pursue the track of this tradition further, we first find it again in some of the Christian writers of the middle ages, viz. in Eugesippus (*De distanc. loc. terr. sanct.*), in William of Tyre (*Histor. rerum a Francis gest.*), and in Marino Sanuto (*De secretis fid. cruc.*). The passages that bear upon the point are brought together in Reland (*Palest.* pp. 265 sq.); and we would simply refer to them, if it were possible for the reader to find his way among the fabulous confusion of the localities in Eugesippus and Sanuto.

The oldest of these citations is from Eugesippus, and is as follows: One part of the country is the land of *Hus*, out of which Job was; it is also called *Sueta*, after which Bildad the Suhite was named. Sanuto tells us where this locality is to be sought. "*Sueta* is the home of Baldad the Suite. Below this city (*civitas*), in the direction of the Kedar-tribes, the Saracens are accustomed to assemble out of Aram, Mesopotamia, Ammon, Moab, and the whole Orient, around the fountain of *Fiale*; and, on account of the charms of the place, to hold a fair there during the whole summer, and to pitch their coloured tents." In another place he says: *fontem Fialen Medan, i.e. aquas Dan, a Saracenis nuncupari.*

Now, since according to an erroneous, but previously prevalent etymology, "the water of Dan " (דָּן מֵי = דָּן יְאֹר) denoted
the Jordan, and since we further know from Josephus (*Bell.*
iii. 10, 7) that the *Phiala* is the small lake of *Râm*, whose subterranean outflow the tetrarch Philip is said to have shown
to be the spring of the Jordan, which comes to light deeper
below, we should have thought the country round about the
lake of Râm, at the south foot of Hermôn, to be the home of
Job and Bildad.   This discovery would be confirmed by the
following statement of Eugesippus (in Reland, *loc. cit.*): "The
river *Dan* flows under ground from its spring as far as the
plain of Meldan, where it comes to light.   This plain is named
after the fair, which is held there, for the Saracens call such an
one *Meldan*.   At the beginning of the summer a large number of men, with wares to sell, congregate there, and several
Parthian and Arabian soldiers also, in order to guard the people
and their herds, which have a rich pasture there in the summer.
The word *meldan* is composed of *mel* and *dan*."   It is indeed
readily seen that the writer has ignorantly jumbled several
words together in the expression *meldan*, as *mê Dan*, "water
of Dan," and *mêdân* or *mîdân*, "market-place;" perhaps even
also *leddân*, the name of the great fountain of the Jordan
in the crater of the *Tell el-Kâdi*.   In like manner, the statement that the neighbourhood of *Phiala*, or that of the large
fountain of the Jordan, might formerly have been a fair of
the tribes, is false, for the former is broken up into innumerable
craters, and the latter is poisoned by the swamp-fevers of the
Hûle; but as to the rest, both Eugesippus and Sanuto seem
really to speak of a tradition which places Job's or Bildad's
home in that region.   And yet it is not so: their tradition
is no other than the Hauranitish; but ignorance of the language and geography of the country, and some accidental
circumstances, so confused their representations, that it is
difficult to find out what is right.   The first clue is given us

by the history of William of Tyre, in which (l. xxii. c. 21) it is said that the crusaders, on their return from a marauding expedition in the Nu*k*ra, wished to reconquer a strong position, the *Cavea Roob*, which they had lost a short time before. "This place," says the historian, "lies in the province of *Suite*, a district distinguished by its pleasantness, etc.; and that Baldad, Job's friend, who is on that account called the Suite, is said to have come from it." This passage removes us at once into the neighbourhood of *Muzêrîb* and the Monastery of Job, for the province of Suete is nothing but the district of Suwêt (ﺻﻮﻳﺖ),[1] the north-western boundary of which is formed by the gorge of the *Wâdi Rahûb*. The *Cavea Roob*, which was first of all again found out by me on my journey in 1862, lies in the middle of the steep bank of that wadi, and is at present called *maghâret Rahûb*, "the cave of R.," or more commonly *mu'allakat Rahûb*, "the swinging cave of R.," and at the time of the Crusades commanded the dangerous pass which the traveller, on ascending from the south end of the Lake of Galilee to *Edre'ât* by the nearest way, has to climb on hands and feet. In another passage (xvi. 9), where the unhealthy march to *Bosrâ* is spoken of, Will. of Tyre says: "After we had come through the gorge of *Roob*, we reached the plain which is called *Medan*, and where every year the Arabs and other oriental tribes are accustomed to hold a large fair." This plain is in the vicinity of *Muzêrîb*, in which the great pilgrim-fair is held annually. We find something similar in xiii. 18: "After having passed Decapolis[2] we came to the pass of *Roob*, and further on into the plain of *Medan*, which stretches far and wide in every direction, and is intersected

---

[1] *Reisebericht*, S. 46; comp. Ritter, *Syr. u. Pal.* ii. 1019 [*Erdk.* xv. Pt. 2, p. 1019].

[2] Here in the more contracted sense, the district of *Gadara*, *Kefârât*, and *Irbid*.

by the river *Dan*, which falls into the Jordan between *Tiberias* and *Scythopolis* (*Bisân*)." This river, the same as that which Sanuto means by his *aquæ Dan* (*Mê Dân*), is none other than the *Wâdi el-Meddân*, called "the overflowing one," because in the month of March it overflows its banks eastward of the *Gezzâr*-bridge. It is extremely strange that the name of this river appears corrupted not only in all three writers mentioned above, but also in Burckhardt; for, deceived by the ear, he calls it *Wâdi Om el-Dhan*.[1] The *Meddân* is the boundary river between the *Suwêt* and *Nukra* plains; it loses its name where it runs into the *Makran*; and where it falls into the valley of the Jordan, below the lake of Tiberias, it is called *el-Muchêbî*.

We have little to add to what has been already said. The *Fiale* of Sanuto is not the Lake Râm, but the round *begge*, the lake of springs of Muzêrîb, the rapid outflow of which, over a depth of sixty to eighty feet, forms a magnificent waterfall, the only one in Syria, as it falls into the Meddân near the village of *Tell Shihâb*.

The unfortunate confusion of the localities was occasioned by two accidental circumstances: first, that both, the springs of the Jordan below *Bâniâs* and the lake of *Muzêrîb*, have a village called *Rahûb* (רחוב) in their vicinity, of which one is mentioned in Judg. xviii. 28 sq., and the other, about a mile below the *Cavea Roob*, is situated by a fountain of the same name, from which village, cavern, and wadi derive their names; secondly, that there, as here, there is a village *Abil* (אָבֵל): that near Dan is situated in the "meadow-district of 'Ijôn" (*Merg 'Ijûn*); and that in the *Suwêt* lies between *Rahûb* and the *Makran*, and was visited by Seetzen as well as by myself. Perhaps the circumstance that, just as the environs of *Muzêrîb* have their *Mîdân*,[2] so the environs of

---

[1] Burckhardt, *Travels in Syr. and Pal.* (ed. Gesenius, S. 392).

[2] The word *el-mîdân* and *el-mêdân* signifies originally the hippodrome,

Bâniás have their *Ard el-Mejâdin*, "region of battle-fields," may also have contributed to the confusion; thus, for example, the country sloping to the west from the *Phiala* towards the Hûle, between *Gubbâtâ ez-zêt* and *Za'úra*, is called, perhaps on account of the murderous encounters which took place there, both in the time of the Crusades and also in more ancient times. It is certainly the ground on which the battle narrated in the book of Joshua, ch. xi., took place, and also the battle in which Antiochus the Great slew the Egyptian army about 200 B.C.

What we have gained for our special purpose from this information (by which not a few statements of Ritter, K. v. Raumer, and others, are substantiated), is not merely the fact that the tradition which places Job's home in the region of *Muzérîb* existed even in the middle ages (which the quotation given above from *Makdeshî*, who lived before the time of the Crusades, also confirms), and even came to the ears of the foreigners who settled in the country as they then passed through the land, but also the certainty that this tradition was then, as now, common to the Christians and the Mussulmans, for the three writers previously mentioned would hardly have recorded it on the testimony of the latter only.[1]

then the arena of the sham-fight, then the place of contest, the battle-field, and finally a wide level place where a large concourse of men are accustomed to meet. In this sense the Damascenes have their *el-mîdân*, the Spanish cities their *almeidân*, and the Italians their *corso*.

[1] [Estôri ha-Parchi, the most renowned Jewish topographer of Palestine, in his work *Caftor wa-ferach*, completed in 1322 (newly edited by Edelmann, published by Asher, Berlin, 1852, S. 49), says דאר איוב lies one hour south of נבו, since he identifies *Nawâ* with the Reubenitish *Nebô*, Num. xxxii. 38, as *Zora'* with יעזר, Num. xxxii. 35 ; so that he explains ארץ עוץ by ארץ יעזר, although he at the same time considers the name, according to Saadia, as one with אלגוטה (*el-Ghuta*). His statements moreover are exact, as one might expect from a man who had travelled for seven years in all directions in Palestine ; and his conclusion, ארץ עוץ היא ארץ קדם לארץ ישראל כנגד טבריא, perfectly accords with the above treatise.—DEL.]

There can be no doubt as to which of these two religions must be regarded as the original mother of this tradition. The Hauranite Christians, who, from their costume, manners, language, and traditions, undoubtedly inherited the country from the pre-Muhammedan age, venerate the Maḵâm perhaps even more than the Muhammedans; which would be altogether impossible in connection with the hostile position of the two religious sects towards one another, and in connection with the zealous scorn with which the Syrian Christians regard the religion of Islam, if the Hauranitish tradition of Job and the Maḵâm were of later, Muhammedan origin. It is also possible that, on a closer examination of the Maḵâm and the buildings about the Sachra, one might find, besides crosses, Greek inscriptions (since they are nowhere wanting in the Nuḵra), which could only have their origin in the time before the occupation of Islam (635 A.D.); for *after* this the Hauranite Christians, who only prolong their existence by wandering from *chirbe* to *chirbe*, have not even built a single dwelling-house, much less a building for religious worship, which was forbidden under pain of death in the treaty of Omar. But in connection with the pre-Islam Monastery of Job, which owed its origin only to the sacred tradition that held its ground in that place, are monumental witnesses that this tradition is pre-Islamic, and has been transferred from the Christians to the Mussulmans, required? We may go even further, and assert that Muḥammed, in the Sur. xxxviii. 41 sqq. of the Korân, had the Hauranitish tradition of Job and the localities near Saʻdîje definitely before his mind.

We must regard the merchandise caravans which the inhabitants of *Tehâma* sent continuously into the "north country," *esh-shâm*,[1] and the return freight of which consisted chiefly of Hauranitish corn, as proof of a regular

---

[1] In Jemen and *Ḥigâz*, Syria may have been called *Shâm* in the earliest times. The name was taken into Syria itself by the immigration of the

intercourse between the east Jordanic country and the west of the Arabian peninsula in the period between Christ and Muhammed. Hundreds of men from Mekka and Medina came every year to *Bosrâ;* indeed, when it has happened that the wandering tribes of Syria, which were, then also as now, bound for Hauran with the *kêl, i.e.* their want of corn, got before them, and had emptied the granaries of Bosrâ, or when the harvests of the south of Hauran had been destroyed by the locusts, which is not unfrequently the case, they will have come into the *Nukra*[1] as far as Nawâ, sometimes even as far as Damascus, in order to obtain their full cargo.

If commerce often has the difficult task of bringing together the most heterogeneous peoples, and of effecting a reciprocal interchange of ideas, it here had the easy work of sustaining the intercourse among tribes that were originally one people, spoke one idiom, and regarded themselves as all related; for

Jemanic tribes of Kudâ'a, and others, because they brought with them the name of Syria that was commonly used in their native land.

[1] The remarkable fair at *Muzêrib* can be traced back to the earliest antiquity, although Bosrâ at times injured it; but this latter city, from its more exposed position, has been frequently laid in ruins. It is·probable that the merchants of Damascus pitched their tents for their *Kasaba, i.e.* their moveable fair, twice a year (in spring and in autumn) by the picturesque lake of Muzêrib. If, with the tradition, we take the *Nukra* to be the home of Job, of the different ways of interpreting ch. vi. 19 there is nothing to hinder our deciding upon that which considers it as the greater caravan which came periodically out of southern Arabia to Hauran (Bosrâ or Muzêrib). *Têmâ* with its well, *Heddâg* (comp. Isa. xxi. 14), celebrated by the poets of the steppe, from which ninety camels *(sâniât)* by turns raise a constantly flowing stream of clear and cool water for irrigating the palms and the seed, was in ancient times, perhaps, the crossing point of the merchant caravans going from south to north, and from east to west. Even under the Omajad Chalifs the Mekka pilgrim-route went exclusively by way of *Têmâ*, just as during the Crusades so long as the Franks kept possession of *Kerak* and *Shôbak.* An attempt made in my *Reisebericht* (S. 93–95) to substitute the Hauranitish *Têmâ* in the two previously mentioned passages of Scripture, I have there (S. 131) given up as being scarcely probable.

the second great Sabæan migration, under 'Amr and his son Ta'labe, had taken possession of Mekka, and left one of their number, Rabî'a ibn Hâritha, with his attendants (the Chuzâ'-ites), behind as lord of the city. In the same manner they had become possessed of Jathrib (el-Medîna), and left this city to their tribes Aus and Chazreg: the remainder of the people passed on to Peræa and took possession of the country, at that time devastated, as far as Damascus, according to Ibn Sa'îd, even including this city. By the reception of Christianity, the Syrian Sabæans appear to have become but slightly or not at all estranged from their relatives in the Higâz, for Christianity spread even here, so that the Cæsars once ventured to appoint a Christian governor even to the city of Mekka. This was during the lifetime of the Gefnite king 'Amr ibn Gebele. At the time of Muhammed there were many Christians in Mekka, who will for the most part have brought their Christianity with the Syrian caravans, so that at the commencement of Islâm the Hauranitish tradition of Job might have been very well known in Mekka, since many men from Mekka may have even visited the Makâm and the Sachra, and there have heard many a legend of Job like that intimated in the Korân xxxviii. 43. Yea, whoever will give himself the trouble to investigate minute commentaries on the Koran, especially such as interpret the Koran from the tradition (hadîth), e.g. the Kitâb ed-durr el-muchtâr, may easily find that not merely Kazwînî, Ibn el-Wardî, and Jâkût, whose observations concerning the Monastery of Job have been given above, but also much older authorities, identify the Koranish fountain of Job with the Hauranitish.

A statement of Eusebius, of value in connection with this investigation, brings us at one stride about three hundred years further on. It is in the Onomastikon, under Καρναείμ, and is as follows: " Astaroth Karnaim is at present (about 310 A.D.) a very large village (κώμη μεγίστη) beyond the

Jordan, in the province of Arabia, which is also called *Bata-næa*. Here, according to tradition (ἐκ παραδόσεως), they fix the dwelling (οἶκος) of Job." On the small map which accompanies these pages, the reader will find in the vicinity of the Makâm the low and somewhat precipitous mound, not above forty feet in height, of *Tell ʿAshtarâ*, the plateau of which forms an almost round surface, which is 425 paces in diameter, and shows the unartistic foundations of buildings, and traces of a ring-wall. Here we have to imagine that *ʿAstarot Karnaim*. Euseb. here makes no mention whatever of the city of *Astaroth*, the ancient capital of *Basan*, for this he does under ᾿Ασταρὼθ ; the hypothesis of its being the residence of king ʿOg, which Newbold[1] set up here, consequently falls to the ground. The κώμη μεγίστη of Eusebius must, in connection with the limited character of the ground, certainly be somewhat contracted ; but the identity of the localities is not to be doubted in connection with the great nearness of the οἶκος (the Makâm).[2] Let us compare another statement that belongs here ; it stands under ᾿Ασταρὼθ Καρναείμ, and is as follows : "There are at the present time two villages of this name in Batanæa, which lie nine miles distant from one another, μεταξὺ ΑΔΑΡΩΝ καὶ ΑΒΙΔΗC." Jerome has *duo castella* instead of two villages, by which at

---

[1] C. Ritter, *Geogr. v. Syr. u Pal.* ii. 819 sqq. [*Erdk.* xv. 2, p. 819 sqq.]. The information of Newbold, which is printed in the *Zeitschr. d. Deutsch. Morgenl. Gesellschaft*, i. 215 sq., is unfortunately little to be relied on, and is to be corrected according to the topography of the mound given above.

[2] A small, desolated stone village, situated a quarter of an hour's journey from the mound of ʿAshtarâ, which however has not a single house of any importance, has two names among the inhabitants of that region, either *Chirbêt ʿIjûn en-Nile* (the ruins near the Nila-springs) or *Chirbêt ʿAshtarâ*, which can signify the ruins of ʿAshtarâ and the ruins near ʿAshtarâ. Since it is, however, quite insignificant, it will not be the village that has given the name to the mound, but the mound with its buildings, which in ancient days were perhaps a temple to Astarte, surrounded by a wall, has given the name to the village.

least the κώμη μεγίστη is somewhat reduced; for that it is one of these two castles[1] can be the less doubtful, since they also regulate the determining of the respective localities. If the reading *ABIΔHC* is correct, only *Abil* (אָבֵל) in the north of *Suwêt* can (since, without doubt, the Arabian names of the places in Hauran existed in Eusebius' day) be intended; and *ΔΔΑΡΩΝ* ought then to be changed into *ΑΔΑΡΩΝ*, in order to denote the large village of *El-hârâ*, on the lofty peak of the same name in the plain of Gêdûr. *El-hârâ* lies to the north, and *Abil* to the south of *'Ashtarâ*. If, however, as is most highly probable, instead of *ABIΔHC* (which form Euseb. does not use elsewhere, for he calls the town of *Abil* Ἀβέλ, and the inscription in *Turra* has the form πόλεως Ἀβέλις), *ABIΔHC* is to be read, which corresponds to the Ἀβιδᾶ of Ptolemy (*ed. Wilberg*, p. 369) and the modern *'Abidin* near *Bêtirrâ*, thus the name of the other village is to be changed from *ΔΔΑΡΩΝ* to *ΑΡΑΡΩΝ* (for which the *Cod. Vat.* erroneously has *ΔΡΑΡΩΝ*), the modern *'Arâr.*[2] *'Abidin*, however, lies nine miles west, and *'Arâr* nine miles east of *'Ashtarâ*.

Now, as to the second village, and its respective castle, which is mentioned in the second citation from the *Onomastikon*, I believe that both Euseb. and Jerome intend to say there are two villages, of which the one has the byname of the other; consequently the one is called *Astarôt* (*Karnaim*), and the other *Karnaim* (*Astarôt*). Twelve miles west of *'Ashtarâ* lies

---

[1] [The meaning of "castle," as defined by Burckhardt, *Travels in Syr.* etc. p. 657, should be borne in mind here. "The name of Kala'at or *castle* is given on the Hadj route, and over the greater part of the desert, to any building walled in and covered, and having, like a *Khan*, a large courtyard in its enclosure. The walls are sometimes of stone, but more commonly of earth, though even the latter are sufficient to withstand an attack of Arabs."—Tr.]

[2] Some, in connection with this word, have erroneously thought of the city of *Edre'ât*, which Eusebius calls Ἀδρά in the immediately preceding article Ἀδραά, and in the art. Ἐδραεί.

the Golanite village of Kornîje (קָרְנָיָה), which in old Kanêtra
I have taken up in my trigonometrical measurements.
We find also a third passage in the *Onomast.* which belongs
here; it is under 'Ιαβώκ in *Cod. Vat.*, under 'Ιδουμαία in
Cod. Leid. and *Vallarsi*, and runs: "According to the view
of a certain one (κατά τινος), this region is the land of *Asitis*
(*Ausitis*), the home of Job, while according to others it is
Arabia (ἡ 'Αραβία) ; and again, according to others, it is the
Land of Sîhôn." Whether genuine or not, this passage
possesses a certain value. If it is genuine, Jerome would
have left it accordingly untranslated, because he would not
be responsible for its whole contents, for he not unfrequently
passes over or alters statements of Eusebius where he believes
himself to be better informed; but, taken exactly, he could
only have rejected the views of those who seek Job's native
country on the *Jabbok* (if the passage belongs to the art. 'Ιαβώκ) or in Edom (if it belongs to 'Ιδουμαία), or in the *Belkâ*,
the land of Sîhôn; but not the view of those who make Arabia
(*Batanæa*) to be *Ausitis*, for the statement of Eusebius with
reference to this point under Καρναείμ he translates faithfully. If the passage is not genuine, it at any rate gives the
very early testimony of an authority distinct from Eusebius
and Jerome in favour of the age of the Hauranitish tradition
concerning Job, while it has only a single (κατά τινος) authority for the view of those who make Edom be Ausitis, and
even this only when the passage belongs to 'Ιδουμαία.
    By means of these quotations from the *Onomastikon*, that
passage of Chrysostom (*Homil. V. de Stud.* § 1, tom. ii. p.
59), in which it is said that many pilgrims from the end of
the earth come to Arabia, in order to seek for the dunghill
on which Job lay, and with rapture to kiss the ground where
he suffered (— — ἀπὸ περάτων τῆς γῆς εἰς τὴν 'Αραβίαν
τρέχοντες, ἵνα τὴν κοπρίαν ἴδωσι, καὶ θεασάμενοι καταφιλή-
σωσι τὴν γῆν), appears also to obtain its right local refer-

ence. This Arabia is certainly none other than that which
Eusebius explains by ἡ καὶ Βαταναία, and that κοπρία or
mezbele to be sought nowhere except near the *Makâm Êjûb.*
And should there be any doubts upon the subject, ought
they not to be removed by the consideration that the proud
structure of the Monastery of Job, with its spring festivals
mentioned above, standing like a Pharos casting its light
far and wide in that age, did not allow either the Syrian
Christians or the pilgrims from foreign parts to mistake the
place, which tradition had rendered sacred, as the place of
Job's sufferings?

There is no monastery whose origin, according to an unimpeachable testimony, belongs to such an early date as that
of the Monastery of Job. According to the chronicles of
the peoples (*ta'rîch el-umem*), or the annals of Hamze el-
Isfahâni (died about 360 of the Hegira), it was built by
'*Amr* I., the second Gefnide. Now, since the first Ghassa-
nitish king (*Gefne* I.) reigned forty-five years and three
months, and '*Amr* five years, the Monastery would have
been in existence about 200 A.D., if we place the beginning
of the Gefnide dynasty in the time 150 A.D. Objections are
raised against such an early date, because one is accustomed
on good authority to assign the origin of monasteries to
about the year 300 A.D. In the face of more certain historical dates, these objections must remain unheeded, for
hermit and monastery life (*rahbanîja*) existed in the country
east of Jordan among the Essenes and other societies and
forms of worship, even before Christianity; so that the latter,
on its appearance in that part, which took place long before
200 A.D., received the monasteries as an inheritance: but
certainly the chronology of the Gefnide dynasty is not reliable. *Hamze* fixes the duration of the dynasty at 616
years; *Ibn Sa'îd,*[1] in his history of the pre-Islamic Arabs, at

[1] Wetzstein, Catal. Arab. MSS. collected in Damascus, No. 1, p. 89.

601 years; and to the same period extends the statement of
Mejánishi,[1] who, in his topography of the *Ka'be*, says that
between the conquest of Mekka by *Ta'lebe* and the rule of
the Kosî in this city was 500 years. On the contrary,
however, *Ibn Jusef*[2] informs us that this dynasty began
"earlier" than 400 years before Islamism. With this statement accord all those numerous accounts, according to which
the "rupture of the dyke" (*sêl el-'arim*), the supposed cause
of the Jemanic emigration, took place rather more than 400
years before Islamism. If therefore, to content ourselves
with an approximate calculation, we make Islamism to begin
about 615 (the year of the "Mission" was 612 A.D.), and the
Gefnide dynasty, with the addition of the "earlier," 415 years
previous, then the commencement of the reign of Gefne I.
would have been 200 A.D., and the erection of the Monastery
shortly before 250.

When the tribe whose king later on built the Monastery
migrated from Jemen into Syria, the Trachonitis was in the
hands of a powerful race of the Kudá'ides, which had settled
there in the first century of our era, having likewise come
out of Jemen, and become tributary to the Romans. This
race had embraced Christianity from the natives; and some
historians maintain that it permitted the *Gefnides* to settle
and share in the possession of the country, only on the condition that they likewise should embrace Christianity. In
those early times, these tribes, of course, with the new religion
received the tradition of Job also from the first hand, from
the Jews and the Jewish Christians, who, since the battle of
the Jewish people with the Romans, will have found refuge
and safety to a large extent in Petræa, and especially in the
hardly accessible Trachonitis. The Nukra also, as the most
favoured region of Syria and Palestina, will have had its

[1] Wetzst. Catal. Arab. MSS. collected in Damascus, No. 24, p. 16.
[2] *Hamzæ Isfahan. Annales, ed. Gottwald,* Vorrede, p. xi.

native population, among which, in spite of the frequent massacres of Syrians and Jews, there will have been many Jews. Perhaps, moreover, the protection of the new Jemanic population of Hauran again attracted Jewish settlers thither; Nawâ[1] at least is a place well known in the Talmud and Midrash, which is mentioned, as a city inhabited by the Jews among those who are not Jews, and as the birth-place of several eminent teachers.[2] Moreover, in Syria the veneration of a spot consecrated by religious tradition is independent of its being at the time inhabited or desolate. The supposed tombs of Aaron near *Petra*, of Hud near *Gerash*, of Jethro (*Su'êb*) in the valley of *Nimrîn*, of Ezekiel in *Melîhat Hiskîn*, of Elisha on the *el-Jeshâ'* mountains, and many other *mezâre* (tombs of the holy, to which pilgrims resort), are frequently one or more days' journey distant from inhabited places, and yet they are carefully tended. They are preserved from decay and neglect by vows, by the spring processions, and especially by the piety of the Beduins, who frequently deposit articles of value near the *mezâre*, as property entrusted to the care of the saint. The Makâm of Job may also have been such a consecrated spot many centuries before the erection of the Monastery, and perhaps not merely to the Jews, but also to the Aramæan and Arab population. The superstitious veneration of such places is not confined among the Semites to a particular religious sect, but is the common heritage of the whole race; and the tra-

---

[1] If *Nawâ* is not also of Jewish origin, its name is nevertheless the old Semitic נָוֶה, "a dwelling" (ch. v. 3, 24, viii. 6, xviii. 15), and not, as *Jâkût* supposes, the collective form of *nawât*, "the kernel of a date."

[2] [No less than three renowned teachers from *Nawâ* appear in the Talmud and Midrash: ר' שִׁילָא דְּנָוֶה, *Schila* of *Nawa* (*jer. Sabbath* cap. ii., *Wajikra rabba* cap. xxxiv., *Midrasch Ruth* on ii. 19a), ר' פְּלַטְיָא דְנָוֶה (*Midr. Koheleth* on i. 4b) and ר' שְׁאוּל דְּנָוֶה (*ib.* on xii. 9a). נוֹה is mentioned as an enemy of the neighbouring town of חַלְמִישׁ in *Wajikra rabba* c. xxiii., *Midr. Echa* on i. 17a, and *Midr. Schir* on ii. 1.—DEL.]

dition of Job in particular was, originally, certainly not Israelitish, but Aramæan.

Job is not mentioned in the writings of Josephus, but we do find there a remarkable passage concerning Job's native country, the land of the Usites, viz. *Ant.* i. 6: "*Aram*, from whom come the *Aramæans*, called by the Greeks *Syrians*, had four sons, of whom the first was named Oὔσης, and pos-- sessed *Trachonitis* and *Damascus*." The first of these two, Trachonitis, has usually been overlooked here, and attention has been fixed only on Damascus. The word *el-Ghûta* (الغوطة), the proper name of the garden and orchard district around Damascus, has been thought to be connected in sound with '*Us*, and they have been treated as identical: this is, however, impossible even on philological grounds. *Ghûta* would certainly be written עוּטָה in Hebrew, because this language has no sign for the sound *Gh* (غ); but Josephus, who wrote in Greek, ought then to have said Γούσης, not Oὔσης, just as he, and the LXX. before him and Eusebius after him, render the city עזה by Γάζα, the mountain עיבל by Γαιβάλ, the village עי by Γαί, etc. In the same manner the LXX. ought to have spoken of a Γαυσῖτις, not Αὐσῖτις, if this were the case. Proper names, also, always receive too definite and lasting an impress for their consonants, as ע and ט, to be easily interchanged, although this is possible with the roots of verbs. Moreover, if the word עוץ had had the consonant צ (ض), Josephus must have reproduced it with τ or θ, not with σ, in accordance with the pronunciation (especially if he had intended to identify עוץ and *Ghûta*). And we see from Ptolemy and Strabo, and likewise from the Greek mode of transcribing the Semitic proper names in the Hau- rânite inscriptions of the Roman period, *e.g.* Μάθιος and Νάταρος for ماضى and نضر, that in the time of Josephus the sound of צ had already been divided into ص and ض; comp. *Abhandl. der Berlin. Acad. d. Wissenschaft*, 1863,

434 APPENDIX.

S. 356 f. Hence it is that Josephus manifestly speaks only of one progenitor Οὔσης, therefore of one tribe; while the word *Ghûta*, often as a synonym of *buq'a* (בִּקְעָה), denotes a low well-watered country enclosed by mountains, and in this appellative signification occurs as the proper name of several localities in the *most widely separated parts of Arabia* (comp. *Jâkût, sub voce*), which could not be the case if it had been = עוץ ארץ.[1] The word *Ausitis* used by the LXX. also has no formation corresponding to the word *Ghûta*, but shows its connection with אֶרֶץ עוּץ by the termination; while the word *Ghûta* rendered in Greek is Γουθατά (in Theophanes Byzant. Γουθαθά), in analogy *e.g.* with the form 'Ρεβλαθά for *Ribla* (Jos. *Ant.* x. 11).[2]

But why are we obliged to think only of Damascus, since Josephus makes *Trachonitis* also to belong to the land of the *Usites?* If we take this word in its most limited signification, it is (apart from the eastern *Trachon*) that lava plateau, about forty miles long and about twenty-eight broad, which is called the *Legâ* in the present day. This is so certain, that one is not obliged first of all to recall the well-known inscription of the temple of *Mismîa*, which calls this city situated in the *Legâ*, Μητροκώμη τοῦ Τράχωνος. From the western border of this *Trachon*, however, the Monastery of Job is not ten miles distant, therefore by no means outside the radius that was at all times tributary to the Trachonites (*Arab el-wa'r*), a people unassailable in their habitations in the clefts of the

---

[1] On the name '*Us*, as the name of men and people, may be compared the proper names '*As* and '*Aus*, together with the diminutive '*Owês*, taken from the genealogies of the Arabs, since the Old Testament is wanting in words formed from the root עוץ, and none of those so named was a Hebrew. In Hebr. they might be sounded עוץ, and signify the "strong one," for the verbal stems عَضّ، عَوّض، عَصّى (comp. عَصَبَ، عَصَرَ، عَصَمَ, and others) have the signif. "to be compressed, firm, to resist."

[2] On this word-formation comp. *Reisebericht*, S. 76.

rocks.[1] According to this, the statement of Josephus would at least not stand in open contradiction to the Hauranitish tradition of Job. But we go further, and maintain that the Monastery of Job lies exactly in the centre of *Trachonitis*. This word has, viz. in Josephus and others, a double signification—a more limited and a wider one. It has the more limited where, together with *Auranitis, Batanæa, Gamalitica,* and *Gaulonitis,* it denotes the separate provinces of the ancient kingdom of *Basan*. Then it signifies the *Trachonitis* κατ' ἐξοχήν, *i.e.* the wildest portion of the volcanic district, viz. the *Legâ,* the Haurân mountain range, the Safâ and Harra of the *Râgil*. On the other hand, it has the wider signification when it stands alone; then it embraces the whole volcanic region of Middle Syria, therefore with the more limited Trachonitis the remaining provinces of Basan, but with the exception, as it seems, of the no longer volcanic *Galadine* (North Gilead). In this sense, therefore, as a geographical notion, Trachonitis is almost synonymous with Basan.

Since it is to the interest of this investigation to make the assertion advanced sure against every objection, we will not withhold the passages in support of it. Josephus says, *Ant.* xv. 10, 3, the district of Hûle (Οὐλαθά) lies between Galilee and Trachonitis. He might have said more accurately, "between Galilee and Gaulonitis," but he wished to express that the great basaltic region begins on the eastern boundary of the Hûle. The word Trachonitis has therefore the *wider* signification. In like manner, in *Bell.* iii. 10 it is said the lake of *Phiala* lies 120 stadia east of Paneion (*Bâniâs*) on the way to the Trachonitis. True, the Phiala is a crater, and therefore itself belongs to Trachonitis, but between it and Bâniâs the lava alternates with the chalk formation of the *H*ermôn, whereas to the south and east of the Phiala it is

<hr>

[1] Comp. Jos. *Ant.* xv. 10, 3; *Zeitschr. für allg. Erdkunde*, New Series, xiii. 213.

everywhere exclusively volcanic; Trachonitis has therefore
here also the *wider* signification. *Ant.* xvii. 2, it is said
Herod had the castle of *Baθύρa* built in Batanæa (here, as
often in Josephus, in the signification of Basan), in order to
protect the Jews who travel from Babylon (*via* Damascus) to
Jerusalem against the Trachonite robbers. Now, since this
castle and village (the *Bêtirrâ* mentioned already), which is
situated in the district of *Gamalitica* on an important ford of
the *Muchêbi* gorge between '*Abidin* and *Sebbûte*, could not be
any protection against the robbers of Trachonitis in the more
limited sense, but only against those of Golan, it is manifest
that by the Trachonites are meant the robbers of Trachonitis
in the *wider* sense.   Aurelius Victor (*De Hist. Cæs.* xxvii.)
calls the Emperor M. Julius Philippus, born in *Bosrâ*, the
metropolis of Auranitis, quite correctly *Arabs ˙Trachonites;*
because the plain of Hauran, in which Bosra is situated, is
also of a basaltic formation, and *therefore* is a part of the
Trachonitis.   The passage of Luke's Gospel, iii. 1, where it
says Herod tetrarch of Galilee, and Philip tetrarch of Ituræa
and Trachonitis, also belongs here.   That Philip possessed not
perhaps merely the Trachonitis (similar to a province assigned
to a man as banishment rather than for administration, pro-
ducing little or no revenue) in the more *limited* sense, but
the whole Basanitis, is shown by Josephus, who informs us,
Ant. xvii. 11, 4 and freq., that he possessed Batanæa (in the
more restricted sense, therefore the fruitful, densely popu-
lated, profitable Nu*k*ra), with Auranitis, Trachonitis, etc.   We
must therefore suppose that in the words τῆς 'Iτουραίας καὶ
Τραχωνίτιδος χώρας in Luke, one district is meant, which
by 'Iτουραίας is mentioned according to the marauding portion of its population, and by Τραχωνίτιδος more generally,
according to its trachonitic formation.[1]   Ioannes Malalas

---

[1] Eusebius in his *Onomast.* also correctly identifies the two words, at
one time under 'Iτουραία, and the other time under Τραχωνῖτις.   After

(*Chronogr. ed. Dindorf,* p. 236), who, as a Syrian born,
ought to be well acquainted with the native usage of the
language, hence calls Antipas, as a perfectly adequate term,
only toparch of Trachonitis; and if, according to his statement (p. 237), the official title of this Herod was the following: Σεβαστὸς Ἡρώδης τοπάρχης καὶ θεσμοδότης Ἰουδαίων
τε καὶ Ἑλλήνων, βασιλεὺς τῆς Τραχωνίτιδος, it is self-evident
that "king of Trachonitis" here is synonymous with king
of Basan. In perfect harmony with this, Pliny says (*H. N.*
v. 18) that the ten cities of Decapolis lay within the extensive
tetrarchies of Trachonitis, which are divided into separate
kingdoms. Undoubtedly Pliny adds to these tetrarchies of
Trachonitis in the wider sense, which are already known to
us, *Galadine* also, which indeed belonged also to the pre-
Mosaic *Basan,* but at the time of Josephus is mostly reckoned
to *Peræa* (in the more limited sense).

On the ground of this evidence, therefore, the land of the
Usites of Josephus, with the exception of the Damascene
portion, was Trachonitis in the wider sense; and since the
Makâm Êjûb is in the central point of this country, this
statement accords most exactly with the Syrian tradition. It
is clear that the latter remains untouched by the extension of

what we have said elsewhere (*Reisebericht,* S. 91 ff.) on the subject,
surely no one will again maintain that the peaceful villages of the plain
of Gêdûr were the abodes of the Ituræans, the wildest of all people (Cic.
Phil. ii. 11; Strabo, xvi. 2). Their principal hiding-places will have been
the Trachonitis in the more restricted sense, but one may seek them also
on the wooded mountains of *Gôlân* and in the gorges of the *Makran.*
That Ptolemy and Josephus speak only of the Trachonites and never of
the Ituræans (in the passage *Ant.* xiii. 11, 3, Ἰδουμαία is to be read
instead of Ἰτουραία), and Strabo, on the other hand, speaks only of the
latter, favours the identity of the two; of like import is the circumstance,
that Pliny (*H. N.* v. 23) makes the inhabitants of the region of Bætarra
(Bêtirrâ) Ituræans, and Josephus (*Ant.* xvii. 2) Trachonites. But in
spite of the identity of the words *Trachonitis* and *Ituræa,* one must not
at the same time overlook the following distinction. If the Trachonites
are called after the country, it must be the description of all the inhabit-

the geographical notion in Josephus, for without knowing
anything more of a "land of the Usites," it describes only a
portion of the same as the "native country of Job;" and
again, Josephus had no occasion to speak of Job in his commentary on the genealogies, therefore also none to speak of
his special home within the land of the Usites. Eusebius,
on the other hand, in his *De Originibus* (ix. 2, 4), refers to
this home, and says, therefore limiting Josephus' definition:
*Hus, Traconitidis conditor, inter Palæstinam et Cœlesyriam
tenuit imperium; unde fuit Iob.*

With this evidence of agreement between two totally independent witnesses, viz. the Syrian tradition and Josephus,
the testimony of the latter in particular has an enhanced
value; for, although connected with the Bible, it nevertheless
avails as extra-biblical testimony concerning the Usites, it
comes from an age when one might still have the historical
fact from the seat of the race, and from an authority of the
highest order. True, Josephus is not free from disfigure-
ments, where he has the opportunity of magnifying his people,
himself, or his Roman patrons, and of depreciating an enemy;
but here he had to do with nothing more than the statement
of the residence of a people; and since the word Οὔσης also

ants of the country, whereas the Iturœans, if they gave the name to the
country, are not necessarily its exclusive population. The whole of the
district of which we speak has a twofold population in keeping with
its double character (rugged rock and fruitful plain), viz. cattle-rearing
freebooters in the clefts of the rocks, and peaceful husbandmen in the
plain; the former dwelling in hair tents (of old also in caves), the latter
in stone houses; the former forming the large majority, the latter the
minority of the population of the district. If writers speak of the *Iturœans*, they mean exclusively that marauding race that hates husbandry;
but if they speak of the *Trachonites*, the connection must determine,
whether they speak of both classes of the population, or only of the
marauding Trachonites (the Iturœans), or of the husbandmen of the
plain (of the provinces of *Batanœa* and *Auranitis*). The latter are
rarely intended, since the peaceful peasant rarely furnishes material for
the historian.

has no similarity in sound with the words *Damascus* and
Trachonitis, that might make a combination with them plaus-
ible, we may surely have before us a reliable historical notice
here, or at least a tradition which was then general (and
therefore also for us important), while we may doubt this in
connection with other parts of the genealogies, where Josephus
seems only to catch at that which is similar in sound as
furnishing an explanation.

But that which might injure the authority of Josephus is
the contradiction in which it seems to stand to a far older
statement concerning *Ausitis*, viz. the recognised postscript
of the LXX. to the book of Job, which makes Job to be the
Edomitish king Jobab. The identification, it may be said, can
however only have been possible because *Ausitis* was in or near
Edom. But the necessity of this inference must be disputed.
It is indeed unmistakeable that that postscript is nothing
more than a combination of the Jews beyond Palestine (probably Egyptio-Hellenistic), formed, perhaps, long before the
LXX.,—such a vagary as many similar ones in the Talmud
and Midrash. From the similarity in sound of ʼ*Ιωβάβ* with
ʼ*Ιώβ*, and the similarity in name of *Ζαρά*, the father of *Jobab*,
with a son of Reʼûël and grandson of Esau (Gen. xxxvi. 13),
Job's descent from Esau has been inferred. That Esau's
first-born was called *Eliphaz* and his son *Temân*, seemed to
confirm this combination, since (in accordance with the custom[1]
of naming the grandson as a rule after his grandfather) *Eliphaz*
the Temanite might be regarded as grandson of that *Eliphaz*,
therefore like Job as great-grandson of Esau and *πέμπτος
ἀπὸ* ʼ*Αβραάμ*. The apparent and certainly designed advantages of this combination were: that Job, who had no pedi-

[1] From this custom, which is called the grandfather's "living again,"
the habit, singular to us, of a father calling his son *jâ abî*, "my father!"
or *jâ bêjî*, "my little father," as an endearing form of address, is
explained.

gree, and therefore was to be thought of as a non-Israelite,
was brought into the nearest possible blood-relationship to
the people of God, and that, by laying the scene in the time
of the patriarchs, all questions which the want of a Mosaic
colouring to the book of Job might excite would be met.
Now, even if the abode of Job were transferred from the land
of 'Us to Edom, it would be only the consequence of his combination with *Jobab*, and, just as worthless as this latter
itself, might lead no one astray. But it does not seem to
have gone so far; it is even worthy of observation, that
מבצרה (from *Bosra*, the Edomite city[1]), being attached to the
misunderstood υἱὸς Ζαρά ἐκ Βοσόῤῥας, Gen. xxxvi. 33, is
reproduced in the LXX. by μητρὸς Βοσόῤῥας, as also that
Job's wife is not called an Edomitess, but a γυνὴ 'Αράβισσα.
And it appears still far more important, that Ausitis lies ἐν
τοῖς ὁρίοις τῆς 'Ιδουμαίας καὶ 'Αραβίας, so far as the central
point of 'Ιδουμαία is removed by the addition καὶ τῆς 'Αραβίας, and Job's abode is certainly removed from the heart of
Idumœa. The *Cod. Alex.* exchanges that statement of the
place, even in a special additional clause, for ἐπὶ τῶν ὁρίων
τοῦ Εὐφράτου, therefore transfers Ausitis to the vicinity of
the Euphrates, and calls the father of Jobab (= Job) Ζαρὲθ
ἐξ ἀνατολῶν ἡλίου (מבני קדם). Nevertheless we attach no
importance to this variation of the text, but rather offer the
suggestion that the postscript gives prominence to the observation: οὗτος (viz. 'Ιώβ) ἑρμηνεύεται ἐκ τῆς Συριακῆς
βίβλου.[2]

---

[1] It need hardly be mentioned that one is not to think of the Hauranitish *Bosrâ* (بصرى), since this name of a city only came into use some
centuries after Christ.

[2] [It is indeed possible that the Hebrew text is meant here, for Philo
usually calls the Hebrew Χαλδαϊστί, and the Talmud describes the
Jewish country-dialect as סורסי ; it is possible, and even more probable,
that it is a Syrian, *i.e.* Aramæan Targum—but not less possible that it
is a Syrian original document. According to Malalas (*ed. Dindorf,*

If we compare the postscript of the LXX. with the legend of Islam, we find in both the Esauitish genealogy of Job; the genealogy of the legend is: Êjûb ibn Zârih (חַרֶת) ibn Reû'îl ibn el-'Aïs ibn Isḥâk ibn Ibrâhîm; and we may suppose that it is borrowed directly from the LXX., and that it reached Arabia and Mekka even in the pre-Islamic times by means of the (Arabian) Christians east of Jordan, who had the Old Testament only in the Greek translation. Even the Arabic orthography of the biblical proper names, which can be explained only on the supposition of their transfer from the Greek, is in favour of this mode of the transmission of the Christian religion and its legends to the people of the Higaz. Certainly there can be no doubt as to an historical connection between the postscript and the legend, and therefore it would be strange if they did not accord respecting the home of Job. The progenitor el-'Aïs (עִיץ), in the genealogy of the legend, is also a remarkable counterpart to the Ausitis ἐν τοῖς ὁρίοις τῆς Ἰδουμ. καὶ Ἀρ., for it is a blending of עִיץ and עִיץ, and it has to solve the difficult problem, as to how Job can be at the same time an Usite and an Esauite; for that Job as an Aïsite no longer belongs to Idumæa, but to the district of the more northern Aramæans, is shown e.g. from the following passage in Mugîr ed-dîn's History of Jerusalem : "Job belonged to the people of the Romans (i.e. the Aïsites[1]), for he sprang

p. 12), Origen understands ἐκ τῆς Συριακῆς βίβλου elsewhere of a Hebrew original, but in c. Celsum iii. 6 he describes the Hebrew language in relation to the Syriac and Phœnician as ἑτέρα παρ' ἀμφοτέρας, and the Homilies on Job in Opp. Origenis, ed. Delarue, ii. 851, say : Beati Iob scriptura primum quidem in Arabia Syriace scripta, ubi et habitabat. —Del.]

[1] We will spare ourselves the ungrateful task of an inquiry into the origin of this 'Aïs and his Protean nature. Biblical passages like Lam. iv. 21, or those in which the readings אֲרָם and אֲדוֹם are doubtful, or the erroneous supposition (Jos. Ant. viii. 7) that the Ben-Hadad dynasty in Damascus is of Edomitish origin, may have contributed to his rise. Moreover, he is altogether one and the same with the Edom of the

from *el-'Ais*, and the Damascene province of *Batanœa* was his property."

The κοπρία of the LXX., at ch. ii. 8, leads to the same result; that it is also found again as *mezbele* in the later legend, is a further proof how thoroughly this accords with the LXX., and how it has understood its statement of the position of *Ausitis*. It may also be maintained here, that it was only possible to translate the words בתוך־האפר by ἐπὶ τῆς κοπρίας ἔξω τῆς πόλεως when "heap of ashes" and "dunghill" were synonymous notions. This, however, is the case only in Hauran, where the dung, as being useless for agricultural purposes, is burnt from time to time in an appointed place before the town (*vid.* ii. p. 152 [1]), while in every other part of Syria it is as valuable and as much stored up as among us. If the LXX. accordingly placed the κοπρία of Job in Hauran, it could hardly represent *Ausitis* as *Edom*.

But how has the Ausitis of the LXX. been transferred hither? Certainly not as the "land of '*Us*" (in the sense of the land of *Basan*, land of *Haurân*), for without wasting a word about it, there has never been such an one in the country east of the Jordan : but as "the land of the Usites" in the sense of the Arabic *diâr 'Us* (dwelling-place of the Usites) or *ard benî 'Us*. A land receives designations of

Jewish tradition : he is called the father of *Rûm*, *Asfar*, *Sôfar*, *Sifûn* (מֶלֶךְ הצפון), and *Nidr (Hamz. Isfah. Ann.* p. ٧٩, l. 18, read نضر for

نصر, and *Zeitschr. d. d. m. Gesellsch.* ii. 239, 3, 6, read *ennidr* for *ennefer*), *i.e.* of the Messiah of the Christians (according to Isa. xi. 1).

[1] Comp. ii. p. 158, note, of the foregoing Commentary. [The Arabic version of Walton's Polyglot translates after the Peschito in accordance with the Hebr. text : "on the ashes (*er-remâd*)," whereas the Arabic translation, of which Tischendorf brought back fifteen leaves with him from the East, and which Fleischer, in the *Deutsch. Morgenl. Zeitschr.* 1864, S. 288 ff., has first described as an important memorial in reference to the history of MSS., translates after the *Hexapla* in accordance with the LXX. : "on the dunghill (*mezbele*) outside the city."—DEL.]

this kind with the settlement of a people in it; they run parallel with the proper name of the country, and in the rule vanish again with that people. These designations belong, indeed, to the geography of the whole earth, but nowhere have they preserved their natural character of transitoriness more faithfully than in the lands where the Semitic tongue is spoken. It is this that makes the geographical knowledge of these countries so extremely difficult to us, because we frequently take them to be the names of the countries, which they are not, and which—so far as they always involve a geological definition of the regions named—can never be displaced and competently substituted by them. In this sense the *land of the Usites* might, at the time of the decay of both Israelitish kingdoms, when the ארם דמשׂק possessed the whole of Peræa, very easily extend from the borders of Edom to the gates of Damascus, and even further northwards, if the Aramæan race of ʿUs numbered many or populous tribes (as it appears to be indicated in כל מלכי ארץ העוץ, Jer. xxv. 20), in perfect analogy with the tribe of *Ghassân*, which during five hundred years occupied the country from the Ælanitic Gulf to the region of *Tedmor*, at one time settling down, at another leading a nomadic life, and Hauran was the centre of its power. By such a rendering the 'Αραβία of the postscript would not be different from the later *provincia Arabiæ*, of which the capital was the Trachonitish *Bostra*, while it was bounded on the south end of the Dead Sea by Edom (*Palæstina tertia*).

But should any one feel a difficulty in freeing himself from the idea that *Ausitis* is to be sought only in the *Ard el-Hâlât* east of *Maʿân*, he must consider that the author of the book of Job could not, like that legend which places the miraculous city of *Iram* in the country of quicksands, transfer the cornfields of his hero to the desert; for there, with the exception of smaller patches of land capable of culture, which we may not bring into account, there is by no means to be found that husbandman's Eldorado, where a single husbandman might find tillage for five hundred (ch. i. 3), yea, for a thousand (ch. xlii. 12) yoke of oxen. Such numbers as these are not to be depreciated; for in connection with the primitive agriculture in Syria and Palestine,—which renders a four years' alternation of crops necessary, so that the fields must be divided into so many portions (called in Hauran *wâgihât*, and around Damascus *auguh*, اوجه), from which only one portion is used annually, and the rest left fallow (*bûr*),—Job required several square miles of tillage for the employment of his oxen. It is all the same in this respect whether the book of Job is a history or poem : in no case could the *Ausitis* be a country, the notorious sterility of which would make the statement of the poet ridiculous.

Our limited space does not admit of our proving the worth which we must acknowledge to the tradition, by illustrating those passages of the Old Testament scriptures which have reference to עוץ and ארץ עוץ. But to any one, who, following the hints they give, wishes again to pursue the investigations, elsewhere useless, concerning the position of the land of the Usites, we might indicate : (1) that עוץ the first-born of Aram (Gen. x. 23) is the tribe sought, while two others of this name—a Nahorite, ch. xxii. 21, and a Horite, ch. xxxvi. 28—may be left out of consideration ; the former because the twelve sons of Nahor need not be progenitors of tribes, and the latter because he belongs to a tribe exterminated by the Edomites in accordance with Deut. ii. 12, 22 : (2) that ארץ העוץ, Jer. xxv. 20, is expressly distinguished from אדום in the 21st verse, and—if one compares the round of the cup of punishment, Jer. ch. xxv., with the detailed prophecies which follow in ch. xlvi.-li., to which it is a proœmium that has been removed from its place—corresponds to דמשק (with H*amât* and *Arpad*), ch. xlix. 23: (3) that there-

fore Lam. iv. 21, where יֹשֶׁבֶת בְּאֶרֶץ עוּץ would be devoid of purpose if it described the proper habitable land of Edom, must
describe a district extending over that, in which the Edomites had established themselves in consequence of Assyria
having led away captive the Israelitish and Aramæan population of the East Jordanic country and Cœle-Syria. In
connection with Jer. xxv. 20 one must not avoid the question
whether עוּץ is the name of the אֲרַם דַּמֶּשֶׂק that has been
missed. Here the migration of the Damascene Aramæans
from Kîr (Am. ix. 7) ought to be considered, the value of
the Armenian accounts concerning the original abode of the
Usites tested, what is erroneous in the combination of קִיר
with the river *Kur* shown and well considered, and in what
relations both as to time and events that migration might
have stood to the overrunning of Middle Syria by the
Aramæan *Sôbæan* tribes (from Mesopotamia) under Hadad-
ezer, and to the seizure and possession of the city of
Damascus by Rezon the *Sôbæan*? Finally, one more tradition might be compared, to which some value may perhaps
be attached, because it is favoured by the stone monuments,
whose testimony we are not accustomed otherwise to despise
in Palestine and Syria. The eastern portal of the mosque of
Benî Uméja in Damascus, probably of the very temple, the
altar of which king Ahaz caused to be copied (2 Kings
xvi. 10), is called *Gêrûn* or the Gerun gate: the portal in
its present form belongs to the Byzantine or Roman period.
And before this gate is the *Gêrûnîje*, a spacious, vaulted
structure, mostly very old, which has been used since the
Mussulman occupation of the city as a *mêda'a*, *i.e.* a place for
religious ablutions. The topographical writings on Damascus
trace these two names back to a *Gêrûn ibn Sa'd ibn 'Ad ibn
'Aus* (עוּץ) *ibn Iram* (אֲרָם) *ibn Sâm* (שֵׁם) *ibn Nûh* (נֹחַ), who
settled in Damascus in the time of Solomon (one version of
the tradition identifies him with *Hadad*, Jos. *Ant.* viii. 7),

and built in the middle of the city a castle named after him, in which a temple to the planet (*kôkeb*) *Mushteri*, the guardian-god of the city, has been erected. That this temple, which, as is well known, under Theodosius, at the same time with the temple of the sun at Baʿlbek, passed over to the Christians, was ·actually surrounded with a strong, fortified wall, is capable of proof even in the present day. In this tradition, which has assumed various forms, a more genuine counterpart of the biblical עוץ appears than that ʿ*Ais* which we have characterized above as an invention of the schools, viz. an ʿ*Aus* (عوض), father of the Adite-tribe which is said to have settled in the Damascene district under that *Gêrûn*, and also ancestor of the prophet *Hûd*, lost to the tradition, whose *makâm* on the mountains of *Suêt* rises far above *Gerash* the city of pillars, this true *Iram dhât el-ʿimâd*, the valley of the Jabbok and the *Sawâd* of Gilead.

It is with good reason that we have hitherto omitted to mention the Ἀισῖται of Ptolemy v. 18 (19). The Codd. have both Ἀισεῖται and Ἀισῖται; different Semitic forms (*e.g.* the

name of the بني خيس, which, according to Jâkût, once

dwelt in the Harra of the *Ragil*) may lie at the basis of this name, only not the form עוץ, which ought to be Οὐσῖται, or at least Αὐσῖται (which no Cod. reads). As to the abodes·of the Ἀισῖται, Ptolemy distributes them under nine greater races or groups of races, which in his time inhabited the Syrian steppe. Three of these had their settlements in the eastern half of the Syrian steppe towards the Euphrates or on its western banks: the Καυχαβηνοί in the north, the Ἀισῖται in the middle, and the Ὀρχηνοί in the south. According to this the Ἀισῖται would have been about between Hît and *Kûfa*, or in that district which is called by the natives *Ard el-Wudjan*, and in which just that race of the Chaldæans might have dwelt that plundered Job's camels.

There we are certainly not to seek the scene of the drama of Job; and if the Edomites were dispersed there (Lam. iv. 21), they were not to be envied on account of their fortune. But if the Αἰσῖται are to be sought there, we may not connect the Καυχαβηνοί with the village of *Cochabe* (كوكبا) on the Hermon (Epiphan. *Hær.* x. 18), in order then to remove the Αἰσῖται, dwelling "below them," to Batanæa.

And now, in concluding here, I have still to explain, that in writing these pages I was not actuated by an invincible desire of increasing the dull literature respecting the ארץ עוץ by another tractate, but exclusively by the wish of my honoured friend that I should furnish him with a contribution on my visit to the *Makâm Êjûb*, and concerning the tradition that prevails there, for his commentary on the book of Job.

As to the accompanying map, it is intended to represent the hitherto unknown position of the Makâm, the Monastery, and the country immediately around them, by comparing it with two localities marked on most maps, *Nawâ* and the castle of *Muzêrib*. The latter, the position of which we determined in 1860 as 32° 44' north lat. and 35° 51' 45" east long. (from Greenwich), lies three hours' journey on horse-back south of the Monastery. The *Wâdi Jarmûk* and *Wâdi Hît* have the gorge formation in common with all other wadis that unite in the neighbourhood of *Zêzûn* and form the *Makran*, which is remarkable from a geological point of view : a phenomenon which is connected with the extreme depression of the valley of the Jordan. For the majority of the geographical names mentioned in this essay I refer the reader to Carl Ritter's *Geographie von Syrien und Palästina*;[1] others will be explained in my *Itinerarien*, which will be published shortly.

[1] Translated by W. L. Gage, and published by T. and T. Clark, Edinburgh, 1866, 4 vols.

THE MODE OF TRANSCRIBING THE ARABIC WORDS.

t = ת, ﺕ; th = ת, ﺙ; $'g$ [soft, the ' over the g has been generally omitted, as liable to be mistaken for an accent in connection with vowels], or, in accordance with the predominant pronunciation, g = ج; h or hh = ح; ch = خ; dh = ذ; z = ז, j; sh or sch = ش; s or ss = צ, ﺹ; d or dd = ﺽ; t or tt = ﻁ, ﻅ; z = ﻅ; ' = ע, ﻉ, $e.g.$ 'Ain = עין, $Gumû'$ = גומע; gh = ﻍ; k (k) or q = ﻕ, ﻕ; k (c) = ﻙ. The exact transcription is sometimes omitted where the word occurs more frequently, $e.g.$ Haurân, Makâm. Instead of ijj and uww are written $îj$ and $ûw$. The vowels a and e correspond to the $Fath$ (פתח), and u and o to the $Damm$; nevertheless the use of o is limited to the emphatic and guttural consonants, including r, while a, according to rule, is subject to this limitation only in nominal forms,—in verbal forms it is also combined with the rest of the consonants; $â$, $ê$ (ei, ai), and $ô$ (au) are = $Fath$ followed by $Elif$, Jod, or Waw, $û$ = $Damm$ followed by Waw.

The sign for $Hamza$ is ', $e.g.$ $mala'a$ = مَلأ (מלא). The $Tenwîn$ (Nunation) is only expressed exceptionally, $e.g.$ '$gelle$ = גֶּלֶּ as it is generally pronounced, especially when the word stands out of its connection as the root form, not '$gellat-un$ (the nunized nominative). Perfect consistency has not been attainable in a book, the printing of which, together with the working in of constantly accumulating material, has occupied nearly two years.

[The consonantal notation is given above according to the variation that has been rendered necessary by the want of casts for printing according to the system adopted by Dr Delitzsch. We were obliged to have recourse to the old notation, which is clumsy and confusing, *e.g.* $hh =$ ﺡ, $tt =$ ﻁ, ﺽ, and in one or two instances a · has been used in the tt thus, $t\!\cdot\!t$, to represent ﺽ (with *Teshdîd*).. This applies to the first volume; but in the second I have adopted a change, which occurred to me later, viz. to use Roman letters among the Italics to represent the stronger consonants, or *vice versâ*, Italics among Roman letters. The advantage of this will be seen more especially in the exact reproduction of geographical names, as by means of it the spelling is not affected, and at the same time the Arabic letters are fairly distinguished. Suffice it to remind the student that the j is to be pronounced as Engl. y, being $=$ ﻱ.

ABBREVIATIONS

Have been rarely used in the translation, and those used are mostly familiar and self-evident. The names of critics are given in full in the earlier part, and though abbreviated, as constantly recurring, need no explanation here. "The Arabic Version referred to is that of the London Polyglot; the Syriac, the ancient Syrian version. *b.* and *j.* in connection with Talmud citations signify respectively the Babylonian and Jerusalem Talmuds; *b.* with the names of persons, *ben* (*bar*), son." The Biblical references are according to the *Hebrew* divisions, *e.g.* Ps. xcii. 11 (10), as also the division of ch. xl. xli.

ERRATUM.

Vol. i. 72, note, *for:* Alters, *read:* early times.—TR.]

INDEX OF TEXTS.

END OF VOL. II.

www.ingramcontent.com/pod-product-compliance
Lightning Source LLC
Chambersburg PA
CBHW052347110726
47901CB00005B/1393